"We are pleased to witness publication of the
Ancient Christian Commentary on Scripture. It is most beneficial for us to learn
how the ancient Christians, especially the saints of the church
who proved through their lives their devotion to God and his Word, interpreted
Scripture. Let us heed the witness of those who have gone before us in the faith."

METROPOLITAN THEODOSIUS
Primate, Orthodox Church in America

"Across Christendom there has emerged a widespread interest
in early Christianity, both at the popular and scholarly level....
Christians of all traditions stand to benefit from this project, especially clergy
and those who study the Bible. Moreover, it will allow us to see how our traditions are
both rooted in the scriptural interpretations of the church fathers while at
the same time seeing how we have developed new perspectives."

ALBERTO FERREIRO
Professor of History, Seattle Pacific University

"The Ancient Christian Commentary on Scripture fills a long overdue need for scholars and
students of the church fathers.... Such information will be of immeasurable
worth to those of us who have felt inundated by contemporary interpreters and novel theories
of the biblical text. We welcome some 'new' insight from the
ancient authors in the early centuries of the church."

H. WAYNE HOUSE
Professor of Theology and Law
Trinity University School of Law

Chronological snobbery—the assumption that our ancestors working without benefit of
computers have nothing to teach us—is exposed as nonsense by this magnificent
new series. Surfeited with knowledge but starved of wisdom, many of us are
more than ready to sit at table with our ancestors and listen to their holy
conversations on Scripture. I know I am.

EUGENE H. PETERSON
Professor Emeritus of Spiritual Theology
Regent College

"Few publishing projects have encouraged me as much as the recently announced Ancient Christian Commentary on Scripture with Dr. Thomas Oden serving as general editor. . . . How is it that so many of us who are dedicated to serve the Lord received seminary educations which omitted familiarity with such incredible students of the Scriptures as St. John Chrysostom, St. Athanasius the Great and St. John of Damascus? I am greatly anticipating the publication of this Commentary."

FR. PETER E. GILLQUIST
Director, Department of Missions and Evangelism
Antiochian Orthodox Christian Archdiocese of North America

"The Scriptures have been read with love and attention for nearly two thousand years, and listening to the voice of believers from previous centuries opens us to unexpected insight and deepened faith. Those who studied Scripture in the centuries closest to its writing, the centuries during and following persecution and martyrdom, speak with particular authority. The Ancient Christian Commentary on Scripture will bring to life the truth that we are invisibly surrounded by a 'great cloud of witnesses.'"

FREDERICA MATHEWES-GREEN
Commentator, National Public Radio

"For those who think that church history began around 1941 when their pastor was born, this Commentary will be a great surprise. Christians throughout the centuries have read the biblical text, nursed their spirits with it and then applied it to their lives. These commentaries reflect that the witness of the Holy Spirit was present in his church throughout the centuries. As a result, we can profit by allowing the ancient Christians to speak to us today."

HADDON ROBINSON
Harold John Ockenga Distinguished Professor of Preaching
Gordon-Conwell Theological Seminary

"All who are interested in the interpretation of the Bible will welcome the forthcoming multivolume series Ancient Christian Commentary on Scripture. Here the insights of scores of early church fathers will be assembled and made readily available for significant passages throughout the Bible and the Apocrypha. It is hard to think of a more worthy ecumenical project to be undertaken by the publisher."

BRUCE M. METZGER
Professor of New Testament, Emeritus
Princeton Theological Seminary

ANCIENT CHRISTIAN
COMMENTARY ON SCRIPTURE

NEW TESTAMENT
VI

ROMANS

EDITED BY

GERALD BRAY

GENERAL EDITOR
THOMAS C. ODEN

InterVarsity Press
Downers Grove, Illinois

227.107

B2 R

InterVarsity Press

P.O. Box 1400, Downers Grove, IL 60515-1426

Internet: www.ivpress.com

E-mail: mail@ivpress.com

InterVarsity Press® is the book-publishing division of InterVarsity Christian Fellowship/USA®, a student movement active on campus at hundreds of universities, colleges and schools of nursing in the United States of America, and a member movement of the International Fellowship of Evangelical Students. For information about local and regional activities, write Public Relations Dept., InterVarsity Christian Fellowship/USA, 6400 Schroeder Rd., P.O. Box 7895, Madison, WI 53707-7895, or visit the IVCF website at <www.intervarsity.org>.

Scripture quotations, unless otherwise noted, are from the Revised Standard Version of the Bible, copyright 1946, 1952, 1971 by the Division of Christian Education of the National Council of the Churches of Christ in the U.S.A., and are used by permission. All rights reserved.

FC Selected excerpts from The Fathers of the Church, 86 volumes. Copyright © 1947-. Used by permission of Catholic University of America Press.

Cover photograph: Scala/Art Resource, New York. View of the apse. S. Vitale, Ravenna, Italy.

Spine photograph: Byzantine Collection, Dumbarton Oaks, Washington D.C. Pendant cross (gold and enamel). Constantinople, late sixth century.

ISBN 0-8308-1356-X

Printed in the United States of America ∞

Library of Congress Cataloging-in-Publication Data

Romans/Gerald Bray, editor.

    p.   cm.—(Ancient Christian commentary on Scripture. New Testament; 6)

    Includes bibliographical references and index.

    ISBN 0-83-8-1491-4 (cloth: alk. paper)

    1. Bible.   N.T. Romans—Commentaries.   I. Bray, Gerald Lewis.

  II. Series.

  BS2665.3.R49   1998

  227'.1077'09—dc21

                                         98-18076

                                         CIP

P	25	24	23	22	21	20	19	18	17	16	15	14	13	12	11	10	9	8	7	6	5	4	3	2	1
Y	26	25	24	23	22	21	20	19	18	17	16	15	14	13	12	11	10	09	08	07	06	05			

Ancient Christian Commentary Project Research Team

General Editor
Thomas C. Oden

Associate Editor
Christopher A. Hall

Translations Projects Director
Joel Scandrett

Editorial Services Director
Susan Kipper

Translation Editor
Dennis McManus

Graduate Research Assistants

Vincent Bacote	*Jeffrey Finch*
Brian Brewer	*Konstantin*
Thomas Buchan	*Peter Gilbert*
Jill Burnett	*Patricia Ireland*
Hunn Choi	*Sergey Kozin*
Meesaeng L. Choi	*Thomas Mauro*
Joel Elowsky	*Wesley Tink*
Bernie Van De Walle	

Computer & Technical Support
Michael Kipper

Administrative Assistant
Judy Cox

Contents

General Introduction

The Ancient Christian Commentary on Scripture has as its goal the revitalization of Christian teaching based on classical Christian exegesis, the intensified study of Scripture by lay persons who wish to think with the early church about the canonical text, and the stimulation of Christian historical, biblical, theological and pastoral scholars toward further inquiry into scriptural interpretation by ancient Christian writers.

The time frame of these documents spans seven centuries of exegesis, from Clement of Rome to John of Damascus, from the end of the New Testament era to A.D. 750, including the Venerable Bede.

Lay readers are asking how they might study sacred texts under the instruction of the great minds of the ancient church. This commentary has been intentionally prepared for a general lay audience of non-professionals who study the Bible regularly and who earnestly wish to have classic Christian observation on the text readily available to them. The series is targeted to anyone who wants to reflect and meditate with the early church about the plain sense, theological wisdom and moral meaning of particular Scripture texts.

A commentary dedicated to allowing ancient Christian exegetes to speak for themselves will refrain from the temptation to fixate endlessly upon contemporary criticism. Rather, it will stand ready to provide textual resources from a distinguished history of exegesis that has remained massively inaccessible and shockingly disregarded during the last century. We seek to make available to our present-day audiences the multicultural, multilingual, transgenerational resources of the early ecumenical Christian tradition.

Preaching at the end of the first millennium focused primarily on the text of Scripture as understood by the earlier esteemed tradition of comment, largely converging on those writers that best reflected classic Christian consensual thinking. Preaching at the end of the second millennium has reversed that pattern. It has so forgotten most of these classic comments that they are vexing to find anywhere, and even when located they are often available only in archaic editions and inadequate translations. The preached word in our time has remained largely bereft of previously influential patristic inspiration. Recent scholarship has so focused attention upon post-Enlightenment historical and literary methods that it has left this longing largely unattended and unserviced.

This series provides the pastor, exegete, student and lay reader with convenient means to see what Athanasius or John Chrysostom or the desert fathers and mothers had to say about a particular text for preaching, for study and for meditation. There is an emerging awareness among Catholic, Protestant and Orthodox laity that vital biblical preaching and spiritual formation need deeper grounding beyond the scope of the historical-critical orientations that have governed biblical studies in our day.

Hence this work is directed toward a much broader audience than the highly technical and specialized scholarly field of patristic studies. The audience is not limited to the university scholar concentrating on the study of the history of the transmission of the text or to those with highly focused philological interests in textual morphology or historical-critical issues. Though these are crucial concerns for specialists, they are not the paramount interests of this series.

This work is a Christian Talmud. The Talmud is a Jewish collection of rabbinic arguments and comments on the Mishnah, which epitomized the laws of the Torah. The Talmud originated in approximately the same period that the patristic writers were commenting on texts of the Christian tradition. Christians from the late patristic age through the medieval period had documents analogous to the Jewish Talmud and Midrash (Jewish commentaries) available to them in the *glossa ordinaria* and catena traditions, two forms of compiling extracts of patristic exegesis. In Talmudic fashion the sacred text of Christian Scripture was thus clarified and interpreted by the classic commentators.

The Ancient Christian Commentary on Scripture has venerable antecedents in medieval exegesis of both eastern and western traditions, as well as in the Reformation tradition. It offers for the first time in this century the earliest Christian comments and reflections on the Old and New Testaments to a modern audience. Intrinsically an ecumenical project, this series is designed to serve Protestant, Catholic and Orthodox lay, pastoral and scholarly audiences.

In cases where Greek, Latin, Syriac and Coptic texts have remained untranslated into English, we provide new translations. Wherever current English translations are already well rendered, they will be utilized, but if necessary their language will be brought up to date. We seek to present fresh dynamic equivalency translations of long-neglected texts which historically have been regarded as authoritative models of biblical interpretation.

These foundational sources are finding their way into many public libraries and into the core book collections of many pastors and lay persons. It is our intent and the publisher's commitment to keep the whole series in print for many years to come.

Thomas C. Oden
General Editor

A Guide to Using This Commentary

Several features have been incorporated into the design of this commentary. The following comments are intended to assist readers in making full use of this volume.

Pericopes of Scripture

The scriptural text has been divided into pericopes, or passages, usually several verses in length. Each of these pericopes is given a heading, which appears at the beginning of the pericope. For example, the first pericope in the commentary on Romans is "1:1-7 Paul and the Gospel." This heading is followed by the Scripture passage quoted in the Revised Standard Version (RSV) across the full width of the page. The Scripture passage is provided for the convenience of readers, but it is also in keeping with medieval patristic commentaries, in which the citations of the Fathers were arranged around the text of Scripture.

Overviews

Following each pericope of text is an overview of the patristic comments on that pericope. The format of this overview varies within the volumes of this series, depending on the requirements of the specific book of Scripture. The function of the overview is to provide a brief summary of all the comments to follow. It tracks a reasonably cohesive thread of argument among patristic comments, even though they are derived from diverse sources and generations. Thus the summaries do not proceed chronologically or by verse sequence. Rather they seek to rehearse the overall course of the patristic comment on that pericope.

We do not assume that the commentators themselves anticipated or expressed a formally received cohesive argument but rather that the various arguments tend to flow in a plausible, recognizable pattern. Modern readers can thus glimpse aspects of continuity in the flow of diverse exegetical traditions representing various generations and geographical locations.

Topical Headings

An abundance of varied patristic comment is available for each pericope of these letters. For this reason we have broken the pericopes into two levels. First is the verse with its topical heading. The patristic comments are then focused on aspects of each verse, with topical headings summarizing the essence of the patristic comment by evoking a key phrase, metaphor or idea. This feature provides a bridge by which modern readers can enter into the heart of the patristic comment.

Identifying the Patristic Texts

Following the topical heading of each section of comment, the name of the patristic commentator is given. An English translation of the patristic comment is then provided. This is immediately followed by the title of the patristic work and the textual reference—either by book, section and subsection or by book-and-verse references. If the notation differs significantly between the English-language source foot-noted and other sources, alternate references appear in parentheses. Some differences may also be due to variant biblical versification or chapter and verse numbering.

The Footnotes

Readers who wish to pursue a deeper investigation of the patristic works cited in this commentary will find the footnotes especially valuable. A footnote number directs the reader to the notes at the bottom of the right-hand column, where in addition to other notations (clarifications or biblical cross references) one will find information on English translations (where available) and standard original-language editions of the work cited. An abbreviated citation (normally citing the book, volume and page number) of the work is provided. A key to the abbreviations is provided on page xv. Where there is any serious ambiguity or textual problem in the selection, we have tried to reflect the best available textual tradition.

Where original language texts have remained untranslated into English, we provide new translations. Wherever current English translations are already well rendered, they are utilized, but where necessary they are stylistically updated. A single asterisk (*) indicates that a previous English translation has been updated to modern English or amended for easier reading. The double asterisk (**) indicates either that a new translation has been provided or that some extant translation has been significantly amended. We have standardized spellings and made grammatical variables uniform so that our English references will not reflect the odd spelling variables of the older English translations. For ease of reading we have in some cases edited out superfluous conjunctions.

For the convenience of computer database users the digital database references are provided to either the Thesaurus Linguae Graecae (Greek texts) or to the Cetedoc (Latin texts) in the appendix found on pages 369-73.

ABBREVIATIONS

ACCS	T. C. Oden, ed. Ancient Christian Commentary on Scripture. Downers Grove, Ill.: InterVarsity Press, 1998-.
ACW	Ancient Christian Writers: The Works of the Fathers in Translation. Mahwah, NJ:Paulist, 1946-.
ANF	A. Roberts and J. Donaldson, eds. Ante-Nicene Fathers. 10 vols. Buffalo, N.Y.: Christian Literature, 1885-1896. Reprint, Grand Rapids, Mich.: Eerdmans, 1951-1956. Reprint, Peabody, Mass.: Hendrickson, 1994.
AOR	P. F. Landes, ed. *Augustine on Romans*. Chico, Calif.: Scholars Press, 1982.
CER	Origen. *Commentarii in Epistulam ad Romanos*. Edited by T. Heither. 5 vols. New York: Herder, 1990-1995.
CSEL	Corpus Scriptorum Ecclesiasticorum Latinorum. Vienna: Tempsky, 1866-.
ELT	S. L. Greenslade, ed. and trans. *Early Latin Theology: Selections from Tertullian, Cyprian, Ambrose, and Jerome*. Library of Christian Classics. Philadelphia: Westminster Press, 1956.
ENPK	H. J. Frede, ed. *Ein neuer Paulustext und Kommentar (A New Pauline Text and Commentary)*. Freiburg, Germany: Herder, 1974.
EPER	Augustine of Hippo. *Expositio Quarundam Propositionum ex Epistula ad Romanos (Exposition of the Epistle to the Romans)*. PL 35 2063-88.
ERIE	Augustine of Hippo. *Epistulae ad Romanos Inchoata Expositio (Rudimentary Exposition of the Epistle to the Romans)*. PL 35 2087-2106.
FC	R. J. Deferrari, ed. Fathers of the Church: A New Translation. Washington, D.C.: Catholic University of America Press, 1947-.
FGFR	*Faith Gives Fullness to Reasoning: The Five Theological Orations of Gregory Nazianzen.* Introduction and commentary by F. W. Morris. Leiden and New York: E. J. Brill, 1991.
IER	Theodoret of Cyr. *Interpretatio epistole ad Romanos*. PG 82 43-226.
LCC	J. Baillie et al., eds. The Library of Christian Classics. 26 vols. Philadelphia: Westminster Press, 1953-1966.
MOT	R. E. Heine, ed. *The Montanist Oracles and Testimonia*. North American Patristic Society Monograph Series 14. Macon, Ga.: Mercer University Press, 1989.
NPNF	P. Schaff et al., eds. A Select Library of the Nicene and Post-Nicene Fathers of the Christian Church. 2 series (14 vols. each). Buffalo, N.Y.: Christian Literature, 1887-1894. Reprint, Grand Rapids, Mich.: Eerdmans, 1952-1956. Reprint, Peabody, Mass.: Hendrickson, 1994.
NTA 15	K. Staab, ed. *Pauluskommentare aus der griechischen Kirche: Aus Katenenhandschriften gesammelt und herausgegeben (Pauline Commentary from the Greek Church: Collected and Edited Catena Writings)*. NT Abhandlungen 15. Münster in Westfalen: Aschendorff, 1933.
OFP	Origen. *On First Principles*. Translated by G. W. Butterworth. London: SPCK, 1936. Reprint, Gloucester, Mass.: Peter Smith, 1973.
OSW	*Origen: An Exhortation to Martyrdom, Prayer and Selected Works*. Mahwah, N.J.: Paulist, 1979.
PCR	M. De Bruyn, ed. *Pelagius's Commentary on Romans*. Oxford: Oxford University Press, 1993.
PDCW	C. Luibheid, trans. *Pseudo-Dionysius: The Complete Works*. Classics of Western Spirituality. Mahwah,

	N.J.: Paulist: 1987.
PETE	A. Souter, ed. *Pelagius's Expositions of Thirteen Epistles of St. Paul*. Texts and Studies 9.1-3. Cambridge: Cambridge University Press, 1922-1931.
PG	J.-P. Migne, ed. Patrologia cursus completus. Series Graeca. 166 vols. Paris: Migne, 1857-1886.
PL	J.-P. Migne, ed. Patrologia cursus completus. Series Latina. 221 vols. Paris: Migne, 1844-1864.
POG	Eusebius. *The Proof of the Gospel*. Translated by W. J. Ferrar. London: SPCK, 1920. Reprint, Grand Rapids, Mich.: Baker, 1981.
SFPSL	S. Brock, trans. *The Syriac Fathers on Prayer and the Spiritual Life*. Kalamazoo, Mich.: Cistercian Publications, 1987.

Introduction to Romans

To help the modern reader to explore Romans through the eyes of the ancient Christian writers, we will examine four preliminary issues:

☐ Who wrote the epistle to the Romans?

☐ Why is the epistle to the Romans important?

☐ How were the quotations used here selected?

☐ How are references presented so as to enable the reader to easily locate the original text and examine it in its context?

Who Wrote the Epistle to the Romans?

On the question of the authorship of Romans, virtually all commentators, both ancient and modern, agree: the author of the epistle was the apostle Paul. Furthermore virtually all agree that Paul wrote it in the later stages of his missionary career, after his famous journeys through Asia Minor and Greece but before his fateful journey to Jerusalem, where he was arrested, put on trial and sent to Rome after having appealed to Caesar. The epistle itself gives us enough information to be able to reconstruct this much, and it seems very likely, also on the basis of internal evidence, that Paul was in Corinth when he wrote it. The exact date of composition is unknown, but it was probably around A.D. 55-57.

Why Is the Epistle to the Romans Important?

The all but unanimous agreement about the authorship of the epistle is matched by an equally widespread consensus concerning its importance. Along with 1 Corinthians, it is one of the longest of Paul's epistles, and furthermore it was written to the church of the capital of the Roman Empire. The epistle is important because of what it tells us about the early days of the Roman church. Paul had not yet visited Rome when he wrote the epistle, but it is clear that he was intending to go there, and to some extent the epistle was a letter introducing him to the leaders of the church at Rome.

Who these leaders were is not clear, although a number of names are given to us in the final chapter. This is a matter of considerable historical interest, because for hundreds of years many scholars in the Western tradition have maintained that the apostle Peter was the first bishop of Rome. Why does Paul nowhere mention him? And if Peter had already brought the Christian gospel to the city, why was it necessary for Paul to write such a letter?

Until the fourth century there is little mention of Peter in any of the commentaries or remarks on the epistle that have come down to us. It was largely after the founding of Constantinople (A.D. 330) that Roman writers began to play on the Petrine origins of their church, probably in an attempt to ensure that Roman primacy would continue to be recognized by the other churches, even after the city had ceased to be the only imperial capital. From the commentaries that have survived, it is obvious that this issue caused some consternation. For if Peter had founded the Roman church, why was it so divided between Jewish and Gentile believers? Why did the Romans need basic Christian teaching from Paul when they had the senior apostle as their bishop? In any case Paul's epistle is the earliest evidence we have for the Christian community in the capital of the Roman Empire. There is no direct evidence in the letter to the Romans of Peter preceding Paul in Rome.

In this epistle Paul develops his views about the relation of Jews and Christians within the history of the covenant. The epistle is therefore also important because of what it tells us about the situation of both Jews and Gentiles within the church. The basic issue can be sketched as follows. Jesus Christ had come as the Savior of humankind, but he had come in the first place to the Jews. His life, ministry and death all took place within an essentially Jewish context. The apostles and their earliest followers were also Jews who believed that in Christ the promises of the Old Testament had been fulfilled for the benefit of the covenant people. But Paul and the other apostles had been led to preach the gospel to Gentiles as well. These Gentiles did not become Jews and saw no need to submit to a legal and ceremonial system that the apostles themselves admitted had been made obsolete by the coming of Christ. How could such people be integrated into a close-knit fellowship of believers, most of whom shared the same cultural assumptions of a Jewish minority living in a hostile pagan environment? Surely Gentiles could not go on living as they had done before if they claimed to worship the one true God.

From the Gentile side, however, the Jewish voices appeared to be arrogant and unreasonable. They were proud of their ancestry. Some claimed to be superior to the new converts, many of whom would have had little or no understanding of the gospel's Old Testament background. How would Gentiles ever feel at home in the church if physical descent from Abraham was a significant advantage, regardless of the spiritual state of those who claimed it? Was it not more important to believe what Abraham believed than to claim physical descent from him?

This was the situation confronting the apostle Paul. He addressed it by saying that each side was partly right and partly wrong and by pointing out that there was a common basis that could unite both into a single church. The Jews were right to emphasize their ancestry and their traditions because these things pointed toward the coming of Christ. Correctly understood and applied, these traditions gave Jews a great advantage in living the Christian life. But Gentiles were also right to insist that claiming descent from Abraham meant nothing if those who did so did not also believe what Abraham believed and did not relate to God in the same way as he had done—by faith.

Faith, says Paul, is the key theological principle that unites both Jews and Gentiles because it is by faith that we are justified, or made right with God. The epistle to the Romans is important because it gave Paul the opportunity to expound the fundamental principles of Christianity. Justification by faith, not by ancestry or the works of the law of Moses, is the starting point for Paul's whole argument. Once this is properly understood the barriers between Jews and Gentiles will melt away, because faith is a matter of the heart, not of the blood. Anyone with faith in Jesus as Lord and Savior is welcome in the Christian community, regardless of his or her background. Naturally, if people who have this faith also happen to have a good knowledge of the Bible (as most Jews did), this is a wonderful gift and will be of great benefit to them. But it is possible to know the Scriptures inside out without believing them, and in that case the knowledge such people have not only is useless but could be harmful as well, insofar as it cuts them off from Christ instead of drawing them to him.

Closely tied to the question of justification is another one, which preoccupies Paul in the later chapters[1] of the epistle. This is the great matter of election and/or predestination. Israel was the chosen people of God, called out from among the nations and given the special privilege and responsibility of being keepers of the divine revelation. The coming of Christ, which implied the opening of salvation to the Gentiles, threw this traditional Jewish belief into confusion. Had Israel ceased to be special in God's sight? Had the promises made to the Jews in the Old Testament been rescinded? Were Gentiles chosen by God, or could they decide for themselves whether or not to follow Christ?

Paul tackled these issues head-on. First, he said that God's plans and promises could never be altered. Therefore the Jews were still God's chosen people. However, the mark of their election was not circumcision or some other outward sign or ritual. It was faith—the same faith that Abraham had. Jews who shared this faith shared in Abraham's election, but others did not. Gentiles who shared Abraham's faith were added to the number of the elect, but the rest were not. The only difference was that at the end of time, after the full number of the elect Gentiles had been gathered in, God would show mercy on the Jews and "all Israel" would be saved. The precise meaning of this continues to be debated. Some scholars think that it includes Gentile believers as well as Jews. Some think that it refers to all Jews, whether they are conscious believers or not. Others think that it refers to those Jews who are elect but who have not yet made a profession of faith in Christ. When they believe, then they will be joined to the existing company of Jewish and Gentile believers, and so "all Israel" will be saved. Whatever the right interpretation is, it is clear that God has not abandoned the Jewish people but still has a purpose for them that will be revealed in due time.

Paul developed his doctrine of election and predestination at great length, but in doing so he shifted the emphasis away from the traditional Jewish understanding of these concepts. For the Jews, election was primarily a matter of national destiny. It was Israel that was chosen, and individual Jews shared in the blessings that special status conveyed by emphasizing how they belonged to the nation. That is why circumcision was so important to them—it was their way of proving that they belonged to the chosen people. For Paul, however, election was primarily a matter of personal faith. You and I are elect if we share the faith of Abraham. Not all of Abraham's descendants inherited the promises; even Abraham's son Ishmael and his grandson Esau were cast out. This shift of emphasis from the national to the personal was fundamental to Paul's gospel, since it was only on that basis that the Gentiles, who were not a nation, could become God's people as the prophet Hosea had foretold.

The fathers of the church understood all this very well, but it must be said that they had great difficulty with the idea that individuals were predestined by God for salvation and even greater difficulty with its logical corollary, that other individuals were chosen by God for damnation (or reprobation, as it is sometimes called). To some this seemed like a denial of human free will, which they were determined to uphold even though the apostle Paul makes it quite clear in Romans 7 that the will of a sinful person is not free—it is in

---

[1]We speak of chapter and verse divisions for convenience, but they were not in the original text. Chapter divisions were made about A.D. 1200 and verse divisions much later.

bondage to sin. Only Augustine (354-430) was prepared to accept the logical consequences of Paul's teaching on this matter, and this led to his famous quarrel with Pelagius. Pelagius was only teaching what many of his contemporaries believed: that people were free to choose or to reject Christ. It was not easy for Augustine to overcome this belief. The Eastern (Greek) church has never accepted this aspect of Augustinian theology, and even the Western (Latin) church has often had to contend with serious opposition. Since the sixteenth century the debate between Jansenists and Molinists in the Roman Catholic Church and between Calvinists and Arminians in the Protestant churches has brought this issue to the fore repeatedly and has demonstrated how difficult it is to resolve the problem.

It is fair, however, to say that this difficulty was felt most acutely by Gentile Christians, and not by Jews like the apostle Paul. He had no trouble believing in election, since it was the only way he could explain the extraordinary survival of the Jewish people. Furthermore, Paul believed that the Gentiles were being grafted into this people and added to its history, a point that was not fully grasped by them until Augustine rewrote their history in his *City of God*. Paul wanted Gentiles to think of Abraham as their ancestor and of Israel as their people because they were united to believing Jews on the common basis of faith in God the Father of our Lord Jesus Christ.

To sum up the debate between the Jews and the Gentiles in the church, it can be said that on the whole the apostle Paul favored the Gentile position as being fundamentally more correct. Once the Jewish Law was seen in relation to the history of grace and Gentiles were admitted to the church on the same basis as Jews, it was hard to see how any absolutely special status could be given to the latter. Unfortunately, special status in the sight of God was what the Jewish case was all about. What Paul was prepared to concede to them was respect. He asked the Gentiles to show consideration for the sensitivities of those who had been chosen even before the coming of Christ and warned them not to be proud, because if the Jews, to whom the promises had been given, were cast out, how much more easily could the same fate befall those who had not been so chosen.

In rendering a modern translation of references to the Jews by Paul and early Christian exegetes, I have sought to avoid the erroneous implication that the modern nuances of racial anti-Semitism were in any way a premise or an insinuation in early Christian texts. When the term "the Jews" is used, as it so often is by Paul in his letter to the Roman Christians, many of whom were Jews, his reference was not to all Jews of all times but to Judaizing Christians who wanted to return Gentile Christians to Jewish practices, or to the pride of Jews over the Law that prevented their becoming open to the gift of forgiveness in Christ, or to those Jewish religious leaders who aggressively opposed the truth of Christianity. These were not racial but religious issues and controversies. In order to avoid these misleading implications we have at times rendered references to the Jews as to the covenant people or the people of Israel or sons of Abraham.

Wherever references to humanity, humankind or the human race are rendered "man" in English translations, I have sought within reason to avoid sexist implications, but this has not always been possible or advisable in a way that will be found acceptable to all audiences. We are pledged not to distort the text by this attempt at avoidance.

A number of other theological themes are tackled in the epistle, most notably the question of eschatology, which is the hope of a future fulfillment in Christ. This idea permeates the epistle, and the apostle Paul repeatedly invokes it as a motive for Christians to continue in faith and responsible behavior in the present. It is sometimes said nowadays that this hope of an imminent second coming of Christ gradually faded away toward the end of the New Testament period, but the evidence of the Fathers does not support this. They regarded the persecutions they had to suffer and the rapid spread of the gospel across the Roman world as signs that the prophecies of the end were about to be fulfilled. If anything, because the eschaton was growing nearer every day, the need for constant vigilance was even greater in their time than it had been at the beginning.

Closely tied up with this idea was the question of the relationship between the primitive church and the state, which Paul deals with briefly in Romans 13. The apostle maintains that the secular authorities were appointed by God and that it is the duty of Christians to obey them in all things lawful. In saying this he was opening up a new area for theological exploration. In Old Testament Israel there was no real separation between the spiritual and the temporal, even though there was a clear distinction in function between the priest and the king. Pagan rulers were appointed by God to fulfill prophecies, as in the cases of Pharaoh, Nebuchadnezzar and Cyrus, but apart from Jeremiah's counsel to the exiles (Jer 29) there is little concept of living permanently under a religiously hostile secular government. From the standpoint of Israelite history, Paul's teaching is extraordinary, and it was soon to be tried to the utmost. It is astonishing to note how the Fathers unanimously support the apostle's position, even under the most extreme provocation from the Roman authorities. Persecution, they came to believe, was a blessing sent from God, and therefore the rulers who brought it were to be thanked, not cursed.

Other matters discussed at length in Romans concern issues of personal holiness, which figure prominently in almost all of Paul's epistles. This was a strong point of the Jews, who had grown accustomed to living separate lives in a pagan environment, although they had to learn that true holiness was a matter of inward conviction, not of outward display. The Gentiles had to learn what it meant to be holy, and in many ways it must have been far more difficult for them to cut themselves off from their pagan neighbors and relatives. But because the call to holiness was the essential preparation for the coming eschaton and the inheritance of eternal life, it could not be shirked. This hope governs everything Paul writes to the Romans, and it is echoed by the Fathers at every turn.

Finally, if faith produces hope for the future, hope must be worked out in a Christian life lived in love. Faith, hope and love are as much pillars of Romans as they are of 1 Corinthians (cf. 1 Cor 13:12). Paul concludes his discussion of Christian behavior on that note: Love of one's neighbor is the true fulfilling of the law, and this remains an obligation for Christians every bit as much as it had always been an obligation for Jews. The person equipped with faith, hope and love will never have to fear for what may happen to him or her, for it is certain that person will inherit the kingdom of God and reign with Christ forever.

How Were the Patristic Quotations Used Here Selected?

The epistle to the Romans has always been among the best known and most frequently quoted New Testament texts. From the patristic period alone there are literally thousands of quotations and allusions, all of which can now be recovered without difficulty, thanks to the possibilities that have been opened up by computer research. The combined resources of the Thesaurus Linguae Graecae and of the Centre de Textes et Documents (Cetedoc) have made it possible to obtain a virtually complete collection of patristic references to Romans which, if they were all reproduced, would take up several volumes. Fortunately, for our purposes the abundance of patristic comment on Romans makes it unnecessary to deal with as much of this sort of material as would be necessary in the case of Mark, for example. Many references are merely passing allusions to the text that shed little or no light on its meaning. Sometimes they are nothing more than quotations that are intended to reinforce a point that has been made on the strength of some other part of Scripture, and more often than we today would like, they are taken out of context.

Indirect allusions to the text of Romans (as distinguished from precise quotations) are almost all that we have to go on for the very earliest period (before A.D. 200), and so a selection of quotations from authors like Justin Martyr, Irenaeus and Tertullian has been given in order to give readers a flavor of how Romans was used before commentary writing became common. These allusions must be used with a certain degree of caution, since in almost every case the writer was making some other point and merely using Romans in order to bolster that argument. For the purposes of this collection an effort has been made to ensure that such references do in fact have a genuine link with Paul's epistle, but even so, readers will be well advised to treat this material with discretion.

We possess a large number of commentaries on the epistle, many of which have survived more or less intact. The first and in some ways greatest of these is the massive work of Origen (c. 185-c. 254), who wrote no fewer than fifteen books on this one epistle. Even in ancient times, this was felt by many to be a bit too much, and in about A.D. 400 a Roman theologian by the name of Rufinus translated the work into Latin, abridging it to a mere ten volumes and adapting it to the needs of Latin-speaking readers. In this form the text has come down to us, although there are enough Greek fragments surviving to enable us to confirm that Rufinus in most cases did not substantially distort the content of Origen's original work.

Origen was prone to two things that modern readers find difficult—digression and allegory. He often interrupts the flow of his commentary to explain (at great length) such matters as the nature of Old Testament priesthood and sacrifice. This is understandable, given the fact that most of his original audience would have had little or no understanding of classical Judaism, but these digressions do take us a long way from Romans. For our purposes it has been necessary to leave most of this material out, although one or two samples have been included in brief form so that the flavor of the original can be grasped.

Allegory is much easier to quote, and it is only fair to Origen that readers should be exposed to his technique in this matter. In principle, Origen did not allegorize those parts of Scripture whose literal sense was clear and acceptable to the moral conscience.[2] Romans, as it happens, tends to fall into this category almost entirely, so there is relatively little allegory, at least when compared with what Origen wrote in his commentaries on parts of the Old Testament. Nevertheless there are times when the influence of Platonism was too strong for him to resist, and we find him, for example, lapsing into allegorical interpretations based on a Platonic body-soul-spirit distinction. We also find frequent references to natural law as opposed to the law of Moses, because Origen preferred the universal character of the former. By interpreting a phrase like "sin against the law" as a reference to natural and not Jewish law, he could extend culpability for sin to the Gentiles and assume a scenario in which the gospel's message of salvation would speak equally to both.

---

[2]Origen looked for a spiritual interpretation of passages of Scripture that portrayed God in anthropomorphic terms.

The specific contribution of Rufinus is most noticeable in the references that occur from time to time to Latin texts and versions of the Scriptures. Origen may have known of some of these, but it is extremely unlikely that he would have made use of them in his original commentary. We may therefore assume that whenever "Origen" refers to something Latin, it is really Rufinus who is speaking. Beyond that it is difficult to say for sure what comes from Rufinus and what does not. No doubt he touched up Origen's text as he went along, but on the whole it seems that the author's original intention has been preserved in translation, so that we can confidently assert that the text as we have it is largely the authentic voice of Origen. There is a good modern German translation (in five volumes, with a sixth containing the Greek fragments still forthcoming) but nothing in English. For this reason quotations from Origen in this book are longer and more frequent than they might otherwise be, since many readers will not have immediate access to the material elsewhere.

After Origen's time, more than a century passed before the next commentary of any significance appeared. A certain Euthalius the Deacon (fourth century?) attempted one but did not get further than a prologue and a list of headings, which does not tell us a great deal. Eusebius of Emesa (d. c. 359) and Acacius of Caesarea (d. 366) both produced commentaries, but these survive now only in fragments. In this edition they have both been cited fairly often, and it is hoped that the selection offered will give a reasonable picture of their work.

The next full-length commentary to appear is by common consent the greatest of them all. It was the work of an unknown scholar, writing in Rome sometime between 366 and 384. He wrote in Latin, and throughout the Middle Ages his identity was merged with that of Ambrose of Milan (d. 397). It was not until Erasmus (1466-1536) examined the text that it became clear that this attribution was a mistake. In reality the commentary on this and on the other Pauline epistles was the work of a much greater scholar than Ambrose, whom Erasmus somewhat punningly chose to call Ambrosiaster, the name by which he has been known ever since.

Ambrosiaster wrote a literal commentary, and he was fully aware of the problems posed by historical and textual criticism. His work can easily stand comparison with modern writings on the subject, so close were his methods to those generally employed today. Who Ambrosiaster was is a matter of speculation, the most intriguing suggestion being that he may have been a monk known as Isaac the Jew, who was a converted Jew in Rome. If that is true, it would certainly explain Ambrosiaster's deep and sympathetic knowledge of Judaism, though we are constrained by lack of evidence from making any definite decision on the question. Whoever he was, he was soon being widely read and imitated, though never altogether successfully. It is a great pity that his work is not available in English translation, and so it is unknown to most readers. For that reason this edition contains rather more of Ambrosiaster than might otherwise be the case, since in effect it is introducing him to a wider reading public for the first time.

Contemporary with Ambrosiaster are a number of Greek commentators whose work survives only in fragments. They are Diodore of Tarsus (d. c. 390), Apollinaris of Laodicea (310-c. 392), Didymus the Blind of Alexandria (313-398) and Severian of Gabala (fl. c. 400). With the exception of Didymus, these all represent the Antiochene school of biblical exegesis, which concentrated heavily on the literal interpretation of the texts and which is full of historical details, textual criticism and so on. The fragmentary nature of the surviving material means that it is impossible to do full justice to them, but the selection presented here will at least give some idea of how these commentators went about their task. Didymus was a partial exception in the sense that he wrote from Alexandria, which was the great rival of Antioch and where an allegorical interpretation of Scripture was more favored. Nevertheless Didymus himself resisted this tendency to a large extent, and the style of his commentary is not noticeably different from that of the others.

The next full-length work to appear in Greek was the sermon series of John Chrysostom (347-407), the famous preacher who became patriarch of Constantinople but who was exiled by the court because of his boldness in criticizing its corruption. Chrysostom has left us thirty-two homilies that compose a verse-by-verse exposition of Romans. Each homily concludes with a long section relating to practical application, most of which has had to be omitted from the present edition. It is, however, readily available in English translation, so that anyone interested in reading the complete text will not have any difficulty finding it. As is to be expected from homilies, Chrysostom's style is more powerfully rhetorical than that of the others. At the same time he was a good historian and critic, and his conclusions about the authorship and dating of Romans are what most commentators would still propose. For a series like this one, which aims to reach pastors and ordinary Christians rather than professional exegetical scholars, he is often the most user-friendly commentator of them all.

About the same time as Chrysostom or slightly later came Theodore of Mopsuestia (350-428), another Antiochene whose work survives only in fragments. Theodore was a truly great commentator, and if his work had survived in toto he would rank with Ambrosiaster or even higher. His feeling for Paul's language and meaning was deep, and his critical sense was acute. His judgments were almost always felicitous, and it is our good fortune that so many of them have survived in the catenae[3] even though the complete text has disappeared.

In the Latin-speaking world, the years around 400 saw a sudden explosion of interest in commentary writing. We have already mentioned Rufinus's translation of Origen, but to that must be added the work of an unknown commentator, who may have been Constantius of Aquileia (fl. c. 405). This is only a guess, but to avoid the vagueness of the word *Anonymous* and to indicate that we are speaking of a single text, we have chosen to use the name "[Pseudo-]Constantius" to indicate selections from this commentary. In general it is brief and to the point, which makes it easy to extract material from.

Similar to this work and evidently dependent on it is the commentary written by the archheretic Pelagius (c. 354-c. 420), which has survived because for many centuries it was thought to have been the work of Jerome. It is important because it allows Pelagius to speak for himself on subjects that were to land him in controversy with Augustine and eventually to lead to his condemnation. What we find is a man of moderate and even mainstream views, though it has to be remembered that the text as we now have it was reworked in the sixth century by both Primasius and Cassiodorus. Pelagius's original text was in specific ways presumably explicitly heretical, but what we have now is unexceptional, even if it is still possible to detect points of disagreement with Augustine.[4] There is a good recent edition and translation into English,

---

[3]"Chains" of quotations selected and anthologized, rather like the present volume.

[4]The corpus of Pelagius is highly controverted. Until 1934 all we had was a corrupted text of his Pauline commentary and fragments quoted by Augustine. R. F. Evans argues that the Pauline commentary was the original work of Pelagius. Since the Pelagian corpus has been so corrupted by a history of redactors, the reader is well advised to not too easily equate the fourth-century Pelagius with later standard stereotypes of the archheresy of Pelagianism. Cf. Adalbert Hamman, Supplementum to Migne PL 1 1959 cols. 1101-1570.

with a full explanation of the history of the commentary (see the bibliography).

By any standard of measurement, Augustine of Hippo (354-430) was the greatest of the Latin fathers, and his reading of Romans was particularly original. He was the most austere of the Fathers in fully accepting the implications of the apostle Paul's teaching on the vexed questions of election and predestination, and this became the hallmark of his later writing. In particular this issue led him into conflict with Pelagius. It is therefore especially disappointing to have to record that although he began to write a commentary on Romans, he never got beyond the introduction. The most systematic exposition of the epistle that we have from him is a series of propositions that deal with the main points of the epistle in a very brief form. These propositions are interesting because they were written at an early stage in Augustine's career, when his views were still not all that different from those of Pelagius.

But of course this only makes the absence of a later, more mature commentary all the more frustrating. What we have are extracts from other works, including a number of letters in which Augustine treats particular verses from Romans without going into the argument of the epistle as a whole. In this edition we have quoted fairly extensively from the Propositions but have also given a wide sampling of his other writings, in order to do justice to the development of his thought. However, the reader is bound to feel somewhat disappointed, in that what would probably have been the most interesting commentary of all was never written.

After Augustine's time there were further commentaries in Greek, of which the most notable was written by Theodoret of Cyr (393-466). This survives, almost uniquely among the Antiochene commentaries, although it is unfortunately not available in English translation. Theodoret was dependent on Theodore of Mopsuestia, and from him we can catch a glimpse of the greatness of the Antiochene tradition. He eschews allegory, concentrates on historical and grammatical details and stays close to the apostle's original intention. His comments are usually helpful and retain their freshness even after the passage of time. Because of all this, we have chosen to offer a fairly extensive selection of his work, so that both he and the tradition he represents may be made more familiar to modern readers.

After Theodoret's time there is the fragmentary Greek commentary of Gennadius of Constantinople (d. 471) and the very incomplete Latin homilies of Luculentius (fifth-sixth centuries), which bring us near the end of the patristic period. Neither of these is especially remarkable, but both are quoted from time to time to give readers some impression of how Romans was being read at the beginning of the Middle Ages.

In addition to the commentaries that are available, there is a wide choice of other patristic works in which particular passages or verses of Romans are mentioned and commented on. In making a selection of them for this volume, two considerations have guided our choice. The first of these is the prominence and representativeness of the writer or source being used. There is little point in quoting obscure authors or writings simply in order to demonstrate a knowledge of their existence. But given that this is often the only way that gives us access to Syriac and Coptic sources, an exception to this rule has been made for them. Otherwise we have preferred to rely on mainstream writers, whose works have entered the spiritual tradition of the church, and who may therefore be taken as more fully representative of patristic thought as a whole.

How Are the References Presented so as to Enable the Reader to Easily Locate the Original Text and Examine It in Its Context?

Gaining access to writings that were produced long ago in ancient languages is never an easy matter, and translations into English do not always help us very much. A number of such translations were made in the nineteenth century, which was a great age of patristic scholarship, but the style of the English is often dated. Modern readers do not want to plow through long sentences full of subordinate clauses and polysyllabic words whose meaning is clear only to those with a classical education. It is also the case that the Fathers wrote to be read aloud, not silently, and they are therefore much more rhetorical in their style than we would be. Sometimes this is attractive, but more often than not the modern reader finds it high-blown and irritating. It can also become unnecessarily repetitive and even disjointed in places, as speech often is.

In this edition, all that has been smoothed out. Contemporary style has been preferred, even when this has meant recasting the literal wording of the original text. Because we are presenting extracts, not complete texts, it has sometimes been necessary to supply bridging material that is not explicitly in the original text but that is either implied by it or is contained there at much greater length. Rather than quoting an entire page merely to retain a particular sentence, we have at times taken the liberty of condensing such paragraphs into a sentence or two, using ellipses so as not to detract from the essence of what the Father in question was really trying to say. Existing English translations have been consulted and used to some extent, but we have felt free to alter them to fit the style and needs of the present edition, so that it is only very occasionally that their wording has been preserved intact. In particular we have tried to establish some consistency in the rendering of theological terms, and whenever possible we have opted for the variants that are normally used by theologians today. All this may cause a certain amount of irritation to the professional scholar, but it should be remembered that the purpose of this commentary is to allow the Fathers to speak to the present generation, not to give people the impression that it is necessary to have a classical Greek or Latin education in order to understand them.

When selections are taken from complete commentaries organized sequentially on a verse-by-verse basis, such as those of Origen, Theodoret or Ambrosiaster, only brief forms of references are given. In many cases these commentaries are untranslated, and we have translated in this series only the portion of them relevant to our editorial premises. It is assumed that anyone wishing to consult the original will have only to look up the relevant chapter and verse of the commentary in question. Hence where the *ad loc*[5] reference appears, the reader may proceed directly to the commentary referred to and consult the specific Scripture text under discussion. This reference will apply only to line-by-line commentaries. Apart from line-by-line commentaries, however, quotations are referenced according to source, either in the original language or translation. Where possible, reference is also made to the best available English translation, though the reader must be warned that what is found in this book is at most a dearchaized adaptation of that and probably not a direct quotation.

Each selection is referenced first by its title and in some cases by its book, chapter and section reference (and subsection where necessary), and then it is footnoted by an abbreviated citation (normally citing the

---

[5]Indicating that the reader can refer to the location of the verse in the line-by-line commentary.

book, volume and page number), usually in its original source and in some cases in translation. For the convenience of computer users, many of the digital database references are provided in the appendix, either to the Thesaurus Linguae Graeca or to the Latin Cetedoc. Some previous English translations have been dearchaized or amended for easier reading. We have in some cases edited out superfluous conjunctions for easier reading.

Furthermore, each group of verses is preceded by a short overview that gives the reader some idea of what the following discussion is about. Where there are notable differences of opinion among the Fathers or where one of them has presented a particularly significant argument, this is also noted, so that readers may be alerted to the particular importance of the selection that follows. The function of the overview in a given pericope is to provide a brief appraisal of all the comments to follow and to show that there is a reasonably cohesive thread of argument among passages taken from diverse sources and generations. We concede that the overview might reasonably be stated by other perceptive interpreters in various ways using other editorial criteria.

Where a selection has no heading, the previous heading applies. In some cases there may be several selections grouped under a single heading. Or when the selection is either very short or very obvious, no heading is included. Headings were selected[6] to identify either a key phrase of the text being commented upon, a key metaphor in the comment or some core idea of the selection.

It remains to be said only that the main purpose of this volume is to edify the communion of saints so that Christians today may be encouraged to examine and appropriate what the writers of an earlier time, many of whom have been canonized by the tradition of the church and all of whom are still worth reading, had to say about one of the greatest letters ever written—the apostle Paul's epistle to the Romans. May God by his grace open the hearts and minds of all who read these texts, and may we, together with them, come to that perfect peace and joy that is the inheritance of the saints in light.

Gerald Bray
Feast of St. Augustine of Hippo

---

[6]By the general editor.

THE EPISTLE TO THE ROMANS

1:1-7 PAUL AND THE GOSPEL

¹Paul, a servant[a] *of Jesus Christ, called to be an apostle, set apart for the gospel of God ²which he promised beforehand through his prophets in the holy scriptures, ³the gospel concerning his Son, who was descended from David according to the flesh ⁴and designated Son of God in power according to the Spirit of holiness by his resurrection from the dead, Jesus Christ our Lord, ⁵through whom we have received grace and apostleship to bring about the obedience of faith for the sake of his name among all the nations, ⁶including yourselves who are called to belong to Jesus Christ;*

⁷To all God's beloved in Rome, who are called to be saints:

Grace to you and peace from God our Father and the Lord Jesus Christ.

a Or *slave*

OVERVIEW: The first seven verses of Romans 1 serve as an introduction to the whole epistle, and the Fathers made many comments on them that nowadays would normally be found in a general preface. They were especially fascinated by the name Paul itself and sought to discern why it had been changed from Saul. The Fathers were also interested in the fact that Paul called himself a servant (slave), which is not surprising given the fact that they were living in a slave-holding society. Nor were they slow to link the apostle's sense of his calling to God's foreknowledge and predestination. This tendency to move from particular details to universal concepts is typical of the ancients generally, and so we must not be surprised to discover that verses like these could be used as a basis for profound theological reflections.

All the Fathers accepted the validity of Old Testament prophecy concerning the coming of Christ, but they were capable of seeing this from many different angles. Some stressed the importance of the gospel as distinct from the coming of Christ in the flesh; others focused on the role of the prophets, and Augustine was concerned to point out that there had been Gentiles as well as Jews who had foretold his coming. Especially from the fourth century onward, the Fathers all emphasized that Christ was the eternal Son of God, because this had by then become the main point in dispute with the Arians. But John Chrysostom was bold enough to point out that in the order of revelation believers came to know the human Christ before they understood that he was God. Romans 1:4 received an enormous amount of attention from the Fathers, because it seemed to suggest that Jesus of Nazareth was merely a man who was "designated" Son of God after his resurrection. All of them took great pains to insist that this was not what Paul meant. Of particular interest in this respect is the lengthy passage from Origen, which obviously has been touched up by Rufinus. In the authentically Origenist part we find that the great biblical scholar was prepared to admit that Joseph could be called the father of Jesus—in an allegorical sense. This use of allegory is the exact opposite of what a modern commentator would suppose, since for moderns it is not the fatherhood of Joseph but the doctrine of the virgin birth of Christ that causes problems and might be regarded as an allegorical reading of those Old Testament texts that are quoted as prophecies of his coming.

Paul received his commission by grace, not because he had any special entitlement to it. Moreover, the word *apostle* had more than one meaning, and it was was not always restricted to a special office as it is in Romans 1:5. Since the gift of God is given to all, all believers from all nations are called to the obedience of faith, even though not all are Jews and not all are apostles. God's love has presented us with grace, and grace with peace. Paul prayed that all who are called might receive the grace of God, by which all believers enjoy salvation, and peace, by which God gives to all the restoration of excellent behavior.

1:1 A Servant of Jesus Christ

CALLED TO BE AN APOSTLE. ORIGEN: The first question which occurs to us concerns the name Paul itself. Why is he, who in Acts[1] was called Saul, now called Paul? In Holy Scripture we find that among the ancients, many names were altered, e.g., Abram was renamed Abraham,[2] Sarai became Sarah,[3] and Jacob became Israel.[4] In the Gospels too, Simon was changed to Peter,[5] and the sons of Zebedee became known as sons of thunder.[6] But these things occurred by divine command, and we read nothing of the sort in the case of Paul. Because of this, some people have imagined that the apostle took the name of Paul, the proconsul of Cyprus, whom he converted to the Christian faith,[7] in the same way that rulers

are in the habit of adding the names of conquered peoples to their titles, e.g., Parthicus would indicate someone who conquered the Parthians, Gothicus a victor over the Goths, and so on. In the same way the apostle would have called himself Paul to indicate that he had conquered the proconsul Paul.

We cannot exclude this reason completely, but given that no such custom can be found in Holy Scripture, we ought rather to seek a solution from the examples which we do have. And indeed we find in the Scriptures that some people have two or even three different names, e.g., Solomon is also called Jedidiah,[8] Zedekiah is also called Mattaniah,[9] Uzziah is also called Azariah,[10] and there are many others in the books of Judges, Samuel and Kings who have double names. But even the Gospels do not abandon this custom, e.g., Matthew was called Levi[11] . . . and Thaddeus sometimes appears as Lebbaeus.[12] Obviously the Gospel writers did not get the names of the apostles wrong, but given that it was the custom of the Hebrews to have two or three names, they gave different names to one and the same man. It seems to us that it is in accordance with this custom that Paul appears to have a second name, and that as long as he was ministering to his own people he was called Saul, which was probably the name his parents gave him, but that when he was writing laws and commandments for the Greeks and other Gentiles, he was called Paul. Scripture makes it clear when it says: "Saul, who is also called Paul,"[13] that the name Paul was not then being given to him for the first time but was already habitual.

But why does Paul call himself a slave, when elsewhere he says: "For you did not receive the spirit of slavery to fall back into fear, but you have received the Spirit of sonship, by which we cry Abba! Father!"[14] . . . We may understand this as an expression of humility . . . and that would not

---

[1]Cf., e.g., Acts 9:1. [2]See Gen 17:5. [3]See Gen 17:15. [4]See Gen 32:28; 35:10. [5]See Mk 3:16; Lk 6:14. [6]See Mk 3:17. [7]See Acts 13:4-12. [8]2 Sam 12:25. [9]2 Kings 24:17. [10]2 Kings 15:32. [11]Lk 5:27. [12]Cf. Mt 10:3. [13]Acts 13:9. [14]Rom 8:15.

be wrong. Nor is the reality of Paul's freedom compromised by this in any way. As he himself says: "Though I am free from all men, I have made myself a slave to all."[15]. . . For he serves Christ not in the spirit of slavery but in the spirit of adoption, for Christ's service is more noble than any freedom.

"Called" is the name given to everyone who believes in Christ and is therefore a general term, although it is applied to each one according to what God has foreseen and chosen in him. He may be called to be an apostle or a prophet or a teacher; as free from a wife or as bound in marriage, and this is determined by the diversity of grace given to everyone, as it is written: "Many are called but few are chosen."[16]

In Paul's case, he was not called to be an apostle in the general sense, but he was also chosen according to the foreknowledge of God to be "set apart for the gospel of God," as he says elsewhere: "God set me apart before I was born and called me through his grace."[17] Heretics wrongly claim that he was set apart from his mother's womb on account of the goodness of his nature, just as from the opposite side of the fence we read in the Psalms of those "sinners who were separated from the womb"[18] because of their evil nature.

But we say that Paul was chosen neither by accident nor because of some natural difference, but he himself attributed the causes of his election to him who knows everything before it happens. . . . For God foresaw that Paul would labor more abundantly than anyone else in the gospel . . . and for that reason Jesus set him apart in his mother's womb for the gospel. Had he been chosen by fate, as the heretics maintain, or by some inherently better nature, he would not have been afraid of being condemned if he failed to preach the gospel.[19]

God's foreknowledge, by which those who will labor and succeed are known, comes first, and his predestination follows afterwards, so that foreknowledge cannot be regarded as the cause of predestination. With men, merits are weighed according to past actions, but with God they are weighed according to future behavior, and anyone who thinks that God cannot see our future just as easily as he can see our past is an unbeliever. COMMENTARY ON THE EPISTLE TO THE ROMANS.[20]

CALLED AS SERVANT AND APOSTLE. EUSEBIUS OF EMESA: Some people argue quite pointlessly as to whether the participle *called* is meant to modify *servant* or *apostle*. It applies to both, since everyone is called, and called equally, both to faith and grace and to election and the apostolic order. PAULINE COMMENTARY FROM THE GREEK CHURCH.[21]

FROM RESTLESSNESS TO REST. AMBROSIASTER: Saul changed his name to Paul, and the change was permanent. Because Saul means restlessness or trial, when he came to faith in Christ he called himself Paul, i.e., rest, because our faith is peace. For whereas previously he had inflicted trials on the servants of God because of his desire to fulfill the law, later he himself endured trials on account of the hope which before he had denied because of his love of Judaism.

In calling himself a "servant of Jesus Christ," Paul shows that he has been delivered from the law, and he puts both names, Jesus and Christ, in order to signify the person of God and man, for in both he is Lord, as Peter the apostle testifies, saying: "He is the Lord of all."[22] And because he is Lord, he is also God, as David says: "For the Lord himself is God."[23] The heretics deny this. Marcion, it seems, denied Christ and his body out of hatred for the law, although he confessed Jesus. The Jews and Photinus denied that Jesus was God out of their zeal for the law. For whenever Scripture says either "Jesus" or "Christ," it sometimes means the person of God and sometimes the person of the man, e.g.: "there is one Lord Jesus Christ, through whom are all things."[24]

---

[15]1 Cor 9:19. [16]Mt 22:14. [17]Gal 1:15. [18]Ps 58:3. [19]1 Cor 9:16. [20]CER 70-88. [21]NTA 15:46. [22]Acts 10:36. [23]Ps 100:3. [24]1 Cor 8:6.

"Called to be an apostle." Because Paul acknowledged the Lord and confessed him he became the perfect servant and shows that he was promoted, saying that he was called to be an apostle, i.e., a messenger sent by the Lord to do his work. By this he shows that he had merit with God because he served Christ and not the law.

"Set apart for the gospel of God." The gospel of God is good news, by which sinners are called to forgiveness. For since as a Pharisee the apostle held a teaching post among the Jews, he now says that he has been set apart from the preaching of Judaism for the gospel of God, so that abandoning the law, he might preach Christ who justifies those who believe in him, which the law could not do. This does not go against the law but affirms it, since the law itself says that this will happen in the future, in the words of Isaiah the prophet: "There will come from Zion one who will break and remove the captivity of Jacob, and this will be a testimony of me, when I shall take away their sins."[25] COMMENTARY ON PAUL'S EPISTLES.[26]

SET APART. APOLLINARIS OF LAODICEA: Paul was set apart and dedicated to evangelism, like the offerings which the law says were set apart for God and for the priests.[27] PAULINE COMMENTARY FROM THE GREEK CHURCH.[28]

CALLED FROM HEAVEN. SEVERIAN: Paul here preaches the divinity of Christ to a world which was ignorant of it. Many people saw the Lord, and others believed in him without seeing, but Paul was called from heaven: "Saul, Saul, why do you persecute me?"[29] He was more highly favored than the other apostles, for the Lord called Peter and James and John and made them his disciples; he did not immediately make or call them apostles. But he made Paul an apostle as soon as he called him. Thus the gospel is preached according to the plan of God. PAULINE COMMENTARY FROM THE GREEK CHURCH.[30]

THE NAME OF PAUL. CHRYSOSTOM: Moses wrote five books, but nowhere did he put his own name to them . . . nor did Matthew, John, Mark or Luke. But St. Paul everywhere in his epistles puts his own name.[31] Why? Because the others were writing to people who were present, and it would have been superfluous for them to have announced themselves when they were present. But Paul sent his writings from a distance and in the form of a letter, and so he had to add his name.

Why did God change his name and call him Paul instead of Saul? It was so that even in this respect he might not come short of the apostles but that he might also have the same preeminence that the chief of the disciples had[32] and on that basis be more closely united with them. Paul also calls himself the "servant" of Christ, and there are many kinds of servitude. One is related to creation, "for all things are thy servants."[33] Another comes from faith[34] and a third is civil subjection, as it says: Moses my servant is dead.[35] Indeed, all the Jews were servants, but Moses in a special way, since his light has shone most brightly in the community. Paul was a servant in all of these senses, and therefore he puts this term first, in the place of greatest dignity.

He says of himself, in all of his epistles, that he is "called," thereby demonstrating his own candor in admitting that it was not because he sought that he found but that when he was called, he came near and obeyed.[36] HOMILIES ON ROMANS 1.[37]

A SERVANT FIRST. THEODORE OF MOPSUESTIA: All things are servants of Christ, and he is Lord of all. Therefore Paul calls himself a servant first of all, thereby encouraging the rest to do likewise. He also recalls the unique lordship of the Son but not in such a way as to deny the lordship of the Father, which is confessed by everybody. In saying that he was set apart, he showed

---

[25]See Is 27:9. [26]CSEL 81.1:9, 11. [27]See Ex 29:24, 26, 28. [28]NTA 15:57. [29]Acts 9:4. [30]NTA 15:213. [31]See 1 Cor 1:1; 2 Cor 1:1; Gal 1:1; Phil 1:1. [32]Mk 3:16. [33]Ps 119:91. [34]See Rom 6:17-18. [35]Josh 1:2. [36]See Acts 9:1-19. [37]NPNF 1 11:338.

that he was not only called but also chosen from among many as useful for the preaching of the gospel. PAULINE COMMENTARY FROM THE GREEK CHURCH.[38]

CALLED AND SET APART. [PSEUDO-]CONSTANTIUS: Just as the names of other saints both in the Old and in the New Testament, e. g., Abraham and Peter and the rest, were changed in accordance with the advance and increase of their merits, so also Paul, as he grew in the grace of God, changed his name. He was a servant not out of fear but out of love, as he himself says: "It is no longer I who live, but Christ lives in me."[39] He reveals that he was not only "called" to the grace of apostleship but "set apart" for preaching to the Gentiles, as he himself records: "We to the Gentiles and they to the circumcision."[40] Called therefore by Christ to the apostleship, he was set apart for preaching to the Gentiles by the Holy Spirit, so that it might be revealed that the Father, Son and Holy Spirit are all of one substance. THE HOLY LETTER OF ST. PAUL TO THE ROMANS.[41]

CALLED FORTH. AUGUSTINE: By these two words, *called* and *set apart*, Paul distinguishes between the church, which is acceptable to God, and the synagogue, whose glory has faded away. The church (i.e., *ecclesia*) is so called because it "calls forth": the synagogue, because it "gathers together." RUDIMENTARY EXPOSITION OF THE EPISTLE TO THE ROMANS 2.1-3, 5.[42]

PAUL'S NEW NAME. PELAGIUS[43]: Do we wonder why he writes *Paul*, given that he was called Saul before? Doubtless he did this following the habit of the saints. When they advanced in virtue they were addressed with a different name, so that they might be new people even in name, e.g., Abraham, Sarah and Cephas.[44] . . . Paul earned the office of an apostle by faithful and matchless service. He was set apart in Acts 13:2. *Gospel* . . . means "good news", i.e., of Christ's birth, suffering, resurrection and ascension into heaven. PELAGIUS'S COMMENTARY ON ROMANS.[45]

THE SALUTATION OF GRACE. THEODORET OF CYR: Civil governors and military commanders put their titles at the beginning of their letters in order to boast and show off. But St. Paul says that he was born out of due time, that he is the chief of sinners and that he is unworthy of his apostleship. Nevertheless, when writing his letters, he starts with the words imposed on him by grace, for the benefit of those who receive them. For when the recipients realized the importance of the person who was writing to them, they would read the letter with greater earnestness and attention. INTERPRETATION OF THE LETTER TO THE ROMANS.[46]

1:2 The Promised Gospel

THE PROMISE OF THE GOSPEL. ORIGEN: You the reader must decide whether this is to be understood simply of the gospel which was promised by God through the prophetic Scriptures or whether this is said in order to distinguish it from another gospel, which John calls "eternal" in the book of Revelation.[47] This gospel will be revealed when the shadow passes and the truth comes, when death will be swallowed up and eternity restored. It seems that those eternal years of which the prophet spoke also belong to this eternal gospel: "I had the eternal years in mind."[48]

It must be understood that what was predicted by the prophets concerning Christ was also predicted concerning the gospel, although the Evangelist Mark seems to make a distinction between Christ and the gospel when he says: "Whoever has left father or mother . . . for my sake or for the gospel."[49] But if promises referring specifically to the gospel are what is required, you will find an abun-

---

[8]NTA 15:113. [39]Gal 2:20. [40]Gal 2:9. [41]*ENPK* 2:19-20. [42]*ERIE*, Migne PL 35 col. 2089. [43]Though he was officially a heretic, Pelagius's commentaries were widely read and preserved for future generations under other names. They were repeatedly edited for orthodoxy and recycled, so that what we have may be regarded as representative of much patristic thought and exegesis, excluding that which is ecumenically censured as Pelagianism. [44]Gen 17:5; Jn 1:42. [45]*PCR* 59. [46]*IER*, Migne PG 82 col. 48. [47]Rev 14:6. [48]Ps 77:5 (LXX 76:5). [49]Mk 10:29.

dance of them in the prophets, to wit: "The Lord will give his word with great power to those who preach the good news,"[50] and: "How beautiful are the feet of those who bring good news."[51] COMMENTARY ON THE EPISTLE TO THE ROMANS.[52]

PROMISED BEFOREHAND. AMBROSIASTER: "Which he had promised." In order to prove that the hope of faith was fulfilled and completed in Christ, Paul says that Christ's gospel was already promised by God beforehand, so that on the basis of the promise Paul could teach that Christ was the perfect author of [eternal] life.

"Through his prophets." In order to show even more clearly that the coming of Christ was a saving event, Paul also indicated the people through whom God gave his promise, so that it might be seen from them just how true and magnificent the promise is. For nobody uses great forerunners to announce some minor thing.

"In the holy scriptures." Paul added this on top of his argument in order to give greater confidence to believers and show his approval of the law. The Scriptures are holy because they condemn sins and because in them is contained the covenant of the one God and the incarnation of the Son of God for the salvation of mankind, by the evidence of numerous signs. COMMENTARY ON PAUL'S EPISTLES.[53]

THROUGH HIS PROPHETS. SEVERIAN: Paul says "his prophets" because there are also prophets of idols, and by the word *his* he distinguishes one type of prophet from another and one gospel from another. For there are many gospels, but they are moral and temporary, whereas that of Christ proclaims in the holy Scriptures the enjoyment of eternal blessedness. These prophets are *his* because they are not of another god but of the Father of Christ. PAULINE COMMENTARY FROM THE GREEK CHURCH.[54]

WORD AS ACT. CHRYSOSTOM: When God is about to do some great thing, he announces it a long time before in order to accustom men's ears

to it, so that when it comes they will accept it. The prophets not only spoke, but they wrote what they spoke; nor did they merely write, but by their very actions they represented what would come, e.g., Abraham when he offered up Isaac;[55] and Moses when he lifted up the serpent,[56] and when he spread out his hands against Amalek,[57] and when he offered the paschal Lamb.[58] HOMILIES ON ROMANS 1.[59]

WHETHER THERE ARE PROPHETS AMONG THE GENTILES. AUGUSTINE: The prophets arose from the Jewish people, and Paul testifies that the gospel, in which believers are justified by faith, had been promised earlier through them. . . . For there are Gentile prophets as well, in whom also are found some things which they heard of Christ and prophesied. This sort of thing is even said about the Sibyl [Virgil, *Eclogues* 4.4] . . . but the writings of the Gentiles, so very full of superstitious idolatry, ought not to be considered holy just because they say something about Christ. RUDIMENTARY EXPOSITION OF THE EPISTLE TO THE ROMANS 3.[60]

NO OTHER CHRIST. PELAGIUS: Paul preaches no other Christ than the Christ whose gospel the prophets promised would go forth from Jerusalem.[61] He declares that they are prophets of God and that the Scriptures which prophesied about Christ are holy. This entire passage contradicts the Manichaeans,[62] for it says that the gospel was promised beforehand through God's prophets and in the Holy Scriptures and that according to the flesh Christ came from the lineage of David, i.e., from the Virgin Mary, just as Isaiah had foretold.[63] PELAGIUS'S COMMENTARY ON ROMANS.[64]

WHY SCRIPTURE IS HOLY. THEODORET OF CYR: The Old Testament is full of predictions of

---

[50]Ps 68:11 (LXX 67:11). [51]Is 52:7. [52]CER 1:90, 94. [53]CSEL 81.1:13. [54]NTA 15:213. [55]See Gen 22:1-19. [56]See Num 21:9; Jn 3:4. [57]See Ex 17:8-13. [58]See Ex 12:1-30. [59]NPNF 1 11:339. [60]ERIE, Migne PL 35 col. 2089. [61]Is 2:3; Mic 4:2. [62]Who demeaned the flesh. [63]Is 7:14. [64]PCR 59.

Christ's coming. Paul did not call them "holy" by accident but, first of all, in order to teach that he recognized that the Old Testament was divinely inspired, and secondly, in order to exclude all other writings. For only the divinely inspired Scriptures are of any use. Indeed, Paul says that they are the image of the promise which was to come. INTERPRETATION OF THE LETTER TO THE ROMANS.[65]

1:3 The Gospel Concerning His Son

SON OF GOD AND OF DAVID. IGNATIUS: I glorify God . . . that you are fully persuaded that our Lord was truly of the seed of David according to the flesh and the Son of God according to the will and power of God. EPISTLE TO THE SMYRNEANS 1.[66]

NEVER A TIME WHEN HE DID NOT EXIST. ORIGEN: Without any doubt, he was made that which he had not previously been according to the flesh. But according to the Spirit he existed beforehand, and there was never a time when he did not exist. COMMENTARY ON THE EPISTLE TO THE ROMANS.[67]

CONCERNING THE SON. AMBROSIASTER: "Concerning his Son." It was fitting, since God promised his own Son to the world, that he should promise him through great men, so that from them it might be known how very powerful the one who was being preached was and so that he might include his future coming in the Holy Scriptures. And what is preached by the Holy Scriptures cannot be shown to be false.

"Who was descended from the seed of David according to the flesh." He who was the Son of God according to the Holy Spirit (that is, according to God, because God is Spirit and without any doubt he is holy), is said to have been made the Son of God according to the flesh by Mary, as it is written: "The Word became flesh."[68] Christ Jesus is both Son of God and Son of Man. As he is truly God, so also he is truly man. For he would not be truly man if he were not of flesh and

soul. Otherwise he would be incomplete. For although he was the Son of God in eternity, he was not known by the creation until, when God wanted him to be revealed for the salvation of mankind, he made him visible and corporeal, because God wanted him to be known through his power to cleanse humans from their sins by overcoming death in the flesh. Therefore he was made of the seed of David. As he was born a king from God before the beginning of time, so also he would acquire birth from a king according to the flesh, being made from a virgin by the work of the Holy Spirit,[69] i.e., born. Thus by the reverence reserved for him because of this fact, he who by his birth was distinguished from the law of nature would be recognized as being more than a man. This had been predicted by Isaiah the prophet: "Behold a virgin will conceive in her womb."[70] Hence when the newborn child appeared to be worthy of honor, a certain providence of God was discerned concerning a future visitation of the human race. COMMENTARY ON PAUL'S EPISTLES.[71]

A GENERATION ACCORDING TO THE SPIRIT. CHRYSOSTOM: Paul is here hinting that there is also a generation of Christ according to the Spirit. Why then did he begin from the flesh, and not from the higher principle? First, it was because that was where Matthew, Luke and Mark started from too. Anyone who wants to lead men by hand to heaven must lead them upward from below. This was the way the actual dispensation [of grace] was ordered. First, they saw Christ as a man on earth, and then later they understood that he is God. His disciple therefore followed the same order in which Christ himself had framed his teaching. Thus the generation according to the flesh comes first, not because it was first in actual fact but because he was leading his hearers upward from one thing to the other. HOMILIES ON ROMANS 1.[72]

---

[65]IER, Migne PG 82 col. 49. [66]ANF 1:86. [67]CER 1:94. [68]Jn 1:1. [69]See Mt 1:20-23. [70]Is 7:14. [71]CSEL 81.1:15. [72]NPNF 1 11:340.

ACCORDING TO THE FLESH. PELAGIUS: Many are sons by grace, but Christ is a son by nature. . . . By adding "according to the flesh" Paul has countered both Photinus and Arius. For if it is true that Christ was made according to the flesh, he most certainly was not made according to the substance of the Word. PELAGIUS'S COMMENTARY ON ROMANS.[73]

1:4 Divine and Human, the Son of God

DESIGNATED SON OF GOD. ORIGEN: Let no one think that we are reading more into this text than the meaning itself permits. For although in Latin translations one normally finds the word *predestined* here, the true reading is *designated* and not *predestined*. For *designated* applies to someone who already exists, whereas *predestined* is only applicable to someone who does not yet exist, like those of whom the apostle said: "For those whom he foreknew he also predestined."[74] . . . Those who do not yet exist may be foreknown and predestined, but he who is and who always exists is not predestined but designated. These things are said by us concerning those who speak blasphemously about the only begotten Son of God and ignoring the difference between *designated* and *predestined* think that Christ is to be numbered among those who were predestined before they existed. But he was never predestined to be the Son, because he always was and is the Son, just as the Father has always been the Father. . . . The apostle makes an essential distinction when he says that "from the seed of David according to the flesh" Christ was made, but as "the Son of God in power according to the Spirit of holiness" he is designated.

And when he says "Son of God" it is not without reason that he adds "in power," indicating by this that in substance he is the Son according to the Spirit of holiness. For Christ is called "the power of God and the wisdom of God."[75] . . . But we want to know what to make of the soul of Jesus, if what is born of the seed of David is according to the flesh and what is designated in power is according to the Spirit of holiness the Son of God

and in the substance of God. The soul, however, is not mentioned either with the flesh, with the Spirit of holiness or with the substance of God's power, although the Savior himself speaks of it elsewhere: "My soul is very sorrowful, even unto death"[76] and: "Now is my soul troubled."[77] Here he means the soul which he laid aside of his own free will, which went down to hell and of which it is said: "Thou dost not leave my soul in hell."[78] It is certain that this soul was not born of the seed of David, for he says that what was born of the seed of David was according to the flesh.

The soul cannot be included with the things which are according to the flesh, nor in that which is designated Son of God in power according to the Spirit of holiness. I think that the apostle is here following his usual custom, knowing that the soul is always midway between the spirit and the flesh. Either it joins itself to the flesh and is made one with the flesh or it associates itself with the spirit and is made one with the spirit. From this it may be concluded that when the soul is united with the flesh, men become carnal, and that when it is united with the spirit, men become spiritual. For this reason, Paul does not mention the soul independently but only as flesh or spirit. For he knows that the soul must necessarily attach itself to one or other of these, as it does in those to whom he says: "But you are in the flesh and not in the spirit,"[79] and: "Whoever joins himself to a harlot is one body with her," calling the harlot here "flesh" or "body," but "whoever joins himself to the Lord is one spirit with him."[80]

Some people come to us raising the most serious problems as to how Christ can be descended from the seed of David when it is clear that he was not born from Joseph, in whom the line of David descends from one generation to the other. Unpleasant as it is to have to argue according to the literal sense of the text, some of our people answer by saying that Mary was already engaged

---

[73]PCR 59-60. His creatureliness did not encompass the essence of the Word. [74]Rom 8:29. [75]1 Cor 1:24. [76]Mt 26:38. [77]Jn 12:27. [78]Ps 16:10. [79]Rom 8:9. [80]1 Cor 6:16-17.

to Joseph and that before they came together, she was found with child by the Holy Spirit. According to the law, she was therefore already united to Joseph's tribe and family.[81] . . . Whether you think this line of argument is valid is up to you, dear reader, to decide!

In our opinion, these things must be understood according to the spiritual or allegorical sense, according to which there is no reason why Joseph should not be called the father of Christ, even though he was not his father. For in the generations recorded by Matthew it is stated that Jehoshaphat begat Joram and Joram begat Uzziah,[82] but in 2 Kings it is said that Jehoshaphat begat Ahaziah and Ahaziah begat Joash and Joash begat Amaziah, and Amaziah begat Azariah, who was also called Uzziah.[83] . . . Matthew therefore left three generations out! The explanation for this is surely not to be sought on the historical level but in conjunction with the spiritual understanding. . . . It is therefore enough for us to say, in answer to our opponents, that just as Jesus is called the son of Joseph even though he did not descend from him, and Uzziah is called the son of Joram even though Joram was not his father, so can we also reckon that Christ was born of the seed of David according to the flesh. What we accept as reason and proof in the case of Joram and Joseph must, we think, be allowed to stand in the case of David as well.

How it is that he who is said to have been made from the seed of David according to the flesh should be the Son of God by his resurrection from the dead is not hard to understand for anyone who has read that it is written: "For it was fitting that he, for whom and by whom all things exist, in bringing many sons to glory, should make the pioneer of their salvation perfect through suffering."[84] Now the end of Christ's sufferings is the resurrection, and after the resurrection "he will never die again; death no longer has dominion over him."[85] And again: "Even though we once regarded Christ from a human point of view, we regard him thus no longer."[86] Thus everything which is in Christ is now the Son of God.

How this all relates to him who is designated Son of God in power is hard for us to understand unless we accept that, because of the indissoluble union of the Word and the flesh, everything which pertains to the flesh may be attributed to the Word also, and everything which pertains to the Word may be attributed to the flesh also. For we often find Jesus referred to in either nature as both Christ and Lord. COMMENTARY ON THE EPISTLE TO THE ROMANS.[87]

BECAUSE OF HIS RESURRECTION FROM THE DEAD. AMBROSIASTER: When Paul speaks about the Son of God he is pointing out that God is Father, and by adding the Spirit of holiness he indicates the mystery of the Trinity. For he who was incarnate, who obscured what he really was, was then predestined according to the Spirit of holiness to be manifested in power as the Son of God by rising from the dead, as it is written in Psalm 84: "Truth is risen from the earth."[88] For every ambiguity and hesitation was made firm and sure by his resurrection, just as the centurion, when he saw the wonders, confessed that the man placed on the cross was the Son of God.[89] . . . Note that Paul did not say "because of the resurrection of Jesus Christ" but "because of his resurrection from the dead," because the resurrection of Christ led to the general resurrection. For this power and victory in Christ appears to be all the greater, in that a dead man could do the same things as he did when he was alive. By this fact he appeared to dissolve death, in order to redeem us. Thus Paul calls him our Lord. COMMENTARY ON PAUL'S EPISTLES.[90]

ACCORDING TO THE SPIRIT OF HOLINESS. CHRYSOSTOM: What is being said here has been made obscure by the complex syntax, and so it is necessary to expound it. What is he actually saying? "We preach," says Paul, "him who was made

---

[81]See Num 36:8-9 [82]Mt 1:8. [83]2 Kings 8:25; 14:1; 15:1, 7, 30, 32, 34. [84]Heb 2:10. [85]Rom 6:9. [86]2 Cor 5:16. [87]CER 94-104. [88]Ps 85:12 (LXX 84:12). [89]See Mt 27:54. [90]CSEL 81.1:16.

of David." But this is obvious. How then is it obvious that this incarnate person was also the Son of God? First of all, it is obvious from the prophets [cf. v. 2], and this source of evidence is no weak one. And then there is the way in which he was born [cf. v. 3], which overruled the rules of nature. Third, there are the miracles which he did, which were a demonstration of much power, for the words *in power* mean this. Fourth, there is the Spirit which he gave to those who believe in him, through whom he made them all holy, which is why he adds: "according to the Spirit of holiness." For only God could grant such gifts. Fifth, there was the resurrection, for he first and he only raised himself, and he also said that this was a miracle which would stop the mouths even of those who believed arrogantly, for he said: "Destroy this temple and in three days I will raise it up."[91] HOMILIES ON ROMANS 1.[92]

IN POWER. [PSEUDO-]CONSTANTIUS: By saying "in power" Paul shows that Christ was conceived not in the normal human way, but that he was procreated from a virgin, without intercourse with a man. He also tells us the time from which he was called to the apostolate, viz., from that time when Christ the Lord was raised from the dead. THE HOLY LETTER OF ST. PAUL TO THE ROMANS.[93]

HUMAN AND DIVINE. AUGUSTINE: Paul had to oppose the unbelief of those who accept our Lord Jesus Christ only according to the man whom he put on but do not understand his divinity, which sets him apart from every other creature. RUDIMENTARY EXPOSITION OF THE EPISTLE TO THE ROMANS 4.[94]

WEAKNESS AND POWER. AUGUSTINE: Christ is the son of David in weakness according to the flesh but Son of God in power according to the Spirit of sanctification. . . . Weakness relates to David but life eternal to the power of God. RUDIMENTARY EXPOSITION OF THE EPISTLE TO THE ROMANS 5.[95]

THE ASSUMPTION OF HUMANITY BY THE WORD OF GOD. AUGUSTINE: Jesus was predestined, so that he who was to be the Son of David according to the flesh should nonetheless be in power the Son of God, according to the Spirit of sanctification, for he was born of the Holy Spirit and the Virgin Mary. This is that unique act, performed in an ineffable manner, the assumption of a man by the Word of God, so that he might truly and properly be called at once the Son of God and the Son of Man—the Son of Man because of the man who was assumed, the Son of God because of the only begotten God who assumed him. ON PREDESTINATION 15.31.[96]

THE GLORIFICATION OF CHRIST. AUGUSTINE: With respect to this predestination Christ was glorified before the foundation of the world, so that as a result of his resurrection from the dead he might have glory at the Father's right hand, where he now sits. Thus, when he saw that his predestined glorification had come, in order that what had already been done by predestination might now also take place in fact, he prayed: "Father, glorify thou me in thy own presence with the glory which I had with thee before the world was made."[97] COMMENTARY ON JOHN 105.8.[98]

THE RESURRECTION. PELAGIUS: Christ was predestined as to the spirit of sanctification, so that because of his incorruptibility he might rise again before anyone else and open the way of resurrection for the children of God. . . . The nature of the resurrection (not of all who rise from the dead but of those who belong to Christ) is prefigured by Christ. PELAGIUS'S COMMENTARY ON ROMANS.[99]

SONSHIP IN POWER AND SONSHIP BY GRACE. CYRIL OF ALEXANDRIA: As Christ was predestined to be the Son of God in power, so we too

---

[91]Jn 2:19. [92]NPNF 1 11:340. [93]ENPK 2:20. [94]ERIE, Migne PL 35 col. 2090. [95]ERIE, Migne PL 35 col. 2091. [96]FC 86:255. [97]Jn 17:5. [98]NPNF 1 7:398. [99]PCR 60.

have been predestined to be sons of God, not however in power but by grace, having been made worthy of such a calling and having received it only by the will of God the Father. There is a big difference here between Emmanuel and us. For even if he was born of the seed of David according to the flesh, and so we can say that the Son of God was one of us in his humanity, still, in power and in truth he is the natural Son, and it is through him that we are made sons as well. . . . We stand in the same relation to him as images do to their original. COMMENTARY ON ROMANS.[100]

RESURRECTION THE PIVOT. THEODORET OF CYR: Before his crucifixion and death the Lord Jesus Christ did not appear to be God either to the Jews or even to the disciples. For they were offended by human things, as when they saw him eating and drinking and sleeping and urinating, and not even his miracles made them change their minds. So, for instance, when they saw the miracle which he performed with the sea, they said: "Who is this, that even the sea and the winds obey him?"[101] . . . But after he rose from the dead and ascended into heaven, and the Holy Spirit came, and after miracles of every kind which they performed by calling on his adorable name, all those who believed recognized that he was God and the only begotten Son of God. INTERPRETATION OF THE LETTER TO THE ROMANS.[102]

CONFIRMATION AS THE SON OF GOD. JOHN OF DAMASCUS: By his miracles and resurrection and by the descent of the Holy Spirit, it was made plain and certain to the world that Christ was the Son of God.[103] ORTHODOX FAITH 4.18.[104]

1:5 Grace and Apostleship

TO FAITH THROUGH GRACE. ORIGEN: Paul says that he has received grace and apostleship through Christ, the mediator between God and men[105]—grace with respect to his patience in many labors and apostleship with respect to his

preaching authority. For Christ was himself called an apostle, i.e., one who was sent by the Father, because he said that he had been sent to preach the gospel to the poor.[106] And everything which is his, he gives to his disciples also. Grace is said to be spread on his lips. For he gives grace to his apostles, by which those who are struggling may say: "I worked harder than any of them, though it was not I but the grace of God which is with me."[107] . . . It was only through the grace which had been given to the apostles that the Gentiles, who were strangers from the covenant of God and from the life of Israel,[108] could believe in the gospel. Through this grace it is said that they came to faith because of the preaching of the apostles, and it is recorded that by the grace given to them the sound of the name of Christ went out into all the world, reaching even those who were at Rome. COMMENTARY ON THE EPISTLE TO THE ROMANS.[109]

ITS POWER MADE CREDIBLE THROUGH DEEDS. AMBROSIASTER: After the resurrection Christ was revealed as the Son of God in power. He gave grace to make sinners righteous and appointed apostles, of whom Paul says here that he is one, so that the apostleship might be granted by the grace of God's gift and not because the apostles were Jews. They received this authority from God the Father through Christ the Lord, so that as representatives of the Lord they might make his teaching acceptable by signs of power. Unbelieving Jews, who had been jealous of this power when they saw it in the Savior, were all the more tormented at seeing it admired by the masses in his servants. For power bears witness to the teaching, so that although what is preached is incredible to the world, it might be made credible by deeds. He says that the apostles have been sent to preach the faith to all nations, that they might obey and

[100]Migne PG 74 cols. 773-76. [101]Mt 8:27. [102]IER, Migne PG 82 col. 52. [103]See Mt 3:16; Mk 1:10; Lk 3:22; Jn 1:32. [104]FC 37:381. [105]1 Tim 2:5. [106]See Lk 4:18. [107]1 Cor 15:10. [108]Eph 2:12. [109]CER 1:106.

be saved, that the gift of God may appear to have been granted not only to the Jews but to all the nations, and that this is the will of God, to have pity on all in Christ and through Christ, by the preaching of his ambassadors. COMMENTARY ON PAUL'S EPISTLES.[110]

NOT OF OURSELVES. CHRYSOSTOM: See the candor of the servant. He wants nothing to be his own but everything to be his master's. And indeed it was the Spirit who gave him this freedom.... Paul says: "We have not achieved the apostleship by ourselves." It was not by much labor and toil that we were given this dignity, but we received grace, and the successful result is a part of the heavenly gift.... It was the apostles' duty to go about and preach, but conviction belonged to God, who worked in them. HOMILIES ON ROMANS I.[111]

GRACE, THEN APOSTLESHIP. AUGUSTINE: Paul preserves the main point of his case very well, so that no one would dare say that he has been led to the gospel because of the merits of his previous life. How could one claim this, when even the apostles themselves ... could not have received their own apostleship unless they had first ... received grace, which cleanses and justifies sinners? RUDIMENTARY EXPOSITION OF THE EPISTLE TO THE ROMANS 6.[112]

SENT BY THE HOLY SPIRIT. PELAGIUS: Paul received grace in baptism and apostleship when he was sent by the Holy Spirit,[113] for *apostle* means "sent" in Greek. The purpose of this was that the Gentiles might submit not to the law but to faith. PELAGIUS'S COMMENTARY ON ROMANS.[114]

1:6 Belonging to Christ

DIFFERENT CALLINGS. ORIGEN: Paul is said to be called to be an apostle, and the Romans are also called, though not to be apostles. Rather they are called to be holy in the obedience of faith. We have already spoken above about the

different callings.[115] COMMENTARY ON THE EPISTLE TO THE ROMANS.[116]

CALLED AND SENT. AMBROSIASTER: This is by the mission of us who are preaching the name of Christ to all the nations, among whom you too have been called, because the gift of God has been sent to all, so that when they hear that they have been called along with others, they will know that they must not act as if they are under the law, since the other nations accepted the faith of Christ without the law of Moses. COMMENTARY ON PAUL'S EPISTLES.[117]

INCLUDING YOURSELVES. APOLLINARIS OF LAODICEA: Paul says this in order to show that the Romans too, made up as they were of all the nations inhabiting the world, rightly accepted the preaching of his message. PAULINE COMMENTARY FROM THE GREEK CHURCH.[118]

THE ROMANS WITH OTHERS. CHRYSOSTOM: Paul does not say that God called the others along with the Romans but the Romans along with the others. HOMILIES ON ROMANS I.[119]

SALVATION TO JEWS AND OTHERS. AUGUSTINE: Paul teaches here that this salvation had come not only to the Jews, as some Jewish Christians thought. RUDIMENTARY EXPOSITION OF THE EPISTLE TO THE ROMANS 6.[120]

APPOINTED. THEODORET OF CYR: Paul tells them here that he is not doing anything improper, nor invading fields assigned to others, for God had appointed him to preach to the Gentiles. INTERPRETATION OF THE LETTER TO THE ROMANS.[121]

1:7 Grace and Peace to the Saints

---

[110]CSEL 81.1:16-17. [111]NPNF 1 11:340. [112]ERIE, Migne PL 35 col. 2092. [113]Acts 13:2. [114]PCR 60. [115]See 1 Cor 12:28. [116]CER 1:106-8. [117]CSEL 81.1:19. [118]NTA 15:57. [119]NPNF 1 11:341. [120]ERIE, Migne PL 35 col. 2092. [121]IER, PG 82 col. 52

GRACE AND PEACE. ORIGEN: The blessing of peace and grace, which the apostle Paul gives to all God's beloved to whom he is writing, is, I think, analogous to the blessing of Noah on Shem and Japheth,[122] which was fulfilled in the Spirit toward all those who were blessed in the same way. It is comparable to the blessing with which Abraham was blessed by Melchizedek[123] and Jacob by his father Isaac,[124] and the twelve patriarchs who were blessed by their father Israel;[125] or the blessing of Moses, with which he blessed the twelve tribes of Israel.[126] I do not think that the blessing of the apostle's, by which he blessed the churches of Christ, is inferior to any of these. . . . The apostle writes in the Spirit of God and blesses in the Spirit. Therefore it is through the same Spirit that those who are blessed by the apostle receive their blessings, as long as those on whom the blessing comes are found to be worthy of it. Otherwise it will happen as it is written: "And if a son of peace is there, your peace shall rest upon him; but if not, it shall return to you."[127] What is written about peace will also be the case with grace, because Paul aligns grace with peace. COMMENTARY ON THE EPISTLE TO THE ROMANS.[128]

FATHER AS GOD, SON AS LORD. TERTULLIAN: I will not speak of gods at all, nor of lords, but I shall follow the apostle, so that if the Father and the Son are both to be invoked, I shall call the Father "God" and invoke Jesus Christ as "Lord." AGAINST PRAXEAS 13.[129]

TO ALL GOD'S BELOVED IN ROME. AMBROSIASTER: "To all God's beloved in Rome, who are called to be saints." Although Paul is writing to the Romans, nevertheless he indicates that he is writing to those who are in the love of God. Who are these, if not those who believe rightly concerning the Son of God? These are the ones who are holy and who are said to have been called. For someone who understands incorrectly is not said to have been called, just as those who act according to the law have not rightly understood Christ and have done injury to God the Father, by

doubting whether there is full salvation in Christ. Therefore they are not holy, nor are they said to have been called.

"Grace to you and peace from God our Father and the Lord Jesus Christ." Paul says that grace and peace are with those who believe rightly. It is grace by which sinners have been cleansed and peace by which former enemies have been reconciled to the Creator, as the Lord says: "Whatever house you enter and they receive you, say: Peace be to this house."[130] And so as to teach that without Christ there is no peace or hope, Paul added that grace and peace are not only from God the Father but also from the Lord Jesus Christ. He says that God is our Father because of our origin, since all things are from him, and that Christ is Lord, because we have been redeemed by his blood and made children of God. COMMENTARY ON PAUL'S EPISTLES.[131]

THE FRUIT OF THE SPIRIT. AMBROSE: There is one grace on the part of the Father and the Son, and there is one peace on the part of the Father and the Son, but this grace and peace is the fruit of the Spirit. THE HOLY SPIRIT 11.125.[132]

FEW ARE CHOSEN. SEVERIAN: Paul does not say "to the saints" lightly—for "many are called but few are chosen"[133] and not all have remained in their calling—but so that he would not be throwing holy things to dogs.[134] . . . According to the heretics, if Christ is the Lord and God is *our* Father, then the Father will be a servant of Christ, for as the son is, so is the father. But it is not like that at all. Paul said that God is our Father, in order to show his grace, and that Christ is Lord, in order that the Romans should not become proud and think that because they too were sons of God they could despise the glory of the Son or raise themselves up beyond what was natural. Paul called God "the Father" because

---

[122]See Gen 9:26-27. [123]See Gen 14:18-19. [124]See Gen 27:26-29; 28:1. [125]See Gen 49:1-28. [126]See Gen 33. [127]Lk 10:6. [128]CER 1:108. [129]ANF 3:608. [130]Lk 10:5. [131]CSEL 81.1:19, 21. [132]FC 44:80. [133]Mt 22:14. [134]Mt 7:6.

he judges no one, but the Son he called "Lord," because he is the judge.[135] He calls God "the Father" so as to point out his guardianship over us. He calls the Son "Lord" so that we might understand that we are called sons by the goodness of God but that Jesus is the true God by nature and our Lord. PAULINE COMMENTARY FROM THE GREEK CHURCH.[136]

CALLED TO BE SAINTS. CHRYSOSTOM: See how often Paul uses the word *called!* . . . And he does so not out of longwindedness but out of a desire to remind them of the benefit which calling brings. For since it was likely that among those who believed there would be some consuls and rulers as well as poor and common men, Paul casts aside inequality of rank and writes to them all under one common heading. But if in the most important and spiritual things everything is laid out as common to both slaves and free men, e.g., the love of God, the calling, the gospel, the adoption, the grace, the peace, the sanctification, etc., how could it be other than the utmost folly to divide those whom God had joined together and made to be of equal honor in the higher things, for the sake of things on earth? For this reason, I presume, from the very start this blessed apostle casts out this mischievous disease and then leads them to the mother of blessings—humility.

"Grace and peace!" Christ told his apostles to make peace their first word when entering into houses.[137] So it is from this that Paul always starts also, for it was no small war which Christ put an end to, but a many-sided and enduring conflict. And it was not because of anything we had done, but by his grace. Since then love presented us with grace and grace with peace . . . he prays over them that they may abide constant and unmoved, so that no other war may ever break out, and he beseeches the God who gave this peace to keep it firmly settled. HOMILIES ON ROMANS 1.[138]

INCLUSION. THEODORE OF MOPSUESTIA: Paul says to all because with Christ everyone is equal. When he says: "to those beloved of God, called to

be holy," he cuts out unbelievers. The forgiveness of sins and the gift of sonship may be what he means by "grace," and the defeat of the invisible enemies, from whom Christ has delivered us, may be what he means by "peace," as well as the refusal of the body to rebel against the reasonings of the soul and godly agreement with one another. PAULINE COMMENTARY FROM THE GREEK CHURCH.[139]

THE SPIRIT'S GIFTS. [PSEUDO-]CONSTANTIUS: "Called to be saints" because he was writing to those who possess the grace of the Holy Spirit, and he therefore preaches that gifts from the Father and the Son are to be bestowed on them. In saying this he is not overlooking the Holy Spirit but showing that the gifts of the Father, Son and Holy Spirit are common to all three. Moreover, Paul the apostle himself frequently demonstrates that the spiritual gifts which are given to men come from the Holy Spirit. THE HOLY LETTER OF ST. PAUL TO THE ROMANS.[140]

EMPHASIZING GOD'S GRACE. AUGUSTINE: Here again Paul has emphasized God's grace rather than the saints' merit, for he does not say "to those loving God" but rather "to God's beloved." RUDIMENTARY EXPOSITION OF THE EPISTLE TO THE ROMANS 7.[141]

FORGIVENESS AND RECONCILIATION. AUGUSTINE: Instead of saying "greetings," Paul says "Grace to you and peace." Grace then is from God the Father and the Lord Jesus Christ, by which our sins, which had turned us from God, are forgiven; and from them also is this peace, whereby we are reconciled to God. Since through grace hostilities dissolve once sins are remitted, now we may cling in peace to him from whom our sins alone had torn us. . . . But when these sins have been forgiven through faith in our Lord Jesus

---

[135]See Acts 10:42; 2 Tim 4:1. [136]NTA 15:213-14. [137]Lk 10:5. [138]NPNF 1 11:341. [139]NTA 15:113. [140]ENPK 2:21. [141]*ERIE*, Migne PL 35 col. 2093.

Christ, we shall have peace with no separation between us and God. RUDIMENTARY EXPOSITION OF THE EPISTLE TO THE ROMANS 8.[142]

RECALLING GOD'S BENEFITS. PELAGIUS: Paul is called to be an apostle to all believers, whom God loves impartially, without showing any preference for Jew or Greek. They are saints because of God's calling, not because of their own holiness. Paul's greeting is designed to recall God's benefits and to pray that they may remain perfect in us, because our sins have been freely forgiven. . . . Paul also insists that Jews and Gentiles live in peace, since both of them have received the same

grace. PELAGIUS'S COMMENTARY ON ROMANS.[143]

PEACE RESTORES VIRTUE. GENNADIUS OF CONSTANTINOPLE: First Paul prays that the Romans might receive the grace of God, by which all believers enjoy salvation. Then he asks for peace, by which God gives to all the restoration of virtue. For the one who accepts the gospel way of life has peace with God. The one who serves him is amenable to everyone. PAULINE COMMENTARY FROM THE GREEK CHURCH.[144]

---

[142]*ERIE*, Migne PL 35 col. 2093. [143]*PCR* 60-61. [144]*NTA* 15:352.

1:8-13 PAUL'S DESIRE TO VISIT ROME

[8]*First, I thank my God through Jesus Christ for all of you, because your faith is proclaimed in all the world.* [9]*For God is my witness, whom I serve with my spirit in the gospel of his Son, that without ceasing I mention you always in my prayers,* [10]*asking that somehow by God's will I may now at last succeed in coming to you.* [11]*For I long to see you, that I may impart to you some spiritual gift to strengthen you,* [12]*that is, that we may be mutually encouraged by each other's faith, both yours and mine.* [13]*I want you to know, brethren, that I have often intended to come to you (but thus far have been prevented), in order that I may reap some harvest among you as well as among the rest of the Gentiles.*

OVERVIEW: The Fathers noted the praise Paul heaped on the Romans and contrasted it favorably with what he said about some of the other churches he wrote to. They were well aware of Rome's importance as the imperial capital and assumed that the reputation of the Roman church had spread across the world because of the city's central political position. Paul longed to visit Rome, but his prayers had so far gone unanswered. Unanswered prayer is an age-old spiritual problem which the Fathers resolved by saying that the real prayer of the Christian is to be con-

formed to God's will. Specific requests might be granted, as in the case of Balaam, but if they were not in the wider purpose of God, they were sure to turn out badly.

Paul's emphasis on the spiritual nature of his own Christian service made a deep impression on the Fathers, who used it as a model for all believers. The spiritual gift Paul desired to give to the Romans was to lead them beyond bondage to the law and into salvation by faith alone. Paul was not coming to Rome to impart new teaching, nor did he wish to lord it over the church. His intentions were both humble and heartwarming, as he desired no more than to share with the Romans and be encouraged by them even as he taught them more of the truth. God's plans for Paul's life overruled the apostle's own desires, which is why he had been prevented from going to Rome. The Fathers emphasized this point much more than Paul's desire to do good when he got there, though that was occasionally mentioned as well. Once more we see the great interest they had in the cosmic ordering of the universe, next to which our individual thoughts and desires count for nothing.

1:8 *The Faith Proclaimed*

THROUGH JESUS CHRIST. ORIGEN: Sometimes the apostle writes in the way he does to the Romans, giving thanks for everyone, but sometimes he just gives thanks without adding "for all of you." If you notice this you will realize that in the places where he gives thanks for everyone, he does not draw attention to any grave faults or sins in them. But where he criticizes people or reproves them, he does not add to his thanksgiving that he gives thanks for them all—see, e.g., 1 Corinthians or Colossians.[1] In Galatians he does not even give thanks at all, because he is surprised that they have so quickly abandoned the gospel that called them and chosen another one instead.[2]

Paul thus begins his letter with thanksgiving. To give thanks to God is to offer him a sacrifice of praise, and therefore he adds "through Jesus Christ," as through a high priest. Anyone who wants to offer a sacrifice to God ought to know that he should offer it through the hands of a priest. But note also this important addition: "(to) my God." This can only be the voice of the saints, whose God he is, as he is the God of Abraham, Isaac and Jacob. No one can say that the Lord God is his if his god is his stomach, or if his god is greed, or if his god is the glory of this life and the pomp of this world or the power of things which are perishing. For whatever anyone wor-

ships more than other things, that is his god.

But let us see what it is that the apostle gives thanks for. "Because," he says, "your faith is proclaimed in all the world." "In all the world," simply understood, means that in many parts of the world, that is of this earth, the faith and religion of those at Rome is preached. But if, as in some passages, the universe is meant here, consisting of heaven and earth and everything in them, it may be understood to mean that the powers, of whom it is said that "they rejoice over one sinner who repents,"[3] rejoice much more over the conversion and the faith of the Romans when the angels who ascend and descend to the Son of Man[4] proclaim it to them. For these powers are amazed at the conversion of the Gentiles and that the sound of the apostles of Christ Jesus has gone out into all the world. Finally, they rejoice even at the sufferings of those in this world, as the apostle says: "We have become a spectacle to the world, to angels and to men."[5]

The verse may also be understood as meaning that this faith which the Romans have is the same faith as, and none other than, that which is proclaimed and believed in all the world and which is preached not only on earth but in heaven as well. For by his blood Jesus reconciled not only those things which are on earth but also those things which are in heaven, and in his name not only earthly powers but also heavenly and infernal ones bow the knee. This is what is meant by preaching the faith in the whole world, through which the entire earth may be subjected to God.

It may be noticed that there is no "second" which corresponds to "first," but we have already explained that Paul's phrases are not always complete. On the other hand, it may be that "first" is picked up by "I want you to know brethren" [in verse 13]. COMMENTARY ON THE EPISTLE TO THE ROMANS.[6]

THE FAITH OF THE CHURCH AT ROME. NOVA-

---

[1]See 1 Cor 1:4; Col 1:3. [2]See Gal 1:1-6. [3]See Lk 15:10. [4]See Jn 1:51. [5]1 Cor 4:9. [6]CER 1:110-14.

TIAN: We have not just recently adopted this particular course of action, nor have these measures against the ungodly suddenly crossed our mind. For with us, the strictness is ancient, the faith is ancient. The apostle would not have praised us so highly by stating: "Your faith is spoken of throughout the whole world," if this strictness of ours had not already been rooted in the faith of those times. LETTER ONE 2.2.[7]

PROCLAIMED ALL OVER THE WORLD. CYPRIAN: This counsel was not recently planned by us, nor have these unexpected protections against the wicked lately surprised us. But this is read of among us as the ancient severity, the ancient faith, the ancient discipline, since the apostle would not have revealed so great praise of us when he said: "because your faith is proclaimed all over the world," if already this vigor had not borrowed the roots of faith from those times; it is a very great crime to have been unworthy of these praises and of glory. LETTER 30.2.[8]

THE CONSPICUOUS ROLE OF ROME. AMBROSIASTER: After finishing his introduction, before all else Paul bears witness to his joy, as the apostle to the Gentiles, that although the Romans ruled the world, they had submitted to the Christian faith, which seemed lowly and stupid to the wise of this world. There were many things about the Romans which he could rejoice in. They were mindful of discipline and eager to do good works, more interested in doing right than in talking about it, which is not far from God's religion. Nevertheless, he says that most of all he rejoices in this, that word of their faith was circulating everywhere. For it seemed to be a wonderful thing, that the lords of the Gentiles should bow before a promise made to the Jews. Even if they did not believe correctly, nevertheless he was pleased that they had begun to worship one God in the name of Christ, and knew that they could advance further. For this reason he reveals his love for them, when he rejoices at their good start and encourages them to go on. He therefore says

that he is giving thanks to God, even though they have not yet received everything, because God is the source of all things. The entire dispensation of our salvation is from God, indeed, but through Christ, not through the law or any prophet. Hence he says that he is giving thanks to God but through Christ, because the report of their faith was an encouragement to many to attribute this very thing to the providence of God through Christ. For either the others who believed rejoiced, having been strengthened by seeing their rulers and brothers established in the faith, or at least those who did not believe could easily have believed by following their example. For the lesser quickly does what he sees being done by the greater. COMMENTARY ON PAUL'S EPISTLES.[9]

FOLLOWING IN PETER'S FOOTSTEPS. THEODORE OF MOPSUESTIA: It seems that Paul begins by giving thanks in his other epistles too, thereby teaching by word and deed those to whom the letter is written that one ought to begin by thanking God, not only for one's own but also for others. But here this salutation has a special importance, because after the teaching of Peter, anyone who wanted to teach them the doctrines of godliness had to show that he accepted Peter's teaching and was not trying to introduce them to anything which went against that. Therefore his praise of the Romans was no accident. Often in his letters he used the salutation as a way of preparing those who would be better disposed toward him as a result of such praise, for the reading of what had been written.

"Through Jesus Christ" had to be added here, not to qualify Christ's ministry, as it seemed to some of the heretics, but because he is the cause of our thanks. Hence the apostle says that he thanks God for them all and that Christ is the cause of his thanksgiving. PAULINE COMMENTARY FROM THE GREEK CHURCH.[10]

---

[7]FC 67:188. Extreme rigorism characterized Novatian's problematic ecclesiology. [8]FC 51:73. [9]CSEL 81.1:21, 23. [10]NTA 15:113-14.

**BOLDNESS IN CARRYING THE WORD EVERY-
WHERE.** CHRYSOSTOM: Paul bears witness to two
excellencies in the Romans—one, that they
believed, and two, that they believed with boldness, and with boldness so great that their reputation spread throughout the world. It was their
faith, not their verbal disputations, nor their
questionings, nor their syllogisms which he
remarked upon. And yet there were many hindrances to their teaching. For having recently
acquired a worldwide empire the Romans were
elated, and they lived in riches and luxury, and
then fishermen brought the preaching there, Jewish fishermen moreover, who belonged to a
nation which was hated and despised by everyone. And these Romans were asked to worship
the crucified one who was brought up in Judea.
Moreover, along with this doctrine, the teachers
proclaimed an ascetic life to men who were used
to luxury and concerned with material comforts.
Those who proclaimed the gospel were poor and
common men of no notable family, and born to
those of no family. But none of these things hindered the progress of the Word, so great was the
power of the crucified to carry the Word everywhere. HOMILIES ON ROMANS 2.[11]

THE FAITH OF THE ROMANS. [PSEUDO-]CON-
STANTIUS: Paul shows that the faith of the
Romans is known to all the churches or at least
that the same faith which the Romans hold is
preached throughout the world by the apostles.
THE HOLY LETTER OF ST. PAUL TO THE
ROMANS.[12]

THE WORLD AMAZED. PELAGIUS: God is the
God of all by nature but of some only by their
own choice and response. . . . Paul calls God his
in this second sense. He thanks God for them all,
not just for the Jews, and praises them prudently,
in order to encourage them to improve. Perhaps
he did this because the whole world stood
amazed that the idolatrous Romans had been
converted . . . but probably he was just praising a
faith which was now evident. PELAGIUS'S COM-

MENTARY ON ROMANS.[13]

KNOWN THROUGHOUT THE WORLD. THE-
ODORET OF CYR: Paul was not saying this in order
to flatter them; he was simply telling the truth.
For it could not be that what was happening at
Rome should not be known all over the world.
After all, it was the capital of the empire. INTER-
PRETATION OF THE LETTER TO THE ROMANS.[14]

PAUL AND THE ROMAN CHURCH. GENNADIUS
OF CONSTANTINOPLE: Paul does not say "through
Jesus Christ" as if he were some kind of interme-
diary, but in the context of giving thanks to God,
says that we do this because of the Lord Christ.
This amazing dispensation which has saved our
race through him has taken us captive, along with
the rest, by the faith we have in him.

Paul does his utmost to win the Romans over,
in case they may be thinking that he has something against them, or that following the tradition of Peter he might be coming to order them
about, and if indeed they are vexed for this sort of
reason, they might refuse to read his letter and
miss out on the blessing it would bring. Therefore, starting with thanksgiving and faith, he
praised them for keeping it pure and firm, as they
all did together, and then with the word *proclaimed* spoke more personally in praise of the city,
and by adding "in all the world" he praised them
greatly and exalted them before going on to talk
about meeting them in person. PAULINE COM-
MENTARY FROM THE GREEK CHURCH.[15]

1:9 Service in the Spirit

YOU WILL BE MY WITNESSES. ORIGEN: God
is witness for his saints, because they also are witnesses for God according to the word of the
prophet Isaiah: "You will be my witnesses and I
am a witness, says the Lord."[16] The Savior also
says to his disciples: "You will be my witnesses in

---

[11]NPNF 1 11:343. [12]ENPK 2:22. [13]PCR 61. [14]IER, Migne PG 82
col. 53. [15]NTA 15:353. [16]Is 43:12 LXX.

Jerusalem, in Samaria and even to the ends of the earth,"[17] according to what is written: "Everyone who acknowledges me before men, I will also acknowledge before my Father."[18]

Let us consider what Paul means when he says: "Whom I serve with my spirit." It seems to me that to serve in spirit is both similar to but also much more than worshiping in spirit, as the Lord said to the Samaritan woman.[19] Paul does not merely worship in spirit—he serves in spirit as well. For it is possible to worship without commitment, but to serve requires personal involvement. Therefore the apostle serves, not in body nor in soul but in the best part of him, i.e., in spirit. . . . The apostle always prefers the spirit and rejects the flesh and the things of the flesh. Similarly he praises the spirit of the law itself and rejects the letter as if it were flesh: "The letter kills, but the spirit gives life."[20]

When Paul says that he prays without ceasing for those to whom he is writing, he is recalling his own instruction and practicing what he has preached.[21] COMMENTARY ON THE EPISTLE TO THE ROMANS.[22]

SERVING IN SPIRIT. AMBROSIASTER: In order to encourage brotherly love, Paul gives God, whom he serves, as a witness, to whom he prays on their behalf, not in keeping the law but in the gospel of his Son, i.e., not in that which Moses the servant handed down but in that which the most beloved Son taught. For the servant is as far from his Lord as the gospel is from the law, not because the law is wrong but because the gospel is better. Therefore Paul serves God in the gospel of his Son in order to show that it is God's will that men should believe in Christ.

"Whom I serve." How? In my spirit, says Paul, not in the circumcision made with hands, nor in new moons, nor in the sabbath or the choice of foods, but in the spirit, that is, in the mind. Because God is a spirit, it is right that he should be served in spirit or in the mind, for whoever serves him in his mind serves him in faith. This is what the Lord said to the Samaritan woman in John.[23]

. . . He prays without ceasing for them, remembering them in his prayers in order to sow brotherly love among them; indeed, he makes this his desire for them. For who would not love someone when he hears that that person remembers him? For if they had willingly listened to the teaching brought to them in the name of Christ by those who were not sent, how much more would they want to listen to him who they knew was an apostle and whose words were accompanied by power! COMMENTARY ON PAUL'S EPISTLES.[24]

SPIRITUAL WORSHIP. THEODORE OF MOPSUESTIA: Paul rightly says "with my spirit," contrasting this with the carnal worship of the Jews in circumcision and sabbatarianism and other such sacrifices, none of which is either spiritual or true. Some have pointed out that the phrase is a simpler way of saying "with my mind and with my will." PAULINE COMMENTARY FROM THE GREEK CHURCH.[25]

THE GOSPEL OF HIS SON. CHRYSOSTOM: Why does Paul call God as his witness? He had to declare to the Romans all his feelings toward them, but he had not yet seen any of them. So he called no human witness but God who enters the heart. For he was saying "I love you," and as evidence of that he mentioned that he was constantly praying for them. This was not self-evident either, so he had recourse to the most trustworthy testimony. Can any of you boast that, when praying at home, he remembers the entire body of the church? I doubt it. But Paul drew near to God on behalf not of one city only but of the whole world, and this not once, twice or three times but continually.

When Paul says "whom I serve with my spirit in the Gospel of his Son," he shows us both the grace of God and his own humility, the grace of God because he entrusted such a great task to

---

[17]Acts 1:8. [18]Mt 10:32. [19]Jn 4:23. [20]2 Cor 3:6. [21]1 Thess 5:17.
[22]CER 1:114-118. [23]See Jn 4:23-24. [24]CSEL 81.1:23, 25. [25]NTA 15:114.

Paul, and his own humility because Paul imputes it all not to his own zeal but to the help of the Spirit. The addition of "the gospel" shows what kind of ministry Paul had. For there are many different kinds of ministry . . . one man serves God and labors by believing and ordering his own life in the right way, another undertakes the care of strangers, and another takes care of those who are in need. Even in the apostle's own time, Stephen's colleagues served God by looking after widows, while others (including Paul) taught the Word and served in the preaching of the gospel.[26] This was the kind of ministry to which he was appointed.

Having spoken above about the gospel of the Father, Paul here says that it is the gospel of the Son. It makes no difference to call it the gospel of the Father or of the Son! Paul had learned from that blessed voice that the things of the Father are the Son's, and the things of the Son are the Father's. For: "all mine are yours and yours are mine."[27]

Praying for them without ceasing is the role of genuine love. Although Paul here seems to be saying only one thing, in fact he is saying four different things. First, he is saying that he remembers; second, that he does so continually; third, that he remembers in his prayers; and fourth, that he remembers to ask great things for them. HOMILIES ON ROMANS 2.[28]

UNCEASING PRAYER. PELAGIUS: Paul serves God with his whole heart and with a ready zeal. . . . He also presents a model of unceasing prayer.[29] PELAGIUS'S COMMENTARY ON ROMANS.[30]

THE GRACE OF THE SPIRIT. GENNADIUS OF CONSTANTINOPLE: When Paul mentioned "his spirit," he was not speaking about the person of the Spirit but about the grace of the Spirit which had been given to him to preach the gospel and by which, once he had been made worthy to be a coworker with God, he was enabled to carry out his work of mission. PAULINE COMMENTARY FROM THE GREEK CHURCH.[31]

1:10 Seeking God's Will

JOURNEYING ACCORDING TO GOD'S WILL. ORIGEN: When Paul says that he is praying that somehow and at some point he may have a successful journey, so that in the will of God he might come to Rome, it must be remembered that since the apostle of God is dedicated to a holy work, that is, to the work of the gospel, he is waiting until by his prayers not only may he have a journey which is successful but also that it might be successful according to the will of God. How much more therefore ought we, whose work and worth are so much less important, to ask God for success on our journey when we have some business to attend to!

Nevertheless, I think that the apostle also wants us to understand that the success of a journey does not always mean that the journey is according to God's will. For Balaam had a successful journey when he went to Balak in order to curse the people of Israel, but this success was not due to God's will.[32] And many people have great success in worldly affairs and rejoice in their prosperity, but such prosperity is not of God's will unless the purpose of our journey is to do his will, as the apostle says here. COMMENTARY ON THE EPISTLE TO THE ROMANS.[33]

HIS DESIRE TO COME TO ROME. AMBROSIASTER: Paul here indicates the point of his prayer for the Romans. He says that he asks God that he might come to Rome in order to encourage them with the will of God, whose gift he preaches. Then when he arrives and is present among them, if something has to be done, it may be done with the will of God. Therefore he prays that for whatever reason an opportunity may be given to him to come to the city, since he was already busy preaching to others, reckoning it a successful journey if he might come by God's will, because the will of God has prepared the way. A success-

---

[26]See Acts 6:1-7. [27]Jn 17:10. [28]NPNF 1 11:344. [29]See 1 Thess 5:17. [30]PCR 61. [31]NTA 15:353. [32]See Num 22:22-35. [33]CER 1:118-20.

ful journey is not to endure the labor of traveling in vain. He asks that God will fill them by calling them to his grace. He speaks with eagerness of mind, for he desires their response, knowing that it will be to their mutual advantage.... For the apostle's fruit is richer if it wins many. For since the joy is greater if the powerful people of this world are converted to Christ, because they are so much more serious enemies, even more are converted thereby, and the fruit of the apostle is richer if he can win many. Thus by God's will the opportunity was given that Paul was arrested and appealed to Caesar, and was sent for a different reason to the city of Rome, by the will of God and in fulfillment of the desire of his will. For when Paul was shipwrecked, God appeared to him and said: "Do not be afraid, Paul. For as you have borne witness to me at Jerusalem, so also will you do at Rome."[34] COMMENTARY ON PAUL'S EPISTLES.[35]

DELAY IN ANSWERING PRAYER. CHRYSOSTOM: You see how much Paul longed to see the Romans, but he did not want to see them if it was not God's will, for his longing was tempered by the fear of God.... This is true love, not as our love, which tends to err in one direction or the other. Either we love no one, or if we do love, we love contrary to what seems good to God, and in both cases we go against the divine law.... For Paul to pray continually and not to give up even when he did not get what he prayed for shows very great love. But to love and yet at the same time to yield to the will of God shows deep reverence.... In this case Paul eventually got what he asked for but not when he asked for it, but this did not upset him. I mention all this so that we might not be upset at not being heard or at being heard only after some delay. For we are not better than Paul, who for good reason confesses that he is thankful in both circumstances. For once he had surrendered to the all-governing hand and submitted to it as far as he was able, like clay in the hand of the potter, he followed wherever God led. HOMILIES ON ROMANS 2.[36]

EVERYTHING ACCORDING TO GOD'S WILL. [PSEUDO-]CONSTANTIUS: Paul shows that he does everything which he does according to the will of God. THE HOLY LETTER OF ST. PAUL TO THE ROMANS.[37]

GOD'S DIRECTION. PELAGIUS: Paul does not find the way propitious unless the will of God, who knows all things, has directed him to a place where he might reap some fruit. For example, we read in Acts that, although he wanted to go to one place, he was directed to another.[38] PELAGIUS'S COMMENTARY ON ROMANS.[39]

ACKNOWLEDGING GOD'S WILL. THEODORET OF CYR: Paul does not simply say that he wants to come to Rome but adds that he wants to come in God's will. For when the salvation of so many people was at stake, St. Paul left nothing unclear but acknowledged God's will in his prayer, for it is only by God's permission that we are worthy to deal with material things and to make choices. Do we not commit everything we have to the divine will on which we depend? INTERPRETATION OF THE LETTER TO THE ROMANS.[40]

1:11 Some Spiritual Gift

IMPARTING SOME SPIRITUAL GIFT. ORIGEN: First of all we must learn that it is an apostolic duty to seek fellowship with our brothers for no reason other than to share some spiritual gift with them if we can, or if we cannot, to receive some spiritual gift from them. Otherwise a desire to visit the beloved is hardly commendable. When Paul says "that I might impart to you some spiritual gift" he seems to imply that there is something which may be called a gift but which is not spiritual. For the gift of faith is undoubtedly spiritual, as is the gift of wisdom, of knowledge, of virginity. But when he speaks of marriage and of virginity, saying: "But each one has his own gift from God, some this one,

---

[34]See Acts 27:24. [35]CSEL 81.1:25, 27. [36]NPNF 1 11:345. [37]ENPK 2:22. [38]Acts 16:7. [39]PCR 61-62. [40]IER, Migne PG 82 col. 58.

some that,"[41] he says that marriage is a gift, since it is written: "The woman was given to the man by God,"[42] but this gift is not, strictly speaking, a spiritual gift. Many other things may also be called gifts of God, e.g., riches and bodily strength, physical beauty and earthly power. These things are also given by God, as Daniel says: "He removes kings and sets up kings,"[43] but they are not spiritual gifts. COMMENTARY ON THE EPISTLE TO THE ROMANS.[44]

GOD'S GIFT TO YOU. AMBROSIASTER: This confirmation requires three persons: God, as helper; the apostle as minister and the people as receiver. Thus he now shows the will of his desire and what his wish for them is. For when he says: "that I might impart some spiritual gift to you," he means that the Romans have followed carnal ideas, because in the name of Christ they have not followed what Christ taught but those things which had been handed down to them by the Jews. But he wants to come to them as quickly as possible in order to take them beyond that tradition and bestow on them a spiritual gift, that he might win them for God, making them partakers of spiritual grace, that they might be perfect in faith and behavior. From this we learn that he had not praised the content of their faith in the preceding verses but their readiness and devotion to Christ. For calling themselves Christians, they acted just as if they were under the law, as that had been handed down to them. For the mercy of God had been given for this reason, that they should cease from the works of the law, as I have often said, because God, taking pity on our weakness, decreed that the human race would be saved by faith alone, along with the natural law.

When he admonishes them in writing and draws them away from carnal thoughts, when he says that his presence is necessary in order to impart a spiritual grace to them, what does this mean? Isn't what he writes also spiritual? He does not want his teaching to be applied in a way he does not intend, for that is what happens with heretics. So he desires to be present with them

and pass on to them the gospel teaching in the precise sense in which he writes it, lest by the authority of his letter their error should be confirmed and not removed. If he were with them he would be able to convince them by power, if words failed to persuade them. COMMENTARY ON PAUL'S EPISTLES.[45]

HIS PRESENCE REQUIRED IN IMPARTING THE GIFT. THEODORE OF MOPSUESTIA: Paul showed by his longing to see them that his desire was genuine, and by his eagerness to share, that the Romans' spiritual gift was not something private but that he himself would be the one who would impart it. PAULINE COMMENTARY FROM THE GREEK CHURCH.[46]

THE CHARACTER OF PAUL'S TEACHING. CHRYSOSTOM: Paul did not travel for no reason, as so many do nowadays, but for a specific and very urgent purpose. And he does not tell them his meaning openly but rather hints at it, for he does not say: "that I may teach you, that I may instruct you, that I may fill up that which is wanting," but: "that I may impart this spiritual gift," showing that it was not his own things which he was giving them but what he had himself received. HOMILIES ON ROMANS 2.[47]

CONFIRMING PETER'S PREACHING. [PSEUDO-]CONSTANTIUS: Paul says that he wants to strengthen the Romans, who held their faith from the preaching of Peter, not because they had received something inferior from Peter but that their faith would be strengthened by the witness and teaching of both apostles. THE HOLY LETTER OF ST. PAUL TO THE ROMANS.[48]

SHARING WHAT HE HAS RECEIVED. THEODORET OF CYR: These words are full of humility. . . . Paul only wants to share what he has himself received. And because the great Peter was the

---

[41]1 Cor 7:7. [42]Prov 19:14. [43]Dan 2:21. [44]CER 1:120-22. [45]CSEL 81.1:27, 29. [46]NTA 15:114. [47]NPNF 1 11:345. [48]ENPK 2:22.

first to have taught them, Paul adds that he merely wants to confirm them in the teaching which has already been given to them and to water the trees which have already been planted. Once again, his speech is full of modesty. INTERPRETATION OF THE LETTER TO THE ROMANS.[49]

1:12 Encouragement in the Faith

ENCOURAGING EACH OTHER'S FAITH. ORIGEN: Those on whom the apostle wishes to bestow spiritual grace for the encouragement of their faith, so that they will no longer be children, nor tossed about by every wind of doctrine[50]—they are the truly blessed. Paul himself received comfort from seeing his work firm and stable, and they are comforted because they share in the apostolic grace. COMMENTARY ON THE EPISTLE TO THE ROMANS.[51]

COMFORT IN THE SAME FAITH. AMBROSIASTER: Paul says that he will be comforted with them insofar as they come to understand spiritual things. Even while he may rejoice in their faith, he nevertheless grieves insofar as they have not received the faith rightly. The apostle was the type to grieve for the faults of others as if they were his own. "And we are comforted by this," he says, "by one and the same faith." In this way the act of comforting is seamless. For it is by the unity of faith that they are brought to maturity in Christ. By this means the ministry of spiritual grace is given through the apostle's preaching of the gospel and produces its own fruit. COMMENTARY ON PAUL'S EPISTLES.[52]

PAUL'S OWN NEED FOR COMFORT. APOLLINARIS OF LAODICEA: Even Paul was not above the need of comfort. For right speech comforts the speaker as well. By this means Paul is teaching his followers not to be proud if they are called to teach. They are not giving what merely belongs to them when they teach. They come to realize that they not only minister to others' needs but that they have needs themselves. For this is the fruit

of the gospel. It is a blessing to those who preach it. PAULINE COMMENTARY FROM THE GREEK CHURCH.[53]

FULL EQUALITY. CHRYSOSTOM: The Romans were undergoing many tribulations. Paul wanted to see them in order to comfort them and also to be comforted by them.... What humility he had! He showed them that he needed them as much as they needed him. By doing this, he put learners in the position of teachers, not claiming any superiority for himself but pointing out that they were fully equal to him.

Now if anyone should say that Paul's comfort was his gladness at the increase of the Romans' faith and that Paul needed this, he would not be mistaken. HOMILIES ON ROMANS 2.[54]

TO GIVE AND TO RECEIVE. THEODORET OF CYR: Paul wanted to receive as well as to give. The eagerness was on both sides. INTERPRETATION OF THE LETTER TO THE ROMANS.[55]

DEFLECTING THE CHARGE OF PRESUMPTION. GENNADIUS OF CONSTANTINOPLE: Paul says this for fear of tripping up his hearers, who might not have known what to say to the prospect of sharing in some spiritual gift. For what could have been lacking in the teaching of Peter? Paul might be accused of criticizing Peter's teaching ... of thinking that he was a greater apostle than Peter, of claiming to be on closer terms with Christ and more beloved by Christ than Peter was. Fearing attacks of this kind, Paul first of all sets out the purpose of his coming, thereby sufficiently refuting the charge of presumption. Then he goes on to say not that he is giving them something but that he is going to share something with them, which is quite different.... Paul reassures them that he has no intention of preaching anything new to them but that he intends to confirm them

---

[49]IER, Migne PG 82 col. 56. [50]See Eph 4:14. [51]CER 1:122. [52]CSEL 81.1:29. [53]NTA 15:58. [54]NPNF 1 11:345-46. [55]IER, Migne PG 82 col. 56.

in what they have already received from Peter. PAULINE COMMENTARY FROM THE GREEK CHURCH.[56]

1:13 Divine and Human Plans

DEALING WITH HINDRANCES. ORIGEN: This sentence contains a rhetorical aside (*hyperbaton*), and the construction is defective. . . . It ought to be joined to the next verse by the words "to whom," so that the phrase reads: "the rest of the Gentiles, Greeks and barbarians, to whom I am under obligation." . . . The whole thing would then read as follows: "Just as I have fruit among the other Gentiles, Greeks and barbarians, wise and foolish, to whom I am under obligation, so also, as much as in me lies, am I eager to preach the gospel also to you who are at Rome, for I am not ashamed to preach the gospel among any people, for the power of God is in it for salvation to all who believe, for the Jew first and for the Greek, for in the gospel the righteousness of God is revealed, which was previously covered by a veil in the law. Now it is revealed in those who come from the faith of the Old Testament to the faith of the new gospel."

So much for the order of the words; now we must examine the apostle's meaning. When Paul says: "I have often intended to come to you," he demonstrates the love which he had for the Romans. But when he adds: "but thus far have been prevented," though indeed it may be thought that he was prevented by God, it is shown by this that it is God's business where each of the apostles ought or ought not to go. It is by a particular dispensation that he appoints some to preach the Word of God and others not, as Paul himself says elsewhere: "When we tried to go into Bithynia, the Spirit of Christ prevented us."[57] . . . But if this phrase refers to the passage where he says that: "Satan hindered us,"[58] he shows clearly that he is constantly struggling in prayer, so that by overcoming the hindrances of Satan he may be given a successful journey in the will of God, to see those who are at Rome.

For he desires and does not cease to pray that he may obtain some fruit from them as he has from the other Gentiles. Thus like one who is acquisitive for many riches, Paul wants to amass some return from his many spiritual investments. He gathers fruit from the Greeks, fruit from the barbarians, fruit from the wise, fruit even from the foolish. For while to some he speaks wisdom as to those who are perfect, to others he says, as if speaking to foolish people, that he wants to know nothing among them except Jesus Christ and him crucified.[59] Some he teaches from the law and the prophets; others he persuades with signs and wonders. COMMENTARY ON THE EPISTLE TO THE ROMANS.[60]

I HAVE OFTEN INTENDED. AMBROSIASTER: Paul here indicates his plan and intention, which he does not doubt that they already know from those brothers who had come to Rome from Jerusalem or the neighboring cities for some reason, perhaps because of their religion, or from Aquila and Priscilla, who would have told the Romans of Paul's intention.[61] As he had often wanted to come but had been prevented, it came about that he wrote them a letter, lest they continue in their unwholesome habits for too long to be easily corrected. He calls them brothers not only because they had been born again but also because there were among them some who believed rightly, however few they may have been. Incidentally, this is why he says that they are "called to be saints."[62] What does it mean to be called to be saints? If they are already saints, how can they be called to be sanctified? This belongs to the foreknowledge of God, because God knows those who will be saints, for those who are already with him are saints and remain called forever. Yet Paul says that he has been prevented up to the time the epistle was written. He was being prevented by God, who could foresee that the Romans were still unpre-

---

[56]NTA 15:353. [57]Acts 16:7. [58]1 Thess 2:18. [59]See 1 Cor 2:6. [60]CER 1:122-26. [61]See Acts 18:1-2; Rom 16:3. [62]Rom 1:7.

pared. So God sent the apostle to other cities more prepared to receive the truth.

While acting in the name of the Savior, they were still prevented by their negligence from being as yet worthy to learn spiritual things.

Paul did not say that he was prevented for no reason. He wanted them to know why he was delayed. He urged them to get ready, so that when they heard that a spiritual grace was to be given to them they would make themselves ready to receive it.

Paul declares that he wants to come to them for their common good, so that they might receive the saving grace of the Spirit, having a reasoned profession of their faith, and that he might have some fruit of his ministry from God, having provoked them to the right faith by the example of the other Gentiles. For one who sees others responding in faith will be more eager to receive it. COMMENTARY ON PAUL'S EPISTLES.[63]

A HARVEST AMONG YOU. APOLLINARIS OF LAODICEA: For the fruit of those who have believed the Word is the benefit to those who hear it. And the Lord says that he has sent the apostles in order to bear much fruit.[64] Indeed, a few gleaners have harvested the entire church. PAULINE COMMENTARY FROM THE GREEK CHURCH.[65]

OFTEN PREVENTED. THEODORE OF MOPSUESTIA: Paul here shows quite clearly that he wanted to go to Rome but that he had often been prevented. At the same time he wants to put them in fear, lest perhaps it was because of their unworthiness that he had been prevented from going to them. PAULINE COMMENTARY FROM THE GREEK CHURCH.[66]

A GODLY MOTIVE. SEVERIAN: There were many who sped to Rome for human reasons. Paul reveals his own chaste desire to go there and that his motive was a godly one. It appears that he longed after the Romans, perhaps because their faith had become an encouragement to all their subject peoples. PAULINE COMMENTARY FROM THE GREEK CHURCH.[67]

YIELDING TO PROVIDENCE. CHRYSOSTOM: Here is an obedience as great as that of slaves and a clear demonstration of Paul's excellent temper. He says he was prevented from coming to them but does not explain why. For he does not pry into the command of his master but simply obeys. And yet one might expect someone to wonder why God prevented a city as conspicuous and great as Rome . . . from enjoying such a teacher, and for such a long time as well. . . . But Paul does not concern himself with such things, yielding instead to the incomprehensible nature of providence. By doing this he shows the right tone of his soul and also teaches us never to call God to account for what happens, even though what is done seems to trouble the minds of many. For it is the master's place to command and the servant's to obey. This is why he says that he was prevented without giving the reason, because he did not know it himself. . . . So if you do not know why something has happened, do not be discouraged, for this is a main feature of faith, to receive what is told to us of God's providence even when we are ignorant of the way in which it is being dispensed. HOMILIES ON ROMANS 2.[68]

PAUL'S PLANS. PELAGIUS: The Romans would have learned of Paul's plans through the brothers who were constantly coming and going. *Prevented* here means "busy," because he was preaching in other provinces. PELAGIUS'S COMMENTARY ON ROMANS.[69]

GOD'S OVERRULING. THEODORET OF CYR: Paul declares both his own plan and God's overruling. For God's grace was fully in control of his life. INTERPRETATION OF THE LETTER TO THE ROMANS.[70]

---

[63]CSEL 81.1:31, 33. [64]See Jn 15:16. [65]NTA 15:58. [66]NTA 15:114. [67]NTA 15:214. [68]NPNF 1 11:346-47. [69]PCR 62. [70]IER, Migne PG 82 col. 56.

Benefits of the Gospel. Gennadius of Constantinople: Paul tells the Romans that it will benefit him to come to them, saying that the nations which received the gospel through him had clearly added to his own riches. Pauline Commentary from the Greek Church.[71]

[71]NTA 15:354.

1:14-17 JUSTIFICATION BY FAITH

[14]*I am under obligation both to Greeks and to barbarians, both to the wise and to the foolish:* [15]*so I am eager to preach the gospel to you also who are in Rome.*

[16]*For I am not ashamed of the gospel: it is the power of God for salvation to every one who has faith, to the Jew first and also to the Greek.* [17]*For in it the righteousness of God is revealed through faith for faith; as it is written, "He who through faith is righteous shall live."*[b]

b Or *The righteous shall live by faith*

Overview: Paul's enthusiasm for the gospel was infectious and his desire to go to Rome strategic, for if the head (capital) of the world were converted, the members of the body (the provinces) would surely follow suit. To pagans, the gospel of a crucified Christ seemed to be madness, but Paul was not ashamed of it, for his message was one not merely of words but of the power to change lives. In the divine plan the Jews were granted a certain priority, but the salvation of the Gentiles was in no sense inferior to theirs. In Christ all human barriers and divisions are overturned, so that God's power may be made plain to everyone. Justification by faith alone is the heart of the Christian gospel, and the Fathers were well aware of this. Centuries before Martin Luther was to make Romans 1:17 the cornerstone of his reformation, they were clearly proclaiming God's free gift to all who believe, whatever their background or previous spiritual history may have been.

1:14 An Obligation to All Nations

Speaking in the Tongues of All Nations. Origen: We must now ask in what sense the apostle is under obligation to Greeks and barbarians, to the wise and to the foolish. What has he received from them that he should be indebted to them? I infer that he is a debtor to the different nations because by the grace of the Holy Spirit he has received the gift of being able to speak in the tongues of all nations, as he himself says: "I speak in tongues more than you all."[1] Given that a man receives the gift of tongues not for himself but for the benefit of those to whom he is called to preach, Paul incurs an obligation to all those whose language he has received as a gift from God. He has incurred an obligation to the wise in that he has received the wisdom hidden in the mystery, which he is to speak to the perfect and to the wise. But how is he indebted to the foolish? In that he has received the grace of patience and longsuffering, for it is the height of patience to be able to endure the furor of the foolish. Commen-

[1]1 Cor 14:18. [2]CER 1:128-30.

tary on the Epistle to the Romans.[2]

Maturing Through Persecution. Origen: We can see how in a short time this religion has grown up, making progress through the persecution and death of its adherents and through their endurance of the confiscation of their property and every kind of torture. And this is particularly miraculous, since its teachers are themselves neither very skillful nor very numerous. But in spite of everything, the Word is now preached in all the world, so that "Greeks and barbarians, wise and foolish" now adopt the Christian faith. On First Principles 4.1.2.[3]

Preaching to All, Greeks and Non-Greeks. Ambrosiaster: Paul says that he is under obligation to those whom he names, because he was sent for the purpose of preaching to everyone. For this reason he states that they are all under obligation to believe in God the Creator, from whom and through whom are all things, for obligation and honor form part of the salvation of the believer. He wrote *Greeks* instead of *Gentiles*," but this includes those who are called Romans, whether by birth or by adoption, and barbarians, who are those who are not Romans, whose race is inimical, and who are not Gentiles. He speaks of those who are wise, because they are learned in worldly sciences and are called wise in the world whether they are stargazers, geometers, mathematicians, grammarians, orators or musicians. Paul shows that none of these things is of any advantage, nor are these people truly wise, unless they believe in Christ. He calls them fools, because in their simplicity they lack knowledge of spiritual things. He testifies that he has been sent to preach to them all. But he says nothing about the Jews, because he is the teacher of the Gentiles.[4] And this is why he says that he is under obligation, because he has accepted this teaching in order to pass it on, and in passing it on, to acquire it himself. Commentary on Paul's Epistles.[5]

Chrysostom: Paul also said this when he was writing to the Corinthians,[6] in order to ascribe everything to God. Homilies on Romans 2.[7]

1:15 Eagerness to Preach the Gospel

Eager to Impart Grace. Ambrosiaster: Paul understood himself to be sent to preach to all nations. Yet he was especially eager to impart the gospel of the grace of God to the Romans, the capital and seat of the empire. For it would be to the benefit and peace of the members if the head were not uncertain. Therefore he opts for the peace of the Romans, that Satan might not get too involved with them, and that he might have even richer fruits of his labor. Commentary on Paul's Epistles.[8]

Temptations Thick as Snowflakes. Chrysostom: What a noble soul was Paul! Having taken on himself a task full of such great danger, a voyage across the sea, temptations, plottings, risings—for it was likely that one who was going to address so great a city, which was under the tyranny of ungodliness, should undergo temptations thick as snowflakes. He lost his life in this way, cut down by a tyrant. Yet still he was ready to undergo great troubles. In fact he was enthusiastic even in travail, even as one in haste. He was in a constant state of preparation. Homilies on Romans 2.[9]

1:16 The Power of God for Salvation

Also to the Greek. Origen: Many attacks were made on the gospel when it was first preached, but Paul learned patience from the prophets who said: "Fear not the reproach of men, and be not dismayed at their revilings."[10] He knew that he should preach the gospel, "not in plausible words of human wisdom but in the power of the Spirit."[11] Therefore, defining what

---

[3]*OFP* 258. [4]See Gal 2:7. [5]CSEL 81.1:33, 35. [6]1 Cor 9:16. [7]NPNF 1 11:348. [8]CSEL 81.1:35. [9]NPNF 1 11:348. [10]Is 51:7. [11]1 Cor 2:4.

the gospel is, he proclaims: "It is the power of God for salvation to everyone who has faith, to the Jew first and also to the Greek." When he says the power of God for salvation he implies that there is another power of God which is not for salvation but for damnation. It may be that it is because of these different powers that right and left are distinguished in God, so that the power for salvation would be identified with the right, and the power by which he condemns would be identified with the left.[12] COMMENTARY ON THE EPISTLE TO THE ROMANS.[13]

THE POWER OF GOD. AMBROSIASTER: For power backed up the teaching of the apostles, so that if what they preached seemed incredible, signs and wonders performed by the apostles were a testimony that they should not be ashamed of what was said to them, because there was so much power in it. For there is no doubt that words must give way before power. Insofar as the Romans' preaching was not backed up by signs, it was without the power of God. Paul is not ashamed of the gospel of God, but the implication is that some whom he is addressing may be ashamed of it. Perhaps what had been handed on to them had come into disrepute, because it had never been confirmed by any testimony and hence had become loosened from apostolic teaching. It is the power of God which calls persons to faith and which gives salvation to all who believe, because it remits sins and justifies, so that one who has been marked with the mystery of the cross cannot be bound by the second death. For the preaching of the cross of Christ is a sign that death has been expelled, as the apostle John says: "The reason the Son of God appeared was to destroy the works of the devil."[14] Thus no believer is bound by death, since he has a sign that death has been conquered.

"To the Jew first and also to the Greek." This means to him who is of the race of Abraham and to him who is from the Gentiles. By *Greek* Paul means Gentile, and by *Jew* he means a descendant of Abraham. For these began to be called Jews only in the time of Judas Maccabeus, who in a

time of destruction resisted the sacrileges of the Gentiles and by trusting in God rallied the nation and defended his people. He was of the sons of Aaron. Therefore, although Paul puts the Jews first because of their ancestors, nevertheless he says that they must also accept the gift of the gospel in the same way as the Gentiles. COMMENTARY ON PAUL'S EPISTLES.[15]

UNASHAMED OF THE CROSS. APOLLINARIS OF LAODICEA: Paul says that even if, in the very largest of cities, the preacher of the cross of Christ will be mocked by the ignorant, he is not to be ashamed. For if the Son of God bore the shame of the cross on our behalf, how could it not be out of place for us to be ashamed at the Lord's suffering for us? PAULINE COMMENTARY FROM THE GREEK CHURCH.[16]

GLORYING IN THE CROSS. CHRYSOSTOM: Paul says that he is "not ashamed," which is not what we usually say of things as glorious as the gospel. Why does he speak like this, when he exults over the gospel even more than he does over heaven? In writing to the Galatians he said: "God forbid that I should glory, except in the cross of our Lord Jesus Christ."[17] How is it then that in this instance he does not even get as far as glory but says only that he is not ashamed? The Romans were most anxious about the things of the world, because of their riches, their empire, their victories, and they thought that their emperors were equal to the gods. . . . While they were so puffed up, Paul was going to preach Jesus, the carpenter's son who was brought up in Judea, in the house of a lower-class woman, who had no bodyguards, who was not surrounded by wealth, but who died as a criminal among thieves and endured many other inglorious afflictions. Since it was likely that the Romans were pretending that they did not know any of these unspeakable things, Paul understates that he is not ashamed, in order to

---

[12]The left hand of God. [13]CER 1:130-32. [14]1 Jn 3:8. [15]CSEL 81.1:35, 37. [16]NTA 15:58. [17]Gal 6:14.

teach them not to be ashamed of Christ either. HOMILIES ON ROMANS 2.[18]

CENSURING THE PAGANS. PELAGIUS: This is subtly intended to censure the pagans who, although they do not hesitate to believe that their god Jupiter turned himself into irrational animals and inanimate gold all for the sake of his monstrous lust, think that we Christians should be ashamed to believe that our Lord was crucified in the flesh he assumed, in order to save his image. . . . At the same time Paul is also bearing in mind those heretics who think that the crucifixion is something unworthy of God, not realizing that nothing is more fitting for the Creator than to care for the salvation of his creatures, particularly as he could not suffer any loss to his own nature, which is not subject to corruption. There is no power greater than the one which overcame death and restored to man the life he had lost,[19] even if this seems like weakness to an unbeliever. PELAGIUS'S COMMENTARY ON ROMANS.[20]

NOT ASHAMED. GENNADIUS OF CONSTANTINOPLE: Those who objected to the Christian gospel ridiculed it, mocking it because of its absurdity. For there is nothing more ridiculous than the word of someone who preaches that the Son of God was born and brought up by Jews, who rejects neither the cross nor death, who says moreover not only that Christ rose from the dead but that he ascended to heaven as Lord of all, that he will raise everyone else from the dead, and other things the apostles preached. The pagans mocked these things and ridiculed them, thinking that they would make the apostles shut up. Therefore St. Paul, feeling obliged to reply to this opinion of the apostles, began his teaching thus: "I am not ashamed of the gospel." PAULINE COMMENTARY FROM THE GREEK CHURCH.[21]

1:17 God's Righteousness Revealed Through Faith

INDIVIDUAL AND CORPORATE FAITH. TERTUL-

LIAN: Where three people are gathered together, there is a church, even if all three are laypersons.[22] For each individual lives by his own faith. ON EXHORTATION TO CHASTITY 7.[23]

THROUGH FAITH FOR FAITH. ORIGEN: The righteousness of God is revealed in the gospel in that no one is excluded from salvation, whether he be a Jew, a Greek or a barbarian. For the Savior says to everyone equally: "Come to me, all who labor and are heavy laden."[24] Concerning "through faith for faith," we have already said that the first people were in the faith, because they believed God and Moses his servant, from which faith they have now gone over to the faith of the gospel. The quotation from Habakkuk[25] means either that the one who lives in the law will also believe the gospel or that the one who believes the gospel will also believe the law and the prophets. For one of these does not have the fullness of life without the other. COMMENTARY ON THE EPISTLE TO THE ROMANS.[26]

SECURE IN THE PROMISE. CYPRIAN: If you are a just man and live by faith, if you truly believe in God, why do you, who are destined to be with Christ and secure in the promise of the Lord, not rejoice that you are called to Christ and be glad that you are free from the devil? TREATISE ON MORTALITY 3.[27]

THE RIGHTEOUSNESS OF GOD REVEALED. AMBROSIASTER: Paul says this because the righteousness of God is revealed in the one who believes, whether Jew or Greek. He calls it "the righteousness of God" because God freely justifies the ungodly by faith, without the works of the law, just as he says elsewhere: "That I may be found in him, not having a righteousness of my own, based on law, but that which is through faith in Christ, the righteousness from God that

---

[18]NPNF 1 11:348. [19]See Heb 2:14. [20]PCR 62-63. [21]NTA 15:354-55. [22]See Mt 18:20. [23]ANF 4:54. [24]Mt 11:28. [25]Hab 2:4. [26]CER 1:132-34. [27]FC 36:201.

depends on faith."[28] He says that this same righteousness is revealed in the gospel when God grants faith to man, through which he may be justified.

The truth and righteousness of God are revealed in this, when a man believes and confesses. The righteousness is of God because what he promised, he gave. Therefore, whoever believes that he has received what God promised through his prophets proves that God is just and is a witness of his righteousness.

"Through faith for faith." What does this mean, except that the faith of God is in him because he promised, and the faith of man is in him because he believes the one who promises, so that through the faith of the God who promises the righteousness of God might be revealed in the faith of the man who believes? For to the believer God appears to be just, but to the unbeliever he appears to be unjust. Anyone who does not believe that God has given what he promised denies that God is truthful. This is said against the Jews, who deny that Christ is the one whom God promised.

"As it is written: 'He who through faith is righteous shall live.' " Paul now moves over to the example of the prophet Habakkuk[29] in order to declare that in the past it was revealed that a just man lives by faith and not by the law, i.e., that a man is not justified before God by the law but by faith. Commentary on Paul's Epistles.[30]

Law and Nature. Acacius of Caesarea: The righteousness of God is revealed in . . . the believer. Paul says that the revelation of righteousness is the approbation of those who do right. Thus he is able to say likewise that wrath is revealed toward those who do the opposite. The Jew has been brought from the faith of the appointed law to the faith which is through Christ and the Gentile from the faith of nature to the same faith in Jesus Christ. Pauline Commentary from the Greek Church.[31]

Life Through Faith. Apollinaris of Laodi-

cea: In place of righteousness by works, which is neither sincere nor life-giving, Paul praised life through faith. The prophet said: "through faith for faith."[32] "If you had believed in Moses," said Jesus, "you would have believed in me also."[33] Pauline Commentary from the Greek Church.[34]

This Righteousness Is Not Ours. Chrysostom: Whoever has become righteous through faith will live, not just in this life but in the one to come as well. Paul does not merely hint at this but adds something else along with it, viz., that such a life will be bright and glorious. For since it is possible to be saved yet still be ashamed (as, for example, criminals whose crimes have been remitted by imperial clemency), Paul adds "righteousness" here so that no one may think like this about salvation. This righteousness is not ours but belongs to God, and in saying this Paul hints to us that it is abundantly available and easy to obtain. For we do not get it by toil and labor but by believing. Then, since his statement does not seem credible, if the adulterer and homosexual, the graverobber and the magician are not only to be suddenly set free from punishment but to be made righteous, and righteous with the righteousness of God, Paul backs up his assertion from the Old Testament.[35] . . . He sends the hearer back to the dispensations of God which took place in the Old Testament . . . showing that both the righteous and the sinners were justified by faith even then.

For since what God gives transcends reason, it is only reasonable that we need faith to understand it. Homilies on Romans 2.[36]

Coming to the Gospel from the Law. [Pseudo-]Constantius: Paul shows that faith may be strengthened in any one through preaching. The first faith, in the law, was to believe in God; the second faith is to believe that Christ is his only begotten Son.

---

[28]Phil 3:9. [29]Hab 2:4. [30]CSEL 81.1:37, 39. [31]NTA 15:53. [32]See Hab 2:4. [33]Jn 5:46. [34]NTA 15:58. [35]See Hab 2:4. [36]NPNF 1 11:349.

"Through faith for faith" therefore means to come to the gospel from the law and to believe that both Old and New Testaments hold that both the Father and Christ are God. THE HOLY LETTER OF ST. PAUL TO THE ROMANS.[37]

THE JUST SHALL LIVE BY FAITH. AMBROSE: It is right for you, my son, to have begun with the law and to have been confirmed in the gospel, from faith to faith, as it is written: "The just shall live by faith." LETTER 47.[38]

AUGUSTINE: What is now the church, prior to the appearance of what will be, lives in toils and afflictions, and in her the just live by faith. QUESTIONS 81.2.[39]

AUGUSTINE: He who claims to be just without faith is a liar. SERMONS FOR THE FEAST OF THE NATIVITY, HOMILY 189.2.[40]

THE RIGHTEOUSNESS BY WHICH THE FAITH-FUL ARE JUST. AUGUSTINE: This righteousness is the grace of the New Testament, by which the faithful are just as long as they live by faith, until by the perfection of righteousness they are brought to the face-to-face vision, as they are also brought to the immortality of the body itself, by the perfection of salvation. THE SPIRIT AND THE LETTER 18.11.[41]

RIGHTEOUSNESS REVEALED TO FAITH. THE-ODORET OF CYR: The righteousness of God is not revealed to everyone but only to those with the eyes of faith. For the holy apostle teaches us that God foresaw this for us from the beginning and predicted it through the prophets, and even before the prophets, had it hidden in his secret will.

Paul quoted Habakkuk for the benefit of the Jews, because he wanted to teach them not to cling to the provisions of the law but to follow the prophets. For many centuries before they had predicted that one day there would be salvation by faith alone.

Then departing from his admonition to the Jews, he accuses everyone else of having brazenly departed from the natural law which the Creator had placed in them.[42] For when God made them, he did not allow them to live like beasts but honored them with reason and gave them the ability to know the difference between good and evil. Those who lived righteous lives before the time of Moses confirm this by their witness. INTERPRE-TATION OF THE LETTER TO THE ROMANS.[43]

REPRISE. GENNADIUS OF CONSTANTINOPLE: What is the overall meaning of the above? It is that our gospel is very great and truly marvelous if you pay careful attention to its power. For through faith in Christ all are saved, those whom the natural law has enlightened and those who follow the written law which was added to it. For when someone is informed about the resurrection from the dead, he learns that he too may share in this by obeying the gospel according to the design of the Savior. And this, says Paul, God had in ancient times announced through Habakkuk the prophet when he said: "The righteous shall live through faith."[44] PAULINE COMMENTARY FROM THE GREEK CHURCH.[45]

---

[37]ENPK 2:23. [38]FC 26:251. [39]FC 70:213. [40]FC 38:21. [41]LCC 8:208. [42]See Rom 1:18. [43]IER, Migne PG 82 col. 57-60. [44]Hab 2:4. [45]NTA 15:355.

1:18-32 GOD'S WRATH AGAINST THE HUMAN RACE

[18]For the wrath of God is revealed from heaven against all ungodliness and wickedness of men who by their wickedness suppress the truth. [19]For what can be known about God is plain to them, because God has shown it to them. [20]Ever since the creation of the world his invisible nature, namely, his eternal power and deity, has been clearly perceived in the things that have been made. So they are without excuse; [21]for although they knew God they did not honor him as God or give thanks to him, but they became futile in their thinking and their senseless minds were darkened. [22]Claiming to be wise, they became fools, [23]and exchanged the glory of the immortal God for images resembling mortal man or birds or animals or reptiles.

[24]Therefore God gave them up in the lusts of their hearts to impurity, to the dishonoring of their bodies among themselves, [25]because they exchanged the truth about God for a lie and worshiped and served the creature rather than the Creator, who is blessed for ever! Amen.

[26]For this reason God gave them up to dishonorable passions. Their women exchanged natural relations for unnatural, [27]and the men likewise gave up natural relations with women and were consumed with passion for one another, men committing shameless acts with men and receiving in their own persons the due penalty for their error.

[28]And since they did not see fit to acknowledge God, God gave them up to a base mind and to improper conduct. [29]They were filled with all manner of wickedness, evil, covetousness, malice. Full of envy, murder, strife, deceit, malignity, they are gossips, [30]slanderers, haters of God, insolent, haughty, boastful, inventors of evil, disobedient to parents, [31]foolish, faithless, heartless, ruthless. [32]Though they know God's decree that those who do such things deserve to die, they not only do them but approve those who practice them.

OVERVIEW: The wrath of God is revealed in the face of sin, not because God is anything other than good, holy and just but because human rebelliousness ensures that these divine attributes will come into conflict with our desires and therefore appear as punishment and retribution for our wrongdoing. The Fathers are sometimes accused of having preached a passionless God who was above such human emotions as wrath (and love, for that matter). But this is not what these readings suggest. God's wrath is a real and conscious response to our moral failure, though we are responsible for its consequences.

God can be known by the human mind, and every form of wisdom is due to divine revelation of one kind or another. The Fathers generally believed in the possibility of coming to a true, albeit limited, knowledge of God by using the resources of the human mind to contemplate the mysteries of the universe. To their way of thinking, this did not open the door to a form of salvation by works. Rather it merely increased the horror of the condemnation that humanity incurred for having turned away from God.

All the understanding of the truth that had been granted to the wisest of the pagans merely increased their condemnation, because they rejected what they knew and turned to the idols of their own imagination instead. Human pride will make even the wisest person a fool. The supposed wisdom of the Egyptians, Greeks and Romans is turned to folly by their idolatry. Idolatry was closely associated with immorality. Fertility cults among the pagans were evidence of this, but the corruption went much deeper. The Fathers were not slow to put the blame for the evils of their time on the errors of paganism. At the same time, they refused to accept the idea that God arbitrarily abandoned those who rebelled against him. Rather they insisted that he left such people alone, so that they would be free to work out the consequences of their disobedience for themselves.

The battle against idolatry was above all a battle for the truth—another instance of how the Fathers raised a particular example to the level of universal principle.

To go against God is to go against nature and to commit the most unnatural sins imaginable. Homosexuality among men was widely practiced, especially among members of the aristocracy and the intellectual class. But true nobility and true intelligence could never practice something that was so clearly contrary to nature, and the Fathers therefore used it as one more example of how corrupt the unbelieving mind had become. The result of sin was to drag people down into ever greater absurdities and a heightened readiness to tolerate other evils. In Romans 1:29-31, Paul defines what he means by sin and shows how extensive it is. The Fathers elaborated his meaning further by showing how these vices interconnect.

To sin is one thing, but to approve of it is far worse. The pagans had corrupted the role of the teacher, which was one of the most highly regarded professions in antiquity. The blind cannot lead the blind. Only those who have been enlightened by the Spirit of God are fit to teach others.

1:18 God's Wrath Against Wickedness

THE RELATION OF TRUTH TO WRATH. TERTULLIAN: Whose wrath? The Creator's, of course!

The truth therefore belongs to the Creator, as does the wrath, which has to be revealed in order to vindicate the truth. AGAINST MARCION 5.13.[1]

AGAINST ALL UNGODLINESS. ORIGEN: Here the wrath of God is said to be revealed not in part but against all ungodliness and wickedness; yet not against all men but only against those who suppress the truth by their wickedness.... Ungodliness refers to sin against God; wickedness, to sin against human beings. Those who suppress the truth by their wickedness sin against both God and humanity. Humans know this truth by the natural and God-given powers of the mind. Enough wisdom is given to them so that they might know what is known of God, i.e., what may be known of God, apprehending the invisible things from those things which can be seen, using the powers of human thought. For this reason God's judgment is just on those who, before the coming of Christ, could have known God but instead turned away from him and fell into worshiping images of men and animals. To sum up: to worship anything at all apart from the Father, Son and Holy Spirit is the offense of ungodliness. COMMENTARY ON THE EPISTLE TO THE ROMANS.[2]

THE REVELATION OF BOTH RIGHTEOUSNESS AND UNRIGHTEOUSNESS. AMBROSIASTER: Just as the righteousness of God is revealed in the one who believes, as I recalled earlier, so ungodliness and unrighteousness are revealed in the one who does not believe. From the very structure of heaven it appears that God is angry with them. For this reason he made the stars so beautiful that from them he might be known as their great and wonderful Creator, and alone be adored. It is written in the eighteenth psalm: "The heavens declare the glory of God, and the firmament shows his handiwork,"[3] and so the human race is made guilty by the natural law. For men could learn this by the law of nature, with the structure

---

[1]ANF 3:457. [2]CER 1:134, 140. [3]Ps 19:1 (LXX 18:1).

of the world bearing witness that God its author ought alone to be loved, which Moses put down in writing.[4] But they became ungodly, not worshiping the Creator, and so unrighteousness appeared in them, in that seeing they suppressed the truth, not confessing the one God. Commentary on Paul's Epistles.[5]

Suppressing the Truth. Apollinaris of Laodicea: This means that although the visible creation was sufficient to reveal the invisible God, they nevertheless abandoned God and deified creatures instead, "suppressing the truth of God in unrighteousness." Pauline Commentary from the Greek Church.[6]

The Opportunity to Repent. Theodore of Mopsuestia: Since the forthcoming punishment of the ungodly and unrighteous has already been decreed, it is essential to walk in the righteousness of faith, in order to avoid the evils to come. Paul rightly said that the wrath of God is being revealed . . . in this present age, when God restrains himself and does not render the full punishment, so as not to remove the opportunity to repent, with the result that either they will turn around and be saved or else they will turn away and have no excuse. Pauline Commentary from the Greek Church.[7]

From Gentler to Dreadful Things. Chrysostom: Notice Paul's discretion, that after encouraging the Romans by the gentler things he turns to the more dreadful ones. For after saying that the gospel is the cause of salvation and life, that it is the power of God, and that it brings forth salvation and righteousness, he mentions what might well make them fear, if they were heedless of it. For since in general most men are drawn not as much by the promise of what is good as by the fear of what is painful, Paul draws them on both sides. It was because of this that God not only promised a kingdom; he threatened hell as well. The prophets spoke to the Jews in the same way, always mingling the evil with the good. Paul changes tack for the same reason, but not arbitrarily. Notice how he puts the good things first and after them the bad ones, in order to show that the former came from the guiding purpose of God but the latter from the wickedness of their backsliding. The prophet also puts the good first: "If you are willing and obedient you shall eat the good of the land, but if you refuse and rebel you shall be devoured by the sword."[8]

"The wrath of God is revealed from heaven" —and this often takes place in famines and plagues and wars, for then each person individually and all in common are punished. What will be new then about this coming judgment? The punishment will be greater and common to all, and it will have a different purpose. For what happens now happens for correction, but then it will be for vengeance. Paul showed this elsewhere when he said: "But when we are judged by the Lord we are chastened, so that we may not be condemned along with the world."[9] Another point is that now many of these things seem to come not from the wrath from above but from human malice. But then the punishment from God will be manifest, when the Judge, sitting upon the terrible tribunal, will order some to be dragged to the furnaces, some to the outer darkness, and some to other inexorable and intolerable punishments. Why then does he not speak as clearly as this . . . but says rather that "the wrath of God is revealed"? This is because his hearers were still new converts, and he wants to win them over by talking in a way they can accept. And besides what is stated here, he seems to me to be aiming at the Greeks. This is why he starts with God's wrath and only afterwards introduces the subject of Christ's judgment.

The ways of ungodliness are many, but the way of truth is only one. Error is something various and multiform and compound, but the truth is one. After speaking of doctrines, Paul speaks of

---

[4]See Deut 6:5; 10:12; 11:1. [5]CSEL 81.1:39. [6]NTA 15:59. [7]NTA 15:115. [8]Is 1:19-20. [9]1 Cor 11:32.

life, mentioning the unrighteousness of humanity. For there are also different kinds of unrighteousness. One is in financial affairs, as when someone deals unrighteously with his neighbor in these, and another in regard to women, when a man leaves his own wife and intrudes upon the marriage of another. . . . Others do not injure wife or property but the reputation of their neighbor, and this too is unrighteousness. Homilies on Romans 3.[10]

Countering Manichean Fantasies on the God of the New Testament.

[Pseudo-]Constantius: If, as the Manichees claim, the God of the Old Testament is cruel because he brings vengeance on sinners, how is it said by the apostle here that vengeance will be brought by the God of the New Testament on the ungodly? From this it appears that the God of the Old and the God of the New Testament are one and the same. The Holy Letter of St. Paul to the Romans.[11]

Reproof of Idolatry. Augustine: Those

whom the apostle reproved knew but did not give thanks and, claiming to be wise, actually became fools and fell into idolatry. For when the apostle spoke to the Athenians, he showed plainly that the wise among the Gentiles had discovered the Creator. . . .[12] He condemned the unbelief of the Gentiles first, in order to show that they could obtain grace if they converted. For it would be unjust for them to suffer a penalty for unbelief but not obtain the reward of faith. Augustine on Romans 3.[13]

To Stun Those Who Rebel. Theodoret of

Cyr: For nature taught them both that God is the Creator of all things and also that they should flee unrighteousness and embrace righteousness. But even when teachers were given to them, they did not live up to this. So God threatened them with future punishment. . . . This punishment is called the wrath of God, not because God punishes people for any emotional reason but in order to stun those who rebel against him. Interpretation of the Letter to the Romans.[14]

Ungodliness and Wickedness. Genna-

dius of Constantinople: Generally speaking there are two main types of sin—discord with God and discord with one's neighbor. Paul mentions them both, putting discord with God first because it is the greater sin, and calling it "ungodliness." He then mentions the second kind of discord, the one with one's neighbor, calling it "wickedness." He even states that our entire race has rightly come under judgment, saying that they have suppressed the truth in wickedness. Nor can they claim to be ignorant, for knowing the truth, they perverted it. . . . And outlining their sins, Paul lists the one against God first, saying that they had clear and plain knowledge about God because God had revealed himself to them. Pauline Commentary from the Greek Church.[15]

1:19 Knowledge of God Is Made Plain

What Can Be Known About God. Origen:

Paul says that what can be known about God is plain to them, thereby revealing that there is something about God which can be known, and something about him which is unknown. Therefore he says that the wrath of God is revealed on those who suppress the truth by their wickedness. If something is revealed it must be brought to our notice from something we have not yet noticed. It appears here that the wrath of God is revealed not to those who are ignorant of the truth but to those who already know the truth, however imperfectly.

The apostle also shows that those things which have come to the wise of this world concerning the knowledge of the truth, have come to them by divine revelation. But when they chase after vain glory, or are praised for ancient errors,

---

[10]NPNF 1 11:350-51. [11]ENPK 2:24. [12]See Acts 17:22-34. [13]AOR 3. [14]IER, Migne PG 82 cols. 60, 61. [15]NTA 15:356-57.

or are silenced by fear of rulers, they become judges of their own damnation. The truth, which they had learned by divine revelation, is either hidden from them by their loss of freedom or else is denied by their wicked behavior.

So also the wrath of God may sometimes appear in the form of that power which is given to the ministers of justice and which applies punishments to sinners, which is what I think is meant in the passage where it is recorded that the wrath of God moved David to order Joab to number the people.[16]

The invisible things of God may be contemplated by the things which have been made. What is unknown about God is the essence of his very nature, which is in my opinion concealed, not only from humanity but even from the angelic creatures. For only God knows whether there has ever been anyone so perfect in his grasp of things that he has been able to attain to a pure knowledge of God's very essence. Nonetheless, we may hope that such may in due time be revealed, for this appears in the words of the Savior: "No one knows the Son, except the Father, and no one knows the Father except the Son and anyone to whom the Son chooses to reveal him."[17] And he would not have added this last phrase if he had not known that there were some to whom God wanted to become revealed. COMMENTARY ON THE EPISTLE TO THE ROMANS.[18]

PLAIN FROM THE STRUCTURE OF THE WORLD. Ambrosiaster: The knowledge of God is plain from the structure of the world. For God, who by nature is invisible, may be known even from things which are visible. For his work is made in such a way that it reveals its Maker by its very visibility, so that what is concealed may be known by looking at what is revealed.[19] This is revealed so that everyone might believe that he is God, who made this cosmos, which is impossible for anyone else to do. COMMENTARY ON PAUL'S EPISTLES.[20]

KNOWN THROUGH CREATION. APOLLINARIS

OF LAODICEA: The energies of the divine being have always been invisible by nature, and they are never revealed to anybody directly, but they are made known through the creation. PAULINE COMMENTARY FROM THE GREEK CHURCH.[21]

THE VOICE OF TRUTH AND BEAUTY. CHRYSOSTOM: God has placed the knowledge of himself in human hearts from the beginning. But this knowledge they unwisely invested in wood and stone and thus contaminated the truth, at least as far as they were able. Meanwhile the truth abides unchanged, having its own unchanging glory.... How did God reveal himself? By a voice from heaven? Not at all! God made a panoply which was able to draw them more than by a voice. He put before them the immense creation, so that both the wise and the unlearned, the Scythian and the barbarian, might ascend to God, having learned through sight the beauty of the things which they had seen. HOMILIES ON ROMANS 3.[22]

THE INVISIBLE MANIFESTED IN THE VISIBLE. [PSEUDO-]CONSTANTIUS: Paul shows that every person who has a normal intellect recognizes in himself some invisible substance which produces different talents and disciplines in human beings. By this means the invisible God is manifested to them in the works which he has done and is still doing. THE HOLY LETTER OF ST. PAUL TO THE ROMANS.[23]

GOD'S EXISTENCE AND JUSTICE PLAIN. PELAGIUS: What can be known about God, i.e., that God exists and that God is just, is plain to their consciences. For every creature knows that it is not God and that it was made by another. PELAGIUS'S COMMENTARY ON ROMANS.[24]

1:20 Creation Displays God's Invisible Nature

---

[16]2 Sam 24:1-2. [17]Mt 11:27. [18]CER 1:134-42. [19]Or what is obscure may be known by what is obvious. [20]CSEL 81.1:39, 41. [21]NTA 15:59. [22]NPNF 1 11:352. [23]ENPK 2:24. [24]PCR 64.

THE PALPABLE TRUTH OF THE SENSES. TERTULLIAN: The objects which are touched by the mind are of a higher nature, since they are spiritual, than those which are grasped by the senses. Since these are corporeal, any superiority they may display lies only in the "objects"—e.g., as lofty ones contrasted with humble—not in the "faculties" of the intellect over against the senses. For how can the intellect be considered sovereign above the senses, when it is these which educate it for the discovery of various truths? It is a fact that these truths are learned by means of palpable forms; in other words, invisible things are discovered by the help of visible ones, even as the apostle says in his epistle. A TREATISE ON THE SOUL 18.[25]

BEHOLDING GOD THROUGH CREATURES. ORIGEN: These things apply to all human beings who possess natural reason. Yet they more specifically apply to those called philosophers, who are wise in the things of this world. Their job is to ponder the creatures of this world and everything which is made in it, and from the things which are seen, to perceive in their minds the things which are invisible. COMMENTARY ON THE EPISTLE TO THE ROMANS.[26]

USE OF THE SENSES UPON SENSIBLE OBJECTS. ORIGEN: From this we infer that all who live on this earth have to begin with the use of the senses upon sensible objects in order to go on from them to a knowledge of the nature of intellectual things. Yet their knowledge must not stop short with the objects of sense. AGAINST CELSUS 7.37.[27]

THE EYES OF THE MIND. NOVATIAN: The human mind, learning to know the hidden things from those which are manifest, may consider in spirit the greatness of the Maker from the greatness of his works, which it sees with the eyes of the mind. THE TRINITY 3.6.[28]

A TRAINING PLACE FOR SOULS. BASIL: You will find that the world was not devised at random or to no purpose, but to contribute to some useful end and to the great advantage of all beings. It is truly a training place for rational souls and a school for attaining the knowledge of God. Through visible and perceptible objects it provides guidance to the mind for the contemplation of the invisible. HOMILY ONE, CREATION OF THE HEAVENS AND EARTH 1.6.[29]

REMINDERS OF THE BENEFACTOR. BASIL: In all things visible, clear reminders of the Benefactor grip us. We shall not give any opportunity for sins, nor shall we leave any place in our hearts for the enemy, if we have God as a dweller in us by our constant remembrance of him. HEXAMERON 3.10.[30]

HIS ETERNAL POWER AND DEITY. AMBROSIASTER: Paul here repeats the same thing in order to teach even more absolutely that, although the power and majesty of God cannot by themselves be seen by the eyes of the creature, they may be known by the work of the structure of the world. In this way he indicts those who lived without law, whether natural or Mosaic. For by the habit of sinning they broke the law of nature, wiping out any memory of him. But they did not want to accept the law, which had been given for their reformation, and thus were doubly condemned.

His power and deity are eternal, so that they are without excuse. So that ungodliness might in no way be excused, Paul added that the power of God and his eternal divinity were known by men, who were prevented by some foolishness from honoring God, who they knew existed and provided for their welfare. COMMENTARY ON PAUL'S EPISTLES.[31]

CREATION FROM NOTHING. AMBROSE: We can find it easy to understand, then, that the Creator of angels, dominions and powers is he who in a moment of his power made this great beauty of the world out of nothing,[32] which did not itself

---

[25]ANF 3:199. [26]CER 1:142. [27]ANF 4:625. [28]FC 67:30. [29]FC 46:11. [30]FC 46:54. [31]CSEL 81.1:41. [32]See Gen 1:1.

have existence and gave substance to things or causes which did not themselves exist. SIX DAYS OF CREATION 1.4.16.[33]

THE HEAVENS DECLARE. CHRYSOSTOM: The prophets also said: "The heavens declare the glory of God."[34] Will the heathen say at the judgment that they were ignorant of God? Did they not hear the heaven sending forth a voice while the well-ordered harmony of all things spoke out more clearly than a trumpet? Did you not see the hours of night and day remaining constantly unmoved, the good order of winter, spring and the other seasons remaining both fixed and unmoved? . . . Yet God did not set so great a system of teaching before the heathen in order to deprive them of any excuse but so that they might come to know him. It was by their failure to recognize him that they deprived themselves of every excuse. HOMILIES ON ROMANS 3.[35]

HIS GLORY BEHELD EVERY DAY. [PSEUDO-] CONSTANTIUS: Because we see the world composed and fashioned by God, in its glory we behold the whole of his work every day. THE HOLY LETTER OF ST. PAUL TO THE ROMANS.[36]

CERTAINTY OF THE INVISIBLE. AUGUSTINE: Invisible things are seen in a special and appropriate way. When they are seen they are much more certain than the objects of the bodily sense, but they are said to be invisible because they cannot be seen by mortal eyes. LETTER 120.[37]

KNOWING THE TRUTH. AUGUSTINE: Notice that Paul does not call them ignorant of the truth but says that they held the truth in iniquity, and he does not fail to answer the obvious question: How could those to whom God had not given the law have a knowledge of the truth? For he says that through the visible things of the creation they reached an understanding of the invisible things of the Creator. THE SPIRIT AND THE LETTER 19.12.[38]

WITHOUT EXCUSE. AUGUSTINE: How does Paul mean that they are without excuse, except by reference to a kind of excuse that usually prompts human pride to voice such protestations as: "If only I had known, I would not have done it." . . . This kind of excuse is taken away from them when a precept is given or when the knowledge of how to avoid sin is made clear to them. GRACE AND FREE WILL 2.2.[39]

VISIBLE THINGS SO SPLENDID. PELAGIUS: God's hidden qualities can be deduced from things which are manifest. For if he made visible things so splendid that some people thought they were gods and tried to maintain that they were eternal, how much more were these people capable of understanding that the one who made these things is everlasting, almighty and boundless? PELAGIUS'S COMMENTARY ON ROMANS.[40]

STUDYING THIS WORLD. GENNADIUS OF CONSTANTINOPLE: He created us with such a nature, placing a mind and reason within us and granting us these things so that by studying this world we might come to a knowledge of the invisible things which are his.

Paul says that they are without excuse in order to shut them up. . . . For God did not deign to reveal himself to human beings in order to give them some excuse but in order to show them that it would be to their advantage to accept him and his mercy. PAULINE COMMENTARY FROM THE GREEK CHURCH.[41]

CREATION PROCLAIMS GOD'S MAJESTY. JOHN OF DAMASCUS: The very creation, by its harmony and ordering, proclaims the majesty of the divine nature. ORTHODOX FAITH 1.1.[42]

1:21 *Futile Thinking and Darkened Minds*

---

[33]FC 42:16. [34]Ps 19:1. [35]NPNF 1 11:352. [36]ENPK 2:25. [37]FC 18:307. [38]LCC 8:209. [39]FC 59:252. [40]PCR 65. [41]NTA 15:357. [42]FC 37:166.

Knowing God They Worshiped Idols.
Ambrosiaster: They were so far from being ignorant that they confessed that there was a single principle from which all things heavenly, earthly and infernal derived their origin, and that there was only one being who decreed what properties and duties would belong to everything by nature. Yet knowing this they did not give thanks. Paul is speaking of the ancients in order to correct his contemporaries and future generations.

Truly this is futility, that knowing the truth they decided to worship something else which they knew was not true, so that hiding from God they might worship idols. A cloud of error covered their hearts. Although they should have honored the Creator all the more from the beautiful things which he made, they clung to what they had, saying that the things which they could see were sufficient for their salvation. Commentary on Paul's Epistles.[43]

The Range of Idolatry. Eusebius of Emesa: It may seem that Paul has simplified his argument against the Greeks, because he condemns idolatry as the only kind of ungodliness. But to those who look more carefully at what he says, things will appear not this way but rather that Paul has broadened his horizons, so as not to overlook any kind of impiety. Pauline Commentary from the Greek Church.[44]

Mistaking What Is Not for What Is.
Apollinaris of Laodicea: It is futile to conceive of nonbeing as if it were being, as do those who worship vanity as if it were God. For this reason their minds have been rendered senseless and darkness has entered their souls. Pauline Commentary from the Greek Church.[45]

They Destroyed the Light That Was in Them. Chrysostom: This is the greatest charge against the heathen, and the second is the fact that they worshiped idols.[46] . . . The heathen tried to get to heaven, but having destroyed the light that was in them, instead entrusted themselves to

the darkness of their own reasoning. They looked for the incorporeal in bodies and for the infinite in creaturely shapes, and so lost their congruity with the light. Homilies on Romans 3.[47]

Applies to the Philosophers. [Pseudo-] Constantius: This applies to Pythagoras, Socrates, Plato, Aristotle, Democritus, Epicurus and all the philosophers who considered themselves wise. The Holy Letter of St. Paul to the Romans.[48]

The Desires of Their Hearts. Augustine: If they had given thanks to God who gave this wisdom, they would not have claimed any credit for their own ideas. Therefore they were given over by the Lord to the desires of their own hearts, and did improper things. Augustine on Romans 4.[49]

The Darkening of the Heart. Augustine: Surely that darkening of the heart was already a penalty and punishment, and by that penalty, that is by the blinding of the heart because of the abandonment by the light of wisdom, they fell into more and more serious sins. On Nature and Grace 22.24.[50]

Worshiping Creatures. Pelagius: Imagining that they could grasp God with their minds, they fell away from their natural instinct and worshiped creatures instead of the Creator. Pelagius's Commentary on Romans.[51]

Different Gods. Caesarius of Arles: In the hearts of the Gentiles, the purest honoring of the one God was changed into the bloody worship of different gods. Sermon 100a.2.[52]

Futile in Their Thinking. Prosper of Aquitaine: It is well known how Greek schools

---

[43]CSEL 81.1:41, 43. [44]NTA 15:46. [45]NTA 15:59. [46]See Jer 2:13. [47]NPNF 1 11:352. [48]ENPK 2:25. [49]AOR 3. [50]FC 86:39. [51]PCR 65. [52]FC 47:93.

and Roman eloquence and the search of the whole world in the quest of the supreme good, with the most penetrating study and outstanding ability, accomplished nothing by their labor except to become "futile in their thinking, and their senseless minds were darkened." GRACE AND FREE WILL 12.4.[53]

No Condemnation for Ignorance. GENNADIUS OF CONSTANTINOPLE: The pagans knew that there was a God, and it is clear that they did not receive judgment because of this. For it was not for want of knowledge that they were condemned, but the opposite. For each one glorified God in the sense that whatever he thought God was, that he served. Thus they corrupted the whole matter by their peculiar and mistaken ideas. They abandoned God's way of knowing him and preferred their own, falling into the deepest imbecility, outdoing themselves in their so-called wisdom by adding to their foolishness, descending to the worship of reptiles and inanimate objects. PAULINE COMMENTARY FROM THE GREEK CHURCH.[54]

1:22 The Wise Became Fools

Claiming to Be Wise. AMBROSIASTER: They imagined that they were wise because they thought they had explored the natural sciences, investigating the courses of the stars and the quantities of the elements, while rejecting the God who made them. Therefore they are fools, for if these things are worthy of praise, how much more is their Creator! COMMENTARY ON PAUL'S EPISTLES.[55]

Senseless Thinking. CHRYSOSTOM: Having some high opinion of themselves and not being patient enough to go the way that God had commanded them, they were immersed in a way of thinking which made no sense. HOMILIES ON ROMANS 3.[56]

Pride Leads to Folly. AUGUSTINE: It is pride

that turns man away from wisdom, and folly is the consequence of turning away from wisdom.[57] ON FREE WILL 24.72.[58]

The Invisible God, Visible Idols. PELAGIUS: They thought they were wise because they had "discovered" how the invisible God can be honored by means of a visible idol! PELAGIUS'S COMMENTARY ON ROMANS.[59]

They Became Fools. THEODORET OF CYR: They increased their guilt by their claim, for in calling themselves wise they showed that in fact they were fools. INTERPRETATION OF THE LETTER TO THE ROMANS.[60]

1:23 The Immortal God, Mortal Beings

Whether the Bodily Image of Man Is the Image of God. ORIGEN: We ought not to overlook this passage. The apostle is not merely complaining about those who worship idols, but he should also be understood to be refuting the Anthropomorphites, who are found inside the church, who say that the bodily image of man is as such the image of God, ignoring the fact that it is written in Genesis that the whole person is created in the image of God,[61] which must be understood as it is interpreted by the apostle, when he said: "You have put off the old man with his behavior and you have put on the new man, which is created according to God."[62] . . . Elsewhere Paul calls this the "inner man" and regards the corrupt bodily image as the "outer man."[63] . . . The mistake of those who think that it is this outer man which is the image of God is therefore obvious. COMMENTARY ON THE EPISTLE TO THE ROMANS.[64]

Body Without Soul. ORIGEN: These people have lowered to a body without soul or sense the

---

[53]FC 7:380. [54]NTA 15:358. [55]CSEL 81.1:43. [56]NPNF 1 11:352. [57]See Prov 11:2; 13:10. [58]LCC 6:214. [59]PCR 65. [60]IER, Migne PG 82 col. 61. [61]See Gen 1:26-27. [62]Col 3:9-10. [63]See Rom 7:22. [64]CER 1:162-64.

identity of the One who gives to all sentient and rational beings not only the power of sentience but also of sensing rationally, and to some even the power of sensing and thinking perfectly and virtuously. On Prayer 29.15.[65]

Exchanging the Immortal God for Images. Ambrosiaster: So blinded were their hearts that they altered the majesty of the invisible God, which they knew from the things which he had made, not into men but, what is worse and is an inexcusable offense, into the image of men, so that the form of a corruptible man was called a god by them, i.e., a depiction of a man. Moreover, they did not dare honor living people with this name but elevated the images of dead men to the glory of God! What great idiocy, what great stupidity, in that they knew they were calling them to their damnation, among whom an image was more powerful than the truth, and the dead were mightier than the living! Turning away from the living God they preferred dead men, among whose number they found themselves.

They so diminished the majesty and glory of God that they gave the title of "god" to the images of things which were small and tiny. For the Babylonians were the first to deify a notion of Bel, who was portrayed as a dead man, who supposedly had once been one of their kings. They also worshiped the dragon serpent, which Daniel the man of God killed and of which they had an image.[66] The Egyptians also worshiped a quadruped which they called Apis and which was in the form of a bull. Jeroboam copied this evil by setting up calves in Samaria, to which the Jews were expected to offer sacrifices.[67] . . . By doing this, those who knew the invisible God did not honor him. They were unable to be wise in the things which are visible. For one who has problems with the big things will not be wise in the little things either. Commentary on Paul's Epistles.[68]

Idolaters Inferior to Their Idols. Gregory Nazianzen: People like this make it hard to tell which was the more contemptible, the wor-

shipers or the worshiped. Perhaps the worshipers by far, since as rational beings and recipients of God's grace, they chose their inferior for patron and better. Oration 28: On God 28.15.[69]

Holding Their Wisdom Up to Ridicule. Chrysostom: Paul's first charge against the heathen was that they failed to find God. His second was that, although they had great and clear means of doing it they did not; the third is that they nevertheless claimed to be wise; the fourth was that not only did they not find the supreme being, they lowered him to the level of devils, stones and wood. Paul also pulls down their pride in 1 Corinthians but not in the same way as here. There it is from the cross that he deals them the blow, saying that the foolishness of God is wiser than men.[70] But here he does not make any comparison, merely holding their wisdom up to ridicule by itself, showing it to be no more than folly and a display of vain boasting.

The heathen ought to have known that God is Lord of all, that he made them out of nothing, that he works by his providence and that he cares about them. For these things are the glory of God. To whom then did they ascribe it? Not even to men, but to an image made like corruptible man! Nor did they stop there but sank to the level of beasts, or rather to the images of beasts. Homilies on Romans 3.[71]

Boastful of Wisdom. Augustine: Here the apostle has in mind the Romans, Greeks and Egyptians, all boastful of their renown for wisdom. The City of God 8.10.[72]

No Similarity Between the Mortal and Immortal. Pelagius: They did not understand that there is no similarity between the mortal and the immortal, the corruptible and the eternal. . . . Here Paul addresses the worshipers of Jupiter,

[65]OSW 159. [66]See Bel 1:26-27. [67]See 1 Kings 12:28-33. [68]CSEL 81.1:45, 47. [69]FGFR 232. [70]See 1 Cor 1:25. [71]NPNF 1 11:352-53. [72]FC 14:39.

who maintain that he was transformed into the likeness of animals and therefore dedicate to him images of the kind in which he satisfied his sexual desire. PELAGIUS'S COMMENTARY ON ROMANS.[73]

1:24 *Dishonoring the Body*

GIVEN OVER TO THE LUST OF THEIR HEARTS. ORIGEN: The details here seem to correspond to the faith of the church, in that for the above-mentioned reasons, for just cause those who in their wickedness suppress the truth revealed by God are abandoned by God, and because they are abandoned they are given over to the desires of their heart. The desires of their heart were that they should disgrace their bodies in uncleanness and abuse and that, with similar lack of discernment toward the worship of God, they should abandon the glory of the incorruptible God for the wicked and base forms of men and animals and think so little of themselves as to live like irrational beasts when in fact they were rational persons.

To those who deny that the good God is also the just judge, we ask what they might say about these words of the apostle: "God gave them up in the lusts of their hearts to impurity, to the dishonoring of their bodies among themselves."

Therefore Marcion and all those of his school who have sprung forth like the offspring of serpents will not dare to touch the answers to these questions, even with the tips of their fingers. Due to this blunder they have already rejected the Old Testament, where such matters are commonplace. But what good did that do them? For they are no less discomfited by similar problems in the New Testament. But we, who say that the one good and just God of the law and prophets and Gospels is the Father of Christ, give the same explanation in the New as in the Old Testament, calling on him who has placed in Zion a stone of stumbling and a rock of offense[74] to reveal to us by the Holy Spirit his own offense and the scandal of the apostolic text, by which irresolute minds appear to be offended. COMMENTARY ON

THE EPISTLE TO THE ROMANS.[75]

HANDED OVER TO UNCLEANNESS. AMBROSIASTER: Paul says that because the Gentiles had deified relics and images of things, so as to dishonor the Creator God, they were given over to illusions. They were given over, not so that they could do what they did not want to do, but so that they could carry out exactly what they desired. And this is the goodness of God.

To "hand over" means to permit, not to encourage or to force, so that they were helped by the devil to carry out in practice the things which they conceived in their lusts. For they never thought of doing anything good. Therefore they were handed over to uncleanness that they might willingly damage each other's bodies with abuse. For even now there are men of this type who are said to dishonor each other's bodies. When the thought of the mind is wrong, the bodies are said to be dishonored. Is not a stain on the body a sign of sin in the soul? When the body is contaminated, nobody doubts that there is sin in the soul. COMMENTARY ON PAUL'S EPISTLES.[76]

GOD GAVE THEM UP. CHRYSOSTOM: "God gave them up" means simply that he left them to their own concoctions. For as an army commander if forced to retreat abandons his deserting soldiers to the enemy, he does not thereby actively push them into the enemy camp but passively withdraws his own protection over them. In the same way, God left those who were not ready to receive what comes from him but were the first to desert him, even though he had fully done his part. After all, he set before them, as a form of teaching, the world. He gave them reason and an understanding capable of perceiving what they needed to understand. Yet the people of that time did not use any of those things in order to obtain salvation, but rather they perverted what they had received into its opposite. What could God

---

[73]PCR 66. [74]See Is 8:14; Rom 9:33. [75]CER 1:144-48. [76]CSEL 81.1:47, 49.

have done about this? Could he have forced them to do what was right? Yes, but that would not have made them virtuous. All he could do then was to leave them to their own devices, which is what he did, so that in that way, if in no other, having tried and discovered the things they lusted after, they might turn away from what was so shameful. HOMILIES ON ROMANS 3.[77]

THE PERMISSION OF GOD. [PSEUDO-]CONSTANTIUS: In saying that God gave them up to their own lusts, Paul is not claiming that God is the direct cause of this but merely that since God did not bring vengeance on them after much longsuffering and patience, he allowed them to act according to their own desires. He did this, wanting them to be converted to repentance. THE HOLY LETTER OF ST. PAUL TO THE ROMANS.[78]

ABANDONED TO THEIR OWN DESIRES. AUGUSTINE: This means that God abandoned them to the desires of their own hearts. For Paul says that they got what they deserved from God. AUGUSTINE ON ROMANS 5.[79]

SIN COMMITTED WILLINGLY. AUGUSTINE: When the evil will receives power to accomplish its purpose, this comes from the judgment of God, in whom there is no unrighteousness. His punishment is carried out in this way as well as in other ways. It is not less just merely because it is hidden. The wicked man only knows that he is being punished when some manifest penalty makes him feel, against his will, the evil of the sin which he committed willingly. THE SPIRIT AND THE LETTER 54.[80]

LEFT TO THEMSELVES. AUGUSTINE: Many are left to themselves, to their own hurt.... A man that has asked for great wealth may have received it to his own hurt. While he was without it he had little to fear; as soon as he has possession of it he has become a prey to the stronger. HOMILIES ON I JOHN 6.8.[81]

ABANDONED BY GOD. THEODORET OF CYR: By "gave them up" Paul means that God permitted this to happen. He simply abandoned them because they had fallen into extreme ungodliness. INTERPRETATION OF THE LETTER TO THE ROMANS.[82]

1:25 Worshiping the Creature, Not the Creator

EXCHANGING THE TRUTH FOR A LIE. AMBROSIASTER: They changed the truth about God into a lie. They gave the name of the true God to these things, which are false gods. Ignoring what rocks and wood and other metals really are, they attributed to them something which does not belong to them. The truth of God is turned into a lie when a rock is called *God*. This fact drove out the God who is true, and since true and false shared a common name, it was easy for the true God to be regarded as false. This is what it means to change what is true into falsehood. For those things were not called *rock* or *wood*, but *God*. This is to worship the creature rather than the Creator, which is what they did. They did not deny God but worshiped a creature as God. In order to justify this, they gave these things the honor due to God, so that their worship rendered dishonor to God. For that reason he hastened to punish them, because although they knew God, they did not honor him "who is blessed for ever. Amen." This is true! COMMENTARY ON PAUL'S EPISTLES.[83]

WORSHIP OF DEVILS. ATHANASIUS: So far did their impiety go that they proceeded to worship devils and proclaimed them as gods, fulfilling their own lusts. ON THE INCARNATION OF THE WORD 11.[84]

TREATING THE IDOL AS TRUTH. THEODORE OF MOPSUESTIA: The truth about God is that he is the true God. But human beings have made idols

---

[77]NPNF 1 11:354. [78]ENPK 2:25-26. [79]AOR 3. [80]LCC 8:238. [81]LCC 8:306. [82]IER, Migne PG 82 col. 64. [83]CSEL 81.1:49. [84]LCC 3:66.

and falsely called them gods. They have transferred the truth of God to idols. In other words, they have changed what could rightly be said and thought about God into a lie by applying it to idols instead. PAULINE COMMENTARY FROM THE GREEK CHURCH.[85]

WORSHIPING THE CREATURE. CHRYSOSTOM: Paul lists out in detail things which were a matter for utter scorn, but the more serious things he dealt with in general terms. . . . Look how strong his condemnation is, for he does not say merely that they served the creature but that they did so more than the Creator, thereby giving fresh force to the charge against them and removing any plea for mitigation.

God is blessed for ever, for even if the heathen treated him insolently, he was not overwhelmed, nor was any harm done to his glory, for he remains forever blessed. It may happen that someone may become philosophical about the insults others heap upon him, yet he does not even feel them. How much less would the true God ignore them and not feel them? For God's nature is imperishable and unalterable. His glory is neither changeable nor erratic. HOMILIES ON ROMANS 3.[86]

SERVING THE CREATURE. AUGUSTINE: For by worshiping and serving the creature rather than the Creator they have not wished to be a temple of the one true God. By wishing to have him along with many other things, they have been more successful in not having him at all than in having him along with many false gods. LETTER 187.29.[87]

PELAGIUS: They not only loved the creature but served it; indeed, anyone who is overwhelmed by a desire for some creature serves that creature.[88] PELAGIUS'S COMMENTARY ON ROMANS.[89]

UNGODLINESS PRODUCES WICKEDNESS. THEODORET OF CYR: Ungodliness is the root of wickedness. These people were deprived of God's grace for both of these things. INTERPRETATION

OF THE LETTER TO THE ROMANS.[90]

SUBJECT TO CORRUPTION. JOHN OF DAMASCUS: Sun and moon are subject to change and variation, as is evident in an eclipse. This refutes the folly of those who worship the creature. Now, anything that is subject to change is not God, for by its very nature it is subject to corruption and change. ORTHODOX FAITH 2.13.[91]

1:26 Dishonorable Passions

NATURAL MALE-FEMALE SEXUALITY VALIDATED. TERTULLIAN: When Paul asserts that males and females changed among themselves the natural use of the creature into that which is unnatural, he validates the natural way. THE CHAPLET 6.[92]

GIVING THEM UP TO GODLESSNESS. ORIGEN: This is the third time that the apostle uses the phrase "God gave them up."[93] Each time he gives reasons for this, but the reasons do not seem to correspond to the causes. . . . It is therefore better to take all three instances together and regard them as a single cause for the abandonment of men to their lusts. . . . And similarly, all of these lusts are found in every case of abandonment. . . . It seems that in these three points the apostle has enumerated every kind of godlessness—one group worships idols, another serves the creation instead of the Creator, and the third has refused to pay attention to God. The first group must be the pagans, the second group includes the wise men and philosophers, while in my opinion, the third group refers to the heretics who either deny God or utter different blasphemies against the Most High. COMMENTARY ON THE EPISTLE TO THE ROMANS.[94]

DISHONORABLE PASSIONS. ORIGEN: Would

---

[85]NTA 15:115. [86]NPNF 1 11:354. [87]FC 30:243. [88]2 Pet 2:19 [89]PCR 66. [90]IER, Migne PG 82 col. 64. [91]FC 37:220. [92]ANF 3:96. [93]See Rom 1:24, 26, 28. [94]CER 1:156-58.

those so condemned not have remained in the lusts of their hearts, even if they had not been given up to them by God? Would they not have fallen into dishonorable passions, even if they had not been given up to them by God? Would they not have fallen into an unfit mind quite apart from being given up to it by God? ON PRAYER 29.12.[95]

WOMEN EXCHANGED NATURAL RELATIONS FOR UNNATURAL. AMBROSIASTER: Paul tells us that these things came about, that a woman should lust after another woman, because God was angry at the human race because of its idolatry. Those who interpret this differently do not understand the force of the argument. For what is it to change the use of nature into a use which is contrary to nature, if not to take away the former and adopt the latter, so that the same part of the body should be used by each of the sexes in a way for which it was not intended? Therefore, if this is the part of the body which they think it is, how could they have changed the natural use of it if they had not had this use given to them by nature? This is why he said earlier that they had been handed over to uncleanness, even though he did not explain in detail what he meant by that. COMMENTARY ON PAUL'S EPISTLES.[96]

TRUE PLEASURE ACCORDING TO NATURE. CHRYSOSTOM: No one can say that it was by being prevented from legitimate intercourse that they came to this pass or that it was from having no means to fulfill their desire that they were driven into this monstrous insanity. . . . What is contrary to nature has something irritating and displeasing in it, so that they could not even claim to be getting pleasure out of it. For genuine pleasure comes from following what is according to nature. But when God abandons a person to his own devices, then everything is turned upside down. Thus not only was their doctrine satanic, but their life was too. . . . How disgraceful it is when even the women sought after these things, when they ought to have a greater sense of shame than men have. HOMILIES ON ROMANS 4.[97]

LEAVING PEOPLE TO THEIR OWN DEVICES. [PSEUDO-]CONSTANTIUS: God gives no one up; the word is used only when he leaves people to their own devices. THE HOLY LETTER OF ST. PAUL TO THE ROMANS.[98]

FORSAKING THE AUTHOR OF NATURE. PELAGIUS: Because of the reasons given above, they were abandoned to their disgraceful behavior. Those who turned against God turned everything on its head. For those who forsook the author of nature could not keep to the order of nature. PELAGIUS'S COMMENTARY ON ROMANS.[99]

WHAT THEY WANTED. OECUMENIUS: God gave them up because that is what they wanted. PAULINE COMMENTARY FROM THE GREEK CHURCH.[100]

1:27 Shameless Acts

MEN CONSUMED WITH PASSION FOR ONE ANOTHER. CYPRIAN: If you were able . . . to direct your eyes into secret places, to unfasten the locked doors of sleeping chambers and to open these hidden recesses to the perception of sight, you would behold that being carried on by the unchaste which a chaste countenance could not behold. You would see what it is an indignity even to see. . . . Men with frenzied lusts rush against men. Things are done which cannot even give pleasure to those who do them. To DONATUS 9.[101]

CHANGING THE NATURAL USE. AMBROSIASTER: It is clear that, because they changed the truth of God into a lie, they changed the natural use (of sexuality) into that use by which they were dishonored and were condemned to the second death. For since Satan cannot make another law, having no power to do so, it must

---

[95]OSW 157. [96]CSEL 81.1:51. [97]NPNF 1 11:355-56. [98]ENPK 2:26. [99]PCR 67. [100]NTA 15:423. [101]FC 36:14-15.

be said that they changed to another order and by doing things which were not allowed, fell into sin.

Paul says that the due penalty comes from contempt of God, and that it is wickedness and obscenity. For this is the prime cause of sin. What is worse, what is more harmful than that sin which deceives even the devil and binds man to death? COMMENTARY ON PAUL'S EPISTLES.[102]

SEVERIAN: Paul did not say this lightly, but because he had heard that there was a homosexual community at Rome. PAULINE COMMENTARY FROM THE GREEK CHURCH.[103]

ABANDONING THE UNITY OF THE SEXES.
CHRYSOSTOM: This is clear proof of the ultimate degree of corruption, when both sexes are abandoned. Both he who was called to be the leader of the woman and she who was told to become a helper to the man now behave as enemies to one another. Notice how deliberately Paul measures his words. For he does not say that they were enamored of one another but that they were consumed by lust for one another! You see that the whole of desire comes from an excess which cannot contain itself within its proper limits. For everything which transgresses God's appointed laws lusts after monstrous things which are not normal.

The normal desire for sexual intercourse united the sexes to one another, but by taking this away and turning it into something else, the devil divided the sexes from each other and forced what was one to become two, in opposition to the law of God. . . . The devil was bent on destroying the human race, not only by preventing them from copulating lawfully but by stirring them up to war and subversion against each other.

Paul goes straight to the source of sexual evil: ungodliness which comes from twisted teaching and lawlessness which is its reward. For since it seemed that the ungodly would not believe him if he spoke of hell and punishment but they might even scorn him, Paul simply states that the punishment came from the lust itself. But if they still

fail to perceive it, do not be surprised. HOMILIES ON ROMANS 4.[104]

UNBRIDLED LUST KNOWS NO LIMIT.
PELAGIUS: Once lust is unbridled, it knows no limit. In the order of nature, those who forgot God did not understand themselves either. PELAGIUS'S COMMENTARY ON ROMANS.[105]

1:28 Base Minds, Improper Conduct

THE FANTASY THAT GOD WOULD LOOK THE OTHER WAY. AMBROSIASTER: Because of the error of idolatry they were handed over to doing evil things with each other, as has already been said. And because they thought they could get away with it and that God would look the other way, and were therefore prone to neglect what they were doing, Paul adds here that they were more and more reduced to idiocy and became ever readier to tolerate all kinds of evils, to the point that they imagined that God would never avenge things which no one doubted were offensive to humanity as well. He now lists all the evils that were added to these, so that if they should be converted to normal reason, they might recognize that these evils befell them because of God's wrath. COMMENTARY ON PAUL'S EPISTLES.[106]

NOT FROM IGNORANCE BUT PRACTICE. CHRYSOSTOM: Here too Paul shows that the heathen were responsible for their own sins, and he deprives them of all excuse. For he says that their evil deeds did not come from ignorance but from willful practice. This is why he did not say "because they did not know God," but rather "they did not see fit to acknowledge God." In other words, their sin was one of a perverted determination of obstinacy more than of a sudden ravishment, and it was not in the flesh (as some heretics[107] say) but in the mind, to whose wicked

---

[102]CSEL 81.1:51, 53. [103]NTA 15:214. [104]NPNF 1 11:356-57. [105]PCR 67. [106]CSEL 81.1:53. [107]Manicheans, who viewed the flesh as such as evil.

lust the sins belonged and from which the fount of evils flowed. For if the mind becomes undiscerning, everything else is dragged off course and overturned. HOMILIES ON ROMANS 5.[108]

PERNICIOUS LUSTS. AUGUSTINE: Whoever follows the pernicious attractiveness of his lusts and tries to push aside those who would stop him heads straight into sin. AUGUSTINE ON ROMANS 6.[109]

GIVEN OVER TO A BASE MIND. PELAGIUS: Not only did they not know God, they did not want to know him. . . . So they were given over to a base mind. PELAGIUS'S COMMENTARY ON ROMANS.[110]

DENYING THE CREATOR. THEODORET OF CYR: If they had wanted to know him, they would have followed the divine laws. But because they denied their Creator, he stopped looking after them. INTERPRETATION OF THE LETTER TO THE ROMANS.[111]

GOD DOES NOT UNILATERALLY DESTROY ANYONE. GENNADIUS OF CONSTANTINOPLE: Paul does not say that God destroyed them because of their loathsome outrages. For God is not responsible for destroying anyone. . . . Paul says rather that God went away from them and left them to their own devices, so that their false understanding of God might appear to be the cause of their evil life. PAULINE COMMENTARY FROM THE GREEK CHURCH.[112]

1:29 Filled with Wickedness

WICKEDNESS THE SOURCE OF OTHER SINS. AMBROSIASTER: Paul put wickedness at the head of the list, because he thought that evil and covetousness depended on it. He then added malice, from which flows envy, murder, strife and deceit. After this he put malignity, which generates gossip and slander. COMMENTARY ON PAUL'S EPISTLES.[113]

THE INTENSITY OF WICKEDNESS. CHRYSOSTOM: Notice how everything here is intensive—"filled" and "with all." Having named maliciousness in general, Paul goes on to discuss the particulars, and these too he mentions in excess—"full of envy," etc. HOMILIES ON ROMANS 5.[114]

VICES LINKED TO EACH OTHER. PELAGIUS: Paul shows that wickedness and evil are the chief causes of the vices. Envy is rightly linked to murder, since it is the chief cause of this crime. Strife exists when something is defended, not by reason but by a proud spirit. Deceit is secret malice covered in flattering speech. Malignity is a wish or a work of malice. PELAGIUS'S COMMENTARY ON ROMANS.[115]

1:30 Things Displeasing to God

HATERS OF GOD. AMBROSIASTER: Because these things were displeasing to God, Paul says that they were hateful to God, and because they are also displeasing to men, he adds that they are insolent, haughty, boastful and inventors of evil, not just followers of it. For, becoming true imitators of their father the devil, they invented the evil of idolatry, through which all the vices in the world originated, as well as the greatest perdition. For the devil, whom Scripture says was a sinner from the beginning,[116] although he gloried in his tyrannical presumption, never dared go so far as to call himself God. For among other things he says to God: "All these things have been given to me,"[117] not: "All these things are from me." In the book of Job the devil asks for power to be given to him,[118] and in the prophet Zechariah he thinks that he can contradict the priest but does not claim power for himself.[119] For this reason the idolaters are even worse, because they proclaim the divinity not only of the elements but also of imaginary things.

---

[108]NPNF 1 11:359. [109]AOR 3. [110]PCR 67. [111]ER, Migne PG 82 col. 65. [112]NTA 15:359. [113]CSEL 81.1:55. [114]NPNF 1 11:360. [115]PCR 67-68. [116]1 Jn 3:8. [117]Lk 4:6. [118]Job 2:6. [119]Zech 3:1.

They were seized with such insolence that they did not even acknowledge their parents, who had given them birth! They rejoiced in their children but despised those by whom they had come into being. COMMENTARY ON PAUL'S EPISTLES.[120]

INVENTORS OF EVIL. CHRYSOSTOM: Classing things which to many seem to be matters of indifference among his accusations of sin, Paul further strengthens his case, going up to the stronghold of their wickedness and styling them "boastful." For although sinning is high-minded, boasting is even worse.... Furthermore, they were "inventors of evil." Not content with the evil which already exists in the world, they went and invented more! Again, this is the behavior of those who are determined and in earnest, not of those who are distracted and forced off course. HOMILIES ON ROMANS 5.[121]

SELF-DESTRUCTION. PELAGIUS: The Scriptures link slander to idolatry by stipulating the same penalty for it—destruction.[122] The haughty are those who want to be more than they are. The devil was like this, and so destroyed himself. For one who seeks to lord it over others will end up beneath them. PELAGIUS'S COMMENTARY ON ROMANS.[123]

1:31 No Feelings for God or Man

HEARTLESS, RUTHLESS. AMBROSIASTER: They were foolish and faithless and had no feelings either for God or for men. That is why they were heartless and ruthless. For someone who is cruel to his own family will be that much more cruel to others! COMMENTARY ON PAUL'S EPISTLES.[124]

TRAITORS TO NATURE. CHRYSOSTOM: Christ himself mentions this as the cause of wickedness, saying: "Because wickedness is multiplied, most men's love will grow cold."[125] Paul says here that they were ... traitors to nature. For most of us have a kind of family feeling to one another, which even the beasts share among themselves.... But

these men became even more ferocious than the beasts. The disorder which resulted in the world by evil teachings he proves to us by these witnesses and clearly shows that in each case the malady came from the negligence of those who were disordered. HOMILIES ON ROMANS 5.[126]

ABANDONING GOD, ABANDONED BY GOD. PELAGIUS: Paul mentions all these sins, set out one by one, with respect to those who have been abandoned by God because they have abandoned him. Let us therefore take care, lest we also be abandoned for embracing one of these evils. PELAGIUS'S COMMENTARY ON ROMANS.[127]

1:32 Doing and Approving Evil

THOSE WHO TAKE PLEASURE IN THOSE WHO DO EVIL. CLEMENT OF ROME: Those who do such things are hateful to God—and not only those who do them but those who take pleasure in those who do them. THE FIRST EPISTLE OF CLEMENT 35.[128]

CONSENT IMPLIES COMPLICITY. AMBROSIASTER: Those who knew by the law of nature that God requires righteousness realized that these things were displeasing to God, but they did not want to think about it, because those who do such things are worthy of death, and not only those who do them but those who allow them to be done, for consent is participation. Their wickedness is double, for those who do such things but prevent others are not so bad, because they realize that these things are evil and do not justify them. But the worst people are those who do these things and approve of others doing them as well, not fearing God but desiring the increase of evil. They do not seek to justify them either, but in their case it is because they want to persuade people that there is nothing wrong in doing them. COMMENTARY ON PAUL'S EPISTLES.[129]

---

[120]CSEL 81.1:55, 57. [121]NPNF 1 11:360. [122]Ex 22:20; Prov 20:13. [123]PCR 68. [124]CSEL 81.1:57. [125]Mt 24:12. [126]NPNF 1 11:360. [127]PCR 68. [128]NF 1:14. [129]CSEL 81.1:61.

Leading Others into Wrong. Apollinaris of Laodicea: Here again we see the innocence of God and the guilt of man and the justice of the judgment which is brought. For men do these things, not being unaware that they are worthy of punishment by God the judge. For it is clear that they are not unaware of this when they judge others and hand those who do such things over to death. For when evil men have knowledge of the good and make use of it as if they are not given over to pleasures, they bear witness that God's creation is good. . . . But those who lead men into wrong, as well as those who follow what is wrong, are both evil. Pauline Commentary from the Greek Church.[130]

The Neglect of Admonition. Basil: Perverted human tradition is the source of great evil for us, in that some sins are denounced while others are viewed with indifference. Crimes like homicide and adultery are the object of a violent but feigned indignation while others, like anger, reviling, drunkenness or avarice, are not considered deserving of even a simple admonition. On the Judgment of God.[131]

Deserving to Die. Severian: When Paul talks about the "judgment of God" he means the just recompense which God gives to everyone according to their deserts. For men know by their natural reasoning that transgressors will be punished by God, but instead of ceasing from their wicked ways they are actually pleased with those who do such things! . . . Therefore God will judge those who do such things as absolutely and without question worthy of death. Pauline Commentary from the Greek Church.[132]

Approving Those Who Practice Evil.

Chrysostom: Having assumed two objections, Paul here removes them. For what reason does anyone have to say that he does not know what he should do? Even if he does not know, he is still to blame, because he has turned away from the God who teaches him. But Paul has shown by many arguments that he does know and transgresses willingly. But is such a person drawn by passion? Why in that case does he cooperate with it and even praise it? For they not only do such things themselves, says Paul, but they "approve those who practice them." Paul thus puts the more serious sin first, in order to get it out of the way (for the one who praises the sin of others is far worse than the one who sins himself), and then he gets ready to deal more firmly with the sinner [in chapter 2]. Homilies on Romans 5.[133]

Consenting to Evil Deeds. Augustine: Whatever they had done they did without compulsion. For when they give their consent to evil deeds, they approve even of things which they did not do themselves. Augustine on Romans 7-8.[134]

Idolatry as the Source of All Wickedness. Pelagius: Even people who did not agree with these doings . . . nevertheless seem to have accepted them, because they agreed to idolatry, which is the source and cause of them all. Pelagius's Commentary on Romans.[135]

Failure of Reproof. Caesarius of Arles: Those who do not admonish adulterers make us suspect that the reason for this failure of reproof is that they commit similar sins themselves. Sermon 42.2.[136]

---

[130]NTA 15:59-60. [131]FC 9:49. [132]NTA 15:215. [133]NPNF 1 11:360. [134]AOR 5. [135]PCR 69. [136]FC 31:210.

2:1-4 GOD'S JUDGMENT IS INEVITABLE

¹Therefore you have no excuse, O man, whoever you are, when you judge another; for in passing judgment upon him you condemn yourself, because you, the judge, are doing the very same things. ²We know that the judgment of God rightly falls upon those who do such things. ³Do you suppose, O man, that when you judge those who do such things and yet do them yourself, you will escape the judgment of God? ⁴Or do you presume upon the riches of his kindness and forbearance and patience? Do you not know that God's kindness is meant to lead you to repentance?

OVERVIEW: Jesus taught his followers not to pass judgment, so that they would not be judged themselves. The apostle Paul repeats this teaching, but the Fathers had various interpretations of it. The question of evil and punishment inevitably raises the problem of God's justice. The Fathers regarded the sins of those who are quick to judge as a sign of pride more than as a form of hypocrisy. Nobody should imagine that he or she is above the judgment of God. Rigorous self-examination should precede our moral evaluation of others. Nobody should assume that because God is slow to punish, he will not do so in the end. If he delays, it is only because he wants to give people time to repent.

2:1 No Excuse for Judging Others

NO EXCUSE. AMBROSIASTER: Paul shows that the man who does evil and consents to others who do it is deserving of death, lest perhaps the one who does it and pretends not to approve of others who do it . . . might think he can be excused, because he can conceal his sin for a time. . . . It is not right to give in to someone who pretends to be better when in fact he is worse. Such a person appears to escape notice and to be worthy of honor, but in fact he will be punished. COMMENTARY ON PAUL'S EPISTLES.[1]

YOU CONDEMN YOURSELVES. CHRYSOSTOM: Paul says this with the rulers of the city in mind, because at that time they ruled the entire world. He was telling them . . . that when they pass sentence on someone they are passing sentence on themselves as well. HOMILIES ON ROMANS 5.[2]

JUDGED BY GOD. [PSEUDO-]CONSTANTIUS: Here it is shown that each person knows that he will be judged by God in what he judges and condemns another man for doing. THE HOLY LETTER OF ST. PAUL TO THE ROMANS.[3]

WHOEVER YOU ARE. AUGUSTINE: Paul is speaking here of sins already committed. And when he says "O man, whoever you are," he includes not only the Gentile but also the Jew who wanted to judge the Gentiles according to the law. AUGUSTINE ON ROMANS 7-8.[4]

PUNISHMENT FOR WICKEDNESS. PELAGIUS: This concerns those who are in a position to pass judgment. Judges and princes are being put on trial. By a natural process everyone pronounces a sentence which fits the crime and knows that righteousness deserves reward while wickedness should be punished. PELAGIUS'S COMMENTARY ON ROMANS.[5]

2:2 The Judgment of God

ONLY GOD KNOWS THE HEART. ORIGEN: The

---

[1]CSEL 81.1:61. [2]NPNF 1 11:360. [3]ENPK 2:26. [4]AOR 5. [5]PCR 69.

judgment of God is to be expected . . . not only for those who do the things which are listed above but for all who have in any way done anything good or evil. What Paul wants to show here is that only God can judge rightly. For there are some crimes committed in which the deed is evil but the intention is not, e.g., when someone accidentally kills someone else. And there are other cases in which the deed may be good but the thought behind it is not, e.g., if someone shows pity not because God has commanded it but in order to win praise from men. And there are still other cases in which thought and deed are so interfused that one cannot distinguish which is good or evil. Given that only God knows the hearts of men and only he can discern the secrets of the mind, only he has the power to judge rightly.

God has judged rightly in the case of those whose iniquities have been forgiven by the grace of baptism, whose sins have been covered by repentance and whose sin has not been imputed to them because of the glory of martyrdom. Rightness of judgment presupposes that the evil person will receive bad things and the good person good ones. Although the gifts and generosity of God do not allow of any dispute, nevertheless we shall show just how right the divine judgment is. It is commonly accepted that a good man should not be punished and that an evil man should not be rewarded with good. Suppose a man has at some point done evil. It is certain that at the time he was doing it he was evil. But if he repents of his previous deeds, turns his mind to the good and does what is right, says what is right, thinks what is right, desires what is right—does not that person seem good to you, and worthy to receive good things? Likewise, if someone is turned from what is good to what is evil, he will be judged now not to be good (which he was but is no longer) but rather evil, which he is now. For the deeds of both a good and an evil man pass away, but they shape and construct the mind of the doer according to their respective quality and leave it either good or bad and accord-

ingly destined to receive either punishment or rewards. Therefore it will be unjust either for a good mind to be punished for evil deeds or for an evil mind to be rewarded for good deeds. Commentary on the Epistle to the Romans.[6]

God Judges the Wicked As They Deserve. Ambrosiaster: This means that we are not unaware that God will judge these people in truth, for we judge them ourselves. If what they do is displeasing to us, how much more will it be so to God, who is truly just and efficient in carrying out his work. . . . Paul is instilling fear, so that although the ungodly say that God does not care, in fact he will judge the wicked and most severely render to each one according to his deserts, not sparing any. Commentary on Paul's Epistles.[7]

Ungodly Despite Knowledge of Creation. Chrysostom: Paul shows that the ungodly had fallen even with a knowledge of God. Such knowledge they had got even from their creation. Homilies on Romans 5.[8]

Judgment Rightly Falls. Theodore of Mopsuestia: "Judgment" means the tribunal and judgment seat of God, and as if to make the condemnation of the wicked certain Paul added "rightly." Pauline Commentary from the Greek Church.[9]

Deflecting the Appearance That Evil Pleases God. Pelagius: If you, a sinner, pass judgment upon a sinner like yourself, how much more will God, who is just, condemn you as unjust? If he did not do so, it might appear that evil is pleasing to him while good is not. But God has no favorites, and he spared neither his friends (the patriarchs) nor his angels when they sinned! Human judgment on the other hand is imperfect in many ways. The integrity of judges is often compromised by love, hate, fear and greed, and occasionally mercy is allowed to overturn the rule

---

[6]CER 1:166-68. [7]CSEL 81.1:63. [8]NPNF 1 11:361. [9]NTA 15:115.

of justice. PELAGIUS'S COMMENTARY ON
ROMANS.[10]

2:3 No Escape from God's Judgment

JUDGMENT BEGINS IN THE HOUSE OF GOD. ORI-
GEN: For this reason it is right for each person to
examine his own conscience first and then debate
the deeds of the person whom he is judging. If
this were to happen, all desire for high ecclesiastical office would vanish from those appointed to
it, if those who want to preside over the people
were more concerned to judge themselves than to
judge others.

No one should imagine that he can escape the
judgment of God, as the prophet also says:
"Whither shall I go from thy Spirit? Or whither
shall I flee from thy presence?"[11] These things
apply most of all to those who preside over the
judgment of the people. Scripture also says elsewhere that "judgment will begin at the house of
God."[12] . . . Therefore judgment begins with the
children of God first of all, for God chastises
everyone whom he accepts into the number of his
children. Indeed, I think that even if it were possible, nobody should try to escape God's judgment,
for not to come to God's judgment is not to come
to improvement, to health or to a cure. COMMEN-
TARY ON THE EPISTLE TO THE ROMANS.[13]

THE ABILITY TO JUDGE. AMBROSIASTER: Paul
does not want them to hope that they can be pardoned, since that would be unjust, when they
have been given the ability to judge evil and
wrongdoing and to avoid it. If they cannot man-
age to avoid it in this life, they will not be able to
escape the judgment of God in the future. For
God, with whom there is neither flattery nor
respect of persons, will judge them on his own
authority.

If someone thinks he ought to be immune
from such punishment, let him say so. But if it is
right that he should not escape, let him trust that
God will judge and judge rightly, and that God,
the Creator of the world, will offer proper atten-

tion and care to his creation. If God had made the
world and then neglected it, he would be called a
bad Creator, because he would be demonstrating
by his neglect that what he had made was not
good. But since it cannot be denied that God
made good things—for it is unworthy and impossible for one who is good to make evil things—it
is necessary to say that he is concerned about
them. It would be a crime and a reproach to him
if he were to neglect the good things which he
had made. Life itself is governed by his servants
the natural elements, who act according to his
pleasure and plan, as the Lord himself says: "he
makes his sun rise on the evil and on the good
and sends rain on the just and on the unjust."[14]
Therefore, if he does all that, will he not take care
to look after what he has made, so as to reward
those who love him and condemn those who
reject him? COMMENTARY ON PAUL'S EPISTLES.[15]

**FALLING INTO THE SAME SINS ONE HAS
ACCUSED OTHERS OF COMMITTING.** CHRY-
SOSTOM: Paul argues that these people, because
they have condemned themselves by their condemnation of others, will not escape the judgment of God. For how can it be reasonable if they
condemn themselves and then expect God to
approve of them and praise them?

Sinning, by itself, is not as serious as falling
into the sins one has accused others of committing. See how Paul makes the whole thing more
serious! For if you punish a person who has committed smaller sins . . . how will God not turn the
tables on you and punish you who have committed greater transgressions? . . . And if you say that
you know you deserve punishment but think that
because God is patient with you that you will
escape it and therefore do not take it seriously,
this is all the more reason to fear and tremble! For
the fact that you have not yet suffered punishment does not mean that you will not suffer it but
that you will suffer more severely if you do not

---

[10]PCR 69. [11]Ps 139:7. [12]1 Pet 4:17. [13]CER 1:170-72. [14]Mt 5:45.
[15]CSEL 81.1:63-65.

repent. Homilies on Romans 5.[16]

Bad Judgment and Evil Men.
[Pseudo-]Constantius: This talks about the bad judgment of evil men who judge according to the law of this world. The Holy Letter of St. Paul to the Romans.[17]

God Persists in Patience. Augustine: Is the fact that some persist in their wickedness any proof that God does not persist in his patience, punishing very few sins in this world, lest we fail to believe in his divine providence and, saving many for the last judgment, to justify his future decree? Letter 153.[18]

2:4 God's Kindness Encourages Repentance

The Riches of God's Kindness. Ignatius: The last times are upon us.[19] Let us therefore be of a reverent spirit and fear the longsuffering of God, lest we despise the riches of his goodness and forbearance. Epistle to the Ephesians 11.[20]

Forbearance Distinguished from Patience. Origen: You can recognize the riches of God's kindness if you consider how many evils men do every day on earth. Almost everyone has fallen away and become worthless, traveling down the wide and broad way of perdition, ignoring the narrow road that leads to eternal life.[21] Yet God lets his sun shine daily on all of them and sends them rain, however much they may blaspheme him. . . . Therefore if anyone despises God's kindness and forbearance and patience, he does not know that he is being encouraged by these things to repent.

Forbearance differs from patience in that it applies more to those who sin because of their weakness and not deliberately, whereas patience is brought to bear in the case of those who sin deliberately, as if to glory in their wrongdoing. But as God has made everything with a certain measure, weight and number, so also his patience has certain limits. Those limits were reached by the people who perished in the flood,[22] as well as by the men of Sodom who were destroyed by fire from heaven.[23] Commentary on the Epistle to the Romans.[24]

Toward Repentance. Ambrosiaster: Paul says this so that no one should think that he has escaped, just because God's goodness has allowed him to go on sinning. Nor should anyone think that God's patience is to be despised, as if he did not care about human affairs, but rather understand that God conceals himself, because his judgment is not promised in this life. It is for the future, so that in the next life the man who did not believe that God is a judge will repent. For in order to reveal the terror of future judgment and that his patience should not be despised, God said: "I have been silent. But shall I be silent for ever?"[25] Thus the man who has been punished and has not repented will repent when he sees the future judgment of God, which he has spurned. Then he who thought that the longsuffering of God's goodness was something to laugh at will not hesitate to beg for mercy. Commentary on Paul's Epistles.[26]

Opportunity to Repent. Chrysostom: God shows us his kindness in order to lead us to repentance, not in order that we might sin even more. If we do not take advantage of this opportunity, the punishment we shall receive will be all the greater. Homilies on Romans 5.[27]

God Desires Repentance. [Pseudo-]Constantius: Here it is clearly shown how God has left the sinner with the desires of his heart. God could stop the sinner altogether from taking vengeance, but he prefers to give time to be converted to repentance. The Holy Letter of St. Paul to the Romans.[28]

---

[16]NPNF 1 11:361. [17]ENPK 2:27. [18]FC 20:283. [19]See 1 Jn 2:18. [20]ANF 1:54. [21]Mt 7:13-14. [22]Gen 7:21-22. [23]Gen 19:24. [24]CER 1:172-74. [25]Is 42:14. [26]CSEL 81.1:65. [27]NPNF 1 11:361. [28]ENPK 2:27.

GOD'S GOODNESS IN WAITING, JUSTICE IN PUNISHING. PELAGIUS: Do you imagine you can act with impunity just because God does not punish immediately. . . . Listen to the words of Scripture: "The Lord is not slow with his promises . . . but is forbearing toward you, not wishing that any should perish but that all should reach repentance."[29] The Lord is good in as much as he waits and just in as much as he punishes. . . . Peo-ple may go far astray because of God's patience, because he does not want to punish sinners immediately. And because he delays, people suppose either that he does not care at all about human affairs or that he overlooks sins. PELAGIUS'S COMMENTARY ON ROMANS.[30]

---

[29]2 Pet 3:9. [30]PCR 69-70.

2:5-11 GOD'S JUDGMENT IS RIGHTEOUS

[5]*But by your hard and impenitent heart you are storing up wrath for yourself on the day of wrath when God's righteous judgment will be revealed. [6]For he will render to every man according to his works: [7]to those who by patience in well-doing seek for glory and honor and immortality, he will give eternal life; [8]but for those who are factious and do not obey the truth, but obey wickedness, there will be wrath and fury. [9]There will be tribulation and distress for every human being who does evil, the Jew first and also the Greek, [10]but glory and honor and peace for every one who does good, the Jew first and also the Greek. [11]For God shows no partiality.*

OVERVIEW: Sinners have turned away from God, and therefore they have brought punishment on themselves. The wrath of God is not an active force directed against the innocent but a permissive retribution aimed solely at the guilty, who deserve it. Sinners are storing up God's judgment on themselves and will get everything they deserve. The righteous will have their reward, which will be far greater than any human comparison could suggest. The wicked will also have their reward, which is the logical and just outcome of their actions. Evil will be meted out proportionately. Believing Jews will get their reward ahead of the Gentiles because they were chosen first. But the Fathers disagreed about the identity of the Jews in verse 9: Was Paul referring to those who believed after the coming of Christ or only to those who hoped for his coming in the Old Testament? To some the latter seemed more logical, since the distinction between Jew and Greek had been abolished in Christ. God does not judge people because of who they are but because of what they do. For this reason Jews and Gentiles will be treated equally.

2:5 Impenitence Heaps Up Judgment

HEAPING UP JUDGMENT. IRENAEUS: Those who depart from God and despise his precepts, and by their deeds bring dishonor on him who made them, and by their opinions blaspheme him who nourishes them, heap up against themselves most righteous judgment. AGAINST HERESIES 4.33.15.[1]

---

[1]ANF 1:511.

Hardness of Heart. Origen: In the Scriptures a hard heart refers to a human mind which, like wax hardened by the cold of wickedness, cannot receive the imprint of God's image. The same thing is called a dull heart elsewhere.[2] Its opposite is a soft heart, which in the Scriptures is called a heart of flesh.[3] . . . When someone knows what is good and does not do it, he is said to be contemptuous of all good things because of the hardness of his heart. For hardness of heart occurs when the mind has no feeling for a refined and spiritual understanding. . . .

The day of wrath will be a day of vengeance and judgment, as is clear from many passages of Scripture. But note that it will also be a day of revelation, when all things are to be revealed.[4] . . . Some people want to know why this day has been fixed for the end of the world, so that everyone who has died from the beginning to the end of time is held over for judgment on the last day. It is certain that the real reasons for this are concealed in the secret mysteries of God, but we shall try to give some explanation for it insofar as it is possible to do so in writing. There are many who, when they leave this life, leave behind them seeds of good or evil that will sprout after their deaths and become occasions either for salvation or for damnation for those who are left behind. I would say, for instance, that this applies to all those philosophers who founded depraved sects which are far from God, or who set up magical sacrileges, or who practiced astrology, not to mention those among us who promoted heresies and false teachings by the books they wrote, or who have brought about divisions, scandals and dissensions in the church. On the other side there is the work of the apostolic writings and the emergence through them of the universal church, conversion to God and the transformation of the entire world. These things will go on to the end of time, and therefore the judgment of God will not be just until the final results are known. This is what the apostle means when he says: "The sins of some men are conspicuous, pointing to judgment, but the sins of others appear later."[5]

It may also be that the saints who are outside the body and who dwell with Christ may be doing something and working on our behalf after the example of the angels, who minister to us for our salvation. On the other hand, perhaps sinners who too have left the body are doing something in line with the disposition of their mind, and no less after the example of the fallen angels. . . . These things too are among the hidden things of God and have not been committed to writing. But they will be made known on the day of wrath and revelation.

Now let us consider what is meant by the just judgment of God, in which he will reward each one according to his works. First of all, we must reject the heretics who say that souls are good or evil by nature and maintain instead that God will reward each one according to his deeds and not according to his nature. Second, believers are to be instructed not to think that it is enough merely to believe [lacking fruit]; they ought to realize that the just judgment of God will reward each one according to his works. . . . Nor are Gentiles to be excluded from this, if they do good. Commentary on the Epistle to the Romans.[6]

Christ Will Judge. Marius Victorinus: Without doubt this is said of Christ, for he himself will judge. Against Arius 1a.17.[7]

Storing Wrath. Severian: When talking about the way they were "storing up" an accumulation of sins, Paul showed that there would also be a greater store of punishment, as a result of the patient endurance of the judge toward those who were suffering so incurably. Pauline Commentary from the Greek Church.[8]

Unaware of Future Wrath. Ambrosiaster: The one who hopes he can get away with his sins not only remains unconvertible and

---

[2]E.g., Mt 13:15. [3]Ezek 11:19. [4]See Mt 10:26. [5]1 Tim 5:24. [6]CER 1:174-86. [7]FC 69:112. [8]NTA 15:215.

intractable but in addition sins more seriously still, sure that there will be no future judgment. He has an impenitent heart, unaware that he is storing up wrath for himself on the day of wrath. COMMENTARY ON PAUL'S EPISTLES.[9]

FOR YOURSELF. CHRYSOSTOM: When a man is neither softened by goodness nor turned back by fear, what can be harder than he is? . . . The true originator of wrath is the one who has stored it up, not the one who judged, as Paul makes plain. For he says "you are storing up wrath for yourself," not "God is storing up wrath for you." HOMILIES ON ROMANS 5.[10]

HARDNESS RESULTS IN WRATH. GENNADIUS OF CONSTANTINOPLE: God's patience toward you gives you the opportunity for every kind of wickedness. Realize clearly therefore that you are storing up wrath for yourself because of your hardness. PAULINE COMMENTARY FROM THE GREEK CHURCH.[11]

CONVERSION TO CHRIST. [PSEUDO-]CONSTANTIUS: Before the revelation of God's righteous judgment comes to you, that day says to everyone: "Behold the man and behold his works." We must be converted to Christ all the more quickly therefore, lest we be deprived of our body by a hard heart and found naked, without the faith of Christ which was promised to us by the Law and the Prophets. THE HOLY LETTER OF ST. PAUL TO THE ROMANS.[12]

WRATH MEANS PUNISHMENT. AUGUSTINE: Whenever Paul talks about the wrath of God he understands it to mean punishment. AUGUSTINE ON ROMANS 9.[13]

REFUSING MERCY. PELAGIUS: Unaware that you are sick, you use the very cure in order to sustain even greater wounds. . . . Rejected kindness leads in the end to severer judgment, so that the man who refused to be touched by mercy is afflicted with punishment. PELA-

GIUS'S COMMENTARY ON ROMANS.[14]

CONCEALING WOUNDS. CAESARIUS OF ARLES: If a person sins once or even twice and then without excuses has recourse to the healing of penance, he will recover his former good condition without any delay. But if he begins to add sin upon sin and prefers to acquire an infection by concealing or defending the wounds of his soul rather than cure them by confession and the performance of penance, it is to be feared that these words of the apostle will be fulfilled in him. SERMON 65.1.[15]

2:6 Judgment According to Works

THE COMING OF THE JUDGE. IGNATIUS: Christ died and rose again, and ascended into heaven to him who sent him, and sat down at his right hand, and will come at the end of time with his Father's glory to judge the living and the dead.[16] EPISTLE TO THE MAGNESIANS 11.[17]

JUST JUDGMENT REVEALED. AMBROSIASTER: Such a person must be punished more severely, even to the point of being tortured in eternal fire,[18] because despite a long stay of execution, not only did he not want to change, but he increased his sinning, adding to his contempt for God. The day of wrath is for sinners, because it is the day on which they will be punished. Therefore the wrath is on those who receive punishment on the day when the just judgment of God is revealed. For it will be revealed and made known, even though it continues to be denied as long as it is in the future. COMMENTARY ON PAUL'S EPISTLES.[19]

APOLLINARIS OF LAODICEA: The Savior says the same thing: "He (the Son) will repay every man for what he has done."[20] Therefore, whatever is said to belong to God also appears to belong to

---

[9]CSEL 81.1:67. [10]NPNF 1 11:362. [11]NTA 15:361. [12]ENPK 2:27. [13]AOR 5. [14]PCR 70. [15]FC 31:312. [16]Cf. Rom 14:9. [17]ANF 1:64. [18]See Mt 3:12; 13:40-42; 25:41; Jude 1:7. [19]CSEL 81.1:67. [20]Mt 16:27.

the Son, which shows that they share a common nature. PAULINE COMMENTARY FROM THE GREEK CHURCH.[21]

PELAGIUS: You are storing up for yourself wrath upon wrath on the day of judgment, which will be revealed at a fixed and certain time. PELAGIUS'S COMMENTARY ON ROMANS.[22]

2:7 Eternal Rewards

GLORY AND HONOR. IRENAEUS: God has given that which is good, and those who do it will receive glory and honor because they have done good when they had it in their power not to do so. But those who do not do it will receive the just judgment of God, because they did not do good when they had it in their power to do so. AGAINST HERESIES 4.37.1.[23]

PATIENCE IN DOING GOOD. ORIGEN: In saying this, Paul indicates that those who desire to do good will have to struggle and will suffer for it. . . . Therefore patience is necessary. COMMENTARY ON THE EPISTLE TO THE ROMANS.[24]

AND IMMORTALITY. AMBROSIASTER: Now Paul predicts the just judgment of God, as he has declared it will be for the good; that is to say, for those who, recognizing that the patience of God is designed partly for concealment and partly for greater revenge on those who do not correct themselves, repent of their previous works and live rightly, armed with confidence in their faith in God that they will not have to wait long before receiving their promised reward of eternal life. For God will give them glory and honor. And to avoid invidious comparisons with this life, where there is another kind of glory and honor, Paul added "immortality," so that people would realize that the glory and honor which they will obtain will be of a different order altogether. . . . For in this life honor and glory are frequently lost, for the one who gives them, what he gives and the one who receives them are all mortal. But on the

day of God's judgment honor and glory will be given to the immortal so that they will be eternal. For this same substance will be glorified by a certain change of properties. Therefore, those who seek eternal life are not merely those who believe correctly but those who live correctly as well. COMMENTARY ON PAUL'S EPISTLES.[25]

ETERNAL REWARDS TRANSCEND ALL WE HAVE BELOW. CHRYSOSTOM: Here Paul stirs up those who had fallen away during the persecutions and shows that it is not right to trust in faith only. For God's tribunal will demand deeds as well. But note that when he talks about what is to come, he cannot say exactly what the blessings will be but talks in general terms of glory and honor. For because the rewards transcend everything which we have here below, there is no image he can use to illustrate them, but instead he takes things which give us a picture of brightness and sets them before us. . . . Glory, honor and life are things men strive for, but what God promises us are much better still because they are incorruptible and immortal. See how he has opened the door to the resurrection of our body by speaking of immortality. . . . For all of us will rise immortal but not all to glory. Some will rise to punishment and others to life. HOMILIES ON ROMANS 5.[26]

PATIENCE IN WELL-DOING. PELAGIUS: The reward for well-doing is awaited with patience because it is not given in this life.[27] The glory is that with which the saints will shine like the sun.[28] Nothing is greater than the honor of the children of God, on account of which they will judge even the angels.[29] PELAGIUS'S COMMENTARY ON ROMANS.[30]

THE REWARD IS ETERNAL. THEODORET OF CYR: Well-doing is for a time, but the reward is eternal. Moreover, eternity applies not only to life

[21]NTA 15:60. [22]PCR 71. [23]ANF 1:519. [24]CER 1:190. [25]CSEL 81.1:67-69. [26]NPNF 1 11:362. [27]See Mt 24:13; 1 Cor 3:14; 2 Cor 5:7. [28]Mt 13:43. [29]1 Cor 6:3. [30]PCR 71.

but to honor, glory and immortality as well. Paul wanted to show that there are many rewards for those who are good. INTERPRETATION OF THE LETTER TO THE ROMANS.[31]

2:8 Unrighteousness Brings Judgment

OBEDIENCE TO UNRIGHTEOUSNESS. THEOPHILUS OF ANTIOCH: To the unbelieving and despisers who obey not the truth but unrighteousness, when they have been filled with adulteries, and fornications and filthiness, and covetousness and unlawful idolatries, there shall be anger and wrath, tribulation and anguish, and at the last everlasting fire shall possess them.[32] You asked me to show you my God—this is my God, and I advise you to fear and trust him. TO AUTOLYCUS 1.14.[33]

WRATH, FURY AND TRIBULATION. AMBROSIASTER: Those who doubt that there will be a future judgment of God through Christ, and who for that reason despise his patience, do all they can to discredit it as being true and certain. For they believe in wickedness. It is wickedness to deny what God has foretold. Paul mentions three things which are fitting punishments for unbelief—wrath, fury and tribulation. The locus of wrath is not in the one who judges but in the one who is judged. God is said to get angry and to take vengeance, but in reality the nature of God transcends such passions. But this is said so that we should believe that God judges sin and that he will finally take revenge. So Paul adds "and fury." This means that God will seek vengeance, adding to his anger in response to the injury which has been done to him. COMMENTARY ON PAUL'S EPISTLES.[34]

WICKEDNESS IS VOLUNTARY. CHRYSOSTOM: Paul deprives those who live in wickedness of any excuse and shows that it is from factiousness and carelessness that they fall into unrighteousness. . . . Their fall is voluntary; their crime is not of necessity. HOMILIES ON ROMANS 5.[35]

THE MEANING OF "FACTIOUS." PELAGIUS: Those who are frequently overcome by hatred and fall into quarreling should be careful and afraid of persisting in so harmful a habit, in case the punishments mentioned are visited upon them. It has already been pointed out[36] that a man is factious when he tries to defend something against his conscience. Such people do not believe the truth of the gospel and approve of wickedness. They have abandoned the Creator and diligently serve the creature instead. "Wrath and fury" are the punishments that God's judgment brings. PELAGIUS'S COMMENTARY ON ROMANS.[37]

2:9 Tribulation for the Evil

TRIBULATION AND DISTRESS. ORIGEN: It is enough for anyone who simply accepts this to interpret it along the lines already mentioned, viz., that God will reward everyone according to his works. . . . But those who think that in the apostolic writings, through which Christ speaks, not one jot or tittle is superfluous will insist that it was not by accident that the apostle added "tribulation and distress" to what he had said earlier. From this a spiritually minded person will understand what the Holy Spirit is saying through Paul . . . that those who from a spirit of contention refuse to accept the truth but instead consort with wickedness will receive wrath and indignation, tribulation and distress, not as God's gift but as a consequence of their own evil deeds, because they have been storing these things up for themselves. COMMENTARY ON THE EPISTLE TO THE ROMANS.[38]

EVIL A MATTER OF UNBELIEF. AMBROSIASTER: "Tribulation" refers to the punishment which the condemned sinner will suffer. Evil is not just a matter of deeds but of unbelief as well. . . . Paul always puts the Jew first, whether he is to be

---

[31]IER, Migne PG 82 col. 69. [32]See Mt 13:42. [33]ANF 2:93. [34]CSEL 81.1:69. [35]NPNF 1 11:362. [36]Rom 1:26. [37]PCR 71. [38]CER 1:200-202.

praised or blamed, because of his privileged ancestry. If he believes he will be all the more honored because of Abraham, but if he doubts he will be treated all the worse, because he has rejected the gift promised to his forefathers. COMMENTARY ON PAUL'S EPISTLES.[39]

THE JEW FIRST. CHRYSOSTOM: Having shown the extreme seriousness of the disease . . . Paul goes on to give the Jew the greater burden in the tribulation. For the Jew has enjoyed a larger share of instruction and so also deserves to suffer a larger share of the punishment if he does wrong. The wiser or mightier we are, the more we will be punished if we sin.[40] HOMILIES ON ROMANS 5.[41]

THE MEANING OF SOUL. PELAGIUS: The apostle threatens the soul with punishment because of heretics[42] who say that only the flesh does wrong and that the soul cannot sin. Or perhaps "soul" refers to the whole man.[43] PELAGIUS'S COMMENTARY ON ROMANS.[44]

THOSE WHO LIVED BEFORE THE INCARNATION. THEODORET OF CYR: Here Paul uses the word *Greek* to refer not to Gentile believers but to those who lived before Christ's incarnation. INTERPRETATION OF THE LETTER TO THE ROMANS.[45]

2:10 Glory and Honor for Those Who Do Good

BELIEVER, JEW AND GENTILE. ORIGEN: Given that Paul puts the Jews first and the Greeks second, both for punishment and for reward, we have to ask who is meant by these terms. If he meant by Jews those who are still under the law and who have not come to Christ, and by Greeks those who are Christians from among the Gentiles, it is clear that he would be going completely against the meaning of the gospel.

It seems to me that the apostle has distinguished three types of people in this passage. First of all, he talks about those who are looking for glory and honor and immortality by patience in well-doing, whom God will reward with eternal life. Patience in well-doing is something which is certainly to be found in those who have endured suffering and struggle for the sake of godliness, and therefore, as we have already explained above, this must be said about Christians, among whom the martyrs are found.

But as I understand it, when Paul mentions Jews and Greeks he is talking about people who in neither case have become believers in Christ. It may happen that among those who are still under the law there will be someone who, because of pressure from his family and friends, has not believed in Christ but nevertheless does what is good, upholds righteousness, loves mercy, preserves chastity and continence, guards modesty and meekness, and does every good work. Although this person does not have eternal life— because despite the fact that he believes that there is only one true God he has not believed in his Son Jesus Christ, whom God has sent—nevertheless it may be that the glory of his works and the peace and honor which they bring may not perish.

But the Greek, that is the Gentile, if he does not have the law, is a law to himself, showing the work of the law in his heart, and motivated by natural reason, as we see that quite a few Gentiles are, either because they uphold righteousness or preserve chastity or maintain prudence, temperance and modesty. Although such a man is cut off from eternal life because he has not believed in Christ, and cannot enter the kingdom of heaven because he has not been born again of water and the Spirit, yet it appears from what the apostle says that he cannot entirely lose the glory, honor and peace of good works. For if it appears, according to what we discussed above, that the apostle condemned the Gentiles on the ground that although they knew God by their natural intelli-

---

[39]CSEL 81.1:69-71. [40]See Lk 12:48. [41]NPNF 1 11:362. [42]Probably Manichaeans. [43]See Gen 46:27; Acts 7:14. [44]PCR 71-72. [45]IER, Migne PG 82 col. 69.

gence they did not glorify him as God, how can we not think that he can and must praise them if they recognize God by their behavior and glorify him? Therefore I do not think it can be doubted that someone who deserves to be condemned because of his evil deeds will also be considered worthy of the reward of good works if he does something good. Consider what the apostle says: "For we must all appear before the judgment seat of Christ, so that each one may receive good or evil, according to what he has done in the body."[46] COMMENTARY ON THE EPISTLE TO THE ROMANS.[47]

RIGHTLY RECOGNIZING THE JEWS. APOLLINARIS OF LAODICEA: Paul is right to put the Jew first here and then the Greek. For those who are closer to the Lord and to his rebukes are honored above others, and they enjoy their rewards more than others. PAULINE COMMENTARY FROM THE GREEK CHURCH.[48]

THREE WOES FOR UNBELIEVERS, THREE BENEFITS FOR BELIEVERS. AMBROSIASTER: Just as Paul mentioned three woes for unbelievers, so now he mentions three benefits for believers: genuine honor as sons of God, unchanging glory and peace. Those who live rightly may be quiet in the future, undisturbed by any commotion. For everyone who keeps himself from wrongdoing has a judge who will be favorable to him. COMMENTARY ON PAUL'S EPISTLES.[49]

BEFORE CHRIST'S COMING. CHRYSOSTOM: Which Jews and Greeks is Paul talking about here? Those before Christ's coming! For he has not yet gotten to the time of grace in the development of his argument but is still dwelling on earlier times. . . . For if there was no difference before, . . . how can there be any now? This is why he puts so much emphasis on this point.

When referring here to Greeks, Paul does not mean those who worshiped idols but those who adored God, who obeyed the law of nature, who kept all the commandments without fail apart

from the Jewish observances, which contribute toward godliness. Melchizedek was one of these people, and so were Job, the Ninevites and Cornelius.

It is on works that punishment and reward depend, not on circumcision and uncircumcision. Paul has already said that the Gentile will not go unpunished, . . . and on this basis he said also that the Gentile would be rewarded. Now he shows that the law and circumcision are superfluous. For in this passage it is the Jews that he is mainly opposing. HOMILIES ON ROMANS 5.[50]

PEACE INDEED. PELAGIUS: Glory is opposed to wrath and honor to displeasure. What Paul called "immortality" above he calls "peace" here. The word *first* is emphatic and means "indeed," because God does not play favorites. Or it may mean first in time but not in honor. PELAGIUS'S COMMENTARY ON ROMANS.[52]

A RIGHTEOUS LIFE. THEODORET OF CYR: God did not promise eternal life to those who worshiped idols but to those who even apart from the law led a Mosaic life, embraced godliness and the worship of God, and were concerned about righteousness. INTERPRETATION OF THE LETTER TO THE ROMANS.[53]

2:11 No Partiality

IN EVERY NATION. ORIGEN: Anyone who doubts this needs only read what Peter said when he went to visit the Gentile Cornelius: "Truly I perceive that God shows no partiality, but in every nation anyone who fears him and does what is right is acceptable to him."[53] We might go even farther and quote what our Lord says in the Gospel: "he who believes in me is not condemned; he who does not believe is condemned already, because he has not believed in the name of the

---

[46]2 Cor 5:10. [47]CER 1:208-16. [48]NTA 15:60, 216. [49]CSEL 81.1:71. [50]NPNF 1 11:363. [51]PCR 72. [52]IER, Migne PG 82 col. 69. [53]Acts 10:34-35.

only begotten Son of God."[54] COMMENTARY ON THE EPISTLE TO THE ROMANS.[55]

NO RACIAL PRIVILEGE. AMBROSIASTER: Paul shows that neither Jews nor Greeks will be rejected by God if they believe in Christ, but that both are justified by faith. Likewise, he says that those who do not believe are equally guilty, since circumcision without faith is worthless but uncircumcision with faith is acceptable. For God does not stick to any privilege of race, so as to accept unbelief on account of ancestors and reject believers because of the unworthiness of their parents. Rather he rewards or condemns each one on his own merits. COMMENTARY ON PAUL'S EPISTLES.[56]

NO PARTIALITY TOWARD PERSONS. CHRYSOSTOM: When Paul says that Jews as well as Gentiles will be punished if they sin, he does not have to argue his case. But when he wants to prove that the Gentile is honored, then he needs a reason for saying so, because it seemed too much to say that someone who knew nothing of the Law

or the Prophets would be honored merely for doing good. . . . God shows no partiality toward persons; he judges actions. Paul says that Jews differed from Gentiles, not in their actions but in their persons only. But it is not for this reason that one is honored and the other disgraced. It is from their works that honor or disgrace will come. He does not say it quite like this though, so as not to rouse the Jews to anger. HOMILIES ON ROMANS 5.[57]

PELAGIUS: Therefore the Gentiles should not be smug about their false ignorance, nor the Jews about their privilege in the law and in the circumcision. PELAGIUS'S COMMENTARY ON ROMANS.[58]

BEING BORN AND DYING AS EQUALS. JEROME: We are all born equal, emperors and paupers, and we die as equals. Our humanity is of one quality. HOMILES ON THE PSALMS 14.[59]

---

[54]Jn 3:18. [55]CER 1:216. [56]CSEL 81.1:71. [57]NPNF 1 11:364. [58]PCR 72. [59]FC 48:106.

2:12-16 GOD'S JUDGMENT IS FAIR

[12]*All who have sinned without the law will also perish without the law, and all who have sinned under the law will be judged by the law.* [13]*For it is not the hearers of the law who are righteous before God, but the doers of the law who will be justified.* [14]*When Gentiles who have not the law do by nature what the law requires, they are a law to themselves, even though they do not have the law.* [15]*They show that what the law requires is written on their hearts, while their conscience also bears witness and their conflicting thoughts accuse or perhaps excuse them* [16]*on that day when, according to my gospel, God judges the secrets of men by Christ Jesus.*

OVERVIEW: Jews and Gentiles will be judged differently: Jews according to the law of Moses and Gentiles according to the law of nature. But the result will be the same: All who refuse to believe

in Christ will be condemned. "Practice what you preach" is the same law for everyone. The Jews were privileged to have the law of Moses, which made God's will clear to them. But Gentiles could discover something of that will for themselves by reading the law of nature and obeying it. The conscience acts as the judge of those who have not received the law of Moses. Those who will be accused here are the heretics and schismatics, who have broken with the faith of the church. Those who will be excused are those who keep the communion of the church intact. The Fathers did not hesitate to evoke the fear of the law when they described the last judgment. On that day there will be perfect confession of the truth and perfect justice, because the imperfections of human courts will be overcome in heaven.

2:12 Two Kinds of Law

WHICH LAW? ORIGEN: When the apostle says that those who are without the law will perish without the law, the question arises as to whether this should be understood only of the law of Moses or whether it should be extended to cover the law of Christ or even some other law under which mortal men may live. Will such a person be judged according to the law under which he has sinned, or will he perish as if he were outside the law because he is outside the law of Moses, even if he lives under some other law? For the apostle Paul himself, when he speaks to those who are outside the law, says that he too is virtually outside the law but adds: "I am not without law, but I am in the law of Christ,"[1] thus showing that although he may not be under the law of Moses he is nevertheless still under law. But whether human laws also belong to this category remains to be seen. COMMENTARY ON THE EPISTLE TO THE ROMANS.[2]

THE LAW OF NATURE. AMBROSIASTER: How can someone sin without the law, when Paul says that everyone is subject to the law of nature? By "law" he means the law of Moses, to which the Jews are bound although they do not believe. The Gentiles are also under the judgment of the natural law, but only insofar as they have chosen not to attach themselves to it. Thus the Gentile unbelievers are doubly in trouble, because they have neither

assented to the law given through Moses, nor have they received the grace of Christ. Therefore it is quite right that they should perish. So just as the person who sins without the law will perish, so also the one who has kept the law without knowing it will be justified. For the keeper of the law maintains his righteousness by nature. For if the law is given not for the righteous but for the unrighteous, whoever does not sin is a friend of the law. For him faith alone is the way by which he is made perfect. For others mere avoidance of evil will not gain them any advantage with God unless they also believe in God, so that they may be righteous on both counts. For the one righteousness is temporal; the other is eternal.

The Gentiles even if they keep the natural law will perish if they do not accept the faith of Christ. For it is a greater thing to confess faith in the one Lord, since God is one, than it is to avoid sinning (for the first of these has to do with God, the second with us). The Jews who live under the law will be accused and judged by the law, insofar as they have not accepted the Christ promised to them in the law. And if you wonder about this, the fate of the Jews will be worse than that of the Gentiles, for it is worse to lose what was promised than not to receive what was not hoped for in the first place. The unbelieving Gentile has not entered the kingdom of God, but the unbelieving Jew has been removed from it. COMMENTARY ON PAUL'S EPISTLES.[3]

THE NEED FOR GRACE. CHRYSOSTOM: Paul says that the Jews have a much greater need of grace than the Gentiles. Because the Jews said that they were justified by the law and therefore did not need grace, Paul shows that they need it even more than the Gentiles, given that they are liable to be punished more severely. HOMILIES ON ROMANS 5.[4]

THE LAW INCREASES PENALTIES. CHRYSOSTOM: Those who lived before the giving of the law

---

[1]1 Cor 9:21. [2]CER 1:220. [3]CSEL 81.1:73. [4]NPNF 1 11:364.

will not receive the same sentence as those after the law. Those sinning after the giving of the law will undergo heavier penalties. HOMILIES ON GENESIS 18.2.[5]

PERISHING WITHOUT THE LAW. THEODORE OF MOPSUESTIA: So as not to appear to be condemning them out of hatred Paul has repeated himself here, saying that those who have sinned without the law will perish without the law and that those under the law will be judged by the law. PAULINE COMMENTARY FROM THE GREEK CHURCH.[6]

MOSAIC LAW AND NATURAL LAW. [PSEUDO-] CONSTANTIUS: This whole section [from verse 6] is addressed to everyone who is bound by natural law, in which the Jews are equally included. But the Jew is given priority over the Greek because in addition to the natural law, he has the law of Moses as well. THE HOLY LETTER OF ST. PAUL TO THE ROMANS.[7]

BELIEVERS WHO SIN UNDER THE LAW. JEROME: The ungodly without the law shall perish forever. But the sinner under the law who comes to faith in God will not perish. The Dialogue AGAINST THE PELAGIANS 1.28.[8]

MEANING OF JUDGMENT. AUGUSTINE: It is generally agreed that *judgment* is the usual expression for eternal damnation. FAITH AND WORKS 23.43.[9]

DISTINGUISHING BETWEEN JEWS AND GEN- TILES. AUGUSTINE: The apostle did not mean to say that those who sin in ignorance will suffer worse punishment than those who know the law. It seems that it is worse to perish than to be judged. Rather the apostle here was merely distinguishing between Jews and Gentiles. GRACE AND FREE WILL 3.5.[10]

PERISHING WITH AND WITHOUT THE LAW. PELAGIUS: "Will perish" means the same thing as

"will be judged," for the man who perishes perishes by God's judgment, and the man who is judged a sinner perishes.[11] Paul puts Jews and Gentiles on the same level when he says that doers rather than hearers of the law are righteous and then adds that the Gentiles will be judged on the day of the Lord. For does anyone doubt that those under the law will perish just as those who lived without the law, unless they have believed in Christ? PELAGIUS'S COMMENTARY ON ROMANS.[12]

2:13 Hearers and Doers of the Law

BELIEF IN CHRIST. AMBROSIASTER: Paul says this because those who hear the law are not justified unless they believe in Christ, whom the law itself has promised. This is what it means to keep the law. For how does someone who does not believe the law keep it, when he does not receive the One to whom the law bears witness? But the one who appears not to be under the law because he is uncircumcised in his flesh, if he believes in Christ, may be said to have kept the law. And he who says he is in the law, i.e., the Jew, because what is said in the law does not penetrate to his mind, is not a doer of the law but a hearer only, for he does not believe in the Christ who is written about in the law, as Philip said to Nathanael: "We have found him of whom Moses in the law and also the prophets wrote."[13] COMMEN- TARY ON PAUL'S EPISTLES.[14]

HEARING AND DOING. CHRYSOSTOM: Well does Paul say "before God," because if they may appear before men to be dignified and to boast of great things, before God it is quite different: only the doers of the law are justified before him. . . . But how is it possible for someone who has not heard to be a doer of the law? Paul insists not only that it is possible but that those who have heard it might not be doers of it. HOMILIES ON ROMANS 5.[15]

---

[5]FC 82:4. [6]NTA 15:116. [7]ENPK 2:28. [8]FC 53:273. [9]FC 27:273. [10]FC 59:255. [11]Ps 37:20. [12]PCR 72. [13]Jn 1:45. [14]CSEL 81.1:75. [15]NPNF 1 11:364.

Practicing What Is Heard. Chrysostom: What benefit is it if, while listening each day, we neglect to practice what we hear? Hence I beseech you, let us be zealous in practicing those very deeds (by no other way, in fact, is it possible to be saved)[16] so that we may also wash away our sins and be granted the Lord's lovingkindness at his own hands, thanks to the grace and mercy of our Lord Jesus Christ. Homilies on Genesis 47.18.[17]

Imperfect Righteousness. Apollinaris of Laodicea: This is not the perfect righteousness according to Christ. About that, Paul says: "By works of the law shall no one be justified."[18] Pauline Commentary from the Greek Church.[19]

Justification and Belief. [Pseudo-]Constantius: God the Father will justify any believer in Christ who has truly obeyed the law. For the reward of his life is justification, which he would have been less able to obtain by the works of the law. Therefore, as I have said, justification is a reward for the believer in Christ. The Holy Letter of St. Paul to the Romans.[20]

Pelagius: Paul explains why the Jews are not better than the Gentiles. We too should be afraid, in case after hearing the law but not doing it we perish along with the Gentiles.[21] Pelagius's Commentary on Romans.[22]

Theodoret of Cyr: The law was given not to tickle our ears but to lead us to good works. Interpretation of the Letter to the Romans.[23]

2:14 Doing What the Law Requires

Letter and Spirit. Origen: The Gentiles need not keep the sabbaths[24] or the new moons or the sacrifices which are written down in the law.[25] For this law is not what is written on the hearts of the Gentiles. Rather it is that which can be discerned naturally, e.g., that they should not kill or commit adultery, that they should not steal nor bear false witness, that they should honor father and mother, etc.[26] It may well be that since God is the one Creator of all, these things are written on the hearts of the Gentiles. . . . For the natural law may agree with the law of Moses in the spirit, if not in the letter. For how would anyone understand by nature that a child should be circumcised on the eighth day?[27] . . . But we who feel that such things must be understood in a spiritual sense believe that we are not merely hearers of the law but doers of it also, being justified not according to the letter of the law, which in any case is so difficult that nobody could ever do it correctly, but according to the Spirit, which is the only way the law can ever be kept. This then is the work of the law which the apostle says even the Gentiles can fulfill. So when they do what the law says, it seems that they have the law written on their hearts by God, "not with ink but with the Spirit of the living God."[28] Commentary on the Epistle to the Romans.[29]

The Natural Law. Ambrose: The Gentiles show the work of the law written in their hearts. There is therefore something like the law of God which exists in the hearts of men. Paradise 8.39.[30]

Keeping the Natural Law. Ambrose: If men had been able to keep the natural law which God the Creator planted in the breast of each one, there would have been no need of that law which, written on stone tablets, enmeshed and entangled the weakness of human nature rather than freed and liberated it.[31] Letter 83.[32]

---

[16]Than by making faith active in love. There is no thought here of works righteousness, by which one might be thought to be saved by works alone, without faith. [17]FC 87:24. [18]Gal 2:16. [19]NTA 15:60. [20]ENPK 2:28. [21]1 Cor 11:32. [22]PCR 72. [23]IER, Migne PG 82 col. 69. [24]In the Pharisaic manner. [25]See Col 2:16-17. [26]See Ex 20; Deut 5. [27]Lev 12:3. [28]2 Cor 3:3. [29]CER 1:228-30. [30]FC 42:314. [31]See Ex 24:12; 2 Cor 3:3. [32]FC 26:464.

**NATURE ACKNOWLEDGING ITS OWN CRE-
ATOR.** AMBROSIASTER: Paul calls the Gentiles
Christians because he is the teacher of the Gentiles, as he says elsewhere: "For I speak to you
Gentiles."[33] These people are uncircumcised and
do not keep new moons or the sabbath or the law
of foods, yet under the guidance of nature they
believe in God and in Christ, i.e., in the Father
and the Son. To keep the law is to acknowledge
the God who gives the law. This is the first part
of wisdom: to stand in awe of God the Father,
from whom all things come, and the Lord Jesus
his Son, through whom all things come. Therefore nature itself acknowledges its Creator by its
own judgment, not by the law but by reason, for
the creature recognizes its Maker in itself. COM-
MENTARY ON PAUL'S EPISTLES.[34]

THE REASONING OF NATURE. CHRYSOSTOM:
When Paul is challenging the pride of Judaism,
he is careful not to appear to be condemning the
law as such. On the contrary, by extolling the
law and showing its greatness he makes good his
whole position. When he says "by nature" he
means "by the reasoning of nature." He shows
that the Gentiles are on better footing than the
Jews. They have not received the law and therefore do not have what seems to give the Jews an
advantage over them. For this reason Paul says
the Gentiles are to be admired, because they did
not need a law, but did all the things which were
written in the law, having its works but not its
letters engraved on their minds. HOMILIES ON
ROMANS 5.[35]

NOT WITHOUT ANY LAW. PELAGIUS: Paul is
referring either to those who were righteous
before the law or to those who even now are
doing some good. He shows that the Gentiles are
not without any kind of law in order to leave
them with no excuse and to take away the glory
which the Jews had by their possession of the law.
PELAGIUS'S COMMENTARY ON ROMANS.[36]

2:15 Conscience Bears Witness

WHAT IS WRITTEN ON THEIR HEARTS? ORI-
GEN: "Written on their hearts" should not be
taken too literally. What Paul calls the heart is
the rational faculty of the soul.

It is also necessary to discuss what Paul means
by the word *conscience*. Is it something distin-
guishable from the heart or from the soul? . . .
Conscience is the spirit which the apostle says is
with the soul, according to which we have been
instructed in the higher things. This spirit or
conscience is linked to the soul as a teacher and
guide to point out what things are best and to
reprove and condemn faults. The apostle was
speaking of it when he said: "What person knows
a man's thoughts except the spirit of the man
which is in him?"[37] COMMENTARY ON THE EPIS-
TLE TO THE ROMANS.[38]

**THE DEFENSE OF CONSCIENCE IN FINAL
JUDGMENT.** AMBROSIASTER: The meaning here
is that those who believe under the guidance of
nature do the work of the law not through the letter but through their conscience. For the work of
the law is faith, which, although it is fully
revealed in the Word of God, also shows itself to
be a law for the natural judgment. Faith goes
beyond what the law commands. Faith trusts in
Christ. These people believe because of the inner
witness of their conscience, because they know in
their conscience that what they believe is right. It
is not disjunctive for the creature to believe and
worship his Creator, nor is it absurd for the servant to recognize his Lord.

Unbelieving Gentiles will be judged first of all
by other believing Gentiles, just as the Lord said
that his disciples would judge the unbelieving
Jews: "They themselves will be your judges."[39] The
unbelief of the Jews will be judged by the faith of
the apostles who, although Jews themselves,
believed in Christ while the rest of their people
rejected him. Similarly the Gentiles will be
accused by their own thoughts if, touched by the

---

[33]Gentile Christians; Rom 11:13. [34]CSEL 81.1:75. [35]NPNF 1
11:364-65. [36]PCR 73. [37]1 Cor 2:11. [38]CER 1:230-32. [39]Mt 12:27.

faith and power of the Creator, they refuse to believe. But if because of some foolishness a man does not think to believe the words or deeds of the Lord, his conscience will defend him on the day of judgment, because he did not think that he was obliged to believe. He will be judged not as an intentional malefactor but as one who was merely ignorant.... It is Christians to whom Paul is referring when he speaks of accusing and excusing on the day of judgment. Those who differ from the true church, either because they think differently about Christ or because they disagree about the meaning of the Bible in the tradition of the church (e.g., Montanists, Novatianists, Donatists and other heretics) will be accused by their own thoughts on the day of judgment. Likewise one who recognizes that the Christian faith is true but refuses to follow it so as not to appear that he has been corrected and who is ashamed to depart from what he has so long held will be accused by his own thoughts on the day of judgment. COMMENTARY ON PAUL'S EPISTLES.[40]

THE CARE OF PROVIDENCE. CHRYSOSTOM: Conscience and reason take the place of the law. By saying this, Paul showed that God made persons independent, giving them the freedom to choose virtue and avoid vice. Do not be surprised that he proves this point, not once or twice but several times. He had to do this in order to counter those who said: "Why did Christ delay his coming so long? Where was this great scheme of providence before Christ came?" ... But even before the law was given the human race enjoyed the care of providence.

Why does Paul insert the words accuse or perhaps excuse? If they have a written law and do what it says, how can their thoughts still accuse them? Paul is not speaking here of the righteous only but of all mankind. For then our thoughts do pass judgment, some excusing us and others accusing. And at that tribunal, one needs no other accuser. HOMILIES ON ROMANS 5.[41]

OUR CONSCIENCE. AUGUSTINE: Compare this

with 1 John [3:20]: "Dearly beloved, if our own hearts condemn us, God is greater than our conscience." AUGUSTINE ON ROMANS 10.[42]

THE WITNESS OF CONSCIENCE. PELAGIUS: Nature produces a law in their hearts through the witness of their conscience. Or it may mean that the conscience testifies to the fact that it has its own law, because even if the sinner is afraid of no one the conscience is worried when he sins and rejoices when that sin is overcome. PELAGIUS'S COMMENTARY ON ROMANS.[43]

2:16 God Judges Our Secrets

JUDGMENT ACCORDING TO MY GOSPEL. TERTULLIAN: If God will judge the secrets of men ... surely the God who will judge is he to whom belong both the law and that nature which is the rule for those who do not know the law. But how will he conduct this judgment? "According to my gospel," says the apostle, "by Christ Jesus." The law and nature are vindicated by the gospel and Christ. AGAINST MARCION 5.13.[44]

ACCUSING AND DEFENDING. ORIGEN: Who can doubt that a trial is properly conducted when there are accusers and defenders and witnesses all present? ... See therefore how on that day, when God will judge the secrets of men, our thoughts will either accuse or defend our soul—not the thoughts which we will have then but the ones which we have now. COMMENTARY ON THE EPISTLE TO THE ROMANS.[45]

CLOTHED IN SINS OR JUST DEEDS. CYRIL OF JERUSALEM: The awe-inspiring countenance of the Judge will compel you to speak the truth. Even if you are silent, it will convict you. You will rise clothed either in your sins or in your just deeds. The Judge himself declared this. CATECHESIS 15.25.[46]

---

[40]CSEL 81.1:75-81. [41]NPNF 1 11:365. [42]AOR 5. [43]PCR 73. [44]ANF 3:457. [45]CER 1:232-34. [46]FC 64:70.

GOD LOOKS INTO THE HEART. APOLLINARIS OF LAODICEA: Men sit as judges of the external things only. It is God who judges things hidden. For Scripture says: "Man looks on the outward appearance, but God looks upon the heart."[47] When Christ judges, then God is the judge. PAULINE COMMENTARY FROM THE GREEK CHURCH.[48]

DUAL ACCUSERS. AMBROSIASTER: There are two thoughts inside a man which will accuse each other—the good and the evil. The good accuses the evil because it has denied the truth. The evil accuses the good because it has not done what it knows to be right. One who knows that the church is good and true but persists in heresy or schism will be judged guilty. Other thoughts will excuse, insofar as one has done what is expedient to do. He will say inwardly: "In my mind I have always thought it expedient to do what I have done. This was my faith." He will have a better case, even though he will still have to be corrected, because his conscience will not accuse him on the day of judgment. This is how the secret things of men will be judged by Jesus Christ our Lord on the day of judgment. COMMENTARY ON PAUL'S EPISTLES.[49]

THE SECRETS OF MEN. CHRYSOSTOM: Paul says the "secrets of men" and not the sins of men, in order to add to their fear. . . . For men sit in judgment on overt acts alone.

If a secret deed of any one of us were brought into the open right now, in the midst of the church, what would we do except pray for death and have the earth swallow us up, rather than have so many witnesses of wickedness? HOMILIES ON ROMANS 5.[50]

BELIEF IN CHRIST NECESSARY TO ESCAPE PUNISHMENT. THEODORE OF MOPSUESTIA: Paul continually preached that there will be a day of judgment and that it will be necessary to have believed in Christ in order to escape punishment. PAULINE COMMENTARY FROM THE GREEK CHURCH.[51]

CONSCIENCE AND THOUGHTS. PELAGIUS: Paul says that there is a mental debate when we decide after long deliberation what we should and should not do. On the day of the Lord we shall be judged by this. This proves that we were not ignorant of good and evil. Or perhaps it means that on the day of judgment our conscience and our thoughts will appear before our eyes like history lessons to be learned; they will either accuse us or excuse us.[52] PELAGIUS'S COMMENTARY ON ROMANS.[53]

---

[47]1 Sam 16:7. [48]NTA 15:60. [49]CSEL 81.1:81. [50]NPNF 1 11:365. [51]NTA 15:116. [52]Ps 49:21. [53]PCR 73.

2:17-29 THE JEWS AND THE LAW

[17]*But if you call yourself a Jew and rely upon the law and boast of your relation to God* [18]*and know his will and approve what is excellent, because you are instructed in the law,* [19]*and if you are sure that you are a guide to the blind, a light to those who are in darkness,* [20]*a corrector of the foolish, a teacher of children, having in the law the embodiment of knowledge and truth—*[21]*you then who teach others, will you not teach yourself? While you preach against stealing, do you steal?*

²²*You who say that one must not commit adultery, do you commit adultery? You who abhor idols, do you rob temples?* ²³*You who boast in the law, do you dishonor God by breaking the law?* ²⁴*For, as it is written, "The name of God is blasphemed among the Gentiles because of you."*

²⁵*Circumcision indeed is of value if you obey the law; but if you break the law, your circumcision becomes uncircumcision.* ²⁶*So, if a man who is uncircumcised keeps the precepts of the law, will not his uncircumcision be regarded as circumcision?* ²⁷*Then those who are physically uncircumcised but keep the law will condemn you who have the written code and circumcision but break the law.* ²⁸*For he is not a real Jew who is one outwardly, nor is true circumcision something external and physical.* ²⁹*He is a Jew who is one inwardly, and real circumcision is a matter of the heart, spiritual and not literal. His praise is not from men but from God.*

OVERVIEW: Jewish boasting based on human ancestry has no place in the kingdom of God. Such people are not really Jews, because they have not understood the spiritual meaning of the covenant that God made with Abraham. In reality those who teach the commandments to others break them daily themselves, thereby causing the name of God to be blasphemed among the Gentiles. The only circumcision that is of any value is the spiritual circumcision of the heart. Outward signs mean nothing by themselves. Therefore Gentiles do not need to be physically circumcised, because if they do what is right, it amounts to the same thing. They will even be in a position to condemn the Jews who are circumcised physically but do not do what they know to be right. Some have received both physical and spiritual circumcision, but the two need not go together. Physical circumcision without the spiritual will lead to greater condemnation, but spiritual circumcision even without the physical leads to eternal life.

2:17 False Boasting

CIRCUMCISION OF THE HEART. ORIGEN: The first thing to notice here is that Paul does not say that the person he is rhetorically addressing is a Jew; only that he calls himself one, which is not at all the same thing. For Paul goes on to teach that the true Jew is the one who is circumcised in secret, i.e., in the heart, who keeps the law in spirit and not according to the letter, whose praise is not from men but from God.[1] But the man who is circumcised visibly in the flesh, observing the law in order to be seen by men, is not a real Jew; such a man only appears to be one. COMMENTARY ON THE EPISTLE TO THE ROMANS.[2]

THREE MEANINGS OF THE NAME JEW. AMBROSIASTER: They are called Jews because it was their ancestral right to be called Israelites. Nevertheless, if we wish to understand everything which is relevant to the case, we must note that the name *Jew* had three different meanings. First, it meant the children of Abraham, who because of his faith was made the father of many nations.[3] Then it refers to Jacob, who because of his increasing faith was called Israel, for the dignity which began with the father was honored in the sons.[4] Third, they are called Jews not so much because of Judah as because of Christ, who was born of Judah according to the flesh, since in Judah it was made known that he would be in Christ. For it is said: "Judah will be your master,"[5] and: "Judah, your brothers praise you."[6] This praise was given not to Judah as such but to Christ, whom nowadays all those whom he deigns to call his brethren praise.... The Jews themselves do not understand the meaning of their name and claim that it refers to the human Judah. COMMENTARY ON PAUL'S EPISTLES.[7]

---

[1]See Mt 23:5. [2]CER 1:238. [3]Gen 17:4-5. [4]Gen 32:28. [5]Judg 20:18. [6]Gen 49:8. [7]CSEL 81.1:81-83.

MISUSING THE GIFT OF THE LAW. CHRYSOS-TOM: The Jew may boast that he is loved by God and honored above all other men. It seems to me that here Paul is gently mocking their unreasonableness . . . because they misused this gift . . . to set themselves up against the rest of mankind and to despise them. HOMILIES ON ROMANS 5.[8]

FALSE PRETENSES. THEODORE OF MOPSUESTIA: This is not to be read as a question, as some people think, but rather as a statement, as if to say: "Not as a true Jew, albeit in secret, but merely claiming to be one and making false pretenses." PAULINE COMMENTARY FROM THE GREEK CHURCH.[9]

BOASTING OF ONE'S RELATION WITH GOD. AUGUSTINE: If a Jew boasts in God in the manner called for by grace, which is given not according to the merits of works but freely, his praise would be of God and not of men. . . . But they thought that they had fulfilled this law of God by their own righteousness, even though they were transgressors of it. And so for them it worked wrath as sin multiplied, committed by those who knew what sin was. Those who did what the law commanded without the help of the Spirit of grace did it through fear of punishment and not out of love for righteousness. THE SPIRIT AND THE LETTER 11.7.[10]

A JEW IN DEED. PELAGIUS: At this point Paul turns to the Jews and says that a man should be a Jew in deed and not merely in name. PELAGIUS'S COMMENTARY ON ROMANS.[11]

2:18 Instructed in the Law

THE LAW AS GUIDE. AMBROSIASTER: It is hardly surprising that a Jew should believe, since he has been taught to do so by the law. It is indeed dangerous for him not to believe if he has the law as his guide. COMMENTARY ON PAUL'S EPISTLES.[12]

AN ADVANTAGE OR A DISADVANTAGE. CHRY-sostom: What seems to be an advantage—being given the law—may turn out to be a disadvantage if one does not keep the law. Paul states this with great accuracy. He does not say "do" but "know," nor does he say "follow" but only "approve." HOMILIES ON ROMANS 6.[13]

APPROVING WHAT IS EXCELLENT. PELAGIUS: The Jew boasts that he alone understands God and knows his will. He approves what is excellent, because what is beneficial by nature is made much more so by the law. PELAGIUS'S COMMENTARY ON ROMANS.[14]

2:19 Deprived of the True Light

BLIND GUIDES. CHRYSOSTOM: Paul does not say that the Jews are really guides to the blind, only that they think they are. . . . Remember what they said in the Gospels to the blind man who had received his sight: "You were born in utter sin, and would you teach us?"[15] HOMILIES ON ROMANS 6.[16]

DEPRIVED OF KNOWLEDGE. PELAGIUS: The blind are those who have been deprived of the light of knowledge. PELAGIUS'S COMMENTARY ON ROMANS.[17]

2:20 Knowledge and Truth

THE EMBODIMENT OF TRUTH. THEODORE OF MOPSUESTIA: By "embodiment" is meant not the form but the substance and the knowledge and the truth, like the one "who was in the form of God."[18] PAULINE COMMENTARY FROM THE GREEK CHURCH.[19]

TEACHING THE FORM OF TRUTH. AMBROSIASTER: These things are true, because this is the task of the law: to teach the ignorant, to subject

---

[8]NPNF 1 11:368. [9]NTA 15:116. [10]LCC 8:203. [11]PCR 73. [12]CSEL 81.1:33. [13]NPNF 1 11:368. [14]PCR 74. [15]Jn 9:34. [16]NPNF 1 11:368. [17]PCR 74. [18]Phil 2:6. [19]NTA 15:116.

the wicked to God, to provoke those who by the worship of idols are ungodly to trust in a better hope by the promise which is given through the law. The teacher of the law is right to glory in these things, because he is teaching the form of truth. But if the teacher does not accept the Expected One whom the law has promised, he glories in vain in the law, to which he is doing harm as long as he rejects the Christ who is promised in the law. In that case he is no more learned than the fools, nor is he a teacher of children, nor is he a light to those who are in the darkness, but rather he is leading all of these into perdition. Commentary on Paul's Epistles.[20]

They Condemn Themselves. Chrysostom: Paul says that they had knowledge and truth not in their conscience, their actions or their well-doing but in the law. After saying this he repeats what he has already said to the Gentiles: In judging others they condemn themselves. Homilies on Romans 6.[21]

Keep the Law in View. Pelagius: One who continually keeps the law in view does not stumble. Pelagius's Commentary on Romans.[22]

2:21 Making a Mockery of One's Faith

On Doing What One Preaches Against. Ambrosiaster: This means: "You who complain about the Gentiles because they are without the law and God are accusing yourself, because you do not believe in the Christ promised by the law but find this belief in those you are complaining about." The Jew does what he preaches should not be done. For by denying the Christ promised to us in the law, he removes faith by false interpretation and thus does what he preaches against. Commentary on Paul's Epistles.[23]

An Indirect Approach. Chrysostom: Sometimes Paul speaks more harshly and sometimes more softly. Here he does not attack them directly . . . but carries on his discourse by way of

questions, getting them to give the answers themselves. Homilies on Romans 6.[24]

Holding the Law in Contempt. Pelagius: Paul says to the Jew: If you rely on the law, why do you not obey it? If you glory in God, why do you dishonor him? If you know his will, why do you not do it? If you approve what is excellent, why do you go after what is harmful? Why do you not look for the right way, if you are a guide for the blind? Surely if you saw it you would walk in it! If you are a light for others, why do you not cast off the works of darkness? As an instructor of the foolish, why have you abandoned the fear of the Lord, which is the beginning of wisdom?[25] As a teacher of children, why are you a child in understanding? If you have the standard of knowledge and truth in the law, why do you not follow it yourself, nor by your evil example allow others to follow it? Why does your life not match your teaching, and why does your behavior make a mockery of your faith? Because you have not kept the law it will happen that not only will the law do you no good, it will condemn you for the greater crime of holding it in contempt. Pelagius's Commentary on Romans.[26]

Pride in the Law Is Pointless. Theodoret of Cyr: Paul shows here and in the next two verses that the Jews had learned little from the law even if they gloried in the letter of it. When they tried to teach others, their deeds contradicted their words, and their pride in the law was pointless. Interpretation of the Letter to the Romans.[27]

2:22 Adulterating God's Word

Robbing the Word of Its Meaning. Origen: These words[28] could equally well be applied

---

[20]CSEL 81.1:83-85. [21]NPNF 1 11:368. [22]PCR 74. [23]CSEL 81.1:85. [24]NPNF 1 11:368. [25]See Ps 111:10. [26]PCR 74. [27]IER, Migne PG 82 col. 73. [28]The Fathers took the term *adultery* broadly and applied it to adulterers of the Word—heretics.

to the heretics who call themselves Christians. . . . Since they rob the Word of God of its true meaning and seduce the minds of their hearers by their perverse interpretation, joining an adulterated kind of faith to the bride of Christ which is the church, this [verse] fits them exactly. Commentary on the Epistle to the Romans.[29]

Adulterers of the Word. Ambrosiaster: The Jew adulterates the law by removing the truth of Christ from it and putting lies in his place. In another of his epistles Paul writes: "They are adulterers of God's Word."[30] A man is sacrilegious when he denies Christ, whom the law and the prophets call God.[31] Did the Jews ever say, "Thou art God and we did not know it"[32] of God the Father, when the entire law proclaims the authority of God the Father, by whom all things are made? But when the Son of God appeared, what he was was hidden and not revealed until after the resurrection. It was then that it was said of him: "Thou art God and we did not know it." Commentary on Paul's Epistles.[33]

The Meaning of Adultery. Pelagius: There is not just one kind of adultery, for you commit adultery if you give anyone other than God what the soul owes exclusively to him.[34] Pelagius's Commentary on Romans.[35]

Robbing Temples. Chrysostom: It was strictly forbidden for Jews to touch any of the treasures deposited in heathen temples, because they would be defiled. But Paul claims here that the tyranny of greed has persuaded them to disregard the law at this point. Homilies on Romans 6.[36]

2:23 Dishonoring God

Preferring Pleasure. Basil: If we prefer a life of pleasure to the life of obedience to the commandments, how can we expect a life of blessedness, fellowship with the saints and the delights of the angelic company in the presence of Christ? Such expectations are truly the fantasies of a

foolish mind. The Long Rules, Preface.[37]

Rejecting Testimony to the Son. Ambrosiaster: The breaker of the law is the one who overlooks the meaning of the law, which speaks of the incarnation and divinity of Christ, and dishonors God by not accepting the testimony which he gave concerning his Son. For the Father said: "This is my beloved Son."[38] Commentary on Paul's Epistles.[39]

Three Dimensions of Dishonor. Chrysostom: Here Paul makes two, or rather three, accusations. First, that they dishonor. Second, that they dishonor that by which they were honored. Third, that they dishonor the One who honored them, which was the depth of ingratitude. And then, so as not to appear to be accusing them off his own bat, he brings in the prophet Isaiah as their accuser.[40] Homilies on Romans 6.[41]

The Offense of Sacrilege. Pelagius: Sacrilege is something committed only against God, because it is a violation of the sacred. Pelagius's Commentary on Romans.[42]

2:24 Blaspheming God

The Name Blasphemed. Tertullian: There is a blasphemy which we must avoid completely, viz., that any of us should give a pagan good cause for blasphemy by deceit or injury or insult or some other matter justifying complaint. It is that blasphemy in which the Name is deservedly blamed, so that the Lord is deservedly angry. But the words "Because of you my Name is blasphemed" seem to cover every blasphemy. So then, are we all lost, since the whole Roman circus assails the Name, for no fault of ours, with its wicked outcries? Shall we stop being Christians

---

[29]CER 1:246. [30]2 Cor 2:17. [31]See Is 45:14-15. [32]Is 45:15. [33]CSEL 81.1:85-87. [34]See Ex 34:14. [35]PCR 75. [36]NPNF 1 11:369. [37]FC 9:229. [38]Mt 3:17. [39]CSEL 81.1:87. [40]See Is 52:5. [41]NPNF 1 11:369. [42]PCR 75.

in order for there to be less blasphemy? No! If the blasphemy continues, we will observe our discipline, not abandoning it, as long as we are being approved and not condemned. The blasphemy which affirms our Christian faith by detesting us because of it is in close proximity to martyrdom. To curse us for keeping our discipline is to bless our Name. On Idolatry 14.[43]

The Name Adorned. Cyprian: Even if the Jews have been alienated from God, because on their account the name of God is blasphemed among the Gentiles, nonetheless they are dear to God. Through their discipline the name of the Lord is adorned with praiseworthy testimony. Letter 13.3.[44]

The Ironic Twist. Origen: What Paul says [in verses 17-23] about the Jews is meant to be taken ironically, since anyone who genuinely relies on the law, glories in God and proves the things which are most useful would be doing the things which are listed here. But [in verse 24] he speaks directly to them, borrowing the words of the prophet Isaiah. Commentary on the Epistle to the Romans.[45]

Because of You. Ambrosiaster: Isaiah the prophet said this because God's name was being blasphemed among the Gentiles when the Jews, by their misdeeds, did not observe the things which were handed down to them but instead gave glory to idols. . . . So also at the time of the apostles, God's name was being blasphemed in Christ, because the Jews, by denying that Christ was God, were blaspheming the Father also, as the Lord said: "Whoever receives me does not receive me, but him who sent me."[46] Therefore God was blasphemed among the Gentiles because when they believed in Christ the Jews tried to persuade them not to call Christ "God." Commentary on Paul's Epistles.[47]

Teaching Others to Blaspheme. Chrysostom: Here Paul makes another double accusa-

tion. The Jews not only commit insolence themselves; they even persuade others to do the same. What then is the use of their teaching, if they cannot teach themselves? . . . But it is much worse than this, for not only do the Jews not teach the law, they actually teach others to blaspheme God, which is the very opposite of the law. Homilies on Romans 6.[48]

Blessing or Blaspheming. [Pseudo-]Constantius: Just as it says that God is "blessed by your good works,"[49] so also he is blasphemed by the Gentiles on account of those who do not live rightly. The Holy Letter of St. Paul to the Romans.[50]

Relying on the Prophets. Pelagius: Paul realized that what he was saying was also to be found in the prophets, which is why he quotes them here.[51] Pelagius's Commentary on Romans.[52]

2:25 Circumcision and the Law

Circumcision of the Heart. Origen: We must examine carefully what this circumcision is which is of value, and what law this is which is profitable if it is kept, so that when we have understood his meaning we may be circumcised as well. . . . Paul teaches in the verses which follow that it is not the circumcision of the flesh which he is talking about but the circumcision of the heart, which is made by the Spirit and not according to the letter, and which receives its praise not from men but from God.

Someone might raise the objection that, if it is true that the circumcision which the apostle regards as being profitable is nothing other than the cleansing of the soul and the rejection of all vices, why does he add here that it is profitable only if you keep the law, since circumcision does

---

[43]ANF 3:69. [44]FC 51:37. [45]CER 1:248. [46]Lk 9:48. [47]CSEL 81.1:87. [48]NPNF 1 11:369. [49]See Mt 5:16. [50]ENPK 2:75. [51]See Ezek 36:20. [52]PCR 75.

not exist apart from the observance of the law? It must be understood that circumcision is not just a matter of rejecting wickedness and ceasing from evil; it is also a matter of doing good and carrying out what is perfect. That is what keeping the law means. For there is no perfection in someone who merely desists from evil; rather it is found in him who does what is good.

Circumcision becomes uncircumcision if, after abstaining from evil, you fail to do what is good. For then you are considered to be an unbeliever. Obviously it is not possible for one who has been physically circumcised to get his foreskin back again, and so this text must be understood figuratively. For if the containment of evil which circumcision signifies is not matched by the works of faith, it is regarded as a form of wickedness. Even in the church, if someone is "circumcised" by the grace of baptism and then becomes a transgressor of the law of Christ, the circumcision of baptism is reckoned to him as uncircumcision, because "faith without works is dead."[53]

Consider also whether in this passage the following interpretation may be accepted, that even after the coming of Christ physical circumcision, observed according to the law, might be said to be of some value to those who keep the law on the same principle as that which obtained at the beginning of our faith, when it was still observed by those who believed in Christ. . . . Now if this (Christian) circumcision were to be turned into uncircumcision, not only would it be of no benefit to anyone, it would call down even greater judgment on the one who by the circumcision of the flesh appeared to be proclaiming the observance of the law but was in fact breaking it. And this judgment would be given by the one who had not submitted to physical circumcision but who nevertheless did the works of the law. Whether this interpretation is to be accepted or not is up to you, the reader, to decide.

Circumcision was of no value to those who thought they could be justified by it, but it was of value to those who thought that they might not come to Christ if they were forbidden to circum-

cise their children. For in the beginning there were some who thought of circumcision mainly as a recognizable symbol of their nationality and kept it up for that reason. They might have been hindered from coming to faith if they had been forbidden to do something which they could not do without. Therefore the apostle says this to them, so as not to close the door of faith to them. COMMENTARY ON THE EPISTLE TO THE ROMANS.[54]

CIRCUMCISION AND LAW. CHRYSOSTOM: Paul accepts the value of circumcision in theory but abolishes it in practice. For circumcision is only useful if the person circumcised keeps the law.. . . But a circumcised person who breaks the law is really uncircumcised, and Paul condemns him without hesitation. HOMILIES ON ROMANS 6.[55]

THE VALUE OF CIRCUMCISION. AMBROSIASTER: An opponent might say: "If circumcision is of value, why was it stopped?" It is only of value if you keep the law. Circumcision may be retained therefore, but if it is to be of any value the law must be observed. So why did Paul prohibit what he shows to be of value if the law is observed?

Paul answers by saying that if the law is not kept, the Jew effectively becomes a Gentile. . . . But to keep the law is to believe in Christ, who was promised to Abraham. Those who are justified by faith have their own merit and are included in the honor shown to the patriarchs. For every mention of salvation in the law refers to Christ. Therefore the man who believes in Christ is the man who keeps the law. But if he does not believe then he is a transgressor of the law because he has not accepted Christ . . . and it is no advantage for him to be called a son of Abraham. COMMENTARY ON PAUL'S EPISTLES.[56]

NEITHER JEW NOR GENTILE FORCED INTO THE PRACTICE OF THE OTHER. AUGUSTINE: The apostle did not say this as if he favored forc-

---

[53]Jas 2:26. [54]CER 1:248-58. [55]NPNF 1 11:370. [56]CSEL 81.1:84.

ing either the Gentiles to remain uncircumcised or the Jews not to adhere to the traditions of their fathers. Rather, he urged that neither group should be forced into the practice of the other but that each person should have the right, not the obligation, to adhere to his own custom. LYING 5.8.[57]

TRUE CIRCUMCISION. PELAGIUS: Circumcision is of value as a sign if righteousness accompanies it; without righteousness the rest is useless. Or this [verse] may mean that circumcision enabled the Jew to live and escape condemnation in childhood before reaching the age of understanding. Or perhaps, because he set it in the context of the law, it is that . . . when the circumcision of the flesh ends, the true circumcision of the heart will come. A man breaks the law when he does not follow what is foretold in it. PELAGIUS'S COMMENTARY ON ROMANS.[58]

2:26 Circumcision, Visible and Invisible

CIRCUMCISED BY GRACE. ORIGEN: We can apply this lesson to our situation in the church as well. For example, let us say that catechumens are still uncircumcised, i.e., Gentiles, and that believers are circumcised by the grace of baptism. Therefore, if a catechumen who has not yet been circumcised by the grace of baptism keeps the law of Christ, he obeys the precepts and commandments. Will he not by analogy with what is written here judge the one who claims to be a believer but does not keep the precepts and despises the law of Christ and his commands? COMMENTARY ON THE EPISTLE TO THE ROMANS.[59]

BECOMING A SON OF ABRAHAM. AMBROSIASTER: Faith in Christ is the righteousness of the law. . . . From this it is clear that if a Gentile believes in Christ he becomes a son of Abraham, who is the father of faith.[60] COMMENTARY ON PAUL'S EPISTLES.[61]

UNCIRCUMCISION COUNTED FOR CIRCUMCI-

SION. AUGUSTINE: Gentiles become members of the house of Israel when their uncircumcision is counted for circumcision, inasmuch as they do not display the righteousness of the law by the cutting of the flesh but keep it in charity of heart. THE SPIRIT AND THE LETTER 46.[62]

BECOMING CIRCUMCISED. CHRYSOSTOM: Look how clever Paul is. He does not say that the uncircumcision overcomes circumcision (for that would have angered the Jews who read his letter) but that the uncircumcision has become circumcision. Next he asks what circumcision really is, and he says that it is well-doing, whereas uncircumcision is evil-doing. Having moved the uncircumcised who does good deeds over to the circumcised and having pushed the circumcised man who leads a corrupt life into the ranks of the uncircumcised, Paul states his preference for the physically uncircumcised. HOMILIES ON ROMANS 6.[63]

WHY CIRCUMCISION WAS INSTITUTED. PELAGIUS: The visible needs the invisible but not the other way round, because the visible is an image of the invisible, while the invisible is the reality itself. Thus, the circumcision of the flesh needs the circumcision of the heart but not vice versa, because the reality does not need the image. . . . If circumcision has no value by itself, why was it instituted?[64] First, in order to distinguish the people of God from among the Gentiles. This is why when they were by themselves in the desert they were not circumcised. Or perhaps so that their bodies might be identified in battle. The reason why they were marked in that part of the body was first so that they would not be disfigured in a part of the body which was open to public view, and second, because the promise of grace would make this part of the body honorable through chastity. Or perhaps it

---

[57]FC 16:63. [58]PCR 75. [59]CER 1:254. [60]See Rom 4:16; Gal 3:7-8. [61]CSEL 81.1:91. [62]LCC 8:230. [63]NPNF 1 11:370-71. [64]See Ex 17:10-11.

was because it signified that Christ would be born from its seed. He was destined to introduce spiritual circumcision, but until he was born, physical circumcision would continue. PELAGIUS'S COMMENTARY ON ROMANS.[65]

2:27 Circumcision and the Law

BREAKERS AND KEEPERS OF THE LAW. ORIGEN: The Jew according to the flesh may keep the law, but only the man who is spiritual, who is a Jew in secret, can fulfill it. Insofar as the former is a transgressor of the law, it is the latter who will be his judge. COMMENTARY ON THE EPISTLE TO THE ROMANS.[66]

THE GENTILE WHO BELIEVES. AMBROSIASTER: The Gentile who believes under the guidance of nature condemns the Jew, to whom Christ was promised through the law and who refused to believe in him when he came. For as much as the Gentile is being prepared for glory for having known the Creator of nature by nature alone, so the Jew deserves to be punished all the more because he did not know Christ the Creator, either by nature or by the law. COMMENTARY ON PAUL'S EPISTLES.[67]

TWO TYPES OF UNCIRCUMCISION. CHRYSOSTOM: Here Paul clearly recognizes that there are two types of uncircumcision—one by nature and the other by will. Here he speaks of the physical uncircumcision and goes on to say that if it keeps the law it will judge the circumcision which breaks it. . . . For this kind of uncircumcision is offended when the law is broken and comes to its defense. . . . It is not the law which is dishonored but the one who disgraces the law. HOMILIES ON ROMANS 6.[68]

LITERAL AND SPIRITUAL CIRCUMCISION. PELAGIUS: This either means that as long as the Jews continue their literal circumcision they reject the spiritual circumcision, or that they will be judged because they have not followed what

the law said, viz., that by believing in Christ they might receive the true circumcision. PELAGIUS'S COMMENTARY ON ROMANS.[69]

2:28 Real Circumcision

THE JEW OUTWARDLY VIEWED. CHRYSOSTOM: Here Paul attacks the Judaizers on the ground that much they do is for outward show. HOMILIES ON ROMANS 6.[70]

THE TRUE JEW. PELAGIUS: This is the true Jew, for everything which was previously done externally was but an image of what was meant to happen internally. PELAGIUS'S COMMENTARY ON ROMANS.[71]

2:29 Spiritual, Not Literal, Circumcision

BEGINNING INWARDLY. ORIGEN: We must realize that in some people these two things go together while in others they do not. For there are some things which have their beginning inside a man and which proceed from there to the outside, but there are other things which start on the outside and work their way inside. What I mean is this. If chastity begins inside a man, there is no doubt that it will manifest itself on the outside of him as well. For it is hardly possible if someone does not commit adultery in his heart that he should do so in his body. But it does not follow from this that if chastity starts as an outward observance that it will necessarily penetrate to the point of inner continence, so that if someone does not commit adultery in his body it will follow immediately that he does not do so in his heart either. Therefore the circumcision of the inner and the outer man must be understood allegorically as meaning that the inner man should not lust in his heart, nor should the outer man surrender to lust in his body, so that he whom the apostle says is no longer in the flesh but in the Spirit, and who mor-

---

[65]PCR 75-76. [66]CER 1:260. [67]CSEL 81.1:91. [68]NPNF 1 11:371. [69]PCR 76. [70]NPNF 1 11:371. [71]PCR 76.

tifies the deeds of the flesh by the Spirit, may be said to be circumcised in the flesh as well.

It is true that he who has been circumcised has given up a part of his flesh to perdition and kept a part of it unharmed. The part that is lost is, I think, what is referred to in the following text: "All flesh is grass, and all its glory is as the flower of the field."[72] But the flesh which is retained is, I think, a type of that flesh of which it is said: "All flesh shall see the salvation of God."[73] It is the task of those ears which can hear to determine which is which. COMMENTARY ON THE EPISTLE TO THE ROMANS.[74]

SPIRIT AND LETTER. HILARY OF POITIERS: The apostle testifies without any hesitation that those who walk according to the teaching of Christ—in the spirit, not in the letter—are the Israel of God. THE TRINITY 5.28.[75]

THE FORESKIN OF YOUR HEART. AMBROSIASTER: It is clear why Paul denies that the circumcision of the flesh has any merit with God. For Abraham was not justified because he was circumcised; rather, he was justified because he believed, and afterward he was circumcised. It is the circumcision of the heart which is praiseworthy before God. To circumcise the heart means to cut out error and recognize the Creator. And because the circumcision of the heart was to come in the future, first Moses said: "Circumcise the hardness of your heart,"[76] and Jeremiah also: "Circumcise the foreskin of your heart."[77] He said this to Jews who were following idols. For there is a veil over the heart which the one who is converted to God circumcises, because faith removes the cloud of error and grants those who are perfect knowledge of God in the mystery of the Trinity, which was unknown in earlier times. The praise of this circumcision is from God but is hidden to men, for it is the merit of the heart which God looks for, not that of the flesh. But the praise of the Jews is from men, for they glory in the circumcision of the flesh, which comes from their ancestors. COMMENTARY ON PAUL'S EPISTLES.[78]

SETTING ASIDE EXTERNAL OBSERVANCES. CHRYSOSTOM: By saying this Paul sets aside everything which is merely of the body. For the circumcision is external, and so are the sabbaths, the sacrifices and the purifications.... The Gentile who does right is more praiseworthy than the Jew who breaks the law. When this is agreed upon, the circumcision of the flesh must be set aside, and the need for a good life is everywhere demonstrated. HOMILIES ON ROMANS 6.[79]

THE WORKS OF THE LAW. THEODORE OF MOPSUESTIA: "Spiritual" here does not refer to the Holy Spirit. For Paul is not talking about those who have been put right by grace but is referring above all to those outside the faith who do the works of the law and who show themselves to be better than those transgressors who are under the law. PAULINE COMMENTARY FROM THE GREEK CHURCH.[80]

UNDERSTANDING THE LAW ACCORDING TO THE SPIRIT. AUGUSTINE: This means that the law should be understood according to the Spirit, and not according to what the letter says. This pertains especially to those who have interpreted circumcision more according to the flesh than according to the Spirit. AUGUSTINE ON ROMANS 11.[81]

CIRCUMCISION OF THE HEART. PELAGIUS: This is foretold in the law: "And the Lord your God will circumcise your heart and the heart of your offspring, so that you will love the Lord your God,"[82] and again: "Circumcise yourselves to the Lord, and remove the foreskin of your heart,"[83] not according to the letter of the law but according to the New Testament, which examines the inner secrets which only God can see. PELAGIUS'S COMMENTARY ON ROMANS.[84]

---

[72]Is 40:6. [73]Is 40:5. [74]CER 1:298-300. [75]FC 25:158. [76]Deut 10:16. [77]Jer 4:4. [78]CSEL 81.1:91, 93. [79]NPNF 1 11:371. [80]NTA 15:116. [81]AOR 5. [82]Deut 30:6. [83]Jer 4:4. [84]PCR 77.

3:1-8 GOD'S FAITHFULNESS

¹Then what advantage has the Jew? Or what is the value of circumcision? ²Much in every way. To begin with, the Jews are entrusted with the oracles of God. ³What if some were unfaithful? Does their faithlessness nullify the faithfulness of God? ⁴By no means! Let God be true though every man be false, as it is written,

"That thou mayest be justified in thy words,
and prevail when thou art judged."

⁵But if our wickedness serves to show the justice of God, what shall we say? That God is unjust to inflict wrath on us? (I speak in a human way.) ⁶By no means! For then how could God judge the world? ⁷But if through my falsehood God's truthfulness abounds to his glory, why am I still being condemned as a sinner? ⁸And why not do evil that good may come?—as some people slanderously charge us with saying. Their condemnation is just.

OVERVIEW: Did the Jews enjoy a special place in God's plan? The Fathers believed that they did, for two reasons. First, they had received the divine oracles before the coming of Christ and therefore had an advantage when the gospel was proclaimed. Second, Jewish Christians were able to claim descent from Abraham and the faithful of the Old Testament. Nevertheless, the Fathers insisted that the salvation of the Gentiles was not inferior to that of the Jews, nor did unbelieving Jews have any advantage over Gentile believers. Human origins do not affect the promises of God. The Fathers pointed out that Jews were human beings like the rest of us. Some of them believed and inherited the promises. Others did not and were cast out. The important thing for everybody, Jews and Gentiles alike, is that we should all believe in Christ.

The problems of evil and God's wrath were issues that preoccupied the Fathers. To them, God was just (righteous) by nature, and this could never change. The snag was that humankind had rebelled against God's righteousness, thereby creating the conflict between good and evil. In such circumstances the presence and sovereignty of good in a world of evil could only appear as wrath, since it is in the nature of justice

to destroy everything that is opposed to it. The fact that God's goodness shines all the more brightly when contrasted with our evil does not justify evil. The early Christians were sometimes accused of being immoral, because of this misunderstanding, and the Fathers were determined to counter such reasoning. To be a Christian is to take on something of the character of God, including his holiness, goodness and righteousness.

3:1 The Value of Circumcision

NOT FOR HUMAN PRAISE OF MAN. CHRYSOSTOM: If Paul means that there is no use in being a Jew or in circumcision, why was that nation called, and why was circumcision given? How does Paul solve this problem? By the same means as he did before: he speaks not of their praises but of the benefits of God. HOMILIES ON ROMANS 6.[1]

3:2 Entrusted with the Oracles of God

THE ORACLES OF GOD FIRST ENTRUSTED TO THE JEWS. ORIGEN: Even though the oracles of God are now entrusted to the Gentiles as well,

[1] NPNF 1 11:372.

they were first entrusted to the Jews, as Paul says. Is he speaking here of the letters and the books or of the meaning and the general gist of the law? For we see many Jews who from infancy to old age never stop studying, yet they never come to a knowledge of the truth. How can it be true that they have some advantage in having been entrusted with the oracles of God first, when they do not understand "what they are saying or the things about which they are making assertions?"[2] . . . It must be understood that these things are being said about Moses, the prophets and others like them, to whom the oracles of God were entrusted, because there can be no doubt that they were Jews and that they had the circumcision. It would also apply to anyone who was wise, an intelligent listener or a gifted counselor. These the Lord is said to have removed from Jerusalem because he was offended by the ungodliness of the people.[3] . . . Even the apostles of Christ and Paul himself, the vessel of election, came from the Jews and from the circumcision. He had far more in every way than those whom he taught who were of the Gentiles. For the oracles of God were entrusted to the Jews.

Note moreover that Paul says that the oracles of God were entrusted to the Jews, not merely the letter of the text. So it is possible for us to understand that those who read but do not understand, as well as those who read but do not believe, have had only the letter entrusted to them, of which the apostle says: "The letter kills."[4] But the oracles of God are entrusted to those who understand and believe what Moses wrote and who believe in Christ, as the Lord said: "If you believed Moses you would believe me, for he wrote of me."[5]

But if the Jew has received more in receiving the letter and something more in the oracles of God, does this mean that those of the Gentiles who have come to Christ are somehow left out? Or is there some way in which they have more than the Jews? Listen to what the Lord says to the Gentile centurion who believed: "Truly I say to you, I have not found such faith even in Israel."[6]

Therefore you see that when it comes to faith, the Gentiles have much more. . . . When it comes to the letter, the Jews have much more in every way, but when it comes to faith, it is the Gentiles who have much more. COMMENTARY ON THE EPISTLE TO THE ROMANS.[7]

THE ORACLES INCLUDE ALL GOOD THINGS.
EUSEBIUS OF EMESA: When Paul says "To begin with," he does not go on to list a second or third item. He means rather that what he begins with is comprehensive of all good things. For what could be better than to believe the words of God? PAULINE COMMENTARY FROM THE GREEK CHURCH.[8]

RACE NO ADVANTAGE, BUT REVELATION IS.
AMBROSIASTER: Although Paul says that there are many things which pertain to the honor and merit of the seed of Abraham, he records only one of them openly, because it is their greatest boast: They were judged worthy to receive the law, by which they learned to distinguish right from wrong. Only after that was it possible for the value of other things to be understood. But as far as the Jews according to the flesh are concerned (that is, the unbelievers among them), Paul shows that the witness of their race is of no advantage to them. But so as not to appear to be treating them all, including the believers among them, badly, he teaches that the law is very useful to Jewish believers, because they are children of Abraham.

For it was to them that the oracles of God were entrusted. It is by the merits of their ancestors that they received the law and were called God's people. . . . Egypt was hit by different plagues because of the wrongs which it did to them.[9] They dined on heavenly manna;[10] they were a terror to all nations, as Rahab the harlot bore witness.[11] Moreover, it was to them that Christ the Savior was promised for their sanctifi-

---

[2]1 Tim 1:7. [3]See Is 3:1-3. [4]2 Cor 3:6. [5]Jn 5:46. [6]Mt 8:10. [7]CER 1:306-10. [8]NTA 15:46. [9]See Ex 7—12. [10]See Ex 16:14-36. [11]See Josh 2:9-11.

cation. Therefore Paul says that in many ways it was useful to the Jews, because they were the children of Abraham and came before the Gentiles. Commentary on Paul's Epistles.[12]

The Jews Entrusted Themselves to the Oracles. Chrysostom: What does *entrusted* mean? It means that the Jews had the law put into their hands because God thought so highly of them that he entrusted them with oracles which came down from on high. I know that some people take the *entrusted* not of the Jews but of the oracles, as if to say: "The law was believed in." But the context does not allow this interpretation. For in the first place he is saying this in order to accuse them and to show that, in spite of the fact that they enjoyed many blessings from above, they still showed great ingratitude. Then look at [verse 3]. If some of the Jews did not believe, how is it that some say that the oracles were believed in? So what does Paul mean? He means that God entrusted the oracles to the Jews, not that the Jews entrusted themselves to the oracles, for the context does not make sense otherwise. Homilies on Romans 6.[13]

[Pseudo-]Constantius: The Jews benefited not because they accepted circumcision in the flesh but because they believed the oracles of God. The Holy Letter of St. Paul to the Romans.[14]

Pelagius: The Jews were at an advantage because the oracles of God were entrusted to them, while nothing was entrusted to the Gentiles. Pelagius's Commentary on Romans.[15]

3:3 The Faithfulness of God

The Faithfulness of God Not Nullified. Origen: The oracles of God were entrusted to the Jews, as we have said above, but some of them did not believe either God or his oracles. Those who did not believe were carnal, as Paul says elsewhere: "The unspiritual man does not receive the

gifts of the Spirit of God, for they are folly to him."[16] But their faithlessness does not nullify the faithfulness of God. By God's faithfulness we understand either the faith which God had when he entrusted his oracles to them or the faith by which those who received the oracles from God believed in him. We are therefore reminded that their faithlessness has not nullified the faithfulness of God, which he has shown to us. Commentary on the Epistle to the Romans.[17]

Cyprian: The sanctity and worth of the confessors (i. e., martyrs) was not shattered because the faith of a few of them was broken. Treatises on the Unity of the Church 22.[18]

Grace Given to Those Who Believed. Ambrosiaster: Paul says this because it was not foreordained that believing Jews would not be thought worthy of receiving what God had promised just because the others were unbelieving, for the promise was such that the gift of grace would be given to those who believed.[19]

Therefore God is not put out because of the unbelief of the Jews and will grant eternal life to their believers, which he promised would be given to those who believed in Christ.[20] Those who did not believe excluded themselves from consideration without doing the rest any injury. Having said this, Paul commends Jewish believers, because it was not their fault that many of their kinsmen refused to believe. Commentary on Paul's Epistles.[21]

God Remains Faithful. Apollinaris of Laodicea: Let it be agreed, Paul says, that God is faithful and true in every case, whereas men have been judged as unfaithful and untrue, so that God by his goodness may conquer the self-righteousness of men by bestowing his own righteousness upon them. Pauline Commentary

---

[12]CSEL 81.1:93, 95. [13]NPNF 1 11:372. [14]ENPK 2:30. [15]PCR 77. [16]1 Cor 2:14. [17]CER 1:314-16. [18]LCC 5:139. [19]See Eph 2:8. [20]See Jn 3:14-15; Acts 13:48. [21]CSEL 81.1:95.

from the Greek Church.[22]

What Does It Matter if Some Were Unfaithful?

What Does It Matter if Some Were Unfaithful? Chrysostom: The unbelief of the Jews does not reflect badly on God but rather shows his honor and love of man to be all the greater, in that God is seen to have bestowed honor on people who would dishonor him. Look how he has revealed them to be guilty of misdeeds because of what they gloried in. The honor God showed to them was so great that even when he saw what the result of it would be, he did not withhold his good will toward them. But the Jews made the honors bestowed on them a means of insulting him who honored them.

Paul said: "What if some of them did not believe?" Wasn't it clear that it was all of them who did not believe? If Paul had told the truth directly he might have appeared to be a severe and hostile accuser. Homilies on Romans 6.[23]

The Promises to Abraham. Pelagius: The faithfulness meant here is that to the promises made to Abraham, to whom it was said that "in your seed all the nations will be blessed."[24] Pelagius's Commentary on Romans.[25]

Unable to Block God's Blessings. Theodoret of Cyr: God knew in advance who would obey the law and who would break it. Therefore those who did not believe were unable to stand in the way of his blessings.[26] Interpretation of the Letter to the Romans.[27]

3:4 Let God Alone Be True

Whether This Makes David and Paul Liars. Origen: If one is to be righteous, one must keep the law in every particular, which is almost impossible for human nature to achieve. Therefore every one is a liar. For since every man is a liar, it follows that on that day when the Lord comes to judgment with men, only he will be justified in what he says. For his words are true in everything, because they are the words of truth.

It should also be understood that this saying, i.e., that every man is a liar, is taken from Psalm 115:28 . . . Now someone might object that if all men are liars, then Paul too, being a man, will also be a liar! But in that case David, who originally said it, would also be a liar, and what he said would be false, just because he was a liar. . . . The whole statement would thus become nonsense, which is absurd! Commentary on the Epistle to the Romans.[29]

Obeying God's Precepts. Cyprian: If every man is a liar and God alone is true, what else ought we servants and bishops of God to do except to reject human errors and lies and to remain in the truth of God, obeying the precepts of the Lord? Letter 67.8.[30]

God Remains Just. Eusebius of Emesa: Even if all men loved a lie before the coming of the truth, the true God nevertheless remained just, holding fast to the things which were proper to God and fulfilling everything which was said that was fitting. Pauline Commentary from the Greek Church.[31]

Whether God Can Lie. Ambrose: Does God tell a lie? He does not. It is impossible for God to tell a lie. Is this an impossibility because of some weakness? Certainly not! How could he be the cause of all things if there were something which he could not cause? What then is impossible to him? Nothing that is difficult for his power but only that which is contrary to his nature. It is impossible, it is said, for him to tell a lie.[32] The impossibility comes not from weakness but from his power and greatness, for truth admits of no lie. Letter 14.[33]

Let God Be True. Ambrosiaster: Because

---

[22]NTA 15:61. [23]NPNF 1 11:372-73. [24]Gen 22:18. [25]PCR 77. [26]IER, Migne PG 82 ad loc. [27]IER, Migne PG 82 ad loc. [28]Ps 116:11. [29]CER 1:316-18. [30]FC 51:238. [31]NTA 15:46. [32]See Num 23:19; Tit 1:2. [33]FC 26:70.

God is true, he gives what he has promised. To fail is human, for the times and the foolishness of nature make man unstable in that he does not have foreknowledge. But God, for whom there is no future, remains unchanging, as he says: "I the Lord do not change."[34] Therefore Paul says that all men are liars, and this is true. For nature is fallible and is not unreasonably called a liar. It may be a liar intentionally or accidentally, but we must not expect God to be like that, for he is perfect and full of good will and will accomplish what he has promised. He even confirms this by the prophetic oracle: "Thou art justified in thy sentence and blameless in thy judgment."[35] COMMENTARY ON PAUL'S EPISTLES.[36]

HOW IS GOD JUSTIFIED? CHRYSOSTOM: Paul is saying something like this: "Even if every one of the Jews was an unbeliever . . . God would only be the more justified." What does the word *justified* mean? It means that if there were a trial and an examination of the things which God had done for the Jews and also of what they had done to him, the victory would be with God, and all the right would be on his side. HOMILIES ON ROMANS 6.[37]

[PSEUDO-]CONSTANTIUS: God is said to be true because he does not give to sinners what he has promised to the saints. THE HOLY LETTER OF ST. PAUL TO THE ROMANS.[38]

THE HERETIC DESTROYS SOULS. JEROME: If everyone who utters a lie has already destroyed his soul, and all of us are liars, are we all going to perish? What Scripture says . . . we should interpret as referring to heretics. . . . The doer of the deed has indeed killed his own soul, but the heretic—the liar—has killed as many souls as he has seduced. HOMILIES ON THE PSALMS 2.[39]

GOD IS TRUE. AUGUSTINE: God in himself is true; you in yourself are a liar—in him you can be true! HOMILIES ON JOHN 1.6.[40]

THOUGH EVERY MAN BE FALSE. PELAGIUS: "Every man" means the majority. Paul's opponents had quoted this text as if David had meant: "For this reason have I sinned, that thou might appear just in judging me." But the true meaning is that God promised to punish sinners without showing favoritism and that some thought his delay in doing so amounted to a lie. God prevails when he judges the deeds of those from whom no one thought vengeance would ever be exacted. Or it may also mean that God has shown that he is concerned about mankind . . . and that he has overthrown those who wrongly suggest that he is not interested in human affairs. PELAGIUS'S COMMENTARY ON ROMANS.[41]

OPPOSITE PATHS. THEODORET OF CYR: Human beings are thus given over to their own free will. Hence they are divided into two groups: those who prefer the worship of God and those who take the opposite path and come to a dire end, corresponding to their choice. INTERPRETATION OF THE LETTER TO THE ROMANS.[42]

3:5 The Justice of God

WHETHER GOD'S WRATH IS UNJUST. ORIGEN: Paul says that it is wrong to say that God is unjust for bringing wrath on men. For how will the one who judges the world be thought to be unjust, when his very title of Judge shows that he does nothing without judgment? And where there is judgment, it follows that there will be justice. For the words *judge* and *judgment* are both derived from *justice*.

The idea being expressed here does not accord with God or with the wisdom of God, but with man and with what has just been said, viz.: "All men are liars."[43]

But it is perfectly logical and right to say that justice is the enemy of unrighteousness, just as

---

[34]Mt 3:6. [35]Ps 51:4. [36]CSEL 81.1:97. [37]NPNF 1 11:373. [38]ENPK 2:31. [39]FC 48:19. [40]LCC 8:264. [41]PCR 77-78. [42]IER, Migne PG 82 col. 77. [43]See Ps 116:11; Rom 3:4.

life is the enemy of death and light is the enemy of darkness. Therefore God, in whom is justice, is said to bring wrath on men, in whom unrighteousness dwells. For justice and unrighteousness are natural enemies. So how could God be regarded as unjust, simply because he is fighting unrighteousness? COMMENTARY ON THE EPISTLE TO THE ROMANS.[44]

WHETHER OUR WICKEDNESS SERVES TO SHOW THE JUSTICE OF GOD. AMBROSIASTER: David had sinned in the case of Uriah the Hittite.[45] Because he knew that the promise would not be given to sinners, he pleaded that the righteousness of the words of God might overrule the judgment which said that the promise should not be given to sinners and that it might sanctify the penitent in order to give him what God had promised he would give to the righteous. To this Paul adds that . . . if God is justified because we are sinners, it would be wrong of him to pardon us on that account. If it can really be said that our wickedness is of some advantage to God, then there is some measure of truth in this reasoning. But it is dangerous to speak like that. God is not unjust if he judges, because our unrighteousness is of no benefit to him. It is not as if he would somehow be justified by our sins or as if he would somehow rejoice at our sins, by which he alone would then appear to be righteous.

This way of thinking suits men but not God, because it does not happen that God should ever be unjust, only man. Nor does our unrighteousness make God righteous if he gives to us sinners what he promised to the saints, for although we are sinners, we are reformed by repentance so that it is not as sinners but as those who have been cleansed[46] that we are readied to receive the promise. COMMENTARY ON PAUL'S EPISTLES.[47]

WHETHER GOD'S JUSTICE EXCEEDS OUR CONCEPTIONS OF JUSTICE. CHRYSOSTOM: What does Paul mean? God honored the Jews, but they dishonored him. This gives God the victory and shows the greatness of his love toward man, in that he continued to honor them in spite of what they were like.

But if this is true of us (someone might say), why am I to be punished when I have contributed to God's victory by dishonoring him? Paul answers this by a corresponding absurdity. In effect, he says that if this man were the cause of God's victory and he was punished as a result, it was an injustice. But if God is not unjust and the man was punished, then he could not have been the cause of God's victory. . . . For God's justice far exceeds what we think of as justice and is based on other ineffable criteria. HOMILIES ON ROMANS 6.[48]

PELAGIUS: Now the apostle begins to answer the objection. It is unjust if God punishes sinners merely in order to appear even more righteous. PELAGIUS'S COMMENTARY ON ROMANS.[49]

DEPRIVED OF GOD'S PROMISES. [PSEUDO-]CONSTANTIUS: It is not that our wickedness increases God's justice, but at that time when we come into judgment with God we shall be deprived of his promises as retribution for not having obeyed his commands. THE HOLY LETTER OF ST. PAUL TO THE ROMANS.[50]

THE SOURCE OF ADVERSITIES. CAESARIUS OF ARLES: When adversities come . . . or when by God's just judgment hostility, dryness or death is imposed, we should attribute this to our sins rather than to God's injustice. SERMON 70.1.[51]

3:6 God Judges the World

THE WHOLE WORLD. ORIGEN: In this passage the word *world* means the people who are in this world, just as we read elsewhere that "the whole

---

[44]CER 2:32-38. [45]See 2 Sam 11:1-27; 1 Kings 15:5. [46]By the mercy of the cross, by pardon in Jesus Christ—not by our own merits or works. [47]CSEL 81.1:99-103. [48]NPNF 1 11:373. [49]PCR 78. [50]ENPK 2:30. [51]FC 31:330.

world is in the power of the evil one."[52] Commentary on the Epistle to the Romans.[53]

Whether Our Sins Are of Some Benefit to God. Ambrosiaster: It is true that it would not have been just if God had judged the world if its sins were of some benefit to him, so that whenever sinners received forgiveness at his nod, God would appear to be good. Then if they had not sinned, according to this reasoning, he would not appear to be righteous. For if they had not sinned there would be nothing to forgive, and God would not be good. But this kind of thinking is absurd! Commentary on Paul's Epistles.[54]

Righteousness and Judgment. [Pseudo-] Constantius: Paul taught after the authority of the Scriptures that God is righteous. Therefore when we come into judgment with him, he demonstrates that it is said by the very meaning of the text that God may rightly wreak vengeance on evildoers. The Holy Letter of St. Paul to the Romans.[55]

Pelagius: By what righteousness will God condemn the unrighteous, if in your opinion human wickedness makes him even more righteous? Pelagius's Commentary on Romans.[56]

3:7 Human Falsehood, God's Truthfulness

Even Through Human Falsehood God's Truthfulness Abounds. Origen: There are many kinds of religion in this world, many schools of philosophy, and many teachings which promote false assertions and are backed up with lying arguments. Those who invent them have a false reputation for wisdom—people of little or no authority. We should recognize them for what they are. Because of them many false statements are commonly accepted as true. The whole world, including religion, is now burdened with lying opinions. Even the elect are being led astray, if you can imagine that. The truth of God is now attacking and refuting every lie. Faith in God's

truth, God's wisdom and God's Word is undercutting all claims of false teaching. By each of these lies which had previously been asserted by men, the truth of God is abounding, by demonstrating their superficiality and by communicating the simple truth of faith in each and every case. In this way, says the apostle, the truth of God abounds through the falsehood of men. Commentary on the Epistle to the Romans.[57]

Whether Evil Is the Cause of Good. Chrysostom: The logic of this argument can easily tend toward the absurdity that good comes out of evil and that evil is the cause of good. In that case, one of two options follows: Either God is clearly unjust in punishing, or if he does not punish, then he gets his victory from our vices. Either of these conclusions is absurd. Homilies on Romans 6.[58]

3:8 Why Not Do Evil?

Twisting Scripture. Clement of Alexandria: These people twist the Scriptures when they read them by their tone of voice, in order to serve their own preferences. They alter some of the accents and punctuation marks in order to force wise and constructive precepts to support their taste for luxury. Stromata 3.39.2.[59]

Why Not Do Evil That Good May Come? Origen: This is an argument raised by unjust people against the Christian faith. They blaspheme us even more by suggesting that because we believe that God's truthfulness abounds in the falsehood of men and that his justice is confirmed by our unrighteousness, we also believe that we should do evil so that good may come of it and that we should tell lies so that God's truthfulness will shine out even more clearly because of it. But in claiming that this is what we think they are

---

[52]1 Jn 5:19. [53]CER 2:44. [54]CSEL 81.1:103. [55]ENPK 2:31. [56]PCR 78. [57]CER 2:44-46. [58]NPNF 1 11:373. [59]FC 85:279.

blaspheming us, as if these things were somehow the logical conclusion of our beliefs. But in fact the logic of our beliefs does not accept this line of reasoning, because we understand that God is a just and true judge. COMMENTARY ON THE EPISTLE TO THE ROMANS.[60]

WHETHER FORGIVENESS ENCOURAGES SIN. AMBROSIASTER: This is why the apostle asked himself this question. The matter was raised by opponents, as if this were the meaning of the preaching of the forgiveness of sins—that they should do evil and good would come of it. That is, they should sin so that by forgiving their sins God should appear to be good, according to what has just been said above. Paul calls this blasphemy and rejects it as a bad interpretation of God's teaching. Faith is not meant to encourage people to sin by preaching that God will ultimately be vindicated. Rather, it gives sinners a remedy so that having recovered their health they may live under the law of God and not sin again. COMMENTARY ON PAUL'S EPISTLES.[61]

CHRYSOSTOM: The people Paul is referring to here are Gentiles who thought in this way themselves. HOMILIES ON ROMANS 6.[62]

WHETHER WITHOUT MY LIES GOD WOULD NOT APPEAR TO BE TRUE. [PSEUDO-]CONSTANTIUS: This is aimed at the Carpocratians, who are the worst of heretics and Gentiles to boot. The text is directed at those who say that unless they sin God's grace will not abound, and unless they tell lies God will not appear to be true. The apostle answers them by saying that if what they think is true, then they should not be judged as sinners. But given that vengeance is wreaked on sinners, Paul says that they have not thought correctly. THE HOLY LETTER OF ST. PAUL TO THE ROMANS.[63]

PELAGIUS: It is not true that, as some people think we say, the more evil we have done, the greater good we shall receive. PELAGIUS'S COMMENTARY ON ROMANS.[64]

ABSTAINING FROM WICKEDNESS. THEODORET OF CYR: This was not the intention of the apostles' teaching. On the contrary, they demanded that everyone abstain from all manner of wickedness. INTERPRETATION OF THE LETTER TO THE ROMANS.[65]

---

[60]CER 2:48-50. [61]CSEL 81.1:103, 105. [62]NPNF 1 11:373. [63]ENPK 2:31. [64]PCR 78. [65]IER, Migne PG 82 col. 80.

3:9-20 HUMAN SINFULNESS

[9]*What then? Are we Jews any better off?[c] No, not at all; for I[d] have already charged that all men, both Jews and Greeks, are under the power of sin,* [10]*as it is written:*
"None is righteous, no, not one;
[11]*no one understands, no one seeks for God.*
[12]*All have turned aside, together they have gone wrong;*
no one does good, not even one."
[13]*"Their throat is an open grave,*

they use their tongues to deceive."

"The venom of asps is under their lips."

[14]*"Their mouth is full of curses and bitterness."*

[15]*"Their feet are swift to shed blood,*

[16]*in their paths are ruin and misery,*

[17]*and the way of peace they do not know."*

[18]*"There is no fear of God before their eyes."*

[19]*Now we know that whatever the law says it speaks to those who are under the law, so that every mouth may be stopped, and the whole world may be held accountable to God.* [20]*For no human being will be justified in his sight by works of the law, since through the law comes knowledge of sin.*

c Or *at any disadvantage?* d Greek *we*

OVERVIEW: In the final analysis there is no difference between Jews and Gentiles, since all have sinned and fallen short of the glory of God. Paul quotes the Scriptures at length to demonstrate this point, and the Fathers echo him. Total depravity was a part of human life from the time Adam fell into sin, and no one escapes its effects. No one has brought goodness to full expression, whether in Sodom, Jerusalem or the church. While in this body, we all behold the good only through a glass darkly. The purpose of the law was to demonstrate the true nature of righteousness in order to show just how far we have all fallen away from it and how hopeless our present condition is. What Paul meant by the law caused some puzzlement among the Fathers. Some argued that Paul was referring to the Old Testament (AMBROSIASTER, CHRYSOSTOM). Others, however, wanted to say that the law referred to here is the law of nature innate in everyone, which condemns through conscience (ORIGEN et al.). Either way the result is the same—the law condemns, and only Christ can save. The law is like a doctor who points out what our disease is and shows how it must be cured. As such it is a good thing, even if it is painful to experience. Although the law can diagnose our illness, it has no power to cure us. Instead it makes us more miserable, since we come to understand what is wrong with us without being able to do anything about it. We may want to escape its clutches, but without the grace of God we lack the power to do so.

3:9 Under the Power of Sin

ALL HUMANITY IS UNDER THE POWER OF SIN. ORIGEN: Here it must be understood that the reference is to all men, whether they are under the written law [of Moses] or the natural law. For we understand that this applies to the Gentiles in the same way as we have already said above.[1] When they begin to do the works of the law by nature and become a law for themselves, then they are reproached by their conscience for the things they do which are contrary to that law. For this reason it seems to me that those who have thought that the law of nature is the law of God and that the law of Moses is merely the written law are correct. If Paul was speaking of the written law, the law of Moses, when he said: "Sin is not imputed when there is no law,"[2] neither Cain[3] nor those who perished in the flood[4] nor those who were burnt with fire at Sodom[5] would have had their sins imputed to them. But since we see that not only did they have their sins imputed

[1]See Rom 1:18-21. [2]Rom 5:13. [3]See Gen 4:1-16. [4]See Gen 7. [5]See Gen 19:1-28.

to them, they also suffered retribution for them, it is clear that Paul was speaking here of the natural law, which with the exception of the early years of childhood, is present in all men. For this reason he was quite right to say that all are under the power of sin. Whence it seems to me that the philosophers were right when they said that every mortal being on coming to the age of discretion, when by the entry of the natural law it might distinguish between good and evil, first of all discovers what is evil and afterward combats it by means of instructions, precepts and warnings, so as to move on to virtue. I think that Paul was agreeing with them when he said: "But when the commandment came, sin sprang to life."[6] . . . It must not be thought that everyone is guilty of all the sins which are listed below. Rather, some are guilty of some of them, and others are guilty of others but in such a way that taken together the whole range of sinfulness is found in the human race. COMMENTARY ON THE EPISTLE TO THE ROMANS.[7]

ALL ARE GUILTY. AMBROSIASTER: Paul is saying: "Why go on talking like this? For we have shown by the examples given that all, Jews and Gentiles alike, are guilty and that the law is being pursued in vain." For Paul first showed that the Gentiles are guilty according to the law of nature and also because they did not accept the law of Moses, for which reason their case is very dire indeed.[8] Then he showed that the Jews were also guilty. While they appeared to be living under God's law and defended their privilege by the merit of their ancestors, they in fact brought the grace of God into disrepute because they rejected the promise made to their ancestors.[9] COMMENTARY ON PAUL'S EPISTLES.[10]

THEODORE OF MOPSUESTIA: Paul's intention here is to say: Come then, after refuting their position, let us demonstrate the greatness of ours. PAULINE COMMENTARY FROM THE GREEK CHURCH.[11]

WHETHER THE JEWS ARE BETTER OFF.

PELAGIUS: Paul finds no reason for saying that the Jews are better than others. . . . Both Jews and Gentiles are under sin—something we not only deduce by reason but also corroborate by the witness of the Jews themselves. PELAGIUS'S COMMENTARY ON ROMANS.[12]

3:10 *None Is Righteous*

COMPARING JERUSALEM, SODOM AND THE CHURCH. ORIGEN: It may appear that there are other scriptural passages which seem to contradict this one by suggesting that some people were righteous, e.g., when it is said of Sodom in relation to Jerusalem: "Sodom is righteous compared with you."[13] But note carefully what Scripture actually says. It does not say that Sodom was righteous but that since Jerusalem had committed so many sins and what it was doing was so awful, Sodom appeared to be righteous by comparison. . . . For this reason, I am afraid that when I look at those of us who are in the church of God and who claim to follow his law and the commands of the gospel, there are not a few unbelievers who appear to be righteous by comparison. COMMENTARY ON THE EPISTLE TO THE ROMANS.[14]

NO ONE HAS BROUGHT GOODNESS TO FULL FRUITION. ORIGEN: That no one has done good, not even one, is a hard saying and difficult to understand. How is it possible that no one, Jew or Greek, has ever done anything good? Are we supposed to believe that nobody has ever shown hospitality, fed the hungry, clothed the naked, delivered the innocent from the hands of the powerful or done anything similar? It does not seem possible to me that Paul was intending to assert anything as incredible as that. I think that what he meant must be understood as follows. If someone lays the foundation for a house and puts up one or two walls or transports some building materials to

---

[6]Rom 7:9. [7]CER 2:60-62. [8]See Rom 2:14. [9]See Acts 6:8—7:53. [10]CSEL 81.1:105. [11]NTA 15:117. [12]PCR 79. [13]See Ezek 16:48. [14]CER 2:62-64.

the site, can he be said to have built the house, just because he has set to work on it? The man who will be said to have built the house is the one who has finished off each and every part of it. So I think that here the apostle is saying that no one has done good in the sense that no one has brought goodness to perfection and completion. If we ask ourselves who is truly good and who has done good perfectly, we shall find only him who said: "I am the good shepherd," and again: "The good shepherd lays down his life for the sheep."[15] Commentary on the Epistle to the Romans.[16]

No Hope Without Christ's Mercy. Ambrosiaster: From unrighteousness Paul goes on to list their evil deeds and even adds some worse ones, in order to show that there was no hope for them unless they cried out for the mercy of Christ, who forgives sins. Commentary on Paul's Epistles.[17]

No, Not One. Pelagius: The psalm from which this quote is taken[18] speaks of the fool. Paul shows that witness to the fool will be fulfilled particularly at the coming of Christ. When he appears, not one righteous person will be found. Pelagius's Commentary on Romans.[19]

3:11 No One Seeks God

Through a Glass Darkly. Origen: Even the apostle Paul himself says that he knows in part and understands in part.[20] So who is there who can make a claim that he understands? For however much he may understand, it will appear that he understands through a glass darkly and that only after he lays aside this earthly body will he see face to face.[21] . . . Thus it is that "no one understands, no one seeks for God." For as long as we are preoccupied with the cares of the body and seek the things of the body, we cannot seek God nor can we think his thoughts. Commentary on the Epistle to the Romans.[22]

The Lameness of Asa. Ambrosiaster: Seek

God. Do not be like Asa the king of Judah, who after receiving many blessings from God fell so far that when he suffered lameness in his feet he would not seek God even though there was a prophet present.[23] Commentary on Paul's Epistles.[24]

Seeking God's Will. Pelagius: One who does not understand does not seek. Or perhaps it is that one does not understand because one does not seek. One seeks for God by enquiring after his will. . . . The sinner has not known the will of his master.[25] "Know me, know my will," as the popular saying goes. Pelagius's Commentary on Romans.[26]

3:12 All Have Gone Wrong

Who Does Good? Origen: It seems to me that Scripture would not say that they had gone wrong if there had not been a time when they were standing in the right way. From this it appears that the original work of God in creating a rational nature was right and that this being was put in the right way by the gift of the Creator himself. But since he turned aside from this to sin, Scripture rightly says that he has gone wrong. Remember how Adam, the first man, was deceived by the serpent and turned aside from the right way of paradise to the fallen and crooked paths of this mortal life.[27] As a consequence therefore, everyone who comes into this world in the following of Adam has gone wrong and become unworthy, just as he did.[28] Commentary on the Epistle to the Romans.[29]

Pelagius: One who does not look for support is bound to fall away and become useless for the work for which he was made. But if there is no one who does good, in what sense does Paul later

---

[15]Jn 10:11. [16]CER 2:70-72. [17]CSEL 81.1:107. [18]Ps 14:1. [19]PCR 79. [20]See 1 Cor 13:9. [21]See 1 Cor 13:12. [22]CER 2:66-68. [23]See 2 Chron 16:12. [24]CSEL 81.1:107. [25]1 Jn 3:6. [26]PCR 79. [27]See Gen 3:1-24. [28]See Rom 5:12. [29]CER 2:68-70.

on accuse those who devour God's people and ruin the needy? For they were not God's people if they did not do good. . . . But this has more to do with the exposition of the psalm than with the apostle's concern here! PELAGIUS'S COMMENTARY ON ROMANS.[30]

FROM BAD TO WORSE. AMBROSIASTER: No one doubts that those who do not look to God for help are inclined to seek help from vain things, and vanity is an idol. Thus they become useless. Once that happens they cannot do good either, for those who have already fallen just go from bad to worse. COMMENTARY ON PAUL'S EPISTLES.[31]

PAUL'S SENSE OF PSALM 14. THEODORE OF MOPSUESTIA: Paul did not treat this passage as if it were prophetic but rather because what David said about transgressors was still a good summary of what was going on in Paul's day. Even now we still cite texts of this kind in our sermons, because what they say can be applied to our congregations. PAULINE COMMENTARY FROM THE GREEK CHURCH.[32]

3:13 The Venom of Asps

IMPURITY ON DISPLAY. ORIGEN: This comes from Psalm 5[:10]. It seems to me that Paul is using this text to describe different types of human sin. The analogy: Every grave contains the uncleanness of the dead body inside. This is why our Lord said in the Gospel that the scribes and Pharisees were whited sepulchres. On the outside they appear to be beautiful, but on the inside they are full of all sorts of uncleanness.[33] But in this passage Paul seems to be revealing something more than this about the sins of those whom he is talking about, because he says that they are an "open" grave, not one which is shut and covered up. Those who were called a closed sepulchre had enough sense of shame not to reveal their sins to the public. But these people are called an open grave because they have their uncleanness and impurity on display, and they are so accustomed

to evil that . . . whenever they open their mouth, instead of speaking the Word of God, the word of life, they open their throat and speak the word of death, the word of the devil, not from the heart but from the grave. Whenever you see a man cursing and swearing, you may be sure that he is one of this type.

"They use their tongues to deceive." "To deceive" means to say one thing and think another. I am not certain that even the justified and the elect are entirely free of this sin. Some commit it more and others less. The only one who is perfect in this respect is the one of whom it is written: "He had committed no sin, and there was no deceit in his mouth."[34] There may be someone who is careful and cautious enough to avoid major failings in this respect, but who is there who does not fall into this trap either from a sense of shame or from neglect? Occasionally things which should be done are overlooked because of forgetfulness, and in order for no blame to appear they are excused in a way which does not correspond to the facts. This is why Peter, realizing that these are all different types of deception, wrote this in his epistle: "Put away all malice and all guile and insincerity and envy and all slander. Like newborn babes, long for pure spiritual milk, that by it you may grow up to salvation."[35]

The bite of the serpent kills the body with its poison. Even a bite of a poisonous word may kill the soul by deception.[36] This may be applied both to those who surround others with slanderous remarks and of those who, by heretical teaching tainted with the poison of the devil, deceive the souls of the simple. COMMENTARY ON THE EPISTLE TO THE ROMANS.[37]

THEIR TONGUES DECEIVE. AMBROSIASTER: Already chained to evil, they wanted if possible to devour the good, so that just as a sepulchre is open to receive corpses, so their throat is open to devour the good. . . . The words of men are like

[30]PCR 79. [31]CSEL 81.1:107. [32]NTA 15:117. [33]See Mt 23:27. [34]Is 53:9. [35]1 Pet 2:1-2. [36]See Ps 140:3. [37]CER 2:72-76.

tiny mice. They speak in order to deceive, and just as poison flows from the lips of a serpent, so trickery and deceit flow from their lips. COMMENTARY ON PAUL'S EPISTLES.[38]

THE VENOM OF DECEPTION. PELAGIUS: The stench of their teaching and flattery contaminates and kills those who listen. This is why a grave is carefully sealed, so that it does not continue to breed disease among the living by its odor. They express one thing with their mouths but another with their hearts. The venom of asps is mentioned because it is supposed to be the most harmful. PELAGIUS'S COMMENTARY ON ROMANS.[39]

3:14 Curses and Bitterness

A MOUTH FULL OF CURSES. ORIGEN: Paul did not say that their lips were full of the poison of asps. For although many may be involved in sins of that kind, there are not many who are totally given over to the harm which that poison can do. On the other hand, there are many whose mouths are full of curses and bitterness. For whose mouth is so pure that he never curses? I am not speaking now of those who deserve to be cursed but of those whom God has not cursed, i.e., the just and innocent. For this vice is so prevalent and so automatic a trait of human weakness, especially with respect to those who are under or inferior to us, that many people would not even think to call it cursing. COMMENTARY ON THE EPISTLE TO THE ROMANS.[40]

HURLING BITTERNESS. AMBROSIASTER: It is clear and obvious that evil people are always throwing curses and bitterness at the good in an attempt to harm and distract them. COMMENTARY ON PAUL'S EPISTLES.[41]

MALICIOUS TALK. PELAGIUS: There is not just one kind of malicious talk. What is said out of malice is without doubt said recklessly. PELAGIUS'S COMMENTARY ON ROMANS.[42]

3:15 Swift to Shed Blood

THE FEET THAT MOVE TO UNDERMINE THE LIFE OF THE SOUL. ORIGEN: This may seem to be an infrequent crime. But we take it to include not only those who shed blood by killing the body but also those who by some deception or other separate the soul from God. . . . For if the one who separates the body from the soul which gives it life is called a murderer, how much more truly will the one who separates the soul from the true life, which is God, be called a murderer?

Feet in this passage refers to the way we live our life, as the prophet says: "My feet had almost stumbled."[43] COMMENTARY ON THE EPISTLE TO THE ROMANS.[44]

SWIFT TO MURDER THE PROPHETS. AMBROSIASTER: Scripture says this about the murder of the prophets, whom they killed without hesitation—"slow to do good but swift to murder."[45] COMMENTARY ON PAUL'S EPISTLES.[46]

PELAGIUS: Either Paul is referring to murderers or he means those who kill souls by flattery, which is why Paul said in the Acts of the Apostles: "I am innocent of the blood of all of you, for I did not shrink from declaring to you the whole counsel of God."[47] PELAGIUS'S COMMENTARY ON ROMANS.[48]

3:16 Ruin and Misery

HURRYING TO DESTRUCTION. AMBROSIASTER: Since they hastened to do evil, Paul called their path a ruinous and unhappy way. COMMENTARY ON PAUL'S EPISTLES.[49]

PELAGIUS: Souls are exhausted and made miserable by their teaching and behavior. PELAGIUS'S COMMENTARY ON ROMANS.[50]

---

[38]CSEL 81.1:107, 109. [39]PCR 79-80. [40]CER 2:76. [41]CSEL 81.1:109. [42]PCR 80. [43]Ps 73:1. [44]CER 2:76-78. [45]See Is 59:7. [46]CSEL 81.1:109. [47]Acts 20:26-27. [48]PCR 80. [49]CSEL 81.1:109. [50]PCR 80.

3:17 *The Way of Peace*

CHRIST OUR PEACE. ORIGEN: Christ is our peace.[51] Therefore the way of peace is the way of Christ, which sinners do not know. COMMENTARY ON THE EPISTLE TO THE ROMANS.[52]

PELAGIUS: Everything which resembles the teaching of God is at peace with him, but everything which is contrary to it is at odds with him. PELAGIUS'S COMMENTARY ON ROMANS.[53]

THE WAY OF HOSTILITY. AMBROSIASTER: Having chosen the way of hostility, along which they were heading toward the second death, they did not want to know about the way which leads to eternal life. This is called the way of peace, because with God as its guardian it will have no disturbance. Those who will the good have this rest with God.[54] COMMENTARY ON PAUL'S EPISTLES.[55]

3:18 *Fear of God*

WHAT OUGHT TO BE FEARED. ORIGEN: If someone is always thinking of what will please or displease God, then it can be said that the fear of God is always before his eyes. But such a person must be experienced and diligently instructed in the law of God so as not to be afraid when there is no reason to fear. For the fear of God must always be placed before our eyes: not the eyes of the flesh—for it is not something visible or corporeal that we are talking about here—but the eyes of the mind, to which an understanding and awareness of the fear of God are evident and by which, as we have said above, we can discover what ought and ought not to be feared. The one who fears God does not fear the powers of this world. COMMENTARY ON THE EPISTLE TO THE ROMANS.[56]

NO FEAR OF GOD. AMBROSIASTER: Since people of this kind have no sense, they have no fear of God. For "the fear of God is the beginning of wisdom," says Solomon.[57] But Scripture did not say that they did not have the fear of God. It said: "There is no fear of God before their eyes." For seeing how evil their works were and not being horrified by them, they are said not to have the fear of God before their eyes. COMMENTARY ON PAUL'S EPISTLES.[58]

PELAGIUS: Paul concludes with the fear of God, because if the people had always kept that before their eyes they would not have transgressed, for a servant will not dare sin when his master is present. PELAGIUS'S COMMENTARY ON ROMANS.[59]

3:19 *The World Held Accountable to God*

THE WHOLE WORLD. ORIGEN: Here we must consider carefully what this law is that speaks to those who are under the law. By what it says to them it deprives them of every excuse, so that they can find no hiding place for their sins. It is this which stops every mouth and makes the whole world accountable to God. Now if we want to take this as referring to the law of Moses, which without doubt spoke only to those who had been circumcised from their mother's womb and had learned what the law was, how is it possible that by that law, which applies to only one nation, every mouth should be stopped and the whole world should be held accountable to God? What have the other nations to do with that law, and why does it affect the entire world? And how is it that a knowledge of sin is said to have originated with the law of Moses, when there were many before his time who were well aware of their sins?

From this it appears that the apostle Paul is not speaking here about the law of Moses but about the natural law which is written on the hearts of men. . . . This natural law speaks to all men who are under that law with the sole excep-

---

[51]See Rom 5:1. [52]CER 2:78. [53]PCR 80. [54]See Jer 6:16; Lk 1:78-79; Rom 8:6. [55]CSEL 81.1:109. [56]CER 2:80. [57]Prov 1:7. [58]CSEL 81.1:111. [59]PCR 80.

tion, it seems to me, of those children who are not yet able to distinguish good from evil. . . .

When Paul says "the whole world" he is not talking about trees and rocks and so on but about the rational animal, i.e., the human being. Anything which is not rational is excluded from consideration in this context. COMMENTARY ON THE EPISTLE TO THE ROMANS.[60]

BOUND IN SIN. AMBROSIASTER: It is clear that the law censures those who did not believe first of all their leader Moses nor their ancestors the prophets, whom they killed, nor the apostles who were their kinsmen according to the flesh, whose blood they spilled. They were always ungodly and rebellious against God, so as to be condemned by the law whose authority they thought should be despised.

Paul says this because with the Jews bound in sin the whole world has become subject to God. For there is no doubt that the pagans were immersed in sins and wickedness and that for that reason the whole world bowed before God in order to obtain forgiveness. The "whole world" means Jews and Gentiles, from whom believers are set apart. Therefore when Paul affirms that the Jews, who had received God's law and to whom the promise had been given, were bound in sin, there is no doubt that all the Gentiles were guilty of death . . . for all have been found guilty and need the mercy of God, whether they be Jews or Gentiles. COMMENTARY ON PAUL'S EPISTLES.[61]

EVERY MOUTH STOPPED. CHRYSOSTOM: Note that Paul was in the habit of referring to the entire Old Testament as "the law" . . . for here he calls a psalm "the law."

When he talks about every mouth being stopped, he does not mean that the purpose of their sinning was to shut them up but that the reason they were rebuked was that they might not sin in ignorance. Furthermore, it was not just the Jews[62] he was referring to but the whole of mankind. HOMILIES ON ROMANS 7.[63]

THE NATURAL LAW. [PSEUDO-]CONSTANTIUS: Paul is talking about the natural law here. THE HOLY LETTER OF ST. PAUL TO THE ROMANS.[64]

UNDER THE LAW. PELAGIUS: In case the Jews might claim that these verses of the psalm were spoken about the Gentiles, Paul indicates that what has been said in the law has been said to those who are under the law. Of course, it is a question as to who is meant by saying that the fool claims that there is no God. The Jews did not say this in words[65] but in deeds, for they claimed to know God but denied it by their behavior. Paul is not talking to the Gentiles here, because he has already made similar statements about them.[66] PELAGIUS'S COMMENTARY ON ROMANS.[67]

3:20 Knowledge of Sin Comes Through the Law

THE LAW REVEALS SIN. CLEMENT OF ALEXANDRIA: The law did not create sin; it revealed it. STROMATA 2.7.34.4.[68]

THE LAW AS GOOD MEDICINE. ORIGEN: Let us see in what way knowledge of sin comes through the law. It comes insofar as we learn through the law what to do and what not to do, what is sin and what is not sin. It is not, as the heretics claim, that God's law is a bad root or a bad tree through which a knowledge of sin comes. Rather the law is like a medicine through which we perceive the true nature of our disease. . . . The medicine itself is good, not least because it enables us to isolate the disease and seek to cure it. COMMENTARY ON THE EPISTLE TO THE ROMANS.[69]

ALL FLESH. AMBROSIASTER: Paul never says that they will not be justified before God because they

---

[60]CER 2:82-90. [61]CSEL 81.1:111, 113. [62]Judaizers in the Pauline environment. There is no implication that the reference is to all Jews of all times. [63]NPNF 1 11:375-76. [64]ENPK 2:32. [65]See Ps 14:1. [66]Cf. 2:12-16 above. [67]CR 80. [68]FC 85:181. [69]CER 2:94.

have not kept the law of righteousness in the commandments but because they have refused to believe the sacrament of the mystery of God, which is in Christ. For God has declared that they should be justified by Christ and not by the law, which may justify for a time, but not before God. Therefore those who keep the law are justified in time, not before God, because faith, by which they are justified before God, is not in them. For faith is greater than the law. The law pertains to us but faith pertains to God. The law has a temporary righteousness, but faith has an eternal one. When Paul says "all flesh" he means every human being . . . but when he says "in the flesh" he means those who are bound by sin. For just as righteousness makes them spiritual, so also sins make them carnal, and they take the name from the deed.

By faith the law is abolished, and faith then follows. What then is this law through which he says that sin is made known? Made known how? It is evident that long before Moses the patriarchs were not ignorant of sin. Joseph was thrown into prison, albeit by the wickedness of others, and both the butler and the baker of Pharaoh were in prison because of their sins.[70] In what way then did sin lie dormant?

In fact, the law has three aspects to it. The first concerns the mystery of God's divinity. The second is what is fitting according to natural law, which forbids sin. And the third is the deeds of the law, e. g., sabbaths, new moons, circumcision, etc. Here Paul refers to the natural law which was partly reformed and partly confirmed by Moses, which made sin known to all who were bound in wickedness. . . . The law shows the coming judgment of God and that no sinner will escape punishment, in case someone who has escaped for a time thinks that the law is an illusion. This is what the law shows: that sin will be dealt with by God. Commentary on Paul's Epistles.[71]

The Law Discloses Sin. Chrysostom: Once more Paul jumps on the law but this time with restraint, for what he says is an accusation not against the law but against the negligence of the covenant people. . . . The law accomplished its task of disclosing sin to them, but then it was their duty to flee it. But since they did not flee it, they brought an even greater punishment on themselves, and the good deeds of the law have just provided an excuse for greater chastisement from God. Homilies on Romans 7.[72]

The Law Itself Does Not Forgive. [Pseudo-]Constantius: The apostle is not contradicting what he said [in 2:15] above ("They show the work of the law in their hearts") when he says: "no human being will be justified . . . by works of the law." He attacks the flesh, whose wisdom cannot submit to the law of God. For the law was able to reveal sin, but it does not reveal its full horror. Then too, the law is bound to punish and does not forgive the repentant sinner. But Christ grants remission of sins to believers and teaches how the vices and the wisdom of the flesh can be eradicated. The Holy Letter of St. Paul to the Romans.[73]

Four Stages of Relation to the Law: Before the Law, Under the Law, Under Grace and at Rest. Augustine: Some think that statements like this are an attack on the law. But they must be read very carefully, so that neither is the law condemned by the apostle nor is free will taken away from man. Therefore, let us distinguish the following four states of human existence: before the law, under the law, under grace and at rest. Before the law we follow the lust of the flesh. Under the law we are dragged along by it. Under grace we neither follow it nor are dragged along by it. At rest[74] there is no lust of the flesh.

Prior to being addressed by the law, we do not struggle, because not only do we lust and sin, we even approve of sinning.

Under the law we struggle but are defeated.

---

[70]See Gen 39:1—40:23. [71]CSEL 81.1:113, 115, 117. [72]NPNF 1 11:375-76. [73]ENPK 2:32. [74]In glory, after the resurrection.

We admit that what we do is evil and that we do not want to do it, but because there is as yet no grace, we are defeated. In this state we discover how far down we lie, and when we want to rise up and yet we fall, we are all the more gravely afflicted. The law is good because it forbids what ought to be forbidden and requires what ought to be required. But when anyone thinks he can fulfill the law in his own strength and not through the grace of his Deliverer, this presumption does him no good but rather harms him so much that he is seized by an even stronger desire to sin and by his sins ends up as a transgressor. So when the man who has fallen realizes that he cannot raise himself, let him cry to his Deliverer for help.

Then comes grace, which can pardon previous sins, give aid to the struggling, supplement justice with love and take away fear. When this takes place, although fleshly desires continue to fight against our spirit in this life and try to lead us into sin, yet our spirit does not give in to these desires because it is rooted in the grace and love of God and ceases to sin. For we do not sin by having these perverse desires but by giving in to them.

These desires arise from the mortality of the flesh, which we inherit from the first sin of the first man, which is why we are born carnal. Nor will they cease until, by the resurrection of the body, we shall obtain the transformation which has been promised to us. Then we shall be in the fourth state, where there is perfect peace. Perfect peace is the state in which nothing will resist us

because we do not resist God. Free will existed perfectly in the first man, but in us, prior to grace, there is no free will which would enable us not to sin but only enough that we do not want to sin. But grace makes it possible not only for us to want to do what is right but actually to do it not in our own strength but by the help of our Deliverer, who at the resurrection will give us that perfect peace which is the consequence of good will. Augustine on Romans 13-18.[75]

RECOGNITION OF SIN. PELAGIUS: By the works of the law Paul means circumcision, the sabbath and the other ceremonies, which had less to do with righteousness than with carnal pleasure. Through the law comes neither forgiveness nor sin itself but rather recognition of sin. Through the law a man realizes what sin is, either because the natural law had been forgotten or because before the written law was given, the lesser sins [i.e., the sins which were more harmful to oneself than others, like lust, drunkenness, etc.] were not recognized as sins. PELAGIUS'S COMMENTARY ON ROMANS.[76]

KNOWLEDGE OF SIN. GENNADIUS OF CONSTANTINOPLE: The purpose of the law, says Paul, is to give us a knowledge of sin not only to forbid the doing of things which are inappropriate but also to punish those who do such things. PAULINE COMMENTARY FROM THE GREEK CHURCH.[77]

---

[75]AOR 5, 7. [76]PCR 81. [77]NTA 15:361.

3:21-31 RIGHTEOUSNESS THROUGH FAITH

[21]*But now the righteousness of God has been manifested apart from law, although the law and the prophets bear witness to it, [22]the righteousness of God through faith in Jesus Christ for all who believe. For there is no distinction; [23]since all have sinned and fall short of the glory of God, [24]they*

are justified by his grace as a gift, through the redemption which is in Christ Jesus, [25]whom God put forward as an expiation by his blood, to be received by faith. This was to show God's righteousness, because in his divine forbearance he had passed over former sins; [26]it was to prove at the present time that he himself is righteous and that he justifies him who has faith in Jesus.

[27]Then what becomes of our boasting? It is excluded. On what principle? On the principle of works? No, but on the principle of faith. [28]For we hold that a man is justified by faith apart from works of law. [29]Or is God the God of Jews only? Is he not the God of Gentiles also? Yes, of Gentiles also, [30]since God is one; and he will justify the circumcised on the ground of their faith and the uncircumcised through their faith. [31]Do we then overthrow the law by this faith? By no means! On the contrary, we uphold the law.

OVERVIEW: In Christ the righteousness of God was made manifest apart from the law. But the Fathers did not agree about the precise meaning of this. Did God reveal himself apart from the natural law or apart from the law of Moses? It seems from the context that the law of Moses is meant, but this forced Origen, for example, to enter into a long explanation as to why this verse does not contradict what he had already said about the natural law. Others gave differing interpretations of what was meant by the righteousness of God. Was it God's mercy, as Ambrosiaster claimed, or was it the new life God gives us in Christ and not a divine attribute as such, as Augustine claimed? This debate still goes on in the church.

Sin is universal and embraces even the saints. Christ has bought us back from sin and the devil and given us justification as a free gift. Christ was sacrificed for us in order to pay the price for our sins by his blood. In this way he fulfilled the Old Testament law and made it redundant. The result of Christ's sacrifice is that now we can receive the righteousness of God, dispensed freely to all who believe in him.

No human being can claim the credit for his or her salvation, because that is a free gift of God's grace. We are justified only by faith, not by works, however good they may be. The principle of justification by faith alone removes any distinction between Jews and Gentiles, since everyone must come to Christ in the same way—by faith. Justification by faith in Christ abolishes the law

but does not discredit it. On the contrary, it fulfills what the law was trying to demonstrate but could not achieve by itself.

3:21 Witness from the Law and the Prophets

NATURAL LAW OR MOSAIC LAW? ORIGEN: We have just said that in the above verses Paul was speaking about the natural law and not about the law of Moses, but now it appears that there can be no doubt that he is referring to the law of Moses, by which the righteousness of God is made manifest through faith in Christ Jesus in all who believe, whether they are Jews or Gentiles, and who are justified not by works but by the grace of God, who has redeemed them in Jesus Christ. Does this mean that our interpretation of the foregoing was mistaken? ...

Just as there is nothing in this verse which makes it possible for us to argue that it is talking about the natural law and not about the law of Moses, so there is nothing in the preceding verses to indicate that they are talking about the law of Moses and not about the natural law. Thus we would argue that just as the foregoing cannot be used to interpret what we now have before us, so neither should our interpretation of it be altered simply because what follows cannot be read in the same way.

Does this mean that the apostle has contradicted himself? There are plenty of people who would like to think so! ... But we shall try to show how this passage does not go against our interpretation of the foregoing one. We have often said, and have expounded this most clearly in the preface, that the apostle mentions many different kinds of law in this epistle, and only the most attentive reader will be able to detect when he is shifting from one to another. . . . The law of nature was able to explain the nature of sin and give us some knowledge of it, but the righteousness of God is above and beyond this, and the human mind is unable to attain it by its natural senses. . . . For this the law of Moses was required, to teach us what God's righteousness is. Do not be surprised that the word *law* is used here in two different senses! . . .

Moreover, there is a way to tell which meaning of the word *law* is intended. The Greek language uses articles in front of proper names. Thus when the law of Moses is intended, the article is used, but when the natural law is meant, the article is omitted. COMMENTARY ON THE EPISTLE TO THE ROMANS.[1]

MADE PERFECT BY THE RIGHTEOUSNESS THAT COMES FROM GOD. APOLLINARIS OF LAODICEA: [The righteousness of God] has not been manifested in opposition to the law but as an increase of good and as the free gift of God, so that we may no longer be judged according to human righteousness, which is always under judgment, but that we may be made perfect by the righteousness which comes from God. For this is the righteousness which comes by faith in Christ to all who believe and which dwells in them all. PAULINE COMMENTARY FROM THE GREEK CHURCH.[2]

THE RIGHTEOUSNESS OF GOD. AMBROSIASTER: It is clear that the righteousness of God has now appeared apart from the law, but this means apart from the law of the sabbath, the circumcision, the new moon and revenge, not apart from the sacrament of God's divinity, because the righteousness of God is all about God's divinity. For when the law held them guilty, the righteous-

ness of God forgave them and did so apart from the law so that until the law was brought to bear God forgave them their sin. And lest someone think that this was done against the law, Paul added that the righteousness of God had a witness in the Law and the Prophets, which means that the law itself had said that in the future someone would come who would save mankind. But it was not allowed for the law to forgive sin.

Therefore, what is called the righteousness of God appears to be mercy because it has its origin in the promise, and when God's promise is fulfilled it is called "the righteousness of God." For it is righteousness when what is promised has been delivered. And when God accepts those who flee to him for refuge, this is called *righteousness*, because wickedness would not accept such people. COMMENTARY ON PAUL'S EPISTLES.[3]

RIGHTEOUSNESS MANIFESTED. CHRYSOSTOM: Paul does not say that the righteousness of God has been "given" but that it has been "manifested," thus destroying the accusation that it is something new. For what is manifested is old but previously concealed. He reinforces this point by going on to mention that the Law and the Prophets had foretold it. HOMILIES ON ROMANS 7.[4]

THE TESTIMONY OF LAW AND PROPHETS. [PSEUDO-]CONSTANTIUS: What he means is that although the righteousness which was to be revealed in Christ was not known in the natural law, it was foretold by the testimony of the law of Moses and by the preaching of the prophets. THE HOLY LETTER OF ST. PAUL TO THE ROMANS.[5]

THAT RIGHTEOUSNESS BY WHICH SINNERS ARE CLOTHED. AUGUSTINE: The righteousness of God is not that by which God is righteous but that with which he clothes man when he justifies the ungodly. To this the Law and the Prophets bear witness. . . . The righteousness of God is not

[1]CER 2:96-104. [2]NTA 15:61. [3]CSEL 81.1:117. [4]NPNF 1 11:376-77. [5]ENPK 2:33.

manifested outside the law, since in that case it could not have been witnessed to in the law. It is a righteousness of God apart from the law because God confers it on the believer through the Spirit of grace without the help of the law. THE SPIRIT AND THE LETTER 15.9.[6]

THE RECOGNITION OF SIN. PELAGIUS: The righteousness which has been given to us freely by God, not acquired by our effort, has been made plain without the written law, and having been hidden in the law has been revealed with greater clarity by the examples of Christ, which are more obvious. The law and the prophets foretold that this righteousness would come in the last times, or perhaps this means that they both bore witness to the recognition of sin. PELAGIUS'S COMMENTARY ON ROMANS.[7]

3:22 The Righteousness of God Through Faith

RIGHTEOUSNESS THROUGH FAITH. AMBROSIASTER: What else comes through faith in Jesus Christ except the righteousness of God which is the revelation of Christ? For it is by faith in the revelation of Jesus Christ that the gift long ago promised by God is acknowledged and received. COMMENTARY ON PAUL'S EPISTLES.[8]

OUR FAITH. CHRYSOSTOM: In order to stop anyone from asking: "How can we be saved without contributing anything at all to our salvation?" Paul shows that in fact we do contribute a great deal toward it—we supply our faith! HOMILIES ON ROMANS 7.[9]

SALVATION IN THE GOSPEL. AUGUSTINE: How could Paul have promised glory, honor and peace to the good works of Gentiles apart from the grace of the gospel? Because there otherwise is no acceptance of persons with God. And because it is not the hearers but the doers of the law who are justified, he argues that all, whether Jew or Gentile, shall alike have salvation in the gospel. THE

SPIRIT AND THE LETTER 44.[10]

IN FAITH, NO DISTINCTION BETWEEN JEW AND GENTILE. PELAGIUS: This refers to the faith by which one believes in Jesus Christ. In this there is no distinction between Jew and Gentile. PELAGIUS'S COMMENTARY ON ROMANS.[11]

FOR ALL WHO BELIEVE. GENNADIUS OF CONSTANTINOPLE: Paul says "for all" meaning first the Jews, in that it was from among them that salvation first arose, and then the Gentiles, in that from the Jews grace had abounded even to them so that now both share in it together. This grace is not given in general but only to those "who believe," but it is common to all these without distinction. PAULINE COMMENTARY FROM THE GREEK CHURCH.[12]

3:23 All Have Sinned

A PROPER FEAR. IRENAEUS: We ought not to be puffed up or severe on those of ancient times, but ought ourselves to fear, lest after we have come to the knowledge of Christ we obtain no further forgiveness of sins. If later we do things displeasing to God, we are shut out of his kingdom. AGAINST HERESIES 4.27.2.[13]

NATURE AND THE LAW HAVE FAILED. SEVERIAN: Paul shows that nature has failed the Gentiles and that both nature and the law have failed the Jews, before going on to mention the grace of the gospel and saying: "What do we have by grace which is special and superior? Faith, made effective by the righteousness of Christ." . . . Paul does not say that all have broken the law but that all have sinned in a general sense. Now the one who is lacking something tries to make up his deficiency. The Jews had the law, but they were lacking the fullness of grace. PAULINE COMMENTARY FROM THE GREEK CHURCH.[14]

---

[6]LCC 8:205. [7]PCR 81. [8]CSEL 81.1:119. [9]NPNF 1 11:377. [10]LCC 8:228. [11]PCR 81. [12]NTA 15:362. [13]ANF 1:499. [14]NTA 15:216-17.

ALL INCLUDES SAINTS. AMBROSIASTER: This includes both Jews and Greeks. For *all* here includes even the saints in order to show that nobody can keep the law without faith. For the law was given in such a way that faith was also embedded in it. This faith looked toward a future salvation. Thus the death of Christ benefits everyone, because it has here in this world taught what is to be believed and observed, and in the future it will deliver everyone from hell. COMMENTARY ON PAUL'S EPISTLES.[15]

NOT TO ELICIT DESPAIR. CHRYSOSTOM: There is no difference at all between the Greek, the Scythian, the Thracian or even the Jew, for all are in the same plight. . . . Even if you have not done the same sins as others, you have still been deprived of God's glory just as they have been, because you are among those who have offended. . . . However, Paul was saying this not to cast them into despair but rather to show the love of the Lord toward man, as he goes on to say [in the following verses]. HOMILIES ON ROMANS 7.[16]

THE GLORY OF GOD. PELAGIUS: All sinners need the glory of God because they do not have their own. PELAGIUS'S COMMENTARY ON ROMANS.[17]

3:24 Redemption in Christ

THE RANSOM OF CAPTIVES. ORIGEN: *Redemption* is the word used for what is given to enemies in order to ransom captives and restore them to their liberty. Therefore human beings were held in captivity by their enemies until the coming of the Son of God, who became for us not only the wisdom of God, and righteousness and sanctification,[18] but also redemption. He gave himself as our redemption, that is, he surrendered himself to our enemies and poured out his blood on those who were thirsting for it. In this way redemption was obtained for believers. COMMENTARY ON THE EPISTLE TO THE ROMANS.[19]

THE DEVIL LOST ALL WHOM HE HAD HELD CAPTIVE. AMBROSIASTER: They are justified freely because they have not done anything nor given anything in return, but by faith alone they have been made holy by the gift of God. Paul testifies that the grace of God is in Christ, because we have been redeemed by Christ according to the will of God so that once set free we may be justified, as he says to the Galatians: "Christ redeemed us by offering himself for us."[20] For he achieved this despite the fierce attacks of the devil, who was outwitted. For the devil received Christ (in hell) thinking that he could hold him there, but because he could not withstand his power he lost not only Christ but all those whom he held at the same time. COMMENTARY ON PAUL'S EPISTLES.[21]

BUYING US BACK. PELAGIUS: We have been justified without the works of the law, through baptism. In this way God has freely forgiven our sins even though we are undeserving. Christ has redeemed us with the blood of his death. . . . For we were all condemned to death, to which Christ handed himself over, though he had no need to, in order to redeem us by his blood. . . . Note also that Christ did not merely buy us but bought us "back," because we were once his by nature, even though we were separated from him by our sins. If we stop sinning, our redemption will indeed be profitable for us. PELAGIUS'S COMMENTARY ON ROMANS.[22]

THE GLORY OF GOD. PROSPER OF AQUITAINE: Grace is the glory of God, not the merit of him who has been freed. GRACE AND FREE WILL 10.2.[23]

3:25 Jesus Christ Is Our Expiation

AN EXPIATION BY CHRIST'S BLOOD. ORIGEN: Although the holy apostle teaches many wonder-

---

[15]CSEL 81.1:119. [16]NPNF 1 11:377. [17]PCR 81. [18]See 1 Cor 1:30. [19]CER 2:110. [20]Gal 3:13. [21]CSEL 81.1:119, 21. [22]PCR 81-82. [23]FC 7:373.

ful things about our Lord Jesus Christ which are said mysteriously about him, in this passage he has given special prominence to something which, I think, is not readily found in other parts of Scripture. For having just said that Christ gave himself as a redemption for the entire human race so that he might ransom those who were held captive by sin . . . now he adds something even more sublime, saying that God put him forward "as an expiation by his blood, to be received by faith." This means that by the sacrifice of Christ's body God has made expiation on behalf of men and by this has shown his righteousness, in that he forgave their previous sins, which they had committed in the service of the worst possible tyrants. God endured this and allowed these things to happen. COMMENTARY ON THE EPISTLE TO THE ROMANS.[24]

NULLIFYING THE SENTENCE. AMBROSIASTER: Paul says this, because in Christ God put forward, i.e., appointed, himself as a future expiation for the human race if they believed. This expiation was by his blood. We have been set free by his death so that God might reveal him and condemn death by his passion. This was in order to make his promise clear, by which he set us free from sin as he had promised before. And when he fulfilled this promise he showed himself to be righteous.

God knew the purpose of his lovingkindness, by which he determined to come to the rescue of sinners, both those living on earth and those who were held bound in hell. He waited a very long time for both. He nullified the sentence by which it seemed just that everyone should be condemned in order to show us that long ago he had decided to liberate the human race, as he promised through Jeremiah the prophet, saying: "I will forgive their iniquity and I will remember their sin no more."[25] And in case it might be thought that this promise was for the Jews only, he said through Isaiah: "My house will be called a house of prayer for all peoples."[26]

For although the promise was made to the Jews, God knew in advance that the ungodly Jews would reject his gift. Therefore he promised that he would allow the Gentiles to share in his grace. In view of this the ungodly negligence of the Jews was thwarted. COMMENTARY ON PAUL'S EPISTLES.[27]

SANCTIFYING ONE'S SOUL. GREGORY OF NYSSA: Christ, being an "expiation by his blood," teaches each one thinking of this to become himself a propitiation, sanctifying his soul by the mortification of his members. ON PERFECTION.[28]

DECLARING GOD'S RICHES. CHRYSOSTOM: Paul calls the redemption an expiation to show that, if the Old Testament type had such power, much more did its New Testament counterpart have it. . . . What does it mean "to show God's righteousness"? It is like declaring his riches not only for him to be rich himself but also to make others rich. . . . Do not doubt, for righteousness is not of works but of faith. HOMILIES ON ROMANS 7.[29]

FOR ALL WHO BELIEVE. PELAGIUS: God has set forth Christ in public so that anyone who wants to be redeemed may draw near to him. Christ performs the work of expiation for all who believe that they need to be set free by his blood. Christ died for our former sins in order to reverse God's judgment, by which he had finally determined to punish us for them. PELAGIUS'S COMMENTARY ON ROMANS.[30]

BOTH PRIEST AND LAMB. THEODORET OF CYR: The mercy seat was gold-plated and placed on top of the ark. On each side was the figure of a cherub.[31] When the high priest approached it, the holy kindness of God was revealed.[32]

The apostle teaches us that Christ is the true mercy seat, of which the one in the Old Testament

---

[24]CER 2:112. [25]Jer 31:34. [26]Is 56:7. [27]CSEL 81.1:121,123. [28]FC 58:105. [29]NPNF 1 11:378. [30]PCR 82. [31]See Ex 25:17-21. [32]See Ex 25:22; 30:6.

was but a type. The name applies to Christ in his humanity, not in his divinity. For as God Christ responded to the expiation made at the mercy seat. It is as man that he receives this label, just as elsewhere he is called a sheep, a lamb, sin and a curse.

Furthermore, the ancient mercy seat was bloodless because it was inanimate. It could only receive the drops of blood pouring from the sacrificial victims. But the Lord Christ is both God and the mercy seat, both the priest and the lamb, and he performed the work of our salvation by his blood, demanding only faith from us.[33] INTERPRETATION OF THE LETTER TO THE ROMANS.[34]

3:26 Justified by Faith in Jesus

AT THIS PRESENT TIME. ORIGEN: God allowed all this so that afterward, that is to say in our time, he might show forth his righteousness. For at the end of the age, in the most recent times, God has manifested his righteousness and given Christ to be our redemption. He has made him our propitiator. If he had sent him as the propitiator at some earlier time, there would have been fewer people whose sins needed propitiating than there are now. For God is just, and therefore he could not justify the unjust. Therefore he required the intervention of a propitiator, so that by having faith in him those who could not be justified by their own works might be justified. These are the presuppositions on which the apostle's exposition here is based.

Paul was right to add "at the present time," because at the moment God's righteousness is revealed for our justification. But when the day of judgment comes, it will be revealed for retribution. COMMENTARY ON THE EPISTLE TO THE ROMANS.[35]

HE JUSTIFIES THOSE WHO HAVE FAITH. AMBROSIASTER: The present time means our time, in which God has given what long before he had promised to give at the time at which he gave it. Paul has rightly said that God gave what he promised in order to be revealed as righteous. For

he had promised that he would justify those who believe in Christ, as he says in Habakkuk: "The righteous will live by faith in me."[36] Whoever has faith in God and Christ is righteous. COMMENTARY ON PAUL'S EPISTLES.[37]

BELIEVERS FOUND RIGHTEOUS. PELAGIUS: Paul wants to show that God had waited for sinners to reform themselves but that they had abused his patience and gone on to greater sins. The believer in Jesus is the only one who has been found righteous, and God has justified him not by works but by faith. PELAGIUS'S COMMENTARY ON ROMANS.[38]

3:27 Faith Excludes Boasting

BOASTING EXCLUDED. AMBROSIASTER: Paul tells those who live under the law that they have no reason to boast basing themselves on the law and claiming to be of the race of Abraham, seeing that no one is justified before God except by faith. COMMENTARY ON PAUL'S EPISTLES.[39]

THE PRINCIPLE OF FAITH. CHRYSOSTOM: Paul is at great pains to show that faith is powerful to a degree which no one ever imagined the law could be. For after saying that God justifies man by faith, he takes up the question of the law again. He does not say: "Where are the good works of the Jews?" but: "Where is their boasting?" Thus he takes every opportunity to demonstrate that it was all talk and that they had no deeds to back them up.

What is "the principle of faith"? This is salvation by grace. Here Paul shows God's power in that he has not only saved, he has also justified and led them to boast in a different way—not relying on works but glorying only in their faith. In saying this Paul is trying to get believing Jews to behave with moderation and to reassure unbelieving Jews so that they might be persuaded to accept his point

---

[33]See Heb 9:1-28. [34]IER, Migne PG 82 ad loc. [35]CER 2:112, 130. [36]Heb 2:4. [37]CSEL 81.1:123. [38]PCR 82. [39]CSEL 81.1:123.

of view. For if the one who has been saved is proud because he abides by the law, he will be told that he has stopped his own mouth, that he has accused himself, that he has renounced any claim to salvation and that he has excluded boasting. But the unbeliever may be humbled by these same means and brought to accept the faith. See how great faith is, in that it has removed us from the former things and does not even allow us to boast of them! HOMILIES ON ROMANS 7.[40]

THE LAW OF FAITH. THEODORE OF MOPSUESTIA: Now you say to me (says Paul), What new law has thrown the old one out? For when the ruler adds to the law, the law is changed. Paul answers: When the law of works came in it did not abolish the former law—on the contrary, it actually contained the former law. But when the law of faith appeared it did abolish the earlier law, having overcome the boasting which came from the law of works. These things have been given to us by the grace of God, which our forefathers, however hard they may have tried, were unable to obtain. PAULINE COMMENTARY FROM THE GREEK CHURCH.[41]

AN IMAGINARY DIALOGUE. [PSEUDO-]CONSTANTIUS: This verse is written in the form of an imaginary dialogue with a Jew. The Jew asks the questions and Paul gives the answers. THE HOLY LETTER OF ST. PAUL TO THE ROMANS.[42]

PELAGIUS: This is addressed to the Jew. The principle of faith is . . . the New Testament, which is God's appointed object of faith. PELAGIUS'S COMMENTARY ON ROMANS.[43]

JUSTIFIED BY MERCY AND GRACE. CYRIL OF ALEXANDRIA: For who will glory, or for what, when everyone has become worthless and gone out of the right way, and nobody does good works anymore? Therefore he says that all glorying is excluded. . . . How? We have acquired the forgiveness of our former sins and have been justified freely by the mercy and grace of Christ.[44]

COMMENTARY ON ROMANS.[45]

A NEW COVENANT. THEODORET OF CYR: By "boasting" Paul means the proud spirits of the Jews and their excessive arrogance. For they thought they were the only ones who enjoyed God's providence. But after the divine grace appeared and spread to all nations, the boasting of the Jews ceased. . . . Paul calls faith a law, recalling the words of the prophet Jeremiah: "Behold, the days are coming, says the Lord, when I will make a new covenant with the House of Israel and the House of Judah, not like the covenant which I made with their fathers."[46] INTERPRETATION OF THE LETTER TO THE ROMANS.[47]

3:28 Faith, Not Works of Law

THE THIEF ON THE CROSS AS JUSTIFIED BY FAITH. ORIGEN: It remains for us who are trying to affirm everything the apostle says, and to do so in the proper order, to inquire who is justified by faith alone, apart from works. If an example is required, I think it must suffice to mention the thief on the cross, who asked Christ to save him and was told: "Truly, this day you will be with me in paradise."[48] . . . A man is justified by faith. The works of the law can make no contribution to this. Where there is no faith which might justify the believer, even if there are works of the law these are not based on the foundation of faith. Even if they are good in themselves they cannot justify the one who does them, because faith is lacking, and faith is the mark of those who are justified by God. COMMENTARY ON THE EPISTLE TO THE ROMANS.[49]

WITHOUT WORKS OF THE LAW. AMBROSIASTER: Paul says that a Gentile can be sure that he is justified by faith without doing the works of the law, e. g., circumcision or new moons or the

---

[40]NPNF 1 11:378-79. [41]NTA 15:117. [42]ENPK 2:34. [43]PCR 83. [44]See Rom 3:24; Gal 2:16-21. [45]Migne PG 74 col. 780. [46]Jer 31:31-32. [47]IER, Migne PG 82 col. 85. [48]Lk 23:43. [49]CER 2:132, 134-36.

veneration of the sabbath. COMMENTARY ON PAUL'S EPISTLES.[50]

THE DOORS OF FAITH OPEN TO THE WORLD. CHRYSOSTOM: Paul does not say a "Jew" or "one under the law" but widens the discussion and opens the doors of faith to the world, saying a "man," i.e., the name common to our race. HOMILIES ON ROMANS 7.[51]

APART FROM WORKS OF THE LAW. THEODORE OF MOPSUESTIA: Paul did not say "we hold" because he was himself uncertain. He said it in order to counter those who concluded from this that anyone who wished to could be justified simply by willing faith. Note carefully that Paul does not say simply "without the law," as if we could just perform virtue by wanting to, nor do we do the works of the law by force. We do them because we have been led to do them by Christ. PAULINE COMMENTARY FROM THE GREEK CHURCH.[52]

[PSEUDO-]CONSTANTIUS: Paul says this because we cannot be justified by the works of the law but only by faith. THE HOLY LETTER OF ST. PAUL TO THE ROMANS.[53]

AUGUSTINE: This must not be understood in such a way as to say that a man who has received faith and continues to live is righteous, even though he leads a wicked life. QUESTIONS 76.1.[54]

FAITH WITHOUT WORKS? PELAGIUS: Some people misinterpret this verse in order to do away with the works of righteousness, saying that faith by itself is enough, even though Paul says elsewhere: "If I have all faith, so as to remove mountains, but have not love, I am nothing."[55] If this seems to contradict the sense of the other [verses], what works did the apostle mean when he said that a man is justified by faith, without works? Obviously, these are the works of circumcision, the sabbath and so on, and not the works of righteousness about which St. James says: "Faith without works is dead."[56] [In this verse]

Paul is speaking about the man who comes to Christ and is saved when he first believes by faith alone. But by adding the works of the law Paul is saying that there are also works of grace which believers ought to perform. PELAGIUS'S COMMENTARY ON ROMANS.[57]

3:29 God of Jews and Gentiles

FATHER OF THOSE WHO KNOW HIM. CLEMENT OF ALEXANDRIA: One righteous person is no different from another righteous person, whether Jew or Greek. For God is not only the Lord of the Jews but of all humanity. He is the Father of all who know him. To live well and according to the law is to live. To live rationally according to reason is to live. Those who lived rightly before the law were classed under faith and judged to be righteous. Those who were outside the law, having lived rightly, on hearing the voice of the Lord . . . may turn and believe with all speed. STROMATA 6.6.[58]

ONE FLOCK OF GOD. TERTULLIAN: Is not all humankind one flock of God? Is not the same God both Lord and Shepherd of all nations?[59] ON MODESTY.[60]

GOD OF LAW AND GOSPEL. ORIGEN: Here Paul gives a short sharp answer to those who would say that there is one God for the Jews and another for the Gentiles, i.e., one God of the law and another of the gospel. COMMENTARY ON THE EPISTLE TO THE ROMANS.[61]

THE GOD OF THE GENTILES. AMBROSIASTER: Undoubtedly there is only one God for everybody. For even the Jews cannot claim that their God is not the God of the Gentiles also, because they believe that the origin of all people is from

---

[50]CSEL 81.1:123. [51]NPNF 1 11:379. [52]NTA 15:117. [53]ENPK 2:34. [54]FC 70:195. [55]1 Cor 13:2. [56]Jas 2:26. [57]PCR 83. [58]ANF 2:491. [59]See Ps 67:1-7; Mic 4:1-3; Rom 16:26; Tob 13:11; 14:7. [60]ANF 4:80. [61]CER 2:140.

the one Adam and that no one who comes willingly to the law may be prevented from accepting it. Some Gentiles actually went with the Israelites into the desert of Egypt, and the Israelites were ordered to accept them as long as they agreed to be circumcised and eat unleavened bread, or the Passover, together with the rest of them.[62] Then again Cornelius, a Gentile who was not judaized, received the gift of God, and it is clear from holy Scripture that he was justified.[63] COMMENTARY ON PAUL'S EPISTLES.[64]

GOD OF ALL. CHRYSOSTOM: Paul shows that the Jews, by trying to put the Gentiles in their place, were insulting God's glory by not allowing him to be the God of all. But if God is God of all, then he takes care of all, and if he takes care of all, then he saves all alike by faith. HOMILIES ON ROMANS 7.[65]

ABRAHAM RIGHTEOUS BEFORE HIS CIRCUMCISION. PELAGIUS: Did God create only the Jews, and is he exclusively concerned with them? For even if the Gentiles sinned, so did the Jews, and even if the Jews repent, so do the Gentiles. If Christ came to the Jews as promised by the law, he came to the Gentiles as well. For the prophets often spoke of the calling of the Gentiles. Paul wants to show the Gentiles that the first saints had not been circumcised and that Abraham was righteous before his circumcision. But he adds "as well," so as not to appear to be excluding the Jews. PELAGIUS'S COMMENTARY ON ROMANS.[66]

3:30 God Justifies Believers Through Their Faith

FAITH PREFIGURED IN THE JEWS. IRENAEUS: We were prefigured in the Jews, and they are represented in us, that is, in the church, and they receive the reward for what they achieved. AGAINST HERESIES 4.22.2.[67]

BOTH JUSTIFIED BY FAITH. ORIGEN: Not only does Paul say that there is only one God for both

Jews and Gentiles, but he adds that this God is the one who justifies the circumcised on the ground of their faith and the uncircumcised through their faith. . . . Neither the circumcision nor the uncircumcision enjoys any advantage in this. COMMENTARY ON THE EPISTLE TO THE ROMANS.[68]

JUSTIFIED IN THE SAME WAY. AMBROSIASTER: By "the circumcised" Paul means the Jews who have been justified by their faith in the promise and who believe that Jesus is the Christ whom God had promised in the law. By "the uncircumcised" he means the Gentiles who have been justified with God by their faith in Christ. Thus God has justified both Jews and Gentiles. For because God is one, everyone has been justified in the same way. What benefit then is there in circumcision? Or what disadvantage is there in uncircumcision when only faith produces worthiness and merit? COMMENTARY ON PAUL'S EPISTLES.[69]

JEROME: Paul shows clearly that righteousness depends not on the merit of man but on the grace of God, who accepts the faith of those who believe without the works of the law. AGAINST THE PELAGIANS 2.7.[70]

ONE GOD. CHRYSOSTOM: There is only one God, who is Lord of all, both Jew and Gentile. Even in ancient times the blessings of providence were shared by both, although in different ways. The Jews had the written law, and the Gentiles had the natural law, but in this they lacked nothing, because if they tried hard enough they could always surpass the Jews in their observance. . . . If there was no difference then, much less is there any now, and this Paul establishes even more firmly by demonstrating that both alike stand in equal need of faith. HOMILIES ON ROMANS 7.[71]

---

[62]See Ex 12:48. [63]See Acts 10:31. [64]CSEL 81.1:123, 125. [65]NPNF 1 11:379. [66]PCR 83-84. [67]ANF 1:494. [68]CER 2:140-42. [69]CSEL 81.1:125. [70]FC 53:306. [71]NPNF 1 11:379.

DISTINGUISHING "THROUGH FAITH" AND "ON THE GROUND OF FAITH." THEODORE OF MOPSUESTIA: Paul says "the ground of their faith" with respect to the Jews because, although they had other ways of seeking righteousness, they could not obtain it except through their faith. When speaking about the Gentiles, he says "through their faith" because this is the only claim to righteousness which they have. PAULINE COMMENTARY FROM THE GREEK CHURCH.[72]

AUGUSTINE: The difference of preposition ("on the ground of" versus "through") does not indicate any difference of meaning but serves simply to vary the phrase. ON THE SPIRIT AND THE LETTER 50.[73]

THE SAME GOD. PELAGIUS: Jews and Gentiles have both believed in the same God and in the same Christ. PELAGIUS'S COMMENTARY ON ROMANS.[74]

3:31 The Law Confirms Faith

CONFIRMING THE LAW THROUGH FAITH. ORIGEN: Whoever does not believe in Christ, of whom Moses wrote in the law, destroys the law. But whoever believes in Christ, of whom Moses wrote, confirms the law through faith, because he believes in Christ.

The Lord himself said: "I have not come to abolish the law but to fulfill it."[75] None of the saints nor even the Lord himself has destroyed the law. Rather its glory, which is temporal and transient, has been destroyed and replaced by a glory which is eternal and permanent. COMMENTARY ON THE EPISTLE TO THE ROMANS.[76]

LAW NOT NULLIFIED. AMBROSIASTER: Paul says that the law is not nullified by faith but fulfilled. For its status is confirmed when faith bears witness that what it said would come has actually happened. Paul says this because of the Jews who thought that faith in Christ was inimical to the law because they did not understand the true

meaning of the law. For Paul does not nullify the law when he says that it must come to an end, because he asserts that at the time it was given it was rightly given, but now it does not have to be kept any longer. In the law itself it is said that a time would come when the promise would be fulfilled and the law would no longer have to be kept. . . . "Behold the days are coming, says the Lord, when I will make a new covenant with the house of Israel and the house of Judah, not like the covenant which I made with their fathers."[77] COMMENTARY ON PAUL'S EPISTLES.[78]

UPHOLDING AND PERFECTING THE LAW. CHRYSOSTOM: Paul's use of the word *uphold* shows that the law was failing. . . . The purpose of the law was to make man righteous, but it had no power to do that. But when faith came it achieved what the law could not do, for once a man believes he is immediately justified. Faith therefore established what the law intended and brought to fulfillment what its provisions aimed for. Consequently faith has not abolished the law but perfected it. HOMILIES ON ROMANS 7.[79]

ABRAHAM JUSTIFIED BY FAITH. [PSEUDO-]CONSTANTIUS: Paul does not contradict what he said above [in verse 27]. What he means by upholding the law is that the law tells me that Abraham was justified not by works but by faith.[80] THE HOLY LETTER OF ST. PAUL TO THE ROMANS.[81]

THE LAW UPHELD BY RIGHTEOUSNESS. AUGUSTINE: How should the law be upheld if not by righteousness? By a righteousness, moreover, which is of faith, for what could not be fulfilled through the law is fulfilled through faith. AUGUSTINE ON ROMANS 19.[82]

FREEDOM OF CHOICE. AUGUSTINE: Do we then

---

[72]NTA 15:118. [73]LCC 8:233. [74]PCR 84. [75]Mt 5:17. [76]CER 2:148, 152. [77]See, e.g., Jer 31:31-32. [78]CSEL 81.1:125, 127. [79]NPNF 1 11:380. [80]Cf. Rom 4:16; Gal 3:2-9; Heb 11:11-19. [81]ENPK 2:34. [82]AOR 7.

make void freedom of choice through grace? God forbid! Rather, we establish freedom of choice. As the law is not made void by faith, so freedom of choice is not made void but established by grace. Freedom of choice is necessary to the fulfillment of the law. But by the law comes the knowledge of sin; by faith comes the obtaining of grace against sin; by grace comes the healing of the soul from sin's sickness; by the healing of the soul comes freedom of choice; by freedom of choice comes the love of righteousness; by the love of righteousness comes the working of the law. Thus, as the law is not made void but established by faith, since faith obtains the grace whereby the law may be fulfilled, so freedom of choice is not made void but established by grace, since grace heals the will whereby righteousness may freely be loved. THE SPIRIT AND THE LETTER 52.[83]

LAW CONFIRMED BY FAITH. AUGUSTINE: The law is confirmed by faith. Apart from faith the law merely commands, and it holds guilty those who do not fulfill its commands, so that it might thereafter turn to the grace of the Deliverer those

groaning in their inability to do what is commanded. QUESTIONS 66.1.[84]

NECESSITY OF THE LAW. PELAGIUS: Is the law which enjoins us to be circumcised unnecessary? Not at all! On the contrary, we enable it to stand firm when we show that what it said is true, viz., that (spiritual) law would follow after (physical) law, (spiritual) testament after (physical) testament, (spiritual) circumcision after (physical) circumcision. PELAGIUS'S COMMENTARY ON ROMANS.[85]

TRUTH AND THE IMAGE OF THE TRUTH. CYRIL OF ALEXANDRIA: On account of his humanity Emmanuel is called a prophet, who following Moses is the mediator between God and humanity. The law was a shadow, but even so it presented an image of the truth. Furthermore, the truth hardly destroys its images; rather it makes them clearer. COMMENTARY ON ROMANS.[86]

---

[83]LCC 8:236. [84]FC 70:140. [85]PCR 84. [86]Migne PG 74 col. 780.

4:1-8 ABRAHAM WAS JUSTIFIED BY FAITH

[1]*What then shall we say about*[e] *Abraham, our forefather according to the flesh?* [2]*For if Abraham was justified by works, he has something to boast about, but not before God.* [3]*For what does the scripture say? "Abraham believed God, and it was reckoned to him as righteousness."* [4]*Now to one who works, his wages are not reckoned as a gift but as his due.* [5]*And to one who does not work but trusts him who justifies the ungodly, his faith is reckoned as righteousness.* [6]*So also David pronounces a blessing upon the man to whom God reckons righteousness apart from works:*

[7]*"Blessed are those whose iniquities are forgiven, and whose sins are covered;*

[8]*blessed is the man against whom the Lord will not reckon his sin."*

e Other ancient authorities read *was gained by*

OVERVIEW: Abraham, the father of the Jewish people, was justified by faith. This faith was reckoned to him as righteousness even before he was circumcised. In fact, he was given circumcision as a sign of the righteousness he already had by faith. If a person could only be justified by works, he would be able to claim that he had earned his reward. But faith is a free gift of God's grace. The prophets of the Old Testament knew this, as David (regarded by the Fathers as a prophet) testifies, calling it a great blessing to be set free from sin. The Fathers used this passage as an opportunity to discourse on the different types and grades of sin, all of which are wiped out in baptism. But it is clear from their remarks that they did not believe that baptism brings immediate spiritual perfection.

4:1 Our Forefather Abraham

ABRAHAM JUSTIFIED BEFORE BEING CIRCUMCISED. AMBROSIASTER: After showing that no one can be justified before God by the works of the law, Paul goes on to say that Abraham could not merit anything according to the flesh either. In saying "the flesh," Paul meant circumcision, because Abraham sought nothing on the basis of his circumcision. For he was already justified before he was circumcised. COMMENTARY ON PAUL'S EPISTLES.[1]

FOREFATHER ACCORDING TO THE FLESH. APOLLINARIS OF LAODICEA: Paul shows from the example of Abraham that faith is not given only to those who are under the law and the circumcision, but also to those who are not circumcised. For Abraham was not justified by his works either, nor did he have any reason to boast, for he was imperfect and apart from God he could do nothing. . . . Abraham our father was justified by faith. Paul calls him the "forefather according to the flesh" of those Israelites who have become sons of God by the Spirit. For Christ was made like them in his birth according to the flesh, and now he has made them like him through his birth

by grace in the Spirit. PAULINE COMMENTARY FROM THE GREEK CHURCH.[2]

FIRST TO BE CIRCUMCISED. CHRYSOSTOM: The Jews kept repeating that Abraham, the friend of God, was the first to be circumcised. Paul wants to show that he was justified by faith. HOMILIES ON ROMANS 8.[3]

[PSEUDO-]CONSTANTIUS: In saying "according to the flesh" Paul reveals that Abraham handed down his flesh but not his soul. THE HOLY LETTER OF ST. PAUL TO THE ROMANS.[4]

PELAGIUS: Paul calls the Jews back to the beginning of circumcision, so that what it originally stood for might be fully understood. PELAGIUS'S COMMENTARY ON ROMANS.[5]

4:2 Boasting in Works or Faith

JUSTIFICATION BY WORKS AND BY FAITH. ORIGEN: This is a rhetorical argument, which goes like this: Someone who is justified by works has nothing to boast of before God. But Abraham did have something to glory in before God. Therefore he was justified by faith and not by works.

In this whole passage it seems that the apostle wants to show that there are two justifications, one by works and the other by faith. He says that justification by works has its glory but only in and of itself, not before God. Justification by faith, on the other hand, has glory before God, who sees our hearts and knows those who believe in secret and those who do not believe. Thus it is right to say that it has glory only before God, who sees the hidden power of faith. But the one who looks for justification by works may expect honor mainly from other persons who see and approve of them.

Let no one think that someone who has faith enough to be justified and to have glory before

---

[1]CSEL 81.1:127. [2]NTA 15:61. [3]NPNF 1 11:385. [4]ENPK 2:35. [5]PCR 84.

God can at the same time have unrighteousness dwelling in him as well. For faith cannot coexist with unbelief, nor can righteousness with wickedness, just as light and darkness cannot live together. COMMENTARY ON THE EPISTLE TO THE ROMANS.[6]

BEFORE GOD. AMBROSIASTER: This is a rhetorical argument. For Abraham indeed does have glory before God, but because of the faith by which he was justified, because nobody is justified by the works of the law in a way which would give him glory before God. And because those who keep the law are still being justified, Paul adds: "If Abraham was justified by works, he has something to boast about, but not before God." COMMENTARY ON PAUL'S EPISTLES.[7]

TWO KINDS OF BOASTING. CHRYSOSTOM: For someone to be justified by faith if he had no works was unusual. But for one who had plenty of good works to delight in being justified not by works but by faith—that was something to cause amazement. It put the power of faith in a new light.

What Paul is saying here is not plain, and so it is necessary to make it clearer. There are two kinds of boasting—one of works and one of faith. . . . Paul's great strength is particularly displayed in this, that he turns the objection around and shows that what seemed to favor the idea of salvation by works (viz., boasting) belonged much more truly to salvation by faith. For the man who boasts in his works is boasting about himself, but the man who finds his honor in having faith in God has a much better reason for boasting, because he is boasting about God, not about himself.[8] . . . To abstain from stealing or murder is a minor accomplishment compared to believing that God can do the impossible. . . . The believer boasts not only because he sincerely loves God but also because he has received great honor and love from him. HOMILIES ON ROMANS 8.[9]

GLORY BELONGS TO GOD. AUGUSTINE: Since

Abraham without the law obtained glory not by the works of the law (as if he could fulfill the law in his own strength), since the law had not yet been given, the glory belongs to God, not to him. For he was justified not by his own merit, as if by works, but by the grace of God through faith. AUGUSTINE ON ROMANS 20.[10]

CARRYING OUT THE ORDINANCES. PELAGIUS: If Abraham was justified because of his circumcision, then God gave him nothing and he could have gloried in what he did to himself. Or it may mean that if Abraham carried out the ordinances, he had glory in his own eyes but not in God's. PELAGIUS'S COMMENTARY ON ROMANS.[11]

BELIEVING ALL THINGS POSSIBLE WITH GOD. CYRIL OF ALEXANDRIA: What can we say to those who insist that Abraham was justified by works because he was ready to sacrifice his son Isaac on the altar?[12] Abraham was already an old man when God promised him that he would have a son and that his descendants would be as countless as the stars of the sky.[13] Abraham piously believed that all things are possible with God and so exercised this faith. God reckoned him to be righteous on this account and gave Abraham a reward worthy of such a godly mind, viz., the forgiveness of his previous sins. . . . So even if Abraham was also justified by his willingness to sacrifice Isaac, this must be regarded as an evident demonstration of a faith which was already very strong.[14] EXPLANATION OF THE LETTER TO THE ROMANS.[15]

REVEALING THE KINDNESS OF GOD. THEODORET OF CYR: The accomplishment of good works honors those who do them, but it does not reveal the kindness of God. Faith, on the other hand, reveals both the love for God of the one

---

[6]CER 2:158-62. [7]CSEL 81.1:129. [8]See Ps 34:2; 44:8; Jer 9:24; 2 Cor 10:17-18; Eph 2:8-10. [9]NPNF 1 11:385-86. [10]AOR 7. [11]PCR 84. [12]See Gen 22:1-14. [13]See Gen 22:17; Heb 11:12. [14]See Heb 11:8-19. [15]Migne PG 74 cols. 780-81.

who believes and God's kindness. INTERPRETA-
TION OF THE LETTER TO THE ROMANS.[16]

4:3 Abraham's Belief

ABRAHAM BELIEVED GOD. IRENAEUS: Abraham
believed that God was the maker of heaven and
earth, the only true God, and he also believed
that God would make his seed as numerous as
the stars of heaven.[17] AGAINST HERESIES 4.5.3.[18]

BELIEVING WHOLLY IN GOD. ORIGEN: Was
Abraham justified just because he had the faith to
believe that he would be given a son? Or was it
also because of all the other things which he had
believed previously? . . . Before this point, Abraham had believed in part but not perfectly. Now,
however, all the parts of his earlier faith are gathered together to make a perfect whole, by which
he is justified. COMMENTARY ON THE EPISTLE TO
THE ROMANS.[19]

HEIRS OF ABRAHAM'S FAITH. AMBROSE: I do not
demand a reason from Christ. If I am convinced
by reason, I deny faith. Abraham believed God.
Let us also believe, so that we who are the heirs of
his race may likewise be heirs of his faith. ON
THE DEATH OF HIS BROTHER SATYRUS 2.89.[20]

THE REWARD OF PRAISE. AMBROSIASTER: Paul
revealed that Abraham had glory before God not
because he was circumcised nor because he
abstained from evil, but because he believed in
God. For that reason he was justified, and he
would receive the reward of praise in the future.
COMMENTARY ON PAUL'S EPISTLES.[21]

**THE POWER OF HIM WHO MADE THE PROM-
ISE.** CHRYSOSTOM: The Master proclaimed that
Abraham was just because he outran the weakness
of his human nature. He strained with his whole
mind toward the power of him who had made the
promise. BAPTISMAL INSTRUCTIONS 8.7.[22]

FAITH COUNTED AS CREDIT FOR ALL SINS.

PELAGIUS: Abraham's faith was so great that his
earlier sins were all forgiven him, and righteousness was counted as credit for every one of them
by faith alone. Later he was on fire with such love
for God that he piled one good work on top of
another. Therefore he has glory in God's eyes.
PELAGIUS'S COMMENTARY ON ROMANS.[23]

4:4 Gift and Due

DISTINGUISHING GRACE AND JUSTICE. ORIGEN:
Faith relies on the grace of the justifier. Works
rely on the justice of the rewarder. When I consider the greatness of Paul's speech, by which he
says that the worker receives what is due to him, I
can hardly persuade myself that there is any deed
which could claim a reward from God as its due.
. . . Therefore, it seems that Paul is really referring
here to evil deeds, of which Scripture frequently
says that they get their due reward.[24] COMMEN-
TARY ON THE EPISTLE TO THE ROMANS.[25]

HE BELIEVES WHAT HE DOES NOT SEE.
AMBROSIASTER: No merit is imputed for reward
to the man who is subject to the law—either to the
law of works, i.e., of Moses, or to the law of nature.
For he who is obliged to keep the law is a debtor. A
necessity is imposed upon him by the law to keep
it whether he wants to or not, so as not to be
guilty, as Paul says in another passage: "Those who
resist will incur judgment."[26] On the other hand,
to believe or not to believe is a matter of choice. No
one can be required to accept something which is
offered as a gift. But he is invited to receive it. He
is not forced but persuaded. He believes what he
does not see but hopes for. This is what glorifies
God. COMMENTARY ON PAUL'S EPISTLES.[27]

WAGES RECKONED AS DUE. AUGUSTINE: Paul
was speaking here of the way wages are given. But

---

[16]*IER*, Migne PG 82 col. 88. [17]See Gen 22:17; Heb 11:12. [18]ANF
1:467. [19]CER 2:166-168. [20]FC 22:236. [21]CSEL 81.1:129. [22]ACW
31:122. [23]PCR 84. [24]E.g., 2 Sam 3:39; Mt 16:27; 2 Tim 4:14; Rev
22:12. [25]CER 2:170. [26]Rom 13:2. [27]CSEL 81.1:129, 131.

God gave by grace, because he gave to sinners so that by faith they might live justly, that is, do good works. Thus the good works which we do after we have received grace are not to be attributed to us but rather to him who has justified us by his grace. For if God had wanted to give us our due reward, he would have given us the punishment due to sinners. AUGUSTINE ON ROMANS 21.[28]

PELAGIUS: An employee must do as he is told, and unless he complies he is dismissed. But if he does what he is told, he has no glory, because a servant who does no more than what he has to is still called unprofitable.[29] Or else he is not given righteousness freely but is paid a wage for prior work. PELAGIUS'S COMMENTARY ON ROMANS.[30]

DISTINGUISHING GIFT AND REWARD. THEODORET OF CYR: The doer of righteousness expects a reward, but justification by faith is the gift of the God of all. INTERPRETATION OF THE LETTER TO THE ROMANS.[31]

4:5 Faith Reckoned as Righteousness

RAIN WATERS THE ROOT AND BEARS FRUIT.
ORIGEN: Faith, which believes in the justifier, is the beginning of justification before God. And this faith, when it is justified, is like a root in the soil of the soul, which the rain has watered, so that as it begins to grow by the law of God, branches appear, which bring forth fruit. The root of righteousness does not spring from works; rather, the fruit of works grows from the root of righteousness, viz., by that root of righteousness by which God brings righteousness to the one whom he has accepted apart from works. COMMENTARY ON THE EPISTLE TO THE ROMANS.[32]

HOW FAITH IS RECKONED AMONG GENTILES.
AMBROSIASTER: This refers to somebody who is bound by sin and who therefore does not do what the law commands. Paul says this because to an ungodly person, that is, to a Gentile, who believes

in Christ without doing the works of the law, his faith is reckoned for righteousness just as Abraham's was. How then can the Jews think that they have been justified by the works of the law in the same way as Abraham, when they see that Abraham was not justified by the works of the law but by faith alone? Therefore there is no need of the law when the ungodly is justified before God by faith alone. COMMENTARY ON PAUL'S EPISTLES.[33]

RIGHTEOUSNESS GREATER THAN REWARD.
CHRYSOSTOM: Think how great a thing it is to be persuaded and have complete confidence that God is able not only to set an ungodly man free from punishment but also to make him righteous and count him worthy to receive these immortal honors. . . . This is what makes a believer glorious—the fact that he enjoys so great a grace and displays such great faith. Note too that the recompense is greater. For the one who works receives his reward, but the one who believes is made righteous. Righteousness is much greater than a reward, because it is a recompense which includes many rewards. HOMILIES ON ROMANS 8.[34]

THE UNGODLY MADE GODLY. AUGUSTINE: God makes the ungodly man godly, in order that he might persevere in this godliness and righteousness. For a man is justified in order that he might be just, not so that he might think it is all right to go on sinning. AUGUSTINE ON ROMANS 22.[35]

THE CONVERSION OF THE UNGODLY.
PELAGIUS: When an ungodly person is converted, God justifies him by faith alone, not for good works which he does not have. On that basis he would have been punished for his ungodly works. But note that Paul does not say one who remains in sin is justified by faith but rather the ungodly,

---

[28]AOR 9. [29]Lk 17:10. [30]PCR 84-85. [31]IER, Migne PG 82 col. 88. [32]CER 2:174-76. [33]CSEL 81.1:131. [34]NPNF 1 11:386-87. [35]AOR 9.

i.e., one who has just come to believe. PELA-GIUS'S COMMENTARY ON ROMANS.[36]

4:6 Righteousness Apart from Works

THE LONGING OF THE RIGHTEOUS. AMBROSI-ASTER: Paul backs this up by the example of the prophet David, who says that those are blessed of whom God has decreed that, without work or any keeping of the law, they are justified before God by faith alone. Therefore he foretells the blessedness of the time when Christ was born, just as the Lord himself said: "Many prophets and righteous men longed to see what you see and to hear what you hear and did not hear it."[37] COMMENTARY ON PAUL'S EPISTLES.[38]

UNEARNED HONOR. PELAGIUS: It is a great blessing to obtain the Lord's grace without the work of the law and penance, as if one were receiving some public honor without having earned it. PELAGIUS'S COMMENTARY ON ROMANS.[39]

FAITH OLDER THAN LAW. THEODORET OF CYR: After demonstrating by the example of the patriarch Abraham that faith is older than the law, Paul quotes a further witness in support of his position, viz., David the prophet and king. INTERPRETATION OF THE LETTER TO THE ROMANS.[40]

4:7 Iniquities Covered

SINS COVERED. AMBROSIASTER: Obviously they are blessed, whose iniquities are forgiven without labor or work of any kind and whose sins are covered without any work of penitence being required of them, as long as they believe.

How can these words apply to a penitent, when we know that penitents obtain the forgiveness of sin with much struggle and groaning? How can they be applied to a martyr, when we know that the glory of martyrdom is obtained by sufferings and pressures? But the prophet, foreseeing a happy time when the Savior comes, calls them blessed

because their sins are forgiven, covered and not reckoned to them, and this without labor or work of any kind. COMMENTARY ON PAUL'S EPISTLES.[41]

IN BAPTISM AND REPENTANCE. [PSEUDO-]CONSTANTIUS: It may be understood that iniquities are forgiven in baptism and that sins are covered by repentance. THE HOLY LETTER OF ST. PAUL TO THE ROMANS.[42]

NOT COUNTED. PELAGIUS: What is forgiven is not retained in the mind, and what is covered does not come to light, and for that reason it is not counted against us. PELAGIUS'S COMMENTARY ON ROMANS.[43]

4:8 Sins Forgiven

INIQUITY FORGIVEN, SIN COVERED, NOT IMPUTED. ORIGEN: Note the order here. First comes the forgiveness of iniquity, then the covering of sin, then the non-imputation of the sin to the sinner. This is the order: First, the beginning of the soul's conversion is the renunciation of evil. Second, the soul begins to do good works, which eventually become more numerous than the evil deeds which preceded them, and in this sense those sins may be said to be covered over. Finally, the soul reaches maturity. Every trace of sin is uprooted from it so that not even the smallest trace of wickedness remains The height of perfect blessedness is promised. The Lord will not impute any sin to the soul.

Wickedness is different from sin in that it applies to things which are done without the law. In Greek the word for this is *anomía*, meaning something which is done without the law. Sin, on the other hand, refers to something which is done against the dictates of conscience and nature. COMMENTARY ON THE EPISTLE TO THE ROMANS.[44]

---

[36]PCR 85. [37]Mt 13:17. [38]CSEL 81.1:131. [39]PCR 85. [40]*IER*, Migne PG 82 col. 88. [41]CSEL 81.1:131, 133. [42]ENPK 2:35. [43]PCR 85. [44]CER 2:176-78.

Three Categories of Sin. Ambrosiaster: "Forgive," "cover," "not reckon"—all amount to one and the same thing. For all three are given and received in the same way.

Paul has three categories to cover the different types of sin. The first category is that of wickedness or ungodliness, in that the Creator is not acknowledged. The second category is that of the more serious sins, and the third is that of the less serious ones. All of these are wiped out in baptism. Commentary on Paul's Epistles.[45]

Sins Forgiven in Baptism. Pelagius: Some people say that sin is forgiven in baptism, covered by penitential works and through martyrdom not counted against us. But others say that when sins have been forgiven in baptism, love for God is increased, which covers a multitude of sins and keeps them from being counted against us as long as daily good works surpass past misdeeds.[46] Pelagius's Commentary on Romans.[47]

Theodore of Mopsuestia: Sinful works are not counted against the faithful. God's love of humanity is the greatest thing that has happened. Pauline Commentary from the Greek Church.[48]

---

[45]CSEL 81.1:133. [46]See 1 Pet 4:8. [47]PCR 85. [48]NTA 15:118.

4:9-12 THE PURPOSE OF CIRCUMCISION

[9]*Is this blessing pronounced only upon the circumcised, or also upon the uncircumcised? We say that faith was reckoned to Abraham as righteousness.* [10]*How then was it reckoned to him? Was it before or after he had been circumcised? It was not after, but before he was circumcised.* [11]*He received circumcision as a sign or seal of the righteousness which he had by faith while he was still uncircumcised. The purpose was to make him the father of all who believe without being circumcised and who thus have righteousness reckoned to them,* [12] *and likewise the father of the circumcised who are not merely circumcised but also follow the example of the faith which our father Abraham had before he was circumcised.*

Overview: Paul returns to his theme, that the blessing of faith is given quite apart from circumcision. The Fathers all echo him in this and merely reinforce what the apostle says about Abraham. Gentiles are invited to receive the blessings of Abraham, the father of all faithful.

4:9 Who Receives the Blessing?

Faith Prior to Circumcision. Origen: If Abraham was justified by faith before he was circumcised, then it is possible for anyone who believes in God to be justified by faith, even if uncircumcised. Commentary on the Epistle to the Romans.[1]

---

[1]CER 2:178.

GENTILES INVITED. AMBROSIASTER: Is this blessedness given to the children of Abraham only or to the Gentiles also? If in those days the Gentiles were not forbidden to come under the law and the promise made to Abraham, how could it be that in the time of Christ they should be prevented from coming to grace, when God has clearly invited them? COMMENTARY ON PAUL'S EPISTLES.[2]

CHRYSOSTOM: Paul shows that the blessing, far from shunning the uncircumcised, was given to the uncircumcised (i.e., Abraham) before circumcision was instituted. HOMILIES ON ROMANS 8.[3]

THE STAGES OF NATURE, LAW AND FAITH. PELAGIUS: Paul means that the blessing is to be found in each of the three periods of nature, circumcision and Christian faith. Everyone agrees that faith was reckoned to Abraham as righteousness. Therefore, what reason discovers about Abraham, we will heed with regard to the rest. PELAGIUS'S COMMENTARY ON ROMANS.[4]

4:10 Abraham's Righteousness Preceded Circumcision

THE FATHER OF ALL UNCIRCUMCISED BELIEVERS. ORIGEN: In that Abraham was justified while he was still uncircumcised, it is obvious that he is the head and father of all uncircumcised believers. COMMENTARY ON THE EPISTLE TO THE ROMANS.[5]

AMBROSIASTER: What did Abraham believe? He believed that he would have a descendant, a son, in whom all the nations would be justified by faith while they were still uncircumcised, as Abraham then was.[6] COMMENTARY ON PAUL'S EPISTLES.[7]

PELAGIUS: Now we must see whether circumcision is born of righteousness or righteousness of circumcision. It must be the former, because Abraham was righteous before he was circum-

cised. PELAGIUS'S COMMENTARY ON ROMANS.[8]

FAITH OLDER THAN CIRCUMCISION. THEODORET OF CYR: Paul demonstrates that faith was not only older than the law, it was older than circumcision as well. INTERPRETATION OF THE LETTER TO THE ROMANS.[9]

4:11 Circumcision as a Sign of Righteousness by Faith

ABRAHAM ACCEPTED CIRCUMCISION AS A SIGN. TERTULLIAN: But you Jews say that Abraham was circumcised. Yes, but he pleased God before his circumcision, and he did not yet observe the sabbath. For he had accepted circumcision as a sign for that time, not as a prerogative title to salvation. AN ANSWER TO THE JEWS 3.[10]

A SIGN OF RIGHTEOUSNESS TO COME. AMBROSIASTER: Abraham received circumcision as a sign of the righteousness of faith. For believing that he would have a son, he received the sign of the thing which he believed, that it might be known that he was justified because of what he believed. Circumcision has no special value; it is just a sign.[11] The children of Abraham received this sign so that it would be known that they were the children of him who had received this sign because he believed in God and so that they would imitate their father's faith and believe in Jesus, who was promised to Abraham. Isaac was born as a type of Christ, for the nations are not blessed in Isaac but in Christ, "for there is no other name under heaven given among men by which we must be saved," says the apostle Peter.[12] COMMENTARY ON PAUL'S EPISTLES.[13]

CHRYSOSTOM: See how the uncircumcised had Abraham as their father before the circumcised came into existence! So if circumcision must be

[2]CSEL 81.1:135. [3]NPNF 1 11:387. [4]PCR 85-86. [5]CER 2:180. [6]Gen 17:6-24. [7]CSEL 81.1:135. [8]PCR 86. [9]IER, Migne PG 82 col. 89. [10]ANF 3:153. [11]Gen 17:10-11. [12]Acts 4:12. [13]CSEL 81.1:135,

honored because it preaches righteousness, uncircumcision is still preeminent, because it came before circumcision in the dispensation of faith. HOMILIES ON ROMANS 8.[14]

CHRYSOSTOM: Paul taught us both that Abraham received circumcision as a sign and that while he was still uncircumcised he gave evidence of righteousness arising from faith. HOMILIES ON GENESIS 39.18.[15]

SEAL OF AN EXISTING RIGHTEOUSNESS.
PELAGIUS: In case anyone says that Abraham was circumcised unnecessarily, Paul argues that it is the sign or seal of an existing righteousness, not of growth in an unfolding righteousness. This righteousness was so perfect that it deserved a seal, for something that is full is always sealed. PELAGIUS'S COMMENTARY ON ROMANS.[16]

THE PURPOSES OF CIRCUMCISION.
SEVERIAN: Circumcision was given for these three reasons: First, to be a sign of faith; second, to mark out the race of Abraham, and third, to be a sign and symbol of good and wise behavior. It was not given in order to produce righteousness but as a sign and seal of the righteousness which was Abraham's by faith. PAULINE COMMENTARY FROM THE GREEK CHURCH.[17]

4:12 Following Abraham's Example

THE FATHER OF THE FAITHFUL.
ORIGEN: After believing, Abraham received circumcision as a sign of the faith which he already had . . . which is how he can also be the father of those who are circumcised, provided that they share the same faith which he had while he was still uncircumcised. COMMENTARY ON THE EPISTLE TO THE ROMANS.[18]

AMBROSIASTER: Paul says this because Abraham by believing became the forefather of the circumcision, but of the heart, not only of those who descended from him but also of those who, from

among the nations, believed in the way he did. He is the father of the Jews according to the flesh, but according to faith he is the father of all believers. COMMENTARY ON PAUL'S EPISTLES.[19]

THE REALITY OF WHICH THE SIGN SPOKE.
CHRYSOSTOM: Circumcision is meaningless if there is no faith within. It is a sign of righteousness, but if there is no righteousness, then there is no sign either. The reason the Jews received a sign was that they might seek diligently for the reality of which the sign spoke. If they had done so, they would not have needed the sign in the first place. Righteousness is not the only thing that circumcision proclaims; it also proclaims that righteousness can be found in an uncircumcised man (e.g., Abraham). In effect, therefore, circumcision proclaims that there is no need of circumcision. HOMILIES ON ROMANS 8.[20]

THE FATHER OF THE RIGHTEOUS.
PELAGIUS: Therefore all the Gentiles who believe are children of Abraham when faith alone is credited to them as righteousness and they too receive the circumcision—of the heart.[21] Or perhaps this verse should be understood like this: Abraham was righteous in uncircumcision so that he could become the father of uncircumcised believers, and he remained righteous once he was circumcised in order to become the father of the righteous who are circumcised. PELAGIUS'S COMMENTARY ON ROMANS.[22]

PREPARED FOR SALVATION BY FAITH.
THEODORET OF CYR: If a Gentile who has not been circumcised follows Abraham's faith, which he manifested before being circumcised, he will not be rejected. For the God of all, since he had foreseen as God that he would gather one people from both Jews and Gentiles and prepare for them salvation by faith, had appointed Abraham

---

[14]NPNF 1 11:388. [15]FC 82:386. [16]PCR 86. [17]NTA 15:217. [18]CER 2:180-82. [19]CSEL 81.1:137. [20]NPNF 1 11:388-89. [21]Deut 10:16; 30:6; Jer 4:4; Rom 2:29. [22]PCR 86.

as their father as well. Paul had demonstrated that Abraham had acquired righteousness by faith before being circumcised and that even after being circumcised he lived not according to the law of Moses but by clinging to his faith. Hence

Paul called him the father of the Gentiles who believe. INTERPRETATION OF THE LETTER TO THE ROMANS.[23]

---

[23]IER, Migne PG 82 cols. 89, 92.

4:13-17 THE PURPOSE OF THE LAW

[13]*The promise to Abraham and his descendants, that they should inherit the world, did not come through the law but through the righteousness of faith.* [14]*If it is the adherents of the law who are to be the heirs, faith is null and the promise is void.* [15]*For the law brings wrath, but where there is no law there is no transgression.*

[16]*That is why it depends on faith, in order that the promise may rest on grace and be guaranteed to all his descendants—not only to the adherents of the law but also to those who share the faith of Abraham, for he is the father of us all,* [17]*as it is written, "I have made you the father of many nations"—in the presence of the God in whom he believed, who gives life to the dead and calls into existence the things that do not exist.*

OVERVIEW: The promises made to Abraham have been inherited by those who share Abraham's faith, not only by those who have received the circumcision given to his physical descendants. Therefore what was promised to Israel has been inherited by the church, and the church will inherit the world.

The law brings not the fulfillment of promises but an awareness of transgression. Origen was aware that transgression existed before the law of Moses was given, and so he applies this verse to the universal law of nature, in spite of the context. The other Fathers concentrate more on the reality of transgression and the hopeless state of those who have nothing but the law of Moses to instruct them. Only faith can bring the fulfillment of God's promises. Faith is not a human work but a free gift from God. Everyone who has received this gift is a descendant of Abraham, whether he has been circumcised or not.

4:13 The Promised Inheritance

THE PROMISE. ORIGEN: Long before Moses ever existed, the Lord appeared to Abraham and said: "Go from your country and your kindred and your father's house to the land that I will show you. And I will make of you a great nation, and I will bless you and make your name great, so that you will be a blessing. I will bless those who bless you, and him who curses you I will curse; and by you all the families of the earth will be blessed."[1] COMMENTARY ON THE EPISTLE TO THE ROMANS.[2]

CHRIST, THE SEED OF ABRAHAM. AMBROSIASTER: It is clear that the law had not yet been

---

[1]Gen 12:1-3. [2]CER 2:192.

given, neither was there as yet circumcision, when the promise was made to Abraham the believer and to his seed, which is Christ, who would cleanse the sins of all.[3] Therefore Abraham was made heir to the world not by the merit earned from keeping the law but by faith. The heir of the world is the heir of the earth, which he obtained in his children. For Christ is the heir of the nations, as David sings: "I will make the nations your heritage and the ends of the earth your possession."[4] COMMENTARY ON PAUL'S EPISTLES.[5]

PELAGIUS: Here Paul calls circumcision the law, because every commandment can be regarded as part of the law. Abraham inherited the world, either because in his seed (viz., Christ) all the nations which were given to him by the Father might be blessed[6] or because the nations would sup with him in the kingdom of heaven.[7] PELAGIUS'S COMMENTARY ON ROMANS.[8]

INHERIT THE WORLD. SEVERIAN: Paul says that the righteous will inherit the world because the ungodly will be thrown out and handed over to punishment on the day of judgment, but the righteous will possess the universe which remains, and will have been renewed, and the good things of heaven and earth will be theirs. PAULINE COMMENTARY FROM THE GREEK CHURCH.[9]

4:14 The Promise Comes Through Faith

RIGHTEOUSNESS IMPUTED TO FAITH. ORIGEN: Paul says that the promise given to Abraham that he should inherit the world did not come from the law but by faith, which was reckoned to him as righteousness. It doubtless follows that everyone who hopes that God's righteousness will be imputed to him hopes for this by faith and not by the law. COMMENTARY ON THE EPISTLE TO THE ROMANS.[10]

AMBROSIASTER: The apostle shows that there is something wicked in hoping for an inheritance by the law. COMMENTARY ON PAUL'S EPISTLES.[11]

THE PROMISE MADE VOID. CHRYSOSTOM: To prevent anyone from saying that it is possible to have faith and to keep the law at the same time, Paul shows that this is impracticable. For one who clings to the law as if it were of saving force dishonors the power of faith. This is why Paul says that faith is made void, i.e., that there is no need of salvation by grace. . . . And without faith, there is no promise of inheritance, which is what scared the Jews most of all, because that is what they really wanted. For the promise was that they should be heirs of the entire world. HOMILIES ON ROMANS 8.[12]

PELAGIUS: If only the circumcised are heirs, God has not fulfilled his promise to Abraham that he would be the father of many nations,[13] and it will seem that the nations believed in God without any reason. PELAGIUS'S COMMENTARY ON ROMANS.[14]

4:15 The Law Brings Wrath

HOW THE LAW BRINGS WRATH. ORIGEN: Paul says that the law brings wrath in order to underline his point, [made in the previous verse,] that it is not the pathway to the inheritance of the promise.

The law which brings transgression cannot be the law of Moses, because there was plenty of transgression before that came into force. Rather, it is the law which dwells in our members and leads us into sin. This is the same law which the apostle says brings wrath. For without a doubt it brings wrath when it leads its captive into sin. But where the law of sin does not obtain, then of course there is no transgression. COMMENTARY ON THE EPISTLE TO THE ROMANS.[15]

HOW FAITH BRINGS JOY. AMBROSIASTER: In

---

[3]Gal 3:16. [4]Ps 2:8. [5]CSEL 81.1:137, 139. [6]See Gen 12:3; Ps 2:8; Gal 3:16. [7]Mt 8:11. [8]PCR 86-87. [9]NTA 15:217. [10]CER 2:194. [11]CSEL 81.1:139. [12]NPNF 1 11:389. [13]Gen 17:4. [14]PCR 87. [15]CER 2:194, 200.

order to show that no man can be justified before God by the law, nor can the promise be given through the law, Paul says that "the law brings wrath." It was given in order to make transgressors guilty. But faith is the gift of God's mercy, so that those who have been made guilty by the law may obtain forgiveness. Therefore faith brings joy. Paul does not speak against the law but gives priority to faith. It is not possible to be saved by the law, but we are saved by God's grace through faith. Therefore the law itself is not wrath, but it brings wrath, i.e., punishment, to the sinner, for wrath is born from sin. For this reason Paul wants the law to be abandoned so that the sinner will take refuge in faith, which forgives sins, that he may be saved.

Paul says that "where there is no law there is no transgression," because once the guilty have been removed from the power of the law and given forgiveness, there is no transgression. For those who were sinners because they had transgressed the law are now justified. For the law of works has ceased, that is, the observance of sabbaths, new moons, circumcision, distinction of foods and the expiation by a dead animal or the blood of a weasel. COMMENTARY ON PAUL'S EPISTLES.[16]

THE OBSTACLE TO INHERITANCE REMOVED. CHRYSOSTOM: The law works wrath and makes those who are under it liable for their transgressions, which is a curse, not a promise! . . . But when faith comes it brings grace with it, and so the promise takes effect. For where there is grace there is forgiveness, and where there is forgiveness there is no punishment. Once punishment is removed and righteousness takes hold from faith, there is no obstacle to our becoming heirs of the promise. HOMILIES ON ROMANS 8.[17]

AUGUSTINE: This applies to the second state of man, when he is under the law. AUGUSTINE ON ROMANS 23.[18]

AUGUSTINE: Paul said this because God's wrath is more severe toward a transgressor who knows

sin by the law and still commits it. GRACE AND FREE WILL 10.22.[19]

THE LAW WEIGHED SINNERS DOWN. PELAGIUS: The law brings wrath because it was ordained for the unrighteous,[20] and it weighed sinners down rather than set them free. . . . Where there is no law there is nothing which can be broken. Or perhaps this means that there is nothing to be punished where the law is not necessary. PELAGIUS'S COMMENTARY ON ROMANS.[21]

4:16 The Promise Depends on Faith

THE PROMISE RESTS ON GRACE. ORIGEN: It might appear from this that faith is not a free gift of God but that it must first be offered to him by man in order for grace to be given in return. But consider what the apostle teaches about this elsewhere. For when he lists the gifts of the Spirit, which he says are given to believers according to the measure of faith, there among the rest he asserts that the gift of faith is also given.[22] Therefore faith is given by grace. . . .

If the promise rested on works, it would not be guaranteed. But now it is guaranteed because it rests on grace, not on works. I think this can be understood to mean that the things of the law are external to us, but the things of grace are internal . . . and therefore they have a firmer foundation. COMMENTARY ON THE EPISTLE TO THE ROMANS.[23]

ONLY BY FAITH IS THE PROMISE MADE ACCESSIBLE TO ALL HUMANITY. AMBROSIASTER: The promise could not be certain to every offspring, that is, to everyone from every nation, unless it was by faith. The source of the promise is faith and not the law, because those who are under the law are guilty, and the promise cannot be given to those who are guilty. For this reason they must first be purified by faith,

---

[16]CSEL 81.1:139, 141. [17]NPNF 1 11:389. [18]AOR 9. [19]FC 59:274. [20]1 Tim 1:9. [21]PCR 87. [22]1 Cor 12:9. [23]CER 2:206-8.

so that they may become worthy to be called the children of God, so that the promise may be certain. For if they say they are children of God when they are still guilty (that is to say, under the law), then the promise is not certain. First the children of God must be set free from sin. So those who are under the law must be rescued from the law in order to deserve to receive the promise, which is all the greater because it is apart from the law. COMMENTARY ON PAUL'S EPISTLES.[24]

THE CERTAINTY AND EXTENT OF THE BLESSING. CHRYSOSTOM: It is not only the law which faith upholds but the promise also.... But the law when kept after its expiry date makes even faith of no effect and blocks the promise. In saying this Paul shows that faith, far from being superfluous, is necessary to the extent that without it there is no salvation.

Here Paul mentions two blessings. The first is that the things which have been given are secured. The second is that they are given to all Abraham's descendants, including the Gentiles who believe and excluding the Jews who do not. HOMILIES ON ROMANS 8.[25]

FORGIVEN BY GRACE. PELAGIUS: The law does not forgive sins but condemns them, and therefore it cannot make all nations children of Abraham, because in the end all must be punished since all are found under sin. But faith makes all believers children of Abraham, because their sins have been forgiven by grace. PELAGIUS'S COMMENTARY ON ROMANS.[26]

SEED OF ABRAHAM NOT MERELY A RACIAL DEFINITION. THEODORET OF CYR: Paul humbled the pride of the Jews by calling all those who imitated Abraham's faith "the seed of Abraham," even if they were of a different race. For if the law punishes those who break it, grace gives forgiveness of sins and confirms the promise of God, giving a blessing to the Gentiles. INTERPRETATION OF THE LETTER TO THE ROMANS.[27]

4:17 God Gives Life to the Dead

LIFE TO THE DEAD. ORIGEN: The dead here are those whose souls have sinned, for Scripture says: "The soul that sins will die."[28] For just as the senses perish in our mortal body so that the body can no longer hear, smell, taste or touch, so also the spiritual senses perish in the soul so that it cannot see God or hear his Word, or sense the sweet odor of Christ, or taste the good Word of God, or handle the word of life. People like that must be said to be dead. This is what we were like when Christ came, but he has given us life by his grace.[29] COMMENTARY ON THE EPISTLE TO THE ROMANS.[30]

PELAGIUS: Abraham is the father of all believers, not just of the nation of Israel. "Life to the dead" is given to those who are dead for the purpose of bearing children, which is the context of the present discussion. PELAGIUS'S COMMENTARY ON ROMANS.[31]

FATHER OF MANY NATIONS. AMBROSIASTER: Paul confirms by quoting the law that Abraham is the father of all who believe, and so the promise is firm if they abandon the law on account of their faith, because the promise of the kingdom of heaven is given to the righteous, not to sinners. Those who are under the law are under sin because all have sinned, and it is not possible for anyone who is under the law to receive grace.

In order to teach that there is one God for all, Paul tells the Gentiles that Abraham believed in God himself and was justified in his sight. The Gentiles also believe in him that they may be justified, and so there is no difference between Jew and Greek in faith,[32] for when the circumcision and the uncircumcision are taken away they are made one in Christ.

Paul invites the Gentiles to share the faith of

---

[24]CSEL 81.1:141. [25]NPNF 1 11:389. [26]PCR 87. [27]IER, Migne PG 82 col. 92. [28]Ezek 18:20. [29]Rom 5:21. [30]CER 2:216. [31]PCR 87. [32]Acts 15:7-9.

Abraham, who believed God while he was still uncircumcised. Now that that faith is preached in Christ, he has been raised from the dead, along with his wife. For when they were already very old they sprang back to life, so that Abraham did not doubt that he would have a son by Sarah, whom he knew to be sterile and who had long since ceased to have her menstrual period. Paul said this so that they would not worry about circumcision or uncircumcision but that they would respond eagerly because of their faith, secure in the knowledge that the one in whom they believe is no other than the one who gives life to the dead, who has the power to bring things which do not exist into being by his will. COMMENTARY ON PAUL'S EPISTLES.[33]

THE RELATION OF FAITH. CHRYSOSTOM: Is God here referring to the fact that Abraham was the father of the Ishmaelites, or the Amalekites, or the Hagarenes?[34] No . . . God is a father not by way of natural relationship but by way of the relation of faith. It is in this sense also that Abraham is the father of us all. HOMILIES ON ROMANS 8.[35]

AUGUSTINE: This means that faith is in the inner man, in the sight of God and not in human display, which is what the circumcision of the flesh is. AUGUSTINE ON ROMANS 24.[36]

OUT OF NOTHING. AUGUSTINE: Everything which God did not beget of himself but made through his Word he made not out of things which already existed but out of what did not exist at all, i.e., out of nothing.[37] THE NATURE OF THE GOOD 26.[38]

---

[33]CSEL 81.1:143, 145. [34]Gen 16:1, 15; 25:12-18; 36:12; Ps 83:6. [35]NPNF 1 11:390. [36]AOR 9. [37]Gen 1:1; Jn 1:3. [38]LCC 6:334.

4:18-25 ABRAHAM'S FAITH AND OURS

[18]*In hope he believed against hope, that he should become the father of many nations; as he had been told, "So shall your descendants be."* [19]*He did not weaken in faith when he considered his own body, which was as good as dead because he was about a hundred years old, or when he considered the barrenness of Sarah's womb.* [20]*No distrust made him waver concerning the promise of God, but he grew strong in his faith as he gave glory to God,* [21]*fully convinced that God was able to do what he had promised.* [22]*That is why his faith was "reckoned to him as righteousness."* [23]*But the words, "it was reckoned to him," were written not for his sake alone,* [24]*but for ours also. It will be reckoned to us who believe in him that raised from the dead Jesus our Lord,* [25]*who was put to death for our trespasses and raised for our justification.*

OVERVIEW: To faith Abraham added hope, even when that flew in the face of reality. In natural terms there was no chance that an old couple like Abraham and Sarah would have children, and yet they did. Hope in the power of God to achieve the impossible is therefore integral to the Christian faith. Abraham's justification was not a private affair. Rather, it was intended to be a model

117

for us. Our faith as Christians is rooted not in belief in the Creator but in the fact that the Creator raised Jesus Christ from the dead. Christ's death and resurrection are the pattern of the Christian life, in which we die to sin in baptism and are born again to a new life of righteousness.

4:18 Believing Against Natural Hope

THE RESURRECTION HOPE. ORIGEN: As always, when the apostle Paul talks about faith, he adds hope as well, and rightly so, for hope and faith are inseparable. . . . Just as Abraham believed against hope, so all believers do the same, for we all believe in the resurrection of the dead and the inheritance of the kingdom of heaven.[1] These appear to go against hope as far as human nature is concerned, but when we take the power of God into consideration, there is no problem. COMMENTARY ON THE EPISTLE TO THE ROMANS.[2]

THE STARS IN THE SKY. AMBROSIASTER: It is clear that since Abraham had no hope of having a son, he believed God and had faith against hope that he would have a son, knowing that with God all things are possible.[3]

The quotation is from Genesis [15:5], where God shows Abraham the stars of the sky and says: "So shall your descendants be," because in believing he was justified. For Abraham believed what seems impossible to the world because it does not occur in the order of nature that old people should have children and know that their seed will increase to such an extent that it will be impossible to count them. Therefore, faith is precious because it believes in the future, even against what it now sees or knows. For it consoles itself in this hope, that it is God who promises. COMMENTARY ON PAUL'S EPISTLES.[4]

IN HOPE HE BELIEVED AGAINST HOPE. PELAGIUS: It was against all natural hope for a hundred-year-old man to believe that his seed would become as numerous as the stars,[5] espe-

cially given that his wife had been barren in her youth and was now as feeble as he was. PELAGIUS'S COMMENTARY ON ROMANS.[6]

THEODORET OF CYR: Abraham believed against the hope of nature but in the hope of the promise of God. INTERPRETATION OF THE LETTER TO THE ROMANS.[7]

4:19 Trusting God, Not the Body

TRUSTING GOD MORE THAN HIS HUNDRED-YEAR-OLD BODY. ORIGEN: This may be understood literally or figuratively. In the literal sense, Abraham did not put his trust in his hundred-year-old body, which was obviously incapable of doing what God had promised him, but rather he trusted in God, the Almighty One who could perform what he had promised even when the laws of human fertility no longer functioned. . . . Figuratively, however, it may be understood in the light of what Paul says elsewhere: "Put to death therefore what is earthly in you."[8] It would be absurd to suggest that what Paul had in this respect was somehow lacking to Abraham. For Abraham also had put his earthly members to death, being neither excited by luxury nor inflamed by lust. . . . Sarah likewise did not suffer from lust or the desires of the flesh. . . . When they heard what God had promised them, they did not consider their own benefit. . . . All these things that would make them rich they regarded as worthless in order that they might win Christ,[9] whose coming they foresaw. COMMENTARY ON THE EPISTLE TO THE ROMANS.[10]

PELAGIUS: Faith takes no aspect of nature into account, because it knows that the one who spoke is almighty. PELAGIUS'S COMMENTARY ON ROMANS.[11]

---

[1]Mt 7:21; 22:31-32; Lk 14:13-14; Jn 5:28-29; 1 Pet 1:5. [2]CER 2:226. [3]Mt 19:26; Mk 10:27. [4]CSEL 81.1:145, 147. [5]Gen 15:5. [6]PCR 87-88. [7]IER, Migne PG 82 col. 93. [8]Col 3:5. [9]See Phil 3:7. [10]CER 2:230-34. [11]PCR 88.

OECUMENIUS: Paul was right to say: "about a hundred," because Abraham was not a hundred but only ninety-nine years old.[12] PAULINE COMMENTARY FROM THE GREEK CHURCH.[13]

4:20 Growing Strong in Faith

TRUSTING THE PROMISE. CHRYSOSTOM: Abraham trusted God even though God gave him no proof, nor even a sign. Rather, there were only mere words promising things which by nature were impossible. HOMILIES ON ROMANS 8.[14]

GLORY TO GOD. AUGUSTINE: Paul says that Abraham "gave glory to God" when he was attacking those who were seeking their own glory in the sight of men by doing the works of the law. AUGUSTINE ON ROMANS 25.[15]

PELAGIUS: Abraham doubted neither the impossibility of old age nor the greatness of the promise. PELAGIUS'S COMMENTARY ON ROMANS.[16]

4:21 Convinced of God's Ability

NO FEAR THAT GOD CANNOT DO THE ENTIRE WORK. AUGUSTINE: God brings about the faith of the Gentiles, because he is able to perform what he has promised. If it is God who produces our faith, acting in a wondrous manner in our hearts so that we believe, surely we should not fear that he cannot do the entire work.[17] PREDESTINATION OF THE SAINTS 2.6.[18]

PELAGIUS: Abraham thanked God as if he had already received the gift. PELAGIUS'S COMMENTARY ON ROMANS.[19]

4:22 Faith Reckoned as Righteousness

HE STRENGTHENED HIS WEAKNESS BY FAITH. AMBROSIASTER: Paul claims that Abraham is worthy of this praise because although he knew that he could not do it himself, he strengthened his weakness by faith, so that he believed that

with God's help he could do what he knew was impossible by the laws of the universe. He was of great merit before God because he believed God over against his own knowledge, not doubting that because he was God he could do things which were impossible according to the world's wisdom.

Paul therefore urges the Gentiles to believe as firmly as Abraham did so that they might receive the promise of God and his grace without any hesitation, secure in the example of Abraham that the praise given to a believer increases if he believes what is incredible and seems to be foolish to the world. For the more foolish what he believes is thought to be, the more honor he will have, and indeed it would be foolish to believe it if it were said to occur without God. COMMENTARY ON PAUL'S EPISTLES.[20]

PELAGIUS: This was because Abraham believed so completely and so steadfastly. PELAGIUS'S COMMENTARY ON ROMANS.[21]

4:23 Not Only for Abraham

A MODEL FOR FAITH. AMBROSIASTER: Paul says that in Abraham a model was given to both Jews and Gentiles, so that by his example we might believe in God and Christ and the Holy Spirit, and that it might be reckoned to us as righteousness. COMMENTARY ON PAUL'S EPISTLES.[22]

4:24 For Our Sake Also

BELIEVING THAT GOD COULD RAISE ISAAC FROM NOTHING. ORIGEN: Note that Paul does not speak of those who believe that God is supreme, or of those who believe that he made heaven and earth, or of those who believe that he made the angels and the other hosts of the heavenly glory. Rather, he speaks of those who believe in the God

---

[12]Gen 17:1, 24. [13]NTA 15:424. [14]NPNF 1 11:390-91. [15]AOR 9. [16]PCR 88. [17]2 Cor 1:20. [18]FC 86:222. [19]PCR 88. [20]CSEL 81.1:147. [21]PCR 88. [22]CSEL 81.1:149.

who raised Jesus Christ from the dead. Did Abraham believe in this God even before he had raised Jesus? . . . Abraham's faith contained within it the form and image of this great mystery. For when he was ordered to sacrifice his only son, he believed that God could raise him up from the dead.[23] Moreover, he did not believe this of Isaac only but also of his seed, which is Christ. COMMENTARY ON THE EPISTLE TO THE ROMANS.[24]

FOR OURS ALSO. AMBROSIASTER: Although what is now believed is different, faith has one and the same gift. Therefore we receive this gift because we believe. And believing that Christ is the Son of God, we are adopted as sons, for God could give no greater gift to believers than to call them sons of God once they had renounced their sins. For we are called "sons of God," but they are not worthy even to be called servants. COMMENTARY ON PAUL'S EPISTLES.[25]

THE FATHER'S WORK THROUGH THE SON. APOLLINARIS OF LAODICEA: The Lord is building his own temple, for the Father raised Christ from the dead in order to do his work through the Son. PAULINE COMMENTARY FROM THE GREEK CHURCH.[26]

IMITATE ABRAHAM'S EXAMPLE. PELAGIUS: We are meant to imitate Abraham's example as if he were our father, just as we imitate the examples of the saints, by which they pleased the Lord. They were tempted so that they might know themselves and so that we might follow them. We shall benefit if we believe as completely that God has raised Christ from the dead as Abraham believed that his body, which was as good as dead, could be made alive in order to produce children. PELAGIUS'S COMMENTARY ON ROMANS.[27]

4:25 Christ Crucified and Resurrected

PUT TO DEATH FOR OUR TRESPASSES. ORIGEN: Paul says this in order to show that we ought to hate and reject the things for which Christ died. For if we believe that he was sacrificed for our sins, how can we not consider every sin to be alien and hostile to us, considering that our Lord was handed over to death because of it? . . .

If we have risen together with Christ, who is our justification, and we now walk in newness of life and live according to righteousness, then Christ has risen for the purpose of our justification. But if we have not yet cast off the old man with all his works but instead live in unrighteousness, I dare to suggest that Christ has not yet risen for our justification, nor has he been sacrificed for our sins. COMMENTARY ON THE EPISTLE TO THE ROMANS.[28]

WE CANNOT BE HELD BY DEATH. AMBROSIASTER: Those who were baptized before Christ's passion received only the remission of their sins. . . . But after the resurrection both those who were baptized before and those who were baptized after were all justified by the set form of faith in the Trinity, and they received the Holy Spirit, who is the sign of believers that they are children of God. . . . For by the Savior's passion death is vanquished. Once it was dominant because of sin, but it does not dare to hang on to those who have been justified by God. COMMENTARY ON PAUL'S EPISTLES.[29]

WHY CRUCIFIED AND RAISED. CHRYSOSTOM: After mentioning the cause of Christ's death, Paul goes on to make the same cause a demonstration of the resurrection. For why was Christ crucified? Not for any sins of his own—and this is plain from the resurrection. For if Christ had been a sinner, how could he have risen from the dead? So if he did rise, it is clear that he was not a sinner. . . . Moreover, Christ did not die in order to make us liable to punishment and condemnation but in order to do good to us. HOMILIES ON ROMANS 9.[30]

---

[23]Gen 22:1-19. [24]CER 2:238-40. [25]CSEL 81.1:149. [26]NTA 15:62. [27]PCR 88. [28]CER 2:244-46. [29]CSEL 81.1:151. [30]NPNF 1 11:395.

Raised for Our Justification.
[Pseudo-]Constantius: Christ was not raised for justice (which would have condemned us) but for our justification. The Holy Letter of St. Paul to the Romans.[31]

Pelagius: Christ wiped away our sins by his death, and, rising again in the same state as the one in which he died, he appeared to believers in order to confirm their righteousness.[32] Pelagius's Commentary on Romans.[33]

His Resurrection Prefigures the General Resurrection. Theodoret of Cyr: Christ underwent suffering for our sins in order to pay our debt and so that his resurrection might prefigure the general resurrection of us all. Interpretation of the Letter to the Romans.[34]

---

[31]ENPK 2:36. [32]Lk 24:36-50. [33]PCR 88. [34]IER, Migne PG 82 col. 93.

5:1-11 PEACE WITH GOD

[1]Therefore, since we are justified by faith, we[f] have peace with God through our Lord Jesus Christ. [2]Through him we have obtained access[g] to this grace in which we stand, and we[h] rejoice in our hope of sharing the glory of God. [3]More than that, we rejoice in our sufferings, knowing that suffering produces endurance, [4]and endurance produces character, and character produces hope, [5]and hope does not disappoint us, because God's love has been poured into our hearts through the Holy Spirit which has been given to us.

[6]While we were still weak, at the right time Christ died for the ungodly. [7]Why, one will hardly die for a righteous man—though perhaps for a good man one will dare even to die. [8]But God shows his love for us in that while we were yet sinners Christ died for us. [9]Since, therefore, we are now justified by his blood, much more shall we be saved by him from the wrath of God. [10]For if while we were enemies we were reconciled to God by the death of his Son, much more, now that we are reconciled, shall we be saved by his life. [11]Not only so, but we also rejoice in God through our Lord Jesus Christ, through whom we have now received our reconciliation.

f Other ancient authorities read let us   g Other ancient authorities add by faith   h Or let us

Overview: Once we are justified by faith we have peace with God and therefore also peace with ourselves, because the spirit within us is no longer at war with the flesh. This does not mean that we have no more trouble or suffering but that, because we are at peace inside ourselves, we are equipped to do battle with the external forces of evil that continue to fight against us. Faith in Christ brings us nearer to God and gives us a greater share in his glory. This in turn produces the hope that what God has begun in us he will bring to completion at the last day. For the Christian, suffering has a positive purpose. Before the fourth century, Christians suffered periodic persecutions for their beliefs. The first fruit of suffering is patience (endurance), which the Fathers perceived as a great good. Endurance forms character and gives us a positive attitude toward the future.

Christ died for us while we were still ungodly, and this is the measure of his love for us. What can we do but respond to him with a similar love? The early Christians had grown accustomed through martyrdom to the idea that innocent people could and would be put to death. But the martyrs were dying for God, who deserved their devotion, whereas Christ died for us, who are undeserving. This is the true miracle of God's love for us. Justification is a work of God. We have been justified by what Christ has done and not by the way we have responded to him. Sinners are enemies of God, but sin is willful disobedience, not some flaw in the created order. God's love is manifested to us in that his Son died for us while we were still sinners. Christians do not dwell on their sins but rather rejoice that they have been delivered from them in and by Christ, who has reconciled us to God. God does not let us down, because he has given us the ultimate gift—his love, manifested by the presence of the Holy Spirit in our hearts.

5:1 Peace with God

THE GUARANTEE OF PEACE. ORIGEN: It is obvious from this that the apostle is inviting everyone who has understood that he is justified by faith and not by works to that "peace which passes all understanding,"[1] in which the height of perfection consists. But let us investigate further in order to see what the apostle means when he talks about peace, and especially about that peace which is through our Lord Jesus Christ. Peace reigns when nobody complains, nobody disagrees, nobody is hostile and nobody misbehaves. Therefore, we who once were enemies of God, following the devil, that great enemy and tyrant, now, if we have thrown down his weapons and in their place taken up the sign of Christ and the standard of his cross,

have peace with God. But this is through our Lord Jesus Christ, who has reconciled us to God through the offering of his blood.

Let us therefore have peace, so that the flesh will no longer war with the spirit, nor will the law of God be opposed by the law of our members. Let there not be in us "yes" and "no," but let us all agree, let us all think alike, let there be no dissension either among ourselves or between us and others outside our ranks, and then we shall have peace with God through our Lord Jesus Christ. But let it most definitely be known that anyone in whom the vice of wickedness is found can never have peace. For as long as he is thinking how he can hurt his neighbor, as long as he seeks after ways of causing harm, his mind will never be at peace.

But if you ask me how a righteous man can have peace when he is attacked by the devil, who maintains his wars of temptation, I would say that such a man has greater peace than anyone else. . . . For the apostle says that we have peace with God knowing full well that war against the devil is a guarantee of peace with God. We shall have even greater peace with God if we continue our active hostility toward the devil and fight against the vices of the flesh. For the apostle James says: "Resist the devil and he will flee from you; draw near to God and he will draw near to you."[2] You see that James too felt that he was getting closer to God by resisting the devil. COMMENTARY ON THE EPISTLE TO THE ROMANS.[3]

FAITH GIVES US PEACE WITH GOD. AMBROSIASTER: Faith gives us peace with God, not the law. For it reconciles us to God by taking away those sins which had made us God's enemies. And because the Lord Jesus is the minister of this grace, it is through him that we have peace with God.[4] Faith is greater than the law because the law is our work, whereas faith belongs to God. Furthermore, the law is concerned with our present life, whereas faith is concerned with eter-

---

[1]Phil 4:7. [2]Jas 4:7-8. [3]CER 2:250-56. [4]Eph 2:14.

nal life. But whoever does not think this way about Christ, as he ought to, will not be able to obtain the rewards of faith, because he does not hold the truth of faith. COMMENTARY ON PAUL'S EPISTLES.[5]

GOD RECONCILED US TO HIMSELF. CHRYSOSTOM: What does it mean to have peace? Some say that it means that we should not fall out with one another because of disagreements over the law. But it seems to me that he is speaking much more about our current behavior. . . . Paul means here that we should stop sinning and not go back to the way we used to live, for that is to make war with God.

How is this possible? Paul says that not only is it possible, it is also reasonable. For if God reconciled us to himself when we were in open warfare with him, it is surely reasonable that we should be able to remain in a state of reconciliation. HOMILIES ON ROMANS 9.[6]

JUSTIFIED BY FAITH ALONE. PELAGIUS: Paul has discussed the point that nobody is justified by works, but all are justified by faith, and he has proved this by the example of Abraham, of whom the Jews claim to be the only children. He has also explained why neither race nor circumcision makes people children of Abraham but only faith, because Abraham was initially justified by faith alone. Now, having concluded this argument, Paul urges both Jews and Gentiles to live at peace, because no one is saved by his own merit, but everyone is saved in the same way, by God's grace. "Peace with God" means either that both sides should submit to God or that we should have the peace of God and not just the peace of the world. PELAGIUS'S COMMENTARY ON ROMANS.[7]

KEEP THE PEACE. THEODORET OF CYR: Faith has given you forgiveness of sins and made you spotless and righteous by the washing of regeneration. Therefore you ought to keep the peace by which you have been united with God. For when

you were still enemies, the only begotten Son of God reconciled you by taking on human flesh and putting sin to death in it. INTERPRETATION OF THE LETTER TO THE ROMANS.[8]

5:2 Standing in Grace

THE DOOR OF TRUTH. ORIGEN: How we have access to grace through our Lord Jesus Christ, the Savior himself tells us "I am the door,"[9] and "No one comes to the Father except by me."[10] . . . This door is the truth, and liars cannot enter in by the door of truth. Again, this door is righteousness, and the unrighteous cannot enter in by it. The Door himself says: "Learn from me, for I am gentle and lowly in heart."[11] So neither the irascible nor the proud can enter in by the door of humility and gentleness. Therefore, if anyone wants to have access to the grace of God which according to the word of the apostle comes through our Lord Jesus Christ and in which Paul and those like him claim to stand, it is essential that he be cleansed of all the things which we have listed above. Otherwise those who do what is contrary to Christ will not be allowed to go in by that door, which will remain closed and keep out those who are incompatible with him.

Why does Paul talk about the hope of glory and not just about the glory itself? After all, Moses saw the glory of God, and so did the people of Israel when God's house was built. But this glory, which was visible, the apostle Paul dared to claim would pass away . . . whereas the hope here is of a glory which will never pass away. It is the glory mentioned in Hebrews[12] in connection with Christ: "He reflects the glory of God and bears the very stamp of his nature." COMMENTARY ON THE EPISTLE TO THE ROMANS.[13]

IF WE STAND. AMBROSIASTER: It is clear that in Christ we have access to the grace of God. For he is the mediator between God and men, who

---

[5]CSEL 81.1:181. [6]NPNF 1 11:396. [7]PCR 89. [8]IER, Migne PG 82 col. 96. [9]Jn 10:9. [10]Jn 14:6. [11]Mt 11:29. [12]Heb 1:3. [13]CER 2:256-60.

builds us up by his teaching and gives us the hope of receiving the gift of his grace if we stand in his faith. Therefore, if we stand (because we used to be flat on the floor) we stand as believers, glorying in the hope of the glory which he has promised to us. Commentary on Paul's Epistles.[14]

Access to Grace. Chrysostom: If God brought us near to himself when we were far off, how much more will he keep us now that we are near! . . . What grace is it to which we now have access? It is being counted worthy of the knowledge of God, being forced to abandon error, coming to a knowledge of the truth, obtaining all the blessings which come through baptism. For the reason he brought us near in the first place was that we might receive these gifts. For we were not reconciled merely in order to receive forgiveness of sins; we were meant to receive countless additional benefits as well. Homilies on Romans 9.[15]

We Rejoice in Hope of What Seems Unbelievable Because of Its Greatness. Pelagius: We have drawn near to God, because previously we were far away from him,[16] and we stand, because previously we were flat on our faces. We rejoice in the hope that we shall possess the glory of God's children. What we hope for is so great that no one would try it on his own, in case it should be regarded as blasphemy, not as hope, and as something which many people think is unbelievable because of its greatness. Pelagius's Commentary on Romans.[17]

5:3 Suffering Produces Endurance

Suffering Not an End in Itself. Origen: The word *rejoice* is sometimes used positively in Scripture and sometimes negatively. . . . For if someone rejoices in his wisdom or strength or riches, he is wrong to do so, but if he rejoices in knowing God and in understanding his judgments of mercy and righteousness, he is right to do so. In this case, Paul says that he rejoices in his

sufferings, not as an end in themselves but because they lead to various virtues of the soul. . . . If suffering produces patience and patience is one of the virtues of the soul, then there is no doubt that suffering must be called not evil or neutral but definitely good. Commentary on the Epistle to the Romans.[18]

Like Exercise for Athletes. Basil: For those who are well prepared, tribulations are like certain foods and exercises for athletes which lead the contestant on to the inheritance of glory. When we are reviled, we bless; maligned, we entreat; ill-treated, we give thanks; afflicted, we glory in our afflictions. Homily 16.[19]

Blessed Are Those Persecuted. Ambrosiaster: Since it is through tribulations that we must enter the kingdom of God, Paul teaches that we should rejoice in them. For suffering added to hope increases our reward. Suffering is the measure of how much hope we have, and it testifies to the fact that we deserve the crown we shall inherit. This is why the Lord said: "Blessed are you when they persecute you and say all kinds of evil things against you on account of God's righteousness. Rejoice and be glad, for your reward in heaven is great."[20] For to despise present sufferings and hindrances and, for the hope of the future, not to give in to pressure has great merit with God. Therefore one should rejoice in suffering, believing that he will be all the more acceptable to God as he sees himself made stronger in the face of tribulation.

Suffering produces endurance as long as it is not the result of weakness or doubt. Commentary on Paul's Epistles.[21]

Suffering Prepares Us for Endurance. Chrysostom: Consider how great the things to come are, when we can rejoice even at things which appear to be distressful. . . . Sufferings are

---

[14]CSEL 81.1:153. [15]NPNF 1 11:396. [16]Eph 2:13. [17]PCR 89. [18]CER 2:268, 274. [19]FC 46:249. [20]Mt 5:11-12. [21]CSEL 81.1:153.

in themselves a good thing, insofar as they prepare us for endurance. HOMILIES ON ROMANS 9.[22]

AUGUSTINE: Paul says this in order to lead us gradually to the love of God, which he says that we have by the gift of the Spirit. He shows us that all those things which we might attribute to ourselves ought to be attributed to God, who was pleased to give us his Holy Spirit through grace. AUGUSTINE ON ROMANS 26.[23]

MINDFUL OF THE END OF SUFFERING.
PELAGIUS: We glory not only in the hope of glory but also in sufferings which are most salutary, being mindful of the greatness of the reward.[24] We should desire to suffer something for the Lord's name so that when sufferings come to an end we may obtain an eternal reward for them. For when we consider the reward, we cannot possibly begrudge the effort needed to be worthy of the reward. PELAGIUS'S COMMENTARY ON ROMANS.[25]

5:4 Endurance Produces Character

ENDURANCE AND HOPE. CLEMENT OF ALEXANDRIA: Endurance is directed toward future hope. Hope is directed toward the reward and restitution of hope. STROMATA 4.22.[26]

STRENGTH THROUGH TESTING. AMBROSIASTER: It is clear that if endurance is of the quality we have said, our character will be quite strong. That there should be hope in someone who has been tried and tested is perfectly reasonable. One who is thus made worthy is sure to receive a reward in the kingdom of God. COMMENTARY ON PAUL'S EPISTLES.[27]

CHARACTER GIVES POWER TO HOPE. CHRYSOSTOM: Endurance produces character, which contributes in some measure to the things which are to come because it gives power to the hope which is within us. Nothing encourages a man to hope for blessing more than the strength of a

good character. No one who has led a good life worries about the future.... Does our good really lie in hope? Yes, but not in human hopes, which often vanish and leave only embarrassment behind. Our hope is in God and is therefore sure and immovable.[28] HOMILIES ON ROMANS 9.[29]

5:5 God's Love Poured into Our Hearts

WHOSE HEARTS? ORIGEN: Whose hearts are those into which God's love has been poured? I believe these are the hearts of those in whom "perfect love has cast out fear"[30] and to whom the spirit of adoption has been given, who cries in their hearts: "Abba, Father!"[31] COMMENTARY ON THE EPISTLE TO THE ROMANS.[32]

HOPE DOES NOT DISAPPOINT. AMBROSIASTER: Hope does not let us down, even though we are considered by evil people to be stupid and naive, because we believe in things which are impossible in this world. For we have in us the pledge of God's love through the Holy Spirit, who has been given to us. COMMENTARY ON PAUL'S EPISTLES.[33]

THE GREATEST GIFT POSSIBLE. CHRYSOSTOM: God has given us the greatest gift possible and in profusion.... What is this gift? It is the Holy Spirit. HOMILIES ON ROMANS 9.[34]

[PSEUDO-]CONSTANTIUS: Clearly Paul is saying here that whatever is given to us by God the Father is given through the Holy Spirit. THE HOLY LETTER OF ST. PAUL TO THE ROMANS.[35]

MORAL PROGRESS. AUGUSTINE: Who can hurt such a man? Who can subdue him? In prosperity he makes moral progress, and in adversity he learns to know the progress he has made. When

---

[22]NPNF 1 11:397. [23]AOR 9. [24]See Jas 1:2. [25]PCR 89. [26]ANF 2:436. [27]CSEL 81.1:155. [28]Ps 146:5-10. [29]NPNF 1 11:397. [30]1 Jn 4:18. [31]Rom 8:15; Gal 4:6. [32]CER 2:278. [33]CSEL 81.1:155. [34]NPNF 1 11:398. [35]ENPK 2:37.

he has an abundance of mutable goods he does not put his trust in them, and when they are taken away he gets to know whether or not they have taken him captive. OF TRUE RELIGION 92.[36]

THE LOVE OF GOD. AUGUSTINE: That God may be loved, the love of God is shed abroad in our hearts, not by the free choice whose spring is in ourselves but through the Holy Spirit, who is given to us. THE SPIRIT AND THE LETTER 5.3.[37]

CONFORMED TO GOD. AUGUSTINE: It is through love that we are conformed to God, and being so conformed and made like to him, and set apart from the world, we are no longer confounded by those things which should be subject to us. This is the work of the Holy Spirit. THE WAY OF LIFE OF THE CATHOLIC CHURCH 1.13.23.[38]

WHY TRIBULATION DOES NOT DESTROY PATIENCE. AUGUSTINE: It is not by ourselves but by the Holy Spirit who is given to us that this charity, shown by the apostle to be God's gift, is the reason why tribulation does not destroy patience but rather gives rise to it. GRACE AND FREE WILL 18.39.[39]

LOVE IS NOT DISMAYED. PELAGIUS: The hope of things to come casts out all confusion. This is why the man who is dismayed by Christ's injunctions lacks hope. The greatness of God's benefits arouses in us greatness of love, which does not know fear or dismay because it is complete.[40] We also learn how God loves us, because he has not only forgiven us our sins through the death of his Son but also given us the Holy Spirit, who already shows us the glory of things to come. PELAGIUS'S COMMENTARY ON ROMANS.[41]

INDWELLING OF THE SPIRIT. OECUMENIUS: It is to be understood that the indwelling of the adorable and thrice-Holy Spirit is found only in our minds and hearts. PAULINE COMMENTARY FROM THE GREEK CHURCH.[42]

GRACE ENABLES THE FULFILLMENT OF LAW. BEDE: The law was indeed given through Moses, and there it was determined by a heavenly rule what was to be done and what was to be avoided, but what it commanded was completed only by the grace of Christ. On the one hand, that law was able to point out sin, teaching justice and showing transgressors what they are charged with. On the other hand, the grace of Christ, poured out in the hearts of the faithful through the spirit of charity, brings it about that what the law commanded may be fulfilled. HOMILIES ON THE GOSPELS 1.2.[43]

5:6 Christ Died for the Ungodly

CHRIST DIED FOR US. ORIGEN: In order to show more fully what power the love which is poured into our hearts by the Holy Spirit has, Paul expounds the way we ought to understand it by teaching us that Christ died not for the godly but for the ungodly. For we were ungodly before we turned to God, and Christ died for us before we believed. Undoubtedly he would not have done this unless either he himself or God the Father, who gave up his only begotten Son for the redemption of the ungodly, had superabundant love toward us. COMMENTARY ON THE EPISTLE TO THE ROMANS.[44]

IF HE DIED FOR ENEMIES, THINK OF WHAT HE WILL DO FOR FRIENDS. AMBROSIASTER: If Christ gave himself up to death at the right time for those who were unbelievers and enemies of God . . . how much more will he protect us with his help if we believe in him! He died for us in order to obtain life and glory for us. So if he died for his enemies, just think what he will do for his friends! COMMENTARY ON PAUL'S EPISTLES.[45]

AT THE RIGHT TIME. PELAGIUS: Why did

---

[36]LCC 6:273. [37]LCC 8:198. [38]FC 56:21. [39]FC 59:295. [40]See 1 Jn 4:18. [41]PCR 90. [42]NTA 15:424. [43]CSEL 110 1:13. [44]CER 2:280-282. [45]CSEL 81.1:157.

Christ die for us when he had no obligation to do so, if it was not to manifest his love at a time when we were still weighed down with the burden of sin and vice? It was the right time, either because righteousness had virtually disappeared and we were weak, or because it was the end of time, or because Christ was dead for the prophesied three-day period.[46] Paul wants to point out that Christ died for the ungodly in order to commend the grace of Christ by considering his benefits and to show how much we, who have been undeservedly loved, ought to love him, and so that we might see whether anything should be valued more highly than one who is so generous and holy. He neither valued his life above us ungodly people nor withheld the death that was indispensable for us. PELAGIUS'S COMMENTARY ON ROMANS.[47]

5:7 Dying for a Good Man

WHAT ABOUT THE MARTYRS? ORIGEN: How can Paul say this when the Bible is full of martyrs? What were they doing? In fact, the martyrs were not dying for other people but for God, and for him anyone would dare to die. But every other death is much harder to endure, even if it is just and in accordance with the law of human nature. COMMENTARY ON THE EPISTLE TO THE ROMANS.[48]

DYING FOR THE UNGODLY. AMBROSIASTER: Christ died for the ungodly. Now if someone will hardly die for a righteous man, how can it be that someone should die for ungodly people? And if someone might dare to die for one good man (or not dare, since the phrase is ambiguous), how can it be that someone would dare to die for a multitude of the ungodly? For if someone dares to die for a righteous or good man, it is probably because he has been touched with some sort of pity or been impressed by his good works. But in the case of the ungodly, not only is there no reason to die for them, but there is plenty to move us to tears when we look at them! COMMENTARY ON PAUL'S EPISTLES.[49]

[Pseudo-]CONSTANTIUS: Many say that in this passage the good man is Christ our God, for whose name some are ready for death and are crowned with martyrdom. THE HOLY LETTER OF ST. PAUL TO THE ROMANS.[50]

PELAGIUS: It is hard to die for a righteous person, because a righteous person is not destined to die. . . . But perhaps one would die for a good person, so that no harm might come to him. PELAGIUS'S COMMENTARY ON ROMANS.[51]

5:8 How God Shows His Love for Us

WHILE WE WERE YET SINNERS. ORIGEN: By saying that Christ died for us while we were yet sinners, Paul gives us hope that we will be saved through him, much more so now that we are cleansed from sin and justified against the wrath which remains for sinners. The One who so loved his enemies that he gave his only Son to die for us will surely be much readier to grant those who have received this gift and been reconciled to him the further gift of eternal life.[52] COMMENTARY ON THE EPISTLE TO THE ROMANS.[53]

GOD SHOWS HIS LOVE. PELAGIUS: God becomes the object of love when he conveys how much he loves us. For when someone does something without obligation, one demonstrates love in a special way. And what would be less of an obligation than that a master who is without sin should die for his faithless servants, and that the Creator of the universe should be hanged for the sake of his own creatures? Note that when the apostle says that believers in Christ were once sinners he means that now they are no longer sinners, so that they may recall how they ought to behave. PELAGIUS'S COMMENTARY ON ROMANS.[54]

5:9 Justified and Saved from Wrath

---

[46]See Mt 26:61; Mk 8:31; 1 Cor 15:4. [47]PCR 90-91. [48]CER 2:284-86. [49]CSEL 81.1:157. [50]ENPK 2:37. [51]PCR 91. [52]Rom 6:23. [53]CER 2:288. [54]PCR 91.

Much More by His Blood Than Our Faith.
Origen: Paul shows by this that neither our faith
without Christ's blood nor Christ's blood without our faith can justify us. Yet of either of these
Christ's blood justifies us much more than our
faith. That is why, in my opinion, having said
above that we are justified by faith, Paul now says
that we are justified by his blood "much more."[55]
Commentary on the Epistle to the
Romans.[56]

Saved by Him from Wrath. Ambrosiaster:
Paul says this, because if God allowed his Son to
be killed for sinners' sake, what will he do for
those who have been justified except save them
from wrath, that is, preserve them unharmed
from the deception of Satan so that they will be
safe on the day of judgment, when revenge will
begin to destroy the wicked. For since the goodness of God does not want anyone to perish, he
has shown mercy on those who deserved death in
order to increase the honor and glory of those
who understand the grace of God. Commentary
on Paul's Epistles.[57]

Preserving the Righteous. Pelagius: If
Christ loved sinners so much, how much more
will he now preserve the righteous! We must be
careful not to make him unclean by our sinning,
as the apostle himself tells the Hebrews.[58]
Pelagius's Commentary on Romans.[59]

5:10 Reconciled by Christ's Death, Saved by His Life

Enmity Overcome. Origen: In saying this Paul
shows that there is no substance which is hostile
to God, as the Marcionites and Valentinians
think, for if something was hostile to God by nature and not simply by will, reconciliation with
him would be impossible. . . .

Christ's death brought death to the enmity
which existed between us and God and ushered
in reconciliation. For Christ's resurrection and
life brought with it salvation to those who

believe, as the apostle said of Christ: "The death
he died he died to sin, once for all, but the life he
lives he lives to God."[60] Christ is said to be dead
to sin—not to his own, for he never sinned, but
dead to sin in that by his death he put sin to
death as well. For he is said to live to God so that
we also might live to God and not to ourselves or
to our own will, so that at the last we may be
saved by his life. Commentary on the Epistle
to the Romans.[61]

Ambrosiaster: The God who acts on behalf of
his enemies will not be able to love his friends
any less than that. Therefore if the death of the
Savior benefited us while we were still ungodly,
how much more will his life do for us who are justified, when he raises us from the dead? Commentary on Paul's Epistles.[62]

Ineffable Benevolence. Basil: There are
many passages of this sort, which set forth with
clarity and splendor the great, ineffable benevolence of God in freely pardoning our sins and
granting us the means and the power of performing righteous acts for the glory of God and his
Christ, in the hope of receiving eternal life
through Jesus Christ our Lord. Concerning
Baptism 1.2.[63]

Chrysostom: There is no one who will save us
except the One who loved us so much that while
we were yet sinners, he died for us. Do you see
what ground this gives for us to hope? For before
this there were two difficulties in the way of our
being saved. First, we were sinners, and second,
our salvation required the Lord's death, something which was quite incredible before it happened and which required enormous love for it to
happen at all. But now that it has happened, the
rest becomes that much easier. Homilies on
Romans 9.[64]

---

[55]Col 1:19-20. [56]CER 2:290. [57]CSEL 81.1:161. [58]Heb 10:29. [59]PCR
91. [60]Rom 6:10. [61]CER 2:294, 298. [62]CSEL 81.1:161. [63]FC 9:360.
[64]NPNF 1 11:398.

SAVED BY HIS DEATH, WE GLORY IN HIS LIFE. PELAGIUS: Sinners are enemies because they show contempt.[65] We were enemies in our deeds but not by nature; we have been reconciled in peace, because by nature we have been united in peace. If we have been saved by Christ's death, how much more shall we glory in his life if we imitate it! PELAGIUS'S COMMENTARY ON ROMANS.[66]

CHRIST'S SUFFERING IN HIS HUMAN NATURE. THEODORET OF CYR: Once more, Paul calls the Lord Christ "the Son," who is both God and man. But it is clear, I think, even to the greatest heretics in which nature his suffering took place. INTERPRETATION OF THE LETTER TO THE ROMANS.[67]

5:11 Rejoicing in Our Reconciliation

NOW RECEIVED OUR RECONCILIATION. ORIGEN: Paul stresses the "now" in order to indicate that our rejoicing is not merely a future hope but also a present experience. COMMENTARY ON THE EPISTLE TO THE ROMANS.[68]

REJOICE IN GOD. AMBROSIASTER: Paul teaches us not only that we should thank God, for the salvation and assurance which we have received, but that we should also rejoice in God through our Lord Jesus Christ, because through his Son the Mediator God has been pleased to call us his friends. Therefore we can rejoice that we have received every blessing through Christ, that through him we have come to know God. As we rejoice in him, let us therefore honor the Son equally with the Father, as he himself bears witness, saying: "That they may honor the Son as they honor the Father."[69] COMMENTARY ON PAUL'S EPISTLES.[70]

SAVED BY GOD'S ONLY SON. CHRYSOSTOM: The fact that we who were such terrible sinners were saved is a very great sign, indicating how much we were loved by him who saved us. For it was not by angels or archangels but by his only begotten Son that God saved us! HOMILIES ON ROMANS 9.[71]

PELAGIUS: Not only shall we have eternal life, but through Christ we are promised a certain likeness to divine glory as well.[72] Paul wants to show that Christ suffered so that we who had forsaken God by following Adam might be reconciled to God through Christ. PELAGIUS'S COMMENTARY ON ROMANS.[73]

---

[65]See Jas 4:4. [66]PCR 91-92. [67]IER, Migne PG 82 col. 97. [68]CER 2:300. [69]Jn 5:23. [70]CSEL 81.1:161, 163. [71]NPNF 1 11:399. [72]See 1 Jn 3:2. [73]PCR 92.

5:12-21 ADAM AND CHRIST

[12]*Therefore as sin came into the world through one man and death through sin, and so death spread to all men because all men sinned—*[13]*sin indeed was in the world before the law was given, but sin is not counted where there is no law.* [14]*Yet death reigned from Adam to Moses, even over those whose sins were not like the transgression of Adam, who was a type of the one who was to come.*

¹⁵But the free gift is not like the trespass. For if many died through one man's trespass, much more have the grace of God and the free gift in the grace of that one man Jesus Christ abounded for many. ¹⁶And the free gift is not like the effect of that one man's sin. For the judgment following one trespass brought condemnation, but the free gift following many trespasses brings justification. ¹⁷If, because of one man's trespass, death reigned through that one man, much more will those who receive the abundance of grace and the free gift of righteousness reign in life through the one man Jesus Christ.

¹⁸Then as one man's trespass led to condemnation for all men, so one man's act of righteousness leads to acquittal and life for all men. ¹⁹For as by one man's disobedience many were made sinners, so by one man's obedience many will be made righteous. ²⁰Law came in, to increase the trespass; but where sin increased, grace abounded all the more, ²¹so that, as sin reigned in death, grace also might reign through righteousness to eternal life through Jesus Christ our Lord.

OVERVIEW: Eve sinned before Adam, but she is not culpable in the way that Adam is because Adam is the head of the human race. The result is that we all have inherited a state of sinfulness from which there is no escape. Even Pelagius denied that there were any truly righteous people left in the world after the fall of Adam. Mortality is the natural consequence of sin, which affects even the smallest children. The existence of sin before the coming of the law was recognized by all the Fathers, but it caused them some difficulty in interpretation. Was there a natural law working in the conscience which would have condemned men long before the law of Moses was given? And what about children and others who were incapable of the sort of reflection that conscience demands? Were they excused from the consequences of sin? These questions were disputed.

Paul's personification of death as a tyrannical ruler struck a chord with the Fathers, who had plenty of experience of both. The Latin text of this verse and some Greek manuscripts had been corrupted by the deletion of the word *not*. This gave Ambrosiaster the opportunity to use his considerable skills of textual criticism, and it is a pity that he came up with the wrong answer. Augustine saw clearly that the text must refer to all sinners, whether or not they imitated Adam's sin. Adam's sin led to the destruction of the entire human race. Christ's free gift of the grace of salva-

tion is greater than Adam's sin. How then can it be that not all are saved? The answer is that Christ's gift is qualitatively greater than Adam's sin, in that it not only restores what people have lost but also gives them an inheritance in heaven that far surpasses that of Adam in Eden. This salvation cannot be universal, however, because that would deny human free will and be untrue to our experience. In Adam only one sin was condemned, but in Christ many sins have been forgiven—another sign that Christ is greater than Adam. Adam's sin brought death, but Christ's forgiveness brings eternal life. Christ's gift to us is far greater than Adam's, but it does not automatically extend to everyone as Adam's did.

There are two spiritual kingdoms in the world. In the first of these, sin is in control. In the second, the grace of God has overcome sin and given those who belong to it the promise of eternal life. The law shed light on sin and therefore increased it by making it more obvious. Grace abounded all the more because it did not merely forgive us our sins but gave us new life as well. Sin is an act of disobedience, which Christ put right by his perfect obedience. Many Fathers found it difficult to accept any concept of what we would call inherited guilt. To most of them disobedience was a personal act, repeated in each individual but not directly inherited from Adam in a way that would make us responsible for his disobedience.

5:12 Death Spread to All People

FROM ONE MAN TO ALL HUMANITY. ORIGEN: Perhaps someone will object that the woman sinned before the man and even that the serpent sinned before her[1] . . . and elsewhere the apostle says: "Adam was not deceived, but the woman was deceived."[2] . . . How is it then that sin seems to have come in through one man rather than through one woman? . . . Here the apostle sticks to the order of nature, and thus when he speaks about sin, because of which death has passed to all men, he attributes the line of human descent, which has succumbed to this death because of sin, not to the woman but to the man. For the descent is not reckoned from the woman but from the man, as the apostle says elsewhere: "For man was not made from woman but woman from man."[3]

In this context the word *world* is to be understood either as the place in which people live or as the earthly and corporeal life in which death has its location. It is to this world, that is, to this earthly life, that the saints say that they are crucified and dead.

The death which entered through sin is without doubt that death of which the prophet speaks when he says: "The soul which sins shall surely die."[4] One might rightly say that our bodily death is a shadow of this death. For whenever a soul dies, the body is obliged to follow suit, like a shadow. Now if someone objects that the Savior did not sin, nor did his soul die because of sin, yet nevertheless his body suffered death, we would answer that the Savior, although he did not himself sin, nevertheless by the assumption of human flesh is said to have become sin. As a result, although he owed his death to nothing else, nor was he bound to anything outside himself, yet for our salvation he voluntarily took on this shadow as part of his incarnation. As he himself said: "I have power to lay my soul down, and I have power to take it again."[5] . . .

The apostle stated most categorically that the death of sin has passed to all men because all have sinned. . . . Therefore even if you say that Abel was righteous, still he cannot be excused, for all have sinned, including him. COMMENTARY ON THE EPISTLE TO THE ROMANS.[6]

DEATH SPREAD. EUSEBIUS OF CAESAREA: Since the apostle said: "By man death entered into the world," it was surely essential that the victory over death should be achieved by man as well, and the body of death be shown to be the body of life, and the reign of sin that before ruled in the mortal body be destroyed so that it should no longer serve sin but righteousness. PROOF OF THE GOSPEL 7.1.[7]

HOW CAN GOD CALL ME BACK EXCEPT HE FIND ME IN ADAM? AMBROSE: Although through one man's sin death has passed to all men, him whom we do not refuse to acknowledge as the father of the human race we cannot refuse to acknowledge as also the author of death. . . . In Adam I fell, in Adam I was cast out of paradise, in Adam I died. How shall God call me back, except he find me in Adam? For just as in Adam I am guilty of sin and owe a debt to death, so in Christ I am justified. ON THE DEATH OF HIS BROTHER SATYRUS 2.6.[8]

WHETHER THROUGH WOMAN OR MAN. AMBROSIASTER: Paul said that all have sinned in Adam even though in fact it was Eve who sinned because he was not referring to the particular but to the universal. For it is clear that all have sinned in Adam as though in a lump. For, being corrupted by sin himself, all those whom he fathered were born under sin. For that reason we are all sinners, because we all descend from him. He lost God's blessing because he transgressed and was made unworthy to eat of the tree of life. For that reason he had to die. Death is the separation of body and soul. There is another death as well, called the second death, which takes place in Gehenna. We do not suffer this death as a result of Adam's sin, but his fall makes it possible for us

---

[1]Gen 3:1-6. [2]1 Tim 2:14. [3]1 Cor 11:8. [4]Ezek 18:4. [5]Jn 10:18. [6]CER 3:44, 50-52. [7]POG 2:52. [8]FC 22:199-200.

to get it by our own sins. Good men were protected from this, as they were only in hell, but they were still not free, because they could not ascend to heaven. They were still bound by the sentence meted out in Adam, the seal of which was broken by the death of Christ. The sentence passed on Adam was that the human body would decompose on earth, but the soul would be bound by the chains of hell until it was released. COMMENTARY ON PAUL'S EPISTLES.[9]

CHRYSOSTOM: Paul inquires as to how death came into the world and why it prevailed. It came in and prevailed through the sin of one man and continued because all have sinned. Thus once Adam fell, even those who had not eaten of the tree became mortal because of him. HOMILIES ON ROMANS 10.[10]

SIN PASSED TO ALL. [PSEUDO-]CONSTANTIUS: If sin entered the world through one human being—Eve—those who say that there was sin in the world before the devil deceived Eve are mad. THE HOLY LETTER OF ST. PAUL TO THE ROMANS.[11]

THE DEATH OF THE SOUL. [PSEUDO-]CONSTANTIUS: "All men sinned" means that they followed the example of Adam. The apostle is here referring to the death of the soul, which is the death Adam suffered when he transgressed, just as the prophet says: "The soul which sins shall surely die."[12] This sin passed to all men, who transgressed the natural law. THE HOLY LETTER OF ST. PAUL TO THE ROMANS.[13]

EVEN CHILDREN. AUGUSTINE: Everyone, even little children, have broken God's covenant, not indeed in virtue of any personal action but in virtue of mankind's common origin in that single ancestor in whom all have sinned. THE CITY OF GOD 16.27.[14]

BORN WITH DEATH. AUGUSTINE: When a man is born, he is already born with death, because he

contracts sin from Adam. TRACTATES ON THE GOSPEL OF JOHN 49.12.2.[15]

AUGUSTINE: If the souls of all men are derived from that one which was breathed into the first man . . . either the soul of Christ was not derived from that one, since he had no sin of any kind . . . or, if his soul was derived from that first one, he purified it in taking it for himself, so that he might be born of the virgin and might come to us without any trace of sin, either committed or transmitted. LETTER 164.[16]

INFANTS SET FREE FROM SIN'S GUILT BY BAPTISM. AUGUSTINE: As infants cannot help being descended from Adam, so they cannot help being touched by the same sin, unless they are set free from its guilt by the baptism of Christ. LETTER 157.[17]

ORIGINAL SIN. AUGUSTINE: These words clearly teach that original sin is common to all men, regardless of the personal sins of each one. AGAINST JULIAN 6.20.63.[18]

AUGUSTINE: All men for whom Christ died died in the sin of the first Adam, and all who are baptized into Christ die to sin. AGAINST JULIAN 6.7.21.[19]

WHETHER THERE ARE EXCEPTIONS. PELAGIUS: Just as through Adam sin came at a time when it did not yet exist, so through Christ righteousness was recovered at a time when it survived in almost nobody. And just as through Adam's sin death came in, so through Christ's righteousness life was regained.[20] As long as people sin as Adam sinned they die. Death did not pass on to Abraham and Isaac, of whom the Lord says: "They all live to him."[21] But here Paul says that all are dead because in a multitude of sinners

---

[9]CSEL 81.1:165, 167. [10]NPNF 1 11:401. [11]ENPK 2:37. [12]Ezek 18:4. [13]ENPK 2:37. [14]FC 14:537. [15]FC 88:249. [16]FC 20:395. [17]FC 20:335. [18]FC 35:375. [19]FC 35:331. [20]1 Cor 15:21-22. [21]Lk 20:38.

no exception is made for a few righteous. . . . Or perhaps we should understand that death passed on to all who lived in a human and not in a heavenly manner. PELAGIUS'S COMMENTARY ON ROMANS.[22]

ALL INCUR PENALTY. CYRIL OF ALEXANDRIA: Death entered into the first man, and into the beginnings of our race, because of sin, and very soon it had corrupted the entire race. In addition to this, the serpent who invented sin, after he had conquered Adam because of the latter's unfaithfulness, opened up a way for himself to enter the mind of man: "They are corrupt . . . there is none that does good."[23] Therefore, having turned away from the face of the most holy God, and because the mind of man willingly inclined towards evil from its adolescence, we lived an absurd life, and death the conqueror devoured us accordingly. . . . For since we have all copied Adam's transgression and thus have all sinned, we have incurred a penalty equal to his. Yet the world was not without hope, for in the end sin was destroyed, Satan was defeated and death itself was abolished. EXPLANATION OF THE LETTER TO THE ROMANS.[24]

NO ONE IS SINLESS BORN. PRUDENTIUS: Such was the soul's first state. Created pure
> Through sordid union with the flesh it fell
> Into iniquity; stained by Adam's sin,
> It tainted all the race from him derived,
> And infant souls inherit at their birth
> The first man's sin; no one is sinless born.

THE DIVINITY OF CHRIST, LINES 909-15.[25]

EACH ONE SENTENCED. THEODORET OF CYR: St. Paul says that when Adam sinned he became mortal because of it and passed both on to his descendants. Thus death came to all men, in that all sinned. But each person receives the sentence of death not because of the sin of his first ancestor but because of his own sin. INTERPRETATION OF THE LETTER TO THE ROMANS.[26]

ALL INHERIT HIS NATURE. GENNADIUS OF

CONSTANTINOPLE: Everyone in the following of Adam has died, because they have all inherited their nature from him. But some have died because they themselves have sinned, while others have died only because of Adam's condemnation—for example, children. PAULINE COMMENTARY FROM THE GREEK CHURCH.[27]

ALL HAVE SINNED IN IMITATION. OECUMENIUS: So that no one can accuse God of injustice, in that we all die because of the fall of Adam, Paul adds: "and so all have sinned." Adam is the origin and the cause of the fact that we have all sinned in imitation of him. PAULINE COMMENTARY FROM THE GREEK CHURCH.[28]

5:13 Sin Preceded the Law

BEFORE WHICH LAW WAS SIN GIVEN? ORIGEN: We have already said on many occasions that in this epistle Paul mentions many different laws, though most often he is discussing the natural law, which also seems to be the case here. For until the natural law comes, sin is indeed dead. Thus it is that at a particular age, when a person begins to be capable of rational thought and to distinguish between right and wrong, good and evil, then sin, which before that time is considered to be dead inside him, is said to revive, because now he has a law inside him which forbids and a reason which shows him what not to do.

Why does Paul say that sin was "in the world" and not that sin was "in men"? The world includes cattle and other animals, not to mention trees and other things like that, but obviously sin does not dwell in them! It seems to me that here the apostle is referring to those men who are capable of reasoning and are subject to natural laws. Those people who have not yet reached the age of reason are not included in this context.

Another argument against those who think

---

[22]PCR 92-93. [23]Ps 14:1. [24]Migne PF 74 col. 784. [25]FC 52:34-35. [26]IER, Migne PG 82 col. 100. [27]NTA 15:362. [28]NTA 15:424.

that this [verse] refers to the law of Moses is that in that case, the devil and his angels would be absolved, because where there is no law, sin would not be imputed. And how, before the law of Moses, would the serpent have been condemned or death have entered the world by the devil's scheming? COMMENTARY ON THE EPISTLE TO THE ROMANS.[29]

IN WHAT SENSE WAS SIN BEFORE THE LAW?

AMBROSIASTER: Before the law was given, men thought that they could sin with impunity before God but not before other men. For the natural law, of which they were well aware, had not completely lost its force, so that they knew not to do to others what they did not want to suffer themselves. For sin was certainly not unknown among men at that time.

How is it then that sin was not imputed, when there was no law? Was it all right to sin, if the law was absent? There had always been a natural law, and it was not unknown, but at that time it was thought to be the only law, and it did not make men guilty before God. For it was not then known that God would judge the human race, and for that reason sin was not imputed, almost as if it did not exist in God's sight and that God did not care about it. But when the law was given through Moses, it became clear that God did care about human affairs and that in the future wrongdoers would not escape without punishment, as they had done up to then. COMMENTARY ON PAUL'S EPISTLES.[30]

BEFORE THE LAW OF MOSES, NOT OF NATURE. DIODORE: Sin was in the world before the law of Moses came, and it was counted, though not according to that law. Rather it was counted according to the law of nature, by which we have learned to distinguish good and evil. This was the law of which Paul spoke above.[31] PAULINE COMMENTARY FROM THE GREEK CHURCH.[32]

LAW DID NOT STOP SIN BUT MADE IT MORE DISCERNIBLE. THEODORE OF MOPSUESTIA: The

coming of the law did not remove sin. On the contrary, even though the law was observed and kept by men, sin continued to increase and the law could do nothing to stop it. . . . So far was the law from being the cure for sin that Paul even says that there would not have been sin at all had there been no law! By "law" Paul means the discernment which comes by both the natural law and the law of Moses. For without this discernment, nobody would be able to call sin by its name, since there would be no way of knowing the difference between good and evil. PAULINE COMMENTARY FROM THE GREEK CHURCH.[33]

SIN NOT COUNTED WHERE THERE IS NO LAW. AUGUSTINE: Paul said this in opposition to those who thought that sin could be taken away through the law. He says that sins were made apparent by the law, not abolished. He says not that there was no sin but only that it was not counted. Once the law was given, sin was not taken away, but it began to be counted. AUGUSTINE ON ROMANS 27-28.[34]

THE NATURAL LAW. [PSEUDO-]CONSTANTIUS: "Before the law" refers to the law of Moses, inferring that sin is not counted where there is no law. This time, however, Paul means the natural law, because of which Cain transgressed[35] and after him those who transgressed the natural law. THE HOLY LETTER OF ST. PAUL TO THE ROMANS.[36]

NOT COUNTED TEMPORARILY. PELAGIUS: The law came to punish sin. Before it came, sinners enjoyed at least the length of this present life with less restraint. Sin indeed existed before the law, but it was not counted as sin because natural knowledge had been almost wiped out. How did death reign, if sin was not counted? You have to understand here that it was not counted "for the time being." PELAGIUS'S COMMENTARY ON ROMANS.[37]

---

[29]CER 3:58, 62-64. [30]CSEL 81.1:167, 169. [31]Rom 2:14. [32]NTA 15:83. [33]NTA 15:118. [34]AOR 9. [35]Gen 4:8. [36]ENPK 2:38. [37]PCR 93.

SIN STRENGTHENED BY LAW. CYRIL OF ALEXANDRIA: The law of Moses was the power constraining the weakness of sinners. It proved to be not the answer to sin but rather a provocation to wrath. For it was necessary for transgressors to undergo the punishments prescribed by the law, and wherever there was transgression, there was also sin. So if sin brought death in its wake, it may undoubtedly be said that death, having been born of sin, was strengthened by this very thing. But when sin was taken away death was also weakened, and it disappeared along with its parent. Therefore there was death in the world until the coming of the law. For as long as the law was valid, the crime of transgression could be laid against those who had fallen, but once the law was removed, the accusation of transgression disappeared as well. Therefore when the guilt ceased, death also came to an end. EXPLANATION OF THE LETTER TO THE ROMANS.[38]

BEFORE THE LAW CAME TO AN END. THEODORET OF CYR: Paul is not, as some think, accusing those who lived before the law but rather everyone together. When he says "before the law" he does not mean before the law began but before the law came to an end, because as long as the law was in control, sin retained its force. INTERPRETATION OF THE LETTER TO THE ROMANS.[39]

SIN COUNTED UNDER THE LAW OF NATURE. OECUMENIUS: When Paul uses the word *sin* here he is thinking primarily of the transgression of the law of Moses and its commandments, e.g., circumcision, sabbath observance, the food laws, etc. Nevertheless, sin in general already existed in human nature, and it was counted. By this I mean things like murder, robbery, child abuse and so on. . . . For there was a law of nature which covered things like that. PAULINE COMMENTARY FROM THE GREEK CHURCH.[40]

5:14 Death Reigned from Adam to Moses

DEATH AS ROBBER. IRENAEUS: But the law given by Moses . . . really took away death's kingdom, showing that death was not a king but a robber, and it revealed death as a murderer. AGAINST HERESIES 3.18.7.[41]

ADAM THE TYPE OF THE SON. IRENAEUS: Paul called Adam "the type of the one who was to come" because the Word, the maker of all things, had formed beforehand for himself the future dispensation of the human race, in union with the Son of God. God predestined that the first man should be of an animal nature with this in view, that he might be saved in the spiritual nature. For since the Word had preexistence as a saving being, it was necessary that what might be saved should also be called into existence, in order that the being who saves should not exist in vain. AGAINST HERESIES 3.22.3.[42]

THE USURPER REIGNED. ORIGEN: It seems to me that Paul's description of death and its power may be compared to the entry of a tyrant who wants to usurp the authority of the legitimate ruler and after seizing the entrance to the kingdom by the treachery of the gatekeeper then tries to get public opinion on his side. To a great extent he succeeds in this and can therefore claim that the kingdom belongs to him. It was during the rule of this tyrant that Moses, a leader chosen by the legitimate ruler, was sent to the occupied peoples in order to revoke the laws of the civil administration and teach them to follow the laws of the true king. . . . This leader did all he could to deliver at least some people from the control of sin and death, and in the end he managed to form a nation composed of those who chose to associate with him. At the command of the king, he instituted sacrifices which were to be offered with a certain solemnity, as was only fitting, and by which their sins would be forgiven.[43] And so at last a part of the human race began to be set free

---

[38]Migne PG 74 col. 784. [39]*IER*, Migne PG 82 col. 100. [40]NTA 15:424. [41]ANF 1:448. [42]ANF 1:455. [43]Lev 1—9, passim.

from the rule of sin and death. . . .

Many manuscripts read that death reigned over even those whose sin was not like that of Adam. If this reading is correct, then it may be said that it refers to that death which has kept souls in hell, and we would understand that even the saints have passed away because of this law of death, even though they were not subject to the law of sin. Therefore it may be said that Christ descended into hell not only in order to show that he could not be held by death but also that he might liberate those who found themselves there not because of the sin of transgression but merely because of their mortal condition. . . .

What did Paul mean when he said that Adam was a type of the one who was to come? Was he speaking of some future man who had not yet come when he was writing, or was he thinking about Christ, who would have been in the future from Adam's point of view but was already in the past when Paul was writing? I do not know how Adam can be regarded as a type of Christ, unless it is by contrast. . . . I think it is better to say that Paul understood Adam as a type of Christ's second coming. Thus just as death has taken control of this age because of the one Adam, and the entire human race has been subjected to mortality, so in the coming age life will reign through Christ, and the entire human race will be blessed with immortality. COMMENTARY ON THE EPISTLE TO THE ROMANS.[44]

ADAM'S EATING NOT COPIED. CYRIL OF JERUSALEM: Paul's meaning is that, although Moses was a righteous and admirable man, the death sentence promulgated upon Adam reached him as well, and also those who came after, even though neither he nor they copied the sin of Adam in disobediently eating of the tree. THE CATECHETICAL LECTURES 15.31.[45]

GREEK AND LATIN MANUSCRIPT DIFFERENCES. AMBROSIASTER: Although sin was not imputed before the law of Moses was given, death nevertheless reigned in the supremacy of its own seizure of power, knowing those who were bound to it. Therefore death reigned in the security of its dominion both over those who for a time escaped punishment and over those who suffered punishment for their evil deeds. Death claimed everyone as its own, because whoever sins is the servant of sin.[46] Imagining they would get away with it, people sinned all the more and were more prone to wrongdoing because the world abetted it as if it were legal. Because of all this Satan rejoiced, knowing that he was secure in his possession of man, who because of Adam's sin had been abandoned by God. Thus it was that death reigned.

Some Greek manuscripts say that death reigned even in those who had not sinned in the way that Adam had. If this is true, it is because Satan's jealousy was such that death, that is, dissolution, held sway over even those who did not sin. . . . Here there is a textual difference between the Latin version and some of the Greek manuscripts. The Latin says that death reigned over those whose sins were like the sin of Adam, but some Greek manuscripts say that death reigned even over those whose sins were not like Adam's. Which of the two readings is the correct one?

What has happened is that somebody who could not win his argument altered the words of the text in order to make them say what he wanted them to say, so that not argument but textual authority would determine the issue. However, it is known that there were Latin-speakers who translated ancient Greek manuscripts which preserved an uncorrupted version from earlier times. But once these problems were raised by heretics and schismatics who were upsetting the harmony of the church, many things were altered so that the biblical text might conform to what people wanted. Thus even the Greeks have different readings in their manuscripts. I consider the correct reading to be the one which reason, history and authority all retain. For the reading of the modern Latin manuscripts is also found in Tertullian, Victori-

---

[44]CER 3:66-78. [45]LCC 4:166. [46]See Jn 8:34.

nus and Cyprian. Thus it was in Judea that the destruction of the kingdom of death began, since God was made known in Judea.[47] But now death is being destroyed daily in every nation, since many who once were sons of the devil have become sons of God. Therefore, death did not reign in everyone but only in those who sinned in the same way that Adam had sinned.

Adam was the type of the one who was to come, because even then God had secretly decided to redeem Adam's sin through the one Christ, as it says in John's Apocalypse: "The Lamb of God which was slain before the foundation of the world."[48] Commentary on Paul's Epistles."[49]

The Fall Applies to All. Acacius of Caesarea: Paul said this in order to contradict those who thought that the Genesis story of the fall applied to nobody but Adam himself. For here he says that all have sinned, even if not exactly in the same way as Adam, and that the Genesis account applies to all men.[50] Pauline Commentary from the Greek Church.[51]

In What Sense Was Adam the Type of Christ? Diodore: Adam was a type of Christ not with respect to his sin or his righteousness—in this respect the two men were opposites—but with respect to the effects of what he did. For just as Adam's sin spread to all men, so Christ's life also spread to all men.[52] Adam was also a type of Christ in another respect. For just as he was the head of Eve, in that he was her husband, so also Christ, being its bridegroom, is the head of the church. Pauline Commentary from the Greek Church.[53]

Falling from and Returning to Paradise. Jerome: In the transgression of Adam we have all through sin been cast out of paradise.[54] The apostle teaches that even in us who were to come later Adam had fallen. In Christ therefore, in the heavenly Adam, we believe that we who through the sin of the first Adam have fallen from paradise now through the righteousness of the

second Adam are to return to paradise. Homilies on the Psalms 66.[55]

Crux of the Typology. Chrysostom: Adam is a type of Christ in that just as those who descended from him inherited death, even though they had not eaten of the fruit of the tree. So also those who are descended from Christ inherit his righteousness, even though they did not produce it themselves. Homilies on Romans 10.[56]

Death the Punishment for All Sin. Theodore of Mopsuestia: Death came to all men not because they committed the same sin as Adam but because they sinned. . . . Death is not just the punishment for one particular sin; it is the punishment for every sin. Pauline Commentary from the Greek Church.[57]

A Type in Reverse. Augustine: This can be understood in two ways: either "in the likeness of Adam's transgression, death reigned," or (as surely it must be read) "death reigned over even those who did not sin in the likeness of Adam's transgression but sinned before the law was given." Thus those who received the law may be understood to have sinned in the likeness of Adam's transgression, because Adam also sinned after having received a law to obey. . . . Adam is the type of the one who was to come but in reverse, for as death came through Adam, so life came through our Lord. Augustine on Romans 29.[58]

Christ's Good Greater Than Adam's Harm. Augustine: Adam is the type of Christ but in reverse, because the good done by Christ to the regenerated is greater than the harm done by Adam to his descendants. Letter 157.[59]

We Sin Like Adam, Even If in a Different Way. [Pseudo-]Constantius: Paul wants to

[47]Ps 76:1. [48]Rev 13:8. [49]CSEL 81.1:169-79. [50]Gen 3:1-24. [51]NTA 15:53. [52]1 Cor 15:45-48. [53]NTA 15:83. [54]Gen 3:23-24. [55]FC 57:68. [56]NPNF 1 11:402. [57]NTA 15:119. [58]AOR 9, 11. [59]FC 11:337.

show that, although death reigned over everyone before the coming of Christ, it was not able to reign without sin. It reigns over even children, who are not bound by the commandment as Adam was. Paul shows that they sin by their natural condition, because of the weakness of the flesh which was not able to keep the law of God. They did not sin in the likeness of the transgression of Adam, because they sinned against the natural law and not against the commandment as Adam did. How can they be said to be bound when they did not sin in the way Adam did, unless this is meant to show that they were unable to keep the law because of the weakness of their flesh? For it is shown that death reigned over even children, who did not sin as Adam did but did other evil things. They are like Adam in that they sinned, even if they did so in a different way. Adam was the type of the one who was to come, viz., Christ. For just as Adam was the first to transgress the commandment of God and thereby to give an example to everyone who wanted to follow suit, so also Christ, by fulfilling the will of God, is an example to those who wish to imitate him. THE HOLY LETTER OF ST. PAUL TO THE ROMANS.[60]

THEODORET OF CYR: Death reigned over even those who did not sin in the likeness of Adam's sin. For even if they did not break the same commandment, they did other things which were wrong. INTERPRETATION OF THE LETTER TO THE ROMANS.[61]

ALTERNATIVE READINGS. PELAGIUS: This may mean that as long as there was no one who distinguished between the righteous and the unrighteous, death imagined that it was Lord over all. Or else it may mean that death reigned not only over those who, like Adam, broke a commandment—like the sons of Noah who were ordered not to eat the life in the blood[62] or the sons of Abraham, on whom circumcision was imposed[63]—but over those who, lacking the com-

mandment, showed contempt for the law of nature. Adam was a type of Christ either because he was made by God without sexual intercourse, just as Christ was born of a virgin by the aid of the Holy Spirit, or he was an antithetical type, that is, as Adam was the source of sin so Christ is the source of righteousness. PELAGIUS'S COMMENTARY ON ROMANS.[64]

5:15 God's Grace Abounded for Many

THE TYPOLOGY CIRCUMSCRIBED. ORIGEN: It makes no difference that Paul said [in verse 12] that sin spread to all, whereas here he says that the grace and gift of God have abounded for many. In Paul's usage, *all* and *many* are almost synonymous. . . . Yet Paul refrains from saying that all will benefit from the free grace of God, because if men had the assurance that they would be saved, they would not fear God and turn away from evil.

[In this verse] Paul starts to explain how Adam may be regarded as a type of Christ. Any close similarity between them is obviously absurd, which is why he insists that "the free gift is not like the trespass." . . . The judgment on Adam was that through his one sin condemnation came to all men. But in sharp contrast to this, through Christ justification is given to all for the many sins in which the entire human race is bound up. COMMENTARY ON THE EPISTLE TO THE ROMANS.[65]

"MANY" AND "ALL" DISTINGUISHED. DIODORE: At first sight it may seem that this verse contradicts what Paul said [in verse 12] above, for there he spoke of death having come to all humanity, whereas here he says only that many have died. In fact there is no contradiction, because death, although it came upon all because we have all sinned, came only to test and to try everyone. Death does not destroy all sinners

---

[60]ENPK 2:39. [61]IER, Migne PG 82 col. 100. [62]Gen 9:4. [63]Gen 17:10. [64]PCR 93-94. [65]CER 3:82-84, 88.

automatically but only those who persist in their sins. By saying that "many died" Paul shows merely that many turned out to be unrepentant in their sins. PAULINE COMMENTARY FROM THE GREEK CHURCH.[66]

THE GIFT UNLIKE THE TRESPASS. AMBROSIASTER: Paul said that Adam was a type of Christ, but in order to assure us that they were not alike in substance, he says that the gift is not like the trespass. The only similarity between them is that just as one man sinned, so one man put things right.

If by the trespass of one man many have died by imitating his transgression, how much more has the grace of God and his gift abounded in those who flee to him for refuge! For there are more who have received grace than who have died because of Adam's trespass. From this it is clear that Paul was not talking about ordinary death, which is common to us all, since everybody dies but not everybody receives grace. Death does not reign in everyone. It only reigns in those who have died because of the sin of Adam, who have sinned by a transgression like his. Paul is talking only about these when he says that although many have died because of Adam's sin, many more have received grace.... For both to those who sinned in a way similar to Adam and to those who did not sin in that way but who were nevertheless confined to hell because of God's judgment on Adam's sin, the grace of God has abounded by the descent of the Savior to hell, granting pardon to all and leading them up to heaven in triumph. COMMENTARY ON PAUL'S EPISTLES.[67]

WHETHER ONE MAN SHOULD BE PUNISHED FOR WHAT ANOTHER DOES. CHRYSOSTOM: What Paul is saying here seems to be something like this. If sin, and the sin of a single man moreover, had such a big effect, how is it that grace, and that the grace of God—not of the Father only but also of the Son—would not have an even greater effect? That one man should be punished on account of another does not seem reasonable, but that one man should be saved on account of another is both more suitable and more reasonable. So if it is true that the former happened, much more should the latter have happened as well! HOMILIES ON ROMANS 10.[68]

THE GIFT EXCELS. AUGUSTINE: The gift excels in two ways: first, because grace abounds much more in that it bestows eternal life even though death reigns in the temporal sphere because of the death of Adam, and second, because by the condemnation of one sin the death of many came about through Adam, whereas by the forgiveness of many sins through our Lord Jesus Christ grace has been given for eternal life. AUGUSTINE ON ROMANS 29.[69]

A COMMON AND NATURAL DEATH. [PSEUDO-] CONSTANTIUS: Here Paul clearly teaches that he is not speaking generally of everyone when he says: "Many died through one man's trespass," because it is not just sinners but the righteous too who die a common and natural death. THE HOLY LETTER OF ST. PAUL TO THE ROMANS.[70]

MISREADING THE ANALOGY. PELAGIUS: The gift is not like the trespass, because one must not give equal value to the type as to the original. Righteousness had more power to bring to life than sin had to put to death. Adam killed only himself and his descendants, whereas Christ freed both those who were then in the body and also succeeding generations. Those who oppose the idea of the transmission of sin try to attack it as follows: "If Adam's sin harmed even those who were not sinners, then Christ's righteousness must help even those who are not believers. For Paul says that people are saved through Christ in the same way or to an even greater degree than they had previously perished through Adam." Secondly, they say: "If baptism washes away that ancient sin, those who are born of two baptized

---

[66]NTA 15:83-84. [67]CSEL 81.1:179-81. [68]NPNF 1 11:402. [69]AOR 11. [70]ENPK 2:40.

parents should not have that sin, for they could not have passed on to their children what they did not possess themselves. Besides, if the soul does not exist by transmission, but only the flesh, then only the flesh carries the transmission of sin and it alone deserves punishment." Declaring it to be unjust that a soul which is born today, not from the lump of Adam, bears so ancient a sin belonging to another, these people say that on no account should it be accepted that God, who forgives a man his own sins, imputes to him the sins of someone else. PELAGIUS'S COMMENTARY ON ROMANS.[71]

ONE MAN. THEODORET OF CYR: Paul calls Jesus a man in this passage in order to underline the parallel with Adam, for just as death came through one man, so the cure for death came through one man as well. INTERPRETATION OF THE LETTER TO THE ROMANS.[72]

WHY THE OBEDIENCE IS GREATER THAN THE DISOBEDIENCE. OECUMENIUS: Christ's obedience was greater than Adam's disobedience in the following sense. Death, which originated with the sin of Adam, had our cooperation in the sins which we all committed, and so it was able to gain control over us. For if men had remained free of all wrongdoing, death would not have been in control. But the grace of Christ has come to us all without our cooperation and shows that the grace of the resurrection is such that not only believers, who glory in their faith, will be resurrected, but also unbelievers, both Jews and Greeks. Something which works in us against our will is therefore obviously greater than something which works in us with our cooperation. PAULINE COMMENTARY FROM THE GREEK CHURCH.[73]

5:16 God's Gift Brings Justification

CHRIST TRANSFORMED MANY SINS INTO RIGHTEOUSNESS. DIODORE: Paul wants to say that it was because of Adam's sin, although it was only one, that God condemned many, on account of the fact that they copied Adam. But the grace of the Lord was measured not according to that one sin but according to the many sins which all had committed. Thus Christ transformed many sins into righteousness. PAULINE COMMENTARY FROM THE GREEK CHURCH.[74]

AMBROSIASTER: There is an obvious difference between the fact that those who have sinned in imitation of Adam's transgression have been condemned and the fact that the grace of God in Christ has justified men not from one trespass but from many sins, giving them forgiveness of sins. COMMENTARY ON PAUL'S EPISTLES.[75]

THE GREATER GOOD OF THE FREE GIFT. CHRYSOSTOM: The free gift is much greater than the judgment.... For it was not just Adam's sin which was done away with by the free gift but all other sins as well. And it was not just that sin was done away with—justification was given, too. So Christ did not merely do the same amount of good that Adam did of harm, but far more and greater good.[76] HOMILIES ON ROMANS 10.[77]

THE ONE GREAT DIFFERENCE BETWEEN GIFT AND TRESPASS. THEODORE OF MOPSUESTIA: There is one great difference between Adam's sin and God's gift in Christ. Adam's sin brought punishment on all those who came after him, and so they died. But the free gift is different. For not only did it take effect in the case of those who came afterward; it also took away the sins of those who had gone before. It is therefore much greater, because where sin harmed those who came after, grace rescued not only those who came after but those who had transgressed before as well. PAULINE COMMENTARY FROM THE GREEK CHURCH.[78]

---

[71]PCR 94. [72]IER, Migne PG 82 col. 101. [73]NTA 15:425. [74]NTA 15:84. [75]CSEL 81.1:181. [76]Is 1:18; 44:22. [77]NPNF 1 11:402-3. [78]NTA 15:119-20.

AUGUSTINE: This is the difference: in Adam one sin was condemned, but by the Lord many sins have been forgiven. AUGUSTINE ON ROMANS 29.[79]

THE EFFECT OF THE GIFT. PELAGIUS: The effect of the gift is greater than that of the sin. From the sin of one righteous man came the judgment of death. Adam never came across all the righteousness which he destroyed, but Christ discharged the sins of many by his grace. Adam was only the model for sin, but Christ both forgave sins freely and gave an example of righteousness. PELAGIUS'S COMMENTARY ON ROMANS.[80]

5:17 Abundant Grace Reigns

WHERE DEATH REIGNED, ABUNDANT GRACE REIGNS. ORIGEN: Not only will death cease to reign in those who receive the abundance of grace, but two additional benefits will be given to them. First, Christ will reign in them by his life, and second, they will reign along with Christ.[81] . . .

It must be noted that Paul speaks of the abundance of grace, because it is not possible for someone who has received only one grace, i.e., who has pleased God in only one thing, to enter the kingdom of heaven. . . . Grace is multiplied and abounds if our conversation is always seasoned with salt[82] and our work is done with the grace of humility and simplicity, and if all that we do is done to the glory of God.[83] COMMENTARY ON THE EPISTLE TO THE ROMANS.[84]

HOW MUCH MORE WILL GRACE REIGN. AMBROSIASTER: Paul says that death reigned, not that it is now reigning. Those who understand the limits of the law—what the future judgment of God will be—have been delivered from its control. Death reigned, because without the revelation of the law there was no fear of God on earth. But the higher meaning is that, since death reigned from Adam to Moses over those who sinned according to the transgression of Adam, how much more will grace reign by the abundance of God's gift of life through the one Jesus

Christ. For if death reigned, why should grace not reign even more, since it has justified far more people than the number over whom death reigned? COMMENTARY ON PAUL'S EPISTLES.[85]

NO TRACE OF DEATH. CHRYSOSTOM: Paul speaks of an abundance of grace to show that what we have received is not just a medicine sufficient to heal the wound of sin, but also health and beauty and honor, and glory and dignity far transcending our natural state. Each of these in itself would have been enough to do away with death, but when they are all put together in one there is not a trace of death left, nor can any shadow of it be seen, so entirely has it been done away with. HOMILIES ON ROMANS 10.[86]

GRACE RECEIVED IN PART, AWAITING FULLNESS. THEODORE OF MOPSUESTIA: Paul shows just how superior grace is to sin, because while death, which came into the world by the sin of Adam, held full sway, the enjoyment of the gift of grace through Christ has been given to us, through which we shall be raised from the dead and in righteousness cease to sin. But we have not yet received it fully; it does not yet hold full sway. We are still waiting for the life to come, even though we now enjoy it in part. PAULINE COMMENTARY FROM THE GREEK CHURCH.[87]

AUGUSTINE: "Much more will those reign" pertains to eternal life; "those who receive the abundance of grace" pertains to the forgiveness of many sins. AUGUSTINE ON ROMANS 29.[88]

PELAGIUS: Righteousness is given through baptism and is not gained by merit. PELAGIUS'S COMMENTARY ON ROMANS.[89]

5:18 Christ's Righteousness Leads to Acquittal

---

[79]AOR 11. [80]PCR 94-95. [81]See also Rev 20:6. [82]See Col 4:6. [83]See 1 Cor 10:31. [84]CER 3:98, 106. [85]CSEL 81.1:183. [86]NPNF 1 11:403. [87]NTA 15:120. [88]AOR 11. [89]PCR 95.

ONE MAN'S TRESPASS. ACACIUS OF CAESAREA: Paul does not mean by this that because one man sinned everybody else had to pay the price for it even though they had not committed the sin, for that would be unjust. Rather he says that from its beginning in Adam humanity derived both its existence and its sinfulness. PAULINE COMMENTARY FROM THE GREEK CHURCH.[90]

OBEDIENCE OVERCAME DISOBEDIENCE. DIODORE: What was Adam's sin? Disobedience.[91] What was Christ's righteousness? Obedience, by which he obeyed the Father in his incarnation and in his suffering for mankind, as the apostle says: "Being found in human form, he humbled himself and became obedient unto death, even death on a cross."[92] Thus obedience overcame disobedience and the worse was condemned by the better. PAULINE COMMENTARY FROM THE GREEK CHURCH.[93]

NO UNIVERSAL ACQUITTAL. AMBROSIASTER: Some people think that because the condemnation was universal, the acquittal will also be universal. But this is not so, because not everyone believes. COMMENTARY ON PAUL'S EPISTLES.[94]

AUGUSTINE: Here Paul returns to his original argument, interrupted [from verse 12]. AUGUSTINE ON ROMANS 29.[95]

NO REBIRTH WITHOUT SPIRITUAL GRACE. AUGUSTINE: No one is born without the intervention of carnal concupiscence, which is inherited from the first man, who is Adam, and no one is reborn without the intervention of spiritual grace, which is given by the second man, who is Christ. LETTER 187.31.[96]

AUGUSTINE: God wants all those to whom grace comes through the righteousness of the One unto justification of life to be saved and come to the knowledge of the truth. AGAINST JULIAN 4.8.42.[97]

WHETHER ALL ARE PUNISHED WHEN NOT

ALL ARE JUSTIFIED. [PSEUDO-]CONSTANTIUS: How is it possible for God to condemn all men by the sin of the one Adam when not all men are justified by the righteousness of Christ? But when Paul says "all" he is not speaking generally but means only a large number of each kind. In other words, everyone who is justified is justified in Christ, just as everyone who is condemned is condemned in Adam, and nobody beyond that will be punished. THE HOLY LETTER OF ST. PAUL TO THE ROMANS.[98]

PELAGIUS: Death reigned, but so also grace reigned through justification. PELAGIUS'S COMMENTARY ON ROMANS.[99]

CONTRACTING THE DISEASE OF SIN. CYRIL OF ALEXANDRIA: What has Adam's guilt got to do with us? Why are we held responsible for his sin when we were not even born when he committed it? Did not God say: "The parents will not die for the children, nor the children for the parents, but the soul which has sinned, it shall die."[100] How then shall we defend this doctrine? The soul, I say, which has sinned, it shall die. We have become sinners because of Adam's disobedience in the following manner. . . . After he fell into sin and surrendered to corruption, impure lusts invaded the nature of his flesh, and at the same time the evil law of our members was born. For our nature contracted the disease of sin because of the disobedience of one man, that is, Adam, and thus many became sinners. This was not because they sinned along with Adam, because they did not then exist, but because they had the same nature as Adam, which fell under the law of sin. Thus, just as human nature acquired the weakness of corruption in Adam because of disobedience, and evil desires invaded it, so the same nature was later set free by Christ, who was obedient to God the

---

[90]NTA 15:53. [91]See Gen 2:15-16; 3:6, 17. [92]Phil 2:8. [93]NTA 15:84. [94]CSEL 81.1:183. [95]AOR 11. [96]FC 30:246. [97]FC 35:205. [98]ENPK 2:40. [99]PCR 95. [100]Deut 24:16.

Father and did not commit sin. EXPLANATION OF THE LETTER TO THE ROMANS.[101]

5:19 Righteousness Through Christ's Obedience

WHY MANY, NOT ALL. ORIGEN: Why does Paul say that many were made sinners and not that all were when it is clear that all have sinned, as he has just said himself? It is one thing to sin and another to be a sinner. A sinner is someone who, as a result of much sinning, has got into the habit and, I would dare say, the enjoyment of it. In the same way, a righteous person is not someone who has done one or two acts of righteousness but rather someone who has become accustomed to acting righteously and has righteousness in him by habit. COMMENTARY ON THE EPISTLE TO THE ROMANS.[102]

AMBROSIASTER: Many sinned by following Adam, but not all. Likewise, many are justified by faith in Christ, but not all. COMMENTARY ON PAUL'S EPISTLES.[103]

THE BENEFITS OF MORTALITY. CHRYSOSTOM: How does it follow that from Adam's disobedience someone else would become a sinner? For surely, if this were so, such a sinner would not deserve punishment, since his sins would not be his own fault. What then does the word *sinners* mean here? To me it seems to mean liable to punishment and condemned to death. Why was this done? Paul does not say, because it was not necessary to his argument. . . . But if you want to know what I think, I would say this: Far from being harmed or condemned, if we think straight, we shall see that we have benefited by becoming mortal, first because it is not an immortal body in which we sin, and second because we have countless reasons for living a religious life. For to be moderate, temperate, subdued and separated from wickedness is what death, by its presence and the fact that we expect it to come, persuades us to do. But following on these or even before

these, mortality has brought many other blessings besides. For it has made possible the crown of martyrdom. . . . In fact, neither death nor the devil himself can do anything to harm us. Immortality is waiting for us, and after being chastened for a little while we shall enjoy the blessings to come without fear.[104] This present life is a kind of school, where we are under instruction by means of disease, suffering, temptations and poverty, as well as other apparent evils, in order to be made fit to receive the blessings of the world to come. HOMILIES ON ROMANS 10.[105]

RIGHTEOUSNESS IS FOR MANY, RESURRECTION FOR ALL. SEVERIAN: Notice that when Paul talks about sin and righteousness he uses the word *many*, for not everyone sinned before the coming of the law, nor has everyone who has received grace been justified—for "many are called, but few are chosen."[106] But when he talks about the death and resurrection of the body, he uses the word *all*. PAULINE COMMENTARY FROM THE GREEK CHURCH.[107]

AUGUSTINE: This is the figure of the future Adam. AUGUSTINE ON ROMANS 29.[108]

BY ONE MAN'S OBEDIENCE. [PSEUDO-]CONSTANTIUS: In this Adam was a type of Christ, because just as by his disobedience death entered the world, so life and resurrection came by the obedience of Christ. THE HOLY LETTER OF ST. PAUL TO THE ROMANS.[109]

PELAGIUS: Just as by the example of Adam's disobedience many sinned, so many are also justified by Christ's obedience. Great therefore is the crime of disobedience, which kills so many. PELAGIUS'S COMMENTARY ON ROMANS.[110]

WHETHER SOME DID NOT SIN. THEODORET

---

[101]Migne PG 74 cols. 788-89. [102]CER 3:112. [103]CSEL 81.1:185. [104]See Mt 25:34; Heb 10:36-37; 2 Macc 7:33. [105]NPNF 1 11:403-4. [106]Mt 22:14. [107]NTA 15:218. [108]AOR 11. [109]ENPK 2:41. [110]PCR 95.

OF CYR: Note that Paul says "many" and "not all," for we find some among the ancients who did not sin, e.g., Abel,[111] Enoch,[112] Melchizedek,[113] the patriarchs and those who succeeded in keeping the law. On the other hand, after the coming of grace, there were many who continued to embrace an unrighteous and wicked life. INTERPRETATION OF THE LETTER TO THE ROMANS.[114]

5:20 Sin Increased, Grace Abounded More

THE INCLINATION TO EXCESS. ORIGEN: What Paul means here is that after the natural law had already been established—the law which he calls the law of the mind, which assents to the law of God—another law arose, the law of our members, which promotes the lusts of the flesh and leads men captive, inclining them to desire and excesses, so that sin may abound in them. . . .

Grace abounded all the more, because not only does it absolve us from the sins which we have already committed, it protects us against sinning in the future. COMMENTARY ON THE EPISTLE TO THE ROMANS.[115]

AMBROSE: When evil had appeared and innocence had been destroyed, there was no one to do good, not even one. The Lord came to restore grace to nature, in fact to give it increase, that where sin abounded, grace might more abound. LETTER 25.[116]

THE HARM OF KNOWING WHAT I CANNOT AVOID. AMBROSE: Sin abounded by the law because through the law came knowledge of sin, and it became harmful for me to know what through my weakness I could not avoid. It is good to know beforehand what one is to avoid, but if I cannot avoid something, it is harmful to have known about it. Thus was the law changed to its opposite, yet it became useful to me by the very increase of sin, for I was humbled. LETTER 83.[117]

THE LAW INCREASED THE TRESPASS. DIODORE: Paul does not mean that the law

increased the incidence of sin but rather that once it was given it uncovered sin and showed that it was more widespread than people had thought. PAULINE COMMENTARY FROM THE GREEK CHURCH.[118]

WHETHER THE LAW SHOULD NEVER HAVE BEEN GIVEN. AMBROSIASTER: An objector might say: "If the law merely served to increase sin, it should never have been given. If there was less sin before the law came, there was no need of the law." Obviously the law was necessary to show that sins, which many thought they could get away with, actually counted before God and so that people might know what they ought to avoid.

How could the law have increased sin, when it warns people not to sin? . . . The law began to show an abundance of sins, and the more it forbade them the more people committed them. That is why it is said that the law was given so that sin might increase. . . .

In order to nullify the pride of Satan, who rejoiced in his victory over man, the just and merciful God decreed that his Son would come to forgive every sin,[119] so that there would be more happiness from the gift of grace than there had been sorrow from the coming of sin. . . . Therefore grace abounded more than sin. COMMENTARY ON PAUL'S EPISTLES.[120]

GRACE ABOUNDED MORE. CHRYSOSTOM: The law was not given in order for sin to abound, for it was given in order to diminish and destroy the offense. But it resulted in the opposite happening, not because of the nature of the law but because of the weakness of those who received it. . . .

Grace abounded much more, because it gave

---

[111]See Gen 4:2-4; Heb 11:4. [112]See Gen 5:22; Heb 11:5. [113]See Gen 14:18-20; Ps 110:4; Heb 6:19—7:10. [114]*IER*, Migne PG 82 cols. 101, 104. Abel, Enoch, Melchizedek and the patriarchs kept the law only by their faith in its future consummation. [115]CER 3:122-24. [116]FC 26:133. [117]FC 26:466. [118]NTA 15:85. [119]See Mt 9:6; 28:18; Mk 2:10; Lk 5:24; Jn 17:1-2. [120]CSEL 81.1:185-89.

us not only remission from punishment but forgiveness from sin as well, and in addition, new life. HOMILIES ON ROMANS 10.[121]

DESIRE GREW THROUGH THE PROHIBITION.
AUGUSTINE: By this Paul has clearly indicated that the Jews did not know by what dispensation the law had been given. It was not given in order to bring life, for grace brings life through faith, but the law was given to show with what great and tight chains those who thought they could fulfill all righteousness in their own strength were bound. So sin abounded, both because desire grew more ardent in the light of the prohibition and because the crime of trespass affected those who sinned against the law. Whoever considers the second of the four states of man will understand this. AUGUSTINE ON ROMANS 30.[122]

AUGUSTINE: Prohibition increased lust. It made it unconquered so that transgression might be added, which did not exist without the law, although there was sin. CONTINENCE 3.7.[123]

AUGUSTINE: Grace means that good works are now performed by those who had earlier done evil; it does not make them continue in evil in the belief that good will be given to them in return. GRACE AND FREE WILL 22.44.[124]

WHY LAW CAME IN. [Pseudo-]CONSTANTIUS: Here Paul is referring to the law of Moses. For the Hebrews had the natural law, and they received the written law, which is why Paul says that it "entered in." For they received the law for greater reward, but when by their negligence they failed to keep it, they fell into greater sin. THE HOLY LETTER OF ST. PAUL TO THE ROMANS.[125]

THE MEDICINE OF CHRIST. CYRIL OF ALEXANDRIA: The law entered in so that the many-sided nature of the fall of those who were under the law might be made clear. Nobody could ever be made righteous because of the weakness of human nature. Rather, everyone condemned themselves

by their own crimes of transgression. The law came as the revealer of our common weakness, so that the human race would appear even more clearly to need the aid of the medicine of Christ. EXPLANATION OF THE LETTER TO THE ROMANS.[126]

A LIGHT TO THE NATIONS. THEODORET OF CYR: Paul says that "the law came in" because he wants to show that God did not leave earlier generations destitute of his providence. But he also gave the law to the Jews, so that by their zeal and dedication to godliness they could act as a light to the other nations.[127] INTERPRETATION OF THE LETTER TO THE ROMANS.[128]

A DEBT OF LOVE. PELAGIUS: The amount of sin has been revealed so that the greatness of grace might be known and so that we might pay back a corresponding debt of love. PELAGIUS'S COMMENTARY ON ROMANS.[129]

5:21 Grace Reigns to Eternal Life

TWO KINGDOMS. ORIGEN: Paul shows that there are two kingdoms in man. In one of these, sin has taken control and leads to death. In the other, grace reigns through righteousness and leads to life. For it is grace which expels and ejects sin from its kingdom, i.e., from our members. COMMENTARY ON THE EPISTLE TO THE ROMANS.[130]

AMBROSIASTER: Sin reigned when it saw that it was driving sinners into death, in which it rejoiced, in much the same way as grace will reign in those who obey God. COMMENTARY ON PAUL'S EPISTLES.[131]

NO LONGER RECEPTIVE TO SIN. THEODORE OF MOPSUESTIA: Paul says that just as sin once

---

[121]NPNF 1 11:404. [122]AOR 11. [123]FC 16:196. [124]FC 59:305. [125]ENPK 2:41. [126]Migne PG 74 col. 792. [127]See Is 42:6-7; 49:6; 60:3. [128]IER, Migne PG 82 col. 104. [129]PCR 95. [130]CER 3:124. [131]CSEL 81.1:189.

ruled us even against our will, because we were so used to it, so now our zeal for God reigns and will reign in us forever. Since we have been made worthy of eternal life through the resurrection and live in true and certain righteousness, we shall no longer be receptive to sin. PAULINE COMMENTARY FROM THE GREEK CHURCH.[132]

[PSEUDO-]CONSTANTIUS: Paul said this because the one who is forgiven more will love more.[133] THE HOLY LETTER OF ST. PAUL TO THE ROMANS.[134]

THE REIGN OF GRACE. PELAGIUS: Just as the reign of sin was established through contempt for the law, so also the reign of grace is established through the forgiveness of many sinners and thereafter through the doing of righteousness without ceasing. PELAGIUS'S COMMENTARY ON ROMANS.[135]

---

[132]NTA 15:121. [133]See Lk 7:47. [134]ENPK 2:41. [135]PCR 96.

6:1-14 DYING TO SIN AND LIVING IN CHRIST

[1]What shall we say then? Are we to continue in sin that grace may abound? [2]By no means! How can we who died to sin still live in it? [3]Do you not know that all of us who have been baptized into Christ Jesus were baptized into his death? [4]We were buried therefore with him by baptism into death, so that as Christ was raised from the dead by the glory of the Father, we too might walk in newness of life.

[5]For if we have been united with him in a death like his, we shall certainly be united with him in a resurrection like his. [6]We know that our old self was crucified with him so that the sinful body might be destroyed, and we might no longer be enslaved to sin. [7]For he who has died is freed from sin. [8]But if we have died with Christ, we believe that we shall also live with him. [9]For we know that Christ being raised from the dead will never die again; death no longer has dominion over him. [10]The death he died he died to sin, once for all, but the life he lives he lives to God. [11]So you also must consider yourselves dead to sin and alive to God in Christ Jesus.

[12]Let not sin therefore reign in your mortal bodies, to make you obey their passions. [13]Do not yield your members to sin as instruments of wickedness, but yield yourselves to God as men who have been brought from death to life, and your members to God as instruments of righteousness. [14]For sin will have no dominion over you, since you are not under law but under grace.

OVERVIEW: God's grace is sufficient to overcome sin, but it does not follow from this that the more we sin, the more grace we shall receive. The Christian is a person who has been born again to a new life—a life of righteousness. Christians die to sin in baptism and are then raised to a new life in Christ. The importance of baptism in this respect can scarcely be exaggerated. By baptism we were sacramentally united to Christ in a death like his, and because of that we have the hope that we shall also share in his resurrection. In baptism we have been crucified with Christ and have therefore died to sin, even though we do not yet share in the fullness of his resurrection.

Christ's death and resurrection were once-for-all events. Christians who put their trust in Christ do not have to worry that they will die a second time and lose their salvation. Christ has put death behind him and now lives for God. In the same way Christians ought to put sin behind them and live for God as well. As inheritors of eternal life, Christians are called to resist the temptations that the body offers and give themselves over to God so that our physical members may become instruments of righteousness instead. Only in this way can a believer live a life worthy of Christ. With the help of the Holy Spirit dwelling in us sin can be overcome, even if it cannot be totally eliminated from us in this life. We certainly have no excuse for falling back into our previous way of life!

6:1 Can We Continue to Sin?

THOSE IN WHOM GRACE ABOUNDS HAVE DIED TO SIN. ORIGEN: This is a rhetorical question which arises from what Paul said [in Romans 5:20] above. . . . He answers it in the next verse, saying that those in whom grace abounds have died to sin. It is clear that someone who has died to sin cannot remain a sinner. COMMENTARY ON THE EPISTLE TO THE ROMANS.[1]

REJECTING THE KINGDOM OF GRACE. AMBROSIASTER: The believer who returns to his former way of life rejects the kingdom of God's grace and returns to sin, i.e., to the pattern of his previous life. For we have received mercy for two reasons: first, that the kingdom of the devil might be removed, and second, that the rule of God might be proclaimed to the ignorant, for it was by this means that we came to desire this dignity. COMMENTARY ON PAUL'S EPISTLES.[2]

AN INDIRECT EXHORTATION. CHRYSOSTOM: Paul is once more starting to exhort his hearers, but he does so indirectly, as if it arose naturally out of his teaching, so as not to appear to be irksome and vexing. HOMILIES ON ROMANS 10.[3]

LIVING FOR GRACE. PELAGIUS: Paul is speaking here of those whom faith found in sin, not of us believers, who have died to sin in order to live for grace. PELAGIUS'S COMMENTARY ON ROMANS.[4]

6:2 Dead to Sin

CAN ONE WHO DIED TO SIN STILL LIVE IN IT? ORIGEN: In order for this point to be clearer, let us inquire as to what it means to live to sin and what it means to die to sin. Just as living for God means living according to God's will, so living for sin means living according to sin's will, as the apostle says [in verse 12] below. To live to sin therefore, means to obey the desires of sin. . . . To die to sin is the opposite of this; it means refusing to obey the desires of sin. . . . If someone dies to sin, it is through repentance that he dies.

Note how carefully Paul has weighed his words when he says: "Can we still live in sin?" To go on in this way means to continue something without interruption. If someone does this it is clear that he has never been converted to Christ. But it sometimes happens not that someone continues in sin but that after having broken with it he goes back to his vomit and becomes most unfortunate, since after having rejected the rule of sin and death and accepted the rule of life and righteousness he returns to the control of sin and death. This is what the apostle calls the shipwreck of faith.[5]

However, although someone may continue in sin, although he may persist in the rule and power of death, nevertheless I do not consider that this rule of death is eternal in the same way that the rule of life and of righteousness is eter-

---

[1]CER 3:126-28. [2]CSEL 81.1:189-91. [3]NPNF 1 11:405. [4]PCR 96. [5]1 Tim 1:19.

nal, particularly as I hear the apostle telling me that death is the last enemy which must be destroyed.[6] For if the eternity of death were analogous to the eternity of life, then death would not be opposed to life but its equal. One eternal is not contrary to another eternal but identical with it. But it is certain that death is contrary to life, and therefore it is certain that if life is eternal, death cannot be eternal as well. For this reason, the resurrection of the dead is necessary. For when the death of the soul, which is the last enemy, is destroyed, then this common death which we have described as the shadow of that one will of necessity be abolished. Then there will be room for the resurrection of the dead, when the rule of death is destroyed along with death itself. COMMENTARY ON THE EPISTLE TO THE ROMANS.[7]

WHAT DYING TO SIN AND LIVING TO GOD MEANS. AMBROSIASTER: To sin is to live to sin, and not to sin is to live to God. Therefore, when the grace of God through Christ and through faith came upon us, we began by the spiritual rebirth of baptism to live to God, and we died to sin, which is the devil. This is what dying to sin means: to be set free from sin and to become a servant of God. Therefore, having died to sin, let us not go back to our earlier evils, lest by living once again to sin and dying to God we should incur the penalty from which we have escaped. COMMENTARY ON PAUL'S EPISTLES.[8]

WHAT IT MEANS TO BE DEAD TO SIN IN BAPTISM. CHRYSOSTOM: Being dead to sin means not obeying it any more. Baptism has made us dead to sin once and for all, but we must strive to maintain this state of affairs, so that however many commands sin may give us, we no longer obey it but remain unmoved by it, as a corpse does. Elsewhere, Paul even says that sin itself is dead . . . in order to show that virtue is easy.[9] But here, since he is trying to rouse his hearers to action, he says that they are the ones who are dead. HOMILIES ON ROMANS 10.[10]

WHEN WE BECOME AN OBSTACLE TO GRACE. AUGUSTINE: Here Paul makes the point that past sins have been forgiven and that in this pardon grace so superabounded that earlier sins were remitted as well. Thus whoever tries to increase sin in order to feel an increase of grace does not understand that he is behaving in such a way that grace can do nothing in him. For the work of grace is that we should die to sin. AUGUSTINE ON ROMANS 31.[11]

AUGUSTINE: Nothing shorter or better could be said. For what more useful gift does the grace of God confer on us than to make us die to sin? LETTER 215.[12]

PELAGIUS: Paul wants the baptized person to be steadfast and virtually perfect. PELAGIUS'S COMMENTARY ON ROMANS.[13]

A NEW LIFE. GENNADIUS OF CONSTANTINOPLE: Carnal people and unbelievers may live like this, but we are totally incapable of it because we have a new life, having died to sin once for all. PAULINE COMMENTARY FROM THE GREEK CHURCH.[14]

6:3 Baptized into Christ's Death

BAPTIZED INTO HIS DEATH. ORIGEN: Paul is saying by this that if we have died to sin then we must necessarily be buried with Christ in baptism, but . . . if we have not died to sin, then we cannot be buried with Christ. For nobody is buried while still alive. Then too, anyone who is not buried together with Christ has not been validly baptized. COMMENTARY ON THE EPISTLE TO THE ROMANS.[15]

WHETHER BAPTISM IS THE DEATH OF SIN. AMBROSIASTER: Paul says this so that we might

---

[6]See 1 Cor 15:26. [7]CER 3:128-34. [8]CSEL 81.1:191. [9]Rom 7:8. [10]NPNF 1 11:405. [11]AOR 11, 13. [12]FC 32:67. [13]PCR 96. [14]NTA 15:365. [15]CER 3:136.

know that once we have been baptized we should no longer sin, since when we are baptized we die with Christ. This is what it means to be baptized into his death. For there all our sins die, so that, renewed by the death we have cast off, we might be seen to rise as those who have been born again to new life, so that just as Christ died to sin and rose again, so through baptism we might also have the hope of resurrection. Therefore, baptism is the death of sin so that a new birth might follow, which, although the body remains, nevertheless renews us in our mind and buries all our old evil deeds. COMMENTARY ON PAUL'S EPISTLES.[16]

WHAT BURIAL WAS TO CHRIST, BAPTISM IS TO US. CHRYSOSTOM: What the cross and burial were to Christ, baptism is to us, though not in all respects. For Christ died and was buried in the flesh, whereas we have died and been buried to sin. HOMILIES ON ROMANS 10.[17]

AUGUSTINE: To be baptized into the death of Christ is nothing else but to die to sin, just as he died in the flesh. AGAINST JULIAN 1.7.33.[18]

[PSEUDO-]CONSTANTIUS: Paul teaches this because we are not under the law but under grace, and therefore we should not sin, because we have died to sin in baptism. THE HOLY LETTER OF ST. PAUL TO THE ROMANS.[19]

SEVERIAN: Since we are baptized we confess that we have died to the world and have been buried to sin and the devil. PAULINE COMMENTARY FROM THE GREEK CHURCH.[20]

THREE BAPTISMS: WATER, THE SPIRIT AND MARTYRDOM. PELAGIUS: Do you not know about this sacrament of baptism? In the Scriptures baptism is received in three ways: with water, with the Holy Spirit (who is also called "fire") and with blood in martyrdom.[21] We who are believers have died with Christ in our baptism. PELAGIUS'S COMMENTARY ON ROMANS.[22]

WE CARRY HIS MORTIFICATION IN OUR BODIES. CYRIL OF ALEXANDRIA: Christ died to sin once, but in that he lives, he lives to God. We have undergone a death like his and have practically been buried together with him. For in that we carry his mortification about in our bodies, we have been buried together with him.[23] EXPLANATION OF THE LETTER TO THE ROMANS.[24]

6:4 Buried into Death, Walking in Newness of Life

THE UNCLEAN SOUL ACTIVELY SINFUL UNTIL REBORN. TERTULLIAN: Every soul, by reason of its birth, has its nature in Adam until it is born again in Christ; moreover, it is unclean as long as it remains without this regeneration, and because it is unclean it is actively sinful and infects even the flesh with its shame, because of their fusion. A TREATISE ON THE SOUL 40.[25]

BAPTISM INTO DEATH. ORIGEN: If we have been buried together with Christ in the way we outlined above, i.e., because we have died to sin, it follows that just as Christ was raised from the dead we shall rise together with him. Just as he ascended into heaven we shall also ascend with him, and just as he sits at the right hand of God, we shall also sit with him, as the apostle himself says elsewhere: (He has) made us sit with him in the heavenly places in Christ Jesus.[26]

Christ rose from the dead by the glory of the Father, and if we have died to sin and are buried together with Christ, and all who see our good works glorify our Father who is in heaven,[27] we shall rightly be said to have risen together with Christ by the glory of the Father so that we may walk in newness of life. For newness of life occurs when we have "put off the old man with his deeds and put on the new man who has been created

---

[16]CSEL 81.1:191. [17]NPNF 1 11:405. [18]FC 35:41. [19]ENPK 2:42.
[20]NTA 15:218. [21]See Lk 12:50. [22]PCR 96. [23]See Col 2:11-12.
[24]Migne PG 74 cols. 792-93. [25]ANF 3:220. [26]Eph 2:6. [27]See Mt 5:16.

according to God"[28] and "who is renewed in the knowledge of God according to the image of him who created him."[29] Nor should you think that this renewal of life, which is said to take place once for all, is enough by itself. Constantly and daily this newness must be renewed, if it can be put that way.[30]

When Paul said: "that we too might walk in newness of life," it seems that he was revealing the spiritual principle that as long as we are making progress we may be said to be walking. For it must not be thought that it is being said that they walk about aimlessly. Rather, those who are making progress will eventually come to the place where they ought to be. COMMENTARY ON THE EPISTLE TO THE ROMANS.[31]

ENTOMBED IN WATER. CYRIL OF JERUSALEM: As Jesus died in taking away the sins of the world, that, by doing sin to death, he might rise in righteousness, so too, when you go down into the water and are, in a fashion, entombed in the water as he was in the rock,[32] you may rise again to walk "in newness of life." THE CATECHETICAL LECTURES 3.12.[33]

BAPTISM A FIGURE OF RESURRECTION. AMBROSE: Baptism is a likeness of death when you go down into the water, and when you rise again it becomes a likeness of resurrection. Thus, according to the interpretation of the apostle, just as Christ's resurrection was a regeneration, so the resurrection from the font is also a regeneration. THE SACRAMENTS 2.7.20.[34]

SPIRITUALLY CLEANSED. AMBROSIASTER: First of all, this means that Christ raised his own body from the dead. For he is the power of God the Father, as he said: "Destroy this temple and I will raise it again in three days."[35] He was saying this about the temple of his own body. . . . It also means that we now have a new way of life which has been given to us by Christ. For by baptism we have been buried together with Christ[36] in order that we may henceforth live according to the life

into which Christ rose from the dead. Therefore baptism is the sign and symbol of the resurrection, which means that we ought to abide in the commandments of Christ and not go back to what we were before. For the person who dies does not sin; death is the end of sin. This is symbolized by water, because just as water cleanses the dirt of the body, so we believe that we have been spiritually cleansed by baptism from every sin and renewed, for what is incorporeal is cleansed invisibly. COMMENTARY ON PAUL'S EPISTLES.[37]

WALKING IN NEWNESS OF LIFE. CHRYSOSTOM: Here Paul hints at the subject of the resurrection along with the duty of a careful walk. In what way? He means: Do you believe that Christ died and that he rose again? If so, then believe that the same will happen to you. . . . For if you have shared in his cross and burial, how much more will you share in his resurrection as well? For now that the greater is done away with (i.e., sin), it is not right to go on doubting about the lesser, viz., the doing away of death. HOMILIES ON ROMANS 10.[38]

SEVERIAN: "Newness of life" means that we have put off the old life of sin and that our rebirth promises a new way of life. PAULINE COMMENTARY FROM THE GREEK CHURCH.[39]

RENOUNCING OUR FORMER LIFE. PELAGIUS: Paul shows that we were baptized so that through the sacrament we are buried with Christ, dying to our sins and renouncing our former life. So just as the Father is glorified in the resurrection of the Son, so too on account of the newness of our lifestyle he is glorified by us all, as long as none of the signs of the old self is recognizable in us. For now we should no longer want or desire anything that those who are not yet baptized and are still

---

[28]Eph 4:22-24; Col 3:9-10. [29]Col 3:10. [30]See 2 Cor 4:16. [31]CER 3:146-50. [32]See Mt 27:60. [33]LCC 4:96. [34]FC 44:290. [35]Jn 2:19. [36]See Col 2:11-12. [37]CSEL 81.1:193. [38]NPNF 1 11:405. [39]NTA 15:218.

trapped in the errors of their old life want or desire. PELAGIUS'S COMMENTARY ON ROMANS.[40]

CYRIL OF ALEXANDRIA: As we have been buried, so we must rise with Christ in a spiritual sense. For if to be buried together with Christ means dying to sin, then it is clear that rising with him means living in righteousness. EXPLANATION OF THE LETTER TO THE ROMANS.[41]

THEODORET OF CYR: The sacrament of baptism itself teaches us to turn away from sin. For baptism is a type of the death of Christ. In it we have become participants in the death and resurrection of Christ. Therefore, because we have shared in Christ's resurrection, we ought to live a new life now. INTERPRETATION OF THE LETTER TO THE ROMANS.[42]

6:5 United in Death and Resurrection

RISING IN THE REALITY OF OUR FLESH. TERTULLIAN: We die figuratively in our baptism, but we shall rise again in reality in our flesh, even as Christ did. ON RESURRECTION OF THE FLESH 47.[43]

PLANTED TOGETHER WITH CHRIST. ORIGEN: In saying that we have been united (i.e., planted together) with Christ, Paul compares the death of Christ to a plant to which we have been joined, so that drawing on the sap of his root our root may bring forth branches of righteousness and bear the fruits of life. If you want to know what plant it is that Scripture says we ought to be planted together with and what type of tree it is, listen to what is said about wisdom: "She is a tree of life to those who hope in her and who trust in her as in the Lord."[44] Therefore it is Christ, the power of God and the wisdom of God, who is the tree of life with whom we must be planted, for by some new and lovely gift of God his death has become for us the tree of life. . . .

Therefore Paul wants us to be planted together in the likeness of Christ's death, so that

we may also be planted together in his resurrection. For "planted together" (i.e., united) must be understood of both. Consider how necessary it was for him to adopt the image of planting. For every plant, after the death of winter, awaits the resurrection of spring. Therefore, if we have been planted in Christ's death in the winter of this world and this present life, so too we shall be found in the coming spring bearing the fruits of righteousness from his root. COMMENTARY ON THE EPISTLE TO THE ROMANS.[45]

UNITED TO HIM BY FAITH. DIODORE: Those who have been validly baptized into Christ's death have been united to him by faith. PAULINE COMMENTARY FROM THE GREEK CHURCH.[46]

UNITED WITH HIM IN THE LIKENESS OF HIS DEATH. AMBROSIASTER: Happily Paul says that we can rise again if we have been united with Christ in the likeness of his death, i.e., if we have laid aside all our wickedness in baptism and, having been transferred into a new life, no longer sin. In this way we shall be like him in his resurrection, because the likeness of his death presupposes a similar resurrection. . . . The likeness does not mean that there will be no difference at all between us, of course. We will be like him in the glory of his body, not in the nature of his divinity. COMMENTARY ON PAUL'S EPISTLES.[47]

REMAINING DEAD TO SIN AFTER BAPTISM. CHRYSOSTOM: Paul says that there are two mortifyings and two deaths. One of them is accomplished by Christ in baptism, and the other it is our duty to effect by earnestness afterwards. For it was Christ's gift that our former sins were buried, but remaining dead to sin after baptism must be the work of our own earnestness, however much we find that God gives us enormous help here as well. For baptism does not just have the

---

[40]PCR 96-97. [41]Migne PG 74 col. 793. [42]IER, Migne PG 82 col. 105. [43]ANF 3:580. [44]Prov 3:18 LXX. [45]CER 3:152-56. [46]NTA 15:85. [47]CSEL 81.1:193-95.

power to obliterate our former transgressions; it also protects us against subsequent ones. HOMILIES ON ROMANS 11.[48]

A DEATH LIKE HIS. CHRYSOSTOM: Paul did not say "in death" but "in a death like his." For both the first and the second are death but not the death of the same thing. The first is the death of the body, the second is the death of sin. BAPTISMAL INSTRUCTIONS 10.10.[49]

PELAGIUS: If we are buried with Christ now, we shall be united with him in his resurrection then, and if we have already become new and been changed in our way of life now, we shall likewise be new and changed in glory then. PELAGIUS'S COMMENTARY ON ROMANS.[50]

UNITED WITH HIM IN A RESURRECTION LIKE HIS. CYRIL OF ALEXANDRIA: Emmanuel gave up his soul for us; he died in the flesh. We also were buried together with him when we were baptized. Does this mean that our flesh died in the same way as his did? Hardly. Come, let me explain in what sense we were buried with him in a death like his. Christ died in the flesh in order to remove the sin of the world, but we do not die to the flesh so much as to guilt, as it is written. Thus now we have to break down the power of sin within us by mortifying our earthly members. . . . As we have died a death like his, so we shall also be conformed to his resurrection, because we shall live in Christ. It is true that the flesh will come to life again, but still we shall live in another way, by dedicating our souls to him and by being transformed into holiness and a kind of glorious life in the Holy Spirit. EXPLANATION OF THE LETTER TO THE ROMANS.[51]

GENNADIUS OF CONSTANTINOPLE: Christ's baptism in the Jordan was a type of the mystery of his resurrection.[52] PAULINE COMMENTARY FROM THE GREEK CHURCH.[53]

METAPHOR OR REALITY? OECUMENIUS: See the

goodness of God. We have died Christ's death metaphorically, but we shall share his resurrection truly. PAULINE COMMENTARY FROM THE GREEK CHURCH.[54]

6:6 No Longer Enslaved to Sin

AMENDMENT OF LIFE. TERTULLIAN: This refers not to our body structure but to our moral behavior. . . . It is not our bodily frame which has been transformed, nor has our flesh endured the cross of Christ. The sinful body is destroyed by amendment of life, not by the destruction of our fleshly substance. ON RESURRECTION OF THE FLESH 47.[55]

THE BODY OF SIN DESTROYED. ORIGEN: I think it should be noticed that when the apostle says something must be destroyed he calls it the body of sin, but when he does not use this expression he refers not to the body of sin but to our own selves, who ought not to be serving sin. He does this to show that if the body of sin were to be destroyed we would not now be serving sin, which however we serve as long as our body is not destroyed and our members on earth are not put to death. . . .

The "sinful body" is our body, for it is written that Adam did not know his wife Eve, nor did he father Cain, until after he had sinned. In the law it is commanded that sacrifices of a pair of turtledoves or two pigeons shall be offered for a newborn child.[56] One of these is a sin offering and the other is a burnt offering. For what sin is this first pigeon offered? How can a newborn child have sinned already? And yet the child has sin, for which the sacrifice is commanded to be offered. . . . For the same reason the church has received a tradition from the apostles to baptize even infants. For they, to whom the secrets of the divine mysteries had been committed, knew that there

---

[48]NPNF 1 11:408. [49]ACW 31:152. [50]PCR 97. [51]Migne PG 74 cols. 793, 796. [52]See Mt 3:13-17; Mk 1:9-11. [53]NTA 15:366. [54]NTA 15:426. [55]ANF 3:580. [56]See Lev 12:8.

are real stains of sin in everyone which must be cleansed by water and the Spirit. It is because of these stains that the body is called a sinful body and not because of sins which the soul in that body may have committed in a previous life, as some who believe in reincarnation like to think. COMMENTARY ON THE EPISTLE TO THE ROMANS.[57]

BASIL: By these words we are taught that he who is baptized in Christ is baptized in his death and is not only buried with Christ and planted together with him but is first of all crucified with him. Thus we are instructed that, as he who is crucified is separated from the living, so also he who has been crucified with Christ in the likeness of his death is completely set apart from those who live according to the old man. CONCERNING BAPTISM 1.2.[58]

OUR OLD SELF CRUCIFIED. AMBROSIASTER: Paul underlines and repeats a good deal in order to teach the baptized that they must not sin and above all that they must not return to idolatry, which is a very serious crime and the root of all errors, lest they lose the grace which they have received through Christ. He calls our former behavior "our old self" because, just as the man who has a pure life through Christ and faith in him is said to be new, so the same man is said to be old through unbelief and evil deeds. Paul says that these deeds have been crucified, which means that they are dead, that the body of sin (i.e., all our misdeeds) has been destroyed. Paul calls all our sins a body, which he says has been destroyed by a good life and by orthodox belief. COMMENTARY ON PAUL'S EPISTLES.[59]

CHRYSOSTOM: Paul does not say that we have been crucified but that we have been crucified "with him," thus linking baptism with the cross. . . . You are dead not in the sense that you have been obliterated but in the sense that now you can live without sin. HOMILIES ON ROMANS 11.[60]

CHRYSOSTOM: Get for yourself none of the things

that are on earth, and do not be active in the affairs of the present life. For your life is hidden now and unseen by those who do not believe, but the time will come when it will be seen. But now is not your time. Since you have died once for all, refuse to mind the things that are on earth. The greatness of your virtue is seen especially when you have prevailed over the arrogance of the flesh and act toward the good things of the world just as if you were dead to this life. BAPTISMAL INSTRUCTIONS 7.22.[61]

NO LONGER SLAVES OF SIN. AMBROSE: Until this price was paid for all men by the shedding of the Lord's blood for the forgiveness of all, blood was required of each man who by the law and the customary rite was following the holy precepts of religion. Since the price has been paid for all after Christ the Lord suffered, there is no longer need for the blood of each individual to be shed by circumcision, for in the blood of Christ the circumcision of all has been solemnized, and in his cross we have all been crucified with him and buried together in his tomb and planted together in the likeness of his death that we may no longer be slaves of sin. LETTER 16.[62]

HE BORE OUR SIN. AUGUSTINE: This refers to Deuteronomy [21:23]: "Cursed be every man hanged from a tree." For as the crucifixion of the old man is symbolized in the cross of the Lord, so the rebirth of the new man is signified in the resurrection. It is clear that according to Paul we are in the place of the old man who is accursed. No one doubts that it was because of him that the Lord was called "sin," because "he bore our sins"[63] and "he was made sin for us,"[64] and "by sin he condemned sin."[65] AUGUSTINE ON ROMANS 32-34."[66]

THE POWER TO RESTRAIN SIN. PELAGIUS:

---

[57]CER 3:160, 164. [58]FC 9:368. [59]CSEL 81.1:195. [60]NPNF 1 11:409. [61]ACW 31:113. [62]FC 26:93. [63]See Jn 1:29; 1 Pet 2:24. [64]2 Cor 5:21. [65]Rom 8:3. [66]AOR 13.

Through baptism you who have been made a member of Christ's body were crucified with Christ.[67] He hangs his innocent body so that you may have the power to restrain your guilty body from sin. Similarly, Moses lifted up the bronze serpent in the wilderness[68] so that every form of wickedness might be torn down, because each vice is a member of the body of sin. Christ was not crucified in part but in whole. Or perhaps we should read this as meaning that our body should be torn away from slavery to sin and that what used to be the property of transgression should now become the property of righteousness, for "everyone who commits sin is a slave to sin."[69] PELAGIUS'S COMMENTARY ON ROMANS.[70]

THE OLD MAN. CYRIL OF ALEXANDRIA: Perhaps some people will think that "the body of sin" is meant to refer to our earthly flesh, which has been joined to the soul as a kind of punishment, in that the soul sinned before bodies were created. Some people think and talk like this, but as it is a pagan idea we must reject it as being incompatible with the truth. Therefore, Paul says that our earthly body is the body of sin and our old man, because it has inherited the necessity of corruption from the old Adam. . . . Moreover, because of its weakness it has contracted a love for wickedness, and thus sin appears in the flesh as a congenital defect.

We were crucified with Christ at the moment when his flesh was crucified, because it somehow included universal human nature in itself, just as universal human nature contracted the sickness of the curse in Adam at the same time that he incurred the curse. EXPLANATION OF THE LETTER TO THE ROMANS.[71]

THEODORET OF CYR: The "old man" does not refer to our nature but to our evil mind. It is this which has been put to death in baptism, so that the body would not continue to serve sin. INTERPRETATION OF THE LETTER TO THE ROMANS.[72]

GENNADIUS OF CONSTANTINOPLE: "Our old self"

refers to our perishable and passible bodies. PAULINE COMMENTARY FROM THE GREEK CHURCH.[73]

6:7 Freed from Sin

THE LIMITS GOD SETS ON SIN. IRENAEUS: God set a limit to man's sin by interposing death and thus causing sin to cease, putting an end to it by the dissolution of the flesh, which should take place in the earth, so that man, ceasing at length to live in sin and dying to it, might begin to live in God. AGAINST HERESIES 3.23.6.[74]

SET FREE. BASIL: He is set free, he is delivered, he is cleansed of all sin, and not sin in word and deed only but also of all irrational movements of the mind. CONCERNING BAPTISM 1.2.[75]

THE DEAD DO NOT SIN. PELAGIUS: *Freed* means "alienated" from sin, for the dead do not sin in any way. "No one born of God commits sin,"[76] for since he has been crucified and all his members are filled with regret, he will hardly be able to sin. PELAGIUS'S COMMENTARY ON ROMANS.[77]

THEODORET OF CYR: Whoever saw a dead man sleeping in some harlot's bed, or bloodying his hands with murder, or doing anything else which is sinful? INTERPRETATION OF THE LETTER TO THE ROMANS.[78]

6:8 We Shall Live with Christ

LIFE WILL COME IN THE FUTURE. ORIGEN: Paul writes that we shall live with him in order to show that, while death works in the present, life will come in the future. COMMENTARY ON THE EPISTLE TO THE ROMANS.[79]

---

[67]See Rom 12:5; 1 Cor 6:15; 12:27; Gal 2:20; 5:24; Eph 5:30. [68]Num 21:9; Jn 3:14. [69]Jn 8:34. [70]PCR 97. [71]Migne PG 74 col. 796. [72]IER, Migne PG 82 col. 105. [73]NTA 15:366. [74]ANF 1:457. [75]FC 9:369. [76]1 Jn 3:9. [77]PCR 97. [78]IER, Migne PG 82 col. 105. [79]CER 3:168.

IF WE HAVE DIED WITH CHRIST. AMBROSI-
ASTER: It is clear that those who have crucified
the body, i.e., the world with its vices and lusts,
die to the world and die together with Christ, and
that they are also conformed to his eternal and
saving life so that they might deserve to be made
like Christ in his glory. But the flesh, i.e., the
body, is crucified in such a way that the lusts
which arise in it as a result of the sin in it, which
comes from the transgression of the first man, are
trampled underfoot. For the devil is crucified in
our flesh; it is he who deceives us through the
flesh. But note how the word *flesh* is sometimes to
be understood as the world, i.e., the elements,
sometimes as the human body and sometimes as
the soul which follows corporeal vices. COMMEN-
TARY ON PAUL'S EPISTLES.[80]

PELAGIUS: If we have not died with him we shall
not live with him, because then we are not his
members. PELAGIUS'S COMMENTARY ON
ROMANS.[81]

THEODORET OF CYR: Those of us who were buried with Christ ought to die to sin, because we
are waiting for the resurrection. INTERPRETA-
TION OF THE LETTER TO THE ROMANS.[82]

6:9 Death Has No Dominion over Christ

CHRIST WILL NEVER DIE AGAIN. ORIGEN: If
Christ were to die again, it follows that those
who have died with him and who will be raised
with him will also die again along with him!
Therefore the apostle makes it clear that Christ
will never die again, so that those who will live
with him may be sure of having eternal life. . . .
    Paul was right to say that "death no longer has
dominion over him." For he will never again give
himself up to the rule of the tyrant, nor will he
again empty himself in order to take the form of a
servant and be made obedient unto death.[83] Nor
will he ever again endure the rule of the tyrant
and of death in the form of a servant, even though
he assumed it voluntarily and not because he was

forced into it. COMMENTARY ON THE EPISTLE TO
THE ROMANS.[84]

HENCE BAPTISM UNREPEATED. PELAGIUS: We
shall not fear the second death if we have died
willingly.[85] Or it may mean: "You cannot be baptized a second time because Christ cannot be crucified for you a second time," as Paul writes to the
Hebrews.[86] He does not say that these people
cannot repent, but he does not allow them to
repeat their baptism. PELAGIUS'S COMMENTARY
ON ROMANS.[87]

CAESARIUS OF ARLES: When death first had
dominion over Christ, it was only with his consent. SERMON 69.2.[88]

DEATH NO LONGER HAS DOMINION. GRE-
GORY THE GREAT: Though Christ is now risen
from the dead, and death has no more power over
him, yet living in himself immortal and incorruptible he is again immolated for us in the mystery of the holy sacrifice. Where his body is eaten,
there his flesh is distributed among the people for
their salvation. His blood no longer stains the
hands of the godless but flows into the hearts of
his faithful followers. DIALOGUES 4.60.[89]

6:10 Christ Died to Sin and Lives to God

HE DIED TO SIN ONCE FOR ALL. TERTULLIAN:
Since Christ died once for all, no one who has
died to Christ since then can live again to sin.
ON MODESTY 17.[90]

KINDS OF DEATH. AMBROSE: In the Scriptures we learn that there are three kinds of death.
The first is when we die to sin and live to God.
Blessed is that death which, escaping from sin
and devoted to God, separates us from what is
mortal and consecrates us to him who is immor-

---

[80]CSEL 81.1:197. [81]PCR 97. [82]IER, Migne PG 82 cols. 105, 108.
[83]Phil 2:7-8. [84]CER 3:172, 180. [85]See Rev 2:11. [86]Heb 6:4. [87]PCR
97-98. [88]FC 31:326. [89]FC 39:273. [90]ANF 4:93.

tal. The second death is the departure from this life.... The third death is that of which it is said: "Let the dead bury their dead."[91] On the Death of His Brother Satyrus 2.36.[92]

Truly Alive Here. Ambrosiaster: Paul shows that in the Savior's resurrection we have the assurance of eternity, to which we shall attain if we live a better life. For whoever lives to God by doing good is truly alive here and now and has eternal life. Commentary on Paul's Epistles.[93]

No Going Back to Sin. Diodore: Paul is saying that if Christ had died for sinners two or three times, there would be no danger in going back to our old sinful ways. But as he only died once, we who have been buried and risen again with him will not die to sin again. There will be no second baptism, no second death of Christ. Therefore we must be careful to stay alive. Pauline Commentary from the Greek Church.[94]

Chrysostom: What does "died to sin" mean? It means that he was not subject to sin but that, in order to destroy it and remove its power, he died for our sin. Do you see how Paul frightens them? For since Christ does not die twice, there is no second washing, so you had better steer clear of any inclination toward sin! Homilies on Romans 11.[95]

Pelagius: Christ carried our sins and suffered for us so that in the future we might not sin. Christ now lives in the glory of his divinity. Pelagius's Commentary on Romans.[96]

6:11 Dead to Sin, Alive to God

Alive to God. Origen: Whoever thinks or considers that he is dead will not sin. For example, if lust for a woman gets hold of me or if greed for silver, gold or riches stirs me and I say in my heart that I have died with Christ ... the lust is immediately quenched and sin disappears.

The addition of "alive to God in Christ Jesus"

does not seem to me to be superfluous. It is as if Paul were saying that we are alive to God in wisdom, peace, righteousness and sanctification, all of which Christ is. Living to God in these is the same as living to God in Christ Jesus. For as nobody lives to God without righteousness, peace, sanctification and the other virtues, so it is certain that no one can live to God except in Christ Jesus. Commentary on the Epistle to the Romans.[97]

Dead to Sin. Hilary of Poitiers: Paul attributes death to sin, i.e., to our body, but life to God, to whose nature it belongs that he lives, so that we must die to our body in order to live in Christ Jesus. While assuming the body of our sin, Christ already lives wholly for God, since he has united the nature that he shared with us in a mutual participation in the divine immortality. The Trinity 9.13.[98]

Freedom from Sin Not Yet Complete. Chrysostom: Paul says: "Consider yourselves" ... because complete freedom from sin is not a reality as yet.... We are told to live for God in Jesus Christ our Lord and to lay hold of every virtue, having Jesus as our ally in the struggle. Homilies on Romans 11.[99]

In Him Our Life Is Hidden with God. Pelagius: As members of Christ you should understand that having died with him once for all you ought now always to live for God in Christ. In him our life is hidden with God, and since we have been clothed with him we should follow his example. Pelagius's Commentary on Romans.[100]

6:12 Do Not Let Sin Reign in Your Bodies

The Same Members. Irenaeus: In these same

---

[91]Mt 8:22; Lk 9:60. [92]FC 22:211-12. [93]CSEL 81.1:197. [94]NTA 15:85. [95]NPNF 1 11:410. [96]PCR 98. [97]CER 3:188. [98]FC 25:334. [99]NPNF 1 11:410. [100]PCR 98.

members in which we used to serve sin and bring forth fruit unto death, God wants us to be obedient unto righteousness, that we may bring forth fruit unto life. AGAINST HERESIES 5.14.4.[101]

LET NOT SIN REIGN IN YOUR MORTAL BODIES. ORIGEN: The apostle declares that all sins are works of the flesh.... Now if it were not in our power that sin should not reign in us, he would not have given us this command. How then is it possible that sin should not reign in our flesh? It is possible if we do what the apostle says—"Put to death what is earthly in you"[102]—and if we always carry around in our body the death of Christ.[103] For it is certain that where the death of Christ is carried around sin cannot reign. For the power of the cross of Christ is such that if it is placed before our eyes and kept faithfully in mind in such a way that the eye of the mind may keep its gaze fixed on the death of Christ, no lust, no desire, no passion and no envy will be able to overcome it. At its presence the whole host of sin and the flesh will always flee.

Why does Paul add that the body is "mortal," when this seems to be obvious? Perhaps, but I think there is a reason for this addition. For Paul was showing by this how it is possible for sin not to reign in our bodies.... If we realize that our body can be put to death and be dead to sin, it may happen that sin will not reign in it. Insofar as it is dead, it is said to be justified from sin. Nor does a dead man lust or get angry or have passions or steal what is not his. Therefore, if we suppress all these desires in our bodies they may be said to be dead to sin. This is what the apostle appears to be telling us by adding the adjective *mortal* in this context. COMMENTARY ON THE EPISTLE TO THE ROMANS.[104]

DIODORE: What sin is this? The sin committed before baptism, of course. PAULINE COMMENTARY FROM THE GREEK CHURCH.[105]

NO ONE IS JUDGED APART FROM HIS BODY. AMBROSIASTER: The body is mortal because of the sin of Adam, but by faith in Christ we believe that it will be immortal. But in order for it to inherit the promise, Paul says that it must not listen to the voice of sin, so that sin may not reign in our mortal body. For it reigns as long as it is in control. But if it does not reign, the body will no longer appear to be mortal, because it dwells in the hope of eternal life. Paul did not say that the body is mortal because it will disintegrate but because of the pain of hell, so that the man who is sent to hell is said to be mortal because whoever hearkens to sin will not escape the second death, from which the Savior has delivered those who believe in him. Therefore, the mortal body refers to the entire human being because those who hearken to sin are said to be mortal. For Scripture says: "The soul which sins shall surely die,"[106] which means the whole human being. For nobody will be judged apart from his body. COMMENTARY ON PAUL'S EPISTLES.[107]

THE ABSURDITY OF REMAINING CAPTIVE. CHRYSOSTOM: It is absurd for those who are being led toward the kingdom of God to have sin ruling over them or for those who are called to reign with Christ to choose to be captives to sin, as if one should throw down the crown from off his head and choose to be the slave of a hysterical woman who comes begging and covered in rags. ... How is it that sin can reign in you? It is not from any power of its own but only from your laziness. HOMILIES ON ROMANS 11.[108]

JEROME: Because men are not my masters, because sin is not my lord—for sin does not reign in my mortal body—I am your servant. HOMILIES ON THE PSALMS 40.[109]

SIN'S REIGN OVERTHROWN. AUGUSTINE: The reign of sin is overthrown and destroyed, partly by such an amendment on the part of men that the

[101]ANF 1:542. [102]Col 3:5. [103]2 Cor 4:10. [104]CER 3:190-96. [105]NTA 15:86. [106]Ezek 18:4. [107]CSEL 81.1:199. [108]NPNF 1 11:410. [109]FC 48:298.

flesh is made subject to the spirit and partly by the condemnation of those who are persevering in sin, in order that they might be so justly restrained that they cannot be troublesome to the righteous, who reign with Christ. COMMENTARY ON THE LORD'S SERMON ON THE MOUNT 1.22.77.[110]

ALLOWING THE EYE TO BE TURNED. AUGUSTINE: We must engage in a constant, daily struggle not to obey those desires which are forbidden or improper. For from this sort of fault it comes about that the eye is turned to where it ought not to look, and if this fault grows strong and prevails, even bodily adultery is carried out, which is committed in the heart as much more quickly as thought is quicker than action and has nothing to hinder or delay it. ON NATURE AND GRACE 38.45.[111]

LIVING AS IF IMMORTAL. PELAGIUS: You should live in your mortal body as if you were immortal. Paul also explains how sin reigns in the body—by obedience and consent. PELAGIUS'S COMMENTARY ON ROMANS.[112]

WITHHOLDING CONSENT TO THE REIGN OF SIN. THEODORET OF CYR: A reign is different from a tyranny in that a tyrant rules without the consent of his subjects, whereas a reign applies in those cases where the subjects have assented to it. Therefore Paul is urging his hearers not to assent any longer to the reign of sin, for the Lord destroyed sin's reign when he took on human flesh. INTERPRETATION OF THE LETTER TO THE ROMANS.[113]

CAESARIUS OF ARLES: Paul did not say: "Let sin not exist," but "Let it not reign." Sin is within you if you take delight in it; it reigns if you consent to it. SERMON 134.3.[114]

GENNADIUS OF CONSTANTINOPLE: Here Paul shows that the reason we no longer sin is not that after baptism we are no longer made of flesh. Up to this point, we claim Christ's perfection by faith

only and not by experience. For we have not yet become impassible or immortal. . . . Therefore Paul does not say: "Do not sin," but rather: "Let not sin reign in your mortal bodies." PAULINE COMMENTARY FROM THE GREEK CHURCH.[115]

6:13 *Yielding to God, Not Sin*

OUR MEMBERS AS INSTRUMENTS OF RIGHTEOUSNESS. ORIGEN: Note carefully the subtle distinctions which Paul makes here. When he talks about yielding to sin, he does not talk about us but about our members. However, when he talks about yielding to God, it is not our members which he mentions but our very selves. By this he means that we must give our souls and our whole persons to God so that, as we present ourselves before him as godly people and cling to him, we shall be making our members instruments of righteousness at the same time. COMMENTARY ON THE EPISTLE TO THE ROMANS.[116]

SUSTAINING A DISPOSITION OF URGENCY. BASIL: This injunction would be successfully carried out, I believe, if we were willing always to keep the same disposition of mind as we had at the time of danger. For surely we realized to some degree the vanity of life, as well as the unreliability and instability of human affairs, which change so easily. And in all likelihood we felt contrition for our past faults and promised that for the future, if we were saved we would serve God with watchful exactitude. LETTER 26.[117]

PROTECTING OUR MEMBERS FROM ABUSE. AMBROSIASTER: Paul shows that the devil fights against us by using our members. For the opportunity is given to him by our sins, so that when God abandons us he acquires the power to deceive and destroy us. Therefore we must protect our members from every work of iniquity so that our enemy may be left defenseless and sub-

---

[110]FC 11:104-5. [111]FC 86:56. [112]PCR 98. [113]IER, Migne PG 82 col. 108. [114]FC 47:253. [115]NTA 15:367. [116]CER 3:196. [117]FC 13:67.

dued. Paul did not say: "Present your bodies," but "Present your members," for a person goes wrong when his members and not his whole body lead him wherever sin dictates.

"Death" in this context means ignorance and unbelief, combined with an evil life, because "life" is to know God through Christ.[118] Just as nobody acquires life without a parent, everyone has obtained life through Christ.[119] Therefore whoever does not recognize that God is the Father of all through Christ is said not to have life, i.e., what he has here on earth does not count as life. For such a person denies himself as long as he thinks he can live without God as his Father. Therefore ignorance and a wicked life are death. For wickedness obtains death, not the death which is common to us all but the death of hell, as I mentioned above. Likewise, knowledge of God the Father and holy behavior are life, not that life which is subject to death but the life of the world to come which is called eternal. For this reason Paul says that you should present yourselves to God, for by knowing him you will go on to salvation. Having turned away from an evil life you will be like people who have risen from the dead.

Such great modesty ought to govern our conduct that our behavior will lead to the righteousness of God, not to earthly righteousness. For the righteousness of this world is without faith in Christ, and without that it is death, not life. Let us then yield our members to him so that he can defend us. For when we yield our members to him through good works, we make ourselves worthy to be aided by God's righteousness, because that righteousness is not given to those who are unworthy to receive it. Where God's righteousness is, there the Holy Spirit dwells and helps our infirmity. Just as we yield our members to sin when we act wrongly, so we yield them to righteousness when we behave rightly, protecting them from all wickedness. COMMENTARY ON PAUL'S EPISTLES.[120]

THE BODY NOT EVIL IN ITSELF. CHRYSOSTOM: The body, like a military weapon, is not in itself

inclined to either vice or virtue. It can go either way, depending on the user. . . . The flesh becomes either good or evil according to the mind's decision, not because of its own nature. HOMILIES ON ROMANS II.[121]

FREELY OFFERING YOUR MEMBERS TO SERVICE. PELAGIUS: Every part of the body can become a weapon of wickedness which will defeat righteousness if it turns its purpose to bad use. At the same time, note that it is by freedom of choice that a man offers his members to the side of his choice. PELAGIUS'S COMMENTARY ON ROMANS.[122]

THEODORET OF CYR: By telling us to yield our members to God as instruments of righteousness, Paul teaches that the body is not evil but the creation of a good God. Therefore if it is properly and correctly controlled by the soul it can serve God. INTERPRETATION OF THE LETTER TO THE ROMANS.[123]

6:14 Under Grace, Not Law

SIN HAS NO DOMINION. ORIGEN: Once again note the subtlety of Paul's language. When he talks about us he says that "sin" will have no dominion over us, but when he talks about Christ he says that it is "death" which will have no dominion over him, for there was room for death in Christ but not sin.

The law of which he speaks here is the law in our members, which is opposed to the law of the mind. It is clear that those who have put to death their members will not be under the law of their members but under the grace of God. If someone wants to read this as referring to the law of Moses, the text will doubtless mean that we are not under the law of the letter, which kills, but under the law of the Spirit, which gives life and

---

[118]See Jn 17:3; 1 Jn 5:13, 20. [119]See Jn 20:31; Rom 6:23. [120]CSEL 81.1:199-201. [121]NPNF 1 11:410-11. [122]PCR 98. [123]IER, Migne PG 82 col. 109.

which Paul here calls grace.[124] Commentary on the Epistle to the Romans.[125]

Under Grace. Ambrosiaster: If we walk according to the commandments which he gives, Paul says that sin will not rule over us, for it rules over those who sin. For if we do not walk as he commands we are under the law. But if we do not sin we are not under the law but under grace. If, however, we sin, we fall back under the law, and sin starts to rule over us once more, for every sinner is a slave to sin. It is necessary for a person to be under the law as long as he does not receive forgiveness, for by the law's authority sin makes the sinner guilty. Thus the person to whom forgiveness is given and who keeps it by not sinning anymore will neither be ruled by sin nor be under the law. For the authority of the law no longer applies to him; he has been delivered from sin. Those whom the law holds guilty have been turned over to it by sin. Therefore the person who has departed from sin cannot be under the law. Commentary on Paul's Epistles.[126]

Grace Both Remits and Protects. Chrysostom: Paul says that unless we sink very low, sin will not get the better of us. For it is not just the law which exhorts us but also grace which has remitted our former sins and protects us against future ones. Homilies on Romans 11.[127]

Live As Though Incapable of Sinning. Theodore of Mopsuestia: Having shown that they should avoid sinning for the sake of future benefits, Paul goes on to add that they should live as though they were incapable of sinning at all. For if the time was coming when they would be transformed and act as sinless people, then here and now they ought to cleanse their minds of any thought of sin and earnestly try to do what is good. Pauline Commentary from the Greek Church.[128]

The Third State: Under Grace. Augus-

tine: This refers to the third state[129] of man, when in his mind he serves the law of God even though his flesh still serves the law of sin. For he does not obey the desire to sin, even though lusts will continue to court him and urge him to surrender until the body is raised to new life and death is swallowed up in victory. Because we do not give in to evil desires we are under grace, and sin does not reign in our mortal bodies. But the man who is controlled by sin even if he wants to resist it is still under the law and not yet under grace. Augustine on Romans 35.[130]

Augustine: Grace causes sin not to have power over you. Therefore do not trust in yourself, lest sin thereby have much more power over you. Continence 5.12.[131]

Grace Enables Action. Augustine: It is not that the law is evil but that it makes those under it guilty by giving commands without providing help to fulfill them. In fact, grace helps one to become a doer of the law, for without such grace one living under the law will be no more than a hearer of the law. Grace and Free Will 12.24.[132]

Grace Ends Sin's Reign. [Pseudo-]Constantius: As long as someone is involved in sins he lives according to the old man, but when he is converted into the right way he is said to be upright. Because it is not impossible for those who have received grace to sin, Paul says: "Let not sin reign in you." But he knows well that those who are under grace are strangers to the many and varied commandments of the law and to their burdens, for the law was given because of the hardness of heart of the Jews. . . . For those who are partakers of the grace of Christ have learned how to overcome their passions and love God and their neighbor, as it is written.[133] The

---

[124]See 2 Cor 3:6. [125]CER 3:198-200. [126]CSEL 81.1:201-3. [127]NPNF 1 11:411. [128]NTA 15:122. [129]Humanity under nature, law, grace and glory are the four states. [130]AOR 13. [131]FC 16:203. [132]FC 59:278. [133]See Lev 19:18; Deut 6:5; Mt 22:37-39; Mk 12:30-31; Lk 10:27.

Holy Letter of St. Paul to the Romans.[134]

You Are Adults. Pelagius: Sin will not overcome you, for you are not children but adults.[135] It is like the teacher who says to a student: "Avoid stylistic errors; you are no longer learning from a primary school teacher but from a professor." Paul offered teaching and example as a way to overcome sin by grace. Pelagius's Commentary on Romans.[136]

Aided by the Spirit. Theodoret of Cyr: In other words, nature is no longer struggling on its own but has the Holy Spirit to help it. Interpretation of the Letter to the Romans.[137]

---

[134]ENPK 2:42-43. [135]See Gal 3:23-26. [136]PCR 98. [137]IER, Migne PG 82 col. 109.

6:15-23 SERVANTS OF RIGHTEOUSNESS

[15]*What then? Are we to sin because we are not under law but under grace? By no means!* [16]*Do you not know that if you yield yourselves to any one as obedient slaves, you are slaves of the one whom you obey, either of sin, which leads to death, or of obedience, which leads to righteousness?* [17]*But thanks be to God, that you who were once slaves of sin have become obedient from the heart to the standard of teaching to which you were committed,* [18]*and, having been set free from sin, have become slaves of righteousness.* [19]*I am speaking in human terms, because of your natural limitations. For just as you once yielded your members to impurity and to greater and greater iniquity, so now yield your members to righteousness for sanctification.*

[20]*When you were slaves of sin, you were free in regard to righteousness.* [21]*But then what return did you get from the things of which you are now ashamed? The end of those things is death.* [22]*But now that you have been set free from sin and have become slaves of God, the return you get is sanctification and its end, eternal life.* [23]*For the wages of sin is death, but the free gift of God is eternal life in Christ Jesus our Lord.*

Overview: Freedom from the law is not a license to sin but the opposite. We have been set free from the law only because under grace we have the spiritual power to live the life that the law models for us but cannot give us. Sin is slavery, and nobody in his right mind would willingly sell himself into that. Righteousness, although it involves obedience, is not slavery but liberation. The essential difference is that the obedience of a righteous person comes from the heart and not from some form of external constraint. In this sense paradoxically we can call ourselves slaves of righteousness. Paul speaks to us in human terms, in order to show that he is not making impossible demands on us. Before we were Christians, we quite happily gave ourselves over to sin, and the only thing we got from that was death. Why then, now that we are Christians and heirs of eternal life, should we find it hard to dedicate ourselves to righteousness, when the reward is eternal life? Those who sin get what they deserve—death. But those who turn to Christ get what they do not deserve—eternal life.

6:15 Grace Disallows Sin

ALREADY UNDER GRACE. ORIGEN: Paul repeats here what he said [in verse 1] above. The only difference is that [in verse 1] he posed the question as if he were speaking to people who had not yet abandoned their sinning, and so he appears to be telling them not to persist in what they had been doing up till then. Here, on the other hand, he seems to be talking to those who have already given up sinning. [In verse 1] he spoke as if abundant grace did not yet exist, but here he speaks as if grace is already present, because "we are not under law but under grace." COMMENTARY ON THE EPISTLE TO THE ROMANS.[1]

NO LONGER UNDER LAW. AMBROSIASTER: Although it was right for the law to be given—for it was given in order to show that those who sinned against it were guilty before God and in order to dissuade people from continuing to sin—yet because of the weakness of its infirmity the human race was unable to restrain itself from sin and had become subject to the death of hell. God was moved by the righteousness of his mercy, by which he always comes to the aid of the human race, and through Christ he provided a way by which he could reward those who were without hope. By forgiving their sins he released them from the law which had held them subject. Restored and made whole again by the help of God, they could reject the sins by which they had previously been held down. Therefore we did not sin in rejecting the law but rather we followed the providence of God himself through Christ. COMMENTARY ON PAUL'S EPISTLES.[2]

NO LICENSE TO SIN. THEODORE OF MOPSUESTIA: I think that Paul is saying this to the Jews because it is the nature of the law to tell us what we should and should not do. If we find ourselves outside the law, there is nothing to stop us from doing what we like, but if there is some way of determining what should and should not be done, then we are back under the law again, and what is said here will easily apply to us. Paul has expressed himself in this seemingly contradictory way because he is saying that since we are free of sin we are no longer under the law. He does not mean that the outpouring of grace has given us license to sin. PAULINE COMMENTARY FROM THE GREEK CHURCH.[3]

PELAGIUS: If you sin, you will not be under grace. PELAGIUS'S COMMENTARY ON ROMANS.[4]

6:16 Slaves of Sin or of Obedience

YOU ARE SLAVES OF THE ONE YOU OBEY. ORIGEN: This is what the apostle is teaching in this passage: that each person has it in his control and in the power of his will to be either a servant of sin or a servant of righteousness. He proves himself to be a slave of whatever side he chooses to obey and of whatever side he inclines toward.

Note that Paul assumes that anyone who yields himself to sin is a slave of sin, but he does not go on to add that anyone who yields himself to righteousness is a slave of righteousness. . . . It would not have been right to phrase it like that, because although God himself does what is righteous he cannot for that reason be said to be a slave of righteousness! On the contrary, he is the Lord of righteousness. Therefore it is not true to say that everyone who does what is righteous is a slave to righteousness in the same way that everyone who sins is a slave to sin. For even the devil himself is a slave to sin, because he departed from the obedience of righteousness and rebelled in the face of Almighty God, for which reason he is called an apostate. COMMENTARY ON THE EPISTLE TO THE ROMANS.[5]

CONFESSING GOD THROUGH OUR ACTIONS.

---

[1]CER 3:200. [2]CSEL 81.1:203. [3]NTA 15:122-23. [4]PCR 99. [5]CER 3:202-4.

AMBROSIASTER: Paul warns us not to say one thing and do another, so that when we are said to be servants of God we should be found by our actions to be servants of the devil. He proclaims that we are servants of the one whose will we do and that it is not fair to confess God as Lord but do the works of the devil. For God himself notices this and attacks it: "This people honors me with their lips, but their hearts are far from me,"[6] and the Lord says in the Gospel: "No man can serve two masters,"[7] and in the law it is written: "God is not mocked."[8] COMMENTARY ON PAUL'S EPISTLES.[9]

THE PERVERTED WILLINGNESS TO REMAIN SLAVES TO SIN. CHRYSOSTOM: Without saying a word about hell or eternal punishment as yet, Paul talks about the shame which comes in this life when people become slaves, and especially when they do so of their own free will, and to sin, of all things, whose wages are the second (i.e., spiritual) death. HOMILIES ON ROMANS 11.[10]

TWO MASTERS UNTHINKABLE. THEODORET OF CYR: Righteousness and sin are mutually incompatible. As the Lord himself said in the holy Gospel: "No man can serve two masters."[11] INTERPRETATION OF THE LETTER TO THE ROMANS.[12]

6:17 Obedient to the Standard of Teaching

SET FREE FROM SLAVERY. ORIGEN: It appears that Paul is saying this to those whose eternal life and spiritual progress are assured. These are the same people of whom he spoke [in 1:8] above. Then he goes on to point out that, to begin with, all men were slaves of sin.... But what follows is said to a few, to those who have been converted.

We all were slaves to sin, but when the standard of teaching was handed down to us and we chose to follow it, not in any which way nor in words only but from the heart, from the mind, with complete devotion, we were set free from the slavery of sin and made servants of righteousness. COMMENTARY ON THE EPISTLE TO THE ROMANS.[13]

OBEDIENT FROM THE HEART. AMBROSIASTER: As it is right to obey Christ, for he is himself righteousness and what he commands is righteous, Paul therefore says that we have become servants of righteousness "from the heart," not from the law. We do this voluntarily and not out of fear, so that our confession of faith might find expression in the judgment of our mind. For by nature we have been led to faith, not by the law, in which standard of teaching we have been made for the rule of God, who created nature. For by nature we know by whom and through whom and in whom we were created. Therefore the standard of teaching is that into which our Creator has led us naturally. This is what he said above: "They are a law unto themselves,"[14] when their own natures see what they believe, that what the law and the Prophets predicted to the Jews concerning Christ is what the Gentiles have confessed from the heart. For this reason Paul gives thanks to the Lord, because when we were still servants of sin we obeyed from the heart, believing in Christ, so that we might serve God not according to the law of Moses but according to the law of nature. COMMENTARY ON PAUL'S EPISTLES.[15]

THE BENEFITS OF FREEDOM FROM SIN. CHRYSOSTOM: After shaming them by mentioning their slavery and alarming them by talking about its rewards, Paul puts the balance right by recalling the benefits which they have received. For by mentioning them he shows that they were set free from very great evils indeed and that this had happened without any labor on their part.... For no human power could have set us free from such great evils, but "thanks be to God," who was willing and able to do such great things. And well he says that they were "obedient from the heart," because they were neither forced nor pressed but came of their own accord, with a willing mind....

[6]Is 29:13. [7]Mt 6:24; Lk 16:13. [8]Gal 6:7. [9]CSEL 81.1:205. [10]NPNF 1 11:412. [11]Mt 6:24; Lk 16:13. [12]IER, Migne PG 82 col. 109. [13]CER 3:206. [14]Rom 2:14. [15]CSEL 81.1:205-7.

This shows that they exercised their free will. Homilies on Romans 11.[16]

Then and Now. Pelagius: We "were" slaves to sin, but we "are" no longer. Pelagius's Commentary on Romans.[17]

Theodoret of Cyr: You who once were slaves to sin have broken away from it by the free will of your mind and have embraced spiritual teaching instead. Interpretation of the Letter to the Romans.[18]

6:18 Slaves of Righteousness

Truth Sets You Free. Origen: What is it which sets us free from sin? Knowledge of the truth, of course! This is what Jesus said to the Jews: "If you believe my word, you will know the truth, and the truth will set you free."[19] Commentary on the Epistle to the Romans.[20]

Reparenting the Orphan. Chrysostom: There are two gifts of God which Paul points out here. First there is the freeing from sin, and then there is the making of slaves of righteousness, which is better than any freedom. For God has done the same as if a person was to take an orphan who had been carried away by savages into their own country, and was not only to free him from captivity but to set a kind father over him and raise him to a very great dignity. This is what has happened in our case. For it was not just that God freed us from our old evils; he also led us into the life of angels. He opened the way for us to enjoy the best life, handing us over to the safekeeping of righteousness and killing our former evils, putting the old man in us to death and bringing us to eternal life. Homilies on Romans 11.[21]

We Have Thrown Off the Yoke. [Pseudo-]Constantius: Paul teaches that we who have been delivered from the burden and chain of the law of Moses ought not to sin, because being redeemed by the grace of Christ we have thrown off the yoke of the law. The Holy Letter of St. Paul to the Romans.[22]

Now Eliminate Opportunities to Sin. Pelagius: This is according to the teaching and example of Christ, who has taught us to get rid not only of sins but also of opportunities to sin. Pelagius's Commentary on Romans.[23]

6:19 Mortal Members, Spiritual Deeds

The Same Zeal for Righteousness As Before for Impurity. Origen: What is there so human, so trivial, so light that no weakness of the flesh can excuse it? . . . It is hardly cause for boasting that someone should serve virtue in the same way as he once served vice. Righteousness ought to be honored much more fully and much more seriously than that! But here Paul says: "I am speaking in human terms," meaning that he requires the same zeal from the convert as was present in him as a sinner. Once your feet ran to the temples of demons; now they run to the church of God. Once they ran to spill blood; now they run to set it free. Once your hands were stretched out to steal what belonged to others; now they are stretched out for you to be generous with what is your own. Once your eyes looked at women or at something which was not yours with lust in them; but now they look at the poor, the weak and the helpless with pity in them. Your ears used to delight in hearing empty talk or in attacking good people; now they have turned to hearing the Word of God, to the exposition of the law and to the learning of the knowledge of wisdom. Your tongue, which was accustomed to bad language, cursing and swearing has now turned to praising the Lord at all times; it produces healthy and honest speech, in order to give grace to the hearers and speak the truth to its neighbor. Commentary on the Epistle to the Romans.[24]

---

[16]NPNF 1 11:412. [17]PCR 99. [18]IER, Migne PG 82 col. 112. [19]Jn 8:31-32. [20]CER 3:210. [21]NPNF 1 11:412-13. [22]ENPK 2:43. [23]PCR 99. [24]CER 3:212-14.

Now Yield Your Members to Righteousness for Sanctification. Origen: But our members must be said to be circumcised if they are devoted to the service of God. But if they go beyond the laws divinely ordained for them, they must be considered uncircumcised. . . . For when our members served iniquity they were not circumcised, nor was the covenant of God in them. But when they began to serve righteousness unto sanctification, the promise which was made to Abraham is fulfilled in them. Homilies on Genesis 3.6.[25]

This Yoke Is Easy. Ambrosiaster: In recalling the weakness of the flesh, Paul wants to say that he is demanding less from us than the worship of God would normally require. . . . In order to remove from us any reason to be afraid of coming to faith, because that might seem to us to be unbearable and rough, Paul commands us to serve God with the same amount of zeal that we previously served the devil. For as we ought to be more willing to serve God than the devil, given that God brings salvation and the devil damnation, yet the spiritual physician does not demand more from us, lest in avoiding the more difficult precepts on account of our weakness we should remain in death. Thus the Lord says: "Take my yoke upon you, for my yoke is easy and my burden is light."[26] Commentary on Paul's Epistles.[27]

In Human Terms. Chrysostom: Paul says that he is speaking in human terms in order to show that he is not making any exorbitant demand, nor even as much as might be expected from someone who enjoyed so great a gift, but rather a moderate and light request. . . . The two masters are very different from each other, but even so, Paul is asking for no more than the same amount of servitude. People really ought to give much more to the service of righteousness, since righteousness is obviously so much bigger and better. But because of their weakness, which he does not ascribe to their free will or to their spirit but to their flesh, Paul is not making any greater demands on them. Homilies on Romans 12.[28]

Let the Flesh Perform Spiritual Deeds. Pelagius: Paul is saying, in effect: "Although you ought to serve righteousness much more than you previously served sin, I nevertheless make allowance for your weakness so that you might serve righteousness just as much as you once served sin." Or perhaps it is this: Whatever the soul does in a carnal fashion is held against the flesh, but if the flesh performs a spiritual deed the whole person becomes spiritual. . . . We offered our members to serve sin; it is not the case, as the Manichaeans say, that it was the nature of the body to have sin ingrained in it. Pelagius's Commentary on Romans.[29]

6:20 Slaves of Sin, Free from God

The "Freedom" That Exists Under Slavery. Origen: Here *free* means "alien," and rightly so. For no one can serve sin and righteousness at the same time, as the Savior said: "No one can serve two masters."[30] Commentary on the Epistle to the Romans.[31]

Freedom from God Is Slavery to Sin. Ambrosiaster: It is clear that whoever is free of God is a slave of sin. For as long as he sins he goes away from God and comes under sin. Commentary on Paul's Epistles.[32]

No Split Allegiances. Chrysostom: In the past you did not split your service between righteousness and sin but were wholly given over to sin. So now that you have come over to the side of righteousness, you should do the same thing and give yourselves over entirely to righteousness, doing nothing at all that is wicked. Homilies on Romans 12.[33]

---

[25]FC 71:99. [26]Mt 11:29-30. [27]CSEL 81.1:207. [28]NPNF 1 11:416. [29]PCR 99. [30]Mt 6:24; Lk 16:13. [31]CER 3:216. [32]CSEL 81.1:209. [33]NPNF 1 11:417.

PELAGIUS: As you are in no way slaves to sin inwardly, you should become free of every sin. PELAGIUS'S COMMENTARY ON ROMANS.[34]

PROSPER OF AQUITAINE: He who serves the devil is free from God, but he who being freed serves God is free from the devil. As a result it is apparent that a false liberty could have been had from a defect of the human will but that a true liberty could not have been received without the help of the liberator.[35] GRACE AND FREE WILL 9.5.[36]

6:21 The Fruits of Sin

THE MEANING OF DEATH. CLEMENT OF ALEXANDRIA: Death is the fellowship of the soul in a state of sin with the body, and life is separation from that sin. STROMATA 4.3.[37]

THE END OF THOSE THINGS IS DEATH. ORIGEN: Someone who turns his heart and mind to righteousness will undoubtedly blush and condemn himself when he thinks back on what he did before, when he was acting under the power of sin, for "the end of those things is death." But what death, I ask? Certainly not the death that is common to us all. . . . Is it perhaps that which is called the death of sin, as when Scripture says: "The soul which sins will surely die."[38] Or should it rather be understood as referring to that death by which we die with Christ to sin and put an end to wickedness and crimes, so that it can be said, as it is here, that death is the end of them? Paul compares fruits with fruits and declares that the fruits of sin for which we are now ashamed because we have been set free from sin and become servants of God end in death, whereas the fruits of righteousness, which lead to sanctification, end in eternal life. COMMENTARY ON THE EPISTLE TO THE ROMANS.[39]

THE DOUBLE MEANING OF DEATH. AMBROSIASTER: What are the fruits of sin? Learning from them what a good life is we are ashamed by the way we lived so wickedly before. And it is not only that the opinion of the pagans is wicked but also the heresy which is found most of all in Phrygia, to which only a morally corrupt person would belong, in which there is no sacrament and Christian piety has died out. Behold a freedom full of sins and bound by wickedness, whose deeds have only shame as their reward and whose end is death! Our departure is the end of this life and its deeds, and either death or life will succeed it. But here the word *death* has a double meaning, for it shifts from one kind of death to another. COMMENTARY ON PAUL'S EPISTLES.[40]

RECOGNIZING YOUR PAST LIFE FOR WHAT IT WAS. CHRYSOSTOM: If even the recollection of your former slavery makes you ashamed, think how much more the reality of it would do so. You have gained in two ways—by being set free from your former shame and by having come to recognize your past life for what it was. HOMILIES ON ROMANS 12.[41]

6:22 Holiness Now, Eternal Life in the Future

THE INJUNCTION AND REWARD WITHIN REACH. TERTULLIAN: Throughout this chapter, while withdrawing our members from unrighteousness and sin and applying them to righteousness and holiness, and transferring the same from the wages of death to the gift of eternal life, Paul undoubtedly promises to the flesh the reward of salvation. Now it would not have been consistent for a rule of holiness and righteousness to be especially enjoined for the flesh if the reward of such a discipline were not also within its reach; nor could even baptism be ordered for the flesh if by its regeneration a course were not inaugurated tending to its restitution. ON RESURRECTION OF THE FLESH 47.[42]

---

[34]PCR 99. [35]See Jn 8:32, 36; 1 Cor 7:22; 2 Cor 3:17. [36]FC 7:372. [37]ANF 2:411. [38]Ezek 18:4. [39]CER 3:218. [40]CSEL 81.1:209. [41]NPNF 1 11:417. [42]ANF 3:580.

NOW IN FULL SERVICE TO GOD. ORIGEN: Paul repeats what he has already said [in verse 18] but with an important difference. There he said that we have become slaves to obedience, which leads to righteousness, but here he says that we have become slaves to God. By saying this, Paul shows that after someone has been set free from sin he ought to serve righteousness and perform all the virtues in the first instance and then ascend by the way of spiritual progress to the point where he becomes a slave of God, even though to be a slave of righteousness is also to be a slave of God. For Christ is righteousness, and to serve Christ is to serve God. Nevertheless, there is a scale of spiritual perfection, and there are different levels of virtue. For this reason Christ is said to reign, because he is righteousness, until such time as the fullness of all virtue is complete in everyone. Then, when the measure of perfection is reached, it is said that he will give up the kingdom to God the Father, so that God may be all in all.[43] COMMENTARY ON THE EPISTLE TO THE ROMANS.[44]

PASSING FROM DEATH TO LIFE. AMBROSIASTER: If when we receive the forgiveness of sins we become imitators of good deeds, we shall acquire holiness and we shall obtain eternal life at the end, for we shall pass from death, which Paul said was the end, to life, which is without end.[45] COMMENTARY ON PAUL'S EPISTLES.[46]

HOLINESS NOW ASSURES ETERNAL LIFE. CHRYSOSTOM: Instead of the shame and death which you deserved before, you now have the hope of attaining holiness and eternal life. Note how Paul says that some things have already been given, while others are still hoped for, but that the former point to the latter. Thus if we can come to holiness now, we can be assured of obtaining eternal life in the future.[47] HOMILIES ON ROMANS 12.[48]

THE RETURN YOU GET IS SANCTIFICATION AND ITS END, ETERNAL LIFE. PELAGIUS: Doubtless there is no blessing in something for which one feels shame when repenting of it. Everyone who comes to know goodness is ashamed of his former actions, but anyone who is ashamed of righteousness is not aware of its fruit.[49] Therefore, those who sin get nothing out of it in the present, and in the future they will reap eternal death. But those who serve God have the gift of the Holy Spirit in the present and eternal life in the future. Or perhaps it should be read like this: what have you got out of doing things which make you feel ashamed whenever you think of them? The return you have already received is that, having been sanctified by baptism, you are alive. PELAGIUS'S COMMENTARY ON ROMANS.[50]

6:23 The Wages of Sin Is Death

KING SIN'S WAGES. ORIGEN: Paul employs a military metaphor to good effect by saying that death is the wage due to those who fight under King Sin. But God does not give his soldiers a wage, as if they have something owing to them. Rather, he gives them the gift of grace, which is eternal life in Christ.

The death being referred to here is not the death which separates the body from the soul but the death by which because of sin the soul is separated from God. COMMENTARY ON THE EPISTLE TO THE ROMANS.[51]

DEATH COMES THROUGH SIN. AMBROSIASTER: Paul says that the wages of sin is death because death comes through sin, and thus whoever refrains from sin will receive eternal life as his reward. Those who do not sin will not undergo the second death.

Just as those who follow sin obtain death, so those who follow the grace of God, that is, the faith of Christ which pardons sins, will have

---

[43]1 Cor 15:24, 28. [44]CER 3:220. [45]See Ezek 36:25-27; Mt 5:43-48; Eph 5:17-18, 25-27; 1 Thess 5:23-24. [46]CSEL 81.1:209. [47]See Ex 19:6; Lev 11:45; 19:2; 20:7, 26; 1 Pet 1:15-16. [48]NPNF 1 11:417. [49]See Heb 12:11. [50]PCR 99-100. [51]CER 3:226, 230.

eternal life.[52] They will therefore rejoice at being dissolved for a time, knowing that they will obtain this life which is free of all care and has no end. It was when he saw this from afar that St. Simeon asked to be released from this world that he might go into peace, that is, into life which allows no disturbance.[53] And he bears witness that this gift is given to us by God through Christ our Lord, so that we should offer thanks to God through no one other than his Son. COMMENTARY ON PAUL'S EPISTLES.[54]

THE LIMITS OF THE WAGE METAPHOR. CHRYSOSTOM: Paul does not parallel "the wages of sin" with "the wages of good deeds" because he wants to show that they were not set free by their own efforts, nor had they done anything to earn their salvation. It was by grace alone that all these things came about.[55] HOMILIES ON ROMANS 12.[56]

DEATH THE REWARD FOR BETRAYING GOD.

[PSEUDO-]CONSTANTIUS: Death is the reward which God offers us for our betrayal of him. THE HOLY LETTER OF ST. PAUL TO THE ROMANS.[57]

THE GIFT OF GOD. PELAGIUS: One who does military service for sin receives death as his wages. Paul does not use the term "wages of righteousness" because there was no righteousness in us before our baptism which God could repay. Righteousness is not obtained by our effort but is a gift of God. PELAGIUS'S COMMENTARY ON ROMANS.[58]

UNMERITED. BEDE: Eternal life is unjustly given for good merits. Rather, merit is first given freely by a benevolent Savior. HOMILIES ON THE GOSPELS 1.2.[59]

---

[53]See Lk 2:25-35. [54]CSEL 81.1:209-11. [55]See Eph 2:8; Tit 3:4-7. [56]NPNF 1 11:417. [57]ENPK 2:44. [58]PCR 100. [59]CSEL 110 1:13.

7:1-6 SET FREE FROM THE LAW

[1]*Do you not know, brethren—for I am speaking to those who know the law—that the law is binding on a person only during his life?* [2]*Thus a married woman is bound by law to her husband as long as he lives; but if her husband dies she is discharged from the law concerning the husband.* [3]*Accordingly, she will be called an adulteress if she lives with another man while her husband is alive. But if her husband dies she is free from that law, and if she marries another man she is not an adulteress.*

[4]*Likewise, my brethren, you have died to the law through the body of Christ, so that you may belong to another, to him who has been raised from the dead in order that we may bear fruit for God.* [5]*While we were living in the flesh, our sinful passions, aroused by the law, were at work in our members to bear fruit for death.* [6]*But now we are discharged from the law, dead to that which held us captive, so that we serve not under the old written code but in the new life of the Spirit.*

OVERVIEW: As long as persons are living their old lives they are bound to the law. But if that tie is broken by death, then the person concerned is free to bind himself or herself to someone or something else—in this case, eternal life in Christ. Without passing through death such a change is impossible, because it would mean serving two masters at once, which is analogous to adultery. The link with sin and the law must be destroyed in order for the new life to begin, but this is precisely what has happened in the case of Christians. For a Christian to go back to the law is the same thing as going back to his or her previous life of sin. Paul's analogy of the woman and her husband is invariably interpreted, as some of the Fathers pointed out, but the general intention of the passage is clear. If we reject Christ and cling to the law, then we shall be tempted by lust and fall into sin. The new life we now live in the Spirit has changed everything. The Fathers laid great stress on this complete alteration of our circumstances. The law was not evil but it was obsolete, and therefore it had to be abandoned.

7:1 Human Law an Argument for Heavenly Things

THE LAW WAS SPIRITUAL. ORIGEN: This is similar to what Paul says later on [in verse 14]: "We know that the law is spiritual." It was not only Paul who knew that the law was spiritual but these people too, who had been taught by it and who were spiritual themselves. . . . Before the coming of Christ there were many Jews who grew in spiritual knowledge and saw God's glory, e.g., Isaiah, of whom John testifies when he says: "Isaiah said this because he saw his glory and spoke of him."[1] COMMENTARY ON THE EPISTLE TO THE ROMANS.[2]

AN EXAMPLE FROM HUMAN LAW. AMBROSIASTER: In order to strengthen their minds in the divine teaching, Paul uses an example drawn from human law, in order once again to argue for heavenly things on the basis of earthly ones, just as

God also is known by the creation of the world. COMMENTARY ON PAUL'S EPISTLES.[3]

MOVING TO GRACE. PELAGIUS: Now Paul begins to point out problems with the law in order to encourage his readers to move over to grace without the fear which belongs to the law. PELAGIUS'S COMMENTARY ON ROMANS.[4]

7:2 The Law of the Letter, the Law of the Gospel

THE LETTER OF THE LAW MUST DIE. ORIGEN: The law of the letter must die so that, free at last, the soul may marry the spirit and receive the marriage of the New Testament. HOMILIES ON GENESIS 6.3.[5]

MOSAIC LAW ILLUMINED BY THE GOSPEL. AMBROSIASTER: This law comes from the gospel, not from Moses or from human justice. For those who learned something from the guidance of nature and those who learned something from the law of Moses have both been made perfect by the gospel of Christ. COMMENTARY ON PAUL'S EPISTLES.[6]

WHEN THE HUSBAND (LAW) DIES, THE WOMAN (SOUL) IS FREE. AUGUSTINE: Note how this analogy is different from the subject it refers to. Paul says that the husband dies, so that the woman, freed from the law of her husband, can marry whomever she likes. Paul compares the soul to the woman and thinks of the husband as the passions of sin which work in our members to produce the fruits of death, which are the offspring worthy of such a marriage. The law is given not to take away sin nor to deliver us from it but to reveal what sin is before grace comes. The result is that those who are placed under the law are seized by an even stronger desire to sin and sin even more because of the trespass. But in

---

[1]Jn 12:41; Is 6:10. [2]CER 3:236-38. [3]CSEL 81.1:213. [4]PCR 100. [5]FC 71:124-25. [6]CSEL 81.1:213.

making this triple analogy—the soul as the woman, the passions of sin as the man and the law as the law of the husband—Paul does not conclude that the soul is set free when its sins are put to death in the way that the woman is set free when her husband is dead. Rather, he says that the soul itself dies to sin and is set free from the law in order that it might belong to another husband, who is Christ. The soul has died to sin, but in a sense sin is still alive. Thus it happens that although desires and certain encouragements to sin remain in us, we do not obey or give in to them because we have died to sin and now serve the law of God. AUGUSTINE ON ROMANS 36.[7]

AS LONG AS THE HUSBAND (LAW) LIVES, SHE REMAINS BOUND. AUGUSTINE: The apostle says that as long as a man lives in sin he lives under the law, just as the woman lives under her husband's law as long as he is alive. QUESTIONS 66.1.[8]

THE LAW (HUSBAND) IS ALREADY DEAD. PELAGIUS: By analogy, Paul calls the commandment of the law a "husband" in order to demonstrate that, without the power to punish, the law (being already dead, as it were) cannot stop us (who have already been put to death) from going over completely to Christ, who has risen from the dead. For the law would quite rightly go on living in us if it could find something in us to punish. PELAGIUS'S COMMENTARY ON ROMANS.[9]

7:3 The Limitations of the Law

MOSAIC MARRIAGE LAW ITSELF FORESHADOWS THE GOSPEL. ORIGEN: Did not the law itself contain a foreshadowing of something like this when it commanded that a widow who was childless (for her husband had been impotent) should marry his brother? For the law of the Spirit is the brother of the law of the letter, and the woman will be better able to bear fruit from him. COMMENTARY ON THE EPISTLE TO THE ROMANS.[10]

"CHRISTIANS" WHO LET THE LAW REMAIN ALIVE IN THEM ARE LIKE ADULTERERS. AMBROSIASTER: For just as a woman is freed by the death of her husband from the law of her husband but not from the law of nature, so also they will be set free by the grace of God from the law by which they were held captive, so that it will be dead for them and they will not be adulterers by being joined to Christianity. For if the law lives in them they are adulterers and have no right to be called Christians, since they will be subject to punishment. Nor will he who is joined to the gospel after the death of the law and later returns to the law be an adulterer to the law but to the gospel. For when the law's authority ceases, it is said to be dead. COMMENTARY ON PAUL'S EPISTLES.[11]

ONCE THE HUSBAND IS DEAD, THE WOMAN IS FREE. PELAGIUS: As long as her husband is alive, a woman must live according to his will alone, but once he is dead and she is married to another man, she should no longer live in the manner of her former husband. PELAGIUS'S COMMENTARY ON ROMANS.[12]

7:4 Dead to the Law

YOU HAVE DIED TO THE LAW. ORIGEN: When we were in the flesh and living according to it, we were unable to serve the newness of the Spirit on account of those sins which the law itself, which was in our members, nourished in order that they might bear fruit to death. . . . But when Christ died for us and we died to sin along with him, we were set free by him from the law of sin in which we were held, and now we can serve the law of God in newness of Spirit and not in the dead form of the law. COMMENTARY ON THE EPISTLE TO THE ROMANS.[13]

THEODORET OF CYR: In order not to offend the Jews or to give those heretics who reject the Old

---

[7]AOR 13, 15. [8]FC 70:138-39. [9]PCR 100. [10]CER 3:246. [11]CSEL 81.1:213-15. [12]PCR 100-1. [13]CER 3:250.

Testament any encouragement, Paul did not say that the law had come to an end but rather that we have died to the law by the saving grace of baptism. INTERPRETATION OF THE LETTER TO THE ROMANS.[14]

YOU ARE NOW FREE TO BELONG TO ANOTHER.

AMBROSIASTER: Since the Savior allowed the devil to crucify his body knowing that this was for us and against him, Paul says that we have been saved by the body of Christ. For to die to the law is to live to God, since the law rules over sinners. Therefore the one whose sins are forgiven dies to the law; this is what it means to be set free from the law. We receive this blessing through the body of Christ, for by giving up his body the Savior conquered death and condemned sin. The devil sinned against him when it killed him even though he was innocent and entirely without sin. For when the devil claims a man for himself because of sin, he is found to be guilty of the thing he accuses him of. Thus it happens that all who believe in Christ are delivered from the law, because sin has been condemned. For sin, which is of the devil, has been conquered by the body of Christ. Now he has no authority over those who belong to Christ, by whom he has been conquered. For because Christ was sinless yet was killed as if he were guilty, he conquered sin by sin—that is to say, he defeated the devil by his own sin. And what he allowed to get into the devil he condemned, thereby destroying the penalty which had been decreed because of the sin of Adam.[15] When he rose again from the dead an image of new life was stamped upon those who believe in him, so that they cannot be bound by the second death. For this reason we have died to the law by the body of Christ. Thus whoever has not died to the law is still guilty, and whoever is guilty cannot escape the second death. . . . Whoever perseveres in the grace of Christ belongs to God and is worthy of the promised resurrection. COMMENTARY ON PAUL'S EPISTLES.[16]

CHRYSOSTOM: Paul's conclusion does not tally with his premise, for what the context would require is: "so the law does not rule over you, for it is dead." Instead of saying this openly, Paul only hints at it by expressing himself the other way round. HOMILIES ON ROMANS 12.[17]

THAT YOU MAY BEAR FRUIT.

PELAGIUS: Paul was reluctant to tell the Jews that the law was dead, but what he dared not say out loud he leaves to be understood. . . . A man bears fruit for God when his works of righteousness like fruit break out in blossom, then grow into fruit, and finally become fully ripe, for no fruit is forever in blossom. PELAGIUS'S COMMENTARY ON ROMANS.[18]

DIED TO THE LAW THROUGH THE BODY OF CHRIST.

THEODORE OF MOPSUESTIA: The phrase "in order that we" should be read as: "and so we shall". . . . For Paul wants to say that once we have been established in this life we shall bear the fruits of righteousness for God,[19] since we have been changed from our behavior under the law.

It is most remarkable that Paul says that we have died not through baptism but through the body of Christ.[20] For Adam was the beginning of this life, and Christ is the beginning of the life to come. So, just as in this life we have everything in common with Adam, so also in the next life we shall have everything in common with Christ, beginning with his resurrection. We are said to be a part of the Lord's body because we share this with him. So just as we have been metaphorically born again by baptism, Paul says that we have become a part of Christ's body by sharing in the resurrection which is typified by baptism. PAULINE COMMENTARY FROM THE GREEK CHURCH.[21]

7:5 The Law Reveals Sin

LIVING IN THE FLESH. AMBROSIASTER: Although

---

[14]IER, Migne PG 82 col. 113. [15]See Gen 3:1-24. [16]CSEL 81.1:215-17. [17]NPNF 1 11:418. [18]PCR 101. [19]See Heb 12:11. [20]See 1 Cor 6:15. [21]NTA 15:124.

he is in the flesh Paul denies that he is "living in the flesh," even though he is in the body. In this passage "living in the flesh" means following something which is forbidden by the law. Therefore "living in the flesh" can be understood in many different ways. For every unbeliever is in the flesh, i.e., is carnal. A Christian living under the law is in the flesh. Anyone who puts his trust in men is in the flesh. Anyone who does not properly understand Christ is in the flesh. If a Christian leads an extravagant life he is in the flesh. Nevertheless, in this passage we should understand "being in the flesh" as meaning that before we believed we were under the power of the flesh. For then we lived under the flesh, i.e., following our carnal desires we were subject to wickedness and sin. For the mind of the flesh is not to understand spiritual things, e.g., that a virgin might conceive without intercourse with a man,[22] that a man may be born again of water and the Spirit,[23] and that a soul delivered from the bondage of the flesh may rise again in it.[24] Anyone who doubts these things is in the flesh.

It is clear that whoever does not believe acts under sin and is led by his captivity to indulge in wickedness and to bear fruit worthy of the second death. When such a person sins, death makes a profit.

This discussion concerns the Jews and all those who say they are Christians yet still want to live under the law. Its purpose is to teach them that they are carnal so that they will abandon the law. Nevertheless, Paul says that the sins which rule over those who commit them in the flesh are revealed by the law; they are not caused by the law. For the law is the yardstick of sin, not its cause, and it makes sinners guilty. COMMENTARY ON PAUL'S EPISTLES.[25]

THE ANALOGY OF THE PERFORMER (SOUL) AND THE SOUR NOTE (SIN). CHRYSOSTOM: You see what we had to gain from our former husband! Paul does not say: "when we were in the law," because that would merely lend a hand to heretics [who wanted to deny the oracles of the

Old Testament] but "when we were in the flesh," that is, when we were living a sinful and carnal life. . . . In order to not accuse the flesh Paul does not say that our members were at work but that sinful passions were at work in our members. This was to show that the origin of the trouble was not in our members but in the thoughts which made use of them. . . . The soul ranks as a performer and the flesh as a harp which produces sound according to the performer's direction. If the tune is discordant, the fault is with the performer, not with the instrument. HOMILIES ON ROMANS 12.[26]

NO LONGER OBEDIENT TO THE FLESH. [PSEUDO-]CONSTANTIUS: A person living in the flesh is one who obeys the will of the flesh and is prevented from obeying the law of God, because he cannot serve two masters.[27] But now, having been taught by the grace of the Holy Spirit how to overcome our passions, we are no longer in the flesh, since we are dead to the law, which does not contain the doctrine of grace.[28] THE HOLY LETTER OF ST. PAUL TO THE ROMANS.[29]

PASSIONS AT WORK IN OUR MEMBERS. PELAGIUS: When we were still living carnally the passion of lust worked in our eyes, and the other passions worked in the rest of our bodies. It was the law which showed us that these passions were sinful, and the severity of the law killed us. PELAGIUS'S COMMENTARY ON ROMANS.[30]

FLESH DOES NOT INHERIT. THEODORE OF MOPSUESTIA: Holy Scripture sometimes calls our human nature "flesh," and sometimes it goes beyond this and includes the concept of mortality as well. . . . In any case, the flesh is never said to inherit or to be capable of inheriting eternal life in the age to come. PAULINE COMMENTARY FROM THE GREEK CHURCH.[31]

---

[22]See Lk 1:34. [23]See Is 44:3; Jn 3:5. [24]See Jn 6:37-40; Rom 8:19-23; 1 Cor 15:12-57. [25]CSEL 81.1:217-19. [26]NPNF 1 11:419-20. [27]See Mt 6:24. [28]See Gal 5:24-25. [29]ENPK 2:44. [30]PCR 101. [31]NTA 15:124.

The Law Does Not Help Us Do What It Requires. Theodoret of Cyr: "In the flesh" means "under the law." Paul calls those laws regarding food, drink, leprosy and so on "flesh." . . . Paul teaches us that before grace came, while we were still under the law, we suffered ever more serious attacks of sin because, although the law showed us what it was we should be doing, it did not give us any help in doing it. Interpretation of the Letter to the Romans.[32]

7:6 Not the Written Law but New Life in the Spirit

New Life in the Spirit. Origen: Some people have wrongly interpreted "the new life of the Spirit" as if it meant that the Spirit himself was new and did not previously exist or teach the prophets of old. Such people do not realize how greatly they are blaspheming! For the same Spirit is in the law as in the gospel. He dwells eternally with the Father and the Son and is eternal just as they are. It is not that he is new but that he makes believers new when he leads them out of their former sins to a new life and a new obedience to the religion of Christ, turning carnal people into spiritual ones.[33] Commentary on the Epistle to the Romans.[34]

Discharged from the Law. Chrysostom: Once again Paul spares the flesh and the law. He does not say that the law was discharged or that sin was discharged but that we were discharged. How did this happen? It happened because the old man, who had been held down by sin, died and was buried.[35] Homilies on Romans 12.[36]

The Old Law Consumed with Age. Ambrosiaster: The law is called the "law of death" because it punishes the guilty and puts sinners to death. It is therefore not evil but righteous. For although evil is inflicted on its victims by the law, the law itself is not evil, because it executes wrath justly. Therefore it is not evil to sinners but just. But to good people it is spiritual.

For who would doubt that it is spiritual to forbid sin? But because the law could not save men by forgiving sin the law of faith was given, in order to deliver believers from the power of sin and bring those whom the law had held in death back to life. For to them it is a law of death and it works wrath in them because of sin.

Although Paul regards the law as inferior to the law of faith, he does not condemn it. . . . The law of Moses is not called old because it is evil but because it is out of date and has ceased to function. . . . The old law was written on tablets of stone, but the law of the Spirit is written spiritually on the tables of the heart that it might be eternal, whereas the letter of the old law is consumed with age.[37] There is another way of understanding the law of the Spirit, which is that, where the former law restrained evil deeds, this law which says that we ought not to sin even in our hearts is called "the law of the Spirit," because it makes the whole person spiritual. Commentary on Paul's Epistles.[38]

Not Under the Old Written Code. Augustine: The law is only a written code to those who do not fulfill it in the spirit of charity to which the New Testament belongs. To Simplician on Various Questions 1.17.[39]

Natural and Written Law. [Pseudo-]Constantius: Here the word *law* means both the natural and the written law. . . . Paul now makes mention of both the written and the natural law, because the written law contains the natural law as well. The Holy Letter of St. Paul to the Romans.[40]

Dead to That Which Held Us Captive. Pelagius: We have died to the sin for which we were held by the law, and now we serve according to the demands of spiritual grace, not according

---

[32]IER, Migne PG 82 col. 116. [33]See 2 Cor 5:17. [34]CER 3:252. [35]See Rom 6:6; Col 3:9-10. [36]NPNF 1 11:420. [37]See 2 Cor 3:3. [38]CSEL 81.1:219-21. [39]LCC 6:385. [40]ENPK 2:44-45.

to the written law. PELAGIUS'S COMMENTARY ON ROMANS.[41]

THEODORE OF MOPSUESTIA: Now everything has changed, Paul says. We have died to this life and are no longer under any obligation to keep the law. Our life no longer has anything in common with that, because we have been renewed by the power of the Spirit and have become different people. We have crossed over from this present life to life eternal and cannot tolerate any captivity of the flesh. . . . What is more, we who follow Christ are much better off than those who are governed by the law. PAULINE COMMENTARY FROM THE GREEK CHURCH.[42]

THEODORET OF CYR: Paul continues in his cautious manner, for he does not say that the law is abolished but rather that we have been set free from it. INTERPRETATION OF THE LETTER TO THE ROMANS.[43]

GENNADIUS OF CONSTANTINOPLE: Paul sets "Spirit" against "letter," "newness" against "oldness," and by these names shows us how different the two things are. [44] PAULINE COMMENTARY FROM THE GREEK CHURCH.[45]

---

[41]PCR 101. [42]NTA 15:125-26. [43]IER, Migne PG 82 col. 116. [44]See 2 Cor 3:6. [45]NTA 15:369.

7:7-13 THE LAW AND THE POWER OF SIN

[7]*What then shall we say? That the law is sin? By no means! Yet, if it had not been for the law, I should not have known sin. I should not have known what it is to covet if the law had not said, "You shall not covet."* [8]*But sin, finding opportunity in the commandment, wrought in me all kinds of covetousness. Apart from the law sin lies dead.* [9]*I was once alive apart from the law, but when the commandment came, sin revived and I died;* [10]*the very commandment which promised life proved to be death to me.* [11]*For sin, finding opportunity in the commandment, deceived me and by it killed me.* [12]*So the law is holy, and the commandment is holy and just and good.*

[13]*Did that which is good, then, bring death to me? By no means! It was sin, working death in me through what is good, in order that sin might be shown to be sin, and through the commandment might become sinful beyond measure.*

OVERVIEW: The law revealed to us that desires that we previously supposed were innocent were in fact culpable. Covetousness is a case in point. Before the law came people were living in a fool's paradise, imagining that everything was all right. But when the law arrived they became aware of how wrong their previous actions had been. In itself the law is holy and shows us what God expects of us.

But because we are sinful, the effect of this is the opposite of the one intended. The devil makes use of this and incites us to sin by transgressing the commandment. The Fathers were well aware of the psychological tendency to find in the commandments of the law a prod to disobedience, and they did not hesitate to bring out this aspect of the matter whenever they could. The law cannot cause death by itself, because it is spiritual by nature. Rather, it is our sin which does this, because we are carnal by nature. The law makes our sin worse because it makes it more obvious.

7:7 Sin Made Known by the Law

WHETHER THE LAW AS SUCH IS SIN. TERTULLIAN: The apostle refrains from any criticism of the law. . . . What high praise of the law we get from the fact that by it the latent presence of sin becomes manifest! It was not the law which led me astray but sin. AGAINST MARCION 5.13.[1]

NO KNOWLEDGE OF SIN. ORIGEN: What Paul is really saying here is this: "Understand what law this is which I am talking about, which if it did not exist, no one would recognize sin." Was it by the law of Moses that Adam recognized his sin and hid himself from the face of God? Was it by the law of Moses that Cain recognized his sin . . . or Pharaoh? . . . This is the law of which we have often spoken, which is written in men's hearts not with ink but with the Spirit of the living God, and which teaches everyone what he should and should not do. This is the law by which a man recognizes his sin. Here Paul says openly that the natural law was unknown to us until we were old enough to know the difference between good and evil and to hear our conscience tell us what it was.[2]

It is not that we did not have sin in us before this, but we did not know what it was. But when natural law and reason implanted itself in us as we were growing up, it began to teach us what was good and forbid us to do what was bad. Thus when it said: "You shall not covet," we learned what we did not previously know, viz., that covetousness is wrong. COMMENTARY ON THE EPISTLE TO THE ROMANS.[3]

LAW DEFINES WHAT SHOULD NOT BE DONE. DIODORE: It is clear from Romans [2:14] that even without the law the Gentiles knew what was required of them. It must therefore be accepted that they knew, though they did not know every-

thing. For there are things which some Gentiles regard as good and proper while others reject them as bad and unlawful. Therefore the giving of the law was necessary to define for us what should and should not be done, outlining for us and showing us what the behavior of a righteous person is. PAULINE COMMENTARY FROM THE GREEK CHURCH.[4]

LEARNING WHAT IT IS TO COVET. AMBROSIASTER: Paul shows that the law is not sin but the yardstick of sin. For Paul demonstrated that sins lie dormant in us and that they will not go unpunished by God. When a man finds this out he becomes guilty and thus does not thank the law. For who would be grateful to someone who tells him that he is running the risk of punishment? But he gives thanks to the law of faith, because the man who was made guilty by the law of Moses has been reconciled to God by the law of faith, even though the law of Moses is just and good in itself (because it is good to show that danger is near). . . .

Paul takes on a particular role in order to expound a general principle. For the law forbids covetousness, but because it is a matter of desire it was not previously thought to be sin.[5] For nothing could be easier than to covet something which belongs to a neighbor; it is the law which called it sin. For to men of the world nothing seems more harmless and innocent than desire. COMMENTARY ON PAUL'S EPISTLES.[6]

GUARDING AGAINST MANICHEAN ANTINOMIANISM. CHRYSOSTOM: Note how Paul gradually shows how the law was not merely an accuser of sin but to some extent its producer as well. This was not from any fault in it but from the disobedience of the Jews . . . for he has taken care to guard against the attacks of the Manichaeans, who accuse the law of being evil in itself. HOMILIES ON ROMANS 12.[7]

---

[1]ANF 3:458-59. [2]See Gal 3:19-25. [3]CER 3:256-58. [4]NTA 15:87. [5]See Ex 20:17; Deut 5:21. [6]CSEL 81.1:223. [7]NPNF 1 11:421.

CONVERTING THE SOUL BY ANXIETY. AUGUSTINE: In this passage [to v. 25], it seems to me that the apostle is portraying himself as a man set under the law and that he speaks in that role.

The law was given not to introduce sin nor to extirpate it but simply to make it known; by the demonstration of sin to give the human soul a sense of its guilt in place of the assurance of its innocence. Sin cannot be overcome without the grace of God, so the law was given to convert the soul by anxiety about its guilt, so that it might be ready to receive grace.... Desire was not implanted in him by the law but was made known to him. To SIMPLICIAN ON VARIOUS QUESTIONS 1.1.[8]

HAD IT NOT BEEN FOR THE LAW. [PSEUDO-] CONSTANTIUS: Paul wants to show that the weakness of the law was not in the attempt to keep it but in human nature. For in saying: "If it had not been for the law, I should not have known sin," Paul assumed the role of a child who is not bound to keep the law because of the weakness of his age, but when he grows up, he knows what the commandments are and begins to be under the law. THE HOLY LETTER OF ST. PAUL TO THE ROMANS.[9]

NOT KNOWN COVETING WITHOUT THE LAW. PELAGIUS: From here on Paul speaks as one who accepts the law, i.e., of one who first comes to know God's commandants while he is still in the habit of breaking them. Paul does not say that without the law he would not have been in the habit of coveting, nor does he say that he would not have done it; rather, he says that he would not have known that coveting was a sin. PELAGIUS'S COMMENTARY ON ROMANS.[10]

THEODORE OF MOPSUESTIA: We often covet the things of this life, not merely food and drink and sex but fame and fortune as well. We have these desires inside us and would never know there was anything wrong with them unless the law told us so. PAULINE COMMENTARY FROM THE GREEK CHURCH.[11]

MAKING SIN KNOWN. CYRIL OF ALEXANDRIA: Paul did not say that he had no sin apart from the law but rather that he was unaware of it. Therefore the law is not the cause of sin but rather the instrument which points it out, making it clear to those who did not know what it was. It did not do this in order that, once sin was made known, those who committed it should continue in what they were doing.... On the contrary, its intention was to convert people to better things by making their sins known to them. EXPLANATION OF THE LETTER TO THE ROMANS.[12]

7:8 Sin Is Dead Without the Law

THINGS FORBIDDEN ARE DESIRED MORE. ORIGEN: I do not know why it is, but things which are forbidden are desired all the more. Thus it happened that although the commandment is holy and just and good, since because it forbids evil it must be good, yet in forbidding covetousness it provoked and inflamed it all the more, with the result that something good wrought death in me. COMMENTARY ON THE EPISTLE TO THE ROMANS.[13]

DIODORE: By "sin," Paul presumably means the devil. For just as Scripture sometimes calls the Savior "life" and "righteousness" because he is the source of life and righteousness,[14] so it calls the opposing power by what it causes—sometimes "sin," sometimes "lie," sometimes "death."[15] PAULINE COMMENTARY FROM THE GREEK CHURCH.[16]

ALL KINDS OF COVETOUSNESS. AMBROSIASTER: By "all kinds of covetousness" Paul means every sin. [In the last verse] he mentioned covetousness according to the law, and now by adding other sins he shows that all covetousness works

---

[8]LCC 6:376-77. [9]ENPK 2:45-46. [10]PCR 102. [11]NTA 15:126. [12]Migne PG 74 col. 301. [13]CER 3:258. [14]See Jn 6:35, 48; 14:6; 1 Cor 1:30. [15]See Jn 8:44; Rom 6:13, 22-23; Heb 2:14; 1 Jn 3:8. [16]NTA 15:87-88.

in man by the impulse of the devil, whom he calls "sin," so that the law was given to man to promote the opposite. For when the devil saw the help provided by the law for man, whom he was delighted to have snared as much by his own sin as by the sin of Adam, he realized that this was done against him. For when he saw man placed under the law he knew that he would escape from his control, for now man knew how to escape the punishment of hell. For this reason his wrath was kindled against man, in order to turn him away from the law and get him to do what was forbidden, so that he would again offend God and fall back into the devil's power.

"Apart from the law sin lies dead." This is to be understood in two ways. First, you should realize that the devil is meant when the word *sin* is used and that it also refers here to sin itself. The devil is said to have died because before the law came he did not conspire to deceive man and was quiet, as if unable to possess him. But, second, "sin was also dead," because it was thought that it would not be reckoned by God. For that reason it was dead as far as natural man was concerned, as if he could sin without being punished. In fact sin was not absent, as I have already indicated, but this was not realized until it became clear by the giving of the law, i.e., that sin would revive. But how could it revive unless it had previously been alive and after the fall of man was thought to be dead when in fact it was still living? People thought that sin was not being reckoned to them, when in fact it was. Thus something which was alive was assumed to be dead. COMMENTARY ON PAUL'S EPISTLES.[17]

SIN FINDS OPPORTUNITY IN THE COMMANDMENT. CHRYSOSTOM: Note how Paul clears the law of all blame. It was sin which took advantage of the commandment and not the law, which increased the covetousness and brought about the opposite of what the law intended. This was caused by weakness rather than by wickedness. For when we desire something but are prevented from obtaining it, all that happens is that the flame of our desire is increased. It was not the law's fault, because the law hindered us and did what it could to keep us away from desire. It was sin, i.e., our own laziness and bad disposition, which used what was good for the opposite. It was not the fault of the physician but rather of the patient who used the medicine wrongly. HOMILIES ON ROMANS 12.[18]

SIN LIES DEAD. AUGUSTINE: Not every sort of lust existed before the prohibition increased it. For since the prohibition increases lust when the Deliverer's grace is missing, it is clear that not all lust existed beforehand. But when, in the absence of grace, lust was forbidden, it grew so much that it reached its own kind of completeness, to the point that it appeared in opposition to the law and added criminal offense to the transgression. When Paul says: "Apart from the law sin lies dead," he does not mean that it does not exist but rather that it lies hidden. He makes this clear [in verse 13]. The law is therefore good, but without grace it only reveals sins; it does not take them away. AUGUSTINE ON ROMANS 37.[19]

AUGUSTINE: By "sin lies dead," Paul means that it is "latent" in us. TO SIMPLICIAN ON VARIOUS QUESTIONS 1.4.[20]

AUGUSTINE: By "sin is dead" the apostle means that it is not "imputed" to us. QUESTIONS 66.4.[21]

SIN DOES NOT LIVE WHERE THERE IS NO LAW. [PSEUDO-]CONSTANTIUS: Just as light in the darkness reveals stumbling stones and pitfalls, similarly the law, by decreeing what must be observed, shows sinners what their sins are, and for this reason we say that the law is good and holy. If sin were dead when there was no law, those who say that sin has come to us by inheritance from Adam would be mad. But Paul says sin was dead because it does not "live" in children, who are without the law, i.e., it is committed

---

[17]CSEL 81.1:223-27. [18]NPNF 1 11:421. [19]AOR 15. [20]LCC 6:377. [21]FC 70:142.

without incurring blame. For a child who curses his parents has sinned, but this sin is "dead," not "alive," because it does not count in his case. THE HOLY LETTER OF ST. PAUL TO THE ROMANS.[22]

THEODORE OF MOPSUESTIA: Paul says that without the law to define it sin would not be effective. Why? Because it is not the deed by itself which is sin but rather doing something when you know that it is wrong. PAULINE COMMENTARY FROM THE GREEK CHURCH.[23]

SINNING IGNORANTLY AND KNOWINGLY.
CYRIL OF ALEXANDRIA: I think that what Paul means here is something like this: Even though the person who sins in ignorance is guilty, there will be a harsher punishment for the one who sins knowingly. EXPLANATION OF THE LETTER TO THE ROMANS.[24]

SEVERIAN: It is not reasonable to condemn completely someone who has sinned in ignorance. But when the law was given and revealed sin, it gave sin power. This was not a condemnation of the law but a punishment of the contempt shown by those who did not keep it. For if it is true that without the law sin lies dead, it is also true that sin is dead when the law is kept. PAULINE COMMENTARY FROM THE GREEK CHURCH.[25]

7:9 The Commandment Came and Sin Revived

SIN REVIVED AND I DIED. BASIL: When the commandment, i.e., the power of the discernment of the good, came, the mind did not prevail over the baser thoughts but permitted its reason to be enslaved by the passions. Then sin revived but the mind died, suffering death because of its transgressions. EXEGETIC HOMILIES 10.5.[26]

DIODORE: If sin "revived" it is clear that it must have been alive at some earlier point and then died. When was that? It was when the devil deceived and defeated Adam, who had received the commandment and knew what transgression meant.[27] Cain too knew that he was sinning, having been commanded not to murder his brother.[28] It was after that that there was no commandment and no law, and so sin was knocked out by the ignorance of those who committed it. PAULINE COMMENTARY FROM THE GREEK CHURCH.[29]

LAW INCREASES AWARENESS. CHRYSOSTOM: This looks like a condemnation of the law, but when you look more closely at it you will find that really it is an encomium in praise of the law. For the law did not give existence to a sin which was not there before; rather, it pointed out what had previously escaped notice. This is why Paul is speaking in praise of the law, since before it came people were sinning without realizing it. If they gained nothing else from the law, at least they became aware that they had been sinning. This is no small point if you want to be delivered from wickedness. If they were not in fact set free, this had nothing to do with the law, which framed everything with that end in view. The accusation lies wholly against their spirit, which was perverse beyond all imagining. HOMILIES ON ROMANS 12.[30]

AUGUSTINE: Nothing can be said to revive if it had not been previously alive. To SIMPLICIAN ON VARIOUS QUESTIONS 1.4.[31]

AUGUSTINE: When he says "I died," Paul means that he realized that he was already dead, because one who sees through the law what he should do but does not do it sins with transgression. QUESTIONS 66.5.[32]

[PSEUDO-]CONSTANTIUS: Paul says that when he was a child he was not bound by the law. If sin revived, that means that it had previously lived at

---

[22]ENPK 2:46. [23]NTA 15:127. [24]Migne PG 74 col. 805. [25]NTA 15:219. [26]FC 46:160. [27]See Gen 2:16-17; 3:1-24. [28]See Gen 4:1-16. [29]NTA 15:88. [30]NPNF 1 11:422. [31]LCC 6:377. [32]FC 70:143.

some point, even before Satan himself rebelled.[33] Paul says that as he grew up he began to be under the law, and the sin which had been dead in him because of his ignorance as a child sprang to life as the law took control. Thus the commandment which was given for life turned out to be a means of death, because of the custom of childhood and the habit of sinning. The Holy Letter of St. Paul to the Romans.[34]

I Was Once Alive Apart from the Law.

Pelagius: Paul means either that he once imagined that he lived as a righteous and free person or that he was alive, at least for the present life. But when the commandment arrived to put an end to forgetfulness, sin was once again recognized, so that everyone who commits it knows that he is dead. Because sin had lived by natural knowledge and died through forgetfulness, it is said to have come back to life through the law. Pelagius's Commentary on Romans.[35]

Cyril of Alexandria: We were not righteous before the law came, but given that sin was dead as long as there was no law to condemn it, we lived having the excuse that we did not know what it was that we ought to be doing. Explanation of the Letter to the Romans.[36]

Theodoret of Cyr: Adam had no fear of death before he sinned. Interpretation of the Letter to the Romans.[37]

7:10 Promising Life, Proving to Be Death

Law, Given for Life, Turned Out to Bring Death.

Ambrosiaster: Man died when he realized that he was guilty before God when he had previously thought that he would not be held accountable for the sins which he committed. It is true that the law was given for life, but because it made man guilty, not only for the sins which he committed before the coming of the law but also for those which he committed afterward, the law which was given for life turned out to bring death

instead. But as I have said, this was for the sinner, because for those who obeyed, it led to eternal life. Commentary on Paul's Epistles.[38]

Chrysostom: If death was the result, the fault lies with those who received the commandment and not with the law, which was leading them to life. Homilies on Romans 12.[39]

Proved to Be Death to Me. [Pseudo-]

Constantius: "Death" is what Paul calls the punishment which sin has brought on us by its deception, holding out to us temporal and earthly things as if they were good and persuading us to transgress the law, which promises eternal life to those who keep it. The Holy Letter of St. Paul to the Romans.[40]

Pelagius: Paul says that he died because then he transgressed knowingly. The commandment which would have led to life had it been kept in fact led to death, because it was disregarded. Pelagius's Commentary on Romans.[41]

The Sentence of Death upon Adam and Eve.

Theodoret of Cyr: As soon as God gave Adam and Eve the commandment concerning the trees, the devil came to Eve in the form of a serpent and lied to her.[42] When she saw the beauty of the fruit she ate of it, being overcome by desire, and broke the commandment. Both she and Adam were immediately placed under sentence of death, for Adam too ate the fruit along with her.[43] Interpretation of the Letter to the Romans.[44]

7:11 Sin Deceives and Kills

Satan as Source of Sin.

Didymus the Blind: The word *sin* does not refer to a particular

---

[33]See Wis 2:24. [34]ENPK 2:47. [35]PCR 102-3. [36]Migne PG 74 col. 805. [37]IER, Migne PG 82 col. 117. [38]CSEL 81.1:227. [39]NPNF 1 11:422. [40]ENPK 2:47. [41]PCR 103. [42]See Gen 3:1-5. [43]See Gen 3:6-19. [44]IER, Migne PG 82 col. 117.

substance but to the manner and life of one who has sinned. . . . Paul calls nothing sin except the one who is the source and begetter of sin, viz., the devil. PAULINE COMMENTARY FROM THE GREEK CHURCH.[45]

SIN, FINDING ITS OPPORTUNITY. AMBROSIASTER: "Sin" in this verse is to be understood as the devil, who is the author of sin. He found an opportunity through the law to satisfy his cruelty by the murder of man, so that as the law threatened sinners, man by instinct always did what was forbidden. By offending God he incurred the penalty of the law, so that he was condemned by that which had been given to him for his own good. For as the law was given to man without his asking for it, it inflamed desires to man's disadvantage in order to stain him even more with sinful lusts, and he could not escape its hands. COMMENTARY ON PAUL'S EPISTLES.[46]

CHRYSOSTOM: Notice yet again how Paul blames sin and clears the law of any accusation. HOMILIES ON ROMANS 12.[47]

SIN DECEIVED ME. AUGUSTINE: Paul means by this that the fruit of a forbidden desire is sweeter. For this reason, sins committed in secret are sweeter, even if this sweetness is deadly. . . . It deceives us and turns into very great bitterness. AUGUSTINE ON ROMANS 39.[48]

AUGUSTINE: Paul means either that pleasure's persuasion to sin is more powerful when something is forbidden or else that, even if a man did do something in accordance with the law's requirements, if there is as yet no faith resting in grace, then he endeavors to attribute this to himself and not to God, and he sins all the more because of pride. QUESTIONS 66.5.[49]

7:12 The Commandment Is Holy, Just and Good

PREPARATORY DISCIPLINE. CLEMENT OF ALEX-

ANDRIA: This is true as far as a sort of training with fear and preparatory discipline goes, leading as it did to the culmination of legislation and finally to grace. WHO IS THE RICH MAN THAT SHALL BE SAVED? 9.[50]

GOODNESS AND JUSTICE CONCUR. ORIGEN: If the law is found to be good, undoubtedly we shall believe that he who gave it is a good God. If, however, it is just rather than good, we shall think of God as a just lawgiver. But Paul the apostle says in no roundabout terms: "The commandment is holy and just and good." It is plain from this that Paul has not learned the doctrines of those [Gnostics] who separate the just from the good. Rather, he had been instructed by that God and illuminated by the Spirit of that God, who is holy and good and just at the same time. ON FIRST PRINCIPLES 2.5.4.[51]

AMBROSIASTER: Paul commends the law in this way so that no doubts about it might remain. COMMENTARY ON PAUL'S EPISTLES.[52]

MOSAIC, NOT NATURAL, LAW. CHRYSOSTOM: Some people say that here Paul is not talking about the law of Moses but rather about the law of nature or of the commandment given in paradise.[53] But surely Paul's aim is to reach beyond the authority of the law of Moses; he has no quarrel with the other two. And rightly so, for it was because the Jews feared the abolition of their law that they so obstinately opposed the working of grace. Moreover, it does not appear that Paul ever called the commandment given in paradise a law, nor has any other writer. Following Paul's logic, let us pursue the argument a little further. Having spoken to the Romans about proper standards of behavior, Paul goes on to say: "Do you not know, brethren—for I am speaking to those who know the law—that the law is binding on a person only

---

[45]NTA 15:3. [46]CSEL 81.1:229. [47]NPNF 1 11:422. [48]AOR 15. [49]FC 70:143. [50]ANF 2:593. [51]OFP 105. [52]CSEL 81.1:229. [53]See Gen 2:16-17.

during his life? But you are discharged from the law."[54] . . . Now if these things had been said about the natural law, we would now be without it. And if that were true, we would be more senseless than the irrational creatures are. But surely this is not so. HOMILIES ON ROMANS 12.[55]

AUGUSTINE: Man needed to be shown the foulness of his malady. Against his wickedness not even a holy and good commandment could avail; by it the wickedness was increased rather than diminished. THE SPIRIT AND THE LETTER 9.6.[56]

PELAGIUS: Contrary to those who attack the law and those who separate justice from goodness, the law is called a good and holy grace as well as a just grace. God is regularly called "good" in the Old Testament[57] and "just" in the New.[58] This contradicts the Marcionites. PELAGIUS'S COMMENTARY ON ROMANS.[59]

HOLY, JUST AND GOOD. THEODORE OF MOPSUESTIA: Paul calls the law "holy" because it gives us the principles on which to tell the difference between good and evil, . . . "just" because after showing us what is good it necessarily points out the punishment for the transgressor, but also "good" because it is the source of good things, showing us what they are and persuading us that they are desirable. PAULINE COMMENTARY FROM THE GREEK CHURCH.[60]

THE LAW IS HOLY. CYRIL OF ALEXANDRIA: The law was holy because it testified that those who kept it were holy, righteous and good and were not guilty of sin in any way whatsoever. EXPLANATION OF THE LETTER TO THE ROMANS.[61]

THE RELATION OF LAW AND CONSCIENCE. THEODORET OF CYR: The law is what was given to Moses; the commandment, what was given to Adam. What Paul praises so highly the average person condemns. For those who have given themselves over to idleness and run away from the works of righteousness blame God for having

given a commandment in the first place. They say that, if God did not know what was going to happen, how can he be God? And if he did know that men would sin but nevertheless gave the commandment, then he is himself the cause of sin. But these people ought to realize that the knowledge of good and evil belongs to all who have the gift of reason. Only those without reason lack the ability to distinguish one from the other. The wolf is vicious, the lion devours, and bears and leopards do the same sort of thing but they have no sense of sin, nor do they have a conscience which is offended by their actions. But men are ashamed even if nobody else sees what they do and are afraid to admit what they have done. For their conscience accuses them. How could this be if they lived without any law? But God gave them a commandment so that they would recognize their own rational nature and fear the lawgiver. Yet they knew that the lawgiver was merciful and that the law was not difficult to keep.

The commandment is "holy" because it teaches what is right. It is "just" because it pronounces the correct sentence on those who break it. But it is also "good" because it prepares eternal life for those who keep it. INTERPRETATION OF THE LETTER TO THE ROMANS.[62]

GENNADIUS OF CONSTANTINOPLE: "Law" and "commandment" are synonymous in this case. The commandment is called "holy" because it takes us away from sin and sets us apart from evil; "just" because with its righteousness it honors those who obey it and punishes those who transgress it; "good" because it leads us to the good, and this because of the goodness given by God. The law is not sin just because it shows me what is evil but the opposite. PAULINE COMMENTARY FROM THE GREEK CHURCH.[63]

7:13 Sin Works Death Through the Law

---

[54]See Rom 7:1, 4. [55]NPNF 1 11:422-23. [56]LCC 8:200. [57]See Ps 73:1. [58]Jn 17:25. [59]PCR 103. [60]NTA 15:128. [61]Migne PG 74 col. 805. [62]IER, Migne PG 82 cols. 120-21. [63]NTA 15:371.

Choosing Death. Didymus the Blind: Here Paul is expounding the person of Adam. For although he had the image of God dwelling in him,[64] he turned away from true life and chose death instead.[65] Moreover, this death was not just the common death of our bodily members but the spiritual death of disobedience as well. Pauline Commentary from the Greek Church.[66]

Whether Goodness Brings Death. Ambrosiaster: Although even before the law came, the devil obtained death for man because of the first sin of Adam, nevertheless, after the law came he found still greater punishments for him in hell, where death followed him. For to have sinned before the coming of the law was a lesser crime than to have sinned after it.

The wording here suggests that a limit was imposed on transgressors when they were forbidden to sin. . . . What the apostle means is that sinning after the law came was much more serious than sinning before it. He means that after the law came the attacks and tricks of Satan grew worse. Commentary on Paul's Epistles.[67]

Shown to Be Sin. Chrysostom: By the very way he accuses sin, Paul shows how excellent the law is. . . . It was the commandment which showed us just how evil sin is. At the same time, Paul also shows how grace is so much greater than the law. Grace is not in conflict with the law; it is superior to it.[68] Homilies on Romans 12.[69]

Sin Working Death in Me. Augustine: Here Paul elaborates on what he said [in verse 8]. It is not that a good thing (i.e., the law) had become death for him but rather that sin worked death through the law's goodness, i.e., that it

became apparent whereas without the law it had lain hidden. For everyone recognizes that he is dead if he cannot fulfill a precept which he recognizes as just, and because of the criminal offense of the trespass he sins even more than he would have if it had not been forbidden. Before the coming of the law the offense was less, because without the law there is no transgression. Augustine on Romans 40.[70]

Sin Revealed Through the Law. Pelagius: The law does not become for me the actual cause of death, but I do when I encounter death by sinning. Sin was revealed through the law, which is itself good, and was also punished by it. Before the law came sin was limited because of ignorance, but when it is committed knowingly these limitations are taken away. Pelagius's Commentary on Romans.[71]

Sinful Beyond Measure. Cyril of Alexandria: Even those who do not know God's will deserve God's punishment because they sin, even if it is in ignorance. Nevertheless, they have some excuse, for when the law is explained to them they will probably excuse themselves in front of those who are under the law, on account of their ignorance. But those who have chosen to sin and do so not out of ignorance have committed a crime of madness and have completely rejected God. Such people are said to be "sinful beyond measure." Someone who sins in ignorance is still sinful, but he is not, nor is he said to be, "sinful beyond measure." Explanation of the Letter to the Romans.[72]

---

[64]See Gen 1:26-27. [65]See Gen 3:17-19. [66]NTA 15:4. [67]CSEL 81.1:231. [68]See Gal 3:21-25. [69]NPNF 1 11:423. [70]AOR 15, 17. [71]PCR 103. [72]Migne PG 74 cols. 805, 808.

7:14-25 THE WEAKNESS OF THE LAW

[14]*We know that the law is spiritual; but I am carnal, sold under sin.* [15]*I do not understand my own actions. For I do not do what I want, but I do the very thing I hate.* [16]*Now if I do what I do not want, I agree that the law is good.* [17]*So then it is no longer I that do it, but sin which dwells within me.* [18]*For I know that nothing good dwells within me, that is, in my flesh. I can will what is right, but I cannot do it.* [19]*For I do not do the good I want, but the evil I do not want is what I do.* [20]*Now if I do what I do not want, it is no longer I that do it, but sin which dwells within me.*

[21]*So I find it to be a law that when I want to do right, evil lies close at hand.* [22]*For I delight in the law of God, in my inmost self,* [23]*but I see in my members another law at war with the law of my mind and making me captive to the law of sin which dwells in my members.* [24]*Wretched man that I am! Who will deliver me from this body of death?* [25]*Thanks be to God through Jesus Christ our Lord! So then, I of myself serve the law of God with my mind, but with my flesh I serve the law of sin.*

OVERVIEW: In Romans 7:15 and the following verses Paul describes the plight of persons who know that they are sinners but who cannot escape from the sins they commit. Most of the Fathers believed that here Paul was adopting the persona of an unregenerate man, not describing his own struggles as a Christian. As far as they were concerned, becoming a Christian would deliver a person from the kind of dilemma the apostle is outlining here. Romans 7:22 would appear to create a difficulty for those who believe that Paul was describing the unregenerate person, but some of the Fathers resolved it by saying that the inmost self was the rational intellect. As far as they were concerned, any rational person would automatically take delight in the law of God because it is supremely rational. The difficulty comes in trying to move from theory to practice. The dilemma of unregenerate persons is insoluble apart from the grace of God given to us in Christ. This sets us free from the law of sin and death and allows us to serve the law of God as right reason dictates.

7:14 *The Law Is Spiritual, We Are Carnal*

THE TEACHER MAY PLAY THE PART OF A

WEAK PUPIL (SOLD UNDER SIN). ORIGEN: Someone who is carnal and sold under sin does not know that the law is spiritual, so how can Paul say this of himself? In fact, when he says that he is carnal and sold under sin he is playing the part of a teacher of the church by taking on the role of the weak, as he said elsewhere: "I became weak to the weak, so that I might win the weak."[1]

We are taught by the Psalms that it was the custom in Holy Scripture for holy men to take on the role of sinners and for teachers to assume the weaknesses of their pupils: "I am utterly bowed down and prostrate; all the day I go about mourning. For my loins are filled with burning, and there is no soundness in my flesh. I am utterly spent and crushed; I groan because of the tumult of my heart."[2] COMMENTARY ON THE EPISTLE TO THE ROMANS.[3]

LAW GIVEN BY THE SPIRIT. DIODORE: The law is spiritual and makes the person who keeps it spiritual as well. It was given by the Holy Spirit so that those who obeyed it might receive the

---

[1] 1 Cor 9:22. [2] Ps 38:6-8. [3] CER 3:270, 282.

Spirit and be cleansed by the law's teaching. Paul was not sold under sin by anyone else but by his own breaking of the law. PAULINE COMMENTARY FROM THE GREEK CHURCH.[4]

PAUL SPEAKS OF MAN PRIOR TO FAITH.
AMBROSIASTER: Paul is speaking here to those who were under the law. For they would not have submitted to it if they did not know that it was spiritual. . . . Paul calls man carnal, because he sins.

To be sold under sin means to trace one's origin to Adam, who was the first to sin, and to subject oneself to sin by one's own transgression. . . . For Adam sold himself first, and because of this all his descendants are subjected to sin.

The law is firm and just and without fault, but man is weak and bound either by his own or by his inherited fault, so that he cannot obey the law in his own strength. COMMENTARY ON PAUL'S EPISTLES.[5]

THE LAW IS SPIRITUAL. CHRYSOSTOM: Not only does Paul clear the law of all blame; he bestows very great praise on it as well. For by calling it spiritual he shows that it is a teacher of virtue and hostile to vice, for this is what being spiritual means—taking people away from any kind of sin. This is what the law did by frightening, admonishing, chastening, correcting and recommending every kind of virtue. How then was sin produced, if the teacher was so admirable? It was from the laziness of the pupils. This is why Paul went on to say that he was carnal, giving us here the portrait of a man as he was under and before the coming of the law. HOMILIES ON ROMANS 13.[6]

AT ONE WITH THE LAW. AUGUSTINE: The law can only be fulfilled by spiritual men, and these only the grace of God can produce. For the man who has been made spiritual like the law will easily do what it commands. He will not be under the law but at one with it. He will also be someone who is not ensnared by temporal goods or frightened by temporal evils. AUGUSTINE ON ROMANS 41.[7]

SOLD UNDER SIN. [PSEUDO-]CONSTANTIUS: At this point Paul reverts to the role of a person who has attained his majority. For when he says: "The law is spiritual," he condemns himself for sinning by the power of his own will. Thus he adds: "But I am carnal, sold under sin," in order to show that although he is free, he has sold himself to sin. THE HOLY LETTER OF ST. PAUL TO THE ROMANS.[8]

PELAGIUS: Paul says he was carnal because, although he accepted the law, he was in the habit of living carnally. PELAGIUS'S COMMENTARY ON ROMANS.[9]

THE STRUGGLE OF SPIRIT AND FLESH. CYRIL OF ALEXANDRIA: The will of the Spirit is one thing, that of the flesh is another. These two wills fight against each other and can never reach agreement. Man is carnal, but the law is spiritual. How then can the law ever become tolerable to those who struggle so hard against the sickness of sin? There is wisdom here, for if a man is carnal he is in some sense captive and reduced to the condition of slavery. EXPLANATION OF THE LETTER TO THE ROMANS.[10]

IN PRAISE OF THE LAW. THEODORET OF CYR: Once again, Paul covers the law with praise. For what could be nobler than what he says about it here? He says in effect that the law was written by the Holy Spirit. Moses was given a share in his grace and thus wrote the law. INTERPRETATION OF THE LETTER TO THE ROMANS.[11]

7:15 Actions Contradict Will

I DO NOT UNDERSTAND MY OWN ACTIONS.

---

[4]NTA 15:88. [5]CSEL 81.1:233-35. [6]NPNF 1 11:427. [7]AOR 17. [8]ENPK 2:2:49. [9]PCR 103. [10]Migne PG 74 col. 808. [11]IER, Migne PG 82 col. 121.

ORIGEN: Paul does not say that the weak man does not know what he is doing but rather that he does not understand why he is doing it.

Here Paul shows that even the man who is carnal and sold under sin may try, by the instinct of natural law as it were, to resist evil, but he is overcome by sin and is subdued unwillingly. This often happens, for example, when someone decides not to react to provocation, but in the end his anger gets the better of him and he gives in to it against his will. In other words, he gets angry when he does not want to get angry. . . . Someone who is not yet spiritual will be defeated in instances like these, even against his own will, because that will is not yet strong or resilient enough to retain control of him even to the point of death in his struggle for truth. COMMENTARY ON THE EPISTLE TO THE ROMANS.[12]

DIODORE: Paul is not condemning himself here but describing the common lot of mankind, which he sees in himself. PAULINE COMMENTARY FROM THE GREEK CHURCH.[13]

SIN MADE CLEAR BY RIGHTEOUSNESS.
AUGUSTINE: This may appear to the less discerning to contradict [verse 13]. How can sin be made manifest if it is not understood? But here "I do not understand" means "I do not approve." For instance, darkness cannot be seen, but it is perceived in contrast to light; in other words, to perceive darkness is not to see it. Likewise sin, because it is not made clear by the light of righteousness, is discerned by not understanding in the way that darkness is perceived by not seeing. "Who understands his own transgressions?[14] AUGUSTINE ON ROMANS 43."[15]

I DO THE VERY THING I HATE. [PSEUDO-] CONSTANTIUS: What does Paul say now? "For I do not understand what I do," that is, he does not want to discern; he does harm but does not want to be harmed. He desires things which are wrong but does not want to be cheated by his own. He

indicates this when he says: "For I do not do what I want," that is, to obtain what is good for me, "but what I hate, that I do," that is, to obtain what is bad for me. . . . Sin is odious to any normal person's judgment; therefore those who commit it either deny it or pretend that it is not evil. THE HOLY LETTER OF ST. PAUL TO THE ROMANS.[16]

PELAGIUS: Paul says that he subjected himself to sin of his own accord and then, as if drunk, he did not know what he was doing. Or perhaps he meant that he did not understand that what he accepted against his will was evil. PELAGIUS'S COMMENTARY ON ROMANS.[17]

SIN IS WILLED. CYRIL OF ALEXANDRIA: It appears that this refers to the ignorant Gentiles, whose thoughts Paul is reproducing. For having consigned their destiny and future to their own lusts even to the point of regarding vain idols as having some power over our lives, they deprive man of his glory, which is the ability to live freely, and to have full and complete control over his own will to do whatever he wishes. . . . It may be that someone who is forced to act against his will cannot be blamed for it, but at the same time no rational person will praise him for his godliness and righteousness either. For why should somebody be praised for doing things against his own will, even if he is forced to do so by a power over which he has no control? EXPLANATION OF THE LETTER TO THE ROMANS.[18]

THEODORET OF CYR: We do not sin from necessity or by compulsion; rather we are overcome by desire and do things which in principle we detest. INTERPRETATION OF THE LETTER TO THE ROMANS.[19]

7:16 *The Law Is Right*

---

[12]CER 3:272. [13]NTA 15:89. [14]See Ps 18:13. [15]AOR 17. [16]ENPK 2:2:49. [17]PCR 103-4. [18]Migne PG 74 cols. 808-9. [19]IER, Migne PG 82 cols. 121, 124.

THE VOICE IS OF ONE UNDER THE LAW, PRIOR TO GRACE. AUGUSTINE: The law is defended against every accusation, but we must be careful not to think that these words deny our free will, which is not true. The man being described here is under the law, before the coming of grace. Sin overpowers him when he attempts to live righteously in his own strength, without the help of God's liberating grace. For by his free will a man is able to believe in the Deliverer and to receive grace. Thus with the deliverance and help of him who gives it, he will not sin and will cease to be under the law. Instead, being at one with the law or in the law, he will fulfill it by the love of God which he could not have done through fear.[20] AUGUSTINE ON ROMANS 44.[21]

WHY I DO WHAT I DO NOT WANT. [PSEUDO-]CONSTANTIUS: If I should want to keep the commandments of the law, which are contrary to the will of the flesh, then according to the flesh I do what I do not want to do, but at the same time, according to the will of the Spirit, I agree that the law of God is spiritual and good. THE HOLY LETTER OF ST. PAUL TO THE ROMANS.[22]

PELAGIUS: Paul says that if he does not want to do the particular evil which he does, at least he agrees with the law, which does not desire evil and prohibits it. But it can also be understood thus: if a man sins, he subjects himself to the severity of the law. PELAGIUS'S COMMENTARY ON ROMANS.[23]

THE LAW IS GOOD. THEODORET OF CYR: Paul says that he learned to hate what he does from the law, and therefore he defends the law and says that it was right. INTERPRETATION OF THE LETTER TO THE ROMANS.[24]

7:17 Sin Dwells Within Us

NO LONGER I THAT DO IT. ORIGEN: The law of nature is introduced as being in agreement with the law of God. . . For if we assent to the law of God according to our will, the evil which we do is no longer ours; rather, it is sin which is at work within us, i.e., the law and will of the flesh, which makes us captive to the law of sin which is in our members.

The kind of person Paul is talking about here is not one in whom Christ does not dwell and who is a stranger to good works but rather someone who has started on the path of wanting to do what is right but has not yet been able to achieve his desires. This kind of weakness exists in those who have accepted the first stages of conversion, but although they want to do everything which is good this desire has not yet prevailed. For instance, someone might decide in himself that it is wrong to get angry and determine not to do it, but since by long custom and daily habit the vice of anger has controlled him, it resists his will and breaks out in the usual way. COMMENTARY ON THE EPISTLE TO THE ROMANS.[25]

SIN DWELLS WITHIN ME. [PSEUDO-]CONSTANTIUS: Paul means by this that it is wrong for a rational man to live like irrational animals, and by the addition of "sin which dwells within me" he taught that he had given himself over totally to the passions of the flesh, which are at enmity with God. THE HOLY LETTER OF ST. PAUL TO THE ROMANS.[26]

SIN BECOMES A HABIT. PELAGIUS: Paul means that he did it willingly before it became a habit. Sin then lived in him as a guest or as one thing inside another . . . in other words, as an accidental quality, not as a natural one. PELAGIUS'S COMMENTARY ON ROMANS.[27]

GENNADIUS OF CONSTANTINOPLE: All this is reminiscent of what was said by the Lord in the Gospels: "The spirit is willing but the flesh is weak."[28] PAULINE COMMENTARY FROM THE GREEK CHURCH.[29]

---

[20]See 2 Tim 1:7. [21]AOR 17. [22]ENPK 2:2:50. [23]PCR 104. [24]IER, Migne PG 82 col. 124. [25]CER 3:274-76. [26]ENPK 2:50. [27]PCR 104. [28]Mt 26:41. [29]NTA 15:373.

7:18 *Willing and Doing*

Nothing Good Dwells Within Me. Ambrosiaster: Paul does not say that the flesh is evil, as some think, but that what dwells in the flesh is not good, i.e., sin. How does sin dwell in the flesh when it is not a substance but the perversion of what is good? Since the body of the first man was corrupted by sin and became dissolvable, this same corruption of sin remains in the body because of the state of transgression, retaining the strength of the divine judgment given in Adam, which is the sign of the devil, at whose prompting Adam sinned. Because of this sin is said to dwell in the flesh, to which the devil comes as if to his own kingdom. For the flesh is sinful and sin remains in it in order to deceive man by evil temptations, so that man will not do what the law commands.

Man can agree that what the law commands is good; he can say that it naturally pleases him and that he wants to do it. But in spite of all that, the power and the strength to carry out his wishes is lacking because he is so oppressed by the power of sin that he cannot go where he wants nor can he make contrary decisions, because another power is in control of him. For man is burdened by his habit of sinning and succumbs to sin more readily than to the law, which he knows teaches what is good. For if he wants to do what is good, habit backed by the enemy prevents him. Commentary on Paul's Epistles.[30]

The Soul Governs the Body. Chrysostom: Paul is not attacking the flesh when he says this. The fact that nothing good dwells in it does not mean that it is evil. . . . Paul is not finding fault with the body but pointing out that the soul is superior to it. It is the soul which governs the body and is responsible for sin, not the flesh. Homilies on Romans 13.[31]

Augustine: It is possible for a good to be performed when there is no yielding to evil lust, but the good is completed or perfected only when evil lust itself no longer exists. Continence 3.6.[32]

Augustine: Paul says that the evil of the flesh is not good but that when this evil has ceased to exist the flesh will still be there, but . . . then it will not be defective or corrupt. Continence 8.19.[33]

Pelagius: Paul does not say that his flesh is not good. The will is there but not the action, because carnal habit opposes the will. Pelagius's Commentary on Romans.[34]

I Cannot Do It. Prosper of Aquitaine: Although Paul has received the knowledge of right willing, he cannot find in himself the power to do what he wills. It is not until he receives a good will as a gift that he finds the power for the virtues which he seeks. Grace and Free Will 4.2.[35]

7:19 *Wanting to Do Good, Doing Evil*

Ambrose: Do you think that anyone with a knowledge of sin can avoid it? Paradise 12.60.[36]

Ambrosiaster: Paul repeats this often in order to make it clear. Commentary on Paul's Epistles.[37]

I Do Not Do the Good I Want. Pelagius: Think of someone who has sworn so much for such a long time that now he does it even when he does not want to. Pelagius's Commentary on Romans.[38]

The Voice Is of One in the Habit of Sinning. [Pseudo-]Constantius: Paul here assumes the role of a person who is in the habit of sinning and who is held bound to the vices of the flesh. The Holy Letter of St. Paul to the Romans.[39]

---

[30]CSEL 81.1:237-39. [31]NPNF 1 11:428-29. [32]FC 16:195. [33]FC 16:211. [34]PCR 104. [35]FC 7:354. [36]FC 42:341. [37]CSEL 81.1. [38]PCR 104. [39]ENPK 2:50.

7:20 Acts of Will

By His Own Fault. Ambrosiaster: Is the sinner compelled to sin by a power outside himself? Not at all. For it was by his own fault that these evil things began, for whoever binds himself to sin voluntarily is ruled by its law. Sin persuades him first, and when it has conquered him it takes control. Commentary on Paul's Epistles.[40]

Willing and Responsibility Remain Ours. Chrysostom: Here Paul clears both the flesh and the soul from responsibility for sin, putting all the blame on the actions themselves. For if the soul does not want to sin it is cleared of guilt, and if it does not perform the action itself the body too is let off the hook. Everything may thus be blamed on the evil moral choice. The essence of the soul and body and that of choice are not the same, for the first two are God's works and the third is a motion from within ourselves which may go in whatever direction we choose to let it. Of course, willing is natural and God-given, but willing in this way is from us and depends on our own mind. Homilies on Romans 13.[41]

What Is Willed Becomes Habit. Pelagius: What was once an act of will has become so habitual that now it is involuntary. Pelagius's Commentary on Romans.[42]

7:21 Evil Lies Close at Hand

Law and Will Agree. Ambrosiaster: Paul says that the law of Moses agrees with his will against sin, which dwells in his flesh and forces him to do something other than what he and the law want to do. Commentary on Paul's Epistles.[43]

Help from a Law. Pelagius: Paul means that he has a law which will help him do good, even though "evil lies close at hand." Pelagius's Commentary on Romans.[44]

Theodoret of Cyr: Paul says that "evil lies close at hand" because our body is mortal and passible, and our soul is sluggish and weak. Interpretation of the Letter to the Romans.[45]

Law Does Not Free from Sin. Cyril of Alexandria: If sin inheres in my flesh and corrupts it, it may well be that the law offers help and gives advice, but even so it does not set me free from sin. Yet for those who are bound by the weakness of sin, it is hardly enough to know that they should be doing better; what they need is the strength to do what is right and in accordance with the law. Explanation of the Letter to the Romans.[46]

7:22 Delight in the Law

The Common Lot of Humanity, Excepting the Faithful. Diodore: Here Paul is describing the common lot of man. For the ordinary person can see in his mind what ought to be done but cannot achieve it. But the man who has believed in Christ with his mind can achieve it with the help of the Holy Spirit. Such a person is therefore called "spiritual." Pauline Commentary from the Greek Church.[47]

I Delight in the Law. Ambrosiaster: Paul says that the mind delights in the things which are taught by the law. This is "our inmost self," because sin does not dwell in the mind but in the flesh. . . . It is prevented from dwelling in the mind by free will. Therefore sin dwells in the flesh, at the door of the soul as it were, so as to prevent the soul from doing what it wants to do. If it dwelt in the mind it would derange it, so that man would not know himself. As it is, he does know himself and takes delight in the law of God. Commentary on Paul's Epistles.[48]

---

[40]CSEL 81.1:239-41. [41]NPNF 1 11:429. [42]PCR 104. [43]CSEL 81.1:241. [44]PCR 104. [45]IER, Migne PG 82 col. 125. [46]Migne PG 74 col. 813. [47]NTA 15:89. [48]CSEL 81.1:241.

AUGUSTINE: See wherein we are free, wherein we are delighted with the law of God. Freedom delights. For as long as you do what is just out of fear, God does not delight you. As long as you do it still a slave, he does not delight you. Let him delight you and you are free. TRACTATES ON THE GOSPEL OF JOHN 41.10.3.[49]

MY INMOST SELF. PELAGIUS: Paul's "inmost self" is the rational and intelligent soul which agrees with the law of God, for its law is to live rationally and not to be led about by the passions of irrational animals.

The outer self, on the other hand, is the body. Its law is the wisdom of the flesh, which instructs one to eat and drink and enjoy the other sensual pleasures. These war against reason, and if they gain the upper hand, subject it to the law of sin. For if it is true that we do what we do not want to do, Paul would not have said that he sees another law in his members, fighting against the law of his mind. He agrees to the law with his mind. PELAGIUS'S COMMENTARY ON ROMANS.[50]

THEODORET OF CYR: The "inmost self" is the mind. INTERPRETATION OF THE LETTER TO THE ROMANS.[51]

7:23 Two Laws at War

TWO LAWS IN STRUGGLE. AMBROSIASTER: Paul mentions two laws here. One of these he sees in his members, i.e., in the outer self, which is the flesh or the body. This law is hostile to us. It wars with his mind, leading him captive in a state of sin and preventing him from getting out of it and finding help. The other law is the law of the mind, which is either the law of Moses or the law of nature which is innate in the mind. This law is attacked by the violence of sin and by its own negligence, for in that it loves evil it subjects itself to sin and is held captive by the habit of sinning. For man is a creature of habit.

For Paul, there are here four kinds of law. The first is spiritual. This is the law of nature, which

was reworked by Moses and made authoritative; it is God's law. Then there is the law of the mind, which agrees with God's law. Third, there is the law of sin, which is said to dwell in man's members because of the transgression of the first man. The fourth appears in our members and tempts us to sin, before retreating. But these four laws can be reduced to two—the law of good and the law of evil. For the law of the mind is the same as the spiritual law or the law of Moses, which is called the law of God. But the law of sin is the same as the law which appears in our members, which contradicts the law of our mind. COMMENTARY ON PAUL'S EPISTLES.[52]

CHRYSOSTOM: Paul calls sin a law not because it establishes good order but because those who are under it obey it completely. HOMILIES ON ROMANS 13.[53]

THE MAN DESCRIBED NOT YET UNDER GRACE. AUGUSTINE: Everyone is bound by carnal habit to the law of sin. Paul says that this law wars against his mind and captures him under the law of sin, by which it may be understood that the man being described here is not yet under grace. For if carnal habit were merely to wage war but not to triumph, there would be no condemnation. Condemnation lies in the fact that we freely submit to and serve depraved carnal lusts. But if such lusts exist and we do not give in to them, then we are not ensnared by them, and are under grace instead. Paul speaks of this grace when he calls upon the Deliverer and pleads for his help, that love might accomplish by grace what fear could not achieve through the law.[54] AUGUSTINE ON ROMANS 45-46.[55]

ANOTHER LAW AT WAR. AUGUSTINE: In this life it cannot happen to anyone that a law warring against the law of the mind should be entirely absent from his members, because that law would still be waging war even if man's spirit were offer-

---

[49]FC 88:146. [50]PCR 104-5. [51]IER, Migne PG 82 col. 125. [52]CSEL 81.1:243. [53]NPNF 1 11:429. [54]See 2 Tim 1:7. [55]AOR 17, 19.

ing it such resistance as not to fall into line with it. The Retractions 1.19.1.[56]

AUGUSTINE: Paul sees another law in his members fighting against the law of his mind. He sees it is there, not remembers that it was there. He is pressed by what is present, not recalling what is past. And he not only sees this law warring against him but even taking him captive to the law of sin, which is (not was) in his members. ON NATURE AND GRACE 55.65.[57]

MAKING ME CAPTIVE. AUGUSTINE: Paul perceives imprisonment where righteousness has not been fulfilled; for when he is delighted with the law of God he is not a prisoner but a friend of the law and thus free, because he is a friend. TRACTATES ON THE GOSPEL OF JOHN 41.11.1.[58]

AUGUSTINE: Look what damage has been done to human nature by the disobedience of the will! ON NATURE AND GRACE 53.62.[59]

OUR PRESENT FIGHT WITH DEAD SINS.
AUGUSTINE: See what a fight we have with our dead sins, as that active soldier of Christ and faithful teacher of the church shows. For how is sin dead when it works many things in us while we struggle against it? What are these many things except foolish and harmful desires which plunge those who consent to them into death and destruction? And to bear them patiently and not give into them is a struggle, a conflict, a battle. And between what parties is this battle if not between good and evil, not of nature against nature but of nature against fault, which is already dead but still to be buried, that is, entirely healed? AGAINST JULIAN 2.9.32.[60]

JEROME: If Paul feared the lusts of the flesh, are we safe? HOMILIES ON THE PSALMS 41.[61]

PELAGIUS: The law of natural conscience, or the divine law which resides in the mind, fights against habitual desires. PELAGIUS'S COM-

MENTARY ON ROMANS.[62]

I SEE IN MY MEMBERS ANOTHER LAW. THEODORE OF MOPSUESTIA: Paul was right to refer to his members here, because sin takes many forms according to the nature of our members. There are sins of the eyes, sins of the tongue, sins of other parts of the body as well. PAULINE COMMENTARY FROM THE GREEK CHURCH.[63]

CAESARIUS OF ARLES: This law in me was born when the former law was transgressed; it was born, I repeat, when the former law was despised. SERMON 177.1.[64]

7:24 The Body of Death

THE REMEDY OF GRACE. AMBROSE: We have a physician—let us follow his remedy! Our remedy is the grace of Christ, and the body of death is our body. Let us therefore be exiled from the body lest we be exiled from Christ. Even if we are in the body let us not follow what is of the body. Let us not neglect the rights of nature, but let us prefer the gifts of grace. ON THE DEATH OF HIS BROTHER SATYRUS 2.41.[65]

WRETCHED MAN THAT I AM! AMBROSIASTER: Paul says that a man born in sin is wretched. For indeed how could man not be wretched when he has succeeded to this inheritance of sin, having this enemy sin with him, through which Satan has access to him? For Adam invented steps by which the despoiler came up to his descendants. Yet the most merciful God, moved by pity, gave us his grace through Christ so that it might be revealed that the human race, once it accepted the forgiveness of sins, might repent and put sin to death. For a man who is pardoned for his sins and cleansed can resist the power of the enemy which is aimed against him, provided that God continues to help

---

[56]FC 11:201. [57]FC 86:73. [58]FC 88:146. [59]FC 86:69. [60]FC 35:95. [61]FC 48:303. [62]PCR 105. [63]NTA 15:132. [64]FC 47:442. [65]FC 22:214.

him. COMMENTARY ON PAUL'S EPISTLES.[66]

LAW AND CONSCIENCE HAVE FAILED. CHRYSOSTOM: The law has failed, and conscience has proved to be unequal to the task, even though it praised what is good and even fought against evil. . . . Where then, is salvation going to come from? HOMILIES ON ROMANS 13.[67]

RENEWED UNDER GRACE. AUGUSTINE: Here Paul begins to describe the man renewed under grace, the third of the four states[68] we distinguished above. AUGUSTINE ON ROMANS 45-46.[69]

THIS BODY OF DEATH. JEROME: Paul uses the term "the body of death" because the body is subject to vices and sickness, disorders and death until it rises in glory with Christ, and what was once fragile clay is purified in the fire of the Holy Spirit into a very solid rock, changing its glory, not its nature. AGAINST RUFINUS 1.25.[70]

THEODORET OF CYR: Paul calls the body a "body of death" because it has been made subject to death and is therefore mortal. The soul, on the other hand, is immortal. INTERPRETATION OF THE LETTER TO THE ROMANS.[71]

WHO WILL DELIVER ME? PELAGIUS: Who will set me free, says Paul, prisoner that I am, from this fatal habit of the body? PELAGIUS'S COMMENTARY ON ROMANS.[72]

SEVERIAN: Having considered the struggle which was taking place in the body against the soul and how man was imprisoned by this, Paul now seeks a way to escape and tries to rescue man, so that the body of death may be transformed into a body of life. . . . For Paul wants his body to be a body of life and not a body of death or of sin. PAULINE COMMENTARY FROM THE GREEK CHURCH.[73]

GENNADIUS OF CONSTANTINOPLE: Paul did not say "bad" or "evil man" but rather "wretched man" . . . for having shown that this person contemplated the good with his mind but was drawn toward evil by the passion of the flesh, he presents him as more deserving of mercy than of punishment. PAULINE COMMENTARY FROM THE GREEK CHURCH.[74]

7:25 Thanks Be to God!

THE VOICE CONTINUES TO PLAY THE ROLE OF THE WEAK MAN IN A GRADUAL PROCESS. ORIGEN: Perhaps someone will say that here the apostle Paul abandons the role of the weak man, which he assumed in the preceding [verses], and talks directly about himself. For he says that he serves the law of God with his mind but the law of sin with his flesh, as if to imply that the power of sin is so great that even an apostle cannot escape it. Moreover, he also said elsewhere: "I pommel my body and subdue it, lest after preaching to others I myself should be disqualified."[75] But someone who takes this interpretation seems to me to be inflicting every soul with despair, because then there would be nobody who did not sin in the flesh. In other words, everyone would be serving the law of sin in the flesh. Rather, it seems to me that here Paul maintains the role he has adopted and plays the part of the weak man, whom we have already described.

It appears that in this passage Paul is teaching us that the mortification of the flesh, of which he has already spoken, is not something which happens overnight but rather is a gradual process, because the force of habit is such and the attraction of sin is so great that, even though our mind may want to do what is right and has decided to serve the law of God, yet the lusts of the flesh continue to urge him to serve sin and obey its laws instead. COMMENTARY ON THE EPISTLE TO THE ROMANS.[76]

I OF MYSELF SERVE THE LAW OF GOD. AMBROSIASTER: "The law of God" means both the law

---

[66]CSEL 81.1:245. [67]NPNF 1 11:430. [68]Nature, law, grace and glory. [69]AOR 19. [70]FC 53:94. [71]IER, Migne PG 82 col. 128. [72]PCR 105. [73]NTA 15:220. [74]NTA 15:374. [75]1 Cor 9:27. [76]CER 3:284-86.

of Moses and the law of Christ. . . . A free mind which has been called back to good habits by the help of the Holy Spirit can repulse evil temptations. For it has recovered its power to resist the enemy. If it is no longer subject then Satan cannot appear uninvited. Flesh, though, has no judgment, nor is it able to discern anything, because it is brute nature. It cannot close the door to the enemy, nor can it come in and persuade the mind to do the opposite to what the mind intends.

Because man consists of both soul and flesh, the part which knows serves God and the part which is mute serves the law of sin. But if man perseveres in the form in which he was created, the enemy would have no power to reach the flesh and persuade it to act against the will of the soul. But because the whole man was not restored to his pristine state by the grace of Christ the sentence pronounced on Adam remains in force, for it would be unjust to abolish a sentence which was rightly pronounced. So although the sentence remains in force, a cure has been found by the providence of God, so that the salvation which man had lost by his own fault might be given back to him. COMMENTARY ON PAUL'S EPISTLES.[77]

EQUIPPED FOR STRUGGLES. CHRYSOSTOM: Christ not only set us free without demanding any payment for his services; he also equipped us for greater struggles in the future. HOMILIES ON ROMANS 13.[78]

WITH MY FLESH I SERVE THE LAW OF SIN. AUGUSTINE: Though his carnal desires still exist, the man who is renewed by grace by not giving in to sin does not serve them. With his mind he serves the law of God, even though with his flesh he serves the law of sin. Paul calls the law of sin the mortal condition which stems from the transgression of Adam, because of which we are born mortal. It is because the flesh has fallen that the lusts of the flesh entice us.[79] AUGUSTINE ON ROMANS 45-46.[80]

UNDER GRACE BUT BATTLING STILL. AUGUS-

TINE: These are the words of one who is now under grace but still battling against his own lust, not so that he consents and sins but so that he experiences desires which he resists. AGAINST JULIAN 6.23.73.[81]

CRUCIFYING THE FLESH. [PSEUDO-]CONSTANTIUS: Paul is right to thank God at this point, because what the law of Moses and the natural law did not teach was taught by our Lord Jesus Christ: to despise the world and to overcome evil. The blessed apostle teaches this when he says: "Those who belong to Christ Jesus have crucified the flesh, with its passions and desires."[82] Here again Paul is speaking in the role of the person who was previously under the law. THE HOLY LETTER OF ST. PAUL TO THE ROMANS.[83]

PAUL STILL SPEAKS NOT OF HIMSELF BUT IN ANOTHER VOICE. PELAGIUS: Grace sets free the man whom the law could not free. Was Paul at this time not yet set free by the grace of God? Of course! This shows that here he is speaking of somebody else. He then reviews the main points in order to conclude his argument. In a sense the carnal person is made up of two people and is divided within himself. PELAGIUS'S COMMENTARY ON ROMANS.[84]

ASKING DELIVERANCE FROM SIN. LIBER GRADUUM: We should be eager to try to become without any sins, asking our Lord to deliver us from sin. LIBER GRADUUM 2.2.[85]

THE RESURRECTED BODY FINALLY FREE. CAESARIUS OF ARLES: The grace of God through Jesus Christ our Lord will free you from the body of this death; it will deliver you from the law of death. But . . . this is going to take place at the resurrection, when you will possess a body in which no evil inclination remains. SERMON 177.4.[86]

---

[77]CSEL 81.1:247. [78]NPNF 1 11:431. [79]See Eph 2:3. [80]AOR 19. [81]FC 35:385. [82]Gal 5:24. [83]ENPK 2:52. [84]PCR 105. [85]SFPSL 56. [86]FC 47:445.

8:1-4 THE FREEDOM OF THE SPIRIT

¹There is therefore now no condemnation for those who are in Christ Jesus. ²For the law of the Spirit of life in Christ Jesus has set me free from the law of sin and death. ³For God has done what the law, weakened by the flesh, could not do: sending his own Son in the likeness of sinful flesh and for sin,ⁱ he condemned sin in the flesh, ⁴in order that the just requirement of the law might be fulfilled in us, who walk not according to the flesh but according to the Spirit.

i Or *and as a sin offering*

OVERVIEW: Christ has released us from condemnation. We now live according to the law of the Spirit, which is the law of God. We not only are forgiven sin but also are given the power to continue to overcome it in Christ. Paul's argument that Christ came "in the likeness of sinful flesh" caused the Fathers considerable concern. On the one hand they wanted to insist, against any hint of Docetism, that Christ was a real human being in a real human body. But on the other hand they also wanted to insist that he was without sin himself. Augustine put it most succinctly: Christ had a human body that was mortal, but he was without sin. Once the law's power is removed it becomes a friend to the faithful, and they desire to fulfill it in its spiritual sense. The Fathers were concerned to underline that the Christian life is not one of license but one of consecration to righteousness.

8:1 No Condemnation for Those in Christ

THOSE WHOLLY IN CHRIST HAVE IN THEM NOTHING WORTHY OF CONDEMNATION. ORIGEN: After having taught what conflict there is in those who are caught in the struggle between a mind which lives according to the law of God and the desires of the flesh which lead them into sin, Paul now goes on to talk not about those who are partly in the flesh and partly in the Spirit but about those who are wholly in Christ. He declares that there is nothing in them worthy of condemnation. COMMENTARY ON THE EPISTLE TO THE ROMANS.[1]

THOSE WHO DO NOT WALK ACCORDING TO THE FLESH. DIODORE: Paul shows here that those who are under the law, because they live according to the flesh, are under sin and condemnation. But those who are in Christ are not under condemnation because they do not walk according to the flesh. PAULINE COMMENTARY FROM THE GREEK CHURCH.[2]

SERVING GOD WITH A DEVOUT MIND. AMBROSIASTER: It is true that there will be no damnation for those who are Christians serving the law of God with a devout mind. COMMENTARY ON PAUL'S EPISTLES.[3]

IN CHRIST WE HAVE THE POWER TO AVOID POSTBAPTISMAL SIN. CHRYSOSTOM: Paul met the difficulty posed by postbaptismal sin by saying that it is due to our laziness. For now that we are in Christ Jesus we have the power to avoid walking after the flesh, but before that it was a difficult task. HOMILIES ON ROMANS 13.[4]

AUGUSTINE: There is no condemnation just because carnal desires exist; it is only if we give in to them and sin that we are condemned.[5] AUGUSTINE ON ROMANS 47.[6]

---

[1]CER 3:286-88. [2]NTA 15:90. [3]CSEL 81.1:251. [4]NPNF 1 11:431. [5]See 1 Cor 10:13; Heb 4:15; 1 Macc 2:52. [6]AOR 19.

PELAGIUS: There is nothing which deserves condemnation in those who have been crucified to the works of the flesh. PELAGIUS'S COMMENTARY ON ROMANS.[7]

GENNADIUS OF CONSTANTINOPLE: Look how great Christ's grace is in that he has set us free from condemnation. PAULINE COMMENTARY FROM THE GREEK CHURCH.[8]

8:2 *The Law of the Spirit Sets Us Free*

THE LAW OF THE SPIRIT OF LIFE. ORIGEN: The law of the Spirit of life is the same thing as the law of God.... For to serve the law of God and to be under the law of the Spirit is to serve Christ. To serve Christ is to serve wisdom, which is to serve righteousness, which is to serve truth and all related virtues. COMMENTARY ON THE EPISTLE TO THE ROMANS.[9]

THE SPIRIT OF LIFE IN JESUS CHRIST. AMBROSIASTER: Paul holds out security for us by the grace of God, so that we should not be tempted by the suggestions of the devil as long as we reject them.... We shall instead be rewarded if we repel the counsels of that sin which remains in us, for it demands great skill to avoid the tricks of the enemy within. "The law of the Spirit of life is the law of faith." For even the law of Moses is spiritual in that it forbids us to sin, but it is not the law of life. It has no power to pardon those who are guilty of the sins which merit death and thus to bring them back to life.... Therefore it is the law in Christ Jesus, that is to say, through faith in Christ, which frees the believer from the law of sin and death.[10] The law of sin, which Paul says dwells in our members, tries to persuade us to sin, but the law of Moses is a law of death, because it puts sinners to death. COMMENTARY ON PAUL'S EPISTLES.[11]

CHRYSOSTOM: "The law of the Spirit of life" is just a way of saying "the Spirit. " For as he calls

sin the "law of sin," so he also calls the Spirit the "law of the Spirit." But Paul also called the law of Moses "spiritual." What is the difference? It is great! For the law of Moses was spiritual, but here we are dealing with the law of the Spirit.... The law of Moses was merely given by the Spirit, but this one gives those who receive it a large measure of the Spirit himself. This is why Paul called it the law of life, in opposition to the law of sin, not to the law of Moses. For when he says that it freed him from the law of sin and death, it is not the law of Moses which he has in mind, because he never calls it the law of sin. In any case, how could he have done so since he had called it "just and holy" on so many other occasions, and destructive of sin as well?[12] Rather, the law of sin is the force which wars against the law of the mind. The grace of the Spirit put a stop to that war by slaying sin and making the contest light for us, putting a victor's crown on our heads at the beginning and then drawing us into the struggle with enough help to win it. Then, as he always does Paul turns from the Spirit to the Son and the Father, showing that we are dependent on the entire Trinity. HOMILIES ON ROMANS 13.[13]

[PSEUDO-]CONSTANTIUS: Those who are in Christ do not serve the lusts of the flesh, and therefore they are not bound to be condemned. THE HOLY LETTER OF ST. PAUL TO THE ROMANS.[14]

PELAGIUS: Note that Paul calls the law "grace." PELAGIUS'S COMMENTARY ON ROMANS.[15]

SET FREE FROM THE LAW OF SIN AND DEATH. THEODORE OF MOPSUESTIA: The apostle says that the resurrection takes place by the working of the Spirit.[16] ... Paul calls the Spirit the "Spirit of life" because the Spirit is the firstfruits of the eternal life which we shall then enjoy. The Spirit has been

---

[7]PCR 105. [8]NTA 15:375. [9]CER 3:288. [10]See Gal 2:16. [11]CSEL 81.1:251. [12]See Rom 7:12. [13]NPNF 1 11:431. [14]ENPK 2:53. [15]PCR 105. [16]See 1 Cor 15:44.

given to us in the hope of immortality, and faith in Christ has permitted us to enjoy him, because he has set us free from death and sin. Clearly Paul is using the things which are to come as evidence for what has been promised to us in Christ. PAULINE COMMENTARY FROM THE GREEK CHURCH.[17]

LEADING A LIFE OF HOLINESS. CYRIL OF ALEXANDRIA: I think it is necessary for an accurate explanation of the meanings which are found here, to say this: Paul calls the lusts of the flesh which lead us into all kinds of wickedness "the law of sin and death." So also he calls the spiritual will, that is, the inclination of the mind to do what is right, "the law of the Spirit of life." . . . This law has not set us free by itself; rather it has restored us to freedom by the merits of Christ. Just as those who have sinned under the law have necessarily been trapped by the snares of death as well, so it is necessary also that those who are not under the law but who have been set free by Christ should lead lives of holiness and show themselves to be above corruption,[18] because they are no longer under the law of death. EXPLANATION OF THE LETTER TO THE ROMANS.[19]

GENNADIUS OF CONSTANTINOPLE: We have been made heirs of a pain-free and immortal life by the free gift of the Spirit and have all become spiritual, being set free from sin and the death which it causes. PAULINE COMMENTARY FROM THE GREEK CHURCH.[20]

8:3 The Son Sent in the Likeness of Sinful Flesh

HIS FLESH NOT ILLUSORY. TERTULLIAN: If the Father "sent his Son in the likeness of sinful flesh," it must not be said that the flesh in which he appeared was illusory. . . . The Son was sent in the likeness of sinful flesh in order to redeem our sinful flesh by a like substance, even a fleshly one, which bore a resemblance to sinful flesh although it was itself free from sin. AGAINST MARCION 5.14.[21]

WHAT THE LAW COULD NOT DO. ORIGEN: In my opinion, Paul here as in many other passages divides the law of Moses into two parts, one of which is carnal and the other spiritual. Moreover, he calls the literal observance of the law its carnal meaning. . . . This observance is both impossible and inadequate. For what is more impossible than observance of the sabbath according to the letter of the law? For it is commanded that no one should go outside his house, nor move away from his place, nor carry any burden.[22] When the Jews, who observed the letter of the law, realized that these things were impossible, they glossed the law in silly and ridiculous ways. . . . And what can I say about the system of sacrifices, which is now totally impossible to observe since there is no temple, no altar and no place to perform the sacrifices? In these instances I would say that the law is not just impossible or inadequate; it is dead!

Paul shows that Jesus had the likeness of sinful flesh but not that he had sinful flesh in the same way we do. For we are all human beings who have been born from the seed of a man who has slept with a woman, and we can only say, along with David, that: "In sin my mother conceived me."[23] But the one who was born without contact with a male but only because the Holy Spirit came upon a virgin and covering her with the power of the Most High gave birth to a spotless body which had the same nature as ours but without the corruption of sin which is passed on by the act of conception. COMMENTARY ON THE EPISTLE TO THE ROMANS.[24]

EUSEBIUS OF CAESAREA: Because God has done what the law could not do, we reject Jewish customs on the ground that they were not meant for us and that it is impossible to accommodate them to the needs of the Gentiles, while we gladly accept that the Jewish prophecies contain predictions

---

[17]NTA 15:133. [18]See Rom 6:17-23; 1 Cor 7:22; Gal 5:1. [19]Migne PG 74 col. 816. [20]NTA 15:375. [21]ANF 3:459. [22]See Ex 20:10; 31:12-17. [23]Ps 51:5. [24]CER 3:294-96.

about ourselves.[25] PROOF OF THE GOSPEL 1.7.[26]

GOD SENT HIS SON IN THE LIKENESS OF SIN-FUL FLESH. AMBROSIASTER: For whom was this impossible? For us of course, because we could not fulfill the commandment of the law, since we were subject to sin. For this reason God sent his Son in the likeness of sinful flesh. It is the likeness of our flesh because, although it is the same as ours is, it was sanctified in the womb and born without sin, neither did he sin in it. Therefore the womb of a virgin was chosen for the divine birth so that the divine flesh might differ from ours in its holiness. It is like ours in origin but not in sinfulness. For this reason Paul says that it is similar to our flesh, since it is of the same substance, but it did not have the same birth, because the body of the Lord was not subject to sin. The Lord's flesh was sanctified by the Holy Spirit in order that he might be born in the same kind of body as Adam had before he sinned. By sending Christ God used sin to condemn sin. . . . For Christ was crucified by sin, which is Satan; hence sin sinned in the flesh of the Savior's body. In this way, God condemned sin in the flesh, in the very place where it sinned. COMMENTARY ON PAUL'S EPISTLES.[27]

HIS FLESH LIKE OURS, EXCEPTING SIN. CHRYSOSTOM: Again it appears as if Paul is criticizing the law, but in reality he is harmonizing it with Christ. The problem with the law was that it was too weak to accomplish what it intended. . . . And even the law's weakness was not its fault but the fault of the flesh, by which he means not the substance itself but the carnal mind.

Just because Paul says that Christ came "in the likeness of sinful flesh," you must not think that his flesh was any different from ours. It was because he called it "sinful" that he added the word "likeness." For Christ did not have sinful flesh but flesh which, though it was like ours by nature, was sinless. From this it is plain that flesh is not sinful by nature. It was not by taking on a different kind of flesh nor by changing ours into something different that Christ caused it to gain

the victory over sin and death.[28] Rather, he allowed the flesh to keep its own nature, giving it the crown of victory and after its resurrection life immortal. HOMILIES ON ROMANS 13.[29]

HE CONDEMNED SIN IN THE FLESH. AUGUSTINE: Here Paul clearly teaches that the precepts of the law were not fulfilled (though they should have been) because those who had the law before grace were given over to worldly goods, from which they were trying to get happiness. Nor did they have any fear except when adversity threatened these goods, and when that happened they easily withdrew from the precepts of the law. Therefore the law grew weaker as its commands went unheeded. This was not the fault of the law but came about through the flesh, because those who went after worldly goods did not love the righteousness of the law but put temporal advantage ahead of it.

And so our deliverer, the Lord Jesus Christ, took on mortal flesh and came in the likeness of the flesh of sin. For death is the reward due to the flesh of sin.[30] Of course the Lord's death was voluntary and not something which he owed. Yet nevertheless the apostle calls the assumption of mortal flesh "sin" even if it was sinless, because when the Savior died he was made sin, so to speak.

But "he condemned sin in the flesh," for the Lord's death ensured that death would not be dreaded, that worldly goods would not be sought and that worldly evils would not be feared by those who had previously been wise in the ways of the world and thus unable to fulfill the commands of the law. AUGUSTINE ON ROMANS 48.[31]

AUGUSTINE: The reason why grace was bestowed on us through our mediator is that we who were polluted by sinful flesh might be purified by the "likeness of sinful flesh." THE CITY OF GOD 10.22.[32]

---

[25]See Acts 15:5-21. [26]POG 1:44. [27]CSEL 81.1:255. [28]See 1 Cor 15:54-57. [29]NPNF 1 11:432. [30]See Rom 5:12. [31]AOR 19, 21. [32]FC 14:156.

DISTINGUISHING SINFUL FLESH AND THE LIKENESS OF SINFUL FLESH. AUGUSTINE: What does sinful flesh have? Death and sin. What does the likeness of sinful flesh have? Death without sin. If it had sin it would be sinful flesh; if it did not have death it would not be the likeness of sinful flesh. As such he came—he came as Savior. He died but he vanquished death. In himself he put an end to what we feared; he took it upon himself and he vanquished it—as a mighty hunter he captured and slew the lion. SERMONS FOR EASTER SEASON, HOMILY 233.3.[33]

HE ASSUMED OUR FLESH. [PSEUDO-]CONSTANTIUS: Paul says here that because of the weakness of the flesh the law could not be fulfilled. When he says: "God sent his Son in the likeness of sinful flesh and for sin," he shows that the Son existed before the incarnation and that he took on flesh which was later bound by sin, though he himself assumed it without sin. Therefore it is said that he came in the likeness of sinful flesh, having assumed flesh, and that he condemned sin in that same flesh, because the flesh which he assumed was holy and free from all knowledge of sin. THE HOLY LETTER OF ST. PAUL TO THE ROMANS.[34]

THE ANALOGY OF SACRIFICIAL VICTIMS BEING GIVEN IN THE NAME OF SIN. PELAGIUS: The law was weakened in the flesh, not in itself. In saying "God sent his Son" Paul counters Photinus, who denied the Son's existence before the incarnation.... The Son took flesh like that of the rest of humanity and "he condemned sin in the flesh," i.e., he overcame like by like. Just as the sacrificial victims which the Jews offered under the law were given in the name of sin, although they had no sin themselves ... so also Christ's flesh, which was offered for our sins, took the name of sin. Some people say that by the sin of the Jews, whereby they killed the Lord, Christ condemned in his humanity the sin of the devil, by which the devil had deceived mankind, as Paul says to the Hebrews: "so that through death he

might destroy him who has the power of death."[35] Or it may mean that through the substance of that flesh which previously was a slave to sin, Christ conquered sin by never sinning himself, and in his flesh he condemned sin to show that it was the will which was on trial, not human nature, which God created in such a way that it could avoid sinning. PELAGIUS'S COMMENTARY ON ROMANS.[36]

WHETHER CHRIST'S BODY WAS MADE OF SINFUL FLESH. CYRIL OF ALEXANDRIA: God forbid that Paul should ever say that Christ's body was made of sinful flesh! Rather, it was in the likeness of sinful flesh, for although it was similar to our bodies it can scarcely be compared with them in the sense that it could not be ill with carnal uncleanness. Even from the womb Christ's body was a holy temple, and no one is afraid to state that in so far as it was flesh, when it attained the age of reason it behaved in the way flesh normally does.[37] Nevertheless, because the Word which sanctifies all things dwelt in his body, the potential for sin was condemned so that the fruit of this blessing might come across into us as well. For we have been transformed into his likeness, not only in spirit but in body also. When Christ dwells in us by the Holy Spirit and the sacramental blessing, then the law of sin is really condemned in us. So it is truly said that what was impossible for the law, which had been weakened by the flesh, became possible through Christ, who condemned and destroyed sin in the flesh so that the righteousness of the law might be fulfilled in us. EXPLANATION OF THE LETTER TO THE ROMANS.[38]

THE SAME NATURE AS WE. THEODORET OF CYR: Christ came "in the likeness of sinful flesh" because, although he took on human nature, he did not assume human sinfulness.... For although he had the same nature as we have, he did not have the same outlook or the same

---

[33]FC 38:220-21. [34]ENPK 2:53-54. [35]Heb 2:14. [36]PCR 106. [37]See Heb 4:15. [38]Migne PG 74 col. 820.

thoughts. For although the law could not accomplish its purpose on account of the weakness of those to whom it was given (for they had a mortal and passible nature), the only begotten Word of God broke the power of sin by taking on human flesh and fulfilled all righteousness, not giving in to the temptations of sin in any way.[39] Interpretation of the Letter to the Romans.[40]

Remaining Without Sin. Caesarius of Arles: By taking upon himself flesh from a sinful substance while remaining without sin, Christ fulfilled all righteousness and condemned sin in the body. This is proved by his conflict with the spirit in the desert, for the devil is overcome not by sheer divine majesty but by a reminder of the commandment, by fasting and by a legal reply.[41] Sermon 11.3.[42]

Bede: He who came in the likeness of sinful flesh—not in sinful flesh—did not turn away from the remedy by which sinful flesh was ordinarily made clean. . . . Not from necessity but by way of example he submitted to the water of baptism, by which he wanted the people of the new law of grace to be washed from the stain of sin.[43] Homilies on the Gospel 1.11.[44]

8:4 Walking According to the Spirit

Three Ways by Which God Condemned Sin. Ambrosiaster: Paul says that sin has been condemned in order that the righteousness of the law given by Moses might be fulfilled in us. For once removed from the power of the law we become the law's friends. Those who have been justified are friends of the law. For how is this righteousness fulfilled in us unless the forgiveness of sins is given to us, so that once we have been justified by the removal of our sins we might serve the law of God with our minds? This is what it means to walk according to the Spirit and not according to the flesh. The devotion of the mind, which is the spirit, will not succumb to the desire of sin,

which sows lusts in the soul by means of the flesh because sin dwells in it. But if sin has been condemned, how can it be indwelling?[45]

Sin has been condemned by the Savior in three different ways. In the first place, he condemned sin in that a person should turn away from it and not sin. Next, sin is said to have been condemned on the cross, because it enacted sin itself. The power by which it held people in hell because of Adam's sin was then taken away. After that it would no longer dare to hang onto anyone who had been signed with the sign of the cross. In the third place, God condemned sin by canceling it out in the case of those who had received forgiveness for their sins. For although a sinner ought to be condemned for his sin, God forgave him and condemned the sin in him instead. So if we follow our Savior's example and do not sin, we are condemning sin. Commentary on Paul's Epistles.[46]

Guarding the Treasure. Chrysostom: Paul shows that it is not only binding on us to keep ourselves from evil deeds but also to be adorned with good. For to give the crown is his prerogative, but to retain it is your responsibility. For Christ has fulfilled the righteousness of the law on your behalf so that you are not subject to its curse. So do not betray so great a gift, but keep this great treasure under guard. For here Paul shows us that baptism will not save us if afterward we fail to display a life worthy of that gift.[47] This is why he returns to the law and defends it. For once we have become obedient to Christ, we must use all ways and means so that its righteousness, which Christ fulfilled, may abide in us and not come to naught. Homilies on Romans 13.[48]

Walking According to the Spirit. Augustine: But since this worldly wisdom has been

---

[39]See Heb 4:15. [40]IER, Migne PG 82 cols. 128-29. [41]See Mt 4:1-11; Mk 1:12-13; Lk 4:1-13. [42]FC 31:64. [43]See Mt 3:13-17; Mk 1:9-11; Lk 3:21-22; Jn 1:29-34. [44]CSEL 110:104. [45]See Jn 8:34-36. [46]CSEL 81.1:257-59. [47]See Rom 6:4-14; Heb 6:1-6. [48]NPNF 1 11:433.

destroyed and removed in the Lord made man, the righteousness of the law is fulfilled when a man walks not according to the flesh but according to the Spirit. Whence it is most rightly said: "I came not to abolish the law but to fulfill it. For love is the fulfilling of the law."[49] Love belongs to those who walk according to the Spirit. For love belongs to the grace of the Holy Spirit.[50] When there was no love of righteousness but only fear, the law was not fulfilled. AUGUSTINE

ON ROMANS 48.[51]

PELAGIUS: Although the law could not be fulfilled in those in whom carnal habit fights back, at least it can be fulfilled in us, who have mortified the flesh according to Christ's example. PELAGIUS'S COMMENTARY ON ROMANS.[52]

---

[49]Mt 5:17; Rom 13:10. [50]See Gal 5:22; 1 Pet 1:22. [51]AOR 21. [52]PCR 107.

8:5-8 THE MIND OF THE SPIRIT

[5]*For those who live according to the flesh set their minds on the things of the flesh, but those who live according to the Spirit set their minds on the things of the Spirit.* [6]*To set the mind on the flesh is death, but to set the mind on the Spirit is life and peace.* [7]*For the mind that is set on the flesh is hostile to God; it does not submit to God's law, indeed it cannot;* [8]*and those who are in the flesh cannot please God.*

OVERVIEW: The Fathers agreed with Paul, but they were not always in agreement on who was "setting their minds on the flesh." For some of the Fathers, this phrase could be applied to new Christians who had not yet progressed very far in their sanctification. For others it meant the Jews. The Fathers were quite clear, however, that "flesh" here refers to a spiritual principle and not to the physical body. The substance of the flesh as such is not censured.

8:5 Mind of the Flesh, Mind of the Spirit

SETTING ONE'S MIND ON THE FLESH. CLEMENT OF ALEXANDRIA: It is possible to think of those who have just recently been instructed in the faith and who are still little ones in Christ as carnal, for he calls those who have already believed by the Holy Spirit "spiritual" and those

newly taught and not yet purified "carnal."[1] He speaks of these latter as carnal with good reason, for like the pagans they still mind the things of the flesh. CHRIST THE EDUCATOR 6.36.[2]

LIVING ACCORDING TO THE SPIRIT. ORIGEN: Those who live according to the flesh are the Jews, whom Paul says are Israel according to the flesh. They know what belongs to the law of the flesh because they interpret the law according to the flesh. Those who live according to the Spirit are the people whom Paul calls Jews in spirit, not in the letter. COMMENTARY ON THE EPISTLE TO THE ROMANS.[3]

PUTTING THE WORLD BEHIND THEM. AMBROSIASTER: Paul says this because whoever obeys the temptation which comes through the flesh knows what the things of the flesh are.... Those who live according to the Spirit are those who have stomped on the lusts of the flesh by attacking sin. They have put the world behind them and although they still walk in the flesh they do not struggle according to the flesh. Their glory is not from men but from God. Dwelling in these spiritual works, they know what the things of the Spirit of God are and walk in his commandments. COMMENTARY ON PAUL'S EPISTLES.[4]

No Disparagement of the Flesh. CHRYSOSTOM: This is not meant to be a disparagement of the flesh. For as long as it keeps its place nothing untoward will happen. But if we let it have its own way in everything and allow the flesh to get out of hand, it will rise up against the soul and then destroy and corrupt everything. This is not because of its own nature but because it is out of proportion, and disorder will ensue. HOMILIES ON ROMANS 13.[5]

Two Substances. PELAGIUS: Man is composed of spirit and flesh. When a man performs carnal deeds he is called "flesh," but when he performs spiritual deeds he is called "Spirit." For when one of these substances brings the other under its control, the subordinate substance in effect loses both its power and its name. For each substance desires what is connected and related to it. PELAGIUS'S COMMENTARY ON ROMANS.[6]

8:6 Life and Peace

Christ Is Life. ORIGEN: Whoever interprets the law according to the flesh, i.e., according to the letter, does not come to Christ, who is life. COMMENTARY ON THE EPISTLE TO THE ROMANS.[7]

Set the Mind on the Spirit. MARIUS VICTORINUS: "To set the mind on the Spirit is life." For error, imprudence and ignorance are impassioned, self-rebellious, self-contradictory. And because of this "to set the mind on the flesh," which is imprudence, is death, because it does not know God. Therefore, "to set the mind on the

Spirit is life and peace." AGAINST ARIUS 3.C.I.[8]

The Supposed Wisdom of the Flesh. AMBROSIASTER: The wisdom of the flesh is death because sin is serious and it is through sin that this death comes. It is called wisdom, even though it is a foolish thing, because to worldly people sins against the law of God which are conceived, whether in thought or in deed, on the basis of what is visible appear as wisdom, especially because those who sin are full of energy and cleverness. The fact that they take so much trouble over it makes them appear wise, even though there is nothing more foolish than sinning. Moreover, there is yet another wisdom of the flesh which, puffed up as it is by earthly reasoning, denies the possibility of miracles. Therefore it laughs at the virgin birth and at the resurrection of the flesh. The wisdom of the Spirit, on the other hand, is true wisdom which leads to life and peace. . . . Paul did not say that the flesh is hostile but rather that "the wisdom of the flesh" is. "The wisdom of the flesh" means, in the first place, any argument about the unknown which men have come up with and, in the second place, a preference for what can be seen. Both these things are hostile to God because they make the Lord of the elements and the Creator of the world equal to what he has made and assert that nothing can happen unless there is a rational cause for it. For this reason they deny that God made a virgin give birth or that he raises the bodies of the dead. They say that it is absurd that God should do anything beyond what man can understand, and therefore he did not do it. . . . These people are so blinded that they do not see how greatly they are insulting God, for the work which he was pleased to do in order that his praise should be proclaimed they condemn and claim is unbelievable and absurd.[9] COMMENTARY ON PAUL'S EPISTLES.[10]

---

[1]See 1 Cor 3:1-4. [2]FC 23:35. [3]CER 3:298. [4]CSEL 81.1:259-61. [5]NPNF 1 11:433. [6]PCR 107. [7]CER 3:300. [8]FC 69:236. [9]See 1 Cor 1:18-31; 2:14. [10]CSEL 81.1:261.

PELAGIUS: Paul says elsewhere that it is human wisdom to repay evil for evil. [11] Such wisdom obtains death because it transgresses the commandment. [12] But the wisdom of the Spirit enjoys peace now because it does not repay in kind, and in the future it will obtain eternal life. PELAGIUS'S COMMENTARY ON ROMANS. [13]

LIFE AND PEACE. GENNADIUS OF CONSTANTINOPLE: "Death" is estrangement and punishment from God; "life" is immortality and "peace" is fellowship with him. PAULINE COMMENTARY FROM THE GREEK CHURCH. [14]

8:7 Hostile to God

THE MIND SET ON THE FLESH. GREGORY OF NYSSA: As long as the flesh lives . . . it is not possible for the pleasing and perfect will of God to be done expeditiously in the life of the believer. ON PERFECTION. [15]

WHETHER FREE CHOICE IS IMPOSSIBLE. CHRYSOSTOM: Paul is not saying that it is impossible for a wicked person to become good but rather that it is impossible for one who continues in wickedness to be subject to God. For a person to change and become good and subject to God is easy. . . . If we give our souls up to the Spirit and persuade our flesh to recognize its proper position, we shall make our souls spiritual as well. But if we are lazy we shall make our souls carnal. For since it was not natural necessity which put the gift into us but freedom of choice, it now rests with us which way we shall choose to go. HOMILIES ON ROMANS 13. [16]

WHY THE "WISDOM" OF THE FLESH IS HOSTILE TO GOD. AUGUSTINE: Paul explains why he said "hostile" so that no one should think that there is some nature derived from an opposing principle which God did not create and which fights against him. An enemy of God is one who does not submit to his law and who behaves this way because of the wisdom of the flesh. This

means that he seeks worldly goods and is afraid of worldly evils. The normal definition of wisdom is to seek what is good and avoid what is evil. Therefore the apostle is right to describe the wisdom of the flesh as the longing for "goods" which do not remain with a man and when there is a fear for losing those things which one day will have to be left behind anyway. Wisdom of this kind cannot submit to the law of God. It must be destroyed so that the wisdom of the Spirit, which does not place its hope in worldly goods nor is afraid of worldly evils, may take its place. For the one nature of the soul has both the wisdom of the flesh when it follows lower things and the wisdom of the Spirit when it chooses higher things, just as the one nature of water freezes in the cold and melts in the heat. AUGUSTINE ON ROMANS 49. [17]

PELAGIUS: The flesh is not in itself hostile to God, as the Manichaeans say, but the carnal mind is. For everything which is not subject is hostile, and anyone who wants to clear himself may sometimes go beyond the limit of the old law. Paul says that this carnal wisdom can never be subject to the law of God in order to call men back from the desires of the flesh. PELAGIUS'S COMMENTARY ON ROMANS. [18]

8:8 The Flesh Cannot Please God

THE SUBSTANCE OF FLESH AS SUCH NOT CENSURED. IRENAEUS: The apostle does not reject the substance of flesh but shows that the Spirit must be infused into it. AGAINST HERESIES 5.10.2. [19]

TERTULLIAN: In these and in similar statements it is not the substance of the flesh which is censured but its actions. ON THE RESURRECTION OF THE FLESH 10. [20]

[11]See Rom 12:16-18; 1 Thess 5:15. [12]See Mt 5:38-48. [13]PCR 107. [14]NTA 15:376. [15]FC 58:104-5. [16]NPNF 1 11:434. [17]AOR 21. [18]PCR 107-8. [19]ANF 1:536. [20]ANF 3:552.

AMBROSIASTER: The wise of this world are in the flesh because they cling to their wisdom, by which they reject God's law. For whatever goes against the law of God is of the flesh, because it is of the world. For the whole world is flesh and every visible thing is assigned to the flesh. COMMENTARY ON PAUL'S EPISTLES.[21]

WHETHER THE FLESH CAN PLEASE GOD.
CHRYSOSTOM: Are we to cut our bodies to pieces in order to please God? Should we become murderers in order to practice virtue? You see what inconsistencies result if we take these words literally! What Paul means by the flesh in this passage is not the essence of the body but a life which is carnal and worldly, serving self-indulgence and extravagance to the full. HOMILIES ON ROMANS 13.[22]

CHRYSOSTOM: Why is this? Is not the speaker himself clad in flesh? Paul does not mean that those clad in flesh are incapable of pleasing God but rather those who put no store by virtue, whose thoughts are totally carnal and who are caught up in pleasures of that kind, paying no attention to their soul, which is incorporeal and intellectual. HOMILIES ON GENESIS 24.6.[23]

JEROME: If all who are carnal cannot please God, how does Paul himself, the speaker, please God? How do Peter and the other apostles and saints,

whom we cannot deny were carnal, please him? . . . It is because they—and we—do not live according to the flesh. We . . . walk about on the earth, it is true, but we are hastening on our way to heaven, for here we do not have a lasting place, but we are wayfarers and pilgrims, like all our fathers.[24] HOMILIES 63.[25]

AUGUSTINE: In the same way, snow cannot tolerate heat. For when snow is heated it melts; it becomes warm as water, but no one can then call it snow. AUGUSTINE ON ROMANS 49.[26]

PELAGIUS: This proves that Paul did not find fault with the flesh itself but with the works of the flesh, because those to whom he was writing were undoubtedly living in the flesh in the physical sense. Once one has given himself over to the flesh (in the spiritual sense) it is impossible to avoid sin. PELAGIUS'S COMMENTARY ON ROMANS.[27]

THEODORET OF CYR: Paul is not telling us to leave the body but to be set free from the wisdom of the flesh. What this means, he tells us in the following verses. INTERPRETATION OF THE LETTER TO THE ROMANS.[28]

---

[21]CSEL 81.1:265. [22]NPNF 1 11:434-35. [23]FC 82:109. [24]See Heb 11:13. [25]FC 57:46. [26]AOR 21. [27]PCR 108. [28]IER, Migne PG 82 col. 129.

8:9-17 THE LIFE OF THE SPIRIT

[9]But you are not in the flesh, you are in the Spirit, if in fact the Spirit of God dwells in you. Any one who does not have the Spirit of Christ does not belong to him. [10]But if Christ is in you, although your bodies are dead because of sin, your spirits are alive because of righteousness. [11]If the Spirit of him who raised Jesus from the dead dwells in you, he who raised Christ Jesus from the

dead will give life to your mortal bodies also through his Spirit which dwells in you.

[12]So then, brethren, we are debtors, not to the flesh, to live according to the flesh—[13]for if you live according to the flesh you will die, but if by the Spirit you put to death the deeds of the body you will live. [14]For all who are led by the Spirit of God are sons of God. [15]For you did not receive the spirit of slavery to fall back into fear, but you have received the spirit of sonship. When we cry, "Abba! Father!" [16]it is the Spirit himself bearing witness with our spirit that we are children of God, [17]and if children, then heirs, heirs of God and fellow heirs with Christ, provided we suffer with him in order that we may also be glorified with him.

Overview: The body is dead because it is mortal, but the spirit is alive if Christ dwells in us. The perspective of the Fathers was eschatological, and they frequently spoke in terms of future fulfillment. The Fathers were intrigued by the juxtaposition of the terms "Spirit of God" and "Spirit of Christ" in Romans 8:9. It was clear to most of them that this is the one Holy Spirit, the third person of the Trinity, and they interpreted the text accordingly. The Holy Spirit who raised Jesus from the dead has the power to give us new life as well. On earth he fills us with the wisdom, peace and righteousness of Christ, but all of this is merely in preparation for the great resurrection on the last day. Romans 8:12 and the following verses were favorites with the Fathers, who viewed them as an outline of the Christian life. To their way of thinking, there was no such thing as a half-hearted Christian. One who was born again must live the new life in anticipation of the resurrection. To be filled with the Holy Spirit is to be made a child of God, not by nature as Christ was but by grace. We are God's children by adoption and are given strength by the Spirit to live the kind of life that is required of those who have been so called. To be a child of God is to be made an heir—the greatest gift God can give us.

8:9 The Spirit of God and of Christ

Whether the Spirit of God and of Christ Are Distinguished. Origen: Is the Spirit of God somehow different from the Spirit of Christ, or are the two one and the same? As far as I can follow the logic of this passage, not to mention what the Savior says of the Holy Spirit in the Gospel, viz., that "he proceeds from the Father"[1] and "he receives of me,"[2] to which he adds by way of explanation: "Father, everything which is mine is yours, and everything which is yours is mine; wherefore I said, that he receives of me."[3] When, I say, I consider the logic of this unity between the Father and the Son, it seems to me that the Spirit of God and the Spirit of Christ are one and the same Spirit.

We can understand this to mean that someone who is not of such a character as to deserve to have the Spirit of Christ is not recognized as belonging to him. . . . It may also be understood to mean that anyone who does not act in the Spirit, who is not prepared for righteousness, for truth, for the proclamation of the Word of God, for the preaching of the kingdom of heaven, for rejecting the letter of the law and for opening up its spirit, for resisting sin, for everything which will prevent him from coming to death, is not Christ's disciple. Commentary on the Epistle to the Romans.[4]

Those in the Spirit. Ambrosiaster: Those who are said to be in the Spirit are not in the flesh if they agree with the apostle John and do not love the world.[5] . . . Paul speaks somewhat ambiguously because those who have been inducted into the law do not yet have a perfect

---

[1]Jn 15:26. [2]Jn 16:14. [3]Jn 17:10. [4]CER 3:306-8. [5]See 1 Jn 2:15-16.

faith, although Paul saw a hope of perfection in them. For this reason he sometimes speaks to them as if they are perfect and sometimes as if they are yet to become perfect. This is why sometimes he praises them and sometimes he warns them, so that if they maintain the law of nature according to what has been said above they will be said to be in the Spirit, because the Spirit of God cannot dwell in anyone who follows carnal things.[6]

Here Paul says that the Spirit of God is the Spirit of Christ, for everything which belongs to the Father belongs to the Son as well. Therefore he says that whoever is subject to the above-mentioned sins does not belong to Christ. Such a person does not have the Spirit of God, even if he has accepted that Christ is God's Son. For the Holy Spirit abandons people for one of two reasons, either because they think carnally or because they act carnally. Therefore he exhorts them to good behavior by the things which he commands. Commentary on Paul's Epistles.[7]

[Pseudo-]Constantius: Here Paul reveals that the Holy Spirit is the Spirit of both the Father and the Son. The Holy Letter of St. Paul to the Romans.[8]

Things Good and Bad. Chrysostom: Some things are good, some are bad and some are indifferent. The soul and the flesh both belong to things indifferent, since each of these may become either good or bad. But the spirit belongs to things which are good and can never become anything else. Likewise, the mind of the flesh, i.e., wickedness, belongs to things which are always bad. Homilies on Romans 13.[9]

You Are Not in the Flesh. Chrysostom: "You are not in the flesh" not because you are not clad in flesh but because in spite of being clad in flesh you rise above the thinking of the flesh. Homilies on Genesis 22.10.[10]

The Sense in Which the Spirit Dwells in

You. Pelagius: You are in the Spirit because you are occupied with spiritual things. The Spirit of God dwells in those in whom his fruit is manifest, as Paul says to the Galatians: "The fruit of the Spirit is love, joy, etc."[11] The Spirit of Christ, who loved his enemies and prayed for them, is the Spirit of humility, patience and all the virtues.[12] Pelagius's Commentary on Romans.[13]

Oecumenius: The Spirit is common to the Father and the Son. Pauline Commentary from the Greek Church.[14]

Severian: By "Spirit of God" Paul here refers to the spiritual gifts of the New Testament. Pauline Commentary from the Greek Church.[15]

8:10 Dead in the Body, Alive in the Spirit

Your Bodies Are Dead Because of Sin. Ambrosiaster: Paul asserts that the bodies of those whom the Holy Spirit has abandoned because of sin are dead, nor does the feeling of their murder touch him, i.e., the Spirit. For the Spirit of God cannot sin. He is given for righteousness in order to make people righteous by his assistance.

If a believer returns to the life of the flesh, the Holy Spirit will leave him and he will die in his unrighteousness. In saying "the body" Paul means that the whole person will die because of sin. Commentary on Paul's Epistles.[16]

Chrysostom: Paul is not saying here that the Spirit is Christ but is showing rather that anyone who has the Spirit has Christ as well. For where the Spirit is, there Christ is also. Wherever one person of the Trinity is present, the whole Trinity is present too. For the Trinity is undivided and has a perfect unity in itself. Homilies on Romans 13.[17]

---

[6]See Job 27:3-4; 1 Cor 2:14. [7]CSEL 81.1:265-67. [8]ENPK 2:55. [9]NPNF 1 11:435. [10]FC 82:76. [11]Gal 5:22. [12]See Mt 5:44; Lk 23:34. [13]PCR 108. [14]NTA 15:427. [15]NTA 15:220. [16]CSEL 81.1:267. [17]NPNF 1 11:436.

AUGUSTINE: Paul calls the body "dead" because it is mortal. Furthermore, it is because of this mortality that the lack of earthly things troubles the soul and arouses certain desires, to which the man who serves the law of God in his mind does not submit and sin. AUGUSTINE ON ROMANS 50.[18]

AUGUSTINE: Paul shows that both life and death exist in a man living in his body—death in his body, life in his spirit. THE CITY OF GOD 20.15.[19]

CARNAL DEATH AND SPIRITUAL LIFE.

PELAGIUS: If you imitate Christ the carnal mind offers no resistance, because it is effectively dead. The spirit lives in order to produce righteousness, for the aim is not just to stop doing carnal things but to start doing spiritual ones. PELAGIUS'S COMMENTARY ON ROMANS.[20]

YOUR SPIRITS ARE ALIVE BECAUSE OF RIGHTEOUSNESS.

THEODORET OF CYR: Paul makes something which was doubtful clear and demonstrates that he is not attacking the flesh but sin. For he decreed that the body was dead to sin, i.e., that it should not sin. But here he calls the soul *spirit*, because it has already become spiritual. He commands it to follow after righteousness, whose fruit is the hope of eternal life. INTERPRETATION OF THE LETTER TO THE ROMANS.[21]

8:11 Life Through the Spirit

HE WHO RAISED CHRIST WILL RAISE YOU.

POLYCARP: But he who raised Christ up from the dead will raise us up also if we do his will and walk in his commandments and love what he loved, keeping ourselves from all unrighteousness, covetousness, love of money, evil-speaking, false witness, "not rendering evil for evil, or railing for railing,"[22] or blow for blow, or cursing for cursing, but being mindful of what the Lord said in his teaching. THE EPISTLE TO THE PHILIPPIANS 2.[23]

TERTULLIAN: The resurrection of the dead implies the resurrection of their bodies. AGAINST MARCION 5.14.[24]

THE TEMPLE OF THE BODY RESTORED TO LIFE.

ORIGEN: If the Spirit of Christ dwells in you, it seems essential that his dwelling place (i.e., your body) will be given back to him and his temple restored.

This is how you can know whether you have the Spirit of Christ or not. Christ is wisdom,[25] so if you are wise according to Christ and know what is his, then by this wisdom you have the Spirit of Christ. Likewise, Christ is righteousness;[26] therefore, if you have the righteousness of Christ, by that righteousness you have the Spirit of Christ. Christ is peace;[27] if you have Christ's peace in you, then through the Spirit of peace you have the Spirit of Christ. So it goes with love, with sanctification and with all that belongs to Christ.[28] The one who has these things may be confident of having the Spirit of Christ in him and can hope that his mortal body will be restored to life on account of the Spirit of Christ dwelling in him. COMMENTARY ON THE EPISTLE TO THE ROMANS.[29]

AMBROSIASTER: Paul repeats here what he has just said. Once again, the word *body* stands for the whole person. COMMENTARY ON PAUL'S EPISTLES.[30]

THE SPIRIT OF THE TRIUNE GOD.

DIODORE: Having already mentioned the Spirit of Christ, Paul refers to him once more, calling him "the Spirit of him who raised Jesus from the dead." By saying that the Spirit of Christ is also the Spirit of the Father, Paul teaches clearly that the Spirit of the Son partakes of the Father's divinity and that their power is one, because they share the same essence as the Father. PAULINE COMMENTARY FROM THE GREEK CHURCH.[31]

---

[18]AOR 21. [19]FC 24:289. [20]PCR 108. [21]IER, Migne PG 82 col. 132. [22]1 Pet 3:9. [23]ANF 1:33. [24]ANF 3:460. [25]See 1 Cor 1:24, 30. [26]See 1 Cor 1:30; 1 Jn 2:1. [27]See Is 9:6; Jn 14:26-27; Eph 2:13-17. [28]See Jn 3:16; 1 Cor 1:30; Eph 3:19; Heb 10:10. [29]CER 3:310, 314. [30]CSEL 81.1:269. [31]NTA 15:92.

Resurrected Life to Your Mortal Bodies. Chrysostom: Here Paul touches once more on the resurrection, since this was the most encouraging hope to the hearer, giving him a sense of security from what happened to Christ. . . . Therefore do not let your body live in this world, so that it may be made alive in the next one! Make it die so that it may never die! For if it goes on living it will die, but if it dies now it will live forever. This is the case with resurrection in general. We must first die and be buried, and then we shall become immortal. This has already been done in baptism. . . . The man who is dead to this life is thus the one who is most truly alive. Homilies on Romans 13.[32]

Finally Made Perfect. Augustine: Paul now explains the fourth of the four states[33] which we mentioned above. But this state is not attained in this life. It belongs to the hope by which we await the redemption of our body, when this corruptible matter will put on incorruption and immortality.[34] Then there will be perfect peace, because the soul will no longer be troubled by the body, which will be revived and transformed into a heavenly substance.[35] Augustine on Romans 51.[36]

Fleshly Annoyances Continue in This Life. Augustine: This is a very explicit witness to the resurrection of the body, and it is sufficiently clear that as long as we are in this life there will be no lack of both the annoyances occasioned by the mortal flesh and some excitations arising from carnal pleasures. For although he who is established under grace serves the law of God with his mind and does not yield, nevertheless, with the flesh he continues to serve the law of sin. Questions 66.7.[37]

The Temple Restored. Pelagius: God will not allow the temple of his Spirit to perish. In the same way as he raised Jesus from the dead he will also restore your body. Pelagius's Commentary on Romans.[38]

8:12 Debtors

The Soul Serving Its Creator. Origen: God did not make us in his image in order for us to be bound to the service of the flesh but rather that our soul, serving its Creator, might make use of the service and ministry of the flesh for that purpose. Commentary on the Epistle to the Romans.[39]

We Are Debtors. Ambrosiaster: It is right and clear that we are not obliged to follow Adam, who lived according to the flesh, and who by being the first to sin left us an inheritance of sin.[40] On the contrary, we ought rather to obey the law of Christ who, as was demonstrated above, has redeemed us spiritually from death. We are debtors to him who has washed our spirits, which had been sullied by carnal sins, in baptism, who has justified us and who has made us children of God.[41] Commentary on Paul's Epistles.[42]

Debtors Not to the Flesh. Chrysostom: Once again, Paul is not speaking here about the nature of the flesh. . . . For in many ways we are indebted to that. We have to give it food, warmth, rest, medicine, clothing and a thousand other things. In order to show us that this is not what he is talking about, Paul adds the words: "to live according to the flesh." . . . It is not to take charge of our life. The flesh must follow, not lead, and it must receive the laws of the Spirit, not seek to control us. Homilies on Romans 14.[43]

Pelagius: The force of this whole argument is to show that the law, which was given for the carnally minded, is not necessary for those who are spiritual. Pelagius's Commentary on Romans.[44]

---

[32]NPNF 1 11:436. [33]Natural, legal, evangelical and glorified. [34]1 Cor 15:53-54. [35]See Ezek 37:1-14; 1 Cor 15:12-55. [36]AOR 21. [37]FC 70:148. [38]PCR 108. [39]CER 3:316. [40]See Gen 3:13-19. [41]See Gal 3:24-26. [42]CSEL 81.1:269-71. [43]NPNF 1 11:440. [44]PCR 108.

Theodoret of Cyr: Since we have obtained salvation from Christ the Lord and have received the grace of the Spirit, we are obliged to serve him. Interpretation of the Letter to the Romans.[45]

8:13 Putting to Death the Works of the Flesh

Cutting Away Fleshly Lusts. Irenaeus: Paul does not prevent them from living their lives in the flesh, for he was himself in the flesh when he wrote to them, but he cuts away the lusts of the flesh which bring death upon a man. Against Heresies 5.10.2.[46]

Put to Death the Deeds of the Body. Origen: Putting to death the deeds of the body works like this: Love is a fruit of the Spirit,[47] but hate is an act of the flesh. Therefore hate is put to death and extinguished by love. Likewise, joy is a fruit of the Spirit,[48] but sadness is of this world, and because it brings death it is a work of the flesh. Therefore it is extinguished if the joy of the Spirit dwells in us. Peace is a fruit of the Spirit,[49] but dissension or discord is an act of the flesh; however, it is certain that discord can be eliminated by peace. Likewise the patience of the Spirit overcomes the impatience of the flesh, goodness wipes out evil, meekness does away with ferocity, continence with intemperance, chastity with license and so on.

By "death" and "life," Paul does not mean physical death and life but the death of sin and eternal life, which everyone who is mature in the Spirit and who has put to death the works of the flesh will attain. But we must also realize that this mortification of the deeds of the flesh comes through patience—not suddenly but step by step. At first they start to wilt in those who have been converted, but then, as they progress in their faith and become more dedicated, the deeds of the flesh not only wilt, they start to die out. But when they reach maturity to the point that there is no longer any trace in them of any sinful thought, word or deed, then they may be reck-

oned to have completely mortified the deeds of the flesh and passed from death to life. Commentary on the Epistle to the Romans.[50]

Adoption as Children of God. Ambrose: It is not strange that one who puts to death the deeds of the flesh will live, since one who has the Spirit of God becomes a son of God.[51] It is for this reason that he is a son of God, so that he may receive not the spirit of slavery but the spirit of the adoption of sons, inasmuch as the Holy Spirit bears witness with our spirit that we are sons of God.[52] Letter 52.[53]

Led by the Holy Spirit. Ambrosiaster: Nothing is truer than this, that if we live according to Adam we shall die. For by sinning Adam was consigned to the flesh and sold himself to sin, for all sin is oriented to the flesh. . . . The body wants to be governed by the law of the spirit, which is why Paul shows that if we are led by the Holy Spirit the acts and desires of the flesh, which are made up by the instigation of the powers of this world, are repressed so as to be unable to act. Then we shall enjoy eternal life. Commentary on Paul's Epistles.[54]

You Will Live. Chrysostom: You can see from this that Paul is not talking about the essence of the body but about the evil deeds which it does. For if we stop doing evil deeds, then our physical bodies will live. Homilies on Romans 14.[55]

Augustine: That we *should* mortify the deeds of the flesh by the Spirit is *required* of us, but that we *may* live is *offered* to us. . . . Shall we therefore agree to say that the mortification of the flesh is not a gift of God and not confess it to be a gift of God, since we hear that it is required of us, with

---

[45]IER, Migne PG 82 col. 132. [46]ANF 1:536. [47]See Gal 5:22. [48]See Gal 5:22. [49]See Gal 5:22. [50]CER 3:318. [51]See Rom 8:14; 1 Jn 3:1. [52]See Rom 8:16. [53]FC 26:278. [54]CSEL 81.1:271. [55]NPNF 1 11:440.

life offered as a reward to us if we have done it? PREDESTINATION OF THE SAINTS 11.22.[56]

AUGUSTINE: When by our spirit we put to death the works of the flesh we are impelled by the Spirit of God, which grants the continence by which we restrain, master and overcome concupiscence. CONTINENCE 5.12.[57]

AUGUSTINE: I have quoted this passage so that I might make use of the apostle's words to deter your free will from evil and to exhort it to what is good. Nor should you on this account glory in man, i.e., in yourselves and not in the Lord. You are not living according to the flesh but are putting the deeds of the flesh to death by the Spirit. GRACE AND FREE WILL 11.23.[58]

YOU WILL DIE. [PSEUDO-]CONSTANTIUS: Here Paul clearly demonstrates that it was not common and natural human death of which he was speaking earlier. In fact he was and is speaking about the death of eternal punishment. For it is not because the flesh is evil and the spirit good that he praises the spirit and condemns the flesh. . . . Rather, he says this wanting to show that for the most part the lusts of our passions belong to the human body, which we share with irrational animals. For just as the other animals on earth are born, so our body is also born; it is our soul which is spiritual, incorporeal, rational and immortal. THE HOLY LETTER OF ST. PAUL TO THE ROMANS.[59]

PELAGIUS: Carnal people cannot preserve righteousness. But you will live if you have replaced the works of the flesh with spiritual deeds. Note that it is the works which are condemned, not the substance of the flesh. PELAGIUS'S COMMENTARY ON ROMANS.[60]

THEODORET OF CYR: Paul does not say that we should mortify the flesh but "the deeds of the flesh," that is, the wisdom of the flesh, the attacks of the passions. For we have the grace of the Spirit

to help us. Eternal life is the fruit of victory. INTERPRETATION OF THE LETTER TO THE ROMANS.[61]

8:14 The Spirit Leads the Children of God

WHETHER THERE ARE MANY SONS, MANY SPIRITS. ORIGEN: The Spirit of God is the same as the Spirit of Christ and the same as the Holy Spirit. But he is also called the Spirit of adoption, as the apostle makes clear in this passage. David spoke of this Spirit also when he said: "Take not thy Holy Spirit from me."[62] There are many sons of God, as Scripture says: "You are gods, sons of the Most High, all of you,"[63] . . . but only one is the Son by nature, the only begotten of the Father, through whom all the rest are called sons. Likewise there are many spirits but only one who truly proceeds from God himself and who bestows on all the others the grace of his name and his sanctification. COMMENTARY ON THE EPISTLE TO THE ROMANS.[64]

HIS TEMPLES. CYPRIAN: If we are the sons of God, if we have already begun to be his temples,[65] if (after receiving the Holy Spirit) we live holily and spiritually, if we have lifted up our eyes from the earth toward heaven, if we have raised our hearts, full of God and Christ, to supernal and divine things, let us do nothing which is not worthy of God and Christ, as the apostle arouses and urges us. JEALOUSY AND ENVY 14.[66]

LED BY THE SPIRIT. CHRYSOSTOM: Note the great honor here. For as believers we do not merely live in the Spirit; we are led by him as well. The Spirit is meant to have the same power over us as a pilot has over his ship or a charioteer over his horses. And it is not only the body but the soul also which is meant to be controlled in this way.

If you put your confidence in baptism to the

---

[56]FC 86:243. [57]FC 16:203. [58]FC 59:276. [59]ENPK 2:56. [60]PCR 108-9. [61]IER, Migne PG 82 col. 133. [62]Ps 51:11. [63]Ps 82:6. [64]CER 4:32. [65]See 1 Cor 3:16. [66]FC 36:304.

point that you neglect your behavior after it, Paul says that, even if you are baptized, if you are not led by the Spirit afterward you will lose the dignity bestowed on you and the honor of your adoption. This is why he does not talk about those who received the Spirit in the past but rather about those who are being led by the Spirit now. HOMILIES ON ROMANS 14.[67]

[PSEUDO-]CONSTANTIUS: Those who live according to the teaching of the Holy Spirit are those who are led by the Spirit of God. THE HOLY LETTER OF ST. PAUL TO THE ROMANS.[68]

PELAGIUS: This applies to all who are worthy to be governed by the Holy Spirit, just as (on the contrary) those who sin are moved by the spirit of the devil, who was a sinner from the beginning.[69] PELAGIUS'S COMMENTARY ON ROMANS.[70]

THEODORE OF MOPSUESTIA: It is clear that these people will live the blessed life with their Father. PAULINE COMMENTARY FROM THE GREEK CHURCH.[71]

DIVINE GRACE AND HUMAN WILLING. PROSPER OF AQUITAINE: Since the Lord prepares the will, he also touches the hearts of his children with fatherly inspirations so that they might do good.... Consequently, we do not think that our free will is lacking, nor do we doubt that, in each and every movement of man's free will, his help is the stronger force. GRACE AND FREE WILL 5.3.[72]

8:15 The Spirit of Sonship

OUR REAL FATHER. CLEMENT OF ALEXANDRIA: We have received the Spirit to enable us to know the one to whom we pray, our real Father, the one and only Father of all, that is, the one who like a Father educates us for salvation and does away with fear. STROMATA 3.11.78.5.[73]

THE SPIRIT OF BONDAGE AND OF ADOPTION.

ORIGEN: It is certain that whoever will become a son of God by the Spirit of adoption will first become a servant of God by the spirit of slavery. For the beginning of service to God is to be filled with the spirit of fear when still a little child [= new convert], since "the fear of the Lord is the beginning of wisdom."[74] ... As long as we remain children in the inner man we hold the Spirit in fear, until we reach the point at which we can rightfully receive the Spirit of adoption as sons and become like the Son and Lord of all. For Paul says: "Everything is yours,"[75] and God has given us everything together with Christ. This is why Paul says that, after we have died together with Christ and after his Spirit comes into us, we no longer receive the spirit of slavery in fear (that is, we do not return to the state of children, and we have completed the first stages of faith), but rather like perfect people we have received the Spirit of adoption, in whom we cry: "Abba! Father!" COMMENTARY ON THE EPISTLE TO THE ROMANS.[76]

DIODORE: In reality, the spirit of slavery and the spirit of sonship were one and the same Spirit, who was given to people according to what they deserved, whether it was good or evil. PAULINE COMMENTARY FROM THE GREEK CHURCH.[77]

THE ASSURANCE THAT DARES TO SAY "ABBA, FATHER." AMBROSIASTER: Paul says this because once we have received the Holy Spirit we are delivered from all fear of evil deeds, so that we might no longer act in such a way as to be afraid once more.[78] Beforehand we were under fear, because once the law was given everyone was considered guilty. Paul called the law "the spirit of fear" because it made people afraid on account of their sins. But the law of faith, which is what is meant by "the Spirit of sonship," is a law of assurance, because it has delivered us from fear by par-

---

[67]NPNF 1 11:440-41. [68]ENPK 2:56. [69]1 Jn 3:8. [70]PCR 109. [71]NTA 15:135. [72]FC 7:358. [73]FC 85:304. [74]Prov 9:10. [75]1 Cor 3:22. [76]CER 4:36, 38. [77]NTA 15:92. [78]See Hag 2:5; 2 Tim 1:7.

doning our sins and thus giving us assurance.[79]

Set free by the grace of God from fear, we have received the Spirit of sonship so that, considering what we were and what we have become by the gift of God, we might govern our life with great care lest the name of God the Father be disgraced by us and we incur all the things we have escaped from.... We have received such grace that we can dare to say to God: "Abba! Father!" For this reason, Paul warns us not to let our trust degenerate into pride. For if our behavior does not correspond to our voice when we cry, "Abba! Father!" we insult God by calling him Father. Indeed, God in his goodness has indulged us with what is beyond our natural capacity. COMMENTARY ON PAUL'S EPISTLES.[80]

CHRYSOSTOM: Paul does not mention the spirit of freedom but passes immediately to the matter of sonship, which obviously includes freedom in it. That much is obvious. However, it is less clear what the spirit of slavery might be. What Paul says here is not only unclear, it is downright perplexing. For the Jews did not receive the Spirit. So what does he mean? It is the letter to which he gives this name, for it was also spiritual, which is why he calls the law, the water from the rock and the manna spiritual as well.[81] ... Paul uses the Hebrew word *Abba* to indicate that sonship given by the Spirit is true sonship. HOMILIES ON ROMANS 14.[82]

THE SPIRIT OF SLAVERY TO FEAR AND TO LOVE. AUGUSTINE: The dispensations of the two Testaments are clearly different. The Old Testament is one of fear; the New Testament is one of love. But, you may ask, what is this spirit of slavery? If the spirit of our adoption as sons is the Holy Spirit, then the spirit of slavery to fear is the one which has the power of death. It is because of this fear that those who lived under the law and not under grace were condemned to slavery for their entire lives. Nor is it surprising that those who went after worldly goods received the spirit of slavery by divine providence ... for this spirit of slavery has nobody in its power unless he has

been handed over by the command of divine providence, since God's righteousness gives every man his due. AUGUSTINE ON ROMANS 52.[83]

AUGUSTINE: The fear of slaves, although it renders belief to the Master, contains no love of righteousness but only the fear of damnation. The cry of sons is "Abba, Father!"—two words, one of which belongs to the circumcision and the other to the uncircumcision. THE SPIRIT AND THE LETTER 56.[84]

AUGUSTINE: Paul is speaking of the fear which was inspired in the Old Testament, lest the temporal be lost which God had promised to those who were not yet his sons under grace but still servants under the law. HOLY VIRGINITY 38.39.[85]

SLAVES FEAR; SONS LOVE. PELAGIUS: The Jews received a spirit which constrained them into service by means of fear. For it is the nature of slaves to fear and of sons to love, as it is written: "The slave shall fear his master, and the son shall love his father."[86] Those who were not willing to work out of the desire of love are compelled by the constraint of fear, but let us perform all things willingly so that we may show that we are sons. He who calls to his father declares himself a son. He ought therefore to resemble his father in character, lest he incur a greater penalty for having assumed the name of his father in vain.[87] PELAGIUS'S COMMENTARY ON ROMANS.[88]

THEODORE OF MOPSUESTIA: The text should be read like this: "You have not received the Spirit; instead you are again in fear of slavery." ... The slavery in question is slavery to the law.[89] PAULINE COMMENTARY FROM THE GREEK CHURCH.[90]

---

[79]See Is 32:17-18; 1 Thess 1:4-5; Heb 10:22. [80]CSEL 81.1:273-75. [81]See Ex 16:15; 17:6; 1 Cor 10:3-4. [82]NPNF 1 11:441. [83]AOR 23. [84]LCC 8:239. [85]FC 27:190. [86]Mal 1:6. [87]See Ex 20:7; Deut 5:11. [88]PCR 109. [89]See Gal 4:24. [90]NTA 15:136.

CYRIL OF ALEXANDRIA: We have been enriched with God's Spirit, for his Spirit has come to dwell in our hearts, and we have taken our place among the children of God and yet have not lost being what we are. For we are men according to nature, even though we cry: "Abba! Father!" LETTER 1.35.[91]

THE SPIRIT OF SONSHIP. NICETA OF REMESIANA: If he is the Spirit of adoption and makes men sons of God, how can he be considered a slave, since no slave can legitimately make another free? POWER OF THE HOLY SPIRIT 4.[92]

BEDE: Through the grace of baptism men can by receiving the Holy Spirit be changed from sons of the devil into sons of God.[93] HOMILIES ON THE GOSPEL 1.12.[94]

8:16 The Spirit Bears Witness

THE SPIRIT BEARING WITNESS WITH OUR SPIRITS. ORIGEN: The Spirit of adoption . . . bears witness and assures our spirits that we are children of God after we have passed from the spirit of slavery and come under the Spirit of adoption, when all fear has departed. We no longer act out of fear of punishment but do everything out of love for the Father. It is right too that the Spirit of God should be said to bear witness with our spirits and not with our souls, because the spirit is our better part. COMMENTARY ON THE EPISTLE TO THE ROMANS.[95]

DIODORE: Paul showed by this that he called the soul "spirit" when it was spiritual, and the gift of the Spirit "Spirit." PAULINE COMMENTARY FROM THE GREEK CHURCH.[96]

AMBROSIASTER: The witness of children is that by the Spirit they should be seen to bear the sign of the Father. COMMENTARY ON PAUL'S EPISTLES.[97]

THE GIFT AND THE GIVER. CHRYSOSTOM: This means that the Comforter bears witness with the gift which he has given us. For it is not merely the gift which speaks but the Comforter who gave the gift as well. HOMILIES ON ROMANS 14.[98]

EVIDENCE OF OUR ADOPTION. PELAGIUS: The evidence of our adoption is that we have the Spirit, through whom we pray in the manner mentioned above; for only sons could receive such a pledge. PELAGIUS'S COMMENTARY ON ROMANS.[99]

HIS SPIRIT AND OURS. THEODORET OF CYR: Paul uses the word *spirit* in two senses. The first is the Spirit of God, the second is our spirit, i.e., through the grace which we have been given. INTERPRETATION OF THE LETTER TO THE ROMANS.[100]

8:17 Fellow Heirs with Christ

GLORIFIED WITH HIM. ORIGEN: The Son of God says to his fellow heirs: "You will also sit on twelve thrones, judging the twelve tribes of Israel."[101] Thus Christ leads his fellow heirs not only into a part of the inheritance but into a sharing of his power. COMMENTARY ON THE EPISTLE TO THE ROMANS.[102]

PROVIDED WE SUFFER WITH HIM. DIODORE: Here "suffer with him" does not mean that we should sympathize and come to the aid of the sufferer, as it usually does in everyday parlance. Christ did not suffer in order to get attention, nor did he undergo weakness in order to gain the sympathy of those who felt sorry for him. To suffer with Christ means to endure the same sufferings that he was forced to suffer by the Jews because he preached the gospel. . . . If we suffer with him we shall be worthy to be glorified with him as well. This glory is the reward of our sufferings and is not to be regarded as a free gift. The free gift is that we have received remission of our

---

[91]FC 76:31. [92]FC 7:27. [93]See 1 Jn 3:8-9. [94]CSEL 110:119. [95]CER 4:38. [96]NTA 15:92. [97]CSEL 81.1:275. [98]NPNF 1 11:442. [99]PCR 109. [100]IER, Migne PG 136 ad loc. [101]See Mt 19:28. [102]CER 4:40.

former sins.[103] PAULINE COMMENTARY FROM THE GREEK CHURCH.[104]

HEIRS OF ONE STILL ALIVE. AMBROSIASTER: Since there is no way that God the Father can be said to have died and Christ the Son is said to have died because of his having become flesh. How is it that he who died is always said to be the heir of the life, when heirs are normally heirs of the dead? But of course Christ died in his humanity, not in his divinity. For with God, which is where our inheritance lies, the Father's gift is poured into his obedient children, so that one who is alive may be the heir of the Living One by his own merit and not by reason of death. . . . What it means to be a fellow heir with Christ we are taught by the apostle John, for among other things he says: "We know that when he appears we shall be like him."[105]. . .

To suffer together with Christ is to endure persecutions in the hope of future rewards and to crucify the flesh with its evils and lusts, i.e., to reject the pleasures and pomp of this world. For when all these things are dead in a man, then he has crucified this world, believing in the life of the world to come in which he believes that he will be a fellow heir with Christ. COMMENTARY ON PAUL'S EPISTLES.[106]

CHILD AND HEIR. CHRYSOSTOM: Notice how Paul gradually increases the attraction of the gift. For it is quite possible to be a child without being an heir. . . . Nor are we simply heirs; we are "fellow heirs with Christ." See how concerned Paul is to bring us ever nearer to the Son! HOMILIES ON ROMANS 14.[107]

ADOPTED INTO THE KINGDOM. AUGUSTINE: By spiritual regeneration we therefore become sons and are adopted into the kingdom of God, not as aliens but as his creatures and offspring. SERMON ON THE MOUNT 23.78.[108]

READY IF NECESSARY TO SUFFER. PELAGIUS: He who is worthy to be a son is worthy to be made an heir of the Father and a coheir with the true Son. This happens if we are ready when it becomes necessary to suffer for him as he suffered for us. PELAGIUS'S COMMENTARY ON ROMANS.[109]

CYRIL OF ALEXANDRIA: Good works can hardly be done without suffering, yet the suffering of the saints is nourished by a great hope. For nothing earthly is promised but rather eternal glory. EXPLANATION OF THE LETTER TO THE ROMANS.[110]

FELLOW HEIRS WITH CHRIST. THEODORET OF CYR: As not every son is an heir of the one who procreated him, St. Paul rightly adds heredity to the adoption of sons. And given that a friend may often receive some inheritance from the Lord, Paul does not omit the word *son* but even adds that we are "fellow heirs with Christ," thereby revealing his ineffable love for mankind. For not all those who have been blessed with saving baptism enjoy these good things, but only those who accept the fellowship of the Lord's sufferings as well. INTERPRETATION OF THE LETTER TO THE ROMANS.[111]

---

[103]See Rom 5:15-18. [104]NTA 15:93. [105]1 Jn 3:2. [106]CSEL 81.1:275-77. [107]NPNF 1 11:442. [108]FC 11:106. [109]PCR 109. [110]Migne PG 74 col. 821. [111]IER, Migne PG 82 col. 136.

8:18-22 THE HOPE OF CREATION

[18]I consider that the sufferings of this present time are not worth comparing with the glory that is to be revealed to us. [19]For the creation waits with eager longing for the revealing of the sons of God; [20]for the creation was subjected to futility, not of its own will but by the will of him who subjected it in hope; [21]because the creation itself will be set free from its bondage to decay and obtain the glorious liberty of the children of God. [22]We know that the whole creation has been groaning in travail together until now.

OVERVIEW: The early Christians were acutely aware of the sufferings of the present time, so it is not surprising to discover that the Fathers paid great attention to Romans 8:18. The future glory was a major expectation in a world beset by warfare, poverty and disease, but this was not their only motivation. They genuinely wanted to leave the temporal sphere and be united with the eternal, and they looked forward to the day when the transitory would give way to the permanent, the shadow to the real. The Fathers were not of one mind about how to interpret "the creation waits with eager longing." To some, Paul seemed to be personifying the inanimate order, as happens in the Old Testament. But to others it seemed that the apostle was referring only to the rational creatures, since they alone would benefit from the revealing of the sons of God. Some of the Fathers viewed creation as human creation, while others viewed the "whole creation" as the natural order grieving over sin, groaning by analogy with human groaning. The Fathers had some difficulty with Romans 8:20, because of their uncertainty about the meaning of the word *futility*. To some it meant sin, to others death, to others corruption. But all were agreed that futility was essentially temporal and that when the fullness of Christ was revealed, it would vanish in the greater light of eternity.

8:18 Present Suffering; Glories to Be Revealed

THE SPIRIT AS PLEDGE OF GLORY TO BE REVEALED. MONTANIST ORACLE: He who has given the cause of the gifts will also give their consequences,[1] and for this reason the Spirit has been said to be the pledge of the glory which will be revealed. TESTIMONIA.[2]

INCOMPARABILITY. ORIGEN: There is nothing which is worthy of comparison with the future glory. For how can what is mortal be compared to what is immortal, what is visible to what is invisible, what is temporal to what is eternal or what is perishable to what is everlasting? COMMENTARY ON THE EPISTLE TO THE ROMANS.[3]

CYPRIAN: Who then does not labor in every way to arrive at such a glory as to become a friend of God, as to rejoice at once with Christ, as to receive the divine rewards after earthly torments and punishments? EXHORTATION TO MARTYRDOM, TO FORTUNATUS 13.[4]

MEDITATE ON GLORY. CYPRIAN: It is fitting for us, meditating upon the glory of this splendor, to endure all afflictions and persecutions because, although the afflictions of the just are many, yet those who trust in God are delivered from them all.[5] LETTER 6.2.[6]

---

[1]The apparent meaning is that God sends the Spirit, who distributes gifts and brings them to fulfillment. [2]MOT 125. [3]CER 4:44. [4]FC 36:343. [5]See 2 Sam 22:3-4; Ps 18:2-3. [6]FC 51:18.

CONSOLED BY HOPE. AMBROSIASTER: This exhortation relates to what we have just read, in which Paul shows that the things which we might suffer at the hands of the wicked here below are small in comparison with the reward which awaits us in the next life. Therefore we ought to be prepared for every eventuality, because the rewards which are promised to us are so great so that our mind may be consoled in tribulation and grow in hope. COMMENTARY ON PAUL'S EPISTLES.[7]

CHRYSOSTOM: Whatever these sufferings may be, they belong to this present life, but the blessings to come stretch out forever. Since Paul had no way of giving a detailed description of these or of putting them before us in human language, he gives them a name which is used of things we especially desire: *glory*. HOMILIES ON ROMANS 14.[8]

CHRYSOSTOM: Even if each day we suffer death, something which nature could not endure even if mind overcomes matter . . . what we endure is nothing compared to the good things we are destined to receive or the glory due to be revealed on our behalf. HOMILIES ON GENESIS 25.23.[9]

NOT WORTH COMPARING. JEROME: Do you dread poverty? Christ calls the poor blessed.[10] Does toil frighten you? No athlete is crowned but in the sweat of his brow. Are you anxious as regards food? Faith fears no famine.[11] Do you dread the bare ground for limbs wasted with fasting? The Lord lies there beside you. Do you recoil from an unwashed head and uncombed hair? Christ is your head. Does the boundless solitude of the desert terrify you? In the Spirit you may walk always in paradise. Do but turn your thoughts there and you will be no more in the desert. Is your skin rough and scaly because you no longer bathe? He that is once washed in Christ has no need to wash again.[12] To all your objections the apostle gives this one brief answer: "The sufferings of this present time are not worth comparing with the glory that is to be revealed in us." LETTER 14.10.[13]

THEIR OWN CONSOLATIONS. AUGUSTINE: The humble and holy servants of God who suffer doubly when temporal evils befall them, because they suffer with the wicked as well as at their hands, have their own consolations and the hope of the world to come. LETTER 111.[14]

HIDDEN GLORY. PELAGIUS: Paul wants to commend future glory so that we may bear present afflictions more easily. Indeed, no human being could ever suffer anything equal to heavenly glory, even if that glory were comparable to this present life. For whatever a man might suffer in dying is no more that what he already deserved to suffer for his sins. But now his sins are forgiven, and in the future he will be granted eternal life, fellowship with the angels, the splendor of the sun and the other things which we have read have been promised for the saints.[15] At the moment, though, this future glory is "hidden with Christ in God,"[16] and "it does not yet appear what we shall be."[17] PELAGIUS'S COMMENTARY ON ROMANS.[18]

THE SAINTS HUMBLE US. BEDE: When we see such extraordinary heirs of the heavenly kingdom suffering so greatly during the time of their mortal exile, what remains for us to do under these circumstances . . . except to humble ourselves all the more in the sight of our benevolent Maker and Redeemer, as we become more clearly aware that we cannot follow them by imitating either their lives or their deaths? HOMILIES ON THE GOSPELS 2.23.[19]

8:19 Creation Waits to Be Restored

CREATION RESTORED. IRENAEUS: God is rich in

[7]CSEL 81.1:277. [8]NPNF 1 11:443. [9]FC 82:142. [10]See Lk 6:20. [11]See Mt 6:25, 31; Lk 12:22. [12]Jn 13:10. [13]LCC 5:300. [14]FC 18:247. [15]See Dan 12:2-3; Mt 13:41-43; Rev 7:9-17. [16]Col 3:3. [17]1 Jn 3:2. [18]PCR 109-10. [19]CSEL 111:239.

all things, and everything is his. It is therefore fitting that the creation itself, having been restored to its primeval condition, should without restraint be under the dominion of the righteous.[20] Against Heresies 5.32.1.[21]

The Revealing. Origen: Paul says this in order to indicate how great and wonderful is the glory which will be revealed both in him and in those who have shared his sufferings. Commentary on the Epistle to the Romans.[22]

Creation Personified as Living. Diodore: The Scriptures often suggest that the visible creation is animate and that the universe has a rational sensibility.[23] Pauline Commentary from the Greek Church.[24]

Chrysostom: Here Paul's discourse becomes more emphatic, and he personifies the creation in the way that the prophets do when they speak of the floods, clapping their hands and so on.[25] Homilies on Romans 14.[26]

In Eager Longing. [Pseudo-]Constantius: When Paul talks here about the creation waiting, he means the rational creation and not, as some think, the irrational or insensible creation which was made in order to serve man and which afterward will perish.... "Creation" refers to Adam and Eve, who are waiting to receive adoption by God. The "eager longing" was shared by Adam and Eve on the one hand and by the angels and the elements, i.e., the heavens, the earth, the sun, the moon and the stars, on the other.... Paul says that Adam and Eve were longing for the day of judgment. The Holy Letter of St. Paul to the Romans.[27]

Alternative Readings. Pelagius: Different interpreters expound this passage in different ways. Some say that the whole creation awaits the time of the resurrection, because then it will be changed into something better. Others say that this refers only to the angelic, rational cre-

ation.[28] Still others say that "creation" refers specifically to Adam and Eve, because they did not sin by themselves but at the temptation of the serpent, who long ago made them subject to corruption when they were exposed to deception in the hope of divine existence.[29] These interpreters say that Adam and Eve will be set free so that they are no longer subject to corruption. But the "whole creation," say these same interpreters, means all those who were righteous up to the coming of Christ, because they too have not yet received and are waiting until God provides something better for us.[30] Not only they, however, but we also, in whom these things have been fulfilled, do not yet hold it in our grasp but endure in hope, although we have seen things which many righteous people have longed to see.[31] Pelagius's Commentary on Romans.[32]

Theodore of Mopsuestia: Paul is referring here to the resurrection on the last day. Pauline Commentary from the Greek Church.[33]

Sons of God Transformed. Cyril of Alexandria: The creation is waiting for the revelation of the sons of God at some point in the future which is still unknown. Who can know when this will be? But by the secret plan of God, which orders all things for the best, it will come to this end. For when the sons of God, who have lived a righteous life, have been transformed into glory from dishonor and from what is corruptible into what is incorruptible, then the creation too will be transformed into something better.[34] Explanation of the Letter to the Romans.[35]

8:20 Creation Subjected to Futility

Not of Its Own Will. Origen: What is this futility to which the creation is said to be subject?

[20]See Is 65:17-25; 1 Cor 6:2-3; 2 Pet 3:13. [21]ANF 1:561. [22]CER 4:48. [23]See Ps 19:1-4. [24]NTA 15:93. [25]See Ps 98:8. [26]NPNF 1 11:444. [27]ENPK 2:57-58. [28]See 1 Pet 1:12. [29]See Gen 3:5. [30]Heb 11:39-40. [31]See Mt 13:17; Lk 10:24. [32]PCR 110. [33]NTA 15:138. [34]See also 1 Cor 15:54. [35]Migne PG 74 col. 821.

It seems to me that this is said about the material and corruptible substance of the body. Likewise with the decay mentioned [in the next verse]. Commentary on the Epistle to the Romans.[36]

Subjected to Futility. Origen: The moon and the stars have been compelled against their will to be subject to futility, as a result of causes long past; yet in the hope of a future reward they do not do their own will but the will of the Creator, by whom they have been appointed to these duties. On First Principles 2.8.3.[37]

Origen: What is the futility to which the creation was subjected? My own opinion is that this is nothing else than the possession of bodies. Even though the bodies of the stars are composed of ether they are nevertheless material. This, it seems to me, is the reason why Solomon arraigns the whole universe as being in a way burdensome: "Vanity of vanities, says the preacher. . . . All is vanity."[38] On First Principles 1.7.5.[39]

Ambrose: Creation itself will also be delivered from its slavery to corruption when the grace of divine reward shines forth. Six Days of Creation 1.6.22.[40]

Ambrosiaster: The subjection of the creation is not for its benefit but for ours. What does it mean to be subject to futility but that what it produces is worthless? For the creation works in order to bring forth corruptible fruit. Corruption therefore is itself futility. Commentary on Paul's Epistles.[41]

Humans Impact Creation. Chrysostom: Paul means by this that the creation became corruptible. Why and for what reason? Because of you, O man! For because you have a body which has become mortal and subject to suffering, the earth too has received a curse and has brought forth thorns and thistles.[42] . . . The creation suffered badly because of you, and it became cor-

ruptible, but it has not been irreparably damaged. For it will become incorruptible once again for your sake.[43] This is the meaning of "in hope." Homilies on Romans 14.[44]

Futility as Transgression. [Pseudo-]Constantius: "Futility" means "transgression," to which Eve was subject not by her own will but by the deception of the serpent, which gave her the hope that she and Adam would become like gods, knowing good and evil.[45] "Subjected" refers to the corruption of mortality, but in the resurrection they will receive the incorrupt nature of the sons of God. The Holy Letter of St. Paul to the Romans.[46]

Pelagius: "Futility" means everything which will someday come to an end. Pelagius's Commentary on Romans.[47]

Whether Creation Understands. Cyril of Alexandria: The visible and tangible creation knows nothing of the promises which have been made to us because it has no understanding of them. For if it should ever happen that the creation acquired some understanding of these things, it would hardly endure such base servitude, nor would it want to be subject to or be on friendly terms with those whose lives bear no good fruit. Nevertheless, Paul says that the creation is subject in hope, for one day the saints and the elect will be saved, and then the yoke which has been imposed on it by God will be removed. . . . In the meantime, the creation groans and in some sense labors and grieves, and if it had any awareness of our works, probably it would burst out crying. Explanation of the Letter to the Romans.[48]

Futility as Corruption. Theodoret of

---

[36]CER 4:50. [37]OFP 127. [38]Eccles 1:2. [39]OFP 63. [40]FC 42:23. [41]CSEL 81.1:279. [42]See Gen 3:18. [43]See Rom 8:21. [44]NPNF 1 11:444. [45]Gen 3:5. [46]ENPK 2:58. [47]PCR 110. [48]Migne PG 74 col. 821.

CYR: "Futility" means corruption. Paul teaches this a little further on when he says that the creation itself will be set free from corruption. He also teaches that all the visible creation has been condemned to mortality because the Creator of all things foresaw the sin of Adam and that he would sentence him to death. INTERPRETATION OF THE LETTER TO THE ROMANS.[49]

8:21 Creation Will Be Freed

THE GLORIOUS LIBERTY. AMBROSE: Paul shows that the grace of the soul is no small thing, for by its strength and power the human race rises to the adoption of sons of God, having in itself that which was given to it in the image and likeness of God.[50] LETTER 51.[51]

CREATION NOT WITHOUT HOPE. AMBROSIASTER: Because the creation cannot contradict its Creator it is subjected because of him, but not without hope. For in its travail it has this comfort, that it will have rest when all those who will believe and for whose sake it was subjected in the first place will have come to faith. COMMENTARY ON PAUL'S EPISTLES.[52]

CHRYSOSTOM: Where man leads the creation will follow, since it was made for man. HOMILIES ON ROMANS 14.[53]

CREATION WILL BE SET FREE. JEROME: When the children of God attain glory, creation itself will be delivered from its slavery. HOMILIES ON THE PSALMS 58.[54]

PELAGIUS: Creation will no longer serve those who have corrupted the image of God. PELAGIUS'S COMMENTARY ON ROMANS.[55]

8:22 Creation Groans

THE ANALOGY OF GROANING. ORIGEN: We must understand this in the same way as we understand Paul's groaning on account of the gos-

pel for those whom he has brought to the light by faith in Christ, or as he said elsewhere: "My little children, with whom I am again in travail until Christ be formed in you!"[56] COMMENTARY ON THE EPISTLE TO THE ROMANS.[57]

AWAITING RELEASE FROM SIN. AMBROSE: The moon toils for you and by reason of the will of God is made subject. . . . It is you who undergo changes of your own volition, not the moon. The moon groans and travails in pain in its changes. You without understanding often find joy in this. The moon frequently awaits your release from sin, so that it may be released from the servitude in which all creation shares. But you place obstacles in the way of your release from sin and to the moon's freedom. The fact that you yourself still await that conversion which fails to come, whereas the moon suffers change, is the result not of the moon's folly but of yours. SIX DAYS OF CREATION 4.8.31.[58]

THE GRIEF OF CREATION. AMBROSIASTER: To groan in travail is to grieve. . . . The elements themselves show forth their works with care, for both the sun and the moon fill the spaces allotted to them not without travail, and the spirit of the animals demonstrates its servitude by loud groanings. All these are waiting for rest and to be set free from their servile labor. Now if this service were of any benefit to God the creation would be rejoicing, not grieving. But every day it watches its labor disappear. Every day its work appears and vanishes. Therefore it is right to grieve, because its work leads not to eternity but to corruption. COMMENTARY ON PAUL'S EPISTLES.[59]

CHRYSOSTOM: Paul says this in order to shame his hearers. He is virtually saying: "Do not be worse than the creation, and do not derive plea-

---

[49]IER, Migne PG 82 cols. 136-37. [50]See Gen 1:26-27. [51]FC 26:273. [52]CSEL 81.1:281. [53]NPNF 1 11:445. [54]FC 48:418. [55]PCR 110. [56]Gal 4:19. [57]CER 4:58. [58]FC 42:155. [59]CSEL 81.1:281-83.

sure from the things of this life. Not only should we not cling to them; we should be groaning at the slowness of our departure from this world. For if this is how the creation behaves, you ought to do so all the more, seeing as you have the gift of reason." HOMILIES ON ROMANS 14.[60]

WHETHER CREATION REFERS TO HUMAN CREATION. AUGUSTINE: This is not to be understood simply as meaning that trees, vegetables, stones and the like sorrow and sigh—this is the error of the Manichaeans—nor should we think that the holy angels are subject to vanity or that they will be set free from the slavery of death, since they are immortal. Here "the creation" means the human race. AUGUSTINE ON ROMANS 53.[61]

AUGUSTINE: Every creature is represented in man, not because all the angels . . . are in him, nor the heaven, earth, sea and all that is in them, but because the human creature is partly spirit, partly soul and partly body. QUESTIONS 67.5.[62]

[PSEUDO-]CONSTANTIUS: Here Paul gives the common designation of "creation" to all the righteous from Adam and Eve up to the time of Christ, saying that they too groaned along with Adam and Eve, desiring to receive the reward of virtue which the Lord had promised to them, viz., the adoption of sons. THE HOLY LETTER OF ST. PAUL TO THE ROMANS.[63]

PELAGIUS: Just as the angels rejoice over those who repent,[64] so they grieve over those who are unwilling to repent. PELAGIUS'S COMMENTARY ON ROMANS.[65]

THEODORE OF MOPSUESTIA: How did the whole creation suffer this? The invisible creatures did it by thinking and feeling; the visible creatures did it by sharing in the thing itself. PAULINE COMMENTARY FROM THE GREEK CHURCH.[66]

---

[60]NPNF 1 11:445. [61]AOR 23. [62]FC 70:153. [63]ENPK 2:59. [64]Lk 15:10. [65]PCR 110. [66]NTA 15:139.

8:23-27 THE HOPE OF GOD'S CHILDREN

[23]*And not only the creation, but we ourselves, who have the first fruits of the Spirit, groan inwardly as we wait for adoption as sons, the redemption of our bodies.* [24]*For in this hope we were saved. Now hope that is seen is not hope. For who hopes for what he sees?* [25]*But if we hope for what we do not see, we wait for it with patience.*

[26]*Likewise the Spirit helps us in our weakness; for we do not know how to pray as we ought, but the Spirit himself intercedes for us with sighs too deep for words.* [27]*And he who searches the hearts of men knows what is the mind of the Spirit, because*[j] *the Spirit intercedes for the saints according to the will of God.*

j Or *that*

OVERVIEW: Christians share in the groaning of creation as it waits for the revelation of God.

This is because we know what is coming and can hardly wait for it to be fulfilled in us. The eschatological perspective of the Fathers is clear from the call to hope, which by definition refers to things we do not yet see. The virtue of patience was dear to the Fathers, as appears from what they have to say about Romans 8:25. Christians were to continue to expect Christ's second coming at any moment, but they were not to despair if he did not return when they expected him. Prayer is effective only when it is offered in the Spirit. This was a major preoccupation of the Fathers, who were acutely conscious of the dangers of unanswered prayer, which might turn people away from their faith. Prayer in the Spirit is prayer according to the will of God, not according to our own desires.

8:23 Awaiting Redemption of Our Bodies

FIRST FRUITS. ORIGEN: Even though because of the fact that we believe in Christ our salvation is assured, nevertheless it still remains something to be hoped for; it has not yet been realized.

There are different ways of interpreting "the first fruits of the Spirit." Just as the first fruits of the threshing floor and the wine press[1] are of the same substance as what follows, is it not also true that the Holy Spirit is the first and best of a multitude of other spirits? So to have the first fruits of the Spirit means to have the Holy Spirit, as opposed to a host of other ministering spirits.

The first fruits may also refer to the many gifts of the Spirit.[2] . . . We apostles, says Paul, have the first fruits of the Spirit, because we were chosen to groan in travail as the Spirit himself does. There is no creature so free of sorrows and sighings that we, who have received the highest and choicest gifts of the Spirit, are not obliged to grieve and sigh over, awaiting the adoption of sons, that is, the perfection of those whom we have been sent to teach and instruct until we see them making enough progress that they deserve to be adopted as sons.

A third possibility is that the first fruits of the Spirit refers to Christ himself, since he is the first born of every creature.[3] COMMENTARY ON THE EPISTLE TO THE ROMANS.[4]

ADOPTION AS SONS. AMBROSE: The adoption as sons is the redemption of the whole body. LETTER 52.[5]

WORLD AS STORMY OCEAN. AMBROSIASTER: For Christians, this world is like the ocean. For just as the sea is whipped up by adverse winds and produces storms for sailors, so also this world, moved by the scheming of wicked men, disturbs the minds of believers. And the enemy does this in so many different ways that it is hard to know what to avoid first, for sources of tribulation are by no means wanting. COMMENTARY ON PAUL'S EPISTLES.[6]

WE OURSELVES GROAN INWARDLY. CHRYSOSTOM: If the first fruits are enough to free us from our sins and give us righteousness and sanctification . . . consider how wonderful the whole inheritance must be. If the creation, devoid as it is of a mind and reason and therefore ignorant of these things, nevertheless groans, much more should we groan as well. Next, so as not to give any comfort to the heretics, he says that we do not groan because of the inadequacies of the present system but because we desire something which is much better. HOMILIES ON ROMANS 14.[7]

AUGUSTINE: Paul now speaks about those of us who already believe. For although we serve the law of God with our spirit (i.e., our mind), our flesh still serves the law of sin for as long as we suffer mortal pains and anxieties. . . . Adoption is already guaranteed for those who believe, but it has been accomplished only spiritually, not physically. The body has not yet received its heavenly transformation, although the spirit, which has turned from its errors to God, has already been

---

[1]See Num 18:27. [2]See 1 Cor 12:4-11. [3]Col 1:15. [4]CER 4:60-62, 66-68. [5]FC 26:281. [6]CSEL 81.1:283. [7]NPNF 1 11:445.

changed through the reconciliation of faith. Therefore even believers still await the revelation which will come in the resurrection of the body. This is the fourth state, when everything will be in perfect peace at eternal rest, completely free of malignant corruption or nagging torment.[8] AUGUSTINE ON ROMANS 53.[9]

[PSEUDO-]CONSTANTIUS: By saying "not only the creation but we ourselves" Paul made it clear that he was not talking about the irrational or insensible creation, which does not partake of the Holy Spirit, but was speaking rather of the saints who pleased God according to the natural law, as well as the disciples of Moses. But the disciples of Christ are said to have the first fruits, the first and most brilliant spiritual gifts by which they impressed the whole world; for there had not been such great grace before the law or in the law of Moses.... By "the redemption of our body," Paul shows that in Christ we are one body. THE HOLY LETTER OF ST. PAUL TO THE ROMANS.[10]

PELAGIUS: Not only do the angels, who are kinder than we are, grieve over these unrepentant people, but we who have the Holy Spirit groan for such people.[11] PELAGIUS'S COMMENTARY ON ROMANS.[12]

THE STRUGGLE CONTINUES. CYRIL OF ALEXANDRIA: The corruptible body weighs down the soul, and the earthly body pulls down a mind full of cares. For as soon as the Spirit comes to dwell in us and turns us to the study of virtue, the love of the flesh jumps up to combat it, and the law in our members, which is prone to silly lusts, begins a bitter struggle. That is why we groan waiting for the liberation of our bodies as a result of the adoption. EXPLANATION OF THE LETTER TO THE ROMANS.[13]

8:24 Hope Is Not Seen

HOPE SEEN IS NOT HOPE. ORIGEN: I have already spoken in general terms about hope, but

here I would add only that Paul teaches us not to expect that in the future life we shall possess any of the things which we can see here and now, for all these things will pass away. COMMENTARY ON THE EPISTLE TO THE ROMANS.[14]

IN THIS HOPE WE WERE SAVED. AMBROSIASTER: By hoping for what God has promised to us in Christ, we have made ourselves worthy of deliverance. Therefore we have been set free in the hope that what is coming in the future is no different from what we believe. COMMENTARY ON PAUL'S EPISTLES.[15]

CHRYSOSTOM: What Paul means is that we are not to expect everything to be given to us in this life, but we are to have hope as well. For the only thing we brought to God was our faith in the promises of what was to come, and it was in this way that we were saved. If we lose this hope, we lose the one thing which we have contributed to our salvation. HOMILIES ON ROMANS 14.[16]

[PSEUDO-]CONSTANTIUS: Here Paul is referring to those who believe in Christ. For when he says that they have the first fruits of the Spirit, he shows that Christians have received the main gifts of the Holy Spirit and have a greater grace than all those saints who had lived before the coming of Christ. THE HOLY LETTER OF ST. PAUL TO THE ROMANS.[17]

SEEING AND HOPING. PELAGIUS: We have not yet seen the things that we were promised, but we live in hope.[18] What we see is not hoped for, but we own it if it belongs to us. Christians have no hope in what can be seen, for we have been promised not what is present but what is to come in the future. PELAGIUS'S COMMENTARY ON ROMANS.[19]

---

[8]See Heb 4:1-13; 4 Ezra 2:34. [9]AOR 25. [10]ENPK 2:59-60. [11]Cf. Mic 7:1-2. [12]PCR 110-11. [13]Migne PG 74 col. 824. [14]CER 4:72. [15]CSEL 81.1:285. [16]NPNF 1 11:446. [17]ENPK 2:60. [18]2 Cor 5:7. [19]PCR 111.

NOT PRESENT, YET CERTAIN. CYRIL OF ALEXANDRIA: We believe that our bodies also will overcome corruption and death. For the time being this is a hope, because it is not yet present, but it is a future certainty. EXPLANATION OF THE LETTER TO THE ROMANS.[20]

8:25 Waiting with Patience

PATIENT WAITING. CYPRIAN: Patient waiting is necessary that we may fulfill what we have begun to be and, through God's help, that we may obtain what we hope for and believe. THE GOOD OF PATIENCE 13.[21]

WE WAIT WITH PATIENCE. AMBROSIASTER: Patience is greatly approved of by God, for by daily waiting it desires the coming of the kingdom of God and does not doubt just because it delays. COMMENTARY ON PAUL'S EPISTLES.[22]

HOPE DISTINGUISHED FROM PATIENCE. CHRYSOSTOM: Hope is feeling confidence in things to come.... The name of *patience* belongs to hard work and to much endurance. But even this he grants to the one who hopes in order to comfort the weary soul. HOMILIES ON ROMANS 14.[23]

AUGUSTINE: Patience trains up the longing. Wait, for he waits. Walk on steadfastly that you may reach the end. He will not leave that place to which you are moving. HOMILIES ON 1 JOHN 4.7.[24]

PELAGIUS: The reward for faith with patience is great, because we believe what we do not yet see,[25] and we are as sure of what we have not yet received as if we have already received it. As Paul says to the Hebrews: "You have need of endurance, so that you may do the will of God and receive what is promised."[26] PELAGIUS'S COMMENTARY ON ROMANS.[27]

THE METAPHOR OF THE EGG. BEDE: The certainty of our hope is prefigured by the egg. No offspring is as yet discernible in the egg, but the birth of the bird to come is hoped for. The faithful do not yet look upon the glory of the fatherland on high in which they believe at the present time, but they await its coming in hope. HOMILIES ON THE GOSPELS 11.14.[28]

8:26 The Spirit Intercedes

THE SPIRIT HELPS IN OUR WEAKNESS. ORIGEN: Just as a sick man does not ask the doctor for things which will restore him to health but rather for things which his disease longs for, so likewise we, as long as we are languishing in the weakness of this life, will from time to time ask God for things which are not good for us. This is why the Spirit has to help us.

The weakness which the Spirit helps us with is our flesh.... Whenever the Holy Spirit sees our spirit struggling with the flesh and being drawn to it, he stretches out his hand and helps us in our weakness. COMMENTARY ON THE EPISTLE TO THE ROMANS.[29]

THE SPIRIT IMPORTUNES. NOVATIAN: The Holy Spirit importunes the divine ears on our behalf "with sighs too deep for words," thereby discharging his duties as advocate and rendering his services in our defense. He has been given to dwell in our bodies and to bring about our sanctification. THE TRINITY 29.16.[30]

THE SPIRIT INTERCEDES ACCORDING TO HIS NATURE. AMBROSIASTER: Our prayers are weak because they ask for things contrary to reason, and for this reason Paul shows that this weakness in us is helped by the Holy Spirit who has been given to us. The Holy Spirit helps because he does not allow anything we ask for before the proper time or against God's wishes to happen.

Paul says that the Spirit intercedes for us not

---

[20]Migne PG 74 col. 824. [21]FC 36:276. [22]CSEL 81.1:287. [23]NPNF 1 11:446. [24]LCC 8:291. [25]See Jn 20:29. [26]Heb 10:36. [27]PCR 111. [28]CSEL 111:130. [29]CER 4:76-78. [30]FC 67:103.

with human words but according to his own nature. For when what comes from God speaks with God, it is obvious that he will speak in the same way as the one from whom he comes speaks. For the Spirit given to us overflows with our prayers in order to make up for our inadequacy and lack of foresight by his actions and to ask God for the things which will be of benefit to us. COMMENTARY ON PAUL'S EPISTLES.[31]

THE GIFT OF PRAYER. CHRYSOSTOM: The Spirit is always there to help us and to do his part.... Since we are ignorant of much that is profitable for us and we ask for things which are not profitable, the gift of prayer used to come into one person in the church, and he would be the person set aside to ask God for the things which would benefit them all. Here the word *Spirit* is the name which Paul gives to the kind of grace and to the soul who receives it and intercedes with God on our behalf. The one who was counted worthy of such a grace as this would stand with great attention, and with many mental groanings he would fall before God, asking the things which were profitable for all. Nowadays, the deacon is a symbol of this, when he offers up the prayers for the people. HOMILIES ON ROMANS 14.[32]

THE DECISIONS OF THE LORD. CHRYSOSTOM: It is not possible, says Paul, for us human beings to have a precise knowledge of everything. So we ought to yield to the Creator of our nature and with joy and great relish accept those things which he has decided on and have an eye not to the appearance of events but to the decisions of the Lord. After all, he knows better than we do what is for our benefit, and he also knows what steps must be taken for our salvation. HOMILIES ON GENESIS 30.16.[33]

WE DO NOT KNOW HOW TO PRAY AS WE OUGHT. AUGUSTINE: It is clear from what follows that Paul is speaking here about the Holy Spirit.... "We do not know how to pray as we

ought" for two reasons. First, it is not yet clear what future we are hoping for or where we are heading, and second, many things in this life may seem positive but are in fact negative, and vice versa. Tribulation, for example, when it comes to a servant of God in order to test or correct him may seem futile to those who have less understanding.... But God often helps us through tribulation, and prosperity, which may be negative if it traps the soul with delight and the love of this life, is sought after in vain.

The Spirit sighs by making us sigh, arousing in us by his love a desire for the future life. "The Lord your God tempts you so that he might know whether you love him,"[34] that is, to make you know, for nothing escapes God's notice. AUGUSTINE ON ROMANS 54.[35]

THE SPIRIT HIMSELF INTERCEDES. AUGUSTINE: The Spirit that intercedes is nothing but the same charity which the Spirit has wrought in you.... Charity itself groans in prayer, and he who gave it cannot shut his ears to its voice. Cast away care, let charity make request, and the ears of God are ready to listen. The answer comes— not what you want but what is to your advantage. HOMILIES ON 1 JOHN 6.8.[36]

AUGUSTINE: The Holy Spirit, who intercedes with God on behalf of the saints, does not groan as if he were in need and experiencing distress. Rather he moves us to pray when we groan, and thus he is said to do what we do when he moves us. AGAINST THE MANICHEES 1.22.34.[37]

AUGUSTINE: We must not deduce from this that either the apostle or those to whom he spoke were unacquainted with the Lord's Prayer. We think that the reason Paul says that we do not know how we should pray ... was because temporal trials and troubles are often useful for curing the swelling of pride or for proving and

---

[31]CSEL 81.1:287-89. [32]NPNF 1 11:446. [33]FC 82:233. [34]Deut 13:3. [35]AOR 27. [36]LCC 8:307. [37]FC 84:82.

testing our patience, and by this proving and testing winning for it a more glorious and precious reward; or for chastising and wiping out certain sins, while we, ignorant of these benefits, wish to be delivered from all trouble. Letter 130.[38]

[Pseudo-]Constantius: We find it difficult to express in words the desire of our prayer, which we have conceived in the heart. This is why Paul adds that the Spirit prays for us with sighs which cannot be uttered. Therefore God, who tries the hearts, knows how much we desire to believe, even if we cannot comprehend it in words. Furthermore, he knows that we ask him for holy things and not for things of this world, according to his will. The Holy Letter of St. Paul to the Romans.[39]

Pelagius: The Spirit helps us in accordance with the hope we have, so that we may request not earthly things but heavenly ones. For our ability is weak unless it is helped by the Holy Spirit. We still see through a glass darkly,[40] and often what we judge to be helpful is actually harmful. Therefore our requests may not be granted by divine providence, as Paul says elsewhere.[41] Pelagius's Commentary on Romans.[42]

Theodoret of Cyr: Do not think that you will be set free by things which are harmful. You do not know what is good for you in the way that God does. Therefore, give yourselves to him who holds the key to the universe. For even if you ask nothing but merely groan under the impulse of the grace which dwells in you, he handles your affairs wisely and will ensure that you get what you need. Interpretation of the Letter to the Romans.[43]

8:27 Interceding According to God's Will

He Who Searches the Heart. Origen: Paul shows here that God pays less attention to the words we use in prayer than he does to what

is in our heart and mind. Commentary on the Epistle to the Romans.[44]

Knows the Mind of the Spirit. Ambrosiaster: It is clear that the prayer of every spirit is known to God, from whom nothing is secret or hidden.[45] How much more then should [the Father] know what the Holy Spirit, who is the same essence as himself, is saying? Commentary on Paul's Epistles.[46]

According to the Will of God. Chrysostom: Paul is here describing the spiritual man who has the gift of prayer. He does not inform God as if God were ignorant but intercedes so that we may learn what it is that we should pray for and to ask God to give us things which are pleasing to him. . . . These prayers are heard, because the man who prays them is doing so "according to the will of God." Homilies on Romans 14.[47]

Spirit as Grace. [Pseudo-]Constantius: It is a custom of holy Scripture to call grace "spirit." So Paul in this passage calls the grace of the Holy Spirit "spirit," which is dispensed and given to us in different ways, as the same apostle says to the Corinthians: "There are many gifts, but there is one Spirit."[48] The Holy Letter of St. Paul to the Romans.[49]

Pelagius: Paul has called a gift of the Spirit "the Spirit." . . . He makes us request with groans which cannot be described, just as God is said to tempt us in order to know, i.e., in order to make us know, what kind of people we are.[50] Even in popular usage the master is said to accomplish what he orders to be done by others, as in statements like "he built a house" or "he wrote a book," though he neither built nor wrote. Pelagius's Commentary on Romans.[51]

[38]FC 18:395. [39]ENPK 2:61. [40]See 1 Cor 13:12. [41]2 Cor 12:7-9. [42]PCR 111. [43]IER, Migne PG 82 col. 140. [44]CER 4:82. [45]See Job 37:16; Acts 15:18; 1 Jn 3:20; 4 Ezra 16:62. [46]CSEL 81.1:289. [47]NPNF 1 11:447. [48]1 Cor 12:4. [49]ENPK 2:61-62. [50]Deut 13:3. [51]PCR 112.

Theodoret of Cyr: "Spirit" here does not mean the substance of the Spirit but rather the grace which is given to believers. By this grace we are encouraged to struggle, we are inflamed to pray more earnestly, and with ineffable sighings we implore God the Savior. The holy apostle wrote this out of the experience of his own suffering. For he himself had asked to be set free from evils, not once or twice but three times, but he did not get what he asked for.[52] Rather, he heard God say: "My grace is sufficient for you, for my power is made perfect in weakness."[53] But when he learned this, he willingly embraced the things which he had asked to be set free from and said: "I will all the more gladly boast of my weaknesses, that the power of Christ may rest upon me."[54] Interpretation of the Letter to the Romans.[55]

The Prompting of the Spirit. Philoxenus of Mabbug: You see that all the good promptings which bring us to repentance result from the activity of the Spirit, and pure prayer, which brings all these good promptings to completion, is also stirred up in our soul as the result of the Spirit's activity. He too, in a hidden way, initially arouses us to groans at the memory of our sins. On the Indwelling of the Holy Spirit.[56]

Caesarius of Arles: By the inspiration of the Holy Spirit in silence, the shouting of the saints is heard in the presence of God. Sermon 97.2.[57]

---

[52]See 2 Cor 12:8. [53]2 Cor 12:9. [54]2 Cor 12:9. [55]IER, Migne PG 82 col. 140. [56]SFPSL 116. [57]FC 47:75.

8:28-39 THE VICTORY OF THE CHRISTIAN

[28]We know that in everything God works for good[k] with those who love him,[l] who are called according to his purpose. [29]For those whom he foreknew he also predestined to be conformed to the image of his Son, in order that he might be the first-born among many brethren. [30]And those whom he predestined he also called; and those whom he called he also justified; and those whom he justified he also glorified.

[31]What then shall we say to this? If God is for us, who is against us? [32]He who did not spare his own Son but gave him up for us all, will he not also give us all things with him? [33]Who shall bring any charge against God's elect? It is God who justifies; [34]who is to condemn? Is it Christ Jesus, who died, yes, who was raised from the dead, who is at the right hand of God, who indeed intercedes for us?[m] [35]Who shall separate us from the love of Christ? Shall tribulation, or distress, or persecution, or famine, or nakedness, or peril, or sword? [36]As it is written,

"For thy sake we are being killed all the day long;
we are regarded as sheep to be slaughtered."

[37]No, in all these things we are more than conquerors through him who loved us. [38]For I am sure that neither death, nor life, nor angels, nor principalities, nor things present, nor things to come, nor powers, [39]nor height, nor depth, nor anything else in all creation, will be able to separate us

from the love of God in Christ Jesus our Lord.

k Other ancient authorities read *in everything he works for good,* or *everything works for good* l Greek *God* m Or *It is Christ Jesus . . . for us*

OVERVIEW: In Romans 8:28 and in the following verses Paul unfolds the great mystery of predestination. Apart from Augustine, who embraced it wholeheartedly, most of the Fathers found it somewhat puzzling to accept the apostle's teaching at face value. They did not want to deny that the world was planned and ordered by God, but neither did they want to suggest that there were some people whom God had predestined to damnation. They were convinced that predestination did not remove human free will. God's call to salvation was generally understood to be universal. The fact that not all responded was their fault entirely and the result of a deliberate choice on their part.

Christians are safe in the love of God and have nothing to fear from anyone. When Christians reflect on the fact that God has already sacrificed his Son for them, they can hardly doubt that he will look after them in the future as well. Nobody can attack the Christian, not even the devil, because Christ has chosen us, he has died for us, and now he intercedes for us at the right hand of the Father. There is no protection greater than that. Romans 8 continues with a long list of potential enemies who would separate us from God if they could, and concludes with Paul's ringing affirmation that the love of God is greater than all of these combined. The Fathers echo his assertion and use the opportunity to explore the full meaning of the things Paul mentions so as to meet the pastoral needs of their flock.

8:28 God Works for Good

IN EVERYTHING GOD WORKS FOR GOOD.
AMBROSIASTER: It is not that God, knowing the intention of their heart and their ignorance, gives them the opposite of what they ask for. Rather he teaches them what ought to be given to people

who love God. This is what the Lord says in the Gospel: "For your Father knows what you need, even before you ask him."[1] Those who are called according to the promise are those whom God knew would believe in the future. COMMENTARY ON PAUL'S EPISTLES.[2]

CHRYSOSTOM: When Paul speaks of "all things" he mentions even the things that seem painful. For if tribulation, or poverty, or imprisonment, or famines, or deaths or anything else should come upon us, God can change them into the opposite. For this is one instance of his ineffable power, that he can make painful things appear light to us and turn them into things which can be helpful.

Paul talks about being called "according to his purpose" in order to show that the calling itself is not enough. . . . The calling was not forced on anyone, nor was it compulsory. Everyone was called, but not everyone obeyed the call. HOMILIES ON ROMANS 15.[3]

CHRYSOSTOM: Even opposition and disappointment are turned into good, which is exactly what happened with this remarkable man, the apostle Paul. HOMILIES ON GENESIS 67.19.[4]

THE TEMPTATION OF JOB. JEROME: When Job lost all his wealth, when he lost his sons, everything seemed to militate against him,[5] but since he loved the Lord, the evils that befell him worked together for his good.[6] The vermin of his body were preparing for him the crown of heaven.[7] Before the time he is tempted, God has never spoken to him; after he is tempted, however, God comes to him and speaks familiarly with him, as a friend with his friend.[8] Let calamity strike, let every kind of disaster fall, as long as

---

[1]Mt 6:8. [2]CSEL 81.1:289-91. [3]NPNF 1 11:452. [4]FC 87:276. [5]See Job 1:13-21. [6]See Job 42:9-17. [7]See Job 7:5. [8]Job 38:1—42:9.

after the catastrophe Christ comes. Homilies on the Psalms 6.[9]

For Those Who Love God. Augustine: There is, in the foreknowledge of God, a predetermined limit and number of saints who love God as he has given them to do through the Holy Spirit poured forth in their hearts, and for them everything works together for good. Letter 186.[10]

Pelagius: Whatever we do or suffer out of love for God will grow into a reward for us.[11] Pelagius's Commentary on Romans.[12;]

Theodore of Mopsuestia: We must not worry if we find that things which we expect to turn out for our good are unexpectedly evil in the present life, because we know that in the end everything works together for good for those who love God. Pauline Commentary from the Greek Church.[13]

Cyril of Alexandria: To be called according to God's purpose is to be called according to the will. But is this the will of the one who calls or the will of those who are called? Naturally, every impulse which leads to righteousness comes from God the Father. Christ himself once said: "No one can come to me unless the Father draws him."[14] Nevertheless it is not wrong to say that some are called according to God's purpose and according to their own intentions as well. Explanation of the Letter to the Romans.[15]

Theodoret of Cyr: This is not true of everyone but only of believers. Nor do things simply work together—they work together for good. If someone asks for something which will not contribute to his good, he will not get it, because it is not good for him to get it. Interpretation of the Letter to the Romans.[16]

8:29 Conformed to the Image of the Son

Whom He Foreknew He Predestined.

Origen: We know that Christ was in the form of God and took on himself the form of a servant also.[17] Which of these two is it that the believer is to be conformed to? . . . In my opinion, new converts are conformed to the image of the servant, and as they progress in the faith, they become conformed to that image which is the image of God.

In Scripture, words like *foreknew* and *predestined* do not apply equally to both good and evil. For the careful student of the Bible will realize that these words are used only of the good. . . . When God speaks of evil people, he says that he "never knew" them.[18] . . . They are not said to be foreknown, not because there is anything which can escape God's knowledge, which is present everywhere and nowhere absent, but because everything which is evil is considered to be unworthy of his knowledge or of his foreknowledge. Commentary on the Epistle to the Romans.[19]

Diodore: This text does not take away our free will. It uses the word *foreknew* before *predestined*. Now it is clear that "foreknowledge" does not by itself impose any particular kind of behavior. What is said here would be clearer if we started from the end and worked backwards. Whom did God glorify? Those whom he justified. Whom did he predestine? Those whom he foreknew, who were called according to his plan, i.e., who demonstrated that they were worthy to be called by his plan and made conformable to Christ. Pauline Commentary from the Greek Church.[20]

Countering the Arian View of First-born. Gregory of Nyssa: For when the Arians say that the "only begotten" God, the Creator of all, . . . is the work and creation and product of

[9]FC 48:48-49. [10]FC 30:208. [11]See Mt 5:12; Lk 6:22-23. [12]PCR 112. [13]NTA 15:141-42. [14]Jn 6:44. [15]Migne PG 74 col. 828. [16]IER, Migne PG 82 cols. 140-41. [17]See Phil 2:6-7. [18]See Mt 7:23; Lk 13:27. [19]CER 4:86-90. [20]NTA 15:95.

God and therefore interpret the phrase "firstborn of every creature" to mean that he is the brother of every creature, taking precedence because of the rights of primogeniture, as Reuben did over his brothers,[21] and that he is placed first not because of his nature but because of the rights of the eldest, this must be said to them first of all— it is not possible for the same person to be the only begotten and the firstborn as well. ON PERFECTION.[22]

FIRSTBORN AMONG MANY BRETHREN.
AMBROSIASTER: Those whom God foreknew would believe in him he chose to receive the promises. But those who appear to believe yet do not persevere in the faith are not chosen by God, because whoever God chooses will persevere.

Christ is rightly called the "firstborn" because he was not made before the rest of creation but begotten, and God has chosen to adopt men as his children following Christ's example. He is the firstborn in the regeneration of the Spirit, in the resurrection from the dead and in the ascension into heaven. Therefore, the firstborn in all things is said to be our brother, because he chose to be born as a man, but he is also Lord, because he is our God. COMMENTARY ON PAUL'S EPISTLES.[23]

CHRYSOSTOM: What a superb honor! For what the only begotten Son was by nature, we have become by grace.[24] Christ in his human nature has become the firstborn of many brethren, even though in his divine nature he remains the only begotten.[25] HOMILIES ON ROMANS 15.[26]

FIRSTBORN, ONLY BEGOTTEN. AUGUSTINE: Not all who are called are called according to God's purpose, for the purpose relates to God's foreknowledge and predestination. God only predestined those whom he knew would believe and follow the call. Paul refers to them as the "elect." For many do not come, even though they have been called, but no one comes who has not been called.

We should understand our Lord as "only begotten" in one sense and as "firstborn" in another. Christ is called "only begotten" because he has no brothers and is the Son of God by nature, the Word in the beginning by whom all things were made.[27] But by his assumption of humanity and by the dispensation of the incarnation, through which even we who are not sons by nature have been called into the adoption of sons, he is said to be the "firstborn" of many brothers.[28] For before him there was no resurrection of the dead . . . but now after him comes the resurrection of many saints, whom he does not hesitate to call "brothers" because he shares in their common humanity. AUGUSTINE ON ROMANS 55.[29]

WHETHER WOMEN WILL CONFORM TO THE IMAGE OF HIS SON. AUGUSTINE: There are some who think that in the resurrection all will be men and that women will lose their sex. This view springs from this text and Ephesians: "Until we all attain to perfect manhood."[30] . . . For my part, I think that those who believe that there will be two sexes in the resurrection are more sensible. THE CITY OF GOD 19.22.17.[31]

PELAGIUS: God's purpose is his plan to save by faith alone those whom he had known in advance would believe, and those whom he freely called to salvation he will glorify all the more as they work toward it. To predestine is the same as to know in advance. Those whom God foresaw would be conformed in life he intended to be conformed in glory[32] so that he might be the firstborn among many brethren.[33] PELAGIUS'S COMMENTARY ON ROMANS.[34]

BEGOTTEN IN HIS DIVINITY, FIRSTBORN IN HIS HUMANITY. [PSEUDO-]CONSTANTIUS: Christ is the firstborn Son of God according to his incarnation and according to the grace that

---

[21]See Gen 29:32; 49:3-4. [22]FC 58:113. [23]CSEL 81.1.291. [24]See Eph 1:4-7; 2 Tim 1:8-10. [25]See Heb 2:5-18. [26]NPNF 1 11.453. [27]Jn 1:1-3. [28]See Col 1:18. [29]AOR 27, 29. [30]Eph 4:13. [31]FC 24:463. [32]Phil 3:21. [33]Col 1:18. [34]PCR 112.

was in him. He intercedes for us not as God but as our High Priest. But when he is called "only begotten,"[35] then it is his divinity which is being referred to. The Holy Letter of St. Paul to the Romans.[36]

Cyril of Alexandria: If as the only begotten he became the "firstborn among many brethren" and yet remains the only begotten, what is the paradox if, although suffering in the flesh according to his humanity, he is known to be impassible according to his divinity? Letter 55.33.[37]

Conformed to the Image of His Son. Theodoret of Cyr: God did not simply predestine; he predestined those whom he foreknew. Paul says everything precisely and writes "conformed to the image of his Son" and not just "conformed to his Son."... For our body is not conformed to Christ's divinity but to his glorified body. It is as a man that Christ is the firstborn; as God he is the only begotten. Nor does Christ as God have brothers. It is as a man that he calls all men his brothers.[38] Interpretation of the Letter to the Romans.[39]

Severian: Paul says "the image of the Son" meaning the Holy Spirit, because just as the Son is the immutable image of the Father, so the Spirit is of the Son. For those who have been made worthy by the Holy Spirit live according to the Spirit and are conformed to the Spirit, who is the image of the Son.[40] Pauline Commentary from the Greek Church.[41]

8:30 Predestined, Called, Justified, Glorified

Distinguishing Many Called from Some Called According to His Purpose. Origen: I understand this, as do most people, to mean that someone who is justified is justified because he has been called, and that someone is called because he has been predestined, and that he is predestined because he has been foreknown. ... Those who think that God's foreknowledge is

limited to knowing what will happen in the future are obviously wrong, for there can be no divine foreknowledge without predestination—the two things go together. ...

But how can it be that all who are called should be justified, when we know that many are called but few are chosen?[42] It seems to me that here we are talking about a different kind of calling. For indeed many are called, but not all are called according to God's purpose. ... It is only those who are called according to his purpose who are justified. Commentary on the Epistle to the Romans.[43]

Ambrosiaster: To "call" is to help somebody who is already thinking about faith or else to address him firmly in the knowledge that he will listen. Commentary on Paul's Epistles.[44]

Those Whom He Called, He Justified. Chrysostom: God justified them by the regeneration of baptism and glorified them by their adoption as sons. Homilies on Romans 15.[45]

Augustine: Are all those who are called justified? "Many are called, but few are chosen."[46] But since the elect have certainly been called, it is obvious that they have not been justified without being called. But not everyone is called to justification; only those "who are called according to his purpose." Augustine on Romans 55.[47]

Augustine: God elected believers in order that they might believe, not because they already believed. Predestination of the Saints 17.34.[48]

Pelagius: Those whom God knew in advance would believe, he called. A call gathers together those who are willing to come, not those who are

---

[35]See Jn 1:14. [36]ENPK 2:62. [37]FC 77:31. [38]See Heb 2:5-18. [39]IER, Migne PG 82 col. 141. [40]See 2 Cor 3:16-18; Gal 4:6. [41]NTA 15:221. [42]Mt 22:14. [43]CER 4:92-98. [44]CSEL 81.1:291. [45]NPNF 1 11:453. [46]See Mt 22:14. [47]AOR 27. [48]FC 86:260.

unwilling. . . . Paul says this because of the enemies of the faith, in order that they may not judge God's grace to be arbitrary. They are called to believe through preaching and are justified through baptism when they believe, and are glorified with spiritual powers now or in the resurrection to come. PELAGIUS'S COMMENTARY ON ROMANS.[49]

CYRIL OF ALEXANDRIA: Jesus said: "Come to me all who labor and are heavy laden, and I will give you rest."[50] He calls everyone to himself, and no one is lacking in the grace of his calling, for when he says everyone he excludes nobody. But those whom he long ago foresaw would come into being he predestined to participate in the future blessings and called them to receive justification by faith in him and not to sin again. EXPLANATION OF THE LETTER TO THE ROMANS.[51]

GOD'S FOREKNOWING DOES NOT IMPLY DIRECT CAUSING. THEODORET OF CYR: Those whose intention God foreknew he predestined from the beginning. Those who are predestined, he called, and those who were called, he justified by baptism. Those who were justified, he glorified, calling them children: "To all who received him, who believed in his name, he gave power to become children of God."[52] Let no one say that God's foreknowledge was the unilateral cause of these things. For it was not foreknowledge which justified people, but God knew what would happen to them, because he is God. INTERPRETATION OF THE LETTER TO THE ROMANS.[53]

8:31 God Is for Us

HOW GOD IS FOR US. ORIGEN: How God can be for us is made clear by what Paul has expounded in the preceding verses. It is because the Spirit of God dwells in us and because the Spirit of Christ, or Christ himself, is in us . . . because we act in the power of God's Spirit, because we have received the Spirit of adoption, because we are children of God, heirs and fellow

heirs of Christ.[54] COMMENTARY ON THE EPISTLE TO THE ROMANS.[55]

WHO CAN BE AGAINST US? AMBROSIASTER: Who would dare attack us when the Judge himself has foreknown us and pronounced us to be suitable? COMMENTARY ON PAUL'S EPISTLES.[56]

CHRYSOSTOM: Paul was saying: "Let me hear no more about the dangers and evils which beset you on all sides. For even if some do not believe in the things to come, still they have not a word to say against the good things which have already taken place, e.g., God's friendship toward you from the beginning, his justifying work, the glory which he gives, and so on."

The world is against us, but . . . in spite of itself it has become the source of endless blessing for us. So in reality nobody is against us! HOMILIES ON ROMANS 15.[57]

PELAGIUS: Paul wants to show that nobody can keep those who love God and who are loved by God from attaining the glory which has been promised, because the perfect love which is in them casts out every reason for mortal fear.[58] PELAGIUS'S COMMENTARY ON ROMANS.[59]

8:32 God Gave His Son for Us

FOR US ALL. ORIGEN: The Father gave up his Son not only for the holy and the great but also for the least and for all everywhere who are members of the church. Therefore anyone who offends the conscience of even the least and weakest of these is said to be sinning against Christ,[60] because he is scandalizing a soul for whom Christ died. COMMENTARY ON THE EPISTLE TO THE ROMANS.[61]

[49]PCR 112-13. [50]Mt 11:28. [51]Migne PG 74 cols. 828-29. [52]Jn 1:12. [53]IER, Migne PG 82 cols. 141-44. [54]See Rom 8:14-17; Gal 4:4-7. [55]CER 4:104. [56]CSEL 81.1:293. [57]NPNF 1 11:453-54. [58]See 1 Jn 4:18. [59]PCR 113. [60]See Rom 14:15, 20-21. [61]CER 4:106.

AMBROSE: Who can grieve because a security especially dear to him has been taken away, when for our comfort the Father delivered his only Son to death for us? ON THE DEATH OF HIS BROTHER SATYRUS 1.4.[62]

GOD DID NOT SPARE HIS SON. AMBROSIASTER: Paul urges us to rest assured on account of our faith by showing us that God gave up his Son to death on our behalf even before we had ceased being sinners, because he knew in advance that we would believe. He says that God long ago decided that all those who believed in Christ would be rewarded. Thus if God is prepared to give us the greatest things, even to the point of sacrificing his own Son on our behalf, how can we not believe that he will give us the lesser things as well? For the believer's rewards are already waiting. Giving them to us is not nearly as difficult as handing Christ over to death for our sake. COMMENTARY ON PAUL'S EPISTLES.[63]

THE TRUTH AND ITS SHADOW. CHRYSOSTOM: Up to this point there was shadow, but now the truth of things is shown to be more excellent. This rational Lamb, you see, was offered for the whole world; he purified the whole world; he freed human beings from error and led them forward to the truth; he made earth into heaven, not by altering the nature of the elements but by transferring life in heaven to human beings on earth. Through him all worship of demons is made pointless; through him people no longer worship wood and stone, nor do those endowed with reason bow down to material things—instead, all error has been abolished and the light of truth has shone brightly on the world. Do you see the superiority of the truth? Do you see what shadow is, on the one hand, and truth on the other? HOMILIES ON GENESIS 47.14.[64]

THE SACRIFICE OF THE SON. [PSEUDO-]CONSTANTIUS: Paul is here attacking the heresy of the Patripassians [who believed that the Father had suffered and died on the cross]. THE HOLY LETTER OF ST. PAUL TO THE ROMANS.[65]

PELAGIUS: God allowed Christ to be handed over in order to preserve the freedom of choice of those who handed him over and to set us an example of patience. How can God have anything dearer to offer us? He offered us his only Son. PELAGIUS'S COMMENTARY ON ROMANS.[66]

THEODORET OF CYR: Would God give us the greater thing but not the lesser? Would he sacrifice his Son but withhold his possessions from us? Note too that there is one person of the Son. His human nature was given for us by his divinity. INTERPRETATION OF THE LETTER TO THE ROMANS.[67]

8:33 God Justifies the Elect

WHO SHALL BRING ANY CHARGE AGAINST GOD'S ELECT? ORIGEN: It seems to me that this must refer to the devil, for apart from Christ, who knew no sin, there is nobody so elect or so great that the devil would not dare to attack.

Note that Paul does not talk about those whom God has called but about God's elect. For unless you are elect and unless you show yourself approved by God in all things, you will have an accuser. For if your case is bad, if your crime restricts you, what can an advocate do for you, even if it is Jesus who intercedes on your behalf? For Jesus is the truth, and the truth cannot lie on your behalf. The advocate can help you only as long as you do not give the accuser grounds for attacking you, so that your previous sins, which were washed away in baptism, will not be imputed to you. But if afterward you sin again and do not wash the sin away by any tears of repentance, you will be giving your accuser grounds to incriminate you, and although Jesus intercedes on our behalf, even he would not call darkness light, or bitterness sweet. COMMEN-

---

[62]FC 22:162. [63]CSEL 81.1:293-95. [64]FC 87:22. [65]ENPK 2:62. [66]PCR 113. [67]IER, Migne PG 82 col. 144.

tary on the Epistle to the Romans.[68]

Ambrosiaster: It is clear that nobody would dare or be able to override the judgment and foreknowledge of God. For who could reject what God has approved, given that nobody is equal to God? Commentary on Paul's Epistles.[69]

It Is God Who Justifies. Ambrosiaster: Paul says that we cannot accuse God, because he justifies us, nor can we condemn Christ, because he loved us to the point of dying for us and rising again to intercede for us with the Father. Christ's prayers on our behalf are not to be despised, because he sits at God's right hand, that is to say, in the place of honor, because he is himself God. So let us rejoice in our faith, secure in the knowledge of God the Father and of his Son, Jesus Christ, who will come to judge us.... The Son is said to intercede because, although he controls everything and is equal to God the Father, we are not to think that the Father and the Son are one and the same person. The Scriptures speak of the distinction of the persons in such a way as to convey the message that the Son is not inferior and that the Father is so called because he is the Father of the Son and because everything comes from him. Commentary on Paul's Epistles.[70]

Chrysostom: Election is a sign of virtue. For if nobody can find fault with the colts which the horsebreaker has selected for the race, someone who pretended to find fault with them would be laughed at. So it is with the souls whom God has selected. Homilies on Romans 15.[71]

Pelagius: Who will dare to charge believers whom God has chosen and shown to be righteous by signs and wonders for previous sins or for disregard of the law's commands?[72] Pelagius's Commentary on Romans.[73]

8:34 Christ Intercedes for Us

Christ Who Died Now Intercedes. Chry-

sostom: Christ did not merely die for us; he now intercedes on our behalf as well.... The only reason why Paul mentioned intercession was to show the warmth and vigor of God's love for us, for the Father is also represented as beseeching us to be reconciled to him.[74] Homilies on Romans 15.[75]

In His Humanity He Died, Arose, Ascended and Intercedes. Pelagius: Paul speaks of Jesus according to the form of the man he assumed, who died and rose again. Now he intercedes for us so that we may go to be with him where he is.[76] The Arians are in the habit of stirring up false accusations on the basis of Christ's intercession, claiming that the one to whom intercession is made is greater than the one who does the interceding. To this one must answer that God does not forget and so does not need to be constantly reminded of those whom he himself chose. Christ intercedes when, as a true and eternal High Priest, he constantly presents and offers as our guarantee to the Father, the man whom he received.[77] Pelagius's Commentary on Romans.[78]

Leo the Great: If the true high priest does not atone for us, using the nature proper to us, and the true blood of the spotless Lamb does not cleanse us, then a true priesthood and true sacrifices do not exist in any other way in God's church, which is the body of Christ.[79] Although he is seated at the right hand of the Father, he performs the sacrament of the atonement in the same flesh which he assumed from the Virgin Mary. Letter 80.[80]

The Son Asks; the Father Grants. Severian: The context shows that there is one person who intercedes and another who receives the

---

[68]CER 4:108-12. [69]CSEL 81.1:295. [70]CSEL 81.1:295-97. [71]NPNF 1 11:454. [72]See Acts 2:22. [73]PCR 113. [74]See 2 Cor 5:20. [75]NPNF 1 11:455. [76]See Jn 14:3. [77]See Heb 6:20. [78]PCR 113. [79]See Heb 7:11-28. [80]FC 34:148-49.

plea. Nor is it improper for the Son to ask and for the Father to grant the request, for thus the complementary relationship between the two persons is maintained. . . . This text teaches us that there is a distinction between the Father and the Son which must not be confused. Pauline Commentary from the Greek Church.[81]

8:35 Troubles Will Not Separate Us from Christ

Who Shall Separate Us? Clement of Alexandria: Let us bear about a deep love for the Creator, let us cleave to him with our whole heart, let us not wickedly waste the substance of reason like the prodigal. Let us obtain the joy laid up, in which Paul, exulting, exclaimed: "Who shall separate us from the love of Christ?" Fragments 11.7.[82]

When in Distress. Origen: Paul says this about those who have been united to Christ in all the ways mentioned above. When tribulation comes, we shall say to God: "Thou hast given me room when I was in distress."[83] If we have distress in the world, arising from the needs of the body, we shall call on the breadth of God's wisdom and knowledge, in which the world cannot distress us. For I shall return to the wide fields of the holy Scriptures and look for the spiritual meaning of God's Word, and there no distress will take hold of me. . . . If I suffer persecution and confess Christ before men, I am certain that he will confess me also before his Father, who is in heaven. Famine cannot disturb me, for I have the bread of life which comes down from heaven and refreshes weary souls; nor can that bread ever be wanting, for it is perfect and eternal. Nakedness does not confound me, because I am clothed with the Lord Jesus Christ.[84] . . . I shall not fear peril, because "God is my light and my salvation; whom then shall I fear?"[85] The earthly sword cannot frighten me because I have "the sword of the Spirit, which is the Word of God."[86] Commentary on the Epistle to the Romans.[87]

Why Persecution? Cyprian: None of these can separate believers; nothing can snatch away those clinging to Christ's body and blood. This persecution is for the examination and evaluation of our heart. God wanted us to be tried and proved, as he has always tried his own, and yet, in his trials, never at any time has his help failed believers.[88] Letter 11.5.[89]

Ambrosiaster: This means: "Who will turn us away from the love of Christ, who has given us such great and innumerable gifts?" No torments will overcome the love of a mature Christian. Commentary on Paul's Epistles.[90]

The Meaning of Tribulation. Chrysostom: Even though it is easy to make a list like this one, each word contains thousands of lines of temptation. "Tribulation," for instance, includes prisons and bonds, calumnies and banishments, and all other such hardships. A single word covers oceans of dangers and reveals to us all the evils which people encounter in life. Homilies on Romans 15.[91]

Augustine: Paul is exhorting his hearers to not be broken by persecution, for perhaps they had been living according to the wisdom of the flesh. Augustine on Romans 57.[92]

Pelagius: After so many and such splendid benefits and promises, what affliction could be so heavy that it might tear us away from love for Christ? In saying "us" Paul is saying that we should all be the sort of Christians that even dangers cannot separate from Christ. Pelagius's Commentary on Romans.[93]

Caesarius of Arles: Good Christians are not separated from Christ even by torture. Tepid and careless ones however, are sometimes separated

---

[81]NTA 15:221. [82]ANF 2:584. [83]Ps 4:1. [84]See Rom 13:14. [85]Ps 27:1. [86]Eph 6:17. [87]CER 4:112-16. [88]2 Cor 12:9. [89]FC 51:32. [90]CSEL 81.1:299. [91]NPNF 1 11:455-56. [92]AOR 29. [93]PCR 114.

from him by idle tales; if they suffer even a slight loss they are immediately scandalized, dare to murmur against God and return to their impious, detestable omens. SERMON 54.2.[94]

8:36 Enduring Persecutions

ALL THE DAY LONG. IRENAEUS: Here the expression "all the day long" means all the time in which we suffer persecution and are killed as sheep. AGAINST HERESIES 2.22.2.[95]

ORIGEN: It is not enough for me to die or be crucified with Christ at one time only but "all the day long," i.e., throughout my entire life. COMMENTARY ON THE EPISTLE TO THE ROMANS.[96]

CHRYSOSTOM: It is possible in one day to die not once or twice but many times. For someone who is always prepared for this will continually receive a full reward. This is what the psalmist hints at when he says "all the day long." HOMILIES ON ROMANS 15.[97]

AS SHEEP TO BE SLAUGHTERED. PELAGIUS: We suffer not for any crime but for the sake of him who said: "Blessed are you when men shall persecute you, etc."[98] This is especially fulfilled in Christians, for we are not permitted to defend ourselves but must endure all attacks with the greatest patience, according to the example of our Lord and teacher, who was led like a sheep to the slaughter.[99] PELAGIUS'S COMMENTARY ON ROMANS.[100]

8:37 More Than Conquerers

RELYING ON GOD'S LOVE. ORIGEN: As long as we rely on God's love, we suffer no feeling of pain. For his love, by which he loved us and drew us to him, makes us not feel the pain and crucifixion of the body. In all these things we are more than conquerors. The bride in the Song of Songs says something similar: "I am wounded with love."[101] In the same way our soul, once it has received

Christ's wound of love, will not feel the wounds of the flesh, even if it gives the body over to the sword. COMMENTARY ON THE EPISTLE TO THE ROMANS.[102]

SHOWING ENDURANCE. BASIL: He conquers who does not yield to those who lead on by force, but he is more than conqueror who voluntarily invites sorrows for a demonstration of his endurance. HOMILIES 22.[103]

CONQUERING WONDROUSLY. CHRYSOSTOM: They did not merely conquer but did so in a wondrous way, so that it might become clear that those who plotted against them were at war with God and not just with men. Look how the Jews were at a loss: "What are we to do with these men?"[104] HOMILIES ON ROMANS 15.[105]

THROUGH HIM WHO LOVED US. PELAGIUS: All these troubles we count as nothing because of him who loved us so much that he even dies for us. And we especially triumph when we die for his name, since it is a light thing to suffer what the Lord first suffered for others. PELAGIUS'S COMMENTARY ON ROMANS.[106]

8:38 Neither Life nor Death

SUPERHUMAN TRIALS. ORIGEN: Here we pass from human temptations to superhuman trials. Of the former Paul says that we can overcome them, but although he does not say this of the latter—for only Christ can conquer them—nevertheless even here there is reason to speak of victory, since even with all the forces of the enemy ranged against us, nothing can separate us from the love of God.

"Death" here refers primarily to the death which separates the soul from the love of God, rather than what we usually think of as death,

---

[94]FC 31:267. [95]ANF 1:390. [96]CER 4:116. [97]NPNF 1 11:456. [98]Mt 5:11. [99]Is 53:7; cf. Acts 8:32. [100]PCR 114. [101]Song 2:5. [102]CER 4:116. [103]FC 46:354. [104]Acts 4:16. [105]NPNF 1 11:456. [106]PCR 114.

which merely separates the soul from the body. "Life" here presumably refers to the life of sin, which is constantly trying to separate us from the love of God.

"Angels" and "principalities" must refer to the devil and his hosts, against whom we have to struggle. "Things present" are the desires of this world, and "things to come" are the trials and temptations which may yet afflict us in this life. The "powers" are spiritual beings rather like angels, who must, however, be distinguished from them. They also fight to separate us from the love of God, but they cannot prevail if that love is rooted and grounded in us. COMMENTARY ON THE EPISTLE TO THE ROMANS.[107]

AMBROSIASTER: These are all the things which have come upon us since we were abducted by the devil.[108] Paul lists them in order to steel us against them if they should appear so that, confident of the hope and help of Christ and armed with faith, we might be able to fight against them.[109] COMMENTARY ON PAUL'S EPISTLES.[110]

I AM SURE. AUGUSTINE: Paul says that he is sure, not merely that he is of the opinion . . . that neither death nor the promise of temporal life nor any of the other things he lists can separate the believer from God's love. No one can separate the believer from God; not someone who threatens death, because he who believes in Christ shall live even if he dies, nor someone who offers earthly life, because Christ gives us eternal life. An angel cannot separate us, because "if an angel comes down from heaven and tells you something other than what you receive, let him be anathema."[111] Nor can a principality, i.e., an opposing power, because Christ has . . . vanquished them in himself.[112] AUGUSTINE ON ROMANS 58.[113]

8:39 Nothing Can Separate Us from God's Love

ELEMENTS ATTACK US. ORIGEN: "Height" and "depth" attack us, as David said: "Many fight

against me from on high,"[114] and "Out of the deep have I called unto thee, O Lord."[115] COMMENTARY ON THE EPISTLE TO THE ROMANS.[116]

CALLING ON THE LORD. ORIGEN: Human nature cannot by itself maintain the struggle against angels and heights and depths and any other creature; but when it has felt the Lord to be present and dwelling within, it will say in the confidence of receiving divine help: "The Lord is my light and my salvation; whom shall I fear?"[117] ON FIRST PRINCIPLES 3.2.5.[118]

SUFFERING FOR CHRIST'S SAKE. CHRYSOSTOM: Paul suffered everything for Christ's sake not in order to obtain the kingdom, nor for any honor, but because of his great love for the Master.[119] But we are not drawn away from the things of this life either by Christ or by the things of Christ. Like snakes or like swine we keep dragging the things of this world along with us in the mire. . . . Yet God even gave up his Son for your sake! HOMILIES ON ROMANS 15.[120]

NOR ANYTHING ELSE. AUGUSTINE: Often vain curiosity about things which are unknowable. . . whether in heaven or in hell separates us from God, unless love triumphs. For love calls us to certain spiritual knowledge not by the vanity of external things but by an inner light.

"Nor anything else in all creation" can be understood in two ways. First, as a visible creature. . . . By this interpretation Paul means that no other creature, i.e., no love of bodies, separates us from God. Or surely it may also mean that no other creature . . . stands between us and God, opposing us and keeping us from God's embrace. For beyond human minds, which are rational, there is no other creature—only God himself. AUGUSTINE ON ROMANS 58.[121]

---

[107]CER 4:118, 122-24. [108]See Gen 3:1-24. [109]See Eph 6:16; 1 Thess 5:8. [110]CSEL 81.1:299. [111]Gal 1:8. [112]Col 2:15. [113]AOR 29. [114]Ps 56:2. [115]Ps 130:1. [116]CER 4:126. [117]Ps 27:1. [118]OFP 219. [119]See Acts 20:24; Phil 3:8. [120]NPNF 1 11:457. [121]AOR 29, 31.

PELAGIUS: I am sure that even if someone threatens us with death, or promises life, or says he is an angel sent from the Lord, or pretends to be the prince of the angels, or gives us some honor in this present life, or holds out the glory of things to come, or works wonders, or promises heaven and staves off hell, or tries to persuade us with deep learning—I am sure that he will never be able to cut us off from the love of Christ.

Paul loved God in Christ. Love for Christ means keeping his commandments.[122] Christ established that brotherly love is an imitation of his own love when he said: "By this will all men know that you are my disciples, if you love one another."[123] So John also says: "If you do not love a brother whom you see, how can you love God, whom you do not see?"[124] PELAGIUS'S COMMENTARY ON ROMANS.[125]

NOTHING SHALL SEPARATE. CAESARIUS OF

ARLES: Spiritual souls are not separated from Christ by torments, but carnal souls are sometimes separated by idle gossip. The cruel sword cannot separate the former, but carnal affections remove the latter. Nothing hard breaks down spiritual men, but even flattering words corrupt the carnal. SERMON 82.2.[126]

PSEUDO-DIONYSIUS: Nothing shall separate the one who believes in truth from the ground of true faith, and it is there that he will come into the possession of enduring, unchanging identity. The man in union with truth knows clearly that all is well with him, even if everyone else thinks that he has gone out of his mind.[127] THE DIVINE NAMES 7.4.[128]

---

[122]Jn 14:5. [123]Jn 13:35. [124]1 Jn 4:20. [125]PCR 114C15. [126]FC 47:8-9. [127]See 1 Cor 1:18-31. [128]PDCW 110.

9:1-13 ISRAEL'S FALL FROM GRACE

[1]I am speaking the truth in Christ, I am not lying; my conscience bears me witness in the Holy Spirit, [2]that I have great sorrow and unceasing anguish in my heart. [3]For I could wish that I myself were accursed and cut off from Christ for the sake of my brethren, my kinsmen by race. [4]They are Israelites, and to them belong the sonship, the glory, the covenants, the giving of the law, the worship, and the promises; [5]to them belong the patriarchs, and of their race, according to the flesh, is the Christ. God who is over all be blessed for ever.[n] Amen.

[6]But it is not as though the word of God had failed. For not all who are descended from Israel belong to Israel, [7]and not all are children of Abraham because they are his descendants; but "Through Isaac shall your descendants be named." [8]This means that it is not the children of the flesh who are the children of God, but the children of the promise are reckoned as descendants. [9]For this is what the promise said, "About this time I will return and Sarah shall have a son." [10]And not only so, but also when Rebecca had conceived children by one man, our forefather Isaac, [11]though they were not yet born and had done nothing either good or bad, in order that God's purpose of election might continue, not because of works but because of his call, [12]she was told, "The elder will serve the younger." [13]As it is written, "Jacob I loved, but Esau I hated."

n *Or Christ, who is God over all, blessed for ever*

Overview: The conscience bears witness to the truth. Paul's love for the Jews and his desire for their salvation was such that he was prepared to wish the impossible: that he should himself be cut off from Christ. Evidently the apostle's hyperbole was subject to misunderstanding, since some of the Fathers felt obliged to reassure their readers that he did not mean what he was saying. Paul's detailed listing of Jewish privileges was respected by the Fathers, but they did not elaborate on them much. It was clear to them that the apostle was referring to the Jews of the Old Testament, not to their own contemporaries, who had rejected Christ. Even in Old Testament times not all of Abraham's children inherited the promise, but only Isaac. Similarly, in the next generation Esau was rejected, but Jacob was chosen. It was therefore impossible to sustain the notion that the promise made to Abraham was ever meant to apply to all his physical descendants. Furthermore, although Isaac was Abraham's natural son, he was born by supernatural means, thereby prefiguring Christ. There is a strong predestinarian note in the account of Jacob and Esau, which the Fathers found difficult to deal with. They were always concerned to insist that Esau had a free choice and that if he had behaved differently, he would not have been rejected. However, they were usually prepared to accept that God knew in advance what would happen, even if he was not the unilateral cause of it, so that there was no real possibility of things turning out otherwise. Only Augustine, and then only in his later writings, was prepared to accept the full implications of divine predestination.

9:1 Speaking the Truth in Christ

I Am Speaking the Truth in Christ. Origen: What Caiaphas said was also true: "It is expedient for you that one man should die for the people and that the whole nation should not perish,"[1] yet this was not the truth in Christ. Therefore the apostle says that he is speaking the truth in Christ, in contrast to that truth which is not in Christ. Commentary on the Epistle to the Romans.[2]

Conscience Bears Me Witness. Pelagius: Because Paul says that his conscience bears him witness, he shows that he is telling the truth, which conscience corroborates in everyone, and he establishes that he is not charged with lying by an accusation from within. Pelagius's Commentary on Romans.[3]

I Am Not Lying. Gennadius of Constantinople: The Jews who opposed the apostles and their message said that one or another of the following propositions must be true. Either the gospel is a lie, or God is a liar. . . . For God promised Abraham that he would bless his offspring, but now he has shown favor to impure and foreign people, i.e., the Gentiles, instead of us. Now if your preaching is a way out of these promises, as you claim, then it is clear that God lied to our ancestors. On the other hand, if it is wrong to speak of God in this way, then you and your message are a lie.

It was to answer this kind of charge that the apostle Paul wanted to work out an alternative position and demonstrate both that the message of the gospel was true and that God was not lying. Pauline Commentary from the Greek Church.[4]

9:2 Sorrow and Anguish

His Love for the Jews. Ambrosiaster: Since it appears that earlier he was speaking against the Jews, who thought that they were justified by the law, Paul now shows his desire and love for them and says that his conscience bears witness in Christ Jesus and in the Holy Spirit. Commentary on Paul's Epistles.[5]

Pelagius: Because Paul intends to proceed against the Jews, he first assures them that he

---

[1]Jn 11:50. [2]CER 132. [3]PCR 115. [4]NTA 15:386. [5]CSEL 81.1:303.

does not speak out of hatred for them, but out of love, for it pains him that they do not believe in Christ, who had come to save them as soon as possible. PELAGIUS'S COMMENTARY ON ROMANS.[6]

UNCEASING ANGUISH IN MY HEART. THE-ODORET OF CYR: The construction here is incomplete. Paul should have added that his unceasing anguish was due to the rejection or unbelief of the Jews. INTERPRETATION OF THE LETTER TO THE ROMANS.[7]

9:3 For the Sake of My Kinsmen

ACCURSED FOR THE SAKE OF MY BRETHREN. ORIGEN: Why be surprised that the apostle desires to be cursed for his brethren's sake, when he who is in the form of God emptied himself and took on the form of a servant and was made a curse for us?[8] Why be surprised if, when Christ became a curse for his servants, one of his servants should become a curse for his brethren? COMMENTARY ON THE EPISTLE TO THE ROMANS.[9]

CUT OFF FROM CHRIST? CHRYSOSTOM: What are you saying, Paul? Do you really want to be cut off from Christ, your beloved one, from whom neither heaven nor hell, nor things visible nor invisible, nor another world as great would separate you? Do you want to be cursed by him? What has happened? Have you changed, have you thrown over your previous love? No, Paul replies, do not worry! On the contrary, I have made my love for him more intense still. HOMILIES ON ROMANS 16.[10]

PAUL'S RELATIONSHIP TO THE JEWS. CHRYSOSTOM: If Paul was willing to become accursed so that others might believe, he ought to have wished it for the sake of the Gentiles as well. But as he wishes it only for the sake of the Jews, it is proof that he did not wish it for Christ's sake, but because of his relationship to them. If he had prayed only for the Gentiles, this would not have been so clear. As it is only for the Jews though, it

is clear proof that he is only as earnest as this because he wants to see Christ glorified in them.

Paul was cut to the heart when he realized the extent to which the Jews had blasphemed God and because he was concerned for God's glory. He wished that he were accursed, if possible, so that they might be saved, their blasphemy might be brought to an end, and God himself might be vindicated from any charge that he might have deceived the offspring of those to whom he had promised gifts. HOMILIES ON ROMANS 16.[11]

CONFESSING HIS SORROW. [PSEUDO-]CON-STANTIUS: Lest anyone think that Paul is here contradicting what he said earlier,[12] what he means is this. He is not now choosing to be accursed and cut off from Christ; rather, he chose that during the time when he persecuted Christ and his church, obeying the will of his brethren and relatives. Now he is confessing his sorrow because, while he has since merited the grace of apostleship, they continue in sin and are deprived of the promise of such great good. THE HOLY LETTER OF ST. PAUL TO THE ROMANS.[13]

"I COULD WISH" AS A PAST REFERENCE. PELAGIUS: Paul wished this at one time, before he became a follower of Christ. . . . But after he recognized the truth, he abandoned those whom he used to love in this way, yet still they do not repent. PELAGIUS'S COMMENTARY ON ROMANS.[14]

9:4 To the Israelites Belongs the Sonship

TO THEM BELONGS THE SONSHIP. ORIGEN: Israel was adopted by God and given the sonship: "When the Most High gave to the nations their inheritance, when he separated the sons of men, he fixed the bounds of the peoples according to the number of the sons of God; for the Lord's portion is his people, Jacob his allotted heritage."[15]

---

[6]PCR 115. [7]IER, Migne PG 82 col. 149. [8]See Phil 2:6-8. [9]CER 4:134. [10]NPNF 1 11:459. [11]NPNF 1 11:460. [12]See Rom 8:35. [13]ENPK 2:63-64. [14]PCR 115. [15]Deut 32:8-9.

"The covenants" and "the giving of the law" seem to be much the same thing. But I think there is this difference between them, that the law was given once, by Moses, but covenants were given frequently.[16] For every time the people sinned and were cast down, they were disinherited. And every time God was propitiated and he called them back to the inheritance of their possession, he renewed the covenants and declared them to be heirs once more.

"The worship" refers to the priestly sacrifices. "The promises" are those which were made to the patriarchs and which are given to all who are called children of Abraham. COMMENTARY ON THE EPISTLE TO THE ROMANS.[17]

PELAGIUS: "The sonship" belongs to the Jews, for of them it was said: "Israel, my firstborn son."[18] They had the old law and the promise of the new law. PELAGIUS'S COMMENTARY ON ROMANS.[19]

9:5 To the Israelites Belong the Patriarchs and Christ

GOD WHO IS OVER ALL. ORIGEN: It is clear from this passage that Christ is the "God who is over all." The one who is over all has nothing over him, for Christ does not come after the Father but from the Father. The Holy Spirit is also included in this, as it is written: "The Spirit of the Lord fills the earth, and whoever contains all things knows every sound."[20] So if the Son is God over all and the Spirit is recorded as containing all things, it is clear that the nature and substance of the Trinity are shown to be one and over all things. COMMENTARY ON THE EPISTLE TO THE ROMANS.[21]

OF THEIR FLESH IS THE CHRIST. AMBROSIASTER: Paul lists so many indications of the nobility and dignity of the Jewish people and of the promises they received in order to deepen his grief for all these things, because by not accepting the Savior they lost the privilege of their fathers and the merit of the promises, and they became

worse than the Gentiles, whom they had previously detested when they were without God. For it is a worse evil to lose a dignity than never to have had it.

As there is no mention of the Father's name in this verse and Paul is talking about Christ, it cannot be disputed that he is called God here. For if Scripture is speaking about God the Father and adds the Son, it often calls the Father God and the Son Lord. If someone does not think that it is said here about Christ that he is God, then let him name the person about whom he thinks it is said, for there is no mention of God the Father in this verse. COMMENTARY ON PAUL'S EPISTLES.[22]

DAVID'S SON IS DAVID'S LORD. AUGUSTINE: The Jews, who held only the first part of this confession, are refuted by the Lord. For when he asked them whose son they said Christ was, they answered "David's."[23] This is true according to the flesh. But concerning his divinity . . . they answered nothing. Therefore the Lord said to them: "Why did David, in the Spirit, call him Lord?"[24] in order that they might realize that they had only confessed that Christ is the son of David and had not said that Christ is Lord of this same David. The first fact is true according to his assumption of flesh, the other according to the eternity of his divinity. AUGUSTINE ON ROMANS 59.[25]

TO THEM BELONG THE PATRIARCHS. PELAGIUS: The patriarchs are Abraham, Isaac and Jacob.[26] Paul writes here against the Manicheans, Photinus and Arius because Christ is of the Jews according to the flesh, and God, blessed forever. PELAGIUS'S COMMENTARY ON ROMANS.[27]

CUT OFF FROM THE HOPE. CYRIL OF ALEXANDRIA: God chose Israel for himself from the

---

[16]See, e.g., Gen 9:8-17; 15:18; 2 Sam 23:5; 2 Kings 23:3. [17]CER 4:136-38. [18]Ex 4:22. [19]PCR 115. [20]Wis 1:7. [21]CER 4:140. [22]CSEL 81.1:305. [23]Mt 22:42. [24]Mt 22:43. [25]AOR 31. [26]See Gen 50:24. [27]PCR 115.

beginning, which is why he called it the first-born. But the Israelites fell because they were proud, wicked and, worst of all, murderers of their Lord. Therefore they perished, for they were rejected and abandoned and excluded from God's company, placed behind even the Gentiles and cut off from the hope promised to their ancestors. EXPLANATION OF THE LETTER TO THE ROMANS.[28]

9:6 God's Word Has Not Failed

NOT ALL DESCENDED FROM ISRAEL BELONG TO ISRAEL. DIODORE: Because the promises which had been given to the Jews had been transferred to the Gentiles, Paul wanted to avoid the charge that God had lied about his promises, and so he shows how God remains faithful. The Scriptures make it clear that it was not those who were Israelites according to the flesh but those who by their godliness showed that they were worthy to be Israelites who were called children of Abraham. PAULINE COMMENTARY FROM THE GREEK CHURCH.[29]

NOT AS THOUGH THE WORD FAILED. [PSEUDO-]CONSTANTIUS: Although the apostle grieves that the Jews have failed to obtain the grace of the promise, he nevertheless shows that the Word of God was not in vain and that the things which were promised are owed not to them who were born of Abraham, Isaac and Israel according to the flesh but to those who keep the faith of the patriarchs and are therefore reckoned to be of their seed. THE HOLY LETTER OF ST. PAUL TO THE ROMANS.[30]

PELAGIUS: Since Paul has said above that he is upset that the people of Israel had been shut out of the kingdom by their own fault, for all these things had belonged to them, he shows here that those who do not believe are not sons of Abraham, lest someone think that he was opposed to all Jews and retort: "Did God then lie to Abraham?" PELAGIUS'S COMMENTARY ON ROMANS.[31]

9:7 Children of Abraham

NOT ALL ARE CHILDREN OF ABRAHAM. DIODORE: Paul wants to say that it is not those who are of Abraham's flesh who are his children, but those who are of the promise, who are godly and just, whom God promised according to his foreknowledge would be children of Abraham, just as Isaac was made righteous by the promise. PAULINE COMMENTARY FROM THE GREEK CHURCH.[32]

NOT ALL ARE WORTHY. AMBROSIASTER: What Paul wants us to understand is that not all are worthy because they are children of Abraham, but only those who are children of the promise, that is, whom God foreknew would receive his promise, whether they are Jews or Gentiles. . . . Abraham believed and received Isaac on account of his faith, because he believed in God.[33] By this the mystery of the future faith was indicated, that they would be brothers of Isaac who had the same faith by which Isaac was born, because Isaac was born as a type of the Savior by the promise. Thus whoever believes that Christ Jesus was promised to Abraham is a child of Abraham and a brother of Isaac. Abraham was told that all the nations would be blessed in his offspring.[34] This happened not in Isaac, but in him who was promised to Abraham in Isaac, that is, Christ, in whom all the nations are blessed when they believe. Therefore the other Jews are children of the flesh, because they are deprived of the promise and cannot claim Abraham's merit, because they do not follow the faith by which Abraham is counted worthy. COMMENTARY ON PAUL'S EPISTLES.[35]

THROUGH ISAAC SHALL YOUR DESCENDANTS BE NAMED. PELAGIUS: Not all Jews are children of Abraham, but some still are; and if not all Israelites are from Israel, then some . . . are from the

---

[28]Migne PG 74 col. 829. [29]NTA 15:96-97. [30]ENPK 2:64. [31]PCR 116. [32]NTA 15:97. [33]See Gen 21:2; Heb 11:11. [34]See Gen 18:18; 22:18. [35]CSEL 81.1:309.

Gentiles. Even so, the sons of Abraham were named in Isaac alone and not in Ishmael, although he too descended from Abraham's line.[36] PELAGIUS'S COMMENTARY ON ROMANS.[37]

DESCENDANTS BY DIVINE GENEROSITY. THEODORET OF CYR: Although it was beyond the capacity of nature, Abraham became a father by divine generosity. Paul says this, even though Ishmael was also Abraham's son and moreover, he was the firstborn.[38] Therefore why do you boast, O Jew, that you are the only one to be descended from Abraham? For if you think that Ishmael does not count because he was the son of a slave, you are wrong. Holy Scripture reckons descent through the father and not through the mother. After all, the holy apostle could have mentioned the children born to Abraham through Keturah and shown that although they were born to a free woman they were not recognized as Abraham's seed. It would also have been easy for Paul to show that the twelve sons of Jacob had different mothers, and four of them were the children of slaves, yet all of them belonged to Israel, and none of them was hurt by his mother's slavery.... Here Paul wanted to insist that it was not the entire race of Abraham which received the blessing. Rather, only one of his sons was blessed, and the others were rejected. INTERPRETATION OF THE LETTER TO THE ROMANS.[39]

9:8 Children of God

CHILDREN OF THE PROMISE. CHRYSOSTOM: Paul does not call them the children of Abraham, but rather "the children of God," thus combining the past with the present and showing that even Isaac was not merely Abraham's son. What Paul means is something like this: Whoever has been born in the way that Isaac was born is a son of God and of the seed of Abraham.... For Isaac was born not according to the law of nature nor according to the power of the flesh but according to the power of the promise. HOMILIES ON ROMANS 16.[40]

CHILDREN OF THE FLESH. PELAGIUS: Ishmael was born of a maidservant by sexual intercourse, but Isaac was begotten by supernatural means from old people, by God's promise.[41] So the promise, which Abraham's faith merited, now makes Christians sons of Abraham, so that Abraham is indeed the father of many nations.[42] PELAGIUS'S COMMENTARY ON ROMANS.[43]

9:9 The Promised Son

THE SON PROMISED. AMBROSIASTER: This prefigures Christ, because Christ was promised to Abraham as a future son, in whom the word of the promise would be fulfilled. COMMENTARY ON PAUL'S EPISTLES.[44]

SARAH SHALL HAVE A SON. CHRYSOSTOM: It is not the children of the flesh who are children of God, but rather even in nature regeneration through baptism from above was sketched out beforehand.... For Sarah's womb was colder than any water, owing to barrenness and old age. ... And just as in her case it happened when her age was past hope, so in this case also it was when the old age of sins had come upon us that Isaac suddenly sprang up in youth, and we all became the children of God and the seed of Abraham. HOMILIES ON ROMANS 16.[45]

AUGUSTINE: This passage [to v. 29] is rather obscure. To SIMPLICIAN ON VARIOUS QUESTIONS 1.2.1.[46]

9:10 Two Different Peoples

JACOB AND ESAU AS TYPES OF BELIEF AND UNBELIEF. AMBROSIASTER: Paul says that Sarah was not the only one to give birth in a typological manner. Rebecca, the wife of Isaac, did the

---

[36]See Gen 16:1-16; 17:18-22. [37]PCR 116. [38]See Gen 16:15-16. [39]IER, Migne PG 82 cols. 152-53. [40]NPNF 1 11:463. [41]See Gal 4:23. [42]See Gal 4:28-31. [43]PCR 116. [44]CSEL 81.1:311. [45]NPNF 1 11:463. [46]LCC 6:385.

same, though in a different way.[47] Isaac was born as a type of the Savior, but Jacob and Esau were born as types of two peoples, believers and unbelievers, who come from the same source but are nevertheless very different. . . . One person represents the entire race, not because he is their physical ancestor but because he shares their relationship to God. There are children of Esau who are children of Jacob, and vice versa. It is not because Jacob is praised that all those descended from him are worthy to be called his children. Nor is it because Esau was rejected that all those descended from him are condemned, for we see that Jacob the deceiver had unbelieving children, and Esau had children who were faithful and dear to God. There is no doubt that there are many unbelieving children of Jacob, for all the Jews, whether they are believers or unbelievers, have their origin in him. And that there are good and faithful children of Esau is proved by the example of Job, who was a descendent of Esau, five generations away from Abraham and therefore Esau's grandson. COMMENTARY ON PAUL'S EPISTLES.[48]

CHOSEN BY GOD. PELAGIUS: Not only are Ishmael and Isaac (who were born of different mothers but the same father) not equal in the sight of God; Jacob and Esau too (who were born of Rebecca by a single conception), were separated in God's sight before they were born, because of their future faith, so that God's plan to choose the good and reject the evil already existed in his foreknowledge.[49] Thus God has now chosen from among the Gentiles those whom he foreknew would believe and has rejected those of Israel whom he foreknew would not believe. Rebecca is thought to have been the first woman to have borne twins; it is because this strange thing has happened to her that she inquires of God.[50] PELAGIUS'S COMMENTARY ON ROMANS.[51]

PELAGIUS: God's foreknowledge does not prejudge the sinner, if he is willing to repent. PELAGIUS'S COMMENTARY ON ROMANS.[52]

THEODORET OF CYR: Paul reinforces here what he said earlier about Sarah and Isaac, in case someone might think that the election depended on the mother. For although Rebecca had twins, only one of them was chosen. INTERPRETATION OF THE LETTER TO THE ROMANS.[53]

9:11 Elect by Grace, Not Merit

THEY HAD DONE NOTHING EITHER GOOD OR BAD. ORIGEN: Paul is saying all this in order to demonstrate that if either Isaac or Jacob had been chosen by God because of their merits and earned justification by the works of the flesh, then the grace which they merited could belong also to those who were descended from them according to flesh and blood. But in fact, since their election was not due to works, but to the purpose of God and the free will of him who called them, the grace of the promises is not fulfilled in the children of the flesh, but in the children of God, that is, in those who are likewise chosen according to God's purpose and adopted as sons. COMMENTARY ON THE EPISTLE TO THE ROMANS.[54]

THAT GOD'S PURPOSE OF ELECTION MIGHT CONTINUE. AMBROSIASTER: Paul proclaims God's foreknowledge by citing these events, because nothing can happen in the future other than what God already knows. Therefore, knowing what each of them would become, God said: "The younger will be worthy and the elder unworthy." In his foreknowledge he chose the one and rejected the other. And in the one whom God chose his purpose remained, because nothing other than what God knew and purposed in him to make him worthy of salvation could happen. Likewise, the purpose of God remained in the one whom he rejected. However, although God knew what would happen, he is not a respecter of persons and condemns nobody before he sins, nor does he reward anyone until he conquers. COM-

---

[48]CSEL 81.1:311-13. [49]See Gen 25:21-26. [50]See Gen 25:22-23. [51]PCR 116. [52]PCR 117. [53]IER, Migne PG 82 col. 153. [54]CER 4:146-48.

mentary on Paul's Epistles.[55]

CHRYSOSTOM: God does not have to wait, as we do, to see which one will turn out good and which one will turn out bad. He knew this in advance and decided accordingly. HOMILIES ON ROMANS 16.[56]

NOT BECAUSE OF WORKS. AUGUSTINE: This moves some people to suppose that the apostle Paul had taken away the freedom of the will, by which we either please God by the good of faithfulness or offend him by the evil of unfaithfulness. These people say that God loved the one and hated the other before either one was born or could have done either good or evil. But we reply that God did this by foreknowledge, by which he knows what even the unborn will be like in the future. But let no one say God chose the works of the man whom he loved, although these works did not yet exist, because he knew in advance what they would be. If God elected works, why does the apostle say that election is not according to works? Thus we should understand that we do good works through love, and we have love by the gift of the Holy Spirit, as the apostle says himself: "God's love has been poured into our hearts through the Holy Spirit which has been given to us."[57]

Therefore no one should glory in his works as if they were his own, for he does them by the gift of God, since love itself works good in him. What then has God elected? If he gives the Holy Spirit, through whom love works good, to whomever he wishes, how does he choose whom to give him to? If he does not choose according to merit, it is not election, for everyone is equal prior to merit, and it is impossible to choose between totally equal things. But since the Holy Spirit is given only to believers, God does not choose works (which he himself bestows), for he gives the Holy Spirit so that through love we might do good works. Rather, he chooses faith.

For unless each one believes in him and perseveres in his willingness to receive, he does not receive the gift of God (i.e., the Holy Spirit), through whom, by an outpouring of love, he is enabled to do good works. Therefore God did not choose anyone's works (which he himself will give) by foreknowledge, but by foreknowledge he chose faith. He chose the one whom he knew in advance would believe in him, and to him he has given the Holy Spirit, so that by doing good works he may attain everlasting life.

Belief is our work, but good deeds belong to him who gives the Holy Spirit to believers. This argument was used against certain Jews who, once they believed in Christ, gloried in the works they had done before receiving grace. They claimed that they had merited the grace of the gospel by these earlier works, even though only a person who has received grace can do good works. Furthermore, grace is such that the call comes to the sinner when he has no merit and prevents him from going straight to his damnation. But if he follows God's call of his own free will, he will also merit the Holy Spirit, through whom he can do good works. And remaining in the Spirit (also by free will) he will merit eternal life, which cannot be marred by any corruption. AUGUSTINE ON ROMANS 60.[58]

BECAUSE OF HIS CALL. AUGUSTINE: No one believes who is not called. God calls in his mercy and not as rewarding the merits of faith. The merits of faith follow his calling; they do not precede it. . . . Unless the mercy of God in calling precedes faith, no one can even believe and thus begin to be justified and to receive the power to do good works. So grace comes before all merit. Christ died for the ungodly. The younger received the promise that the elder should serve him from the God who called him and not from any meritorious works of his own. TO SIMPLICIAN ON VARIOUS QUESTIONS 1.2.1.[59]

THOUGH NOT YET BORN. AUGUSTINE: We know that children not yet born have done noth-

---

[55]CSEL 81.1:313. [56]NPNF 1 11:464-65. [57]Rom 5:5. [58]AOR 31, 33. [59]LCC 6:391.

ing either good or evil in their own life, nor have they any merits from a previous life, which no individual can have as his own. They come into the miseries of this life, their carnal birth according to Adam involves them at the moment of their nativity in the contagion of the primal death, and they are not delivered from the penalty of eternal death which a just verdict passing from one lays upon all unless they are born again in Christ through grace. LETTER 217.[60]

PELAGIUS: Perhaps this happened so that it might be shown that even from a set of twins the one who does not believe is abandoned. PELAGIUS'S COMMENTARY ON ROMANS.[61]

9:12 Good Works Produced by Grace

JACOB HAD NO MERITORIOUS WORKS BEFORE HE WAS BORN. AUGUSTINE: No one could say that Jacob had conciliated God by meritorious works before he was born, so that God should say this of him. . . . Nor had Isaac conciliated God by any previous meritorious works, so that his birth should have been promised. . . . Good works do not produce grace, but are produced by grace. TO SIMPLICIAN ON VARIOUS QUESTIONS 1.2.3.[62]

PELAGIUS: Here Paul shows that the people who came afterward belonged to the promise after the manner of Isaac. PELAGIUS'S COMMENTARY ON ROMANS.[63]

9:13 Choosing One, Rejecting Another

THE FOREKNOWLEDGE AND JUSTICE OF GOD. AMBROSIASTER: These things are said of the Jews . . . for not all who are called children of Abraham deserve to be so called, as I have already pointed out. Therefore Paul restricts his grief to the fact that he discovered that it was long ago predicted that not all would believe, and he grieves for them only because they refused to believe out of jealousy. They had the opportunity, however, as Paul

demonstrates. At the same time, there was no point in grieving over those who were not predestined to eternal life, for God's foreknowledge had long ago decreed that they would not be saved. For who would cry over someone who is long dead? But when the Gentiles appeared and accepted the salvation which the Jews had lost, Paul's grief was stirred, but this was mainly because they were the cause of their own damnation.

God knew those who would turn out to be people of ill will and he did not number them among the good, although the Savior said to the seventy-two disciples whom he chose as a second class and who later abandoned him: "Your names are written in heaven."[64] But this was because of justice, since it is just that each person should receive his reward. For because they were good they were chosen for this service, and their names were written in heaven for the sake of justice, as I have said. But according to foreknowledge they were among the number of the wicked. For God judges according to his justice, not according to his foreknowledge. Thus he said to Moses: "If someone sins against me, I shall delete him from my book."[65] The person who sins is deleted according to the justice of the Judge, but according to his foreknowledge his name was never in the book of life. The apostle John described these people as follows: "They went out from us but they were never of us, for if they had been of us they would have remained with us."[66] There is no respect of persons in God's foreknowledge.[67] For God's foreknowledge is that by which it is defined what the future will of each person will be, in which he will remain, by which he will either be condemned or rewarded. Some of those who will remain among the good were once evil, and some of those who will remain among the evil were once good. COMMENTARY ON PAUL'S EPISTLES.[68]

---

[60]FC 32:86. [61]PCR 116. [62]LCC 6:387-88. [63]PCR 117. [64]Lk 10:20. [65]Ex 32:33. [66]1 Jn 2:19. [67]See Acts 10:34-35. [68]CSEL 81.1:313-17.

WHETHER GOD HATES NOTHING HE HAS MADE. AUGUSTINE: If God hated Esau because he was a vessel made for dishonor, how could it be true that God hates nothing which he has made? For in that case, God hated Esau, even though he had made him as a vessel for dishonor. This knotty problem is solved if we understand that God is the Maker of all creatures. Every creature of God is good. Every man is a creature as man but not as sinner. God is the Creator both of the body and of the soul of man. Neither of these is evil, and God hates neither. He hates nothing which he has made. But the soul is more excellent than the body, and God is more excellent than both soul and body, being the maker and fashioner of both. In man he hates nothing but sin. Sin in man is perversity and lack of order, i.e., a turning away from the Creator, who is more excellent, and a turning to the creatures which are inferior to him. God does not hate Esau the man, but he does hate Esau the sinner. TO SIMPLICIAN ON VARIOUS QUESTIONS 1.2.18.[69]

[PSEUDO-]CONSTANTIUS: In this passage Paul conflates Genesis [25:23-25] with Malachi [1:1-2], both of which he regards as being equally the Word of God. THE HOLY LETTER OF ST. PAUL TO THE ROMANS.[70]

PROPHECY FULFILLED IN REBECCA'S DESCENDANTS. PELAGIUS: The apostle shows that what had been told to Rebecca was fulfilled in her descendants.[71] PELAGIUS'S COMMENTARY ON ROMANS.[72]

THEODORET OF CYR: Thus God chose Isaac and rejected Ishmael and the children of Keturah.[73] So also he chose Jacob over Esau, even though both were formed together in the womb. Why be surprised then, if God does the same thing nowadays, by accepting those of you who believe and rejecting those who have not seen the light? INTERPRETATION OF THE LETTER TO THE ROMANS.[74]

GENNADIUS OF CONSTANTINOPLE: It was many years after the event that Scripture testified to this in the words of the prophet Haggai [Malachi].[75] Paul added this quotation because he wanted to show that God's judgment is just, for while it was in accordance with his foreknowledge, the lives of both men later followed these different paths. PAULINE COMMENTARY FROM THE GREEK CHURCH.[76]

---

[69]LCC 6:399-400. [70]ENPK 2:66. [71]See Gen 25:23. [72]PCR 117. [73]See Gen 25:1-4; 1 Chron 1:32. [74]IER, Migne PG 82 col. 153. [75]Mal 1:2-3. [76]NTA 15:390.

9:14-21 PREDESTINATION AND FREE WILL

[14]*What shall we say then? Is there injustice on God's part? By no means!* [15]*For he says to Moses, "I will have mercy on whom I have mercy, and I will have compassion on whom I have compassion."* [16]*So it depends not upon man's will or exertion, but upon God's mercy.* [17]*For the scripture says to Pharaoh, "I have raised you up for the very purpose of showing my power in you, so that my name may be proclaimed in all the earth."* [18]*So then he has mercy on whomever he wills, and he hardens the heart of whomever he wills.*

[19]*You will say to me then, "Why does he still find fault? For who can resist his will?"* [20]*But who*

are you, a man, to answer back to God? Will what is molded say to its molder, "Why have you made me thus?" [21]Has the potter no right over the clay, to make out of the same lump one vessel for beauty and another for menial use?

OVERVIEW: The fact that God punishes some and not others is hard to understand, but it is not unjust. Here we meet the problem of the baptized who do not follow Christ in later life. As far as Augustine was concerned, such people had no claim to inherit eternal life, though he could not explain why God allows such apostasy to happen. God is free to show mercy to whomever he wishes, and his decisions are never unjust. God's choosing is not based on human merit. Ultimately it is a mystery understood by God alone.

God can use even the hardest heart to serve his purposes, as was the case with Pharaoh. The idea that the Egyptian monarch might have repented is dismissed by saying that he was so far gone in sin that it would have been inconceivable. God's approach to Pharaoh was not unjust, because Pharaoh was a sinner. Mercy is never automatic and cannot be taken for granted by anyone. God's will can never be resisted, but it is always holy and just whether we understand it or not. Few passages in the New Testament are more strongly predestinarian than Romans 9:19-21, and we can sense that some Fathers were uncomfortable with them. Once more it is Augustine who draws the logical conclusion and says that since the entire clay of the human race was corrupted in Adam, it is only by the mercy of God that any of us can be redeemed. Adam's exercise of his free will effectively removes ours. These selections differ as to the voice of the speaker, whether Paul's or a rhetorical opponent's, and as to the extent to which the metaphor of the vessel allows for free will.

9:14 God Is Just

THE CASE OF BAPTIZED CHILDREN WHO LATER BECOME APOSTATES. AUGUSTINE: What is to be said of infants who receive the sac-rament of Christian grace, as is usual at that age, and thus undoubtedly have a claim to eternal life and the kingdom of heaven if they die at once, whereas if they are allowed to grow up, some become even apostates? Why is this, except that they are not included in that predestination and calling according to his purpose which is without repentance? Why some are included and others are not can be for a hidden reason but not for an unjust one. LETTER 149.[1]

WHETHER GOD MAKES SOME PEOPLE EVIL. PELAGIUS: Paul was afraid that because he had argued that racial privilege is of no consequence in God's sight, or in case the Jews understood him to be saying that already at that time it was indicated that later people would be better people, they might think that he meant that God makes some people good and others evil, because, in the judgment of the Jews, it was unjust to punish those who had not voluntarily sinned, Paul also calls to mind the contrary texts which they usually used to support this view, and after replying to these examples with brief objections he shows that they should not be understood as they understand them. PELAGIUS'S COMMENTARY ON ROMANS.[2]

CAESARIUS OF ARLES: Why does God not scourge all men mercifully in such a way so as not to allow anyone to be hardened against him? Either this is to be ascribed to the wickedness of those who have deserved to become hardened, or it is to be referred to the inscrutable judgments of God, which are often hidden but are never unjust. SERMON 101.5.[3]

9:15 God Dispenses Mercy and Compassion

---

[1]FC 20:256. [2]PCR 117. [3]FC 47:101.

**MERCY NOT DISPENSED ACCORDING TO
HUMAN STANDARDS.** APOLLINARIS OF LAODI-
CEA: It is not unjust for God to have mercy on
those he wishes to have mercy on but not on others. For, as Paul says, God demonstrates through
Moses what his mercy was like. He does not dis-
pense mercy according to human standards, but
according to the wisdom of God. For we are
shown mercy not because of our own works but
because of God, who has the power to show
mercy. PAULINE COMMENTARY FROM THE GREEK
CHURCH.[4]

FOREKNOWLEDGE AND MERCY. AMBROSIASTER:
This means that God will have mercy on those
whom he knows will be converted and remain
with him. . . . He will show mercy to those who,
after they have sinned, return to him with a right
heart. It is God's to give or to not give. He calls
the ones whom he knows will obey and does not
call those whom he knows will not obey. COM-
MENTARY ON PAUL'S EPISTLES.[5]

CHRYSOSTOM: God was telling Moses[6] that it was
not his to know who was deserving of God's love
towards man; rather, Moses was to leave that up
to God. If that was true for him, how much more
is it true for us! HOMILIES ON ROMANS 16.[7]

**I WILL HAVE COMPASSION ON WHOM I WILL
HAVE COMPASSION.** AUGUSTINE: God was merciful to us in the first place in that he called us
while we were still sinners . . . and he continues to
have mercy on us now that we believe. How does
God have mercy a second time? He gives his Holy
Spirit to the man who believes and asks for him.
And having given the Spirit God will then have
compassion on those to whom he has already
shown compassion. That is to say, he will make
the believer compassionate so that he may do
good works through love. Let no one take the
credit for acting compassionately, since it was by
the Holy Spirit that God gave him this love,
without which no one can be compassionate.[8]

God did not elect those who had done good

works, but those who believed, so that he might
enable them to do good works. It is our part to
believe and to will and his part to give to those
who believe and will the ability to do good works
through the Holy Spirit, by whom the love of
God is poured out in our hearts in order to make
us compassionate. AUGUSTINE ON ROMANS 61.[9]

[PSEUDO-]CONSTANTIUS: God says this to
Moses.[10] Referring to the passage the apostle
shows that God's compassion will be shown to
those who believe in Christ. THE HOLY LETTER
OF ST. PAUL TO THE ROMANS.[11]

PELAGIUS: This means: "I will have mercy on him
whom I have foreknown will be able to deserve
compassion, so that I have already had mercy on
him." PELAGIUS'S COMMENTARY ON ROMANS.[12]

9:16 Not by Human Will or Exertion

UNLESS THE LORD BUILDS. ORIGEN: This must
be understood in the light of what David says in
the psalm: "Unless the Lord builds the house,
those who build it labor in vain. Unless the Lord
watches over the city, the watchman stays awake in
vain."[13] From this we learn that it is not because
the builder sits idly by that God builds the house
for him but because he works and expends as
much labor and care as lies within human power,
but yet it belongs to God to remove all the obstacles and bring the work to completion. Thus, man
is called to work as hard as he can, but God will
crown the work with success. Therefore it is godly
and right for a man to leave the completion of his
work to God and not to another human being.
Likewise, Paul sowed and Apollos watered but
God gave the increase, "so neither he who plants
nor he who waters is anything, but only God who
gives the growth."[14] In the same way, we can say
that "it depends not upon man's will or exertion

---

[4]NTA 15:67. [5]CSEL 81.1:319. [6]Ex 33:19. [7]NPNF 1 11:466. [8]See
Gal 5:22. [9]AOR 33, 35. [10]See Ex 33:19. [11]ENPK 2:67. [12]PCR 117.
[13]Ps 127:1. [14]1 Cor 3:6-7.

but upon God's mercy." COMMENTARY ON THE EPISTLE TO THE ROMANS.[15]

DIODORE: God is not unjust simply because he does not give everyone what they deserve. PAULINE COMMENTARY FROM THE GREEK CHURCH.[16]

THE EXAMPLE OF SAUL AND DAVID. AMBROSIASTER: When Saul asked forgiveness for his sin he did not receive it, but David, when he confessed his sin, did receive forgiveness.[17] However, it cannot be said on this basis that God judged unjustly by granting forgiveness to the one and withholding it from the other. For the one who looks on the heart knows in what spirit the penitent is making his request and whether it deserves to be heard. And although it is dangerous to try to figure out God's judgment, yet in the case of unbelievers, who reap the reward of their own minds, it cannot be said that God's judgment is unjust.

Look at the stories of Saul and David and ask yourself what happened to them after God's judgment. Did Saul do what was right after he was refused mercy? Did he prove that God's judgment was unjust? Did David after receiving mercy turn his back on God? Or did he remain in him from whom he received mercy? COMMENTARY ON PAUL'S EPISTLES.[18]

MAN'S WILL AND RUNNING. JEROME: It is clear from this passage that the willing and running are ours, but the fulfillment of our willing and running belongs to the mercy of God. So it is that free will is preserved as far as our willing and running is concerned and that everything depends on the power of God as far as the fulfillment of our willing and running is concerned. AGAINST THE PELAGIANS 1.5.[19]

IT DEPENDS UPON GOD'S MERCY. AUGUSTINE: Paul does not take away the freedom of the will but says that our will is not sufficient unless God helps us, making us compassionate so that we

might do good works by the gift of the Holy Spirit. . . . We cannot will unless we are called, and when we will after our calling neither our will nor our striving is enough unless God gives strength to our striving and leads us where he calls. It is therefore clear that it is not by willing nor by striving but by the mercy of God that we do good works, even though our will (which by itself can do nothing) is also present. AUGUSTINE ON ROMANS 62.[20]

[PSEUDO-]CONSTANTIUS: From here to [verse 19] the apostle Paul assumes the role of devil's advocate, saying that we do not have it in us to do either good or evil, but that this is found only in the will of God. The actual words of the devil's advocate are taken from Isaiah.[21] THE HOLY LETTER OF ST. PAUL TO THE ROMANS.[22]

PELAGIUS: The Jewish argument here goes like this: "It does not depend on the one who wills or on the one who runs; God has mercy on whomever he wills and hardens whomever he wills." The apostle, though, does not take away what we possess in our own will. . . . For if the Jewish argument is correct, why does Paul run, as when he says: "I have finished the race,"[23] and why does he urge others to run?[24] For this reason it is understood that here Paul takes the role of the one who questions (and refutes), not of the one who denies. PELAGIUS'S COMMENTARY ON ROMANS.[25]

9:17 Human Intent Shows God's Power

GOD'S KNOWING AND FOREKNOWING OF HUMAN INTENTIONALITY. ORIGEN: It is certain that God not only knows everyone's intention and will but that he foreknows them as well. Thus knowing and foreknowing, the good and just dispenser uses the motives and intention of each one in order to accomplish the works which

---

[15]CER 4:152-54. [16]NTA 15:98. [17]1 Sam 15:24-31; 2 Sam 12:13. [18]CSEL 81.1:321. [19]FC 53:239. [20]AOR 35. [21]See Is 29:16; 45:9. [22]ENPK 2:67. [23]2 Tim 4:7. [24]See 1 Cor 9:24. [25]PCR 117-18.

the mind and will of each person has chosen. COMMENTARY ON THE EPISTLE TO THE ROMANS.[26]

PHARAOH RAISED UP TO SHOW GOD'S POWER. AMBROSIASTER: This Pharaoh (this was a royal title among the Egyptians and not a personal name, just as the rulers of Rome are called *Caesars*), was guilty of a great many crimes and unfit to live. He would never repent or in any way earn the right to live with God. But if anyone thought that God had made a mistake or that he was unable to take revenge on Pharaoh, let him listen to what God says. . . . Pharaoh was used by God in order that many signs and plagues might be revealed through him.[27] Even though he was really dead, he appeared to be alive for a short while so that all those who were without God might be frightened by the punishment and the torments which they saw being inflicted on him and confess the one true God, by whom this revenge was being wreaked. In the same way the ancient physicians used to open up the bodies of people who deserved to die, while they were still alive, in order to find out what the causes of their disease might be and thus by punishing the dying bring saving health to the living. COMMENTARY ON PAUL'S EPISTLES.[28]

GOD'S PATIENCE WITH PHAROAH. CHRYSOSTOM: God endured Pharaoh for long time in the hope that he might repent, but even when he did not do so God was patient with him in order to display his own goodness and power, even if Pharaoh gained nothing from it. HOMILIES ON ROMANS 16.[29]

WHETHER PHAROAH'S HARDNESS OF HEART WAS UNWILLED. AUGUSTINE: We read in Exodus [10:1] that Pharaoh's heart was hardened, so that he was not moved even by clear signs. Therefore, because Pharaoh did not obey the commands of God he was punished. No one can say that this hardness of heart came upon Pharaoh undeservedly; it came by the judgment of God

who was giving him just punishment for his unbelief. Nor should it be thought that Pharaoh did not obey because he could not, on the ground that his heart had already been hardened. On the contrary, Pharaoh had deserved his hardness of heart by his earlier unbelief.

For in those whom God has chosen it is not works but faith which is the beginning of merit, so that they might do good works by the gift of God. And in those whom he condemns unbelief and unfaithfulness are the beginning of punishment, so that by that very punishment they are permitted to do what is evil.[30] AUGUSTINE ON ROMANS 62.[31]

PELAGIUS: The Jews explain this passage in the wrong way as well. It is expounded by Christian interpreters in one of two ways. First, there are those who say that since each one will be punished when the measure and degree of his sins is complete . . . and Pharaoh had exceeded his limit, God desired to make an example of him for the benefit of others . . . so that God's people might come to know his justice and power and neither dare to sin nor fear their enemies. The same thing that happened to Pharaoh happens when a doctor, seeking the cure for an illness, discovers a remedy in the course of torturing someone who has already been condemned to death for committing many crimes or when a judge, although he could punish a guilty man immediately, afflicts him first with various torments in order to rouse everyone's fear.

Second, there are those who say that Pharaoh was hardened by God's patience, for after a plague from God was over Pharaoh became harder, and although God knew that Pharaoh had not repented he nevertheless wanted to show his forbearance even toward him. PELAGIUS'S COMMENTARY ON ROMANS.[32]

OECUMENIUS: God's power is patience, and it is a

---

[26]CER 4:154. [27]See Ex 7:1—12:30. [28]CSEL 81.1:323-25. [29]NPNF 1 11:468. [30]See Rom 1:28. [31]AOR 35. [32]PCR 118-19.

very great power indeed. For who would not be overawed by the enormous patience of God? For he says that it is for this reason that he has agreed to let Pharaoh rule, that it may be shown how patient he is. PAULINE COMMENTARY FROM THE GREEK CHURCH.[33]

9:18 God's Mercy and Human Unbelief

WHETHER PHAROAH'S HEART WAS HARD-ENED APART FROM HIS OWN RECALCI-TRANCE. ORIGEN: Pharaoh's heart was hardened in the following way: God did not want to punish him immediately and completely. Although Pharaoh's wickedness was enormous, God in his patience did not withdraw the possibility of conversion from him. Instead he struck him lightly at first and then gradually increased the blows. But although God acted with patience, Pharaoh was hardened by that very thing and became even more angry with God and contemptuous of him. . . . Therefore it is not that God hardens whom he wills, but rather that whoever is not softened by his patience is thereby automatically hardened. COMMENTARY ON THE EPISTLE TO THE ROMANS.[34]

APOLLINARIS OF LAODICEA: Someone may object that Pharaoh cannot have been hardened, nor can anyone else who falls into sin, since in that case they would not be guilty of the hardening which has come upon them. But in saying this, O Man, you are going beyond yourself and seeking the secret reason for this inequality in God. There is no injustice here, the apostle said, because the refusal to show mercy on a sinner is due to the foreknowledge of the divine wisdom and not to some judicial reward. In this respect the apostle goes on to say that it is not up to men to sound the hidden depths of God,[35] for the message of salvation is properly administered to all, whether mercy is shown to them or not. PAULINE COMMENTARY FROM THE GREEK CHURCH.[36]

AMBROSIASTER: Here Paul assumes the role of an

objector who makes these assumptions. COMMENTARY ON PAUL'S EPISTLES.[37]

HOW GOD'S MERCY IS RELATED TO ONE'S WILLED FAITH OR UNFAITH. AUGUSTINE: He enables the one on whom he has mercy to do good, and he leaves the one whom he hardens to do evil. But that mercy is the result of the prior merit of faith, and that hardening is the fruit of prior unbelief, so that we do good deeds by the gift of God and evil deeds because of his punishment. Yet in either case free will is not taken away from man, whether it is to believe in God, so that mercy on us might follow, or to disbelieve in him, so that punishment on us might be the result. AUGUSTINE ON ROMANS 62.[38]

AUGUSTINE: Why does the Father not teach all people in order that they might come to Christ, unless it is that all those whom he teaches, he teaches because of mercy, but those whom he does not teach, he does not teach because of judgment? PREDESTINATION OF THE SAINTS 8. 14.[39]

AUGUSTINE: You must believe that the man whom God permits to go astray and to become hardened has deserved this evil, while in the case of the man upon whom he has mercy, you must acknowledge with an unswerving faith that this is a case of the grace of God, who is rendering not evil for evil but good for evil. GRACE AND FREE WILL 23.45.[40]

WHETHER GOD CAUSES WICKEDNESS. PELAGIUS: If this is understood to mean that God has mercy on whom he wills and hardens whom he wills because there is enough wickedness, then your argument will be lost, viz., the argument that not you but the will of the Lord, to which there can be no opposition, is the cause of your sins. The very nature of God's justice opposes

---

[33]NTA 15:428. [34]CER 4:158. [35]See Rom 11:33. [36]NTA 15:68. [37]CSEL 81.1:325. [38]AOR 35. [39]FC 86:234-35. [40]FC 59:307.

this reasoning. Pelagius's Commentary on Romans.[41]

9:19 Resisting God's Will

Who Can Resist His Will? Origen: It is certain that no one can resist God's will, but it is good for us to remember that his will is just and right. Whether we are good or bad depends on our will, but it is God's will that the bad person is destined to punishment and the good person is destined to glory. Commentary on the Epistle to the Romans.[42]

Ambrosiaster: Paul teaches us first that nobody can resist God's will because he is more powerful than anyone else. Next he teaches us that God is the Father of all and therefore does not want anyone to suffer evil. What God has made he wants to remain unharmed. Commentary on Paul's Epistles.[43]

Paul's Persistent Way of Pressing Questions. Chrysostom: Paul does everything he can to embarrass the questioner. He does not answer him right away either, but prefers to shut him up with a further question.... This is what a good teacher does. He does not follow his pupils' fancy everywhere but leads them to his own mind and pulls up the thorns, and then puts the seed in and does not immediately answer all the questions put to him. Homilies on Romans 16.[44]

Augustine: Having given his conclusion [in the last verse] Paul plays devil's advocate by asking a rhetorical question.... He responds to this question in a sensible way so that we might understand that the basic rewards of faith and of unbelief are made plain only to spiritual people and not to those who live according to the earthly man. Likewise with the way God in his foreknowledge elects those who will believe and condemns unbelievers. He neither elects the ones because of their works nor condemns the others because of theirs, but he grants to the faith of the ones the ability to do good works and hardens the unbelief of the others by deserting them, so that they do evil. This understanding, as I have said, is given only to spiritual people and is very different from the wisdom of the flesh. Thus Paul counters his inquirer so that he may understand that he first must put away the man of clay in order to be worthy to investigate these things by the Spirit. Augustine on Romans 62.[45]

9:20 Answering Back to God

Who Are You to Answer God? Origen: I do not think that, if you are a faithful and discreet servant of God and want to understand and admire the wisdom of the Lord, he will say to you: "Who are you?" . . . If we want to know something of the secret and hidden things of God and if we are not people of lusts and contentions, then let us inquire faithfully and humbly into the judgments of God which are contained more secretly in holy Scripture. For even the Lord said: "Search the Scriptures,"[46] knowing that these things are applicable not to those who are busy with other matters and only hear or read the Bible from time to time, but to those who with a pure and simple heart endeavor to open up the holy Scriptures by their labor and constant attention. I know well enough that I am not one of them! But anyone who is, let him seek and he will find. Commentary on the Epistle to the Romans.[47]

Origen: Such a rebuke does not refer to one who is faithful and lives a good and righteous life and has confidence towards God.... This rebuke is not for the faithful and the saints but for the unfaithful and the ungodly. On First Principles 3.1.22.[48]

Ambrosiaster: It is a great indignity and presumption for a man to answer back to God—the

---

[41]PCR 119. [42]CER 4:158. [43]CSEL 81.1:325-27. [44]NPNF 1 11:467. [45]AOR 35, 37. [46]Jn 5:39. [47]CER 4:160-62. [48]OFP 205-6.

unjust to the just, the evil to the good, the imperfect to the perfect, the weak to the strong, the corruptible to the incorrupt, the mortal to the immortal, the servant to the Lord, the creature to the Creator! COMMENTARY ON PAUL'S EPISTLES.[49]

THE FAITHFUL FREELY YIELD TO THE POTTER'S HANDS. CHRYSOSTOM: Paul says this in order not to do away with free will but rather to show to what extent we ought to obey God. We should be as little inclined to call God to account as a piece of clay is. We ought to abstain not only from complaining or questioning but from even speaking or thinking about it at all, and instead we should become like that lifeless matter which follows the potter's hands and lets itself be shaped in whatever way the potter wills. HOMILIES ON ROMANS 16.[50]

AUGUSTINE: As long as you are just a creature, says Paul, like this lump of clay, and you have not been led to spiritual things, so that as a spiritual man you might judge all things and be judged by no one, it is right for you to hold back from this kind of inquiry and not to answer back to God. For everyone who wants to know God's plan ought first to be received into his friendship, and this is only possible for spiritual people who already bear the image of the heavenly. AUGUSTINE ON ROMANS 62.[51]

PELAGIUS: Some people say that Paul is still speaking here in the role of those who object, because to say that nobody can oppose the will of God, who has mercy on one and who hardens another, and to add that nobody should criticize God amounts to the same thing. But others say that from here on the apostle replies that, even if there were a reason for them to make an accusation, they ought not to talk back to their Creator, for in comparison with God, we are like a piece of pottery in the hands of the potter.[52] PELAGIUS'S COMMENTARY ON ROMANS.[53]

THIS VESSEL CANNOT RIGHTLY SCOLD THIS

POTTER. [PSEUDO-]CONSTANTIUS: Now the apostle lunges out at the man who was contradicting him [in the above verses], showing that it is of God's own will and decision. . . . There is no difference in the clay which the potter molds in his hand. He can make whatever kind of vessel he wants to, and the vessel cannot answer back and say how it would prefer to be made. But here, in words like "resist" and "find fault with God's will," he shows the free will of the one who dares to draw back from the will of God. THE HOLY LETTER OF ST. PAUL TO THE ROMANS.[54]

THEODORE OF MOPSUESTIA: How can the thing which is made blame its Maker for the construction of its own nature? Everything must be content with its own nature, whatever that may be. PAULINE COMMENTARY FROM THE GREEK CHURCH.[55]

WHY HAVE YOU MADE ME THUS? THEODORET OF CYR: If you did not have your own independence, and if you did not choose what you do by your own free will, you would have to be quiet in the way that inanimate objects are and simply acquiesce in what is given to you. But as it is you have reason, and you can both describe and do the things which are shown to you. Instead you do not like what has happened and are trying to investigate the causes of the divine plan. INTERPRETATION OF THE LETTER TO THE ROMANS.[56]

9:21 The Potter's Right Over the Clay

NATURE OF THE VESSEL. TERTULLIAN: The vessel is the flesh, because it was made of clay by the breath of God,[57] and only afterward was it clothed with the coat of skin. ON THE RESURRECTION OF THE FLESH 8.[58]

FIT ONLY FOR MENIAL USE. ORIGEN: Remem-

[49]CSEL 81.1:327. [50]NPNF 1 11:467. [51]AOR 37. [52]See Is 64:8; Jer 19:11. [53]PCR 119. [54]ENPK 2:68. [55]NTA 15:146. [56]IER, Migne PG 82 cols. 156-57. [57]Cf. Gen 2:7. [58]ANF 3:550.

ber the incident in Jeremiah when the prophet went down to the potter's house and found him reworking a clay vessel which was spoiled, as it seemed good to him to do. Then the Lord said: "O house of Israel, can I not do with you as this potter has done? Behold, like the clay in the potter's hand, so are you in my hand, O house of Israel."[59] It seems to me that no more need be said on the subject. . . .

Someone who does not cleanse himself and does not wash away his sins by repentance is a vessel fit only for menial use. If he goes on and increases in wickedness so that his mind is hardened and his impenitent heart ends up despising everything God commands, then he will no longer be fit even for menial use but will become a vessel fit only for destruction. COMMENTARY ON THE EPISTLE TO THE ROMANS.[60]

ORIGEN: If both the saved and the lost come from one lump of clay, then the nature of their souls will be not different but the same. ON FIRST PRINCIPLES 3.1.23.[61]

WHETHER THIS POTTER FOREKNEW WHAT THIS VESSEL WOULD DO. DIODORE: Do not dare to condemn God or imagine that he showed mercy on one and hardened another by accident, for it was according to the power of his foreknowledge that he gave each one his due. Nor is he guilty because he knew in advance what would happen, but rather each of those who was foreknown in this way is responsible for his own actions, whether good or evil. PAULINE COMMENTARY FROM THE GREEK CHURCH.[62]

THE LIMITS OF THE POTTER ANALOGY. AMBROSIASTER: The substance of the clay is the same, but the will of the potter is different. Likewise God made us all of the same substance and we all became sinners, but he had mercy on one and rejected another, not without justice. The potter has only a will, but God has a will and justice to go with it. For he knows who ought to be shown mercy, as I have already said. COMMEN-

TARY ON PAUL'S EPISTLES.[63]

THE SAME LUMP. CHRYSOSTOM: God does nothing at random or by mere chance, even if you do not understand the secrets of his wisdom. You allow the potter to make different things from the same lump of clay and find no fault with him, but you do not grant the same freedom to God! . . . How monstrous this is. It is not on the potter that the honor or dishonor of the vessel depends but rather on those who make use of it. It is the same way with people—it all depends on their own free choice. HOMILIES ON ROMANS 16.46.[64]

HAS THE POTTER NO RIGHT OVER THE CLAY? AUGUSTINE: As long as you are a potter's vessel, you must first be broken by the iron rod of which it was said: "You will rule them with a rod of iron, and you will break them as a potter's vessel."[65] Then, when the outer man is destroyed and the inner man is renewed, you will be able, rooted and grounded in love, to understand what is the length and breadth and height and depth, to know even the overwhelming knowledge of the love of God.[66] So because from the same lump of clay God has made some vessels for noble use and others for ignoble, it is not for you, whoever you are who still lives according to this lump (that is, who are wise by the standards of earthly sense and the flesh), to dispute what God has decreed. AUGUSTINE ON ROMANS 62.[67]

AUGUSTINE: First comes the clay which is fit only to be thrown away. We must begin with this but need not remain in it. Afterward comes what is fit for use, into which we can be gradually molded and in which, once molded, we can remain. This does not mean that everyone who is wicked will become good but that no one becomes good who was not once wicked. What is true is that the sooner a man makes a change in himself for the better, the sooner he has a right to be called what

---

[59]Jer 18:6. [60]CER 4:162-64. [61]OFP 206. [62]NTA 15:99. [63]CSEL 81.1:327-29. [64]NPNF 1 11:468. [65]Ps 2:9. [66]Eph 3:18-19. [67]AOR 37.

he has become. THE CITY OF GOD 15.1.[68]

AUGUSTINE: Given that our nature sinned in paradise, we are now formed through a mortal begetting by the same divine providence, not according to heaven but according to earth, i. e., not according to the spirit but according to the flesh, and we have all become one mass of clay, i.e., a mass of sin. QUESTIONS 68.3.[69]

THE FREE WILL OF THE FIRST MAN. AUGUSTINE: If this lump of clay were of such indifferent value that it deserved nothing good any more than it deserved anything evil, there would be reason to see injustice in making of it a vessel unto dishonor. But when through the free will of the first man alone, condemnation extended to the whole lump of clay, it is undoubtedly true that if vessels are made of it unto honor, it is a question not of justice not forestalling grace, but of God's mercy. If however, vessels are made of it unto dishonor, this is to be attributed to God's justice, not to his injustice—a concept which can hardly exist with God! LETTER 186.[70]

AUGUSTINE: It would seem unjust that vessels of wrath should be made unto destruction if the whole lump of clay has not been condemned in Adam. The fact that men become vessels of wrath at birth is due to the penalty they deserve, but that they become vessels of mercy at their second birth is due to an undeserved grace. LETTER 190.[71]

THEODORE OF MOPSUESTIA: Whoever heard of a clay pot made for menial use blaming the potter for the way it was made and demanding to be remolded for some better purpose?[72] PAULINE COMMENTARY FROM THE GREEK CHURCH.[73]

CYRIL OF ALEXANDRIA: It is not possible to say on the basis of this [verse] that there are different types of human nature, nor does holy Scripture claim that some people have been made cruel or obdurate or even vessels of honor and wickedness, nor does it attribute this kind of nature to them. Rather, it should be understood to mean that some men are made like clay vessels and that we use them either for honor or for dishonor.[74] EXPLANATION OF THE LETTER TO THE ROMANS.[75]

THE MENIAL PATH CHOSEN. THEODORET OF CYR: Those who are called vessels for menial use have chosen this path for themselves. . . . This is clear from what Paul says to Timothy: "If anyone purifies himself from what is ignoble, then he will be a vessel for noble use, consecrated and useful to the master of the house, ready for any good work."[76] INTERPRETATION OF THE LETTER TO THE ROMANS.[77]

---

[68]FC 14:415. [69]FC 70:161. [70]FC 30:204. [71]FC 30:276. [72]See Is 45:9. [73]NTA 15:146. [74]See 2 Tim 2:20-21. [75]Migne PG 74 col. 837. [76]2 Tim 2:21. [77]IER, Migne PG 82 col. 157.

9:22-33 THE CHOSEN PEOPLE

[22]*What if God, desiring to show his wrath and to make known his power, has endured with much patience the vessels of wrath made for destruction,* [23]*in order to make known the riches of his glory for the vessels of mercy, which he has prepared beforehand for glory,* [24]*even us whom he has called, not from the Jews only but also from the Gentiles?* [25]*As indeed he says in Hosea,*

"Those who were not my people
I will call 'my people,'
and her who was not beloved
I will call 'my beloved.'"
[26]*"And in the very place where it was said to them, 'You are not my people,'*
they will be called 'sons of the living God.'"
[27]*And Isaiah cries out concerning Israel: "Though the number of the sons of Israel be as the*
sand of the sea, only a remnant of them will be saved; [28]*for the Lord will execute his sentence upon*
the earth with rigor and dispatch." [29]*And as Isaiah predicted,*
"If the Lord of hosts had not left us children,
we would have fared like Sodom and been made like Gomorrah."
[30]*What shall we say, then? That Gentiles who did not pursue righteousness have attained it,*
that is, righteousness through faith; [31]*but that Israel who pursued the righteousness which is based*
on law did not succeed in fulfilling that law. [32]*Why? Because they did not pursue it through faith,*
but as if it were based on works. They have stumbled over the stumbling stone, [33]*as it is written,*
"Behold, I am laying in Zion a stone that will make men stumble,
a rock that will make them fall;
and he who believes in him will not be put to shame."

OVERVIEW: God's patient calling was to Gentiles as well as to Jews, as the Old Testament prophesied. It was never intended that all the Jews would be saved, since even Isaiah had predicted that only a remnant would be left. It is futile to pursue after righteousness by works. The Jews tried it and failed, whereas the Gentiles were saved in spite of themselves. It is a matter of faith. Those who have faith will be saved; those who lack it will be rejected, however hard they may try. The stumbling stone on which the Jews tripped up was Christ. They were so busy pursuing their own righteousness that they failed to notice God's provision for them.

9:22 God's Patient Endurance

DESIRING TO SHOW HIS WRATH. ORIGEN: I am astonished when I examine the Holy Spirit's purpose in the Scriptures. For he says that the wrath of God, which is foreign to his nature, will be made known to men . . . but that his goodness and mercy, which are proper to his nature, will be concealed and hidden. . . . Why should God reveal his wrath to men and conceal his mercy? No doubt it is because God knows that the human race is weak and prone to fall through negligence, and that it is therefore better for them to be under the fear of wrath than to relax in the hope of God's mercy and forgiveness. COMMENTARY ON THE EPISTLE TO THE ROMANS.[1]

GOD ENDURED WITH MUCH PATIENCE. AMBROSIASTER: This means that unbelievers are made ready for punishment by the will and long-suffering of God, which is his patience. For although he has waited a long time for them, they have not repented. He has waited a long time so that they should be without excuse,[2] for God knew all along that they would not believe. COMMENTARY ON PAUL'S EPISTLES.[3]

SELF-CHOSEN VESSELS OF WRATH. CHRYSOSTOM: Why are some people vessels of wrath and

---

[1]CER 4:170. [2]See Rom 1:20; 2 Pet 3:15. [3]CSEL 81.1:329.

others vessels of mercy? It is by their own free choice. God, being very good, shows the same kindness to both. For it was not only to those who were saved that God showed kindness but to Pharaoh also, as far as he deserved. For both Pharaoh and God's people had the advantage of God's patience. And if Pharaoh was not saved it was because of his own will, since God had done as much for him as he had done for those who were saved. HOMILIES ON ROMANS 16.[4]

AUGUSTINE: Paul has sufficiently demonstrated that the hardness of heart which came to Pharaoh came as the just deserts of his earlier unbelief. Yet God patiently endured his unbelief until the time came for him to mete out his punishment. God did this in order to correct those whom he had decided to set free from error and to lead them by calling them back to reverence and godliness, offering his aid to their prayers and sighings. AUGUSTINE ON ROMANS 63.[5]

MADE FOR DESTRUCTION. [PSEUDO-]CONSTANTIUS: God desires a response, because his patience and goodness makes those who have their own will live either as vessels of wrath or as vessels of mercy. Here the apostle deprives them of any reason to start sinning. Despite God's patience they have not been converted to the right way. They are being prepared for destruction because it is always unjust to endure sinners and allow the evil things which they do to go unpunished. Therefore, just as punishment is being prepared for sinners, so eternal glory is being prepared for those who fear God.[6] THE HOLY LETTER OF ST. PAUL TO THE ROMANS.[7]

THEY PREPARED THEMSELVES FOR DESTRUCTION. PELAGIUS: God put up with Pharaoh for a long time while Pharaoh blasphemed and oppressed his people with hard labor and even had ordered that innocent little children be put to death.[8] By filling up the quota of their sins, people like Pharaoh become vessels worthy of wrath, and by their own doing they prepare themselves

for destruction. PELAGIUS'S COMMENTARY ON ROMANS.[9]

ALL ARE TESTED TO BE FINALLY SHOWN FOR WHAT THEY ARE. THEODORE OF MOPSUESTIA: What Paul is saying is this: God has made this present life one of struggles and not of reward, and he agrees that wicked men and good ones alike will be tested in both good and bad things in order to have an exact touchstone for the predestination of each person. In this way those who are good will follow the path of virtue and will cling to it through all the changes of life, neither boasting in the good times nor being unable to bear reverses. Wicked people, on the other hand, will in all circumstances be shown to be lovers of evil, ignorant of the reason for their good fortune when they enjoy it and exaggerating the wretchedness of their condition when they suffer grief. God gives each of these what they deserve in the next life. PAULINE COMMENTARY FROM THE GREEK CHURCH.[10]

WHETHER GOD LITERALLY HAS THE PASSION OF WRATH. OECUMENIUS: Of course God is not subject to the passion of wrath. It is when he does what we do when we are angry that he calls it "wrath," so that we will understand what he means. PAULINE COMMENTARY FROM THE GREEK CHURCH.[11]

9:23 The Riches of God's Glory

TO MAKE KNOWN THE RICHES OF HIS GLORY. ORIGEN: The riches of God are made known when his mercy is shown toward those who are rejected by men and who are downtrodden, who put their hope not in their own riches or in their own strength but in the Lord.[12] COMMENTARY ON THE EPISTLE TO THE ROMANS.[13]

[4]NPNF 1 11:469. [5]AOR 37. [6]See Rom 2:7-9; 1 Pet 5:10. [7]ENPK 2:69C71. [8]See Ex 1:8-16. [9]PCR 119. [10]NTA 15:147. [11]NTA 15:429. [12]See Ps 18:25; 103:11. [13]CER 4:170-72.

Prepared Beforehand for Glory. Ambrosiaster: It is God's patience and long-suffering that, just as he prepares the wicked for destruction, so also he prepares the good for their reward. For the good are those who have the hope of faith. God preserves everyone knowing what the destiny of each will be. Therefore, it is a sign of his patience that those who have been rescued from evil or who persevere in good works he prepares for glory. Commentary on Paul's Epistles.[14]

Chrysostom: The Jews reproached the Gentiles because the latter were saved by grace, and they thought that by making this accusation they would bring shame on them. But Paul sets this insinuation aside, because if this brought glory to God, how much more would it bring glory to those through whom God was glorified? Homilies on Romans 16.[15]

Good in Benefits, Just in Punishment. Augustine: In giving to some what they did not deserve God obviously wanted his grace to be gratuitous and therefore genuinely grace, and in not giving it to all he showed what all deserved. He is good in the benefit given to certain people and just in the punishment of others but good in all things, for it is good when that which is deserved is given, and just in all things, as it is just when that which is not merited is given without injury to anyone. Gift of Perseverance 12.28.[16]

Caesarius of Arles: We who were vessels of wrath through our first birth have deserved to become vessels of mercy through the second one. The first birth brought us forth unto death, but the second one recalled us to life. All of us were temples of the devil before baptism, but after baptism we were made ready to become temples of Christ. Sermon 229.[17]

9:24 Jews and Gentiles Called by God

Those Whom He Has Called. Ambrosi-

aster: God has called those whom he has prepared for glory, who he knew would persevere in faith, whether they are near at hand or far away. Commentary on Paul's Epistles.[18]

The Potter's One Lump. Augustine: God did not call all the Jews but only some of them. Nor did he call all the Gentiles but only some of them. From Adam has sprung one mass of sinners and godless men, in which both Jews and Gentiles belong to one lump, apart from the grace of God. If the potter out of one lump of clay makes one vessel for honor and another for dishonor, it is clear that God has made of the Jews some vessels for honor and others for dishonor, and similarly of the Gentiles. To Simplician on Various Questions 1.2.19.[19]

Pelagius: Since even then some of the Egyptians left with the children of Israel ... so too now God has called not only Jews but also Gentiles to faith. Pelagius's Commentary on Romans.[20]

9:25 Now Called and Loved

The Calling of the Gentiles. Ambrosiaster: It is clear that this was said about the Gentiles, who once were not God's people, but afterward, to the chagrin of the Jews, received mercy and are called God's people. Once they were not loved, but when the Jews fell away they were adopted as children and are now loved, so that where once they were not called God's people, now they are called children of the living God. Commentary on Paul's Epistles.[21]

Chrysostom: Hosea obviously was speaking about the Gentiles here. Homilies on Romans 16.[22]

Augustine: The gist of the entire argument

---

[14]CSEL 81.1:329. [15]NPNF 1 11:469. [16]FC 86:296. [17]FC 66:173. [18]CSEL 81.1:331. [19]LCC 6:401-2. [20]PCR 120. [21]CSEL 81.1:331. [22]NPNF 1 11:469.

leads to this conclusion. Paul taught that we do good by the mercy of God and that the Jews who had received the gospel should not glory in their works, thinking that they had deserved this and not wanting it to be given to the Gentiles. In Paul's mind, the Jews should cease from such pride and understand that if we are called to faith not through our own works but by the mercy of God and if it is given to those who believe to do good, then they should not begrudge the Gentiles this mercy as if it had been given to the Jews on the ground of prior merit, which is nothing. Augustine on Romans 64.[23]

Not Beloved. Theodoret of Cyr: This passage originally applied to Jews, not to Gentiles. . . . It meant that God's people would lose their status and be called "Not my people" and "Not beloved." But then God promised that the rejected Jews would be called back again. Thus from having been God's people and then rejected they would return. . . . The Gentiles, on the other hand, would become God's people for the first time, having never been his people before. Interpretation of the Letter to the Romans.[24]

9:26 Sons of the Living God

They Will Be Called Sons. Chrysostom: Even if this was said about those Jews who believed and not about the Gentiles, the argument still stands. For if those who had received so many benefits and then had become hard-hearted and estranged and had lost their identity as a people were turned around, . . . what is there to prevent those who were originally aliens from being called and counted worthy of the same blessings if only they obey? Homilies on Romans 16.[25]

[Pseudo-]Constantius: Paul is referring to the Gentiles who would believe in Christ. The Holy Letter of St. Paul to the Romans.[26]

Pelagius: Those who think that this is not Paul talking but the Jews interpret it to mean: "God

saved as many as he wished, so that he chose even Gentile idolaters who had never served God, and called few from Israel, as Isaiah testifies." Pelagius's Commentary on Romans.[27]

9:27 A Remnant Will Be Saved

Isaiah Cries Out. Ambrosiaster: Paul says this because Isaiah was crying out for those who would believe in Christ. It is these who are the true Israel. . . . The others have gone away from the law because they have not believed in him whom the law promised would alone be sufficient for salvation. Therefore they became apostate, because by not accepting Christ they became lawbreakers. Therefore, of that great number only those who God foreknew would believe have been saved. Commentary on Paul's Epistles.[28]

Chrysostom: Not content with Hosea, Paul quotes Isaiah as well. . . . He does not say that all are to be saved either, but only those who are worthy. Homilies on Romans 16.[29]

Other Sheep Not of This Fold. Augustine: This shows that the Lord is the cornerstone, uniting both walls in himself. Hosea's testimony is spoken of the Gentiles, but the Lord unites both Jews and Gentiles, according to what he said in the gospel about the latter: "I have other sheep that are not of this fold; I must bring them also and they will heed my voice. So there shall be one flock, one shepherd."[30] Augustine on Romans 65.[31]

Only a Remnant Saved. Augustine: If by remnant . . . we are to understand not election of the justified to eternal life but election of those who are to be justified, that kind of election is truly hidden and cannot be known by us, who must regard all men as parts of a single lump of

---

[23]AOR 37. [24]IER, Migne PG 82 col. 160. [25]NPNF 1 11:469. [26]ENPK 2:70. [27]PCR 120. [28]CSEL 81.1:333. [29]NPNF 1 11:469. [30]Jn 10:16. [31]AOR 39.

clay. If some claim to be able to know it, I must confess my own weakness in this matter. To Simplician on Various Questions 1.2.22.[32]

Pelagius: Here Isaiah showed that only a few Jews would believe. Pelagius's Commentary on Romans.[33]

9:28 The Lord Will Execute His Sentence

Done in Christ. Ambrosiaster: This has been done in Christ, who said: "Moses wrote about me."[34] Commentary on Paul's Epistles.[35]

With Dispatch. Chrysostom: What this means is that salvation will come quickly, and it depends on very few words. There is no need to make a big palaver of it or get involved with the vexation of the works of the law. Homilies on Romans 16.[36]

Pelagius: The historical sense is that, just as I shorten and finish off a sentence, so God will accomplish this with all speed. But in prophecy, the shortened sentence is understood to mean the New Testament, because everything is briefly summarized in it. Pelagius's Commentary on Romans.[37]

9:29 A Seed

Abraham's Seed. Origen: What children are these that the Lord has left? No doubt this means what the apostle expounds elsewhere, when he says that it was said to Abraham: "I shall give this land to you and to your seed."[38] He did not say "to your seeds," as if to many, but to your seed, as if to one, and that one is Christ.[39]

Nor was it an accident that Isaiah called the remnant a seed. It was so called because it was meant to be sown in the earth and bear much fruit. In this way he teaches that Christ must also be sown, that is, buried in the earth, from which he would rise and bear fruit in the whole multitude of the church. Commentary on the Epistle to the Romans.[40]

Ambrosiaster: This seed, which alone remains reserved for the conversion of the human race is Christ and his teaching, as he himself said: "The seed is the Word of God."[41] Therefore what was long ago promised to us who have been delivered from the burden of the law remains for our redemption, so that by receiving the forgiveness of sins we might not be punished by the law and perish as Sodom did. Commentary on Paul's Epistles.[42]

As Isaiah Predicted. Chrysostom: This prophecy was actually fulfilled in the captivity, when most of the people were taken away and perished, with only a few being saved.[43] Homilies on Romans 16.[44]

Pelagius: *Predicted* is a good choice of words, because the same thing as he mentioned [in verses 27-28] was written even earlier.[45] God did not allow a few righteous people to perish along with a host of the ungodly.[46] Or this text may mean that this would have happened had Christ, Abraham's offspring, not been sent to set the people free. The interpretation of the objectors, however, is that it would have happened, unless God had wished to call at least a few from among the Jews. Pelagius's Commentary on Romans.[47]

Oecumenius: This may also be said of Christ, which is how Cyril of Alexandria interpreted it. Pauline Commentary from the Greek Church.[48]

9:30 Attaining Righteousness Through Faith

Righteousness Implanted in the Gentiles Who Did Not Pursue It. Origen: It is

---

[32]LCC 6:405. [33]PCR 120. [34]Jn 5:46. [35]CSEL 81.1:333. [36]NPNF 1 11:470. [37]PCR 120. [38]Gen 17:8. [39]See Gal 3:16. [40]CER 4:180. [41]Lk 8:11. [42]CSEL 81.1:335. [43]See 2 Kings 24—25; 2 Chron 36; Jer 52. [44]NPNF 1 11:470. [45]Is 1:9. [46]See Gen 18:20; 19:29. [47]PCR 120. [48]NTA 15:429.

one thing to pursue righteousness and another to have it implanted within. A person who tries by much teaching and reading to obtain something is said to pursue it. . . . In this sense, the Gentiles, who did not have the tables of the law or the written Word, cannot be said to have pursued righteousness. Nevertheless, they had it in them because the natural law had taught it to them. Therefore, they were close to that righteousness which is of faith, that is, to Christ. COMMENTARY ON THE EPISTLE TO THE ROMANS.[49]

AMBROSIASTER: God is the true and lasting righteousness, if he is acknowledged. For what is more righteous that to know God the Father, from whom all things come, and Christ his Son, through whom all things come? Therefore the first part of righteousness is to acknowledge the Creator, and the next part is to keep what he commands. COMMENTARY ON PAUL'S EPISTLES.[50]

CHRYSOSTOM: Paul means that the Gentiles did not go to particular trouble to acquire righteousness, in the way that the Jews did. HOMILIES ON ROMANS 16.[51]

ALTERNATIVE READINGS ACCORDING TO VOICE. PELAGIUS: If this is spoken in the person of the apostle, Paul here once again imagines that the Jews might say: "If it is not true, as we say, that it does not depend on the one who wills or on the one who runs, why have the Gentiles found righteousness, which they never sought before, while Israel could not find it, although they have always sought it?" But if the whole of the above thought belongs to the objectors, the apostle is here replying and summarizing the issue by saying: "What shall I say to these objections which are presented to us except that the Gentiles believed as soon as they were called and that the Jews refused to believe?" Righteousness is by faith, and the Jews refused to believe. PELAGIUS'S COMMENTARY ON ROMANS.[52]

9:31 Israel Did Not Fulfill the Law

PURSUIT LACKING FULFILLMENT. ORIGEN: Israel pursued the law of righteousness according to the letter but did not fulfill the law. What law? No doubt the law of the Spirit. COMMENTARY ON THE EPISTLE TO THE ROMANS.[53]

FAITH FULFILLS THE LAW. AMBROSIASTER: Faith is the fulfilling of the law. It is because the Gentiles have faith that they appear to fulfill the whole law. But the Jews, who out of envy did not believe in the Savior, because they claimed the righteousness which is commanded in the law, i.e., the sabbath, circumcision, etc., did not come to the law. In other words, they did not fulfill the law, and those who do not fulfill the law are guilty of it. COMMENTARY ON PAUL'S EPISTLES.[54]

PELAGIUS: Paul explains once again why the Jews did not find righteousness. Having wrongly gloried in their works they refused to believe and rejected grace on the ground that they were righteous already. PELAGIUS'S COMMENTARY ON ROMANS.[55]

9:32 Stumbling Over the Law of Faith

BASED ON WORKS. ORIGEN: The apostle would never say that they did not fulfill the law which they pursued, which they had and held in their hands. Rather he is explaining why Israel was unable to fulfill the law. It was because they relied on works, not on faith. COMMENTARY ON THE EPISTLE TO THE ROMANS.[56]

AMBROSIASTER: The Jews rejected faith, which as I have said is the fulfillment of the law, and instead claimed that they were justified by works, that is, by the sabbath, the new moons, circumcision and so on. They forgot that Scripture says that "the just shall live by faith."[57] COMMENTARY ON PAUL'S EPISTLES.[58]

---

[49]CER 4:182. [50]CSEL 81.1:337. [51]NPNF 1 11:470. [52]PCR 120-21. [53]CER 4:182. [54]CSEL 81.1:337. [55]PCR 121. [56]CER 4:182-84. [57]Hab 2:4. [58]CSEL 81.1:339.

[PSEUDO-]CONSTANTIUS: Paul says this because the Jewish people, thinking that they could be justified by the works of the law, were unable to come to the law of righteousness, that is to say, to faith in Christ. THE HOLY LETTER OF ST. PAUL TO THE ROMANS.[59]

THE STUMBLING STONE. PELAGIUS: The man who sees a stone does not stumble, but the blind man dashes himself against it. This is what happened to the Jews, who were blinded by their hatred and crucified Christ because they did not recognize him. PELAGIUS'S COMMENTARY ON ROMANS.[60]

THEODORE OF MOPSUESTIA: It is impossible to be justified by the works of the law because it would be necessary to keep the whole law, which is not possible. But anyone who sins (which is inevitable) lies under the judgment of the law. PAULINE COMMENTARY FROM THE GREEK CHURCH.[61]

GENNADIUS OF CONSTANTINOPLE: Paul calls the Lord Christ a stumbling stone because those who did not accept the new covenant in him stumbled over him and by their unbelief fell from the grace of justification which was given to men through him. PAULINE COMMENTARY FROM THE GREEK CHURCH.[62]

9:33 A Stumbling Stone

PREDICTION OF THE PASSION. TERTULLIAN: It was fitting that the mystery of the passion should be set forth in predictions, for the more incredible it was, the more likely it was to have been a stumbling stone if it had been openly predicted. AN ANSWER TO THE JEWS 10.[63]

THE STONE THE BUILDERS REJECTED. AMBROSIASTER: There are many passages of Scripture where Christ is portrayed as a rock or a stone. The prophet Daniel calls him a stone which detaches itself without hands from the mountain, hitting and threatening all the kingdoms and fill-

ing the whole earth.[64] This clearly refers to Christ. And in the law the rock from which the waters flowed is called Christ, as the apostle Paul himself testifies.[65] And the apostle Peter says to the Jews: "This is the stone which the builders rejected."[66]

The Jews did not want to compare Christ's words with his deeds lest perhaps they might recognize that it was not absurd for him to say that he had come down from heaven. . . . This was the rock of offense as far as the Jews were concerned. The rock was undoubtedly the human flesh of the Savior. It detached itself without hands, because it was made of a virgin by the Holy Spirit without the participation of a male. COMMENTARY ON PAUL'S EPISTLES.[67]

CHRYSOSTOM: This is said not of the Jews only but of the entire human race. . . . The wonder is that the prophet speaks not only of those who will believe but also of those who will not believe. For to stumble is to disbelieve. HOMILIES ON ROMANS 16.[68]

THE ROCK OF OFFENSE. PELAGIUS: It was foretold that Christ would be the stumbling stone and the rock of offense precisely because many take offense at his birth and death.[69] . . . Nobody who believes, not just the Jew, will be put to shame by former sins. PELAGIUS'S COMMENTARY ON ROMANS.[70]

PAYING ATTENTION TO THE PROPHETS. THEODORET OF CYR: People stumble when they stop paying attention to where they are going and look elsewhere. This is what happened to the Jews. Because they were so busy adding extras to the law, they failed to notice the stone which the prophets predicted. INTERPRETATION OF THE LETTER TO THE ROMANS.[71]

---

[59]ENPK 2:71. [60]PCR 121. [61]NTA 15:149. [62]NTA 15:395. [63]ANF 3:165. [64]See Dan 2:31-45. [65]See 1 Cor 10:4. [66]Ps 118:22; Acts 4:11. [67]CSEL 81.1:341. [68]NPNF 1 11:471. [69]See Mt 13:57; Mk 6:3. [70]PCR 121. [71]IER, Migne PG 82 col. 164.

10:1-11 CHRIST THE ONLY SAVIOR

¹Brethren, my heart's desire and prayer to God for them is that they may be saved. ²I bear them witness that they have a zeal for God, but it is not enlightened. ³For, being ignorant of the right-eousness that comes from God, and seeking to establish their own, they did not submit to God's righteousness. ⁴For Christ is the end of the law, that everyone who has faith may be justified.

⁵Moses writes that the man who practices the righteousness which is based on the law shall live by it. ⁶But the righteousness based on faith says, Do not say in your heart, "Who will ascend into heaven?" (that is, to bring Christ down) ⁷or "Who will descend into the abyss?" (that is, to bring Christ up from the dead). ⁸But what does it say? The word is near you, on your lips and in your heart (that is, the word of faith which we preach); ⁹because, if you confess with your lips that Jesus is Lord and believe in your heart that God raised him from the dead, you will be saved. ¹⁰For man believes with his heart and so is justified, and he confesses with his lips and so is saved. ¹¹The scripture says, "No one who believes in him will be put to shame."

OVERVIEW: Paul does everything he can to find something good to say about the Jews, but in the end he is forced to admit that even their good qualities have been distorted because of their un-belief. Christ brings the law to an end, but this is recognized and realized only in those who believe in him. Those who reject him and cling to the law are destroyed along with the law they trust in. The Fathers were unwilling to accept the idea that a person could be saved by keeping the law. They therefore interpreted Romans 10:5 to mean that the law would keep people safe in this life but would not grant them safe passage into eter-nity.

Those who know Christ by faith understand that he is everywhere but above all that he is present in our hearts and on our lips. There is no need to go in search of him but only to do what he commands. A Christian is saved by confessing Christ—a notion that came to be understood as confessing the creed from the heart at baptism. Those who believe in Christ will be rewarded on the day of judgment, when others will be pun-ished. Jews and Gentiles will be treated alike, for it is those who call on the name of the Lord who will be saved.

10:1 Praying That the Jews Will Be Saved

NO HATRED FOR JUDAISM. AMBROSIASTER: Since Paul wants to liberate the Jews from the law, which is a veil over their faces, but does not want to appear to desire this out of any hatred for Judaism, he shows his love for them and says many good things about the law. But he teaches that the time for obeying the law has come to an end and by doing this bears witness that he is concerned for them, if only they will listen to him and not assume that he is their enemy. COMMEN-TARY ON PAUL'S EPISTLES.[1]

MY HEART'S DESIRE AND PRAYER. CHRYSOS-TOM: Paul continues to demonstrate his deep-seated good will toward the Jews.... He even does his best to find excuses for them, but in the end he is overcome by the nature of the facts and cannot do so. HOMILIES ON ROMANS 17.[2]

AUGUSTINE: Here Paul begins to speak of his hope for the Jews, lest the Gentiles in their turn become condescending toward them. For just as

---

¹CSEL 81.1:343. ²NPNF 1 11:472.

the pride of the Jews had to be countered because they gloried in their works, so also with the Gentiles, lest they become proud at having been preferred over the Jews. AUGUSTINE ON ROMANS 66.[3]

PELAGIUS: Here Paul shows that he prays for his enemies not only with the tongue but also with the heart.[4] PELAGIUS'S COMMENTARY ON ROMANS.[5]

10:2 A Zeal for God

ZEAL FOR GOD BUT NOT ACCORDING TO KNOWLEDGE. ORIGEN: If someone has a love for God but does not know that love must be patient, kind, not envious, not acting wrongly, not puffed up, not ambitious, not seeking its own and so on; if he does not have these things in his love but only loves God in his emotions, then it may rightly be said of him that he has a love for God but not according to knowledge. COMMENTARY ON THE EPISTLE TO THE ROMANS.[6]

AMBROSE: I know that you [Emperor Theodosius I] are God-fearing, merciful, gentle and calm, that you have the faith and fear of God in your heart, but often some things escape our notice. Some people have a zeal for God but not according to knowledge. Care must be taken . . . lest this condition steal upon pious souls. LETTER 2.[7]

CHRYSOSTOM: Should not the Jews be excused if they have erred because of some misguided zeal? Notice how Paul goes on to remove this excuse from them. HOMILIES ON ROMANS 17.[8]

PELAGIUS: The Jews are zealous in pursuing the law, but they do not understand that Christ came according to the law and that they cannot be justified by the law. Indeed, it is risky to do something without knowledge, because it often turns out contrary to what was expected. PELAGIUS'S COMMENTARY ON ROMANS.[9]

PRAISE WITH A HOOK. THEODORET OF CYR: Paul adds criticism to his praise, just as food sometimes contains a hook, so that they might derive some benefit from what he had to say. INTERPRETATION OF THE LETTER TO THE ROMANS.[10]

GENNADIUS OF CONSTANTINOPLE: Having once been one of them himself, Paul understood and bore witness that the Jews fought against the gospel out of zeal for God, yet it was a zeal uninformed by true knowledge. PAULINE COMMENTARY FROM THE GREEK CHURCH.[11]

10:3 Ignorance of Righteousness from God

WHETHER THEIR IGNORANCE WAS DUE TO MALICE. AMBROSIASTER: Paul says that the Jews did not accept Christ because they were mistaken, not because there was any malice on their part. COMMENTARY ON PAUL'S EPISTLES.[12]

CHRYSOSTOM: Once again, ignorance would seem to be an excuse for pardoning them. But it turns out to lead only to a stronger accusation. . . . It was from small-mindedness and a desire for power that they erred rather than from ignorance, and even their own righteousness was not based on keeping the law. HOMILIES ON ROMANS 17.[13]

SEEKING TO ESTABLISH THEIR OWN RIGHTEOUSNESS. AUGUSTINE: Paul said this about the Jews who because of their self-confidence rejected grace and as a result did not believe in Christ. The Jews, he says, seek to establish a righteousness of their own that comes from the law, not that the law was established by them but rather that they had placed their righteousness in the law which comes from God by supposing that they were able to fulfill this law by themselves. For they were ignorant of the righteousness of God, not that

---

[3]AOR 39. [4]See Is 29:13; Mt 5:44; 15:8. [5]PCR 121. [6]CER 4:192-94. [7]FC 26:8. [8]NPNF 1 11:472. [9]PCR 121-22. [10]IER, Migne PG 82 col. 164. [11]NTA 15:395. [12]CSEL 81.1:345. [13]NPNF 1 11:472.

righteousness whereby God is righteous but the one which comes to man from God. GRACE AND FREE WILL 12.24.[14]

[PSEUDO-]CONSTANTIUS: By "their own righteousness" Paul means the law of the Pharisees. For the sacrifices of the law and the other things which were a shadow of the truth, which were to be fulfilled in Christ, ceased to operate once he had come. But this they did not want to believe. The apostle was right to talk of their own righteousness, because it was not of God but of themselves. THE HOLY LETTER OF ST. PAUL TO THE ROMANS.[15]

THEY DID NOT SUBMIT. PELAGIUS: Because the Jews did not know that God justifies by faith alone and because they thought they were righteous by the works of a law they did not keep, they refused to submit themselves to the forgiveness of sins, to prevent the appearance of having been sinners, as it is written: "But the Pharisees, rejecting God's purpose for themselves, refused to be baptized with John's baptism."[16] PELAGIUS'S COMMENTARY ON ROMANS.[17]

THEODORET OF CYR: When Paul talks about the Jews' own righteousness he means their inappropriate way of keeping the law. For they were trying to keep something which was already out of date. INTERPRETATION OF THE LETTER TO THE ROMANS.[18]

10:4 Christ Is the End of the Law

THE INTENT OF THE LAW. CLEMENT OF ALEXANDRIA: The Jews did not understand the intention of the law and so failed to practice it. They made up their own version and thought that that was what the law intended. They had no faith in the prophetic power of the law. They followed the bare letter, not the inner meaning—fear, not faith. STROMATA 2.9.42.5.[19]

THE END OF THE LAW. IRENAEUS: How is

Christ the end of the law if he is not also the cause of it? For he who has brought in the end also created the beginning. AGAINST HERESIES 4.12.3.[20]

ORIGEN: Christ is the end of the law, but only for those who believe. Those who do not believe and who do not have Christ do not have the end of the law and therefore cannot come to justification. COMMENTARY ON THE EPISTLE TO THE ROMANS.[21]

NOVATIAN: There was indeed a time long ago when attention was to be paid to these shadows and figures prescribing abstinence from foods pronounced good in their creation but forbidden by the law. When Christ, "the end of the law," came, he cleared up all the ambiguities of the law and all those things which antiquity had shrouded in mystery. JEWISH FOODS 5.1-2.[22]

APOLLINARIS OF LAODICEA: Christ furnishes believers with holy righteousness, because he is "the end of the law," and the law prepared the way for Christ by showing that he was the fulfillment of it, the salvation of mankind.[23] PAULINE COMMENTARY FROM THE GREEK CHURCH.[24]

EVERYONE WHO HAS FAITH MAY BE JUSTIFIED. CHRYSOSTOM: There is only one righteousness, which finds its fulfillment in Christ.... Even someone who has failed to keep the law properly will be righteous if he has Christ ... but the man who does not have Christ is a stranger to the law as well. HOMILIES ON ROMANS 17.[25]

PELAGIUS: On the day that one believes in Christ it is as if one has fulfilled the whole law. PELAGIUS'S COMMENTARY ON ROMANS.[26]

SEVERIAN: This does not mean that Christ is a

---

[14]FC 59:277. [15]ENPK 2:71-72. [16]Lk 7:30. [17]PCR 122. [18]IER, Migne PG 82 col. 164. [19]FC 85:187. [20]ANF 1:476. [21]CER 4:198. [22]FC 67:151. [23]See Rom 1:16. [24]NTA 15:69. [25]NPNF 1 11:472. [26]PCR 122.

part of the law but rather that he is the beginning of a new life. The law has come to an end; it has ceased. PAULINE COMMENTARY FROM THE GREEK CHURCH.[27]

GENNADIUS OF CONSTANTINOPLE: Christ fulfilled the law's purpose by granting the righteousness which comes by faith in him to all those who accepted him. PAULINE COMMENTARY FROM THE GREEK CHURCH.[28]

10:5 Righteousness Based on Law

SHALL LIVE BY IT IN THIS LIFE. ORIGEN: Moses did not say that the man who practices the righteousness of the law will live forever but only that he will live by it in this life.[29] For Christ is the end of the law, as the apostle says, and without Christ it is impossible to fulfill the righteousness of the law.[30] COMMENTARY ON THE EPISTLE TO THE ROMANS.[31]

JEROME: Scripture says not that he will find life through the law, in the sense that through it he will live in heaven but that he will find life through it to the extent that what he will reap what he deserves in this world.[32] SERMONS ON THE GOSPEL OF MARK 76.[33]

THE ONE WHO PRACTICES THE LAW'S RIGHTEOUSNESS. AMBROSIASTER: Paul says this because the righteousness of the law of Moses did not make people guilty as long as they kept it. COMMENTARY ON PAUL'S EPISTLES.[34]

DIODORE: Paul says that the man who fulfilled the law would enjoy the good things promised by it, that is to say, "a land flowing with milk and honey."[35] PAULINE COMMENTARY FROM THE GREEK CHURCH.[36]

CHRYSOSTOM: In fact this has proved to be impossible, and therefore the law's righteousness has failed those who tried to keep it. HOMILIES ON ROMANS 17.[37]

NO ONE KEEPS THE LAW PERFECTLY WITHOUT CHRIST. PELAGIUS: Moses distinguished between two kinds of righteousness, the righteousness of faith and the righteousness of works. The latter justifies the suppliant by deeds, but the former justifies by belief alone. . . . In this age no one keeps the law perfectly without Christ. Believing in him is also implied in the law. On account of this passage some think that the Jews have earned only this present life by the works of the law, but the words of the Lord show that this is not true. When he was asked about eternal life the Lord stipulated the commandments of the law: "If you would enter life, keep the commandments."[38] From this we understand that one who kept the law at that time had everlasting life.[39] PELAGIUS'S COMMENTARY ON ROMANS.[40]

ALL COMMANDMENTS REQUIRED. GENNADIUS OF CONSTANTINOPLE: Comparing the law with the glory of grace, Paul says that even Moses could not have been justified by the law unless he fulfilled all the commandments of the law. PAULINE COMMENTARY FROM THE GREEK CHURCH.[41]

10:6 Righteousness Based on Faith

CONTRASTING TWO KINDS OF RIGHTEOUSNESS. [PSEUDO-]CONSTANTIUS: Wanting to demonstrate the difference between the righteousness of the law and the righteousness of faith, the apostle calls Moses as his witness. Moses said of the righteousness of the law that the man who practiced it would live by it. But concerning the righteousness of faith, he says: "Do not say in your heart, 'Who will ascend into heaven?'" which means: Do not doubt but believe the command which Christ will announce in the future, when he will come to give you right-

---

[27]NTA 15:222. [28]NTA 15:395. [29]See Lev 18:5. [30]See Gal 2:16. [31]CER 4:198-200. [32]See Lev 18:5; Gal 3:12. [33]FC 57:137. [34]CSEL 81.1:345. [35]Ex 3:8. [36]NTA 15:101. [37]NPNF 1 11:473. [38]Mt 19:17. [39]As distiniguished from both Origen and Jerome above. [40]PCR 122. [41]NTA 15:395.

eousness by faith. THE HOLY LETTER OF ST. PAUL TO THE ROMANS.[42]

MOSES AS GOD'S MOUTHPIECE. THEODORET OF CYR: These are the words not of Moses but of the God of all things, who was using Moses as his mouthpiece. INTERPRETATION OF THE LETTER TO THE ROMANS.[43]

10:7 No Limitations on Christ

CHRIST NOT LIMITED TO A PARTICULAR PLACE. ORIGEN: We are not to think that Christ is in heaven in such a way as to be absent from the depths. . . . Furthermore, if someone should go down into the depths in his mind and thought, thinking that Christ is contained there and that he can somehow be called back from the dead . . . let him realize that he ought to think of Christ as he thinks of the Word, the truth and the righteousness of God. These things are not limited to a particular place but are present everywhere, nor can they be called up from the lower depths, but they can be grasped only by the mind and the intellect. COMMENTARY ON THE EPISTLE TO THE ROMANS.[44]

WITHOUT DOUBT. AMBROSIASTER: The quotation is from Deuteronomy [30:12], but the last phrase is the apostle's own addition. He says that someone who does not doubt about the hope which is in Christ has the righteousness of faith. COMMENTARY ON PAUL'S EPISTLES.[45]

DESCENT AND ASCENT. DIODORE: The Word of God leaves believers in no doubt either about the descent of the Lord from heaven for our sake or about the resurrection from the dead and the ascent into heaven. PAULINE COMMENTARY FROM THE GREEK CHURCH.[46]

10:8 The Word of Faith Is Near Us

THE WORD IS NEAR YOU. ORIGEN: Here we have to bear in mind the important distinction

between what is possible in theory and what is realized in practice. . . . Christ, who is the Word of God, is potentially near us and near everyone, but this is only realized in practice when I confess with my mouth that Christ is Lord and when I believe in my heart that God has raised him from the dead. COMMENTARY ON THE EPISTLE TO THE ROMANS.[47]

ORIGEN: By this Paul indicates that Christ is in the heart of all men by virtue of his being the Word or reason [logos] embedded in all things by sharing in which all men are rational. ON FIRST PRINCIPLES 1.3.6.[48]

FAITH NOT FOREIGN TO OUR NATURE. AMBROSIASTER: This is said in Deuteronomy [30:14] in order to show that belief [in Christ] is not all that foreign to our mind or to our nature. Even though we cannot see him with our eyes, what we believe is not out of harmony with the nature of our minds and our way of speaking. COMMENTARY ON PAUL'S EPISTLES.[49]

PELAGIUS: Historically speaking, Moses said this about the law, but the apostle applies it to Christ, because the law was neither in heaven nor in the abyss. Or it may mean that Paul is ordering them to meditate constantly on the law[50] so that they may find Christ in it.[51] The "word of faith which we preach" is the New Testament. PELAGIUS'S COMMENTARY ON ROMANS.[52]

10:9 Confessing Jesus Is Lord

AUGUSTINE: The creed builds up in you what you ought to believe and confess in order to be saved. SERMONS FOR THE RECENT CONVERTS, HOMILY 214.1.[53]

PELAGIUS: The testimony of the heart is the con-

---

[42]ENPK 2:72. [43]IER, Migne PG 82 col. 165. [44]CER 4:202. [46]5SEL 81.1:347. [46]NTA 15:101. [47]CER 4:204. [48]OFP 35. [49]CSEL 81.1:347. [50]See Ps 1:2. [51]See 2 Tim 3:14-17. [52]PCR 122. [53]FC 38:130.

fession of the mouth. "You will be saved" from past transgressions, not from future ones. Pelagius's Commentary on Romans.[54]

10:10 Belief and Confession

Consistency Needed. Ignatius: It is better for a man to be silent and be a Christian than to talk and not be one. . . . Men believe with the heart and confess with the mouth, the one unto righteousness, the other unto salvation. It is good to teach, if the teacher also does what he says. Epistle to the Ephesians 15.[55]

Heart and Mouth. Ambrose: With these twin trumpets of heart and mouth we arrive at that holy land, viz., the grace of resurrection. So let them always sound together in harmony for us, that we may always hear the voice of God. Let the utterances of the angels and prophets arouse us and move us to hasten to higher things. On the Death of His Brother Satyrus 2.112.[56]

The Rule of Faith. Ambrosiaster: What Paul previously spoke about he now makes clear. The rule of faith is to believe that Jesus is Lord and not to be ashamed to confess that God raised him from the dead and has taken him up to heaven with his body, whence he will come again. Commentary on Paul's Epistles.[57]

Chrysostom: The understanding must be strongly fixed in pious faith, and the tongue must herald forth by its confession the solid resolution of the mind. Baptismal Instructions 1.19.[58]

The Simplicity of Confession. Augustine: The innumerable and multiple rites by which the Jewish people had been oppressed have been taken away, so that in the mercy of God we might attain salvation by the simplicity of a confession of faith. Augustine on Romans 67.[59]

A Consistent Profession. Augustine: Did not almost all those who disowned Christ in the presence of their persecutors keep in their hearts what they believed about him? Yet, for not making with their mouth profession of faith unto salvation they perished, except those who repented and lived again. Against Lying 6.13.[60]

Baptismal Profession. Augustine: This condition is fulfilled at the time of baptism, when faith and profession of faith are all that is demanded for one to be baptized. The Christian Life 13.[61]

Augustine: This profession of faith is the creed which you will be going over in your thoughts and repeating from memory. The Creed 1.[62]

Augustine: We who expect to reign in everlasting righteousness can only be saved from this wicked world if while for our neighbor's salvation we profess with our lips the faith which we carry about in our heart, we exercise a pious and careful vigilance to see that this faith in us is not sullied in any point of belief by the deceitful snares of heretics. Faith and the Creed 1.1.[63]

Pelagius: If faith avails for righteousness and confession for salvation, there is no distinction between the Jew who believes and the Gentile who believes. Pelagius's Commentary on Romans.[64]

10:11 No Shame for Believers

Adam Hid Himself. Origen: If no one who believes in him will be put to shame, it is clear that those who sin will be, just as Adam sinned and was ashamed and hid himself.[65] So whoever incurs the shame of sin obviously does not believe. Commentary on the Epistle to the Romans.[66]

---

[54]PCR 123. [55]ANF 1:55. [56]FC 22:249. [57]CSEL 81.1:349. [68]ACW 31:30. [59]AOR 39. [60]FC 16:139. [61]FC 16:36. [62]FC 27:289. [63]FC 27:315. [64]PCR 123. [65]See Gen 3:8-10. [66]CER 4:208.

The Day of Judgment. Ambrosiaster: On the day of judgment, when everything will be examined and all false opinions and teachings will be overthrown, then those who believe in Christ will rejoice, seeing it revealed to all that what they believed is true and what was thought to be foolish was wise. For they will look at others and see that they alone are glorified and wise, when they had been considered contemptible and crazy. This will be the real test, when rewards and condemnation are decreed.[67] Commentary on Paul's Epistles.[68]

The Penitent Thief. [Pseudo-]Constantius: Take for instance that thief who was crucified next to Christ and who confessed Christ with his heart and his mouth (the two parts of him which were free)[69] and thus deserved to hear the reply: "Today you will be with me in Paradise."[70] The Holy Letter of St. Paul to the Romans.[71]

Believers Not Put to Shame. Pelagius: This applies not only to the Jews but to everyone. Do not put believers to shame, therefore, on account of their former actions, since the Scripture says that they cannot be put to shame. Pelagius's Commentary on Romans.[72]

Cyril of Alexandria: Israel ought not to suppose that salvation by faith is a blessing peculiar to it. For Scripture says that everyone who calls on the name of the Lord will be saved, whether Jew or Gentile, whether slave or free.[73] The universal God saves everyone without distinction, because all things belong to him. Thus we say that all things are recapitulated in Christ.[74] Explanation of the Letter to the Romans.[75]

---

[67]See Mt 12:36-37. [68]CSEL 81.1:349. [69]See Lk 23:42. [70]Lk 23:43. [71]ENPK 2:73. [72]PCR 123. [73]See Joel 2:32; Zech 13:9; Acts 2:21. [74]Eph 1:10. [75]Migne PG 74 col. 844.

10:12-21 HEARING THE GOSPEL

[12]For there is no distinction between Jew and Greek; the same Lord is Lord of all and bestows his riches upon all who call upon him. [13]For, "every one who calls upon the name of the Lord will be saved."

[14]But how are men to call upon him in whom they have not believed? And how are they to believe in him of whom they have never heard? And how are they to hear without a preacher? [15]And how can men preach unless they are sent? As it is written, "How beautiful are the feet of those who preach good news!" [16]But they have not all obeyed the gospel; for Isaiah says, "Lord, who has believed what he has heard from us?" [17]So faith comes from what is heard, and what is heard comes by the preaching of Christ.

[18]But I ask, have they not heard? Indeed they have; for

"Their voice has gone out to all the earth,
and their words to the ends of the world."

[19]Again I ask, did Israel not understand? First Moses says,

"I will make you jealous of those who are not a nation;
with a foolish nation I will make you angry."
[20]*Then Isaiah is so bold as to say,*
"I have been found by those who did not seek me;
I have shown myself to those who did not ask for me."
[21]*But of Israel he says, "All day long I have held out my hands to a disobedient and contrary people."*

OVERVIEW: Preaching is essential if people are to believe in Christ, since otherwise they will never hear of him. This is the justification for the missionary and teaching ministry of the church. Preaching is necessary, but it is not universally effective, since some of those who hear still refuse to believe. As always, there is no difference between Jews and Gentiles: among both there are some who believe and some who do not. The Jews knew but refused to believe, so God turned to the Gentiles. This made the Jews jealous but did little to bring them to repentance.

10:12 No Distinction Between Jews and Gentiles

NO DISTINCTION. AMBROSIASTER: Paul says that in general everyone is lumped together because of unbelief or else exalted together because of their belief, because apart from Christ there is no salvation in God's presence, only punishment or death. For neither the privileges of their ancestors nor the law can do the Jews any good if they do not accept the merit and promise made to them. Neither do the Gentiles have anything to boast about in the flesh, if they do not believe in Christ. . . .

Paul says that God bestows his riches not on those who believe but on those who call upon him, so that after believing the mind will not cease to ask God for what it has been taught to ask the Lord for. COMMENTARY ON PAUL'S EPISTLES.[1]

HE BESTOWS HIS RICHES. CHRYSOSTOM: Christ finds his wealth in the salvation of our souls. BAPTISMAL INSTRUCTIONS 11.26.[2]

LORD OF ALL. PELAGIUS: There is one Lord of all, who abounds in mercy and possesses salvation, with which he is generous to all.[3] PELAGIUS'S COMMENTARY ON ROMANS.[4]

10:13 Calling on the Lord

THE NAME OF THE LORD. AMBROSIASTER: God himself, when he was seen by Moses, said to him: "My name is the Lord."[5] This is the Son of God, who is said to be both a messenger and God. The Son is not to be confused with the Father from whom all things come, but is to be acknowledged as the One through whom all things come and to whom all things belong.[6] He is called God because the Father and the Son are one.[7] He is also called an angel, because he was sent by the Father to announce the promised salvation. COMMENTARY ON PAUL'S EPISTLES.[8]

EVERYONE. CHRYSOSTOM: The words "Everyone who believes"[9] point out faith, but the words "Everyone who calls upon" point out confession. HOMILIES ON ROMANS 17.[10]

BEGINNING AND PERFECTING. AUGUSTINE: By faith in Jesus Christ is granted to us both possession of the little beginning of salvation and its perfecting, which we await in hope. THE SPIRIT AND THE LETTER 51.[11]

10:14 Calling, Believing, Hearing

---

[1]CSEL 81.1:349-51. [2]ACW 31:169. [3]See Ps 85. [4]PCR 123. [5]Ex 6:2-3; cf. Ex 3:13-14. [6]See Rom 11:36; Heb 2:10. [7]See Jn 10:30; 17:21; 1 Cor 8:6. [8]CSEL 81.1:351-53. [9]Rom 10:11. [10]NPNF 1 11:472. [11]LCC 8:235.

ACCEPTING OR REJECTING. AMBROSIASTER: As I said above, you have to believe first if you are going to have the faith to ask for anything. It is obvious that Christ cannot be believed in if he is not obeyed. It is likewise clear that whoever rejects a preacher does not accept the one who sent him either. COMMENTARY ON PAUL'S EPISTLES.[12]

REJECTION OF UNIVERSAL GRACE. APOLLINARIS OF LAODICEA: Paul says that salvation by the calling of the Lord is common to all but that the above mentioned rejection of this universal grace hardened the Jews, making them unable to receive the common good. As a result the mission and the message did not go to them but to the Gentiles, along with the hearing, the faith and the calling. For just as the light is by nature common to all but becomes something else to those who are blinded, so that the blind cannot see the sun, nor can the deaf hear the message when it is proclaimed, so those who have been sent to preach to the Jews have had little effect. They cannot hear the message because they have become deaf to God's calling. PAULINE COMMENTARY FROM THE GREEK CHURCH.[13]

WITHOUT A PREACHER. AUGUSTINE: The preaching of predestination should not hinder the preaching of perseverance and progress in faith, so that those to whom it has been given to obey should hear what they ought to hear. For how will they hear without a preacher? GIFT OF PERSEVERANCE 14.36.[14]

WHO CAN CALL UPON GOD? AUGUSTINE: Those who believe rightly believe that they may call on him in whom they have believed and may be strong to do what they have learned in the precepts of the law, since faith obtains what the law commands. LETTER 157.[15]

PROMISE TO ALL NATIONS, NOT ALL PERSONS. AUGUSTINE: God sends his angels and gathers together his elect from the four winds, that is, from the whole world.[16] Therefore, the church must necessarily be found among the nations where it does not yet exist, but it does not necessarily follow that all who live there will believe. The promise was to all nations but not to all men of all nations, for not all have faith. LETTER 199.48.[17]

PELAGIUS: Here we have an objection raised by the Jews concerning the Gentiles, viz. , that they could not call upon God. PELAGIUS'S COMMENTARY ON ROMANS.[18]

THE CREED'S PURPOSE. CAESARIUS OF ARLES: This is why you first learned the creed. Here is a rule of your faith which is both short and long—short in the number of words, long because of the weight of the thoughts. SERMON 147.1.[19]

10:15 Preaching the Good News

THE BEAUTY OF THE PREACHER'S FEET. ORIGEN: It seems to me that there is some difficulty with this [verse]. For if we understand it to mean that nobody preaches because nobody is sent . . . then it would appear that the reason they are not saved is ultimately the fault of Christ for not having sent them.

But it is better for us to understand this as follows. It is as if the apostle were saying: "We, the heralds and preachers of Christ, would not be able to preach, nor would we have any power to proclaim, if he who sent us were not also present with us. So if you do not want to listen to us when we preach, that is your problem, if hearing you do not believe, and not believing, you do not call on him, and not calling on him, you are not saved."

The beauty of the preacher's feet must be understood in a spiritual, not in a physical sense. For it would make a mockery of the apostle's meaning to suppose that the feet of the evange-

---

[12]CSEL 81.1:353. [13]NTA 15:69. [14]FC 86:304-5. [15]FC 20:324. [16]See Mt 24:31; Mk 13:27. [17]FC 30:396. [18]PCR 123. [19]FC 47:312.

lists, which can be seen with the physical eye, should be regarded as beautiful in themselves. . . . Only those feet which walk in the way of life can make this claim. Given that Christ said that he is the way, you should understand that it is the feet of those evangelists who walk according to that way which deserve to be called beautiful. COMMENTARY ON THE EPISTLE TO THE ROMANS.[20]

THE WAY OF PEACE. AMBROSIASTER: Nobody can be a true apostle unless he is sent by Christ, nor will he be able to preach without a mandate to do so, for his testimony will not reflect his signs of power.

Paul quotes the prophet Nahum.[21] By talking about feet he means the coming of the apostles who went round the world preaching the coming of the kingdom of God. For their appearance enlightened mankind by showing them the way toward peace with God, which John the Baptist had come to prepare.[22] This is the peace to which those who believe in Christ are hastening. Then St. Simeon, seeing the discord in the world, rejoiced at the coming of the Savior, saying: "Lord, now let your servant depart in peace,"[23] because the kingdom of God is peace, and all discord is taken away when everyone bows the knee to the one God. COMMENTARY ON PAUL'S EPISTLES.[24]

HOW TO PREACH UNLESS ONE IS SENT? APOLLINARIS OF LAODICEA: It is clear even from the prophets that it is impossible to believe if nobody preaches the gospel. PAULINE COMMENTARY FROM THE GREEK CHURCH.[25]

DISBELIEVING THE PROPHET AND THE APOSTLES. CHRYSOSTOM: Paul is saying that by disbelieving, the Jews are not disbelieving the apostles only but also the prophet Isaiah, who foretold many years before that they would be sent to preach the gospel. HOMILIES ON ROMANS 18.[26]

ESSENTIAL TEACHING. THEODORE OF MOPSUESTIA: If the heralds of these things are deemed

worthy of such great admiration, how essential and how advantageous a thing the teaching of the apostles must be. PAULINE COMMENTARY FROM THE GREEK CHURCH.[27]

10:16 Not All Believe

NOT ALL HEEDED THE GOSPEL. ORIGEN: Not all the Gentiles have believed the gospel nor have all the Jews, but many have, and many more Gentiles have believed than Jews. In this passage, "who has believed really means few have believed." . . . Isaiah here is speaking prophetically in the person of the apostles, to whom the work of preaching was entrusted. It was they, when they saw how few believers there were in Israel, who exclaimed: "Lord, who has believed what he has heard from us?" COMMENTARY ON THE EPISTLE TO THE ROMANS.[28]

PELAGIUS: The prophets were never sent to the Gentiles. If not all those to whom the prophets were sent obeyed, how much less those to whom no one was sent! PELAGIUS'S COMMENTARY ON ROMANS.[29]

THEODORE OF MOPSUESTIA: The first part of this [verse] ought to be read as a question to which the second part is the apostle's answer. . . . There is nothing surprising about this, for Isaiah also testifies to the small number of believers.[30] PAULINE COMMENTARY FROM THE GREEK CHURCH.[31]

10:17 Faith Comes From What Is Heard

SOMETHING MUST BE SAID. AMBROSIASTER: It is obvious that unless something is said, it can neither be heard nor believed. COMMENTARY ON PAUL'S EPISTLES.[32]

---

[20]CER 4:218-420. [21]Nahum 1:15; see also Is 52:7. [22]See Is 40:3; Mt 3:3; Mk 1:3; Lk 3:4. [23]Lk 2:29. [24]CSEL 81.1:353-55. [25]NTA 15:71. [26]NPNF 1 11:478. [27]NTA 15:152. [28]CER 4:226-28. [29]PCR 123. [30]See Is 10:21-22; 11:11. [31]NTA 15:152. [32]CSEL 81.1:355.

FAITH COMES BY HEARING. CHRYSOSTOM: The Jews were forever seeking a sign[33] . . . but Isaiah promised them no such thing. Rather, it was by hearing that they were to believe. HOMILIES ON ROMANS 18.[34]

PELAGIUS: From here on we have the apostle's reply to the above questions. PELAGIUS'S COMMENTARY ON ROMANS.[35]

THEODORE OF MOPSUESTIA: It is perfectly clear to us, says Paul, following the voice of the prophet and what we have said, that there can be no faith without teaching, and the teaching of godliness is impossible unless it shows the truth about God. PAULINE COMMENTARY FROM THE GREEK CHURCH.[36]

JOHN OF DAMASCUS: Faith comes by hearing, because when we hear the holy Scriptures we believe in the teaching of the Holy Spirit. This faith is made perfect by all the things which Christ has ordained; it believes truly, it is devout and it keeps the commandments of him who has renewed us. For he who does not believe in accordance with the traditions of the catholic church or who through untoward works holds communion with the devil is without faith. ORTHODOX FAITH 4.10.[37]

10:18 Preaching to All the World

TERTULLIAN: Who else have the nations of the world believed in but Christ, who has already come? AN ANSWER TO THE JEWS 7.[38]

ORIGEN: This passage, taken from Psalm 19[:4], must refer to the Gentiles. COMMENTARY ON THE EPISTLE TO THE ROMANS.[39]

THEIR VOICE HAS GONE OUT TO ALL THE EARTH. AMBROSIASTER: They heard but they did not want to believe. For there are some who, in spite of the fact that they hear, do not believe. For they hear but do not understand, because

their heart is blinded by wickedness.[40] . . . If the sound of the gospel has gone out to the entire world, it is not possible that the Jews have not heard it, and so none of them can be pardoned from the sin of unbelief. COMMENTARY ON PAUL'S EPISTLES.[41]

CHRYSOSTOM: If the ends of the world have heard, how can the Jews claim that they have not? HOMILIES ON ROMANS 18.[42]

PELAGIUS: Paul wants this passage to be understood allegorically to refer to the cries of the prophets. PELAGIUS'S COMMENTARY ON ROMANS.[43]

THEODORE OF MOPSUESTIA: It is clear that Paul did not put this here as a kind of prophecy but rather as a statement of what was actually going on at the time. PAULINE COMMENTARY FROM THE GREEK CHURCH.[44]

10:19 Israel's Lack of Understanding

MOSES FORESAW THE FOOLISHNESS OF GRACE. ORIGEN: Having just spoken of the Gentiles Paul goes on, as is his custom, to talk about Israel as well. His intention is to demonstrate by suitable quotations that Israel has no excuse for its rejection of Christ.

In this passage it is true that Moses the friend of God wanted to attach blame to the people of God, but he also foresaw in the Spirit that if someone wants to be wise in this world he must become foolish, in order to be wise in the sight of God.[45] COMMENTARY ON THE EPISTLE TO THE ROMANS.[46]

AUGUSTINE: By calling a people "foolish" Paul explained what he meant by "those who are not a

---

[33]See Mk 8:11-12; 1 Cor 1:22. [34]NPNF 1 11:479. [35]PCR 123. [36]NTA 15:152. [37]FC 37:348. [38]ANF 3:157. [39]CER 4:230. [40]See Is 6:10; Jn 12:40. [41]CSEL 81.1:355-57. [42]NPNF 1 11:479. [43]PCR 123. [44]NTA 15:153. [45]See Is 29:14; 1 Cor 1:19-25. [46]CER 4:232-34.

people," viz., a foolish people ought not to be called a people at all. But he says that the Jewish people will be angered by the Gentiles' faith, because they have received what the Jews have rejected. . . . Even though entire peoples were foolish idol worshipers, they nevertheless put away their paganism by believing. Thus Paul said: "If a man who is uncircumcised keeps the precepts of the law, will not his uncircumcision be regarded as circumcision?"[47] Thus he means: "I will make you jealous of those who once were not a people but were made a people," because although they were once a foolish idol-worshiping people, they put aside their paganism through their faith in Christ.[48] AUGUSTINE ON ROMANS 68.[49]

I WILL MAKE YOU JEALOUS. AMBROSIASTER: Paul means here that of course Israel knew. . . . They all heard but they did not all believe.

The jealousy of the Jews arose from their envy at seeing a people which earlier had been without God and barbarous claim the Jewish God as their own and receive the promise which had originally been made to the Jews. . . . Nothing destroys a man so much as jealousy, which is why God made it the avenger of unbelief, because that is a great sin. COMMENTARY ON PAUL'S EPISTLES.[50]

DID NOT ISRAEL UNDERSTAND? CHRYSOSTOM: Israel ought to have known even on the basis of Moses alone how to tell who were the true preachers, not merely from the fact that they believed, nor from the fact that the preachers spoke of peace, nor from the fact that they brought glad tidings of good things, nor from the fact that the word was sown in all the world, but from the ironic fact that their inferiors, the Gentiles, were receiving greater honor than they had. HOMILIES ON ROMANS 18.[51]

PELAGIUS: Israel did not understand that the Gentiles were to be called to faith. Moses is first because the prophets after him spoke of the salvation of the Gentiles. Before they believed in God,

they were not God's people. Therefore it is as if he says: "I shall call those who are not my people, and they will believe in me in order to provoke you, so that although you should have been better than they are, you will be glad to be their equals." It is just as if someone has a disobedient son and in order to reform him gives half his inheritance to his slave, so that when he finally repents he may be glad if he deserves to receive even that much. PELAGIUS'S COMMENTARY ON ROMANS.[52]

10:20 Found by Those Who Did Not Seek

ORIGEN: From the context, it is obvious that this must refer to the Gentiles. COMMENTARY ON THE EPISTLE TO THE ROMANS.[53]

ISAIAH SPEAKING IN THE ROLE OF CHRIST. AMBROSIASTER: Having made us aware of the words of Moses to talk about the rejection of the Jews, Paul here adds the testimony of the prophet Isaiah in order to make his point clearer still. . . . Isaiah here is speaking in the role of Christ. COMMENTARY ON PAUL'S EPISTLES.[54]

ENQUIRING OF IDOLS. PELAGIUS: The Gentiles did not enquire after God in the law but after idols in ignorance. They asked not of God but of demons through the augurs, astrologers and haruspices of the idols. PELAGIUS'S COMMENTARY ON ROMANS.[55]

10:21 God Held Out His Hands

UNDERSTANDING THE PASSAGE. ORIGEN: The Hebrew text does not contain the words *and contrary*, but here the apostle has followed the Septuagint and quoted the passage as they understood it.[56] COMMENTARY ON THE EPISTLE TO THE ROMANS.[57]

---

[47]Rom 2:26. [48]See 1 Cor 12:2; 1 Thess 1:9. [49]AOR 39. [50]CSEL 81.1:357-59. [51]NPNF 1 11:479. [52]PCR 123-24. [53]CER 4:236. [54]CSEL 81.1:359-61. [55]PCR 124. [56]This selection shows that Origen was comparing the Hebrew Bible and the Greek Septuagint as he worked through Paul's prophetic reference. [57]CER 4:238.

SHELTERING THE DISOBEDIENT. JEROME: The hands of the Lord lifted up to heaven were not begging for help but were sheltering us, his miserable creatures. HOMILIES ON THE PSALMS 68.[58]

HELD OUT MY HANDS. AMBROSIASTER: Here *Israel* refers to the Israel of the flesh, those who are children of Abraham but not according to faith. For the true Israel is spiritual and sees God by believing in him. "All day long" means "always."

This passage may also refer to the Savior, who held out his hands on the cross to plead forgiveness for those who were killing him.[59] COMMENTARY ON PAUL'S EPISTLES.[60]

DIODORE: It appears from the holding out of his hands that God is calling the people to himself. It is also a sign pointing toward the form of the cross. PAULINE COMMENTARY FROM THE GREEK CHURCH.[61]

CHRYSOSTOM: Throughout the period of the old dispensation, God held out his hands to the Jews to call them and draw them to himself. HOMILIES ON ROMANS 18.[62]

PELAGIUS: The same prophet who made promises of this sort to the Gentiles issues similar warnings here to the Jews, so that you may know that both were foretold. The holding out of the hands means, allegorically, the cross. PELAGIUS'S COMMENTARY ON ROMANS.[63]

---

[58]FC 57:83. [59]See Lk 23:34. [60]CSEL 81.1.36. [61]NTA 15:102. [62]NPNF 1 11:480. [63]PCR 124.

11:1-10 THE REMNANT OF ISRAEL

[1]*I ask, then, has God rejected his people? By no means! I myself am an Israelite, a descendant of Abraham, a member of the tribe of Benjamin.* [2]*God has not rejected his people whom he foreknew. Do you not know what the scripture says of Elijah, how he pleads with God against Israel?* [3]*"Lord, they have killed thy prophets, they have demolished thy altars, and I alone am left, and they seek my life."* [4]*But what is God's reply to him? "I have kept for myself seven thousand men who have not bowed the knee to Baal."* [5]*So too at the present time there is a remnant, chosen by grace.* [6]*But if it is by grace, it is no longer on the basis of works; otherwise grace would no longer be grace.*

[7]*What then? Israel failed to obtain what it sought. The elect obtained it, but the rest were hardened,* [8]*as it is written,*

"God gave them a spirit of stupor,
eyes that should not see and ears that should not hear,
down to this very day."
[9]*And David says,*

"Let their table become a snare and a trap,
a pitfall and a retribution for them;

*10let their eyes be darkened so that they cannot see,
and bend their backs for ever."*

OVERVIEW: The present situation of the Jews is bleak, but that does not mean that God has rejected them. Paul himself was a Jew, and God would preserve a remnant among them for the future as he had already done in the past. The remnant of Israel will be saved by grace just as the Gentiles are now. Just when Elijah thought he was alone he learned that seven thousand had not bowed the knee to Baal. So there remains in Israel a remnant chosen by grace. God blinded the Israel of works and made it deaf because of its unbelief. This terrible fate had been predicted in the Old Testament.

11:1 Part of Israel Saved

I MYSELF AM A DESCENDANT OF ABRAHAM. AMBROSIASTER: Since Paul has shown that the people of Israel did not believe, now, in order that it should not be thought that he has said that they were all unbelievers, he shows that God has not rejected the inheritance which he promised to the descendants of Abraham. For he would not have promised them a kingdom if he knew that none of them would believe. . . . By using himself as an example, he shows that the part of Israel which God foreknew would be saved had in fact been saved and that the part which had been consigned to perdition because of its constant unbelief might yet be saved. COMMENTARY ON PAUL'S EPISTLES.[1]

HAS GOD REJECTED HIS PEOPLE? CHRYSOSTOM: God has not rejected his people, because Paul himself was one of them. If God had cast them off, he would not have chosen one of them as the one to whom he entrusted all his preaching, the affairs of the world, all the mysteries and the whole message of salvation. HOMILIES ON ROMANS 18.[2]

REMNANT OF ELECTION. DIODORE: Fearing

once again that exaggerating the rejection of the Jews might lead to a choice of disobedience, Paul turns to the small remnant of the election—the apostles and their fellow believers. PAULINE COMMENTARY FROM THE GREEK CHURCH.[3]

AUGUSTINE: This refers to what Paul said above.[4] Only those Jews who have believed in the Lord will be counted as descendants. AUGUSTINE ON ROMANS 69.[5]

HUMBLING AND ENCOURAGEMENT. PELAGIUS: Because Paul had by this point humbled them far enough, he now encourages the Jews in the way a good teacher would, so as not to provoke them unduly. God has not rejected everyone, and not forever, but only those who do not believe, as long as they do not believe. Paul reminds them that if God had rejected all the Jews, he too would have been rejected. PELAGIUS'S COMMENTARY ON ROMANS.[6]

CYRIL OF ALEXANDRIA: Wisely, Paul does not make the plight of Israel appear worse than it is. Even though he says that the nation is struggling in its blindness, he manages to say something positive at this point. EXPLANATION OF THE LETTER TO THE ROMANS.[7]

THEODORET OF CYR: Paul says that, if God had rejected his people, he would have been one of those rejected as well. INTERPRETATION OF THE LETTER TO THE ROMANS.[8]

OF THE TRIBE OF BENJAMIN. THEODORE OF MOPSUESTIA: Paul has mentioned not only his first ancestor but also the head of his tribe in

---

[1]CSEL 81.1:361-63. [2]NPNF 1 11:481. [3]NTA 15:102. [4]Rom 9:6-9. [5]AOR 39, 41. [6]PCR 124. [7]Migne PG 74 cols. 844-45. [8]IER, Migne PG 82 col. 172.

order to show that he is not fabricating his claim. PAULINE COMMENTARY FROM THE GREEK CHURCH.[9]

THEODORET OF CYR: Paul could have supported his statement by referring to the 3,000 who believed at Jerusalem and to the many thousands spoken of by St. James,[10] not to mention all those Jews of the diaspora who believed the message. But instead he uses himself as an example. INTERPRETATION OF THE LETTER TO THE ROMANS.[11]

11:2 A Remnant Foreknown

NONE OF THEM IS LOST. AMBROSIASTER: This is what the Savior says: "Father, I have kept those whom thou didst give to me, and none of them is lost but the son of perdition."[12] COMMENTARY ON PAUL'S EPISTLES."[13]

WHOM HE FOREKNEW. AUGUSTINE: Predestination is sometimes designated by the name of foreknowledge, as here, where "he foreknew" can only mean "he predestined," as the context of what follows demonstrates. GIFT OF PERSEVERANCE 18.47.[14]

NO OCCASION FOR PRIDE. PELAGIUS: God has not rejected those whom he knew in advance would believe. Paul eliminates any occasion for pride among the Gentiles, in case they become boastful because so few of the Jews believed. PELAGIUS'S COMMENTARY ON ROMANS.[15]

11:3 A Lone Voice

I ALONE AM LEFT. DIODORE: Paul takes these words of Elijah and applies them by analogy to the Savior, in that only a remnant obtained the grace of the promise. PAULINE COMMENTARY FROM THE GREEK CHURCH.[16]

PELAGIUS: The prophets knew only the things which had been revealed to them by the Lord.

That is why the king, uncertain of mind, asked Jeremiah if, at the time at which he spoke with him, a word of the Lord had come to him.[17] . . . Elijah was unaware that there were others besides himself who worshiped God.[18] PELAGIUS'S COMMENTARY ON ROMANS.[19]

11:4 The Hidden Faithful

SEVEN THOUSAND HAVE NOT BOWED THE KNEE TO BAAL. AMBROSIASTER: This is clear, for Paul shows that not only Elijah remained as one devoted to God who did not worship idols, but that there were many who remained faithful to God, just as there were not a few Jews who believed in Christ. COMMENTARY ON PAUL'S EPISTLES.[20]

PELAGIUS: If so many men were hidden from the prophet, how much more are you unaware of how many Jews have been saved and are to be saved! PELAGIUS'S COMMENTARY ON ROMANS. [21]

THEODORET OF CYR: Elijah did not know about these 7,000 until God revealed their existence to him.[22] So it is not unbelievable that you too are ignorant of how many Jews have believed in the Savior. INTERPRETATION OF THE LETTER TO THE ROMANS.[23]

11:5 A Remnant Chosen by Grace

CHOSEN BY GRACE. ORIGEN: The fact that Paul adds the words "chosen by grace" seems to me to be significant. He could have said simply that there is a remnant saved by grace, but by adding "chosen" he indicates that there is grace both with and without election. For everyone who is saved has doubtless been saved by grace, but those who have been saved by the election of grace seem to

---

[9]NTA 15:154. [10]Acts 21:20. [11]IER, Migne PG 82 col. 172. [12]Jn 17:12. [13]CSEL 81.1:363. [14]FC 86:316. [15]PCR 124-25. [16]NTA 15:102. [17]See Jer 37:17. [18]See 1 Kings 19:18. [19]PCR 125. [20]CSEL 81.1:363. [21]PCR 125. [22]See 1 Kings 19:18. [23]IER, Migne PG 82 col. 172.

me to be more perfect than the others. For just as Israel includes all those who are descended from the nation of Israel as well as those who worship God with a pure mind and sincere heart, so we may also assume that all who come to faith in Christ come by grace. But those in whom the gift of grace is adorned with the works of virtue and purity of heart will be said to be saved not only by grace but by the election of grace. COMMENTARY ON THE EPISTLE TO THE ROMANS.[24]

CALLED TO SALVATION. ORIGEN: Not only the Gentiles are benefited by the coming of Christ but also some who belong to the divine race, many of whom have been called to salvation. ON FIRST PRINCIPLES 4.2.6.[25]

BROUGHT TO THE KNOWLEDGE OF THE LORD. EUSEBIUS OF CAESAREA: The remnant of the Jews has proclaimed the sign of the Lord to all the Gentiles and has joined to God in one people, drawn to him, the souls of the Gentiles which are brought out of destruction to the knowledge of the Lord. PROOF OF THE GOSPEL 2.3.[26]

WHOM GOD FOREKNEW. AMBROSIASTER: Even though many have fallen away, those whom God foreknew have remained in the promise of the law. For those who have accepted Christ as he was promised in the law have remained in the law, but those who rejected Christ have fallen away from it. COMMENTARY ON PAUL'S EPISTLES.[27]

AT THE PRESENT TIME THERE IS A REMNANT. AUGUSTINE: The "remnant" refers to the Jews who have believed in Christ. Many of them did believe in the days of the apostles, and even today there are some converts, though very few. THE CITY OF GOD 17.5.[28]

GRACE, NOT MERIT. AUGUSTINE: The election of which the apostle speaks is according to grace, not merit. PREDESTINATION OF THE SAINTS 16.33.[29]

PELAGIUS: Just as all did not perish then, so too some are saved now. The election of grace is faith just as works are the election of the law. Otherwise, what sort of election is it where there is no difference in merit? PELAGIUS'S COMMENTARY ON ROMANS.[30]

11:6 Grace Rather Than Works

IF BY GRACE, NO LONGER ON THE BASIS OF WORKS. AMBROSIASTER: It is clear that because grace is the gift of God there is no reward due for works, but it is granted freely because of the free mercy which intervenes.[31] COMMENTARY ON PAUL'S EPISTLES.[32]

DIODORE: Grace shows the love for mankind of the one who gives it, but works demand compensation according to what they are worth. PAULINE COMMENTARY FROM THE GREEK CHURCH.[33]

GRACE SAVES THE WILLING. CHRYSOSTOM: If we are all saved by grace, some might argue, why is everyone not saved? Because they did not want to be is the answer. For grace, even though it is grace, saves the willing, not those who refuse it and turn away from it.[34] HOMILIES ON ROMANS 18.[35]

GRACE EMPOWERS WORKS. AUGUSTINE: Grace is given not because we have done good works but in order that we may have power to do them, not because we have fulfilled the law but in order that we may be able to fulfill it. THE SPIRIT AND THE LETTER 16.10.[36]

SAVED FREELY. PELAGIUS: In case the Jews replied to Paul about those concerning whom the word comes to Elijah: "They were righteous; why

---

[24]CER 4:246. [25]OFP 281-82. [26]POG 1:91. [27]CSEL 81.1:365. [28]FC 24:38. [29]FC 86:258. [30]PCR 125. [31]See Gal 2:15-16. [32]CSEL 81.1:365. [33]NTA 15:102. [34]See Mt 22:3; Lk 13:34; Acts 7:51; Heb 3:8, 12. [35]NPNF 1 11:483. [36]LCC 8:206.

were these sinners chosen?" the apostle adds that they too are saved freely just as the Gentiles are. PELAGIUS'S COMMENTARY ON ROMANS.[37]

LAW AND GRACE INCOMPATIBLE. GENNADIUS OF CONSTANTINOPLE: The apostle has expressed himself in this way . . . because he wants to show that the law and grace are completely incompatible and that the two of them can never go together. Of necessity, one must drive the other out.[38] PAULINE COMMENTARY FROM THE GREEK CHURCH.[39]

11:7 Failure to Obtain the Promise

WHAT ISRAEL SOUGHT. DIODORE: What was Israel seeking? The promise that they would be made sons and heirs of the universe.[40] PAULINE COMMENTARY FROM THE GREEK CHURCH.[41]

THEY FAILED TO OBTAIN WHAT WAS PROMISED. [PSEUDO-]CONSTANTIUS: The promises were made to the Jews, that Christ would come to save them from their sins, but since he came and they did not believe, Paul says: "Israel failed to obtain." THE HOLY LETTER OF ST. PAUL TO THE ROMANS.[42]

PELAGIUS: Israel as a whole has not obtained righteousness because it did not seek it by faith but thought that it was justified solely by works of the law, even though it disregarded the greatest commandments of the law. That is why the Savior censures those who strain at a gnat but swallow a camel.[43] PELAGIUS'S COMMENTARY ON ROMANS.[44]

CYRIL OF ALEXANDRIA: Israel tried to find righteousness in the type which was the law but did not obtain it. However, those who were sealed were elected and did obtain it on account of their belief, being justified by their faith. The rest were blinded, being hardened and rebellious. EXPLANATION OF THE LETTER TO THE ROMANS.[45]

THEODORET OF CYR: The elect are those who believed. . . . The rest were hardened because of their unbelief. INTERPRETATION OF THE LETTER TO THE ROMANS.[46]

11:8 Failure to See and Hear

SOURCE OF THE QUOTE. ORIGEN: I have not been able to find the source of this quotation. If someone consults holy Scripture more carefully than I have done and finds it, let him say so.[47] COMMENTARY ON THE EPISTLE TO THE ROMANS.[48]

TWO KINDS OF BLINDNESS. AMBROSIASTER: These are the carnal Israelites who thought they were justified by the law and did not realize that they were justified by faith before God, because through the law they were all guilty.

Those who were blinded were those who were unable to see the way of truth which in their wickedness they had rejected and gone away from so that they could no longer come to the grace of salvation. The examples taken from the prophets reveal that there are two kinds of blind people. The first kind consists of those who are blinded forever, who will never be saved. These people are of such evil will that they knowingly say that they do not know what they hear. . . . The second type consists of those who, although they try to live according to the law, do not accept the righteousness of Christ. These people are doing this not out of the envy of an evil will but by an erroneous imitation of the tradition of their ancestors. They are blinded for a time, for although they ought to recognize the great works of Christ which cannot be ignored. . . . They have forgotten God and follow human opinions instead. COMMENTARY ON PAUL'S EPISTLES.[49]

---

[37]PCR 125. [38]See Rom 6:14; Gal 2:21; 5:4. [39]NTA 15:398. [40]See Gal 4:4-7. [41]NTA 15:102. [42]ENPK 2:74. [43]See Mt 23:24. [44]PCR 125. [45]Migne PG 74 col. 848. [46]IER, Migne PG 82 col. 173. [47]The passage is a mixed quotation from Is 29:10 and Deut 29:4. [48]CER 4:252. [49]CSEL 81.1:365-71.

A Spirit of Stupor. Apollinaris of Laodicea: This quotation was taken directly from the Hebrew by the apostle himself. The Septuagint edition has "God has put a spirit of stupor in you." The version of Aquila more clearly has "virulence" and that of Symmachus has "pride." . . . In effect, because of the ignorance of the people, the prophetic writings will be a sealed book to them, and they will be incapable of reading them. Pauline Commentary from the Greek Church.[50]

Gennadius of Constantinople: The spirit of stupor prevented them from making the hard choice of repentance and conversion. Pauline Commentary from the Greek Church.[51]

Addressed to Both Believers and Sinners. Pelagius: The rest were hardened through unfaithfulness, as it is written: "Unless you believe, you will not understand."[52]

It is God's prerogative to give them the spirit of stupor which they desired, for they have always disbelieved the words of God. If they had wanted to have a spirit of faith they would have received it. But even today Christians who doubt the resurrection reward or Gehenna have sought a similar spirit for themselves, for in this passage the prophet was addressing both believers and sinners. Pelagius's Commentary on Romans.[53]

11:9 A Snare and Retribution

A Textual Note. Origen: The trap is not mentioned either in the Hebrew or in the Septuagint.[54] We have recorded these things about the order of the words and the quality of the witnesses consulted in order to show by these details that the authority of the apostle does not rely on the texts of the Hebrews nor does it always retain the words of the translators, but rather it expounds the meaning of the Scriptures in whatever words are most suitable. Commentary on the Epistle to the Romans.[55]

Let Their Feast Become a Snare. Ambrosiaster: He curses the feast of the wicked because the innocent are often deceived there. They are tricked into coming to dinner so that they may be ruined. Commentary on Paul's Epistles.[56]

Chrysostom: This means: Let their comforts and all their good things change and perish, and let them be open to attack from all sides. Homilies on Romans 19.[57]

Pelagius: The table is where they rejoiced at the death of Christ while they ate the passover. Pelagius's Commentary on Romans.[58]

Theodore of Mopsuestia: Paul is using these words not as a prophecy but as a statement from the Scriptures which backs up what he has already said about the Jews, and at the same time he shows that there is nothing new under the sun. Pauline Commentary from the Greek Church.[59]

11:10 Eyes Darkened, Backs Bent

Origen: God will do this because it is better not to know anything at all than to know something badly. Commentary on the Epistle to the Romans.[60]

Chrysostom: Do these words need any interpretation? Are they not plain to everyone? Homilies on Romans 19.[61]

Their Eyes Darkened. Augustine: Behold mercy and judgment—mercy on the elect, who have obtained the righteousness of God, but judgment upon the others who have been blinded. And yet the former have believed because they willed it, while the latter have not believed because they have not willed it. Hence mercy and judgment were executed in their own

---

[50]NTA 15:72. [51]NTA 15:399. [52]Is 7:9. [53]PCR 125. [54]This is not true; Ps 69:22. [55]CER 4:254. [56]CSEL 81.1:369. [57]NPNF 1 11:487. [58]PCR 126. [59]NTA 15:155. [60]CER 4:256. [61]NPNF 1 11:487.

wills. PREDESTINATION OF THE SAINTS 6.11.[62]

THEIR BACKS BENT. [PSEUDO-]CONSTANTIUS: Their backs were bent forever by the burden of their sins so that they would not be forgiven unless they believed. THE HOLY LETTER OF ST. PAUL TO THE ROMANS.[63]

PELAGIUS: This prophecy speaks of those who gave the Savior vinegar and gall to drink. [64] PELAGIUS'S COMMENTARY ON ROMANS.[65]

---

[62]FC 86:231. [63]ENPK 2:75. [64]See Mt 27:34. [65]PCR 126.

11:11-24 THE OLIVE TREE AND THE BRANCHES

[11]*So I ask, have they stumbled so as to fall? By no means! But through their trespass salvation has come to the Gentiles, so as to make Israel jealous.* [12]*Now if their trespass means riches for the world, and if their failure means riches for the Gentiles, how much more will their full inclusion mean!*

[13]*Now I am speaking to you Gentiles. Inasmuch then as I am an apostle to the Gentiles, I magnify my ministry* [14]*in order to make my fellow Jews jealous, and thus save some of them.* [15]*For if their rejection means the reconciliation of the world, what will their acceptance mean but life from the dead?* [16]*If the dough offered as first fruits is holy, so is the whole lump; and if the root is holy, so are the branches.*

[17]*But if some of the branches were broken off, and you, a wild olive shoot, were grafted in their place to share the richness*° *of the olive tree,* [18]*do not boast over the branches. If you do boast, remember it is not you that support the root, but the root that supports you.* [19]*You will say, "Branches were broken off so that I might be grafted in."* [20]*That is true. They were broken off because of their unbelief, but you stand fast only through faith. So do not become proud, but stand in awe.* [21]*For if God did not spare the natural branches, neither will he spare you.* [22]*Note then the kindness and severity of God: severity toward those who have fallen, but God's kindness to you, provided you continue in his kindness; otherwise you too will be cut off.* [23]*And even the others, if they do not persist in their unbelief, will be grafted in, for God has the power to graft them in again.* [24]*For if you have been cut from what is by nature a wild olive tree, and grafted, contrary to nature, into a cultivated olive tree, how much more will these natural branches be grafted back into their own olive tree.*

o Other ancient authorities read *rich root*

OVERVIEW: The Jews have stumbled, but they have not fallen away completely. Moreover, God has used their tragedy for good, in that because of it the gateway of salvation has been opened to the

Gentiles. The Gentiles have been shown mercy because of the stumbling of the Jews, but they must be careful not to boast. The Jews belonged to the divine olive tree by nature, but because of their unbelief they have been broken off. The Gentiles have been grafted in from a wild olive tree, but it follows that if they turn away from Christ, they too will be cast off, and all the more readily because they did not belong in the first place. The Fathers recognized that Paul was humbling both Jews and Gentiles in their different ways, and warned against presumption on the goodness of God.

11:11 Salvation for Gentiles Comes Through the Jews' Stumbling

THEY HAVE NOT STUMBLED SO AS TO FALL.
ORIGEN: Note that Paul distinguishes between stumbling and sinning on the one hand and falling on the other. For he envisages a cure for stumbling and sinning but not for falling. . . . This is why he denies that Israel has fallen. . . . For the Israelites, although they rejected their redeemer and stoned and persecuted those who were sent to them, nevertheless still contain a remnant within them. For they have the witness of the law even if they do not believe or understand it. They also have the imitation of God even if it is not according to knowledge. COMMENTARY ON THE EPISTLE TO THE ROMANS.[1]

THROUGH THEIR TRESPASSES. CHRYSOSTOM: After showing that the Jews were guilty of evils without number, Paul devises something in mitigation. Note that he accuses them on the basis of the prophets but modifies the condemnation by his own words. For nobody will deny that they have sinned greatly.[2] But let us see if the fall is of such a kind as to be incurable. . . . No, it is not! HOMILIES ON ROMANS 19.[3]

AMBROSIASTER: Paul says here what I have recorded above, that these people have not fallen into unbelief in such a way as to make their ulti-

mate conversion impossible. COMMENTARY ON PAUL'S EPISTLES.[4]

SALVATION HAS COME TO THE GENTILES.
AUGUSTINE: Paul says that the Jews have not fallen but rather that their fall was not pointless, since it led to the salvation of the Gentiles. The Jews did not sin only to fall as a punishment but so that their fall might serve the salvation of the Gentiles.[5] Paul even begins to praise the Jewish people for this fall of unbelief, in order that the Gentiles should not become proud, seeing that the fall of the Jews was so important for their own salvation. On the contrary, the Gentiles ought to be all the more careful, lest they too should grow proud and fall also. AUGUSTINE ON ROMANS 70.[6]

PELAGIUS: Once more, Paul explains the position of the Jews. They have not fallen away completely and beyond hope. God loved them so much that the Gentiles were called for their salvation, so that when the Jews saw that the Gentiles were being allowed into the kingdom of God, they might perhaps repent more easily. PELAGIUS'S COMMENTARY ON ROMANS.[7]

CYRIL OF ALEXANDRIA: I marvel at your kindness, Paul, and the way in which you so artfully craft the words of the divine dispensation. You assert that the Gentiles were called not because the Israelites had lost all hope of salvation after they had stumbled on Christ the stumbling stone but rather that they would imitate those who were so unexpectedly accepted by God, that they would recognize their wickedness, that they would want to understand better than before and that they would accept the redeemer. EXPLANATION OF THE LETTER TO THE ROMANS.[8]

11:12 Riches for the Gentiles and the World

---

[1]CER 4:266-70. [2]See Is 2:2. [3]NPNF 1 11:488. [4]CSEL 81.1:371. [5]See Zech 2:11. [6]AOR 41. [7]PCR 126-27. [8]Migne PG 74 col. 848.

Their Failure Means Riches for the Gentiles. ORIGEN: Consider the wisdom of God in this. For with him not even sins and lapses are wasted, but whenever someone rejects freedom of his own accord, the dispensation of divine wisdom makes others rich by using the very failing by which they have become poor. . . .

Now indeed, until all the Gentiles come to salvation the riches of God are concentrated in the multitude of believers, but as long as Israel remains in its unbelief it will not be possible to say that the fullness of the Lord's portion has been attained. The people of Israel are still missing from the complete picture. But when the fullness of the Gentiles has come in and Israel comes to salvation at the end of time, then it will be the people which, although it existed long ago, will come at the last and complete the fullness of the Lord's portion and inheritance. COMMENTARY ON THE EPISTLE TO THE ROMANS.[9]

Their Full Inclusion. AMBROSIASTER: It is clear that the world will be even richer in good people if those who have been blinded are converted. COMMENTARY ON PAUL'S EPISTLES.[10]

Consolation in Distress. CHRYSOSTOM: Even if the Jews had fallen a thousand times, the Gentiles would not have been saved unless they had shown faith. Likewise, the Jews would not have perished unless they had been unbelieving and disputatious. Here Paul is consoling the Jews in their distress, giving them reason to be confident of their salvation if they were to change. HOMILIES ON ROMANS 19.[11]

Gentiles Should Not Look Down upon Jews. [PSEUDO-]CONSTANTIUS: Writing to the Romans, the apostle warns the Gentiles not to look down on the Jews, because a remnant of them will be saved in the future.[12] THE HOLY LETTER OF ST. PAUL TO THE ROMANS.[13]

Jews Can Benefit Gentiles. PELAGIUS: If the transgression of the Jews benefitted you to the extent that without the works of the law you were made coheirs with them, and if the few Jews who believed called all of you to salvation, how much more could they benefit you with instruction if they all believed! PELAGIUS'S COMMENTARY ON ROMANS.[14]

11:13 Paul's Ministry

My Ministry. ORIGEN: What is more worthy than to magnify the ministry which one has received by the providence of God? For the man who ministers well magnifies his ministry, while on the other hand the one who has ministered negligently and unworthily dishonors his ministry and draws unfavorable comment on it. COMMENTARY ON THE EPISTLE TO THE ROMANS.[15]

Apostle to the Gentiles. AMBROSIASTER: Paul is showing the Gentiles here how much he loves the Jews. For he magnifies his ministry, by which he is the apostle of the Gentiles, if by loving his own people he wins them to the faith as well. For he is more honored still if he wins to eternal life those to whom he has not been sent. For he who finds his lost brothers will have the greatest honor with his parents. COMMENTARY ON PAUL'S EPISTLES.[16]

Honoring His Ministry. PELAGIUS: Paul wants to show that he is especially anxious to save the Jews. As long as he is in the body he will honor his ministry, striving to save many of them by his example.[17] PELAGIUS'S COMMENTARY ON ROMANS.[18]

11:14 Seeking to Save Fellow Jews

My Fellow Jews. ORIGEN: By his attentive care and close attention to the teaching of the Gentiles and by making their behavior worthy of eternal

---

[9]CER 4:272-74. [10]CSEL 81.1:373. [11]NPNF 1 11:489. [12]See Is 10:22; Rom 9:27; 11:5. [13]ENPK 2:76. [14]PCR 127. [15]CER 4:278. [16]CSEL 81.1:373. [17]See 2 Cor 5:6-8. [18]PCR 127.

life, Paul is inviting and provoking the Jews who see these things and who are his kinsmen according to the flesh to imitate those who are progressing in the faith of God. It is the glory of his ministry that he can use the teaching of the Gentiles to reach some of his own people as well. COMMENTARY ON THE EPISTLE TO THE ROMANS.[19]

CHRYSOSTOM: Paul appears to be blaming the Gentiles and to be humbling their conceits, but he gives a gentle provocation to the Jews as well. He tries to veil their great ruin, but he cannot do so because the facts are too clear. HOMILIES ON ROMANS 19.[20]

PELAGIUS: Paul will always present himself to the Jews in such a way that they will want to imitate him.[21] PELAGIUS'S COMMENTARY ON ROMANS.[22]

SO AS TO MAKE ISRAEL JEALOUS. THEODORET OF CYR: Paul evangelized the Gentiles of necessity, addressing himself to them and showing that the prophets had predicted this many centuries before.[23] His aim was to make the Jews jealous and thus encourage some of them to come to salvation also. INTERPRETATION OF THE LETTER TO THE ROMANS.[24]

11:15 *Life from the Dead*

WHAT WILL THEIR ACCEPTANCE MEAN? AMBROSIASTER: This is why Paul worked so hard for the conversion of the Jews, since the handicap of their blindness will be removed at the time when their sin is paid for, so that they might receive the free exercise of their will. COMMENTARY ON PAUL'S EPISTLES.[25]

OTHERS GAINED FROM THEIR SINS. CHRYSOSTOM: This also condemns the Jews, because although others gained from their sins, they did not profit from the good works of others. HOMILIES ON ROMANS 19.[26]

PELAGIUS: What was the occasion for the reception of the Gentiles but that they came to life because of the death of the Jews? Or it may mean from among the Jews that were dead, Christ and the apostles have become life to the Gentiles. Or perhaps if those whom Christ sets free from death contribute to your life. PELAGIUS'S COMMENTARY ON ROMANS.[27]

THEODORET OF CYR: Note how diplomatically Paul phrases his statements. On the one hand he teaches those who already believe not to think too highly of themselves, and on the other hand he extends a hand to those Jews who do not believe, showing them that they could obtain salvation through repentance. In the following [verses] he develops this theme more clearly. INTERPRETATION OF THE LETTER TO THE ROMANS.[28]

11:16 *Root and Branch*

THE WHOLE LUMP. DIODORE: "First fruits" and "root" both refer here to the patriarchs, the lawgiver and the prophets. "Lump" and "branches" refer to the whole of the Jewish people. PAULINE COMMENTARY FROM THE GREEK CHURCH.[29]

AMBROSIASTER: It is clear that they are one and the same substance, so it is impossible for the offering to be holy and the lump unclean, given that the offering comes from the lump. Thus Paul shows that those whose ancestors believed cannot be regarded as unworthy to receive the faith, for if some of the Jews have believed, why can it not be said that the others may also believe? COMMENTARY ON PAUL'S EPISTLES.[30]

THE ROOT OF FAITH. [PSEUDO-]CONSTANTIUS: Here the "first fruits" refers to Christ and the

---

[19]CER 4:282. [20]NPNF 1 11:489. [21]See 1 Cor 9:22. [22]PCR 127. [23]See Is 42:6; 49:6; 66:19; Mal 1:11. [24]IER, Migne PG 82 col. 176. [25]CSEL 81.1:373. [26]NPNF 1 11:489. [27]PCR 127. [28]IER, Migne PG 82 col. 176. [29]NTA 15:104. [30]CSEL 81.1:375.

"whole lump" to the Jewish people, of whom Christ was, according to the flesh. The root refers to Abraham, for he is called the "father of many nations" on account of his faith, and the branches are those who, coming after him, held the same faith as he did. THE HOLY LETTER OF ST. PAUL TO THE ROMANS.[31]

CHRIST AS FIRST FRUITS. THEODORE OF MOPSUESTIA: By "first fruits" Paul means Christ, because he was selected out of the entire race of the Jews; by "root" he means Abraham, from whom the race descended. PAULINE COMMENTARY FROM THE GREEK CHURCH.[32]

THEODORET OF CYR: The "first fruits" refers to Christ in his human nature, the root is Abraham the patriarch and the branches of the olive tree are the Jews who descended from the root. INTERPRETATION OF THE LETTER TO THE ROMANS.[33]

GENNADIUS OF CONSTANTINOPLE: Paul calls the Lord Christ the "first fruits," because he was one of them according to the flesh, and through his resurrection he became the first to claim the inheritance. PAULINE COMMENTARY FROM THE GREEK CHURCH.[34]

11:17 A Wild Branch Grafted to a Good Tree

A WILD OLIVE SHOOT. CLEMENT OF ALEXANDRIA: The graft uses as soil the tree in which it is engrafted. Now all the plants sprouted forth simultaneously in consequence of the divine order. Wherefore also, though the wild olive is wild, it crowns the Olympic victors. . . . Now we see that the wild trees attract more nutriment because they cannot ripen. The wild trees therefore have less power of secretion than those that are cultivated. And the cause of their wildness is the absence of the power of secretion. The engrafted olive accordingly receives more nutriment from its growing in the cultivated one, and it gets accustomed, as it were, to secrete the

nutriment, becoming thus assimilated to the fatness of the cultivated tree. STROMATA 6.15.[35]

PROGRESS BY FAITH. IRENAEUS: If the wild olive takes kindly to the graft . . . it becomes a fruit bearing olive. . . . So likewise men shall be spiritual if they progress by faith to better things and receive the Spirit of God and bring forth the fruit. AGAINST HERESIES 5.10.1.[36]

THE BAD ROOT GRAFTED INTO A GOOD TREE. AMBROSIASTER: If some Jews have not believed, then they have been cut out of the promise. . . . The Gentiles, who were from a bad root, were grafted into a good tree, which is the opposite of what happens in agriculture, where it is the good branch which is grafted onto a bad root.[37] COMMENTARY ON PAUL'S EPISTLES.[38]

SHARING THE RICHNESS OF THE OLIVE TREE. PELAGIUS: The branches were not broken off for your sake, but you were grafted in because they were broken off. You were an olive shoot, to be sure, but a wild and uncultivated one. "The richness of the olive tree" is the root of their fathers, the richness of Christ. PELAGIUS'S COMMENTARY ON ROMANS.[39]

THEODORET OF CYR: "The riches of the olive tree" means the teaching of righteousness. INTERPRETATION OF THE LETTER TO THE ROMANS.[40]

11:18 The Root Supports the Branches

THE ENGRAFTED BRANCH NEED NOT STRUGGLE AGAINST ITS ROOT. JEROME: Whenever I see a synagogue, the thought of the apostle always comes to me—that we should not boast against the olive tree whose branches have been broken off but rather fear. For if the natural branches have been cut off, how much more we who have

[31]ENPK 2:77. [32]NTA 15:158. [33]IER, Migne PG 82 col. 177. [34]NTA 15:400. [35]ANF 2:507. [36]ANF 1:536. [37]See Eph 2:12-13. [38]CSEL 81.1:375. [39]PCR 127. [40]IER, Migne PG 82 col. 177.

been grafted on the wild olive should fear, lest we become like them. HOMILIES ON THE PSALMS 11.[41]

DO NOT REJOICE AT THE MISFORTUNE OF OTHERS. AMBROSIASTER: It displeases God if someone rejoices at the misfortune of others, as Solomon says.[42] In any case, the Jews were not rejected for the sake of the Gentiles. Rather, it was because they were rejected that they gave an opportunity for the gospel to be preached to the Gentiles. If you boast against those onto whose root you have been grafted, you insult the people who have accepted you so that you might be converted from bad to good. You will not continue like that if you destroy the thing on which you stand. COMMENTARY ON PAUL'S EPISTLES.[43]

PELAGIUS: Do not rejoice in the fall of the Jews, or else you will hear that they do not abide through you but you through them and that you do not supply them with life, but they supply you.[44] PELAGIUS'S COMMENTARY ON ROMANS.[45]

11:19 Grafted into the Good Tree

GRAFTED INTO THE GOOD OLIVE TREE. CYRIL OF JERUSALEM: When you were stripped you were anointed with exorcised olive oil, from the topmost hairs of your head to the soles of your feet, and became partakers of the good olive tree, Jesus Christ. Cuttings from the wild olive tree, you were grafted into the good olive tree and became partakers of the richness of the true olive tree. THE MYSTAGOGICAL LECTURES 2.3.[46]

DO NOT BOAST. AMBROSIASTER: A believing Gentile says that he can rejoice that the Jews did not believe, saying that their condemnation made room for the Gentiles. But the Jews were not condemned by God in order to let the Gentiles in. They condemned themselves by rejecting God's gift, and by doing that they gave the Gentiles an opportunity to be saved. Paul wants to stop this boasting, so that we might rejoice in our salvation

rather than insult the weak. For the man who insults a sinner is easily deceived. COMMENTARY ON PAUL'S EPISTLES.[47]

11:20 Broken Off by Unbelief

ORIGEN: Who is the one from whom they have been broken off but he in whom they have not believed?[48] COMMENTARY ON THE EPISTLE TO THE ROMANS.[49]

THAT THEY TOO MIGHT RETURN TO THEIR ROOTS. AMBROSIASTER: You ought to thank God for his gift in Christ and not insult them but rather pray that, if their wickedness has led to your salvation, they too might return to their roots. Then you will please God who has shown you mercy, for he called you so that by making them jealous of you he might bring them to grace as well. COMMENTARY ON PAUL'S EPISTLES.[50]

THEY IN EFFECT BROKE THEMSELVES OFF. CHRYSOSTOM: It was not God who cut them off but rather they broke themselves off and fell.... You see what a great thing man's free choice is, how great the working of the mind is. For none of these things is immutable, neither your good nor their evil. HOMILIES ON ROMANS 19.[51]

THE PURSUIT OF WISDOM NOT BROKEN OFF. PELAGIUS: Some interpreters, who do not understand this passage and do not consider the reason for which or the people to whom the apostle is speaking, think that the pursuit of wisdom is forbidden by this text. But if this is so Paul will seem to contradict himself in the eyes of these interpreters, since here he is forbidding what elsewhere he asks of the Lord, that the Ephesians and others may receive.[52] PELAGIUS'S COMMENTARY ON ROMANS.[53]

---

[41]FC 48:89. [42]See Prov 24:17. [43]CSEL 81.1:375-77. [44]See Jn 4:22. [45]PCR 127-28. [46]FC 64:162. [47]CSEL 81.1:377. [48]See Jn 5:45-46; Rom 11:31. [49]CER 4:294. [50]CSEL 81.1:377. [51]NPNF 1 11:492. [52]Eph 3:14-21; Phil 1:9-11; Col 1:9-15. [53]PCR 128.

11:21 *Judgment and Grace*

BASIL: Judgment will be in accordance with grace, and the Judge will make examination of how you have used the graces bestowed upon you.[54] HOMILY 20.[55]

PELAGIUS: If God did not spare those who sprang from the holy root because of their unbelief, how much less will he spare you if you sin! PELAGIUS'S COMMENTARY ON ROMANS.[56]

11:22 *God's Kindness and Severity*

FORGIVENESS AND REJECTION. AMBROSIASTER: Paul testifies that God is good to the Gentiles because, although they followed idols and deserved to die, he waited for them in his patience, and even though they did not seek him, he called them and forgave their sins. But God is severe toward the Jews and has even blinded them because they rejected God's gift. Here Paul is referring to those Jews who because of their wickedness have been permanently blinded. For this reason he says that they have fallen, whereas the others whom I mentioned above have not fallen, even though they have sinned, because Paul shows that they have been blinded for a time. But God has been severe to these, because they have become eternally blind and apostate. COMMENTARY ON PAUL'S EPISTLES.[57]

SALVATION COMES FROM GRACE. CHRYSOSTOM: Paul does not point to human works but to the goodness of God as a reminder to us that our salvation comes from God's grace and to make us tremble. HOMILIES ON ROMANS 19.[58]

MERCIFULLY GRAFTED IN. PELAGIUS: "Severity" is shown against those who assert that there are two Gods, one righteous and another good; and against those who deny that God punishes sinners. . . . But you were mercifully grafted in, through faith which has been bestowed upon you by the kindness of God. PELAGIUS'S COMMENTARY ON ROMANS.[59]

COUNTED WORTHY THROUGH FAITH. THEODORE OF MOPSUESTIA: Paul is telling us that we ought to learn from both these things and consider how great God's love for us is, that we should have been counted worthy through faith. We ought to become ever more eager to live a godly life bearing in mind how God rejected them because of their unbelief and do everything in our power not to fall in the same way. PAULINE COMMENTARY FROM THE GREEK CHURCH.[60]

11:23 *God's Power*

WITH GOD ALL THINGS ARE POSSIBLE. PELAGIUS: If either of you changes you will experience severity and they will receive kindness.[61] Humanly speaking, it is impossible to restore withered cuttings, but with God all things are possible and even easy.[62] PELAGIUS'S COMMENTARY ON ROMANS.[63]

THEODORET OF CYR: Paul shows what an easy matter this would be for God to accomplish. INTERPRETATION OF THE LETTER TO THE ROMANS.[64]

11:24 *God Is Able to Recover His Own*

THE TWO TREES. AMBROSIASTER: The olive tree represents faith, whereas the wild olive refers to wickedness. COMMENTARY ON PAUL'S EPISTLES.[65]

WHAT FAITH CAN ACCOMPLISH. CHRYSOSTOM: If faith could do what was contrary to nature, how much more will it be able to accomplish that which is according to nature. For if the Gentile, who was cut off from his natural fathers

---

[54]See Is 2:4; 51:5; Ezek 18:30; Lk 12:48; 4 Ezra 16:67. [55]FC 9:480. [56]PCR 128. [57]CSEL 81.1:379. [58]NPNF 1 11:492. [59]PCR 128. [60]NTA 15:158. [61]See 2 Chron 7:14. [62]See Mt 19:26. [63]PCR 128. [64]IER, Migne PG 82. [65]CSEL 81.1:381.

and came, contrary to nature, to Abraham, how much more will God be able to recover his own! HOMILIES ON ROMANS 19.[66]

FOLLOW THE GOODNESS OF THE ROOT. [Pseudo-]Constantius: In this passage Paul says that the Gentiles have been grafted against nature onto the root, that is, onto the faith of the patriarchs, and that being grafted on in this way they do not bear fruit of their own kind, according to the nature of the tree, but they follow the goodness of the root onto which they have been grafted. THE HOLY LETTER OF ST. PAUL TO THE ROMANS.[67]

GRAFTED AGAINST NATURE. Pelagius: Their

fathers had fallen away from nature because they had forgotten the law of nature, and when their habits had become fixed through repeated sinning, they came to be bitter and unproductive, as it were, by nature.

"And grafted, contrary to nature." . . . It is against nature to graft a wild olive tree into a cultivated olive tree, because the branch usually alters the effectiveness of the root. The root does not change the effectiveness of the branches to conform to its character. PELAGIUS'S COMMENTARY ON ROMANS.[68]

---

[66]NPNF 1 11:493. [67]ENPK 2:78. [68]PCR 129.

11:25-36 GOD'S FINAL PLAN FOR ISRAEL

[25]*Lest you be wise in your own conceits, I want you to understand this mystery, brethren: a hardening has come upon part of Israel, until the full number of the Gentiles come in,* [26]*and so all Israel will be saved; as it is written,*

"The Deliverer will come from Zion,
he will banish ungodliness from Jacob";
[27]*"and this will be my covenant with them*
when I take away their sins."

[28]*As regards the gospel they are enemies of God, for your sake; but as regards election they are beloved for the sake of their forefathers.* [29]*For the gifts and the call of God are irrevocable.* [30]*Just as you were once disobedient to God but now have received mercy because of their disobedience,* [31]*so they have now been disobedient in order that by the mercy shown to you they also may*[p] *receive mercy.* [32]*For God has consigned all men to disobedience, that he may have mercy upon all.*

[33]*O the depth of the riches and wisdom and knowledge of God! How unsearchable are his judgments and how inscrutable his ways!*

[34]*"For who has known the mind of the Lord,*
or who has been his counselor?"
[35]*"Or who has given a gift to him*
that he might be repaid?"

[36]For from him and through him and to him are all things. To him be glory for ever. Amen.

p Other ancient authorities add *now*

OVERVIEW: The hardening of Israel is partial and temporary. When the full number of the Gentiles has been saved, the Jews who have been chosen will repent and believe. All the elect faithful of Israel will be saved. Everything that happens has a purpose in the plan of God. He allowed the world to sink into disobedience in order to be able to show how great his mercy is. The depths of his wisdom are impenetrable, but we know that in the end everything that happens is for our good and is consistent with the holiness and justice of God.

11:25 Understanding a Mystery

JEWS BELIEVE IN CHRIST. CHRYSOSTOM: Part of the Jewish people have been blinded, but not all, for many of them already have believed in Christ. HOMILIES ON ROMANS 19.[1]

UNTIL THE FULL NUMBER OF GENTILES COMES IN. [PSEUDO-]CONSTANTIUS: Here Paul shows that, as the complement of the Gentiles comes into faith in Christ, the rest of the Jewish people will be stirred by jealousy and a desire to follow suit, and believing in Christ they will be saved. But in the meantime the apostle ranks the Gentiles ahead of the Jews in the faith for the reason that even if some of the Jews believed in Christ, they still followed the precepts of the law of Moses. But afterward they too, following the example of the Gentiles, began to maintain the Christian faith in its fullness. THE HOLY LETTER OF ST. PAUL TO THE ROMANS.[2]

NO CONCEIT. PELAGIUS: All that follows is designed to prevent the Gentiles from being filled with pride toward the Jews. It is a secret unknown to mankind why the Gentiles were saved, because Israel's blindness in fact furnished the occasion for their salvation. The blindness continued until the Jews saw that the Gentiles were being saved, since all were called to salvation. PELAGIUS'S COMMENTARY ON ROMANS.[3]

ELIJAH WILL COME AND RESTORE ISRAEL. THEODORET OF CYR: Paul insists that only a part of Israel has been hardened, for in fact many of them believe. He thus encourages them not to despair that others will be saved as well. After the Gentiles accepted the gospel, the Jews would believe, when the great Elijah would come to them and bring them the doctrine of faith. The Lord himself said as much: "Elijah will come and will restore all things."[4] INTERPRETATION OF THE LETTER TO THE ROMANS.[5]

11:26 A Deliverer from Zion

ALL ISRAEL WILL BE SAVED. ORIGEN: What "all Israel" means or what the fullness of the Gentiles will be only God knows along with his only begotten Son and perhaps a few of his friends, as he said: "I no longer call you servants but friends, for I have made known to you everything which I have heard from my Father."[6] COMMENTARY ON THE EPISTLE TO THE ROMANS.[7]

DIODORE: What does it mean to say that "all Israel will be saved?" Just as we say that the whole world and all the nations are being saved because everywhere and among all nations there are those who are coming to faith, so also "all Israel will be saved" does not mean that every one of them will be but that either those who were understood by Elijah or those who are scattered all over the world will one day come to faith. PAULINE COMMENTARY FROM THE GREEK CHURCH.[8]

---

[1]NPNF 1 11:493. [2]ENPK 2:78-79. [3]PCR 129. [4]Mt 17:11; Mk 9:12. [5]IER, Migne PG 82. [6]Jn 15:15. [7]CER 4:304. [8]NTA 15:104.

SET FREE BY GRACE. AMBROSIASTER: God will give them back the free exercise of their will so that, because their unbelief did not spring from malice but from error, they may be put right and afterward be saved....

Paul quotes Isaiah in order to prove that God has reserved a gift for them, in order to teach that they can be set free by the same grace by which the believing Jews have already been set free, because he is not empty but always full of grace. COMMENTARY ON PAUL'S EPISTLES.[9]

A TRUER ISRAEL. AUGUSTINE: Not all the Jews were blind; some of them recognized Christ. But the fullness of the Gentiles comes in among those who have been called according to the plan, and there arises a truer Israel of God ... the elect from both the Jews and the Gentiles. LETTER 149.[10]

PELAGIUS: Some interpreters regard all these events as future. To them one must reply: Then this prophecy ... must still take place, and Christ will come again to set them free. If they have been blinded temporarily by God and not by themselves, what will become of those who are now perishing as unbelievers? PELAGIUS'S COMMENTARY ON ROMANS.[11]

ISRAEL CALLED AT THE END. CYRIL OF ALEXANDRIA: Although it was rejected, Israel will also be saved eventually, a hope which Paul confirms by quoting this text of Scripture. For indeed, Israel will be saved in its own time and will be called at the end, after the calling of the Gentiles. EXPLANATION OF THE LETTER TO THE ROMANS.[12]

DEFINING "ALL ISRAEL." THEODORET OF CYR: "All Israel" means all those who believe, whether they are Jews, who have a natural relationship to Israel, or Gentiles, who are related to Israel by faith. INTERPRETATION OF THE LETTER TO THE ROMANS.[13]

SALVATION INDISPUTABLE. GENNADIUS OF

CONSTANTINOPLE: When their sins are taken away and forgiven their salvation will be clear and indisputable. PAULINE COMMENTARY FROM THE GREEK CHURCH.[14]

11:27 Fulfilling the Covenant

MY COVENANT WITH THEM. AMBROSIASTER: The covenant will always be there, however long it takes for them to believe. For this is the Lord Jesus, who has promised to come from heaven in order to set the human race free. Every day he forgives the sins of those who turn to God, nor does he condemn unbelievers straightaway but waits for them, knowing that they may come to a knowledge of God. COMMENTARY ON PAUL'S EPISTLES.[15]

WHEN I TAKE AWAY THEIR SINS. CHRYSOSTOM: God's covenant will be fulfilled not when they are circumcised, nor when they do the other deeds of the law, but when they obtain forgiveness of sins. If this has been promised but has not yet happened in their case, nor have they enjoyed the forgiveness of sins in baptism, nevertheless it will certainly come to pass. HOMILIES ON ROMANS 19.[16]

PELAGIUS: This new covenant Jeremiah promised which only those who are new, whose sins have been wiped away, will receive.[17] PELAGIUS'S COMMENTARY ON ROMANS.[18]

11:28 Beloved for the Sake of Their Ancestors

RECEIVED WITH JOY. AMBROSIASTER: However seriously the Jews may have sinned by rejecting the gift of God, and however worthy they may be of death, nevertheless, because they are the children of good people, whose privileges and many

---

[9]CSEL 81.1:383. [10]FC 20:253. [11]PCR 129-30. [12]Migne PG 74 col. 849. [13]IER, Migne PG 82 col. 180. [14]TA 15:401. [15]CSEL 81.1:383. [16]NPNF 1 11:493. [17]See Jer 31:31-34. [18]PCR 130.

benefits from God they have received, they will be received with joy when they return to the faith, because God's love for them is stirred up by the memory of their ancestors. COMMENTARY ON PAUL'S EPISTLES.[19]

CHRYSOSTOM: When the Gentiles believed, the Jews became even more obnoxious. But even now God has not stopped calling the Gentiles. He is waiting for all of them who are to believe to come in, and then the rest of the Jews will come as well. HOMILIES ON ROMANS 19.[20]

PELAGIUS: They are Paul's enemies because he preaches Christ to the Gentiles. But if they believe they are beloved, i.e., doubly blessed. PELAGIUS'S COMMENTARY ON ROMANS.[21]

11:29 God's Call Is Irrevocable

WHETHER SORROW IS REQUIRED. AMBROSIASTER: It is usually thought that those who have sinned badly by not accepting the promise of God cannot receive mercy if they do not demonstrate their sorrow, because those who have sinned badly cannot be forgiven without tears and wailing. But Paul shows that these things are not required at the start, because God's gift freely pardons sins in baptism. COMMENTARY ON PAUL'S EPISTLES.[22]

IRREVOCABLE. AUGUSTINE: For God to order his future works in his foreknowledge, which cannot be deceived or changed, is entirely (and nothing other than) to predestine. But just as he whom God has foreknown to be chaste, although this may be unclear to him, acts in such a way as to be chaste, so he whom God has predestined to be chaste, although this may be unclear to him, does not, simply because he hears that by God's gift he will be what he will be, fail to act so as to be chaste. Indeed, his charity is delighted, and he is not puffed up as if he had not received it. Not only is he not hindered from the work of charity by the

preaching of predestination, but on the contrary he is helped in this task, so that when he glories he may glory in the Lord.[23] GIFT OF PERSEVERANCE 17.[24]

THE PROMISE HOLDS. PELAGIUS: If they believe, their sins will not be counted against them, because God does not repent that he made a promise with Abraham's descendants. Or it may mean if they believe they will be saved without the anguish of penance. PELAGIUS'S COMMENTARY ON ROMANS.[25]

SAUL AND SOLOMON ARGUE FOR REVOCABILITY. THEODORET OF CYR: Paul says this in order to encourage the Jews. In fact, of course, God did revoke the good gifts which he gave . . . King Saul, for example, who received spiritual grace which later deserted him.[26] Likewise Solomon, who received peace through the kindness of God, but after his transgression was deprived of grace.[27] And then there are the Jews themselves, who always had their prophets to take care of them but who at the present time have been deprived of them. INTERPRETATION OF THE LETTER TO THE ROMANS.[28]

11:30 Mercy Through the Jews' Disobedience

MERCY UNDESERVED. PELAGIUS: You did not believe when the Jews did, and now you have received mercy, but not because you have deserved it. PELAGIUS'S COMMENTARY ON ROMANS.[29]

CLEANSED BY THE SAME GRACE. CYRIL OF ALEXANDRIA: Paul shows that both Jews and Gentiles were guilty of the same thing and that they were likewise cleansed by one and the same grace. EXPLANATION OF THE LETTER TO THE ROMANS.[30]

---

[19]CSEL 81.1:385. [20]NPNF 1 11:493. [21]PCR 130. [22]CSEL 81.1:385. [23]See 1 Cor 1:31. [24]FC 86:311. [25]PCR 130. [26]See 1 Sam 15:26; 28:6. [27]See 1 Kings 11:6-13. [28]IER, Migne PG 82 col. 181. [29]PCR 130. [30]Migne PG 74 cols. 849-52.

11:31 Mercy Shown to the Jews

That They May Also Receive Mercy.

Ambrosiaster: Paul recalls the unbelief of the Gentiles so that being ashamed of it they may not insult the Jews who have not believed but rejoice when they accept the promise of God. Commentary on Paul's Epistles.[31]

Pelagius: Christ is the mercy of the Gentiles.[32] They have been such unbelievers that they too are justified not by their works but in mercy, as you are.[33] Pelagius's Commentary on Romans.[34]

11:32 God's Mercy on All

Consigned All to Disobedience. Ambrosiaster: From earliest times all nations lived in ungodliness and ignorance because they were without God.[35] For this reason the law was revealed, by which the worst ones could be restrained. But by the activity of the adversary sins began to multiply, so that through the commandment man was considered more guilty still. Then God, who in the mercy of his goodness always takes care of human creation, seeing that even without the law sin still existed and that by the law it could not be wiped out, decreed that he would require only faith, by which the sins of all men might be abolished. Thus although man had no ground for hope through the law, he was nevertheless saved by the mercy of God. To consign everything to disobedience means that this decree comes as a gift from God at a time when everyone was laboring in unbelief, so that grace might appear to be the freest of all rewards. Therefore nobody should boast, for the one who is proud of his ignorance is to be pitied. Commentary on Paul's Epistles.[36]

Jerome: This is complete righteousness in man, not to impute any virtue that he can attain to himself but rather to the Lord, the giver. Against the Pelagians 13.[37]

Augustine: The apostle did not mean by these words that God would not condemn anybody. What he meant is made clear by the context. Paul was speaking about those Jews who would one day believe. The City of God 21.24.[38]

Not Consigned Without Their Choice.

Pelagius: God has not imprisoned them by force, but for a good reason he has confined all those whom he found in unbelief, i.e., all Jews and Gentiles. He confined the Jews because previously they were only sinners, not faithless as well. But since they have not believed Christ they are equal to the Gentiles and receive mercy in the same way. God does all this so that he may have mercy on them all. Pelagius's Commentary on Romans.[39]

Whether Convicted or Consigned. The-

odoret of Cyr: Paul has put "consigned" here instead of "convicted." For God convicted the Gentiles, who had received the natural law and had created things to teach them the knowledge of God yet had not benefited from either the one or the other. He also convicted the Jews, who had received more teaching still (for besides nature and the creation they had also received the law and the prophets, who taught them what they needed to know) and had become liable to even greater punishments as a result. But God was pleased to offer salvation to each of them, even though basically they deserved to perish, if only they would believe. Interpretation of the Letter to the Romans.[40]

Consigned by Divine Permission, Not by Divine Action. John of Damascus: This is not to be taken in the sense of God acting but in the sense of God permitting, because of free will and because virtue is not forced. Orthodox Faith 4.19.[41]

---

[31]CSEL 81.1:387. [32]See Tit 3:5. [33]See Lam 3:22. [34]PCR 130. [35]See, e.g., Gen 6:5. [36]CSEL 81.1:387-89. [37]FC 53:247. [38]FC 24:393. [39]PCR 130. [40]IER, Migne PG 181. [41]FC 37:384.

11:33 God's Unsearchable Ways

HOW UNSEARCHABLE HIS WAYS. TERTULLIAN: Whence this outburst of feeling? Surely from the recollection of the Scriptures, which he had been previously turning over, as well as from his contemplation of the mysteries which he had been setting forth above, in relation to the faith of Christ coming from the law. AGAINST MARCION 24.[42]

ORIGEN: Paul did not say that God's judgments were hard to search out but that they could not be searched out at all. He did not say that God's ways were hard to find out but that they were impossible to find out. For however far one may advance in the search and make progress through an increasingly earnest study, even when aided and enlightened in the mind by God's grace, he will never be able to reach the final goal of his inquiries. ON FIRST PRINCIPLES 4.3.14.[43]

GUIDED BY ANGELS. NOVATIAN: The world, this chariot of God and all that is therein, is guided by the angels and the stars. Although their movements are varied—bound nevertheless by fixed laws—we see them guided to their goals according to the time measured out to them. So may we deservedly cry out with the apostle as we admire the Maker and his works: "O the depth of the riches and wisdom and knowledge of God! How unsearchable are his judgments and how inscrutable his ways!" THE TRINITY 8.11.[44]

THE DIVINE MYSTERIES. GREGORY OF NYSSA: Paul examined . . . the unclear and hidden aspects of the divine mysteries and through suggestive phrases revealed the illuminations which came to him from God concerning the understanding of what is incomprehensible and unsearchable. ON PERFECTION.[45]

THE DEPTH OF THE RICHES. AMBROSIASTER: God knew from the beginning what man's behavior and works would be like, in that the human race could not be saved only by the severity of his justice nor could it reach perfection only by his mercy. So at a particular time he decreed what should be preached, whereas before that time he allowed each person to decide for himself, because righteousness was recognized under the guidance of nature. And because the authority of natural righteousness was weakened by the habit of sin, the law was given so that the human race would be held back by the fear engendered by the revealed law. But because they did not restrain themselves and were counted guilty under the law, mercy was proclaimed, which would save those who took refuge in it but would blind those who rejected it for a time. During that time this mercy would invite the Gentiles, who earlier on had not wanted to follow the law given to Moses, to share in the promise, so that the Jews might become jealous of their salvation and because of that jealousy turn again to the source of the root, which is the Savior. This is "the depth of the riches and wisdom and knowledge of God," who by his many-sided providence has won both Jews and Gentiles to eternal life. COMMENTARY ON PAUL'S EPISTLES.[46]

STRUCK WITH AWE. CHRYSOSTOM: After going back to former times and looking back to God's original dispensation of things, whereby the world has existed up to the present time, and having considered the special provision which he had made for all eventualities, Paul is struck with awe and cries aloud, making his hearers feel confident that what he is saying will come to pass. HOMILIES ON ROMANS 19.[47]

PELAGIUS: Paul praises the wisdom of God, who according to his foreknowledge waited until all were in need of mercy in order to take from everyone the glory that derives from unfounded boasting in works. The judgments of God are a

---

[42]ANF 3:460. [43]OFP 311. [44]FC 67:41. [45]FC 58:105. [46]CSEL 81.1:389. [47]NPNF 1 11:494.

great deep,[48] for they cannot be clearly grasped. PELAGIUS'S COMMENTARY ON ROMANS.[49]

A KNOWING BEYOND EVERY WAY OF KNOWING. PSEUDO-DIONYSIUS: It is in this sense that one says of St. Paul that he knew God, for he knew that God is beyond every act of mind and every way of knowing. LETTER 5.[50]

11:34 Knowing the Mind of the Lord

THE NATURE OF CREATURES. ORIGEN: This refers to creatures, but the other members of the Trinity are excepted because they have nothing in common with the nature of creatures. COMMENTARY ON THE EPISTLE TO THE ROMANS.[51]

GOD'S KNOWING NOT MEASURABLE BY US. AMBROSIASTER: It is clear that only God knows everything and it is only he who lacks nothing, because everything comes from him. No one can understand or measure this knowledge, because the inferior cannot comprehend what is superior to it. Jewish believers could not understand that the salvation of the Gentiles could be God's plan and will. Likewise, it seemed unlikely and incredible to the Gentiles that the Jews, who had not believed, could be converted or accepted as believers. COMMENTARY ON PAUL'S EPISTLES.[52]

GOD'S WISDOM NOT DERIVED. CHRYSOSTOM: God does not get his wisdom from anyone else but is himself the fountain of all good things.[53] HOMILIES ON ROMANS 19.[54]

THE MIND OF THE LORD. PELAGIUS: Previously nobody knew it, but at the time of writing Paul certainly knew it, as he indicated to others when he said: "We have the mind of the Lord."[55] PELAGIUS'S COMMENTARY ON ROMANS.[56]

11:35 God Cannot Be Repaid

GOD DEVISED ALL THINGS. CHRYSOSTOM: God himself devised all things, created all things

and worked all things together. He is rich and had no need to receive anything from anyone else. HOMILIES ON ROMANS 19.[57]

UNWARRANTED BOASTING. PELAGIUS: Who has done something beforehand, so that instead of magnifying God's mercy, he boasts that he has received what he deserved? PELAGIUS'S COMMENTARY ON ROMANS.[58]

THE WHOLE OF SALVATION IS A GIFT. PROSPER OF AQUITAINE: No good work comes from the dead; nothing righteous from the ungodly. Their whole salvation is gratuitous and is therefore the glory of God, so that he who glories may glory in him of whose glory he has stood in need. GRACE AND FREE WILL 10.[59]

11:36 All Things Are from God

THE FATHER FROM WHOM AND THE SON THROUGH WHOM AND THE SPIRIT TO WHOM. ORIGEN: You see how here, [as in the previous verses,] Paul indicates the mystery of the Trinity. For when he says from him and through him and to him, this corresponds to the one God and Father, from whom are all things, and our one Lord Jesus Christ, through whom are all things.[60] Likewise he says that all things are revealed by the Spirit of God, thus indicating that the providence of the Trinity is present in everything. When he talks about the height of riches he means the Father, from whom all things come; when he talks about the height of wisdom he means Christ, who is the wisdom of God; and when he talks about the depth of knowledge he is referring to the Holy Spirit, who knows the deep things of God.

Paul adds "forever" to indicate that the perfection of all things is not bound by time but will extend to eternity and even be increased. He fur-

[48]Ps 36:6. [49]PCR 130. [50]PDCW 265. [51]CER 4:316. [52]CSEL 81.1:391. [53]See 1 Cor 2:16. [54]NPNF 1 11:495. [55]1 Cor 2:16. [56]PCR 130-31. [57]CSEL 81.1:391. [58]PCR 131. [59]FC 7:373. [60]1 Cor 8:6.

ther adds "Amen" so that we might understand that we are coming to that blessedness through him, of whom it is written in the Apocalypse: "These are the words of the Amen."[61] COMMENTARY ON THE EPISTLE TO THE ROMANS.[62]

ORIGEN: Paul declares that God is the beginning of the substance of all things by the words "of him" and the bond of their subsistence by the expression "through him" and their final end by the term "to him."[63] AGAINST CELSUS 6.65.[64]

NOVATIAN: All things exist by God's command, so that they are "from him"; they are set in order by his Word and therefore "through him." Finally, all things have recourse to his judgment so that, while they long for freedom "in him," after corruption has been done away with they appear to be recalled "to him." THE TRINITY 3.7.[65]

GREGORY OF NYSSA: What person who believes that he lives "from him and through him and to him" will dare to make the One who encompasses in himself the life of each of us a witness of a life which does not reflect him? ON PERFECTION. [66]

BEGINNING, CONTINUING AND CONSUMMATING PROVIDENCE. AMBROSE: "From him" means the beginning and origin of the substance of the universe, i.e., by his will and power.... "Through him" means the continuation of the universe; "unto him" means its end. SIX DAYS OF CREATION 5.19.[67]

THE SAVING WORK OF THE TRIUNE GOD. AMBROSIASTER: By saying this Paul revealed a meaning which had been hidden from the world. For because God is the Creator of all things, everything comes from him. And because everything comes from him, it comes through his Son, who is of the same substance and whose work is the Father's work as well.... And because what is from God and through God is then born again in the Holy Spirit, everything is in him as well, because the Holy Spirit is from God the Father,

which is why he knows what is in God.... Here Paul laid bare the mystery of God, which he said above should not be unknown to them. COMMENTARY ON PAUL'S EPISTLES.[68]

AUGUSTINE: Paul is referring to the Trinity when he says this. FAITH AND THE CREED 16.[69]

COUNTERING ARIANISM. PELAGIUS: From him all creation received its beginning, through him it is governed, and in him are all things contained, whereas he is not contained by any created thing. He alone should receive glory, for it is from him that we live and move.[70]

At the same time, this passage also contradicts the Arians when it is said that it is one and the same God from whom and through whom all things are revealed to have been made, since the Evangelist indicated that in the beginning everything was made through the Word.[71] The apostle here teaches that what the Evangelist testifies concerning the Son should be understood and believed of the Father, through the mystery of the unity. PELAGIUS'S COMMENTARY ON ROMANS.[72]

IN HIM ARE ALL THINGS. THEODORET OF CYR: God himself made all things and he rules in perpetuity over everything which he has made. Everyone ought to turn to him, to thank him for what they asked for and to put their trust in him for the future. They ought to honor him as well. In this way the holy apostle shows that there is no difference between the prepositions *from* and *through*, as if the former, which might mean something greater, should apply to the Father and the latter, which might mean something less, to the Son. In fact, both apply equally to both persons. INTERPRETATION OF THE LETTER TO THE ROMANS.[73]

JOHN OF DAMASCUS: "In him are all things" not

---

[61]Rev 3:14. [62]CER 4:316-18. [63]See Heb 9:14. [64]ANF 4:603. [65]FC 67:30-31. [66]FC 58:107. [67]FC 42:18. [68]CSEL 81.1:391-93. [69]LCC 6:361. [70]See Acts 17:28. [71]See Jn 1:1-3. [72]PCR 131. [73]IER, Migne PG 82 col. 184.

only because he has brought them from nothing into being but because it is by his operation that all things he made are kept in existence and held together. Living things, however, participate more abundantly, because they participate in the good both by their being and by their living. But rational beings, while they participate in the good in the aforementioned ways, do so still more by their very rationality. For in a way they are more akin to him, although of course he is immeasurably superior to them. ORTHODOX FAITH 4.13.[74]

---

[74]FC 37:354.

12:1-8 LIVING SACRIFICES

[1]*I appeal to you therefore, brethren, by the mercies of God, to present your bodies as a living sacrifice, holy and acceptable to God, which is your spiritual worship.* [2]*Do not be conformed to this world*[q] *but be transformed by the renewal of your mind, that you may prove what is the will of God, what is good and acceptable and perfect.*[r]

[3]*For by the grace given to me I bid every one among you not to think of himself more highly than he ought to think, but to think with sober judgment, each according to the measure of faith which God has assigned him.* [4]*For as in one body we have many members, and all the members do not have the same function,* [5]*so we, though many, are one body in Christ, and individually members one of another.* [6]*Having gifts that differ according to the grace given to us, let us use them: if prophecy, in proportion to our faith;* [7]*if service, in our serving; he who teaches, in his teaching;* [8]*he who exhorts, in his exhortation; he who contributes, in liberality; he who gives aid, with zeal; he who does acts of mercy, with cheerfulness.*

q Greek *age*   r Or *what is the good and acceptable and perfect will of God*

OVERVIEW: Having expounded the basic principles of his doctrine Paul now goes on to teach its moral consequences for the Christian life. The body is to become a living sacrifice, totally dedicated to the pursuit of righteousness. The Fathers found any number of ways that this principle could be applied and were not slow to expound them in detail. To understand God's will correctly it is first necessary to have a renewed mind. Once that is achieved it will be possible not merely to know God's will but to do it as well. It is up to individuals to know their own proper place in the kingdom of God and not to seek after things they have not been given. Spiritual gifts are distributed among the body of believers in order that they may see their need of each other and help each other grow in grace. *Service* was originally understood as a generic term, though later it came to be restricted to liturgical functions. The Fathers generally understood the gift of prophecy to mean the preaching and exposition of the Scriptures, not the revelation of new messages from God, though that was not excluded. Exhortation was regarded as a form of preaching or teaching designed to encourage the faint-hearted. Charitable giving was held to be of the essence of the faith and encouraged accordingly.

12:1 *Living Sacrifices*

New Life Manifested in Our Bodies. Origen: Paul says that the sacrifice is living because it has eternal life in it, which is Christ. Elsewhere he says: "We always carry in the body the death of Jesus so that the life of Jesus may also be manifested in our bodies."[1] He calls it holy because the Holy Spirit dwells in it, as he says elsewhere: "Do you not know that you are God's temple and that the Spirit of God dwells in you?"[2] Commentary on the Epistle to the Romans.[3]

Origen: The divine Word wants you to offer your flesh to God in purity, with the understanding of your reason. Homilies on Leviticus 1.5.1.[4]

Holy and Acceptable to God. Gregory of Nyssa: How can the person who is conformed to this age, who is not transformed in the newness of his mind and who does not walk in the newness of this life but instead follows the life of the old man, obey Paul, who commanded you to present your body as a sacrifice living, holy and pleasing to God? How can you be a priest for God, having been anointed for this very purpose of offering a gift to God, not a gift that is completely alien or fraudulent because it consists of what is external to you but a gift which is truly yours because it consists of what is internal to you, which is the man inside you helping you to be perfect and blameless according to the word of the Lamb, free from all stain and dishonor?[5] How will you place these offerings before God if you do not listen to the law which forbids an unholy man to be a priest? On Virginity 23.[6]

A Living Sacrifice. Jerome: Idolatry is not confined to casting incense upon an altar with finger and thumb or to pouring libations of wine out of a cup into a bowl. Covetousness is idolatry, or else the selling of the Lord for thirty pieces of

silver was a righteous act.[7] Lust involves sacrilege, or else men may defile with common harlots those members of Christ which should be "a living sacrifice, acceptable to God." Epistles 14.5.[8]

Not Bodies but Sins of the Body Sacrificed. Ambrosiaster: Paul pleads with them through the mercy of God, by which the human race is saved. . . . This is a warning that they should remember that they have received God's mercy and that they should take care to worship the one who gave it to them.

God's will is our sanctification,[9] for bodies subject to sin are considered not to be alive but dead, since they have no hope of obtaining the promise of eternal life. It is for this purpose that we are cleansed from our sins by God's gift, that henceforth we should lead a pure life and stir up the love of God in us, not making his work of grace of no effect. For the ancients killed sacrifices which were offered in order to signify that men were subjected to death because of sin. But now, since by the gift of God men have been purified and set free from the second death, they must offer a living sacrifice as a sign of eternal life. For now it is no longer the case that bodies are sacrificed for bodies, but instead of bodies it is the sins of the body which must be put to death.[10] Commentary on Paul's Epistles.[11]

How the Body Becomes a Sacrifice. Chrysostom: How is the body to become a sacrifice? Let the eye look on no evil thing, and it has already become a sacrifice.[12] Let the tongue say nothing filthy, and it has become an offering.[13] Let your hand do nothing evil, and it has become a whole burnt offering.[14] But even this is not enough, for we must have good works also.[15] The hand must do alms, the mouth must bless those who curse it, and the ears must find time to listen

---

[1] 2 Cor 4:10. [2] 1 Cor 3:16. [3] CER 5:26. [4] FC 83:37. [5] See Rom 8:9-11; 1 Cor 3:16-17; 2 Cor 13:5; Col 1:27. [6] FC 58:74. [7] See Mt 26:14-16; 27:3-10. [8] LCC 5:295. [9] 1 Thess 4:3. [10] Jn 8:34-36. [11] CSEL 81.1:393-95. [12] See Mt 5:29; 6:22; 18:9; Mk 9:47. [13] See Prov 10:31; 18:21; Jas 3:5-6. [14] See Is 56:2. [15] See 2 Tim 2:21.

to the reading of Scripture.[16] Sacrifice allows of no unclean thing. It is the first fruits of all other actions. HOMILIES ON ROMANS 20.[17]

AFLAME WITH DIVINE LOVE. AUGUSTINE: If the body, which is less than the soul and which the soul uses as a servant or a tool, is a sacrifice when it is used well and rightly for the service of God, how much more so is the soul when it offers itself to God? In this way, aflame in the fire of divine love and with the dross of worldly desire melted away, it is remolded into the unchangeable form of God and becomes beautiful in his sight by reason of the bounty of beauty which he has bestowed upon it. THE CITY OF GOD 10.6.[18]

FROM DOCTRINE TO MORALS. [PSEUDO-] CONSTANTIUS: Up to this point Paul has expounded doctrine. Now he goes on to teach morals. THE HOLY LETTER OF ST. PAUL TO THE ROMANS.[19]

NOT ANIMALS SACRIFICED BUT OUR OWN BODIES. PELAGIUS: Because Paul has already mentioned the mind of the Lord, he now instructs them how they ought to conduct themselves so that they are worthy to have the mind of the Lord.[20] They possessed nothing greater than the mercy of God because they had been set free by it. They were to present their bodies, not those of animals, as under the law, which (in spite of the fact that they were a symbolic offering) were nevertheless offered up healthy and unblemished. The living sacrifice was to be pure and free from the total death of sin. It should be pleasing only to God, not to other people. Every good work pleases God if it is done in a reasonable manner. For one is deprived of one's reward if, for example, one fasts for public notice, for then one is performing a good deed in a foolish way.[21] And the same applies to all vices that border on virtues. PELAGIUS'S COMMENTARY ON ROMANS.[22]

AS IF WE HAD RISEN. THEODORET OF CYR: Paul has already exhorted us to make our mem-

bers instruments of righteousness and to present ourselves before God as if we had risen from the dead.[23] But here he exhorts us to make our members a sacrifice, and one which he describes as "living." He does not command us to kill our bodies but demands that they should be dead to sin.[24] INTERPRETATION OF THE LETTER TO THE ROMANS.[25]

THE LIVING SACRIFICE OF RATIONAL CREATURES. GENNADIUS OF CONSTANTINOPLE: As the fullness of God's mercies toward us is limitless, I am obliged and I challenge us all to be set apart and offered to God as a complete sacrifice. For the present sacrifice does not lead to death, as did that under the law, but by making us holy it leads to eternal life, because it is pleasing to God and the offering of rational creatures is much more valuable than that of dumb ones. PAULINE COMMENTARY FROM THE GREEK CHURCH.[26]

PRIESTLY OFFERING. PHILOXENUS OF MABBUG: Just as with the former law of Moses, all the priests . . . must first offer a rational sacrifice to God for themselves, and only then for the people. In his prayer, the priest asks in the first place for forgiveness of his own sins and a cleansing of his own soul and body from all sinful thoughts and actions. Then each priest offers these prayers to God in accordance with the measure of his own purity of soul. ON THE INDWELLING OF THE HOLY SPIRIT.[27]

I APPEAL TO YOU. LUCULENTIUS: The difference between asking and appealing is that we ask about unimportant matters but appeal about important ones. . . . Our bodies are sacrifices because the flesh is put to death. They are living sacrifices, because the Spirit has given them life. COMMENTARY 3.[28]

---

[16]See Mt 5:44; 22:29; Mk 12:24; Jn 5:39; 2 Tim 3:16. [17]NPNF 1 11:496. [18]FC 14:126*. [19]ENPK 2:80. [20]See 1 Chron 28:9; 1 Cor 2:16; Phil 2:5; Sir 6:37. [21]See Mt 6:16. [22]PCR 131-32. [23]Rom 6:13. [24]See Rom 6:2, 11. [25]IER, Migne PG 82 col. 185. [26]NTA 15:403. [27]SFPSL 110. [28]Migne PL 72 col. 811.

THE SAME GLORY. BEDE: If we display our bodies as a living sacrifice, holy and pleasing to God, he will with heavenly condescension deign to see to it that we are rewarded with the same glory as those who have given their bodies up to death for the Lord's sake. HOMILIES ON THE GOSPELS 2.21.[29]

12:2 Transformed by a New Mind

BE TRANSFORMED. ORIGEN: By this Paul shows that there is one form of this world and another of the world to come. If there are those who love this present life and the things which are in the world, they are taken up with the form of the present age and pay no attention to what is not seen. But the things which are not seen are eternal,[30] and they are being transformed and re-newed in the form of the age to come. For this reason the world does not acknowledge them but hates them and persecutes them.[31] But the angels of God, who belong to the age to come, see that form.

"Be transformed by the renewal of your mind" tells us what form is guilty, for every soul once had the form of wickedness. But the apostle's words urge us to cast that off and to be reformed in the likeness of the individual virtues, so that once the face of our heart is revealed we may be transformed by God's image and contemplate his glory. . . . Our mind is renewed by the practice of wisdom and reflection on the Word of God and the spiritual understanding of his law. The more one reads the Scriptures daily and the greater one's understanding is, the more one is renewed always and every day.[32] I doubt whether a mind which is lazy toward the holy Scriptures and the exercise of spiritual knowledge can be renewed at all.

Many people think they know what God's will is, and they are mistaken. Those who do not have a renewed mind err and go wrong. It is not every mind but only one which is renewed and conformed (as I say) to the image of God which can tell whether what we think, say and do in particular instances is the will of God or not.

"What is the will of God, what is good and acceptable and perfect." If we read this according to the Latin manuscripts, the meaning is as follows: Because the will of God is something good and acceptable and perfect, there is no doubt that it is pleasing to God. For God cannot will anything which is not good, and if something is good and perfect, then it must be pleasing to God. But if we read this according to the Greek manuscripts, i.e., "that you may prove that the will of God is good and acceptable and perfect," it can also be interpreted in the same sense. Yet something else may be felt in these words, viz., that God's will is always good but that we do not always deserve to receive what is good by his will, nor what is acceptable and perfect. For example, when Saul was anointed king it was according to God's will, but it was not acceptable or perfect. For God was angry at the people because they refused to have him as their king, and he ordered a man to be set over them as king.[33] . . . Thus from time to time God's will gives us what we want and desire, but the man who is renewed in his mind must ask whether this will of God is good and acceptable and perfect, and not more likely to indulge our lusts than to serve our needs. COMMENTARY ON THE EPISTLE TO THE ROMANS.[34]

THE PERFECT WILL OF GOD. APOLLINARIS OF LAODICEA: This is what the prophet Jeremiah meant when he talked about writing the law of God on the heart.[35] For in the pursuit of God the spiritually minded heart will know what is good and acceptable and perfect, and it will only like the things which are pleasing to God. Filled with the goodness of the good Father it will want to do his will and will try to encourage everyone to do good.

However, it is not enough merely to do good; one must resist evil as well. For it is the rejection of evil which represents true progress toward the good. PAULINE COMMENTARY FROM THE GREEK CHURCH.[36]

---

[29]CSEL 81.1:219. [30]2 Cor 4:18. [31]See Mt 5:10-11; Jn 15:19-20. [32]See Mt 22:29; Mk 12:24; Jn 5:39; Acts 17:10-11; 2 Tim 3:16. [33]1 Sam 8:4-22. [34]CER 5:30-36. [35]See Jer 32:37-44. [36]NTA 15:75-76.

GREGORY OF NYSSA: The perfect will of God is that the soul be changed by reverence, having been brought to the full flower of its beauty by the grace of the Spirit, which attends to the sufferings of the person who undergoes the change. ON THE CHRISTIAN MODE OF LIFE.[37]

THAT YOU MAY PROVE WHAT IS THE WILL OF GOD. CHRYSOSTOM: The fashion of this world is groveling and worthless, and temporal as well. It has nothing noble or uplifting about it but is wholly perverted. The second part [of the verse] may mean either that we should be renewed, in order to learn what is expedient for us, or that if we learn what is expedient for us we shall be renewed. Either way, God wills what is expedient for us, and whatever he wills is by definition expedient for us. HOMILIES ON ROMANS 20.[38]

HOW DEFORMITY DESIRES CONFORMITY. AUGUSTINE: Those who are moved . . . to turn again to the Lord out of that state of deformity wherein worldly desires conformed them to this world must receive from the Lord their reformation. THE TRINITY 14.22.[39]

THE RENEWED MIND. PELAGIUS: Do not be like the children of the world, you who have been made children of God, but renew your mind, by which the body is governed and all the members are directed. Thus even the movements of the body will be renewed, so that you may be able to recognize the will of God and his mind, for these are revealed only to a renewed mind. PELAGIUS'S COMMENTARY ON ROMANS.[40]

THE FORM OF THIS WORLD. THEODORET OF CYR: Paul calls the things of this present life "forms," e.g., wealth, power and every other splendor. But reality is what is yet to come, which will be stable and eternal. INTERPRETATION OF THE LETTER TO THE ROMANS.[41]

12:3 According to the Measure of Grace

EACH ACCORDING TO THE MEASURE OF FAITH. ORIGEN: In his usual way, the apostle says that he is speaking by the grace which has been given to him and not by the power of human persuasion, nor by philosophy. . . . There is an enormous difference between speaking by grace and speaking by human cleverness. Many people speak with a smooth voice and a clever style but do not edify their audience. They cannot get anyone to obey them, because they do not practice what they preach. People like that are not speaking by grace, which was given to Paul.

Everyone ought to know what the measure is of the grace which has been given to him, for which he has been prepared by his faith.[42] One person receives grace from God to be wise in the work of charity, or in the service of visiting or toward the needs of the poor, or concerning the care of the sick, or the defense of widows and children, or hospitality. For God has apportioned these to each person according to the measure of his faith. But suppose someone has received grace in order to be wise about one of these things but does not understand the measure of the grace which has been given to him and wants to know more about the wisdom of God, the word of doctrine, the meaning of deeper knowledge, for which he has not received grace. He does not want to learn so much as to teach what he does not know. Because he does not know enough, he wants to know more than he ought to know. COMMENTARY ON THE EPISTLE TO THE ROMANS.[43]

BASIL: Paul clearly allots to each one the form of ministry which is right for him and forbids him to encroach on another's territory when he says this.[44] CONCERNING BAPTISM 2.8.[45]

AMBROSIASTER: Here Paul teaches us that we ought to know that the bounds of righteousness must not be transgressed, so that not only will it

---

[37]FC 58:131. [38]NPNF 1 11:497. [39]LCC 8:119. [40]PCR 132. [41]IER, Migne PG 82 col. 185. [42]See Eph 4:7; 1 Cor 12:7. [43]CER 5:38, 46. [44]See 1 Cor 12:4-31. [45]FC 9:410.

be of service to us but it will not harm anyone else either. COMMENTARY ON PAUL'S EPISTLES.[46]

CHRYSOSTOM: Paul addresses these words not to one group of people only but to everyone. The governor and the governed, the slave and the free, the ignorant and the wise, the woman and the man, the young and the old—all are included. The law is the Lord's and is therefore common to everyone. HOMILIES ON ROMANS 20.[47]

NOT THINK MORE HIGHLY OF YOURSELVES THAN YOU OUGHT. PELAGIUS: Since Paul is about to disallow human wisdom that goes beyond the law, he declares that he is not speaking his own mind but by the authority of a spiritual gift. He is writing to all those who are priests or teachers, whose example the others follow.

One who searches into matters of which the law does not speak is trying to be *wiser*. That is why Solomon says: "Do not enquire after things higher than yourself and do not search after things greater than yourself but think always on the things that God has commanded you."[48] Note that Paul calls the Holy Spirit *God*, for to the Corinthians he declares that the Holy Spirit apportions gifts to each person as he wishes.[49] A charismatic power, which only believers receive, is to be regarded as a measure of faith. PELAGIUS'S COMMENTARY ON ROMANS.[50]

THEODORET OF CYR: In the Gospel the Lord decreed that those who possessed humility were first among the blessed: "Blessed are the poor in spirit, for theirs is the kingdom of heaven."[51] Paul laid this command on everyone, rich and poor, servant and master. INTERPRETATION OF THE LETTER TO THE ROMANS.[52]

THINK WITH SOBER JUDGMENT. GENNADIUS OF CONSTANTINOPLE: Paul said this in criticism of those brothers who were running after charismatic gifts. God did not give us his gift in order that we should hate each other or that spiritual things should become an excuse for warfare, but

so that we should enjoy harmony and friendship and the common salvation of all. None of you has anything by right, but the one who is worthy of the greatest, as well as the one who is worthy of the least of the charismatic gifts, has been given it by God. Knowing this he ought to use it according to the measure of his faith. PAULINE COMMENTARY FROM THE GREEK CHURCH.[53]

12:4 One Body, Many Members

ONE BODY. ORIGEN: One person gives all his energy to the wisdom of God and the teaching of the Word; he is the eye of the whole body. Another, as we said above, looks after the needs of the brethren and of the poor; he is the hand of the holy body. Another is an attentive listener to the Word of God; he is the ear of the body. Another is busy admonishing the slack, comforting the suffering and aiding those in need; he is without any doubt called the foot of the body of the church. Each of these has his special task, but none can function properly without the others.[54] COMMENTARY ON THE EPISTLE TO THE ROMANS.[55]

MEMBERS NEED EACH OTHER. AMBROSIASTER: By using the example of the body, Paul teaches that it is impossible for any one of us to do everything on our own, for we are members of each other and need one another. For this reason we ought to behave toward one another with care, because we need each other's gifts.[56] COMMENTARY ON PAUL'S EPISTLES.[57]

MANY MEMBERS HAVE DIFFERENT FUNCTIONS. CHRYSOSTOM: Paul says not that one person received more and another less of God's gifts but only that they are different. We all have different functions, but the body is one and the same. HOMILIES ON ROMANS 21.[58]

---

[46]CSEL 81.1:395. [47]NPNF 1 11:499. [48]Sir 3:22. [49]1 Cor 12:11, 28. [50]PCR 132. [51]Mt 5:3. [52]IER, Migne PG 82 col. 188. [53]NTA 15:403. [54]See Rom 12:6-8; 1 Cor 12:4-31. [55]CER 5:48. [56]See 1 Cor 12:25-26. [57]CSEL 81.1:397. [58]NPNF 1 11:501.

THE HARMONY OF VARIED BODILY FUNC-TIONS. PELAGIUS: Paul exhorts them to live in harmony by comparing them with the body, in case they are not roused by the fact that they have received different gifts. For as individuals they could not have had all the gifts, for then they might have become proud. . . . Nor could they all have the same gift, for then the likeness of the body of Christ would not be present among us. PELAGIUS'S COMMENTARY ON ROMANS.[59]

12:5 One Body But Members of Each Other

MEMBERS ONE OF ANOTHER. CLEMENT OF ROME: Why do we divide and tear to pieces the members of Christ and raise up strife against our own body, and why have we reached such a height of madness as to forget that "we are members one of another?"[60] THE FIRST EPISTLE OF CLEMENT 46.[61]

ONE BODY IN CHRIST. AMBROSIASTER: This is what it means to love Christ, that we should encourage one another to live in a way which corresponds to the way in which the body is made perfect in Christ. COMMENTARY ON PAUL'S EPIS-TLES.[62]

[PSEUDO-]CONSTANTIUS: Paul says that there are many members in the one body, on account of the many different ministries which there are. THE HOLY LETTER OF ST. PAUL TO THE ROMANS.[63]

UNITY AND CHARITY. LEO THE GREAT: The bond of our unity cannot be firm unless the bond of charity has tied us together in indivisible solidarity. . . . It is the connection of the entire body which makes for one health, one beauty.[64] And this connection requires the unanimity of the entire body, but especially it demands harmony among the bishops. LETTER 14.[65]

12:6 Using Our Gifts

THE MEANING OF PROPHECY. ORIGEN: "Proph-

ecy" refers to the content of the apostle's teaching, not to the means by which it is taught. COMMENTARY ON THE EPISTLE TO THE ROMANS.[66]

THE GIFT OF PROPHECY. APOLLINARIS OF LAODICEA: Paul is saying here that if someone has the gift of prophecy, then he has the greatest gift, after that of apostleship. For God placed in the church first apostles and second prophets,[67] and thus such a person, knowing that the apostleship comes first, ought to recognize the limitations of prophecy and accept that he is a servant who must follow the rule of service laid down by his superiors, just as the hands must do the bidding of the head. PAULINE COMMENTARY FROM THE GREEK CHURCH.[68]

DIODORE: "Prophecy" means primarily the explanation of things which are unclear, whether future or past, whether present or hidden. "Prophecy" may also refer to the interpretation of a prophet's words. PAULINE COMMENTARY FROM THE GREEK CHURCH.[69]

HAVING GIFTS THAT DIFFER. BASIL: No one has the capacity to receive all spiritual gifts, but the grace of the Spirit is given proportionately to the faith of each one. THE LONG RULES 7.[70]

AMBROSIASTER: Paul begins with prophecy, which is the first proof that our faith is rational, for believers prophesied when they received the Spirit. This is given in proportion to the recipient, that is, as much as is necessary for the purpose for which it is given. COMMENTARY ON PAUL'S EPISTLES.[71]

ACCORDING TO THE GRACE GIVEN. CHRYSOS-TOM: Although prophecy is a grace, it does not flow forth freely at random but is given only

---

[59]PCR 132. [60]1 Cor 10:17. [61]ANF 1:17. [62]CSEL 81.1:397. [63]ENPK 2:80. [64]See Gal 3:28; Eph 4:11-13. [65]FC 34:66. [66]CER 5:60. [67]1 Cor 12:28. [68]NTA 15:76-77. [69]NTA 15:106. [70]FC 9:250. [71]CSEL 81.1:397.

in proportion to our faith. Homilies on Romans 21.[72]

[Pseudo-]Constantius: Not according to the faith which is from us but according to the faith which has been given and granted to each person from God. The Holy Letter of St. Paul to the Romans.[73]

If Prophecy, in Proportion to Faith.
Pelagius: The gift does not depend upon us but upon the one who gives it.[74] The glory to come is promised to all who believe, but the person who has a heart so pure that he deserves it receives the charismatic power which God has chosen for him even in this life.

If we receive prophecy, it is according to faith, not the law. Or perhaps this means that faith deserves it. For each one receives as much as he believes. Pelagius's Commentary on Romans.[75]

Theodoret of Cyr: It is to be understood that . . . we each must use our gifts for the benefit of one another. . . . Prophecy does not refer only to the prediction of future events but also to the knowledge of things which have been hidden. Interpretation of the Letter to the Romans.[76]

Gennadius of Constantinople: "In proportion to our faith" not only applies to prophecy but may be extended by analogy to all the gifts. Pauline Commentary from the Greek Church.[77]

12:7 Service and Teaching

Serving and Teaching in Proportion to Faith.
Origen: These things must both be done "in proportion to our faith," as Paul says [in the previous verse]. For many who received this ministry claimed to know more than they ought to know and, puffed up with pride or lost in their fantasies, they fell headlong. Commentary on the Epistle to the Romans.[78]

If Teachers, in Your Teaching.
Apollinaris of Laodicea: The teacher must remain in subjection to the prophets, according to the established order, for the prophets are second (after the apostles) and the teachers are third.[79] In fact, teachers are interpreters of the prophetic word, because they have heard and understood it with their ears and seen it with their eyes. For the prophets themselves called those whom they had taught to serve in the ministry of teaching. Pauline Commentary from the Greek Church.[80]

If Service, in Your Serving.
Ambrosiaster: The minister is strengthened for the service of the church to the extent that he believes he ought to serve, lest he labor beyond his faith and exhaust himself in serving to his ruin. . . . Likewise Paul says that the teacher is aided in his teaching so that he will be inspired to transmit the divine doctrine to the extent that he has the faith to teach. Commentary on Paul's Epistles.[81]

Chrysostom: The word *service* is comprehensive, covering everything from the apostleship itself to any spiritual function. It is indeed the name of a particular office [viz., the diaconate], but here it is used in a general sense. Homilies on Romans 21.[82]

Pelagius: "Service" refers to the office of elder or deacon. Pelagius's Commentary on Romans.[83]

Theodoret of Cyr: "Service" means the preaching of the Word; "teaching" means instruction in the commands of God. Interpretation of the Letter to the Romans.[84]

12:8 Exhortation, Giving, Aid and Mercy

Effective Exhortation.
Origen: Exhorta-

---

[72]NPNF 1 11:501. [73]ENPK 2:80. [74]See 1 Cor 12:28. [75]PCR 133. [76]IER, Migne PG 82 col. 188. [77]NTA 15:404. [78]CER 5:62. [79]1 Cor 12:28. [80]NTA 15:77. [81]CSEL 81.1:399. [82]NPNF 1 11:501-2. [83]PCR 133. [84]IER, Migne PG 82 col. 188.

tion is a kind of teaching or word by which afflicted souls are enlightened by the words of holy Scripture which are carefully adapted and collected together for that purpose. For despair often comes when the tribulations of the soul are too many, and it is not an easy matter to put this right with mere words, however polished and plausible they may be. But if the word has the power of God in it, then it penetrates the heart and offers comfort, giving hope to the despairing soul. COMMENTARY ON THE EPISTLE TO THE ROMANS.[85]

DIODORE: "Exhortation" means the type of sermon in which we call those who are still in ignorance to faith in Christ. We do not at that point lay out the full meaning of the Christian life but give them the hope that if they believe in Christ they will enjoy everlasting blessings. PAULINE COMMENTARY FROM THE GREEK CHURCH.[86]

DESCRIBING THE GIFTS. AMBROSIASTER: The exhorter is helped in the same way as the above and is prepared by the Spirit to have the grace to provoke, for he stirs up the brethren to do good and unbelievers to accept the faith. The contributor is likewise given a spirit of generosity so that he will not stop giving.

He who takes care of his brethren will receive vigilance and authority in proportion to his faith. . . . Likewise, he who does acts of mercy according to his intention will do it with a cheerful heart and not as if somebody was twisting his arm to do it. COMMENTARY ON PAUL'S EPISTLES.[87]

LIBERALITY, ZEAL, CHEERFULNESS. CHRYSOSTOM: Exhortation is a form of teaching. . . . In giving Paul looks for liberality;[88] in showing mercy, for cheerfulness; in caregiving, for diligence. For it is not just with money that Paul wants us to help those in need but with words, deeds, in person and in every other way. HOMILIES ON ROMANS 21.[89]

---

[85]CER 5:62-64. [86]NTA 15:106. [87]CSEL 81.1:399-401. [88]See 2 Cor 9:7-9. [89]NPNF 1 11:502.

12:9-21 LOVE

[9]Let love be genuine; hate what is evil, hold fast to what is good; [10]love one another with brotherly affection; outdo one another in showing honor. [11]Never flag in zeal, be aglow with the Spirit, serve the Lord. [12]Rejoice in your hope, be patient in tribulation, be constant in prayer. [13]Contribute to the needs of the saints, practice hospitality.

[14]Bless those who persecute you; bless and do not curse them. [15]Rejoice with those who rejoice, weep with those who weep. [16]Live in harmony with one another; do not be haughty, but associate with the lowly;[s] never be conceited. [17]Repay no one evil for evil, but take thought for what is noble in the sight of all. [18]If possible, so far as it depends upon you, live peaceably with all. [19]Beloved, never avenge yourselves, but leave it[t] to the wrath of God; for it is written, "Vengeance is mine, I will repay, says the Lord." [20]No, "if your enemy is hungry, feed him; if he is thirsty, give him

drink; for by so doing you will heap burning coals upon his head." ²¹Do not be overcome by evil, but overcome evil with good.

s Or *give yourselves to humble tasks*   t Greek *give place*

OVERVIEW: Love is the fulfilling of the law and the ultimate goal of all our labors. Deep love for one another is the hallmark of the Christian fellowship at all times. Love must be accompanied by zeal and service if it is to be effective. Christians are called to rejoice because of their hope of eternal salvation, to be patient in times of suffering and persecution, and to pray without ceasing. In all these things the eschatological dimension of hope governs everything the Fathers say on the subject. The early Christians understood that persecution elicits spiritual growth, and therefore they ought to bless their persecutors. Christian pastoral care must be marked by sympathy and understanding for others but also by wisdom to know which reaction is the appropriate one at any given moment. Humility and peaceableness are the universal marks of a Christian. Christians repay evil with good and never seek revenge, which belongs to God alone. The Fathers believed that if Christians did good to their enemy they would be shaming the enemy into repentance. The coals of fire were understood as a kind of punishment that would burn away all rebellion and malice and prepare the enemy to receive Christ. The Christian demonstrates the superiority of good over evil by refusing to succumb to bitterness, even when provoked.

12:9 *Holding to the Good*

LET LOVE BE GENUINE; HATE WHAT IS EVIL.
ORIGEN: I think that any love without God is artificial and not genuine. For God, the Creator of the soul, filled it with the feeling of love, along with the other virtues, so that it might love God and the things which God wants. But if the soul loves something other than God and what God wants, this love is said to be artificial and invented. And if someone loves his neighbor but does not warn him when he sees him going astray

or correct him, such is only a pretense of love.

Perhaps it seems odd to find hatred listed among the virtues, but it is put here of necessity by the apostle. Nobody doubts that the soul has feelings of hatred in it; however, it is praiseworthy to hate evil and to hate sin.[1] For unless a person hates evil he cannot love, nor can he retain the virtues. For example, if someone intends to preserve chastity, he cannot keep it safe unless he hates and despises immodesty. COMMENTARY ON THE EPISTLE TO THE ROMANS.[2]

HOLD FAST TO WHAT IS GOOD. CHRYSOSTOM: If you have love, you will not notice the loss of your money, the labor of your body, the toil of your words, your trouble or your ministering, but you will bear everything courageously. HOMILIES ON ROMANS 21.[3]

PELAGIUS: Complete purity should dwell in the Christian, just as God is pure light,[4] for it is typical of slaves to dissemble.[5] And let us love not only in word but in deed and in truth,[6] so that if it were necessary we would even die for one another.[7] PELAGIUS'S COMMENTARY ON ROMANS.[8]

12:10 *Showing Affection and Honor*

LOVE ONE ANOTHER. POLYCARP: "Stand fast therefore in these things and follow the example of the Lord," being firm in the faith and immovable, in love of the brotherhood kindly affectioned to one another, "partners with the truth," forestalling one another "in the gentleness of the Lord," despising no one. THE EPISTLE TO THE PHILIPPIANS 10.[9]

---

[1]See Ps 97:10; Prov 8:13; Amos 5:15. [2]CER 5:66-68. [3]NPNF 1 11:502. [4]See 1 Jn 1:5-7. [5]See 2 Cor 6:4-6; 1 Tim 1:5-7. [6]See 1 Jn 3:18. [7]See Jn 15:13. [8]PCR 133-34. [9]ANF 1:35.

AMBROSIASTER: Brotherly love is useless unless it is mutual.[10] COMMENTARY ON PAUL'S EPISTLES.[11]

CHRIST DIED FOR THE UNGODLY. ORIGEN: It happens that we hate things we ought not to, just as we love things we ought not to. We are ordered to love our brothers, not to hate them. If you think that someone is ungodly, remember that "Christ died for the ungodly."[12] And if you think that because your brother is a sinner you do not have to love him, remember that "Christ Jesus came into this world to save sinners."[13] But if he is righteous, then he is much more worthy of love, for "God loves the righteous."[14] COMMENTARY ON THE EPISTLE TO THE ROMANS.[15]

HONOR THE NEIGHBOR. CHRYSOSTOM: You should love one another because you are brothers and have been born from the same spiritual womb.[16] . . . There is nothing which makes friends so much as the earnest endeavor to overcome one's neighbor by honoring him. HOMILIES ON ROMANS 21.[17]

WITH BROTHERLY AFFECTION. PELAGIUS: You should love one another as if you had been born of the same mother. If we always observed this injunction we would maintain love and patience. For if we considered ourselves less than everyone else we would neither insult anyone gratuitously nor be deeply hurt if someone insulted us. PELAGIUS'S COMMENTARY ON ROMANS.[18]

12:11 *Serving the Lord*

AGLOW WITH THE SPIRIT. ORIGEN: The expression "aglow with the Spirit" proves that the Word of God is hot and fiery. ON FIRST PRINCIPLES 2.8.3.[19]

NOT LUKEWARM. AMBROSIASTER: This means that we should not be lukewarm in doing God's work or the law, as God says in the Revelation of John: "Because you are lukewarm, I shall spit you out of my mouth."[20] Daily meditation removes

laziness and makes people vigilant. COMMENTARY ON PAUL'S EPISTLES.[21]

NEVER FLAG IN ZEAL. CHRYSOSTOM: Love by itself is not enough; there must be zeal as well. For zeal also comes out of loving and gives it warmth, so that the one confirms the other. For there are many who have love in their mind but who do not stretch out their hand. This is why Paul calls on every means he knows to build up love. HOMILIES ON ROMANS 21.[22]

PELAGIUS: Do not become slow and lazy in God's work out of concern for the world. The Lord does not love those who are unresponsive and is nauseated by those who are lukewarm.[23] If we are resistant to the world we then manifestly glow with the Spirit, doing all things not for the world or its vices but for the Lord. PELAGIUS'S COMMENTARY ON ROMANS.[24]

DO NOT QUENCH THE SPIRIT. THEODORET OF CYR: *Spirit* is the word Paul uses here for "grace." . . . He does the same thing elsewhere when he says: "Do not quench the Spirit."[25] The Spirit is quenched in those who are unworthy of grace. INTERPRETATION OF THE LETTER TO THE ROMANS.[26]

12:12 *Joy, Patience and Constancy*

REJOICE IN HOPE. ORIGEN: The person who does not look at what can be seen but eagerly waits for what cannot be seen is the one who rejoices in hope.[27] COMMENTARY ON THE EPISTLE TO THE ROMANS.[28]

BE PATIENT IN TRIBULATION. AMBROSIASTER: Even if the times do not allow us to speak publicly about our faith, nevertheless we must rejoice

---

[10]See Jn 13:34-35. [11]CSEL 81.1:403. [12]Rom 5:6. [13]1 Tim 1:15. [14]Ps 146:8. [15]CER 5:68, 70. [16]See 1 Thess 4:9-10. [17]NPNF 1 11:503. [18]PCR 134. [19]OFP 123. [20]Rev 3:16. [21]CSEL 81.1:403. [22]NPNF 1 11:503. [23]See Rev 3:15-16. [24]PCR 134. [25]1 Thess 5:19. [26]IER, Migne PG 82 col. 189. [27]See Rom 5:2. [28]CER 5:72.

in tribulation, for this sadness brings joy. . . .
With the joy of hope we can endure tribulation,
knowing that the things which are promised to
those who suffer are much greater. Prayer is
essential if we are to survive tribulation! Commentary on Paul's Epistles.[29]

Tribulation as Fuel for the Spirit. Chrysostom: All these things are fuel for the fire of
the Spirit. . . . There is nothing which makes the
soul so courageous and venturesome for anything
as a good hope. Homilies on Romans 21.[30]

Augustine: We rejoice in hope in order to look
forward to the rest to come and so conduct ourselves cheerfully in the midst of toils. Letter
55.[31]

Pelagius: Bear everything for the sake of the joy
of the hope to come. Pelagius's Commentary
on Romans.[32]

Constant Help. Gennadius of Constantinople: God's mercy does not abandon you in
these circumstances, but you are constantly
and everywhere helped by him in all things.
Pauline Commentary from the Greek
Church.[33]

12:13 Caring for the Saints and Offering Hospitality

Practice Hospitality. Origen: We must not
look on the saints as beggars but see them as people who have needs like our own.

The practice of hospitality does not simply
mean that we should entertain those who come to
us. It means also that we should go out and invite
others to come in.[34] Commentary on the Epistle to the Romans.[35]

Diodore: The point here is that we should honor
the saints and take care of their needs until they
no longer have them. Pauline Commentary
from the Greek Church.[36]

Ambrosiaster: The imitator and lover of the
saints will practice hospitality following the
examples of Abraham and Lot as righteous men.[37]
Commentary on Paul's Epistles.[38]

Contribute to the Needs of the Saints.
Pelagius: Provide for those who need the services of others for a while, because they neglect
their own affairs for the sake of Christ. Practice
hospitality, because the saints did this too, e.g.,
Abraham and Lot, who detained even guests who
were reluctant to stay.[39] Pelagius's Commentary on Romans.[40]

Theodore of Mopsuestia: Paul says that it is
right for us always to remember the saints, to
regard their needs as our own, and thus to lighten
their suffering.[41] Pauline Commentary from
the Greek Church.[42]

Theodoret of Cyr: It is not just guests that Paul
calls saints but also those (wherever they may
come from) who are in any kind of need. Interpretation of the Letter to the Romans.[43]

Gennadius of Constantinople: Paul calls the
believers "saints" because they have been called to
be holy. Pauline Commentary from the Greek
Church.[44]

12:14 Blessing Persecutors

Bless Those Who Persecute You. Origen:
Paul does not want those who believe in Christ to
curse but rather to speak and to pray for good
things so that they may be thought to be servants
of a good Lord and disciples of a good Master. . . .
What the apostle says here refers to when we are
provoked by our enemies or afflicted by harm.
Paul warns us not to repay curses with curses but

[29]CSEL 81.1:405-7. [30]NPNF 1 11:504. [31]FC 12:280. [32]PCR 134.
[33]NTA 15:405. [34]See Lk 14:12-14. [35]CER 5:72-74. [36]NTA 15:106.
[37]See Gen 18:1-5; 19:1-3. [38]CSEL 81.1:407. [39]See Gen 18:1-5;
19:1-3. [40]PCR 134. [41]See 1 Pet 4:8-9. [42]NTA 15:162. [43]IER, Migne
PG 82 col. 192. [44]NTA 15:405.

to do what he says he himself did, as he wrote: "When reviled, we bless."[45] Commentary on the Epistle to the Romans.[46]

Overcome Anger with Praise. Ambrosiaster: God makes Christians new people in every respect, so that here too he wants to take away from us the habits of anger which are common to everyone, so that instead of cursing others in anger, which we once did so easily, we might rather overcome our anger and bless them, so that the Lord's teaching might be praised.[47] Commentary on Paul's Epistles.[48]

Bless, Do Not Curse Them. Chrysostom: Those who persecute us are conveyors of a reward to us. If you are levelheaded, there will be another reward after that one which you will earn yourself. For your enemy will let you get a reward for persecution, but you will earn a further reward by blessing him, because by doing so you will be demonstrating a very great sign of love for Christ. Just as the man who curses his persecutor shows that he is not pleased to be suffering this for Christ's sake, he who blesses his persecutor shows the greatness of his love.[49] Homilies on Romans 22.[50]

Transform the Persecutors. Gennadius of Constantinople: Paul wants them to exhibit such brotherly love that those who want to persecute them will have no excuse for doing so.[51] Pauline Commentary from the Greek Church.[52]

Curse as Prophecy. Caesarius of Arles: How can the Scriptures, which forbid us to curse, contain so many curses themselves? Those curses are not spoken by a person who desires their fulfillment but merely foretell the fact. They do not want this to befall sinners, but because they will doubtless come to pass these curses are proved to be prophecies. Sermon 48.2.[53]

12:15 Rejoicing and Weeping

Rejoice with Those Who Rejoice. Origen: Here we must make a clear and appropriate distinction. For the joys of Christians are not to be linked with every sort of joy, nor are our tears to be connected with just any sort of tears. For if I see people rejoicing because they have made a lot of money, or acquired a lot of property, or gained worldly honor, I ought not to rejoice with them, because I know that sorrow and tears follow joys of that kind.

Therefore we ought to rejoice only with those whom we see doing a work which deserves to be written in heaven, whether it is a work of righteousness, of charity, of peace or of mercy.... Likewise, if we see people turn from error, leave the darkness of ignorance behind and come to the light of truth and the forgiveness of sins, we ought to rejoice with them.[54]

Likewise, in weeping with those who weep we ought not to weep with those who are mourning their dead or losses in this world.... Our tears ought not to be joined with theirs; rather we should weep for someone who is weeping for his sins, who after doing wrong is converted to repentance and who is washing his error in tears. We ought to weep with someone who groans at finding himself in this position and wants to return to Christ, and his holy desire is consoled by an outpouring of tears.[55] Commentary on the Epistle to the Romans.[56]

Weep with Those Who Weep. Ambrosiaster: If you weep with an unbeliever, you may provoke him to accept the Lord's teaching.[57] Commentary on Paul's Epistles.[58]

Feeling Compassion. Chrysostom: Paul wants us to be penetrated with the warmth of friendship. This is why he goes on to say that we are not merely to bless but that we are to feel

---

[45]1 Cor 4:12. [46]CER 5:74-76. [47]See Mt 5:43-45; Lk 6:35. [48]CSEL 81.1:407. [49]See 1 Thess 5:15. [50]NPNF 1 11:506. [51]See Prov 25:21-22. [52]NTA 15:405. [53]FC 31:244. [54]See Ps 13:5-6; 40:16; 68:3; 71:23; 97:12; Is 25:9; 61:10; Mt 5:11-12; Lk 15:6. [55]See Jer 30:15; 4 Ezra 2:3. [56]CER 5:76-78. [57]See Sir 3:27. [58]CSEL 81.1:409.

compassion for their pains and sufferings whenever we happen to see them fall into trouble. HOMILIES ON ROMANS 22.[59]

THE TEARS OF OUR LORD. PELAGIUS: The Lord was brought to tears by the tears of Mary, to give us an example.[60] For do not suppose that he wept for Lazarus, whom he would bring back to life, nor because of the unbelief of those who again and again did not believe him when he performed wonders. But now we do the opposite— we weep over those who rejoice and rejoice over those who weep. For if someone has been praised, we are unhappy. If someone has fallen, we leap for joy. When we behave in this way we show that we do not belong to the body of Christ, we who do not grieve for a member who has been cut off but are enemies of our own side and friends of the opposite side, who do not grieve when the strongest men of our battle line fall and do not rejoice if we see them fighting bravely, even though we ourselves are not mighty in battle. PELAGIUS'S COMMENTARY ON ROMANS.[61]

12:16 Living in Harmony

DO NOT BE HAUGHTY. ORIGEN: The conceited person is stupid in his own arrogance, nor can he know the wisdom of God if he clings to his own foolishness as if it were wisdom.[62] COMMENTARY ON THE EPISTLE TO THE ROMANS.[63]

GOD RESISTS THE PROUD. AMBROSIASTER: To be haughty is pride, which is how the devil fell. . . . Solomon says that "God resists the proud."[64] Put pride aside and make other people's cares your own so that you might be acceptable to God. COMMENTARY ON PAUL'S EPISTLES.[65]

ASSOCIATE WITH THE LOWLY. CHRYSOSTOM: Here again Paul insists on humility, which is how he started this whole exhortation. For since there was a probability that the Romans would be high minded because of the greatness of their city and for many other reasons, he keeps drawing off the

sickness of pride. . . . There is nothing so likely to cause schisms in the church as vanity. . . .

If a poor man comes into your house, behave like him and do not put on airs because of your riches.[66] In Christ there is no rich or poor. Do not be ashamed of him because of his outward dress, but receive him because of his inward faith. If you see him in sorrow, do not hesitate to comfort him, and if he is prospering, do not feel shy about sharing in his pleasure. . . . If you think you are a great person, then think others are also. If you think they are humble and lowly, then think the same of yourself. HOMILIES ON ROMANS 22.[67]

PELAGIUS: Regard one another as you regard yourselves. The person who desires to avenge his wrongs by himself thinks proud thoughts and does not agree to things humble, i.e., to humiliation. Do not boast of human wisdom, but be fools to the world so that you may be wise in the Lord. PELAGIUS'S COMMENTARY ON ROMANS.[68]

NEVER BE CONCEITED. THEODORET OF CYR: "Never be conceited" means: Be ready to accept the advice of others. INTERPRETATION OF THE LETTER TO THE ROMANS.[69]

12:17 Do Not Repay Evil

TERTULLIAN: This precept is absolute. ON PATIENCE 10.[70]

REPAY NO ONE EVIL FOR EVIL. ORIGEN: If as some people think it is wrong to do evil but not wrong to repay it, it may be just but it is still a similar sin, or in my opinion, even a worse one. For the one who does evil to begin with may perhaps not realize that what he has done is wrong. But the one who repays evil and who is moved by thoughts of revenge has already admitted that he

---

[59]NPNF 1 11:507. [60]See Jn 11:33-35. [61]PCR 135. [62]See Prov 26:12. [63]CER 5:80. [64]Prov 3:34; Jas 4:6; 1 Pet 5:5. [65]CSEL 81.1:409. [66]See Lk 14:7-11; Jas 2:5. [67]NPNF 1 11:507. [68]PCR 135. [69]IER, Migne PG 82 col. 192. [70]ANF 3:713.

knew it was wrong to do it. . . . Note that the apostle does not tell us to do what is pleasing to everyone. But we should do what is right whether other people like it or not. COMMENTARY ON THE EPISTLE TO THE ROMANS.[71]

AMBROSIASTER: The law said: "Love your neighbor and hate your enemy,"[72] but the Lord says: "Unless your righteousness exceeds the righteousness of the scribes and the Pharisees, you will not enter the kingdom of God."[73] Therefore, in order for this to be the case, it is taught that we should not repay evil with evil.[74] COMMENTARY ON PAUL'S EPISTLES.[75]

TAKE THOUGHT FOR WHAT IS NOBLE IN THE SIGHT OF ALL. CHRYSOSTOM: Paul means this: As far as possible, play your part and give nobody, either Jew or Gentile, any cause for fighting.[76] But if you see the faith suffering anywhere, do not put harmony above truth. Make a noble stand, even to the point of death. And even then, do not be at war in your soul or of an adverse temper, but concentrate on the things themselves. HOMILIES ON ROMANS 22.[77]

CHRYSOSTOM: If you find fault with someone who is plotting against you, why expose yourself to the same accusation? HOMILIES ON ROMANS 22.[78]

PELAGIUS: It is human wisdom if you seek to repay your enemies in turn, for it is foolishness in this world if, having been struck, you offer the other cheek as well.[79] But if you have such great patience and humility, you will be found praiseworthy not only in the Lord's eyes but also in the eyes of all people. Take care not to act so that you seek to please not God but only other people. PELAGIUS'S COMMENTARY ON ROMANS.[80]

12:18 Live Peaceably with Others

IF POSSIBLE, LIVE PEACEABLY. ORIGEN: The

apostle here gives a very balanced command because he knows perfectly well that peace depends on both parties, and the other party may well be hostile and block peace. What he asks is that our mind should always be ready for peace and that the blame for any discord should lie with the other side and not with us.

Of course there are times when this command cannot be applied; for example, we cannot have peace and fellowship with evil. It is one thing to love people but quite another to love crimes. Whoever loves people loves God's creatures, but whoever loves crimes loves the inventions of the devil. Therefore, those who are perfect will love the sinner but hate his sin. COMMENTARY ON THE EPISTLE TO THE ROMANS.[81]

AMBROSIASTER: Paul wants everyone who serves God's righteousness to be peaceful. . . . The person who is not peaceful is the one who has rejected the law of God and who follows his own law instead. . . . Even if the other person is not a lover of peace, you should want to be peaceful insofar as you can be. COMMENTARY ON PAUL'S EPISTLES.[82]

PELAGIUS: Inasmuch as you can, be at peace with everybody . . . desiring their conversion and salvation.[83] PELAGIUS'S COMMENTARY ON ROMANS.[84]

THEODORET OF CYR: If someone blesses those who persecute him and does not harm those who do him harm, how will he attract hatred or revenge on himself? INTERPRETATION OF THE LETTER TO THE ROMANS.[85]

GENNADIUS OF CONSTANTINOPLE: Paul says that he wants Christians to have the right spirit, even if others think differently. PAULINE COMMENTARY FROM THE GREEK CHURCH.[86]

[71]CER 5:80-82. [72]Lev 19:17-18. [73]Mt 5:20. [74]See 1 Thess 5:15. [75]CSEL 81.1:411. [76]See Ps 34:14; Heb 12:14. [77]NPNF 1 11:508. [78]NPNF 1 11:508. [79]See Mt 5:39. [80]PCR 135. [81]CER 5:82. [82]CSEL 81.1:413. [83]Heb 12:14. [84]PCR 135-36. [85]IER, Migne PG 82 col. 192. [86]NTA 15:406.

12:19 *Vengeance Belongs to God*

Dealing with Anger. Origen: There are two ways of dealing with the anger which comes when we are offended. The first is to hold back and let it pass, for once the fury of rage has subsided it will not return, and we can learn to swallow it. The second way is to give it to God and store up the wrath against the day of judgment, when God will reward each person according to his works. For if we avenge ourselves, there is not much we can do apart from demanding an eye for an eye or a tooth for a tooth,[87] or else insulting others as they have insulted us. But if we reserve these things to the vengeance of God, he will without doubt punish them far more severely than we ever could. Commentary on the Epistle to the Romans.[88]

Leave It to the Wrath of God. Diodore: Paul uses the word *wrath* to describe God's punishment, not because it is some kind of passion in God but because men would find it difficult to understand God's judgment if they did not hear it compared to wrath. For since men respond to those who sin against them in wrath and anger, Scripture uses the same words to describe God's reaction, because then the average person can hear and understand it. Pauline Commentary from the Greek Church.[89]

Do Not Let Another's Wrath Draw You into Sin. Ambrose: This is written lest another's wrath draw you into sin when you want to offer resistance, when you want to be avenged. You can take the fault from him and from yourself if you decide to yield to the other. Letter 59.[90]

Never Avenge Yourselves. Ambrosiaster: Paul warns us to avoid anger, especially because so often anger is the chief cause of sin. Someone who is motivated by wrath will demand more than the cause of the sin merits or will put himself out to do more harm while seeking revenge.... In the end he will destroy someone when he could have corrected and restored him instead.

Paul forbids us to seek revenge not only from those under us but also from those who are our equals or superiors.... We are not to seek to avenge ourselves against brethren who may have sinned against us but rather to commit everything to God's judgment, so that an enemy will find no way of promoting or advancing what is against our interest while we are too angry to notice what is happening.

Paul quotes Proverbs [25:22] to back up his point. If we do not do what God teaches, he will show us contempt. But if we give revenge over to God it benefits us in two ways: it overcomes our anger and tends toward our perfection and justification in God's sight. Commentary on Paul's Epistles.[91]

Vengeance Is Mine. Chrysostom: What the injured man most desires to see is revenge, and God will give it to him in full measure, provided that he does not try to avenge himself. Leave it to God to follow up the wrongs done to you. Homilies on Romans 22.[92]

Pelagius: I will avenge the wrong, says the Lord, as my own, not as yours. Pelagius's Commentary on Romans.[93]

12:20 *Burning Coals*

Heap Burning Coals upon His Head. Origen: The Lord himself commanded the same thing in the Gospels.[94] For insofar as we do good to our enemies and do not repay evil for evil, we store up wrath for them on the day of judgment, as I have just said.... Jeremiah [Isaiah] says: "You have coals of fire; sit on them for they will help you."[95] Perhaps here also these coals of fire which are heaped on the head of an enemy are

[87]See Ex 21:24; Lev 24:20; Deut 19:21; Mt 5:38-48. [88]CER 5:84. [89]NTA 15:106. [90]FC 26:358-59. [91]CSEL 81.1:415. [92]NPNF 1 11:508. [93]PCR 136. [94]Mt 5:42. [95]Is 47:14 LXX.

heaped for his benefit. For it may be that a savage and barbarous mind, if it feels our good will, our kindness, our love and our godliness, may be struck by it and repent, and he will swear that as his conscience torments him for the wrong which he has done, it is as if a fire were enveloping him. COMMENTARY ON THE EPISTLE TO THE ROMANS.[96]

CONTAINING VIOLENCE. DIODORE: Paul is not suggesting that we do anything wicked; on the contrary, he is wisely and cleverly checking and containing the violence of the one who is angry. PAULINE COMMENTARY FROM THE GREEK CHURCH.[97]

DO GOOD. AMBROSIASTER: Paul teaches us not just to let God take revenge but also to give good things to our enemies, so that we may demonstrate that we do not have these enemies because of anything we have done. Rather, we are trying to get them to desist from evil by doing them service. If by their ungodliness they continue in their evil ways, our service to them will lead to punishment for them. . . . Thus the Lord not only forbids us to repay our enemies in kind but also exhorts us to seek friendship by acts of kindness, both because that serves to mature us and because it is a means of winning others to eternal life.[98] COMMENTARY ON PAUL'S EPISTLES.[99]

SWEPT UP IN VENGEANCE. CHRYSOSTOM: Paul said this in order to humble the wrongdoer by fear and to make the person wronged more ready to act, through hope of receiving some reward. For the one who has been wronged, when he is feeble, is not so much taken with his own goods as with the vengeance which he wants to wreak on the person who has hurt him. There is nothing so sweet as to see an enemy chastised. HOMILIES ON ROMANS 22.[100]

PROVOKING THE ABUSER TO REPENTANCE. AUGUSTINE: This may seem to many people to contradict what the Lord teaches, that we should love our enemies and pray for those who persecute us,[101] or the apostle's own statements [in verses 14 and 17] above. For how can it be love to feed and nourish someone just in order to heap coals of fire on his head, assuming that "coals of fire" means some serious punishment? Therefore we must understand that this means that we should provoke whoever does us harm to repentance by doing him a good turn. For the coals of fire serve to burn, i.e., to bring anguish to his spirit, which is like the head of the soul, in which all malice is burnt out when one is changed for the better through repentance. These coals of fire are mentioned in the Psalms: "What should be given to you or what appointed to you, for your deceitful tongue? Sharp arrows of the warrior with devouring burning coals."[102] AUGUSTINE ON ROMANS 71.[103]

JEROME: He who avenges himself is not worthy of the vengeance of the Lord. AGAINST RUFINUS 3.2.[104]

SOFTENED BY CHARITY. JEROME: We are not to revile and condemn our enemy, as the world does, but rather we are to correct him and lead him to repentance so that, being won over by our good deeds, he may be softened by the fire of charity and may cease to be an enemy. AGAINST THE PELAGIANS 1.30.[105]

JEROME: If someone does you a wrong and in return you do him good you will be heaping coals of fire on his head. In other words, you are curing him of his vices and burning out his malice, in order to bring him to repentance. HOMILIES ON THE PSALMS 41.[106]

IF THE ENEMY IS HUNGRY, FEED HIM. [PSEUDO-]CONSTANTIUS: In this passage Paul teaches that we ought to imitate God, who causes

---

[96]CER 5:86. [97]NTA 15:107. [98]See Mt 5:38-48. [99]CSEL 81.1:415-17. [100]NPNF 1 11:508-9. [101]Mt 5:44. [102]Ps 120:3-4. [103]AOR 41. [104]FC 53:164. [105]FC 53:276. [106]FC 48:313*.

his sun to rise on the good and the evil,[107] for by feeding our enemy and giving him something to drink we provoke him to peace or even to reconciliation. But if he persists in his wickedness, he will bring down fire on his head. THE HOLY LETTER OF ST. PAUL TO THE ROMANS.[108]

DO NOT SHOW MERCY SO AS TO ALLOW SOMETHING WORSE TO OCCUR. PELAGIUS: Do not deny your enemy what God denies no one, even if he is a godless blasphemer.[109] When he realizes that coals have been heaped upon him through your undeserved mercy, he may shake them off, that is, repent, and may love you whom at one time he hated. Otherwise it is not mercy but cruelty, if you show mercy so that something worse might befall him, for whom you are called to intercede to the Lord.[110] PELAGIUS'S COMMENTARY ON ROMANS.[111]

DEAD COALS MADE ALIVE. LUCULENTIUS: Some people give their enemies food and drink in order to inflict coals of fire, that is, punishments, on them. But whoever does that does not love his enemy as himself. It is not for that reason that we are supposed to give our enemy food and drink but rather to convert him to us. For as he detested us before, he will now start to love us. The person who loves his enemy in this way will heap coals of fire on his head, that is, the love which comes from charity. Coals in themselves are dead, but when they meet someone who is alive they are set on fire. COMMENTARY 5.[112]

12:21 Overcome Evil with Good

HOW EVIL GROWS. ORIGEN: It is the nature of evil to increase and grow by similar acts, rather like adding fire to fire. COMMENTARY ON THE EPISTLE TO THE ROMANS.[113]

OVERCOMING EVIL WITH GOOD. AMBROSIASTER: It will do us much good if we refrain from evil. The person who appears to be overcome by evil for a time in fact may be overcoming evil, just as the Savior overcame evil by not resisting it. Evil works against itself, and when it is overcome it thinks that it has won! Our enemy acts in such a way as to divert us from our purpose, looking for an opportunity to make us sin. Therefore if we are provoked by him and do not reply in kind, we overcome him with good. Therefore we do not resist, in order to serve the good by ignoring the demands of justice for retribution. COMMENTARY ON PAUL'S EPISTLES.[114]

DO NOT BE OVERCOME BY EVIL. CHRYSOSTOM: After giving the wronged person what he wants, Paul goes on to give him advice of a higher tone, telling him not to be overcome with evil. For he knew that even if the enemy was a brute he would not go on being an enemy once he was fed. . . . To overcome evil with good is true victory.[115] HOMILIES ON ROMANS 22.[116]

INTERIOR FREEDOM. AUGUSTINE: The evil man who is overcome by good is set free, not from an exterior, foreign evil but from an interior, personal one, by which he is more grievously and ruinously laid waste than he would be by the inhumanity of any enemy from without. LETTER 138.[117]

THEODORET OF CYR: Revenge is mean-spirited. True victory is returning good for evil. INTERPRETATION OF THE LETTER TO THE ROMANS.[118]

---

[107]Mt 5:45. [108]ENPK 2:81. [109]See Mt 5:45; Lk 6:35. [110]See Mt 5:44. [111]PCR 136. [112]Migne PL 72 col. 822. [113]CER 5:88. [114]CSEL 81.1:417. [115]See 1 Pet 3:9. [116]NPNF 1 11:509. [117]FC 20:45. [118]IER, Migne PG 82 col. 193.

13:1-7 SUBMISSION TO THE AUTHORITIES

[1]Let every person be subject to the governing authorities. For there is no authority except from God, and those that exist have been instituted by God. [2]Therefore he who resists the authorities resists what God has appointed, and those who resist will incur judgment. [3]For rulers are not a terror to good conduct, but to bad. Would you have no fear of him who is in authority? Then do what is good, and you will receive his approval, [4]for he is God's servant for your good. But if you do wrong, be afraid, for he does not bear the sword in vain; he is the servant of God to execute his wrath on the wrongdoer. [5]Therefore one must be subject, not only to avoid God's wrath but also for the sake of conscience. [6]For the same reason you also pay taxes, for the authorities are ministers of God, attending to this very thing. [7]Pay all of them their dues, taxes to whom taxes are due, revenue to whom revenue is due, respect to whom respect is due, honor to whom honor is due.

OVERVIEW: The problem of church-state relations was an acute one for the early Christians. How could they accept that a government that persecuted them had been ordained by God? Nevertheless, the Fathers consistently supported the New Testament idea that the civil authorities were divinely ordained within their own sphere. They had every right to exercise restraint on the body but not the soul. Christian obedience out of conscience must be serious in the temporal realm, but if the secular ruler transgressed his authority, it was the duty of believers to attest the truth by peaceful means. Secular rulers are entitled to punish criminals, and Christians accept this. Likewise, they obey the law of the land, paying their taxes and respecting those in authority, whether they agree with them or not.

13:1 Authority Instituted by God

GOD WILL JUDGE THOSE WHO ABUSE AUTHORITY. ORIGEN: What does Paul mean when he says that "there is no authority except from God?" Is an authority which persecutes the children of God, which attacks the faith and which undermines our religion, from God? We shall answer this briefly. Nobody will deny that our senses—sight, sound and thought—are given to us by God. But although we get them from God, what we do with them is up to us.... God will judge us righteously for having abused what he gave us to use for good. Likewise, God's judgment against the authorities will be just, if they have used the powers they have received according to their own ungodliness and not according to the laws of God. COMMENTARY ON THE EPISTLE TO THE ROMANS.[1]

THE ILLUSION OF REVOLT. APOLLINARIS OF LAODICEA: "Judas the Galilean revolted in the days of the census,"[2] says Gamaliel in the Acts of the Apostles, and "drew away some of the people after him," refusing to obey the order of the Romans and register their goods, for which reason Quirinius had been sent to Syria.... But as Judas's decision was the cause of domestic murders and of a rebellion against the authorities which did much harm to the people, it seems to me that here the apostle is condemning any attempt to imitate him based on the illusion that it is a godly thing to disobey rulers. He has a good deal to say about this, condemning it as a mistaken way of thinking. PAULINE COMMENTARY FROM THE GREEK CHURCH.[3]

---

[1]CER 5:92-94. [2]Acts 5:37. [3]NTA 15:78.

THROUGH ME KINGS REIGN. DIODORE: The book of Proverbs teaches us that kings do not come to rule apart from the dispensation and will of God: "Through me kings reign and princes decree justice."[4] PAULINE COMMENTARY FROM THE GREEK CHURCH.[5]

NO RULER SAVED BY POWER. BASIL: The ruler is saved not through much power but through divine grace. EXEGETIC HOMILIES 15.9.[6]

EARTHLY LAW AS TUTOR FOR RIGHTEOUSNESS. AMBROSIASTER: As Paul has already ordered that the law of heavenly righteousness be followed, he now commends earthly law as well, so as not to appear to be slighting it. For if the earthly law is not kept, the heavenly law will not be kept either. The earthly law is a kind of tutor, who helps little children along so that they can tackle a stronger degree of righteousness. For mercy cannot be imputed to anyone who does not seek righteousness.

Therefore, in order to back up the authority and fear of the natural law, Paul bears witness to the fact that God is the author of both and that the ministers of the earthly law have God's permission to act, so that no one should despise it as a merely human construction. In effect, Paul sees the divine law as being delegated to human authorities. COMMENTARY ON PAUL'S EPISTLES.[7]

BE SUBJECT TO THE GOVERNING AUTHORITIES. CHRYSOSTOM: Paul has a good deal to say on this matter in his other epistles also, placing subjects under their rulers in the same way that household servants are under their masters. He does this to show that Christ did not introduce his laws for the purpose of undermining the state but rather so that it should be better governed.

He does not speak about individual rulers but about the principle of authority itself. For that there should be rulers and ruled and that things should not just lapse into anarchy, with the people swaying like waves from one extreme to the other, is the work of God's wisdom. HOMILIES ON ROMANS 23.[8]

NO SECULAR AUTHORITY OVER FAITH. AUGUSTINE: Most rightly, Paul warns against anyone who is puffed up with pride by the fact that he has been called by his Lord into freedom and become a Christian, and therefore thinks that he does not have to keep the status given to him in the course of this life or submit to the higher powers to whom the government of temporal things has been confided for a time. For because we are made of soul and body and as long as we are in this life we make use of temporal things as a means of living this life, it is fitting that, as far as this life is concerned, we be subject to the authorities, i.e., to the people who with some recognition administer human affairs. But as far as the spiritual side is concerned, in which we believe in God and are called into his kingdom, it is not right for us to be subject to any man who seeks to overturn in us the very thing which God has been pleased to grant us so that we might obtain eternal life.

So if anyone thinks that because he is a Christian he does not have to pay taxes or tribute nor show the proper respect to the authorities who take care of these things, he is in very great error. Likewise, if anyone thinks that he ought to submit to the point where he accepts that someone who is his superior in temporal affairs should have authority even over his faith, he falls into an even greater error. But the balance which the Lord himself prescribed is to be maintained: "Render unto Caesar the things which are Caesar's but unto God the things which are God's."[9] For although we are called into that kingdom where there will be no power of this world, nevertheless, while we are on the way there and until we have reached that state where every principality and power will be destroyed, let us put up with our condition for the sake of human affairs,

---

[4]Prov 8:15. [5]NTA 15:107. [6]FC 46:243. [7]CSEL 81.1:417-19. [8]NPNF 1 11:511. [9]Mt 22:21.

doing nothing falsely and in this very thing obeying God, who commands us to do it, rather than men. Augustine on Romans 72.[10]

Secular Authority from God, Even If Unjust. Pelagius: This is an argument against those who thought that they were obliged to use their Christian freedom in such a way that they gave honor or paid taxes to nobody. Paul wants to humble such people in any way he can, so that they will not suffer reproach on account of their pride instead of on account of God.

It seems that Paul is speaking of secular authorities, not all of whom will be just, even if they received their authority from God. . . . The ruler is set up by God to judge with righteousness, so that sinners might have reason to be afraid should they sin. Pelagius's Commentary on Romans.[11]

Obey Insofar As Obedience Is Consistent with Godliness. Theodoret of Cyr: Even priests, bishops and monks must obey the commands of secular rulers. Of course, they must do so insofar as obedience is consistent with godliness. If the rulers demand something which is ungodly, then on no account are they allowed to do it.

The holy apostle teaches us that both authorities and obedience depend entirely on God's providence, but he does not say that God has specifically appointed one person or another to exercise that authority. For it is not the wickedness of individual rulers which comes from God but the establishment of the ruling power itself. . . . Since God wants sinners to be punished, he is prepared to tolerate even bad rulers. Interpretation of the Letter to the Romans.[12]

13:2 Resisting Authority Incurs Judgment

Not Applicable to Persecutors of the Faith. Origen: This injunction does not apply in the case of authorities who persecute the faith. It only applies to those who are going about their

proper business. Commentary on the Epistle to the Romans.[13]

The Obedience of Subjects. Basil: True and perfect obedience of subjects to their superior is shown not only by their refraining from every untoward action in accordance with his advice but also by their not doing even what is approved without his consent. An Ascetical Discourse.[14]

Those Who Resist Will Incur Judgment. Diodore: Those who disobey the king have committed a crime and will face judgment. Pauline Commentary from the Greek Church.[15]

Combating the Reputation of Subversiveness. Chrysostom: In saying this, Paul was more likely to draw civil governors who were unbelievers to accept the Christian faith and to persuade believers to obey them. For it was commonly rumored in those days that the apostles were guilty of plotting sedition and revolution, aiming in all that they did and said at the subversion of the received institutions. However, when we see that Christ's command is that we should obey the authorities, all rumors of this kind will be shown to be false. Homilies on Romans 23.[16]

Sidestepping the Law. Ambrosiaster: Paul writes this against those who believe that because of their own power they cannot be apprehended and so therefore they can play fast and loose with the law. He shows them that this is the law of God and that those who by some subterfuge escape it for a time will not escape God's judgment. Commentary on Paul's Epistles.[17]

Pelagius: As it was said to Rahab: "Whoever goes outside will be responsible for himself."[18] Pelagius's Commentary on Romans.[19]

---

[10]AOR 41, 43. [11]PCR 136-37. [12]IER, Migne PG 82 col. 193. [13]CER 5:94. [14]FC 9:218. [15]NTA 15:108. [16]NPNF 1 11:512. [17]CSEL 81.1:419. [18]Josh 2:19. [19]PCR 137.

13:3 *Rulers to Enforce Good Conduct*

Insofar As a Divine Command Not Violated. Basil: It is right to submit to higher authority whenever a command of God is not violated thereby. The Morals 79.1.[20]

The Task of Rulers. Ambrosiaster: Rulers here are kings who are created in order to correct behavior and prevent bad things from happening. They have the image of God, because everyone else is under one head. Commentary on Paul's Epistles.[21]

Praise Comes from God, Not Authorities. Augustine: This can upset some people, when they think that Christians have often suffered persecution by these authorities. They say: "Were these Christians not doing good, since not only did the authorities not praise them, they punished and killed them!" The apostle's words must be carefully considered. He does not say: "Do what is good and the authorities will praise you," but: "Do what is good and you will have praise from him." Whether someone in authority approves what you do or persecutes you, "you will have praise from him," either when you win it by your obedience to God or when you earn your crown by persecution. Augustine on Romans 73.[22]

No Fear of One in Authority. Pelagius: The wicked should be afraid of the authorities, but the good have no reason to fear, for they come into glory if they are killed unjustly. Paul says: "Take my advice and you will never be afraid." Condemnation of the wicked is in itself commendation of the good.[23] Pelagius's Commentary on Romans.[24]

13:4 *Rulers as Servants of God*

The Human Judge Acts as God's Servant for Your Good. Origen: In what sense is a judge in this world the servant of God? . . . It seems to me that this question is answered by that passage in the Acts of the Apostles where the decision was taken to impose only certain ritual obligations on Gentile believers.[25] They were told to abstain from eating what had been sacrificed to idols, from blood and from fornication, but nothing was said about murder, adultery, theft, homosexuality or other crimes which are punished by both divine and human laws. Now if what was explicitly forbidden to the Gentiles was all they had to do, then it would seem as if these other things were all right. But look at how the Holy Spirit has organized everything. Because these other crimes are already punished by secular laws, it seemed superfluous to add a divine prohibition as well. All that he decreed concerned matters which seemed right from the divine point of view but which were not covered by human laws. It is in this way that a human judge acts as a servant of God. For God wants these crimes to be punished by human judges and not by representatives of the church. Commentary on the Epistle to the Romans.[26]

Tutors Ordained. Ambrosiaster: Since God has ordained that there will be a future judgment and he does not want anyone to perish, he has ordained rulers in this world who, by causing people to be afraid of them, act as tutors to mankind, teaching them what to do in order to avoid future punishment. Commentary on Paul's Epistles.[27]

Making Virtue Easier. Chrysostom: The civil power makes virtue easier for the Christian by chastising the wicked, by benefiting and honoring the good and by working together with the will of God. For this reason he is even given the name of "God's servant." . . . Even when he administers punishment, it is God's will that he is carrying out. Homilies on Romans 23.[28]

---

[20]FC 9:196. [21]CSEL 81.1:419. [22]AOR 43. [23]See 1 Pet 2:14. [24]PCR 137. [25]Acts 15:23-29. [26]CER 5:94-96. [27]CSEL 81.1:421. [28]NPNF 1 11:512.

FOR YOUR GOOD. AUGUSTINE: When Paul says: "He is God's servant for your good," though it be for his own evil, this should be understood in the same way as the above. AUGUSTINE ON ROMANS 73.[29]

[PSEUDO-]CONSTANTIUS: By saying that the ruler is "God's servant for your good," Paul shows that we must obey the authorities in those things which are right but not in things which are unlawful or which go against the faith. THE HOLY LETTER OF ST. PAUL TO THE ROMANS.[30]

THAT NONE PROFIT FROM SIN. PELAGIUS: The authorities are concerned for your safety. They also have the responsibility to see to it that if you sin you do not profit thereby, because God does not love the wicked and hates all who "work iniquity."[31] PELAGIUS'S COMMENTARY ON ROMANS.[32]

13:5 Subject for the Sake of Conscience

PUNISHMENT FOR CRIMES. ORIGEN: Paul tells the church not to do anything against the princes and powers of this world so that it may live in peace and quiet. For if the church rebels . . . then it will be punished, not because of its faith but because of its crimes, and instead of dying for a worthy cause people will die for an unworthy one. COMMENTARY ON THE EPISTLE TO THE ROMANS.[33]

BE SUBJECT. AMBROSIASTER: One must be subject . . . because of the coming judgment, for whoever escapes now will be punished then, his own conscience accusing him. COMMENTARY ON PAUL'S EPISTLES.[34]

AVOID GOD'S WRATH. CHRYSOSTOM: What is the meaning of "not only to avoid God's wrath"? It means not only because you resist God by not being subject, nor only because you are bringing great evils on yourself both from God and from the ruler, but also because the ruler is a benefactor to you in things of the utmost importance, because he brings you peace and the blessings of

civil institutions. States receive countless blessings through these authorities, and if they were taken away, everything would go to pieces. HOMILIES ON ROMANS 23.[35]

FOR THE SAKE OF CONSCIENCE. AUGUSTINE: This is helpful for understanding that because of this life we must be subject and not offer resistance if anyone wants to take something from us, if it is in his power to do so, because authority has been given to him over temporal things, which will pass away. We are not to be subject in those good things which remain forever but only in the needs of this age.

But when he says "one must be subject," lest anyone submit to the authorities halfheartedly and not from pure love, Paul adds: "not only to avoid . . . wrath but also for the sake of conscience." That is to say, you should not submit simply to avoid the authority's anger, which can be done by pretense, but so that you might be assured in your conscience that you are doing this out of love for him. For you submit at your Lord's command. AUGUSTINE ON ROMANS 74.[36]

[PSEUDO-]CONSTANTIUS: Those who do wrong and who live in opposition to the commandments, are subject to the authorities for their punishment, but those who live rightly are subject for conscience's sake, because the things which they are commanded to do are just and good. THE HOLY LETTER OF ST. PAUL TO THE ROMANS.[37]

PELAGIUS: You must be subject, not only because the authorities can become angry even without cause but also so that you may not be condemned for the consciousness of some sin. PELAGIUS'S COMMENTARY ON ROMANS.[38]

THEODORET OF CYR: "For the sake of conscience" means "in order to do what is right." INTERPRE-

---

[29]AOR 43. [30]ENPK 2:82. [31]See Ps 5:6. [32]PCR 137. [33]CER 5:100. [34]CSEL 81.1:421. [35]NPNF 1 11:513. [36]AOR 43. [37]ENPK 2:82-83. [38]PCR 137.

tation of the Letter to the Romans.[39]

13:6 *Paying Taxes*

Bearing Witness Through Taxes to the Benefits of Civil Order. Chrysostom: Paul is saying here that we bear witness to the benefits which the ruler gives us by paying him a salary. The taxation system may seem to be burdensome and annoying, but Paul turns it into proof that rulers care for their people. Why, after all, do we pay taxes to the emperor? Is it not because he provides for us? We would not have paid it in the first place if we did not know that we are the ones who benefit from this government. It was for this reason that the men of old agreed that rulers should be maintained by the people, because they neglect their own affairs in order to devote themselves entirely to the public welfare, spending all their energy in order to protect us. Homilies on Romans 23.[40]

Rendering What Is Due. Pelagius: Taxes can also mean taxes for the priests, which were set up for them by God.[41] Or this may mean that you pay taxes to rulers because, in possessing the world, you subjected yourselves to them willingly. Paul calls them "God's servants," so that people might render to them what they owe,[42] lest it seem that Christ taught his followers pride. Pelagius's Commentary on Romans.[43]

13:7 *Paying What Is Due*

Keeping Free of Idolatry. Tertullian: So far as concerns the honors due to king or emperor, we have a clear ruling to be subject in all obedience, according to the apostle's command, to magistrates and princes and those in authority, but within the limits of Christian discipline, i.e., so long as we keep ourselves free of idolatry. On Idolatry 15.[44]

Taxes to Whom Taxes Are Due. Origen: The authorities demand taxes on our property

and revenue from our business transactions. What can I say? Jesus Christ himself was obliged to pay taxes, not because he owed anything but so as not to cause scandal.[45] If he who owed nothing to Caesar and who had every right to refuse to pay taxes nevertheless agreed to pay them, who are we to refuse to do so? Commentary on the Epistle to the Romans.[46]

Giving Honor. Ambrosiaster: Giving honor to the powers that be in this world may have the effect that, if they see the humility of Christ's servants, they may praise rather than curse the gospel's teaching. Commentary on Paul's Epistles.[47]

Respect to Whom Respect Is Due. Chrysostom: Paul urges the people to give their rulers not only money but honor and fear as well. Fear in this context means very great honor, not the kind of fear which comes from a bad conscience. Homilies on Romans 23.[48]

Revenue to Whom Revenue Is Due. Pelagius: Even alms can be called a due.[49] Revenue is ours to give to those who are passing by or to those who are seated by the roadside while we pass by.... Fear as well as honor must be given to those who are your superiors but only honor to your peers. Pelagius's Commentary on Romans.[50]

Theodore of Mopsuestia: "Taxes" refers to property taxes; "revenue" refers to sales taxes. Pauline Commentary from the Greek Church.[51]

Gennadius of Constantinople: "Taxes" and "revenue" are the same thing. Pauline Commentary from the Greek Church.[52]

---

[39]*IER*, Migne PG 82 col. 196. [40]NPNF 1 11:513. [41]See Ex 30:11-16; Lev 7; Num 31:25-54. [42]See Mt 22:21. [43]PCR 137-38. [44]LCC 5:100-101. [45]Mt 17:25-26. [46]CER 5:104. [47]CSEL 81.1:423. [48]NPNF 1 11:513. [49]Sir 4:8. [50]PCR 138. [51]NTA 15:162. [52]NTA 15:408.

13:8-14 THE FULFILLMENT OF THE LAW

[8]*Owe no one anything, except to love one another; for he who loves his neighbor has fulfilled the law.* [9]*The commandments, "You shall not commit adultery, You shall not kill, You shall not steal, You shall not covet," and any other commandment, are summed up in this sentence, "You shall love your neighbor as yourself."* [10]*Love does no wrong to a neighbor; therefore love is the fulfilling of the law.*

[11]*Besides this you know what hour it is, how it is full time now for you to wake from sleep. For salvation is nearer to us now than when we first believed;* [12]*the night is far gone, the day is at hand. Let us then cast off the works of darkness and put on the armor of light;* [13]*let us conduct ourselves becomingly as in the day, not in reveling and drunkenness, not in debauchery and licentiousness, not in quarreling and jealousy.* [14]*But put on the Lord Jesus Christ, and make no provision for the flesh, to gratify its desires.*

OVERVIEW: The only debt we should owe others is the debt of love, which is the underlying basis of all the commandments. Christian conduct is governed by the expectation of Christ's return and the last judgment. Now that Christ has come the light of that day has already dawned, and it will not be long before the final consummation will come. Casting off the works of darkness and making no provision for the flesh, we are called to put on Christ, ready to bear arms for the reign of light.

13:8 Owe Only a Debt of Love

SIN AS DEBT. ORIGEN: In many cases debt is equivalent to sin. Paul therefore wants us to owe nothing on account of sin and to steer clear of debts of this kind, retaining only the debt which springs from love, which we ought to be repaying every day. COMMENTARY ON THE EPISTLE TO THE ROMANS.[1]

LOVE THE NEIGHBOR. AMBROSIASTER: Paul wants us to have peace with everyone and love the brethren. Then we shall not owe anybody anything.

He who loves his neighbor has fulfilled the law

of Moses. The commandment of the new law is that we should love our enemies also.[2] COMMENTARY ON PAUL'S EPISTLES.[3]

FULFILL THE LAW. CHRYSOSTOM: Love is a debt which you owe to your brother because of your spiritual relationship to him. . . . If love departs from us, the whole body is torn in pieces. Therefore love your brother, for if you can fulfill the law by befriending him, then the benefit you receive puts you in his debt. HOMILIES ON ROMANS 23.[4]

CHARITY ACCOMPLISHES WHAT FEAR COULD NOT DO. AUGUSTINE: Paul shows that the fulfillment of the law is found in love, i.e., in charity. Thus also the Lord says that the whole law and prophets depend on these two precepts, the love of God and neighbor.[5] So he who came to fulfill the law gave love through the Holy Spirit, so that charity might accomplish what fear could not. AUGUSTINE ON ROMANS 75.[6]

LOVING THE PATTERN OF RIGHTEOUSNESS IN THE PERSON. AUGUSTINE: The only way of

---

[1]CER 5:104. [2]See Mt 5:44; Lk 6:27, 35. [3]CSEL 81.1:423. [4]NPNF 1 11:514. [5]See Mt 22:37-39; Mk 12:30-31; Lk 10:27. [6]AOR 43, 45.

cleaving to that pattern[7] is by love. If we love another whom we believe to be righteous, we cannot but love the pattern itself, which shows us what the righteous soul is, in order that we too may become righteous. Indeed, if we did not love the image of God in him, we would have no love for the person, since our love for him is based on the pattern. Yet so long as we ourselves are not righteous, our love of the pattern is not enough to make us righteous. THE TRINITY 8.9.[8]

EVERYONE WITHOUT DISTINCTION IS YOUR NEIGHBOR. PELAGIUS: Do not fail to repay debts. Only the debt of love should remain, because it can never be paid in full. According to the parable of the Lord, who bids us show mercy to everyone without distinction, we must think of every person as our neighbor.[9] Paul mentioned love first because he was writing to the faithful and dealing with behavior proper to righteousness. PELAGIUS'S COMMENTARY ON ROMANS.[10]

13:9 Loving One's Neighbor

THE RELATION OF LOVE AND LAW. ORIGEN: If you love somebody, you will not kill him. Nor will you commit adultery, steal from him or bear false witness against him. It is the same with all the other commands of the law: love ensures that they are kept. COMMENTARY ON THE EPISTLE TO THE ROMANS.[11]

LOVE FULFILLS LAW. AMBROSIASTER: Moses wrote all this in order to reform the natural law. . . . Although there may be other laws which Paul has not mentioned, love is the fulfillment of them all. For if the human race had loved from the beginning, there would never have been any wickedness on earth. For the result of unright-eousness is discord. COMMENTARY ON PAUL'S EPISTLES.[12]

LOVE YOUR NEIGHBOR AS YOURSELF. CHRYSOSTOM: The beginning and the end of virtue is love. . . . But Paul is not looking merely for love;

he wants it to be an intense love. For he does not say merely: "Love your neighbor," but adds: "as yourself." Christ himself said that the law and the prophets hang upon this.[13] HOMILIES ON ROMANS 23.[14]

CHRYSOSTOM: Note that love has two excellent qualities: it abstains from evil and does good deeds. HOMILIES ON ROMANS 23.[15]

THE LAW WRITTEN ON THE HEART. AUGUSTINE: This law is not written on tables of stone but is shed abroad in our hearts through the Holy Spirit who is given to us.[16] THE SPIRIT AND THE LETTER 29.15.[17]

GOD'S LOVE POURED OUT ON THE NEIGHBOR. AUGUSTINE: No one loves his neighbor unless he loves God, and by loving him as himself, to the limit of his ability, he pours out his love on him so that he too may love God. But if he does not love God, he loves neither himself nor his neighbor. LETTER 20.[18]

THE SUM OF THE COMMANDMENTS. PELAGIUS: The whole of righteousness is summed up in the love of one's neighbor. Unrighteousness is born when we love ourselves more than others. For one who loves his neighbor as himself not only does him no wrong but also does him good. He knows how much he wishes both aspects to be done with regard to himself. PELAGIUS'S COMMENTARY ON ROMANS.[19]

THEODORET OF CYR: If a man is well disposed by love for another person, he will not kill the one he loves, nor will he rape his wife, nor will he steal goods or do anything which might harm them. INTERPRETATION OF THE LETTER TO THE ROMANS.[20]

---

[7]The pattern is the image of God in every person. [8]LCC 8:49. [9]See Lk 10:29-37. [10]PCR 138. [11]CER 5:106. [12]CSEL 81.1:429. [13]Mt 22:39. [14]NPNF 1 11:514. [15]NPNF 1 11:514. [16]See 2 Cor 3:3. [17]LCC 8:217. [18]FC 12:46. [19]PCR 138. [20]IER, Migne PG 82 col. 196.

Abstain from Evil, Do Good. Theodore of Mopsuestia: Every law either forbids evil or tells us to do good. Legislators pass the first kind of law in order that we should not harm one another and the second kind in order that we should help one another as far as possible. But they are all summed up in the one command that we should love our neighbor. Pauline Commentary from the Greek Church.[21]

13:10 Love Fulfills the Law

The Single Author of Gospel and Law. Ambrosiaster: Paul is using the words of the law to arrive at the meaning of the gospel. Therefore when he records the fulfilling of the law he ties it to the gospel, demonstrating that both have a single author. Yet in the time of Christ it was necessary to add something, viz., that we should love our enemies as well as our neighbors. . . . What does it mean to love an enemy, except to choose not to hate him any longer and to seek to do him no harm? . . . For the Lord himself on the cross prayed for his enemies[22] in order to demonstrate what the fullness of righteousness, which he had taught, actually was. Commentary on Paul's Epistles.[23]

The Rule of Love. Augustine: The rule of love is that one should wish his friend to have all the good things he wants to have himself and should not wish the evils to befall his friend which he wishes to avoid himself.[24] He shows this benevolence to all men. No evil must be done to any. Love of one's neighbor works no evil. Let us then love even our enemies as we are commanded, if we wish to be truly unconquered. Of True Religion 87.[25]

The Love We Owe. [Pseudo-]Constantius: The apostle clearly said that we must render to each person what he is due but that we are bound only by the need to love one another. Therefore if we always give our brethren the love which we owe them, we shall always be linked together in mutual love. The Holy Letter of St. Paul to the Romans.[26]

Withholding Food from the Neighbor May Kill. Pelagius: Even not to do good is wrong. For if one sees that one's neighbor is in danger of starvation, does one not kill him if, while one has an abundance, one does not give him food, though one has not used up one's own provisions?[27] For anyone who is able to help someone close to death in whatever situation of need kills that person if he does not come to his aid. Pelagius's Commentary on Romans.[28]

Love Is the Fulfilling of the Law. Caesarius of Arles: Therefore, whatever you do, do it for the love of Christ, and let the intention or end of all your actions look to him. Do nothing for the sake of human praise but everything for the love of God and the desire for eternal life. Then you will see the end of all perfection, and when you have reached it you will want nothing more. Sermon 137.1.[29]

13:11 The Nearness of Salvation

When We First Believed. Diodore: When we realized what the advantages of good works are, the message of salvation became easier to understand than it was when we first believed. For when we believed in Christ we did not immediately acquire an exact understanding of what we should be doing, nor was it clear to us what we should stop doing and what we should continue doing. Pauline Commentary from the Greek Church.[30]

Wake from Sleep. Ambrosiaster: Paul says that the time has come when we must hasten to obtain our reward. This is what it means to wake up from sleep—to do good as if it were day, i.e.,

---

[21]NTA 15:163. [22]See Lk 23:34. [23]CSEL 81.1:425-27. [24]See Mt 7:12; Lk 6:31. [25]LCC 6:270. [26]ENPK 2:83. [27]See Jas 2:15-16. [28]PCR 138-39. [29]FC 47:270. [30]NTA 15:108.

openly. . . . It is clear that if we live well after baptism and strive for love we are not far from the reward of the promised resurrection. For the good life of a Christian is the sign of future salvation. For when a person is baptized he is forgiven but not rewarded. Later, as he walks in newness of life, he is near to eternal life. COMMENTARY ON PAUL'S EPISTLES.[31]

FULL TIME TO AWAKE. CHRYSOSTOM: The time is short. . . . The day of resurrection and of the terrible judgment is fast approaching. . . . If you have done everything that was asked of you and are prepared for it, then you have nothing to fear, but if you have not, then look out! Paul is not trying to frighten his hearers but to encourage them, so as to detach them from their love of the things of this world. It was not unlikely that at the beginning of their endeavors they would be more dedicated and slacken off as time went on. But Paul wants them to do the opposite—not to slacken as time goes on but to become even more dedicated. For the nearer the King is, the more they ought to be ready to receive him. HOMILIES ON ROMANS 23.[32]

THE ACCEPTABLE TIME. AUGUSTINE: This relates to 2 Corinthians [6:2]: "Behold, now is the acceptable time, now is the day of salvation." Paul means by this the time of the gospel and the opportunity to save all those who believe in God. AUGUSTINE ON ROMANS 76.[33]

GROW UP! PELAGIUS: It is the hour for you to strive for that which is more perfect and complete, for you should not always be children and infants. . . . Let us together rise from the sleep of idleness and ignorance, for now the knowledge of Christ shines forth. With the increase of knowledge our salvation is nearer than it was when we first believed. PELAGIUS'S COMMENTARY ON ROMANS.[34]

TRUE SALVATION. THEODORE OF MOPSUESTIA: "Our salvation" means the general resurrection

on the last day, for it is then that we shall enjoy true salvation. PAULINE COMMENTARY FROM THE GREEK CHURCH.[35]

ON THE THRESHOLD OF THE RESURRECTION. GENNADIUS OF CONSTANTINOPLE: Every day the end comes closer, and we are already on the threshold of the resurrection. PAULINE COMMENTARY FROM THE GREEK CHURCH.[36]

13:12 Putting on the Armor of Light

THE SON AND THE PROMISES. CLEMENT OF ALEXANDRIA: By "day" and "light" he designates figuratively the Son, and by "the armor of light" he means the promises. STROMATA 4.22.[37]

CAST OFF WORKS OF DARKNESS. ORIGEN: This may be understood in both a universal and in a particular sense. In the first instance, the light is dawning everywhere, and the reign of darkness over the world is rapidly coming to an end. . . . In the second instance, if we have Christ in our hearts he gives us light. Therefore if the reason of knowledge drives away our ignorance and if we turn away from unworthy deeds and do what is right, we are in the light and are walking honestly as if in the day. COMMENTARY ON THE EPISTLE TO THE ROMANS.[38]

OPPORTUNITIES MAY BE LOST. DIODORE: The "day" is the time of this life which remains to us, in which we can do good works. The "night" is the future, in which it will no longer be possible to work. Then we shall lie in the darkness, having lost the chance to do good works. PAULINE COMMENTARY FROM THE GREEK CHURCH.[39]

THE ARMOR OF LIGHT. AMBROSIASTER: "Night" means the old man,[40] who is renewed through baptism. Paul says that he has passed

---

[31]CSEL 81.1:427-29. [32]NPNF 1 11:517. [33]AOR 45. [34]PCR 139. [35]NTA 15:163. [36]NTA 15:409. [37]ANF 2:435. [38]CER 5:112. [39]NTA 15:109. [40]See Rom 6:6; Eph 4:22; Col 3:9.

away like the night and that the day is near, i.e., the sun of righteousness, by whose light the truth appears to us so that we may know what to do. For before we were in the dark, being ignorant of Christ. But when we learned of him the light rose on us and we passed from the false to the true.

The "darkness" refers to carnal sins, which are done by worldly enticements. . . . But to "put on the armor of light" is to do good deeds. COMMENTARY ON PAUL'S EPISTLES.[41]

BEARING ARMS FOR THE REIGN OF LIGHT.

CHRYSOSTOM: The day is calling us to get ready for the battle. Do not be afraid at the thought of bearing arms. It is a heavy and distasteful duty when we have to bear a visible suit of armor, but in this case it is desirable and worth it. For the arms we are called to bear are those of the light! HOMILIES ON ROMANS 24.[42]

THE DAY IS AT HAND. AUGUSTINE: Paul said this, yet look at how many years have passed since then! Yet what he said was not untrue. How much more probable it is that the coming of the Lord is near now, when there has been such an increase of time toward the end! LETTER 77.[43]

WALKING IN THE LIGHT. [PSEUDO-]CONSTANTIUS: The apostle urges us to put off the works of darkness embedded in the torpor of sleep and walk in the light, that is, in good works. THE HOLY LETTER OF ST. PAUL TO THE ROMANS.[44]

DARKNESS AS IGNORANCE. PELAGIUS: Paul likens knowledge to the day and ignorance to the night, in accordance with what Hosea says: "I have likened your mother to the night; my people have become as those who have no knowledge."[45] Let us therefore cast off the works of ignorance and put on the armor of light, that is, works of light. PELAGIUS'S COMMENTARY ON ROMANS.[46]

THE MEANING OF DAY AND NIGHT. THEODORE OF MOPSUESTIA: By "day" Paul means the time since the coming of Christ, for his appearing has

made it much easier to tell the difference between good and evil. "Night" refers to the time before his coming. PAULINE COMMENTARY FROM THE GREEK CHURCH.[47]

THEODORET OF CYR: "Night" refers to the time of ignorance, whereas "day" refers to the time after the Lord's coming. INTERPRETATION OF THE LETTER TO THE ROMANS.[48]

13:13 Proper Conduct

WORKS OF THE FLESH. ORIGEN: These are the works of darkness, which are also called the "works of the flesh," in which people bind their flesh to luxury and uncleanness rather than to holiness or the Lord. "Reveling" refers to dishonorable and extravagant banqueting, which inevitably is prone to sexual immorality. . . . "Quarreling and jealousy" are really acts of the mind, but like everything else here, they are called acts of the flesh. COMMENTARY ON THE EPISTLE TO THE ROMANS.[49]

CONDUCT OURSELVES BECOMINGLY AS IN THE DAY. JEROME: Let us live our lives in the same way now as we are going to live in the day, that is, in the future world. HOMILIES ON THE PSALMS 46.[50]

REVELING AND DRUNKENNESS. AMBROSIASTER: It is true that people do not sin in public, so let us behave as if we were constantly in the public eye. For there is nothing more public than the truth. . . .

Crimes are hatched in large supplies of wine, and many kinds of lust are stirred up. Therefore banquets of this kind are to be avoided. . . . Debauchery is another result of this sort of thing. Paul was right to warn them against quarreling and jealousy, because both of these things lead to

---

[41]CSEL 81.1:429-31. [42]NPNF 1 11:517. [43]FC 12:373. [44]ENPK 2:84. [45]Hos 4:5-6. [46]PCR 139. [47]NTA 15:163. [48]IER, Migne PG 82 col. 197. [49]CER 5:112-14. [50]FC 48:345.

enmity. Commentary on Paul's Epistles.[51]

Restraint of Excess. Chrysostom: Paul does not forbid alcohol; he is opposed only to its excessive use. Nor does he prohibit sexual intercourse; rather, he is against fornication. What he wants to do is to get rid of the deadly passions of lust and anger. Therefore he does not merely attack them but goes to their source as well. For nothing kindles lust or wrath so much as excessive drinking. Homilies on Romans 24.[52]

As in the Day. Pelagius: Just as the light of day keeps everyone from doing what he would freely do at night, so too, knowledge keeps us from ignoring the commands of the law. A revel is a luxurious banquet, but we have a spiritual feast.[53] Moreover, that drunkenness is ruinous and an occasion for debauchery is further proved by the fact that Paul has added "licentiousness." That quarreling and jealousy are also objects of reproach is demonstrated both here and by many other examples.[54] Pelagius's Commentary on Romans.[55]

13:14 Conformed to Christ

Modest Dress. Clement of Alexandria: Let the wife always make use of a plain dress, dignified, softer than that allowed her husband but not one that offends grossly against modesty nor one made with a view only to softness. Let the clothes be in keeping with the person's age, with the individual himself, the place, his character and occupation. The apostle well advises us: "Put on the Lord Jesus Christ, and make no provision for the flesh, to gratify its desires." Christ the Educator 3.11.56.[56]

Put On Christ. Origen: We have often said that Christ is wisdom, righteousness, holiness, truth and all the other virtues. Therefore anyone who has acquired these has put on Christ. For if all these are Christ, then the person who has them must of necessity have Christ as well. Whoever has them will not bother about the flesh. The apostle

speaks here with some care, because he knows that we must take some thought for the needs of the flesh. It is the excesses and lusts of the flesh, not its basic needs, which must be avoided. Commentary on the Epistle to the Romans.[57]

Origen: The Lord Jesus Christ himself . . . is said to be the clothing of the saints. On First Principles 2.3.2.[58]

Diodore: This means that we should imitate Christ in what we do and show him to others in the way we behave. Pauline Commentary from the Greek Church.[59]

Wearing the Wedding Garment. Ambrosiaster: Paul wants everything the law forbids not to be desired, or if it is desired, to be overcome. . . . To put on Christ means to cut oneself off from every sin and wickedness, so that at the wedding banquet one will not be found without a new garment and be shamefully thrown out into the darkness. Commentary on Paul's Epistles.[60]

Not to Gratify Excessive Desires. Chrysostom: Here Paul no longer speaks of works, but rather he rouses his hearers to greater things. When he was speaking of vice he talked about its works, but now that he is speaking about virtue, he does not speak about works but about armor. . . . Even more strikingly, he talks about the Lord Jesus Christ as the garment we are to put on, for whoever is clothed with him has all virtue.

When Paul says "make no provision for the flesh," he is not speaking of necessities but of excess. That is why he adds the qualifying phrase: "to gratify its desires." Homilies on Romans 24.[61]

Make No Provision for the Flesh. Augustine: Provision for the flesh is not to be con-

---

[51]CSEL 81.1:431. [52]NPNF 1 11:518. [53]See 1 Cor 14:26. [54]See, e.g., Jas 3:14. [55]PCR 139. [56]FC 23:244. [57]CER 5:114. [58]OFP 85. [59]NTA 15:109. [60]CSEL 81.1:433. [61]NPNF 1 11:518.

demned if it has to do with the needs of bodily health. But if it is a question of unnecessary delights or luxuries, a person who enjoys the delights of the flesh is rightly chastised. For in that case he makes provision for the desires of the flesh, and "he who sows in the flesh will reap corruption in the flesh."[62] AUGUSTINE ON ROMANS 77.[63]

WALK AS HE WALKED. PELAGIUS: Christ alone should be seen in us, not the old self,[64] for "one who says he abides in Christ should walk as he walked."[65] PELAGIUS'S COMMENTARY ON ROMANS.[66]

EXPECTING RESURRECTION. THEODORE OF MOPSUESTIA: Paul wants to say that by the regeneration of baptism we have been conformed to Christ and become members of the one body of the church, of which he is the head, and so we must put him on in the understanding of what we are expecting, in that we hope to share in his resurrection. PAULINE COMMENTARY FROM THE GREEK CHURCH.[67]

---

[62]Gal 6:8. [63]AOR 45. [64]See Rom 6:6 above. [65]1 Jn 2:6. [66]PCR 140. [67]NTA 15:164.

14:1-8 THE WEAK AND THE STRONG

[1]As for the man who is weak in faith, welcome him, but not for disputes over opinions. [2]One believes that he may eat anything, while the weak man eats only vegetables. [3]Let not him who eats despise him who abstains, and let not him who abstains pass judgment on him who eats; for God has welcomed him. [4]Who are you to pass judgment on the servant of another? It is before his own master that he stands or falls. And he will be upheld, for the Master is able to make him stand.

[5]One man esteems one day as better than another, while another man esteems all days alike. Let every one be fully convinced in his own mind. [6]He who observes the day, observes it in honor of the Lord. He also who eats, eats in honor of the Lord, since he gives thanks to God; while he who abstains, abstains in honor of the Lord and gives thanks to God. [7]None of us lives to himself, and none of us dies to himself. [8]If we live, we live to the Lord, and if we die, we die to the Lord; so then, whether we live or whether we die, we are the Lord's.

OVERVIEW: Those who are weak in faith must be accepted and integrated into the fellowship, though they should refrain from passing judgment on others. It is up to the strong to show humility and encourage the weak to grow in the faith. Eating certain foods or observing certain holy days may be matters of indifference, but they should not be allowed to disrupt Christian fellowship. God alone is the judge of the heart.

Whether "the weak" referred to the vegetarian, the sick, those under the law or the immature in faith was disputed. Christians are called to consider the feelings of others in everything they do, remembering that they are answerable to Christ for everything. Giving thanks in everything the baptized faithful live and die to the Lord.

14:1 Welcome the Weak in Faith

WELCOME THOSE WEAK IN FAITH. ORIGEN: A man who is weak in his faith is to be accepted and not rejected. For it is one thing to be weak in faith but quite another to be an unbeliever altogether. An unbeliever has no faith at all, but one who is merely weak has doubts about certain aspects of the faith. COMMENTARY ON THE EPISTLE TO THE ROMANS.[1]

LOVE IS NOT INDIFFERENCE. APOLLINARIS OF LAODICEA: As far as matters of indifference are concerned, Paul says that it does not matter whether we do them or not, but when it comes to loving our neighbor, they cease to be matters of indifference.[2] Any regulation concerning food is a matter of indifference, because everything has been sanctified by the power of Christ. But not everyone is so strong in his faith that he is in no danger of being corrupted by these things. Whether we injure such a person or do not injure him is not to be regarded as a matter of indifference, but we are to take great care to ensure that no one loses his soul by eating something which he thinks it might be wrong to eat. PAULINE COMMENTARY FROM THE GREEK CHURCH.[3]

"WEAKNESS" RELATED TO THE DISPUTE OVER EATING MEATS. AMBROSIASTER: As I mentioned in my prologue to the epistle, those who led the Romans to faith had mixed it up with the law because they were Jews, which is why some of them thought that they should not eat meat. But others, who followed Christ apart from the law, thought otherwise, that it was permissible to eat meat, and for this reason there were disputes among them. The apostle tried to solve these disputes by arguing that the person who abstained from eating gained no advantage in the sight of God, nor did the one who ate lose anything thereby. He says that the person who is afraid to eat because the Jews had forbidden it is weak. He wants this person to be left to his own judgment, so as not to be hurt and depart from that love which is a mother of souls. COM-

mentary on Paul's Epistles.[4]

NOT JUDGING ANOTHER'S HEART. AUGUSTINE: Paul says that we should receive the weak man in order that we might support his weakness by our strength. Neither should we criticize his opinions by daring to pass judgment on someone else's heart, which we do not see. AUGUSTINE ON ROMANS 78.[5]

WHY SOME ATE VEGETABLES ONLY. [PSEUDO-]-CONSTANTIUS: Paul calls "weak in faith" those who thought that meats which were being sold in the markets of that time had been sacrificed to idols, and for that reason they ate only vegetables, thinking that that way they would not be polluted. THE HOLY LETTER OF ST. PAUL TO THE ROMANS.[6]

THE CHALLENGE OF WEAKNESS. CHRYSOSTOM: Paul points out that the person in question here is not healthy and that he must be received because he needs a lot of attention, because of his infirmity. Furthermore, he makes it appear that the weak man's error is of such a nature that the others, although they do not share his weakness, are nevertheless disconcerted by it and liable to fall into uncertainty themselves. HOMILIES ON ROMANS 25.[7]

NOT FOR DISPUTES OVER OPINIONS. PELAGIUS: From here on Paul indirectly begins to upbraid those who thought they were strong and who therefore ate meat without restraint. Paul tells them not to judge others according to their opinions when the law does not judge them. PELAGIUS'S COMMENTARY ON ROMANS.[8]

THOSE WHO KEEP THE LAW. THEODORET OF CYR: The weak were those who continued to observe the law. INTERPRETATION OF THE LETTER TO THE ROMANS.[9]

---

[1]CER 5:116. [2]Rom 13:9. [3]NTA 15:78. [4]CSEL 81.1:433. [5]AOR 45. [6]ENPK 2:84. [7]NPNF 1 11:522. [8]PCR 140. [9]IER, Migne PG 82 col. 200.

Cultural Sensitivity. Gennadius of Constantinople: Who would be so inhumane as to lay aside any sympathy for the weak and trample on them, not even offering them the help they need in adversity? Paul makes this an absolute command and accompanies it with the teaching that the law and all the behavior it entailed has been abolished in Christ. Yet he was conscious that the ethnic heritage weighed more heavily on the Jew, who felt that he would be sinning against his brothers if he went against the law. Pauline Commentary from the Greek Church.[10]

14:2 Abstaining or Eating

The Food of the Word. Origen: Given that the law of Moses says nothing about eating vegetables, it is clear that the apostle has a deeper meaning in view here. What he is really talking about is the food of the Word of God. The man who is weak in faith is one who cannot fully accept what the Word of God teaches. Compare what the apostle says elsewhere: "Solid food is for the mature, for those who have their faculties trained by practice to distinguish good from evil."[11] . . . Thus the man who believes that he can eat anything is not stuffing himself with food . . . but is showing himself able to understand the secret things of the Spirit, which because of his faith he believes he can eat through grace. Commentary on the Epistle to the Romans.[12]

Everything God Creates Is Good. Ambrosiaster: The faithful reader of Scripture will not doubt that everything which is given for human use is fit to be eaten, for it says in Genesis that everything which God created is good.[13] Therefore nothing is to be rejected, for neither Enoch, who was the first to please God, nor Noah, who alone was found righteous at the time of the flood, nor Abraham, who was the friend of God, nor Isaac nor Jacob, both righteous men and friends of God, nor even Lot, nor any other righteous men are said to have abstained from these things.

If someone thinks it right to be a vegetarian he

is not to be persuaded to eat meat, because if he ignores his own principles and eats with reluctance he will appear to be sinning. Commentary on Paul's Epistles.[14]

What Comes Out of One's Mouth Defiles, Not What Goes In. Augustine: At that time many people who were strong in their faith and who knew the Lord's teaching, that it is what comes out of the mouth which defiles a man, not what goes into it, were eating whatever they liked with a clear conscience. But some weaker ones abstained from meat and wine, so as to avoid unknowingly eating foods which had been sacrificed to idols.[15] At that time the Gentiles sold all sacrificed meat in the butcher shops, poured out the first fruits of the wine as a libation to their idols and even made some offerings in the wine presses. Augustine on Romans 78.[16]

The Relation of Faith to What One Eats. Pelagius: Some people have a faith so strong that it is not disturbed. Some are worn out by abstinence, or else they are elderly. Others are weak because of their youth or the lusts of the flesh. Paul is not speaking here of the Jews, as some suppose, but of those who abstain, for the Jews do not eat meats even if they are clean according to the law, but only vegetables.

Another possible interpretation is this: If you become fainthearted because you know another person who has decided to eat only vegetables and you hesitate to eat meat because of his faith, do not judge the other man's decision or ask him what has been left to individual discretion. But if you take offense and do not want to eat meat, set a limit for yourself and do the better thing—eat only vegetables—so that everyone may be stirred to abstinence by your agreeableness in this matter rather than be annoyed and offended and thereby merely strengthened in their resolve to go on eat-

---

[10]NTA 15:410. [11]Heb 5:14. [12]CER 5:118-20. [13]See Gen 1:31. [14]CSEL 81.1:433-35. [15]See Acts 15:29; 21:25; 1 Cor 8:1-13; 10:25-31. [16]AOR 45.

ing meat. For you cannot condemn someone if he is acting in faith or does it because of his health or old age. PELAGIUS'S COMMENTARY ON ROMANS.[17]

NOT SHAMING THOSE OF ANOTHER CULTURE. THEODORET OF CYR: Those who would eat anything were obviously Gentiles. Some people say that converted Jews shamed these Gentiles not only into abstaining from meat which had been sacrificed to idols but from any kind of meat whatever. INTERPRETATION OF THE LETTER TO THE ROMANS.[18]

14:3 Do Not Pass Judgment

NOT PASSING JUDGMENT. ORIGEN: Paul wants harmony to prevail in the church between those who are more mature and those who are less. COMMENTARY ON THE EPISTLE TO THE ROMANS.[19]

NOT ABSTAINING. CLEMENT OF ALEXANDRIA: We are not to abstain completely from different kinds of food but only not to be preoccupied with them. We are to eat what is set before us, as a Christian should, out of respect to our host. THE INSTRUCTOR 2.1.[20]

PERSONAL CHOICE. AMBROSIASTER: What we eat or do not eat is a matter of personal choice and therefore it should not become a matter for argument. COMMENTARY ON PAUL'S EPISTLES.[21]

THE STRONG SHOULD NOT DEMEAN THE WEAK. CHRYSOSTOM: Paul does not say that the one who eats should simply ignore the one who abstains, nor does he suggest that the latter should not be blamed and put right. All he is saying is that the stronger ones should not look down on the weak or be contemptuous of them. Likewise, those who abstain are not to pass judgment on those who eat. For just as the strong mocked the weak, claiming that they had no faith, that they were not really saved and that

they were Judaizers, so the others thought that the strong ones were lawbreakers and gluttonous. Since these were probably mostly Gentiles, Paul adds that God has welcomed them. HOMILIES ON ROMANS 25.[22]

ON NOT DESPISING ANOTHER CULTURE'S CUSTOMS. AUGUSTINE: The apostle instructed those who ate such food with a clear conscience not to despise the weakness of those who abstained. . . . And he told the weak not to condemn as polluted those who consumed such meat and wine. . . . For the strong insisted on despising the weak, and the weak did not hesitate to condemn the strong. AUGUSTINE ON ROMANS 78.[23]

KEEPING THE BALANCE. AUGUSTINE: Paul wanted to keep the balance, by which scandals are avoided, between those who fast on Saturday and those who do not, so that the one who eats would not despise the one who does not eat, and the one who fasts would not judge the one who eats. LETTER 36.[24]

NOT TAKING OFFENSE. PELAGIUS: These people took offense at each other. Those who did not eat judged those who ate as carnal, and those who ate ridiculed those who did not eat as fools and considered them to be superstitious. But God called the one, just as he called the other. PELAGIUS'S COMMENTARY ON ROMANS.[25]

14:4 Judged by the Master

A SPIRIT OF DEVOTION. AMBROSIASTER: The servant is not guilty whether he eats or not, as long as he does what he does in a spirit of devotion. COMMENTARY ON PAUL'S EPISTLES.[26]

PASSING JUDGMENT ON ANOTHER'S SERVANT. DIODORE: A servant of Christ is anyone whom

---

[17]PCR 140-41. [18]IER, Migne PG 82 col. 200. [19]CER 5:120. [20]ANF 2:239. [21]CSEL 81.1:435. [22]NPNF 1 11:522. [23]AOR 45. [24]FC 12:157. [25]PCR 141. [26]CSEL 81.1:435-37.

Christ has accepted. He is then no longer under the law. Who are you, therefore, to judge someone by the law when he is a stranger to it? PAULINE COMMENTARY FROM THE GREEK CHURCH.[27]

IN GOD'S SERVICE WE ARE JUDGED BY GOD. CHRYSOSTOM: It is not because someone does things which are worthy of escaping judgment that we are not to judge, but because the person in question is another man's servant—not ours but God's. It is up to God to decide what to do. HOMILIES ON ROMANS 25.[28]

WHO ARE YOU TO PASS JUDGMENT? AUGUSTINE: Paul says this so that, when something might be done with either good or bad motives, we should leave the judgment to God and not presume to judge the heart of someone else, which we do not see.[29] But when it comes to things which obviously could not have been done with good and innocent intentions, it is not wrong if we pass judgment. So in the matter of food, where it is not known what the motive in eating it is, Paul does not want us to be judges, but God. But in the case of that abominable immorality where a man had taken his stepmother, Paul taught us to judge.[30] For that man could not possibly claim that he committed such a gross act of indecency with good intentions. So we must pass judgment on things which are obviously wrong. AUGUSTINE ON ROMANS 79.[31]

GOD ALONE IS JUDGE OF THE HEART. AUGUSTINE: These men were of a mind to pass judgment with regard to things which may indeed be done with a bad intention but which may also be done with an upright, simple and magnanimous motive. Although they were men, they wanted to judge the secrets of the heart—secrets of which God alone is the judge. SERMON ON THE MOUNT 2.18.59.[32]

JUDGING THE LAW. PELAGIUS: What authority do you have to judge someone whom the law does

not judge? This is why James says: "He who judges his brother judges the Law";[33] in other words, he judges himself to be wiser than the law. Nevertheless, Paul himself judged those who broke the commandments and gave others the power to judge.[34] A man either lives or dies according to his own master. PELAGIUS'S COMMENTARY ON ROMANS.[35]

14:5 All Days Alike

ESTEEMING ALL SCRIPTURE TEXTS (SYMBOLICALLY, ALL DAYS) ALIKE. ORIGEN: According to the spiritual interpretation, which we have already expounded in the case of food, the word *day* is used to mean a portion of holy Scripture in which the doctrine of godliness and faith is contained. For it is the day which enlightens the mind, which drives away the darkness of ignorance. The day has Christ, the sun of righteousness, in it. If one person dedicates himself to the study of holy Scripture and discovers the true meaning of every day, so that not one jot or tittle of the law escapes him, then it can be said that he "esteems all days alike." Another person may not have reached that point but still has enough to be able to understand the basic tenets of the faith. Therefore both are to give thanks to God, according to the apostle's teaching. One understands and enjoys everything, whereas another does not understand everything but will nevertheless be saved by confessing the little that he does know. COMMENTARY ON THE EPISTLE TO THE ROMANS.[36]

FASTING OUT OF FEAR. CHRYSOSTOM: Here it seems to me that Paul is giving a subtle hint about fasting. For it is probable that those who fasted were always passing judgment on those who did not, and it is likely that some of those

---

[27]TA 15:109. [28]NPNF 1 11:523. [29]See Mt 7:1; 1 Cor 4:5; Jas 4:12. [30]1 Cor 5:1-5. [31]AOR 45, 47. [32]FC 11:170. [33]Jas 4:11. [34]1 Cor 5:3-5; 6:2-3. [35]PCR 141. [36]CER 5:124-26. As all foods are useful for physical growth, so all Scriptures are useful for spiritual growth. So every day, every food, every text enables growth.

who fasted did so on particular days. . . . Paul releases those who fasted out of fear from their bondage by saying that it was something which was basically indifferent. HOMILIES ON ROMANS 25.[37]

THE INCONSTANCY OF HUMAN JUDGMENT AS DISTINGUISHED FROM DIVINE. AUGUSTINE: At the moment, and without any deeper consideration, it seems to me that this is said about God and man, not about two men. He who judges on alternate days is man, who can judge one way today and another way tomorrow. . . . But the One whose judgment is the same every day is the Lord. . . . But let everyone dare to judge only insofar as is granted to human intelligence or at least to his own. AUGUSTINE ON ROMANS 80.[38]

CERTAIN DAYS TO ABSTAIN FROM MEAT. [PSEUDO-]CONSTANTIUS: Paul is saying that there are some people who at certain times of the year abstain from meat but that there are others who have decided they must abstain from meat for their entire lives. THE HOLY LETTER OF ST. PAUL TO THE ROMANS.[39]

BECOMING FULLY CONVINCED IN ONE'S OWN MIND. PELAGIUS: Therefore Paul is speaking here about fasting and abstinence, which are not treated under a fixed provision of the law. Each individual should do whatever he sees fit in the light of his desire to share in the reward. Thus it follows that in a matter of this kind one should simply do what he himself has judged to be better. PELAGIUS'S COMMENTARY ON ROMANS.[40]

OECUMENIUS: This is not to be made an article of faith, as Paul himself says. PAULINE COMMENTARY FROM THE GREEK CHURCH.[41]

14:6 Honoring and Thanking God

EITHER VIEW MAY HONOR GOD. CHRYSOSTOM: Paul continues his exposition [from the pre-

vious verse]. The issue at stake is not a fundamental one. Both sides are acting for God's sake, and both end up by giving him thanks. Thus the difference between them turns out to be a minor one. Nevertheless, Paul aims a blow at the Judaizers, because he accepts the validity of all foods. HOMILIES ON ROMANS 25.[42]

KEEPING THE DAY FOR THE LORD. AUGUSTINE: When someone observes the day well, he keeps the day for the Lord. To judge the day well means you are not to despair over the future correction of the person whose guilt might appear now to be clean. AUGUSTINE ON ROMANS.[43]

EATING IN HONOR OF THE LORD. PELAGIUS: The man who fasts for God's sake and not on account of other people observes the day for the Lord.[44] He eats for God's sake so that he may have strength to preach the gospel, for which every convert should thank God. This man is not devoted to his own stomach but to the salvation of others.[45]

But it is also true that by the example of the one who does not eat meat many are saved and return thanks to God. For one who gives thanks with the voice gives thanks alone, but one who gives thanks in deed as well as voice gives thanks with many others. PELAGIUS'S COMMENTARY ON ROMANS.[46]

14:7 No One Lives or Dies to Himself

NO ONE DIES TO HIMSELF. ORIGEN: We must not please ourselves but rather assume the example of Christ, who alone died to sin, so that by imitating him we too might become strangers to sin and die to it. We do not have this example of living in ourselves, but we get it from Christ.[47] COMMENTARY ON THE EPISTLE TO THE ROMANS.[48]

---

[37]NPNF 1 11:523. [38]AOR 47. [39]ENPK 2:86. [40]PCR 141. [41]NTA 15:431. [42]NPNF 1 11:524. [43]AOR 47. [44]See Mt 6:18. [45]See 1 Cor 10:31-32. [46]PCR 141-42. [48]CER 5:128.

The Will to Live for Oneself. Ambrosiaster: A man would be living for himself if he did not act according to the law. But whoever is controlled by the brake of the law is not living for himself but for God, who gave the law so that it might be possible to live according to his will. Likewise, whoever dies dies to God, for he is the Judge who will either condemn or reward him. Commentary on Paul's Epistles.[49]

Death as Apostasy. Chrysostom: This means that we are not free. We have a master who wants us to live and not die, and to whom life and death matter more than they do to us.... For if we die, we do not die to ourselves alone but to our master as well. By "death," Paul means apostasy from the faith. Homilies on Romans 25.[50]

Pelagius: No believer lives for himself or dies for himself, because "Christ has died for all, so that those who live no longer live for themselves but for him."[51] Pelagius's Commentary on Romans.[52]

14:8 Living or Dying, We Are the Lord's

Baptism as Burial. Origen: Here "death" refers to the death which we die when we are buried with Christ in baptism, and "life" is the life we live in Christ, having died to sin and become strangers to this world.[53] Commentary on the Epistle to the Romans.[54]

Living to the Law. Chrysostom: One who is living under the law cannot be living to Christ as well. Homilies on Romans 25.[55]

We Live to the Lord. Pelagius: Therefore, we must take care that we do not live for ourselves in eating or die on account of others in fasting. Pelagius's Commentary on Romans.[56]

We Are the Lord's. Theodore of Mopsuestia: If we live, it is Christ's life that we live; if we die, we die with him, under his custody. Pauline Commentary from the Greek Church.[57]

---

[49]CSEL 81.1:437. [50]NPNF 1 11:524. [51]2 Cor 5:15. [52]PCR 142. [53]See Gal 2:20; Col 3:3. [54]CER 5:128. [55]NPNF 1 11:524. [56]PCR 142. [57]NTA 15:164.

14:9-18 PRINCIPLES AND PRACTICE

[9]For to this end Christ died and lived again, that he might be Lord both of the dead and of the living.

[10]Why do you pass judgment on your brother? Or you, why do you despise your brother? For we shall all stand before the judgment seat of God; [11]for it is written,

"As I live, says the Lord, every knee shall bow to me,
and every tongue shall give praise[u] to God."

[12]So each of us shall give account of himself to God.

[13]Then let us no more pass judgment on one another, but rather decide never to put a stumbling block or hindrance in the way of a brother. [14]I know and am persuaded in the Lord Jesus that nothing is unclean in itself; but it is unclean for any one who thinks it unclean. [15]If your brother is being

injured by what you eat, you are no longer walking in love. Do not let what you eat cause the ruin of one for whom Christ died. ⁶So do not let your good be spoken of as evil. ⁷For the kingdom of God is not food and drink but righteousness and peace and joy in the Holy Spirit; ⁸he who thus serves Christ is acceptable to God and approved by men.

u Or *confess*

OVERVIEW: We are in no position to pass judgment on one another, because in the final analysis we shall all stand before the judgment seat of God. No food is unclean. But some people are not convinced of this, and if we offend their consciences we are guilty of causing them to stumble. Christians must be prepared to give way on these secondary matters in order that peace and harmony may be preserved in the church. Those who know better can keep their knowledge to themselves, and God will respect them for it. But to force someone to go against his or her conscience is to lead that person into sin. Do not let what you eat cause the ruin of one for whom Christ died.

14:9 Lord of the Dead and the Living

CHRIST'S RULE OVER CREATION. ORIGEN: There are some people who think that Christ had to die in order to become the Lord of the dead and that he had to rise again in order to become the Lord of the living. But I think this assertion can be refuted as follows. Christ's rule over all creation consists of two parts. First, by virtue of his majesty and power as the Creator of all things who rules the universe, he has everything in subjection, not only good and holy minds and spirits but also rebellious ones and those whom the Scriptures call "the wicked angels."[1] In this sense he is known as the Almighty, as John says in his Apocalypse: "Thus says the one who is and who was and who is to come, the Almighty."[2]

Second, given that so good a Son of so good a Father does not want rational spirits to bend to the obedience of his law by force but waits for them to come voluntarily, so that they will seek

what is good freely and not of necessity,[3] he persuades them by teaching them rather than by commanding them and by inviting them rather than by forcing them. Thus he was pleased to go even to the point of death, in order to leave an example of new life and a way of dying for those who want to die to sin and evil. Christ is therefore Lord of both the living and the dead—of the living, because he is the head of those who by the example of his resurrection look for a new and heavenly life here on earth, and of the dead, because these same people bear the death of Christ about in their bodies[4] and mortify their members which are on earth.[5] COMMENTARY ON THE EPISTLE TO THE ROMANS.[6]

TO THIS END CHRIST DIED. AMBROSIASTER: The creation was made by Christ the Lord, but because of sin it has become separated from its maker and taken captive. But God the Father sent his Son from heaven to earth to teach his creation what to do in order to escape the hands of its captors, so that his work should not perish. For this reason he allowed himself to be killed by his enemies, so that by going down to hell he could condemn sin, because he was killed as an innocent man, and liberate those whom the devil held there. Therefore, since he showed the way of salvation to the living and offered himself for them and also delivered the dead from hell, he is Lord of both the living and the dead. For he has turned the lost into his servants. COMMENTARY ON PAUL'S EPISTLES.[7]

---

[1]Lk 8:2. [2]Rev 1:18. [3]See Deut 30:19; Is 1:19-20; Jer 11:8; Mt 23:37; 2 Cor 5:20. [4]2 Cor 4:10. [5]Col 3:5. [6]CER 5:128-32. [7]CSEL 81.1:439.

NOTHING ESCAPES HIS LORDSHIP. CHRYSOSTOM: Look how Christ takes care of the dead. If he is concerned about the departed, it is clear that he will be concerned about the living as well. For nothing escapes his lordship.... Christ put down his own life for our salvation. Having gone to so much trouble and expense, he is not likely to consider us as being of no value. HOMILIES ON ROMANS 25.[8]

THE RETURN OF CHRIST. PELAGIUS: The coming of Christ will find people alive and will bring the dead back to life.[9] It does not matter whether he brings you back to life or finds you alive, as long as you appear righteous before him. PELAGIUS'S COMMENTARY ON ROMANS.[10]

14:10 All Stand Before God's Judgment

ON JUDGING AND DESPISING. ORIGEN: This reflects the behavior of those who have advanced a little way in knowledge but reject and refuse to instruct those who are less able to attain this higher understanding. Others show how unskilled and rebellious they are by judging (by accusing and condemning) those who are trying to obtain a knowledge which is higher and deeper than what they are capable of understanding. The apostle wants to reprove the blame which attaches to both of these by ordering the first group not to reject or despise the less advanced and the others not to think of themselves as superior when in fact they have no ability to judge them.... The judgment seat of God is the same thing as the judgment seat of Christ, to which Paul refers when writing to the Corinthians.[11] COMMENTARY ON THE EPISTLE TO THE ROMANS.[12]

CHRYSOSTOM: At first sight, Paul seems to be attacking the stronger here, but he is also laying into the legalists, by calling their attention to the great benefit which they have received in Christ and to the terror of the judgment to come. HOMILIES ON ROMANS 25.[13]

ALL WILL BE JUDGED. PELAGIUS: By what authority do you condemn your brother as a voracious glutton? For what reason do you despise him, as if he were weak or his fast were pointless?[14] The Lord will judge our consciences to see with what sort of desire and intention we did what we did. PELAGIUS'S COMMENTARY ON ROMANS.[15]

WHY DESPISE YOUR BROTHER? THEODORE OF MOPSUESTIA: "Why do you pass judgment on your brother?" was said to the Jews. "Why do you despise your brother?" was said to the Gentiles. Neither of you should do either, says Paul, because you are under obligation to maintain Christ's standards of behavior in your life. PAULINE COMMENTARY FROM THE GREEK CHURCH.[16]

THEODORET OF CYR: Paul addresses these words to the Jews. INTERPRETATION OF THE LETTER TO THE ROMANS.[17]

GENNADIUS OF CONSTANTINOPLE: Once again Paul takes up his earlier theme and by adding the word *brother* shows how inappropriate this kind of judging is. PAULINE COMMENTARY FROM THE GREEK CHURCH.[18]

14:11 Confessing God's Name

ALL WILL KNEEL. AMBROSIASTER: For having been killed, the future Judge rose from the dead, and therefore he rightly said: "As I live."[19] ... For not only do I live, but I will come to judge, and my enemies will confess my name and kneel before me, acknowledging that I am God from God. COMMENTARY ON PAUL'S EPISTLES.[20]

PELAGIUS: This shows that we must all account for our actions to the Lord alone. PELAGIUS'S COMMENTARY ON ROMANS.[21]

---

[8]NPNF 1 11:524. [9]See Acts 17:31. [10]PCR 142. [11]2 Cor 5:10. [12]CER 5:132-34. [13]NPNF 1 11:525. [14]See Rom 14:3. [15]PCR 142. [16]NTA 15:165. [17]IER, Migne PG 82 col. 201. [18]NTA 15:411. [19]Is 49:18. [20]CSEL 81.1:441. [21]PCR 142.

So Do Not Cause Divisions. Chrysostom: Be careful when you see the Master sitting on his judgment seat, and do not make schisms or divisions in the church by breaking away from grace and running back to the law. For the law belongs to Christ as well. Homilies on Romans 25.[22]

14:12 Accountable to God

Giving Account Before God. Polycarp: If we ask the Lord to forgive us we should also forgive,[23] for we stand before the eyes of the Lord God, and "we must all stand before the judgment seat of Christ," and "each must give account of himself." The Epistle to the Philippians 6.[24]

Each One Accountable. Ambrosiaster: Since we are not going to give account of each other, says Paul, let us not condemn one another over the issues mentioned above. Commentary on Paul's Epistles.[25]

To Christ. Chrysostom: It is not the law which will demand an account from us but Christ. You see from this how Paul has released us from the fear of the law. Homilies on Romans 25.[26]

Admonition Still Required. Pelagius: We shall account to God for those things about which the law is silent. But if we do not rebuke someone when we see him sinning, we shall also give an account to the Lord for that.[27] Pelagius's Commentary on Romans.[28]

14:13 Do Not Be a Stumbling Block

Never Be a Stumbling Block. Chrysostom: Consider the great punishment we shall suffer if we give offense at all. If the thing concerned was against the law and some people rebuked others wrongly, Paul forbade them to do so, in order not to cause a brother to stumble and fall. If we give offense without having anything to put right, what treatment will we deserve? For if not saving others is a crime (as is demonstrated by the man who buried his one talent), what will be the result if we offend him as well? But you may say: What if he brings the offense on himself, by being weak? Well, this is precisely why you ought to be patient. For if he were strong, he would not require so much care. Homilies on Romans 25.[29]

Pelagius: From here on, Paul subtly begins to recommend abstinence and says that even though those who eat are strong, they ought to abstain in case the weak are subjected to a stumbling block by their example. Pelagius's Commentary on Romans.[30]

Gentiles Must Not Deliberately Upset the Jews. Theodore of Mopsuestia: Paul is saying this to the Gentiles, even if it appears that he is speaking to the Jews. . . . For the Gentiles at Rome were doing many things deliberately in order to upset the Jews, partly because they were the majority in the church and partly because they were of a higher social class. Pauline Commentary from the Greek Church.[31]

14:14 Nothing Is Unclean

The Faithful Enjoy the Blessing of Food Offered in Their Original Creation. Novatian: It is evident that all these foods enjoy again the blessings they received at their creation, now that the law has ended. We must not return to the legal prohibition of foods commanded for certain reasons and which evangelical liberty, setting us free from its bondage, has now discontinued. Jewish Foods 5.6.[32]

With Faith Nothing Is Unclean. Diodore: This means that nothing is common or

---

[22]NPNF 1 11:525. [23]See Mt 6:14-15; 18:35; Mk 11:25-26; Lk 17:3-4. [24]ANF 1:34. [25]CSEL 81.1:441. [26]NPNF 1 11:525. [27]See 2 Tim 4:2. [28]PCR 142. [29]NPNF 1 11:525. [30]PCR 142. [31]NTA 15:166. [32]FC 67:152.

unclean when eaten with faith in Christ. PAULINE COMMENTARY FROM THE GREEK CHURCH.[33]

CHRYSOSTOM: Nothing is unclean by nature, but it becomes so by the spirit in which a person uses it. HOMILIES ON ROMANS 25.[34]

THE TENDER CONSCIENCE. PELAGIUS: Paul is not saying here that there is anything which is unclean but that for someone with a tender conscience things do become unclean, for even after coming to faith in Christ he is still judging according to Jewish custom. PELAGIUS'S COMMENTARY ON ROMANS.[35]

WHAT DEFILES. CYRIL OF ALEXANDRIA: Christ had said: "Not what goes into the mouth defiles a man but what comes out of the mouth—this defiles a man."[36] This applies to food as well. EXPLANATION OF THE LETTER TO THE ROMANS.[37]

14:15 Causing a Brother's Ruin

WALKING IN LOVE. ORIGEN: Although Paul establishes the principle that nothing is unclean in itself, and he gives complete freedom to believers to eat whatever they like, nevertheless he proceeds to restrict that freedom for the sake of building up the freedom of brotherly love. COMMENTARY ON THE EPISTLE TO THE ROMANS.[38]

BASIL: The Christian must serve everyone who is upset with him in every way, at least insofar as he can. THE MORALS 5.3.[39]

AMBROSIASTER: In another epistle Paul says: Food is meant for the stomach and the stomach for food, and God will destroy both one and the other.[40] Since God does not care one way or the other about food, Paul tells us to maintain a spirit of charity, by which God has seen fit to deliver us from sin. COMMENTARY ON PAUL'S EPISTLES.[41]

WHEN ANOTHER IS INJURED BY WHAT YOU EAT. CHRYSOSTOM: You see how far Paul bends in the name of charity, endeavoring to draw the erring brother by yielding to him so as not to hurt him. For even when he has freed him from his fears, he does not drag or force him but leaves him to his own decision. Abstaining from food is not in the same category as seriously injuring somebody by what you eat.

Do you not value your brother enough even to purchase his salvation at the price of abstaining from certain types of food? Christ did not refuse to become a servant and even to die for him, but you will not even give up your food in order to save him! HOMILIES ON ROMANS 26.[42]

DO NOT LET WHAT YOU EAT CAUSE THE RUIN OF ONE FOR WHOM CHRIST DIED. CHRYSOSTOM: One who ruins his brother has subverted peace and harmed joy in a way which is more serious even than stealing money. What is worse is that although another has saved him, you have wronged him and ruined him. HOMILIES ON ROMANS 26.[43]

THINKING OF ANOTHER'S GOOD. PELAGIUS: Paul did not say that a brother is distressed because of fasting but because of food; therefore you should not incite or constrain anyone by the example of what you eat. If your neighbor eats something which is not good for him against his will, you are no longer loving him as yourself if you are not thinking of his good as much as of your own. PELAGIUS'S COMMENTARY ON ROMANS.[44]

THE SEQUENCE OF PAUL'S ARGUMENT. GENNADIUS OF CONSTANTINOPLE: Look at how wonderfully Paul develops his argument. He starts off at the bottom, by referring to food. Then he goes on to call the person who is sinned against a

---

[33]NTA 15:110. [34]NPNF 1 11:529. [35]PCR 142-43. [36]Mt 15:11. [37]Migne PG 74 col. 852. [38]CER 5:150-52. [39]FC 9:79. [40]1 Cor 6:13. [41]CSEL 81.1:443. [42]NPNF 1 11:529. [43]NPNF 1 11:530. [44]PCR 143.

"brother." Then he calls what has been done to him "destruction." Fourth, he says that this outrage has been committed against someone "for whom Christ died." Fifth, he says that someone who does this causes godliness to be blasphemed, and sixth, that we have not come to faith in Christ in order to be able to enjoy this or that but in order to be able to share in righteousness, which means in sinlessness, peace and joy. Pauline Commentary from the Greek Church.[45]

14:16 Causing Good to Be Spoken of as Evil

A Spiritual Interpretation of "Good Is Spoken of as Evil." Origen: How is it possible for what is good to us to be spoken of as evil? "What is good to us" refers here to the spiritual interpretation of the law, avoiding the ungodly and foolish teachings of the heretics and of those engaged in false philosophy concerning unclean and polluted food. This is what is enjoined by the spiritual law. But a Jew, for example, or one of the so-called Encratites might think that in order to believe in Christ it is necessary to practice celibacy or abstinence from certain types of food and might quote Scripture in support of this. If you then insist that in order for such a person to be saved or to come to Christ he must eat everything, including the food from which he abstains, the good element in the spiritual law is blasphemed, because he will think that eating such food is an essential part of our faith, when in fact it is a matter of indifference. Commentary on the Epistle to the Romans.[46]

Blaspheming God's Teaching. Ambrosiaster: Since God's teaching is good and salutary, it should not be blasphemed, because of something trivial. Yet it is blasphemed when doubts are cast on the goodness of God's creation. Commentary on Paul's Epistles.[47]

Oecumenius: Even if you are teaching correctly, your argument may become the cause of blas-

phemy. Pauline Commentary from the Greek Church.[48]

Do Not Cause Good Doctrine to Be Spoken Evil of. Chrysostom: By "what is good to you" Paul means either their faith, or the hope of reward in the hereafter, or the perfection of their religious state. For it is not just that you fail to do anything to help your brother, Paul says, but you even cause the doctrine itself, the grace of God and his gift, to be spoken evil of. Homilies on Romans 26.[49]

Do Not Flaunt Christian Freedom. Pelagius: What is good is our freedom, which we have in the Lord, so that everything is clean to us. We should not use our freedom in such a way that we appear to be living for the stomach and for feasts. Pelagius's Commentary on Romans.[50]

Avoid Causing Another's Destruction. Theodoret of Cyr: Paul is saying that he praises their faith but does not want it to become the cause of cursing and damnation. Interpretation of the Letter to the Romans.[51]

14:17 Righteousness, Not Food and Drink

Finally Righteousness Will Be Our Food and Drink. Origen: Just as there is no marriage in heaven,[52] so there is no eating and drinking there either. All that will be over and done with and will have no place there. Rather there will be "righteousness and peace and joy in the Holy Spirit." Therefore, Paul urges us to concentrate on those things and to realize that we already have their substance here below, which we shall take with us when we go to the heavenly kingdom. Peace and righteousness and whatever else we acquire from the Holy Spirit will be our food and drink in the kingdom of heaven. Com-

---

[45]NTA 15:412. [46]CER 5:160. [47]CSEL 81.1:445. [48]NTA 15:431. [49]NPNF 1 11:530. [50]PCR 143. [51]IER, Migne PG 82 col. 204. [52]Mt 22:30.

MENTARY ON THE EPISTLE TO THE ROMANS.[53]

CLEMENT OF ALEXANDRIA: He who eats of this meal, the best of all, will possess the kingdom of God, fixing his gaze on the holy assembly of love, the heavenly church. CHRIST THE EDUCATOR 2.1.[54]

AUGUSTINE: By "the kingdom of God" Paul means the church, in which God reigns. LETTER 36.[55]

[PSEUDO-]CONSTANTIUS: Here Paul shows clearly that the kingdom of heaven does not have corporeal food and drink but that everyone lives in a spiritual way there. THE HOLY LETTER OF ST. PAUL TO THE ROMANS.[56]

WE ARE NOT JUSTIFIED BY FOOD. PELAGIUS: We are not justified by food. But one should also note that Paul did not say that "fasting and temperance" are not the kingdom of God but rather food and drink. The gifts of the Holy Spirit are more easily maintained through abstinence, for where there is righteousness (by loving one's neighbor as oneself) there is also peace, and where there is peace there is also spiritual joy, because distress and trouble always arise out of discord. PELAGIUS'S COM-

MENTARY ON ROMANS.[57]

THEODORE OF MOPSUESTIA: We ought to laugh at those who think that after the resurrection we shall eat and drink, when Paul's words so clearly say the opposite. PAULINE COMMENTARY FROM THE GREEK CHURCH.[58]

14:18 Approved by God and Men

ACCEPTABLE TO GOD. AMBROSIASTER: The man who is acceptable to God is approved by men. Why? Because he has accepted the gift through which he appears worthy in the sight of God. COMMENTARY ON PAUL'S EPISTLES.[59]

APPROVED BY MEN. CHRYSOSTOM: Men will approve of such a person, not so much because of his perfect state but because of his devotion to peace and good relations. HOMILIES ON ROMANS 26.[60]

PELAGIUS: No one can doubt that a person like this is holy. PELAGIUS'S COMMENTARY ON ROMANS.[61]

---

[53]CER 5:162. [54]ANF 2:238. [55]FC 12:152. [56]ENPK 2:87. [57]PCR 143. [58]NTA 15:166. [59]CSEL 81.1:447. [60]NPNF 1 11:530. [61]PCR

14:19-23 HARMONY IN THE CHURCH

[19]*Let us then pursue what makes for peace and for mutual upbuilding.* [20]*Do not, for the sake of food, destroy the work of God. Everything is indeed clean, but it is wrong for any one to make others fall by what he eats;* [21]*it is right not to eat meat or drink wine or do anything that makes your brother stumble.*[v] [22]*The faith that you have, keep between yourself and God; happy is he who has no reason to judge himself for what he approves.* [23]*But he who has doubts is condemned, if he eats, because he does not act from faith; for whatever does not proceed from faith is sin.*[w]

v Other ancient authorities add *or be upset or be weakened*   w Other authorities, some ancient, insert here Ch 16.25-27

Overview: By offending the weak we condemn ourselves. Do nothing that would cause another to stumble. Let all that you do be for the neighbor's upbuilding. Do not judge harshly. Let your actions proceed from the premise of faith, not sin.

14:19 Pursue Peace and Mutual Upbuilding

Mutual Upbuilding. Ambrosiaster: Since disapproval leads to discord, Paul teaches us to be peaceful and to avoid arguments over eating or not eating. Instead, he encourages us to follow the way of upbuilding.[1] Commentary on Paul's Epistles.[2]

Pursue Peace. Chrysostom: This applies to both sides equally. The one must become peaceable and the other must not destroy his brother. Without peace it is impossible to edify anyone. Homilies on Romans 26.[3]

Do Not Judge Each Other. Pelagius: Let us not judge one another in matters of this kind. Abstinence is edification; food, on the other hand, even if it does not ruin anybody, edifies no one. Pelagius's Commentary on Romans.[4]

14:20 Do Not Destroy the Work of God

Everything Is Created Unblemished. Origen: Cleanliness and uncleanness inhere not in the things themselves but rather in the minds and thoughts of those who use them. Commentary on the Epistle to the Romans.[5]

The True Banquet of the Word. Clement of Alexandria: It is the mark of a silly mind to be amazed and stupefied at what is presented at vulgar banquets after having enjoyed the rich fare which is in the Word of God. Christ the Educator 2.1.[6]

Food Made for Human Life. Ambrosiaster: Man is the work of God by creation, and again by his renewal in regeneration, and food is

God's work as well. But man was not made for food; food was made for man, which is very different! Commentary on Paul's Epistles.[7]

The Work of God Destroyed Because of Food, Not Upbuilt. Chrysostom: Here "the work of God" means the salvation of a brother. For these people were so far away from building others up that they were prepared to destroy what God had made, and not for any great matter but for something very trivial.

It is not the eating which is unclean but the intention behind it. If you have not put that right but forced him to eat anyway, you have done it to no purpose and have made everything worse. Thinking that something is unclean is not as bad as tasting it when you think it is unclean. In that case you are committing two errors: first, by increasing his opposition by your quarrelsome attitude, and second, by getting him to taste what to him is unclean. As long as you have not persuaded him, do not try to force him. Homilies on Romans 26.[8]

The Work of God. Pelagius: The "work of God" means "a human being, created by God." Paul repeats what he said above [in verse 14], lest it appear that he is condemning creation. What is clean in itself becomes wrong if someone else takes offense on his account. Pelagius's Commentary on Romans.[9]

Oecumenius: God did his work on the cross, but now you are destroying it. Pauline Commentary from the Greek Church.[10]

14:21 Do Not Make a Brother Stumble

Assessing Abstinence from Meat and Wine. Origen: Eating meat and drinking wine are matters of indifference in themselves. Even

---

[1]See Eph 4:11-12. [2]CSEL 81.1:447. [3]NPNF 1 11:530. [4]PCR 143-44. [5]CER 5:168. [6]ANF 2:240. [7]CSEL 81.1:447. [8]NPNF 1 11:530. [9]PCR 144. [10]NTA 15:431.

wicked people may abstain from these things, and some idol worshipers in fact do so, for reasons which are actually evil. Likewise quite a few heretics enjoin similar practices. The only reason abstinence of this kind is good is that it may help to avoid offending a brother. COMMENTARY ON THE EPISTLE TO THE ROMANS.[11]

VOLUNTARY USE. AMBROSIASTER: Although the issue involves only meat, Paul adds drink here as well, in order to nurture those who abstain from both of these things, so that they will not be hurt by those who eat and drink, on the ground that it is lawful to do so. Paul gives them peace of mind by telling them to make their own decision and putting an end to the disagreement through which the dispute had arisen. No one will dispute that either option is legitimate in itself. For the creation was given for voluntary use. There is no necessity imposed on anybody, one way or the other. COMMENTARY ON PAUL'S EPISTLES.[12]

DO NOTHING THAT MAKES ANOTHER STUMBLE. CHRYSOSTOM: If you force him he will be immediately destroyed and will condemn you, strengthening himself all the more by refusing to eat. But if you yield to him, then he will love you and will not suspect you as a teacher, and afterward you will discover that you have gained the power of sowing in him the right views. But once he starts hating you, you have closed the door to reason. Do not compel him therefore, but refrain for his sake, not because the thing is unclean but because he is offended, and then he will love you all the more. HOMILIES ON ROMANS 26.[13]

[PSEUDO-]CONSTANTIUS: In this passage Paul praises abstinence from meat and wine, but much more he warns us that we must abstain from food and drink which has been sacrificed to idols, so as not to cause scandal to our brother. THE HOLY LETTER OF ST. PAUL TO THE ROMANS.[14]

14:22 Keeping One's Faith to Oneself

HAPPY IS ONE WHO PERSEVERES IN DOING GOOD. ORIGEN: This person should keep his faith to himself and not try to impose it on others. . . . It is reward enough to have God's approval.

There are many people who start off with good intentions, e.g., they decide they are going to live a celibate life, but in the course of time, either by negligence or desire, what they originally decided to do gets spoiled and corrupted. He is an unhappy person, therefore, who pronounces himself defeated in what he has tried to do, for he judges and condemns himself. A happy person is one who perseveres and thus has no reason to judge or to reprove himself for what he does. COMMENTARY ON THE EPISTLE TO THE ROMANS.[15]

NO NEED TO JUDGE OTHERS. AMBROSIASTER: This means that if you are happy to eat because you know that everything God made is good, there is no need to judge anyone else. Rather, you should be at peace with your brother, for this is what God wants. COMMENTARY ON PAUL'S EPISTLES.[16]

RESIST VANITY. CHRYSOSTOM: It seems to me that here Paul is gently warning the stronger ones against the temptation of vanity. He does not want them to go around boasting of their superiority but to be happy with having a clear conscience. HOMILIES ON ROMANS 26.[17]

BY OFFENDING THE WEAK WE CONDEMN OURSELVES. AUGUSTINE: This should be read in connection with [verse 16] above. . . . Let us make good use of what we have, lest we sin against our brothers by creating a stumbling block for the weaker ones. For when we offend the weak we condemn ourselves by the very good by which we approve ourselves when this faith pleases us. AUGUSTINE ON ROMANS 81.[18]

---

[11]CER 5:170-72. [12]CSEL 81.1:449-51. [13]NPNF 1 11:531. [14]ENPK 2:87. [15]CER 5:174-76. [16]CSEL 81.1:451 [17]NPNF 1 11:531.

DO NOT WEAKEN ANOTHER'S FAITH BECAUSE OF WHAT YOU EAT. PELAGIUS: If you consider yourself faithful in this matter, eat in such a way that nobody is weakened by your example. The man who, in demonstrating his own strength, does not think of himself but of the salvation of the weak, is truly blessed.[19] PELAGIUS'S COMMENTARY ON ROMANS.[20]

14:23 What Is Not of Faith Is Sin

ALL THAT IS NOT OF FAITH IS SIN. BASIL: If "all that is not of faith is sin, and faith comes by hearing, and hearing by the Word of God," then everything outside holy Scripture, not being of faith, is sin. THE MORALS 80.22.[21]

EITHER/OR. GREGORY OF NYSSA: Every word or deed or thought which does not look to Christ looks completely to the adversary of Christ. For it is not possible for what is outside of light or life not to be completely in darkness or death. . . . The person outside of Christ rejects him by what he thinks, does or says. ON PERFECTION.[22]

RESPECT CONSCIENCE. AMBROSIASTER: It is true that if someone thinks it wrong to eat but does so anyway, he is condemned. For he makes himself guilty when he does what he thinks he ought not to.

If someone acts against his better judgment in a matter of conscience, then Paul says that it is a sin.[23] COMMENTARY ON PAUL'S EPISTLES.[24]

CHRYSOSTOM: Once again, Paul shows what great harm people do if they force people to do things which go against their conscience. When a person does not feel sure or believe that something is clean, how can he do other than commit sin? HOMILIES ON ROMANS 26.[25]

ONE WHO INCREASES DOUBT IS CONDEMNED. [PSEUDO-]CONSTANTIUS: If one person has doubts about another and says: "If this man has eaten he has obviously been condemned," then it is clear that he has no faith. . . . For it is not of faith if you condemn someone else because while you are fasting he is eating. THE HOLY LETTER OF ST. PAUL TO THE ROMANS.[26]

PELAGIUS: Whatever destroys another is not of faith and is therefore sin. PELAGIUS'S COMMENTARY ON ROMANS.[27]

---

[18]AOR 47. [19]See Is 57:14; 1 Jn 2:10. [20]PCR 144. [21]FC 9:204. [22]FC 58:120. [23]See Jn 8:9; 1 Tim 1:5; Heb 13:18; Sir 14:2. [24]CSEL 81.1:451. [25]NPNF 1 11:531. [26]ENPK 2:87. [27]PCR 144.

15:1-13 LOVING EACH OTHER

[1]We who are strong ought to bear with the failings of the weak, and not to please ourselves; [2]let each of us please his neighbor for his good, to edify him. [3]For Christ did not please himself; but, as it is written, "The reproaches of those who reproached thee fell on me." [4]For whatever was written in former days was written for our instruction, that by steadfastness and by the encouragement of the scriptures we might have hope. [5]May the God of steadfastness and encouragement grant you to live in such harmony with one another, in accord with Christ Jesus, [6]that together you may with

one voice glorify the God and Father of our Lord Jesus Christ.

[7]*Welcome one another, therefore, as Christ has welcomed you, for the glory of God.* [8]*For I tell you that Christ became a servant to the circumcised to show God's truthfulness, in order to confirm the promises given to the patriarchs,* [9]*and in order that the Gentiles might glorify God for his mercy. As it is written,*

"Therefore I will praise thee among the Gentiles,

and sing to thy name";

[10]*and again it is said,*

"Rejoice, O Gentiles, with his people";

[11]*and again,*

"Praise the Lord, all Gentiles,

and let all the peoples praise him";

[12]*and further Isaiah says,*

"The root of Jesse shall come,

he who rises to rule the Gentiles;

in him shall the Gentiles hope."

[13]*May the God of hope fill you with all joy and peace in believing, so that by the power of the Holy Spirit you may abound in hope.*

OVERVIEW: Christ suffered reproach and did not seek his own advantage. This is the pattern of the Christian life: pleasing God first and others accordingly, not fearing to be weak to win the weak. The Scriptures were written to be understood and followed, and so to give us hope and patience. Christians are called to live in harmony, which is achieved by mutual self-sacrifice in imitation of Christ. When Gentiles see the unity of the church, they will be persuaded of the truth of the gospel and believe. Christians look to the future in hope and confidence.

15:1 Bearing with the Weak

WINNING THE WEAK. ORIGEN: Paul appears from this to be calling himself strong, just as he says in 1 Corinthians: "To the weak I became weak, that I might win the weak."[1] COMMENTARY ON THE EPISTLE TO THE ROMANS.[2]

LET THE WEAK TEST YOUR STRENGTH. CHRYSOSTOM: What Paul says is this: If you are strong, then let the weak test your strength. HOMILIES ON ROMANS 27.[3]

BECOMING WEAK. PELAGIUS: If you really are strong, Paul says, do as I did and become weak in order to win the weak.[4] PELAGIUS'S COMMENTARY ON ROMANS.[5]

THEODORE OF MOPSUESTIA: Once again, Paul is speaking to the Gentiles, who looked down on the Jews because they kept the law. PAULINE COMMENTARY FROM THE GREEK CHURCH.[6]

15:2 Edifying Our Neighbor

TO EDIFY. ORIGEN: We ought to please God first, then our neighbor. But perhaps someone will say that Paul is contradicting himself here, because elsewhere he says: "If I please men, then I am not a servant of Christ."[7] . . . In answer to

---

[1]1 Cor 9:22. [2]CER 5:182. [3]NPNF 1 11:535. [4]1 Cor 9:22. [5]PCR 144. [6]NTA 15:168. [7]Gal 1:10.

this it must be said that it is one thing to try to please others in order to get their praise and quite another to please them in order that one's own life might be blameless, so that those who meet us may be edified by what they see and hear. We are not called to please others by doing things which are against faith, honor and piety.... Note that Paul himself says this, when he adds that in pleasing our neighbor the purpose is to edify him. Commentary on the Epistle to the Romans.[8]

Care for the Poor. Chrysostom: If you are rich and powerful, do not please yourself but look after the poor and needy, because that way you will enjoy true glory and be doing much service besides. Homilies on Romans 27.[9]

Not Seeking My Own Advantage. Pelagius: Let us be commended not by ourselves but by our neighbors, just as Paul sets his own example before us elsewhere when he says: "Just as I try to please all men in everything I do, not seeking my own advantage but that of many, that they may be saved."[10] For nobody can build up another person if he has not first attracted him by his good life. But those who do their own will, because they are seeking their own advantage, are pleasing themselves. Paul indicates how and why we should please, so that we do not do it for worthless glory. Pelagius's Commentary on Romans.[11]

15:3 Christ Pleased God, Not Himself

Christ Did Not Please Himself. Origen: Christ did not please himself nor did he think it was robbery to be equal with God,[12] but wanting to please men, that is, to save them, he suffered the reproaches of those who reproached God, as it is written. Commentary on the Epistle to the Romans.[13]

Christ's Pleasure in Doing the Will of the One Who Sent Him. Ambrosiaster: In the sixty-eighth Psalm [LXX] the Savior says that he did not come to please himself but God the

Father. For because he said: "I did not come down from heaven to do my will but the will of him who sent me,"[14] the Jews objected and put him to death as a sinner. Therefore the psalmist puts himself in Christ's place and says: "The reproaches of those who reproached thee fell on me."[15] Commentary on Paul's Epistles.[16]

Chrysostom: Paul always points to Christ's self-sacrifice when he asks us to make sacrifices.[17] Homilies on Romans 27.[18]

Christ Suffered Reproach. Pelagius: An imitator and disciple of Christ does not seek his own advantage. Christ died for the salvation of others and bore the most bitter reproach.... But whatever insults are cast, not only upon Christ but also upon the saints for God's sake, are cast upon God himself. Pelagius's Commentary on Romans.[19]

Not As I Will. Theodoret of Cyr: Remember the words of Christ's prayer concerning his passion: "Father, if it be possible, let this cup pass from me; nevertheless, not as I will but as thou wilt."[20] Interpretation of the Letter to the Romans.[21]

15:4 The Scriptures Encourage Hope

For Our Instruction. Origen: This is similar to what Paul says elsewhere: "these things were written down for our instruction."[22] ... "Encouragement of the Scriptures" is given not to those who neither believe nor understand them but only to those who do. Commentary on the Epistle to the Romans.[23]

The Scriptures Enable Hope and Patience. Chrysostom: These things were

[8]CER 5:186-88. [9]NPNF 1 11:535. [10]1 Cor 10:33. [11]PCR 144-45. [12]Phil 2:6. [13]CER 5:188-90. [14]Jn 6:38. [15]Ps 69:9. [16]CSEL 81.1:455. [17]See 1 Cor 5:7; Eph 5:1-2. [18]NPNF 1 11:535. [19]PCR 145. [20]Mt 26:39. [21]IER, Migne PG 82 col. 209. [22]1 Cor 10:11. [23]CER 5:190-94.

written so that we might not fall away, for we have many battles to fight, both inward and outward. But being comforted by the Scriptures we can exhibit patience, so that by living in patience we might dwell in hope. For these things produce one another—hope brings forth patience, and patience, hope. HOMILIES ON ROMANS 27.[24]

THE ENCOURAGEMENT OF THE SCRIPTURES.
PELAGIUS: No Scripture is written without reason, for the merits and temptations of the righteous contribute to our edification, because they so very obviously lived for God. Through the encouragement of the Scriptures we await with great patience the hope which is to come. . . . Those who enjoy the encouragement of the law cannot be moved by any temptation. By the examples of patience and encouragement which have been written down, we may hope for encouragement both in present temptations and . . . in the future. For it is great cause for encouragement if we know that our Lord and his saints have already borne the things which we suffer. PELAGIUS'S COMMENTARY ON ROMANS.[25]

15:5 Living in Harmony

LIVE IN HARMONY. ORIGEN: Here Paul is blessing the Romans in the manner of the patriarchs and prophets. . . . It is a great blessing that they should all understand and think alike. If you want to know just how great it is, look at what the Savior said in the Gospel: "If two or three of you agree, whatever they ask will be done for them by God."[26] . . .

This unanimity must be "in accord with Christ Jesus," for of course it is possible to conspire together for evil. COMMENTARY ON THE EPISTLE TO THE ROMANS.[27]

GREATER LOVE HAS NO MAN THAN THIS.
AMBROSIASTER: As if he had been sent for their salvation, the apostle charges the people with a good wish, praying that God may grant them a common understanding of his wisdom according

to Christ Jesus, so that they may be wise in the teaching of Christ. For then they will be able to please God by following the example of the Lord, who said: "Greater love has no man than this, that a man should lay down his life for his friends"[28] and his brethren, and with one voice and one confession magnify God the Father in Christ. COMMENTARY ON PAUL'S EPISTLES.[29]

IN ACCORD WITH CHRIST. CHRYSOSTOM: Love wants us to think of one another as we think of Christ. And to show that it is not mere love that he requires Paul adds, as always: "in accord with Christ Jesus." HOMILIES ON ROMANS 27.[30]

THE GOD OF STEADFASTNESS. [PSEUDO-] CONSTANTIUS: By "the God of steadfastness" Paul means the Holy Spirit. THE HOLY LETTER OF ST. PAUL TO THE ROMANS.[31]

PELAGIUS: The God of steadfastness is the Holy Spirit, who grants that with one mind, in accordance with Christ, we may glorify the God and Father of our Lord Jesus Christ. His steadfastness is meant to lead to repentance, and his encouragement is for those who have already repented.

We are to live in harmony, so that each one may seek the salvation of the other as if it were his own, just as Christ saved everyone from death by his own death. PELAGIUS'S COMMENTARY ON ROMANS.[32]

GODLY CONSENSUS. THEODORET OF CYR: Paul adds "in accord with Christ Jesus" in order to show that he is not praying for them to live in unbounded harmony but rather in a godly consensus. INTERPRETATION OF THE LETTER TO THE ROMANS.[33]

15:6 Glorifying God with One Voice

---

[24]NPNF 1 11:536. [25]PCR 145. [26]Mt 18:19. [27]CER 5:194-98. [28]Jn 15:13. [29]CSEL 81.1:457. [30]NPNF 1 11:536. [31]ENPK 2:88. [32]PCR 145-46. [33]IER, Migne PG 82 col. 209.

THE WHOLE BODY UNITED. CHRYSOSTOM: He wants us to do this not just with one mouth but with one mind also. The whole body is united into one, and Paul concludes his address with another doxology, in which he gives the utmost encouragement to unanimity and concord. HOM-ILIES ON ROMANS 27.[34]

WITH ONE MIND. PELAGIUS: God is truly glorified when we praise him with one mind and with one voice. PELAGIUS'S COMMENTARY ON ROMANS.[35]

15:7 Welcoming One Another

BIND YOURSELVES TO ONE ANOTHER. CHRY-SOSTOM: Let us obey this command and bind ourselves closely to one another. For it is no longer just the weak that he is encouraging, but everyone. If someone wants to break relations with you, do not do the same with him. . . . Rather, display even more love toward him, that you may draw him to you. For he is a member of the body, and when a member is cut off we must do everything we can to unite it again and then pay more attention to it. HOMILIES ON ROMANS 27.[36]

BEARING BURDENS AS DID GOD. PELAGIUS: For the sake of God's honor bear one another's burdens.[37] . . . If God took us upon himself while we were ungodly,[38] how much more should we, who are like one another, support each other! PELAGIUS'S COMMENTARY ON ROMANS.[39]

UNITED IN LOVE. CYRIL OF ALEXANDRIA: We are all one body and members one of another.[40] Christ obliges us to be united with one another in the bonds of charity. EXPLANATION OF THE LET-TER TO THE ROMANS.[41]

15:8 Confirming the Promises to the Patriarchs

IDENTIFYING WITH AND TRANSCENDING CIR-CUMCISION. ORIGEN: There are two ways in which "Christ became a servant to the circumcised." First, he was himself circumcised and so identified himself with them.[42] Second, he fulfilled the promises of the law, so that now neither those who are circumcised nor Gentile believers are obliged to keep it any more. COMMENTARY ON THE EPISTLE TO THE ROMANS.[43]

TO CONFIRM THE PROMISES TO THE PATRI-ARCHS. CHRYSOSTOM: When Paul says that "Christ became a servant to the circumcised" he means that by coming to fulfill the law, by being circumcised and born of the seed of Abraham, Christ undid the curse, held back God's wrath and made those who were meant to obtain the promises fit to receive them.[44] . . . It was because you had transgressed the law that Christ came to fulfill it, not so that you might then keep it but so that he might confirm to you the promises which were made to the fathers, which the law had caused to be suspended because you offended and were unworthy of the promise. HOMILIES ON ROMANS 28.[45]

THE WORD SPOKEN FIRST TO ISRAEL. AUGUS-TINE: Paul said this so that the Gentiles would understand that the Lord Christ had been sent to the Jews and so they would not be proud. Since the Jews rejected what had been sent to them, it happened that the gospel was also preached to the Gentiles, as is most clearly written in the Acts of the apostles, when the apostles say to the Jews: "It was necessary that the Word of God should be spoken first to you. Since you . . . judge yourselves unworthy . . . behold, we turn to the Gentiles."[46]

It also agrees with the Lord's own testimony, when he said: "I was sent only to the lost sheep of the house of Israel"[47] and: "It is not right for the children's bread to be thrown to the dogs."[48] If the Gentiles think carefully, they will realize by their

---

[34]NPNF 1 11:536. [35]PCR 146. [36]NPNF 1 11:537. [37]Gal 6:2. [38]See Rom 5:6. [39]PCR 146. [40]See Rom 12:4-5; 1 Cor 10:17. [41]Migne PG 74 col. 353. [42]Lk 2:21. [43]CER 5:200. [44]See Gal 3:13. [45]NPNF 1 11:538. [46]Acts 13:46. [47]Mt 15:24. [48]Mt 15:26.

own faith, by which they now believe that to the pure all things are pure, that they should not offend those Jewish converts who, perhaps from weakness, dare not touch certain kinds of meat, fearing that it has been in contact with idols. AUGUSTINE ON ROMANS 82.[49]

NOW JEWS AND GENTILES CALLED TO BE ONE. PELAGIUS: Once more Paul urges both Jews and Gentiles to unity with each other. He agrees with the Jews that Christ was promised to them and came to them first and that the Gentiles were called later on, because of God's mercy. Nevertheless, both peoples have now been made into one. PELAGIUS'S COMMENTARY ON ROMANS 82.[50]

15:9 The Gentiles Glorify God

THE GENTILES RECEIVE MERCY. AMBROSIASTER: It is written in the seventeenth psalm [LXX][51] that the Gentiles will be admitted to the grace of God in order to receive salvation. For this is the voice of Christ, which predicted what would happen in the future. COMMENTARY ON PAUL'S EPISTLES.[52]

GLORIFY GOD BY MANIFESTING UNITY. CHRYSOSTOM: It was by mercy alone that the Gentiles were saved; hence they were bound to glorify God. It is a glory to God when they are blended together and united, when they offer praise with one mind, when they bear the weaker and when they do not neglect the member who has been cut off. HOMILIES ON ROMANS 28.[53]

PELAGIUS: Paul deprives the Jews of presumption when he teaches that it was foretold that the Gentiles would be saved, even though this was not announced to them. Christ accepts those Gentiles who have received mercy because they too belong to his body. PELAGIUS'S COMMENTARY ON ROMANS.[54]

15:10 Gentiles Rejoice with Jews

GENTILES CALLED TO REJOICE WITH JEWS.

CHRYSOSTOM: Paul has given this and the following Scriptures in order to show that we ought to be united and glorify God. He wanted to humble the Jews, that they might not lift themselves up over the Gentiles, given that all the prophets called them. He also wanted to humble the Gentiles, by showing them that they had a greater grace to be thankful for. HOMILIES ON ROMANS 28.[55]

PELAGIUS: These Gentiles have been brought to salvation along with God's people, the Jews. PELAGIUS'S COMMENTARY ON ROMANS.[56]

15:11 Gentiles Praise God

JEWS AND GENTILES FELLOW HEIRS. AMBROSIASTER: God long ago decreed in Psalm 116 that by the intervention of his mercy Jews and Gentiles would be united.[57] The Gentiles would be granted grace to become fellow heirs with the Jews, who by the grace of God were long ago named as his people. While the Jews were noble, the Gentiles were ignoble, but now by God's mercy the Gentiles have been made noble as well, so that all may rejoice together by acknowledging the truth. COMMENTARY ON PAUL'S EPISTLES.[58]

PELAGIUS: The Gentiles must praise God because they have been brought to salvation. PELAGIUS'S COMMENTARY ON ROMANS.[59]

15:12 Gentiles Hope in Christ

THE ROOT OF JESSE. AMBROSIASTER: In order to give the Gentiles greater assurance and a surer hope, Paul backs up God's decree with many examples.

Why is Christ said to be from the root of Jesse and not from the root of Boaz,[60] a righteous man, or of Obed?[61] It is because he is said to be the Son

---

[49]AOR 47, 49. [50]PCR 146. [51]Ps 18:49. [52]CSEL 81.1:461. [53]NPNF 1 11:539. [54]PCR 146. [55]NPNF 1 11:539. [56]PCR 146. [57]See Ps 117:1 LXX. [58]CSEL 81.1:461-63. [59]PCR 147. [60]See Ruth 2:1—4:22. [61]See Ruth 4:17-22; 1 Chron 2:12.

of David on account of the kingdom, and just as he was born of God to be king, so also he was born of David according to the flesh. Therefore, the root of Jesse is the tree of David, which bore fruit on the branch which is the Virgin Mary, who gave birth to Christ. COMMENTARY ON PAUL'S EPISTLES.[62]

IN HIM THE GENTILES SHALL HOPE.

PELAGIUS: Jesse was the father of David, from whose seed, through Mary, Christ was born [cf. 1:3].... It is thus proved to the Jews that their Messiah has already come, because it is clear that all the Gentiles hope in Christ. PELAGIUS'S COMMENTARY ON ROMANS.[63]

15:13 Abounding in Hope

ALL JOY AND PEACE. ORIGEN: Precisely how all this can be fulfilled so that they may be filled with all joy and peace is hard to say, especially since the apostle himself, when talking about the gifts of the Spirit, says that he knows in part and prophesies in part.[64] But I think that believers can have the fullness of peace when they are reconciled to God the Father by faith.... For if someone who believes is armed with the power of the Holy Spirit, it is certain that he will always have the fullness of joy and peace. COMMENTARY ON THE EPISTLE TO THE ROMANS.[65]

IN BELIEVING. CHRYSOSTOM: In other words,

may you get rid of your heartlessness toward one another and not be cast down by temptations. You will achieve this by abounding in hope, which is the cause of all good things and comes from the Holy Spirit. It is not just from the Spirit, though, because you must do your part also. That is why Paul adds the words "in believing." HOMILIES ON ROMANS 28.[66]

THE TRIUNE GIFT IS ONE. [PSEUDO-] CONSTANTIUS: Here Paul shows that because God does not fill anyone with the gift of grace apart from the power of the Holy Spirit, the gift of the Father and of the Holy Spirit is one and the same. THE HOLY LETTER OF ST. PAUL TO THE ROMANS.[67]

ABOUND IN HOPE. PELAGIUS: All the joy of believers should be in the hope to come. Where there is peace, all is joy. However, there is no joy in discord but only widespread sorrow.... Hope rests in the signs and wonders of the Holy Spirit. PELAGIUS'S COMMENTARY ON ROMANS.[68]

THE GOD OF ALL HOPE. GENNADIUS OF CONSTANTINOPLE: By "the God of all hope" Paul means that God has blessed us with the hope of things to come. PAULINE COMMENTARY FROM THE GREEK CHURCH.[69]

---

[62]CSEL 81.1:463. [63]PCR 147. [64]1 Cor 13:9. [65]CER 5:206-8. [66]NPNF 1 11:539. [67]ENPK 2:89. [68]PCR 147. [69]NTA 15:415.

15:14-22 THE APOSTLE TO THE GENTILES

[14]*I myself am satisfied about you, my brethren, that you yourselves are full of goodness, filled with all knowledge, and able to instruct one another.* [15]*But on some points I have written to you very boldly by way of reminder, because of the grace given me by God* [16]*to be a minister of Christ*

Jesus to the Gentiles in the priestly service of the gospel of God, so that the offering of the Gentiles may be acceptable, sanctified by the Holy Spirit. [17]In Christ Jesus, then, I have reason to be proud of my work for God. [18]For I will not venture to speak of anything except what Christ has wrought through me to win obedience from the Gentiles, by word and deed, [19]by the power of signs and wonders, by the power of the Holy Spirit, so that from Jerusalem and as far round as Illyricum I have fully preached the gospel of Christ, [20]thus making it my ambition to preach the gospel, not where Christ has already been named, lest I build on another man's foundation, [21]but as it is written,

"They shall see who have never been told of him,
and they shall understand who have never heard of him."

[22]This is the reason why I have so often been hindered from coming to you.

OVERVIEW: Paul praises the Roman church, not because it is perfect but because in many ways it sets an example for others. All the more reason, therefore, to go on toward perfection, so that this example may be the best it can possibly be. In admonishing the Romans on certain points, Paul is fulfilling the ministry given to him by God. The Fathers noted how wisely he did this, not alienating his hearers in the process. Paul takes time in Romans 15:17 to remind the Romans of the mighty work God has done through him. The Fathers respected his many achievements and held them up as a sign of his God-given authority. At Romans 15:22 Paul returns to a theme he has already mentioned in the opening chapter—the fact that he has so far been prevented from going to Rome. The Fathers were concerned to point out that he was not hindered by the devil but by the wider plan of God, who wanted to make use of him elsewhere. Paul's calling is authenticated by the signs and wonders accomplished by the Spirit in his mission to the Gentiles.

15:14 Paul Encourages His Readers

THE RELATIVITY OF HUMAN GOODNESS. ORIGEN: This fullness is relative. Paul and those like him are full of goodness, etc., in comparison with their fellow believers, but naturally they are still vastly inferior to the perfection of God. COMMENTARY ON THE EPISTLE TO THE ROMANS.[1]

EXHORTING ONE ANOTHER. AMBROSIASTER: These are words of encouragement. By praising them he is exhorting them to better understanding and behavior. For one who sees himself praised develops the works he has been given, so that the things which are said might be true. Therefore he did not say that they should teach one another but that they should exhort one another. Exhortation normally occurs when it becomes clear that something is undermining the mind or that it has grown slack. The rest is clear and needs no explanation. COMMENTARY ON PAUL'S EPISTLES.[2]

SATISFIED ABOUT YOU, MY BRETHREN. CHRYSOSTOM: This applies to the exhortation just given [in the preceding verses]. It is as if Paul was saying: "It was not that you were cruel or haters of your brethren that I gave you that exhortation to receive and not to neglect or destroy the work of God. For I am aware that you are full of goodness." HOMILIES ON ROMANS 28.[3]

THE ENCOURAGEMENT OF PRAISE. PELAGIUS: As a good teacher Paul rouses the people to further progress by praising them, so that they might blush for not being the sort of people the apostle thought they were. He is careful not to appear as if he has sternly rebuked the quarrel-

---

[1]CER 5:208. [2]CSEL 81.1:465. [3]NPNF 1 11:542.

some, the dissident or the foolish. PELAGIUS'S COMMENTARY ON ROMANS.[4]

15:15 A Reminder

BECAUSE OF THE GRACE GIVEN ME BY GOD.
AMBROSIASTER: Paul says he has been given authority by the grace of God, to embolden him to write to all the Gentiles, exhorting and confirming their calling in Christ, so that he might show his concern in the service of the gospel as a teacher of the Gentiles and so that their sacrifice might be reckoned acceptable because of their sanctification in the Holy Spirit. For whatever is offered with a pure faith and a sober mind is purified by the Holy Spirit. COMMENTARY ON PAUL'S EPISTLES.[5]

WRITTEN BOLDLY. CHRYSOSTOM: Note how humble and how wise Paul is. He cut deep in the first part of his discourse, and after obtaining what he wished, now he turns to kindliness. Even without the rest of what he said, his confession of boldness would be enough to calm their anger.... He often does this in his epistles,[6] but here even more than usual. For the Romans were of a higher rank than the others, and Paul had to bring them down to size. HOMILIES ON ROMANS 29.[7]

[PSEUDO-]CONSTANTIUS: In this passage Paul is either humbling himself or else is saying that he is bold enough to preach to those who already possessed the preaching of Peter. THE HOLY LETTER OF ST. PAUL TO THE ROMANS.[8]

PELAGIUS: Paul means: "I had greater confidence to write because I knew that you were sensible people, ready to accept a reasonable argument." ... Paul wrote to them not because of earthly obligations or to earn praise but to discharge the task he had received. PELAGIUS'S COMMENTARY ON ROMANS.[9]

BY WAY OF REMINDER. THEODORE OF MOP-

SUESTIA: Paul is telling them that he has not received anything new or wonderful which he is writing to teach them. Rather, he is just reminding them of things they have already learned. PAULINE COMMENTARY FROM THE GREEK CHURCH.[10]

15:16 In Service of the Gospel

JUSTIN MARTYR: We are the true high priestly people of God ... for everywhere among the Gentiles well-pleasing and pure sacrifices are presented to God. DIALOGUE WITH TRYPHO 116.[11]

IN THE PRIESTLY SERVICE OF THE GOSPEL.
ORIGEN: The priests had to make sure when they offered sacrifices that there were no blemishes on the sacrificial victim nor faults of any kind, so that the sacrifice might be acceptable and pleasing to God.[12] So also the one who makes a sacrifice of the gospel and preaches the Word of God must ensure that there is no blemish in his preaching, nor fault in his teaching, which might make him blameworthy at the judgment.[13] Rather, he ought first of all to sacrifice himself, to strangle his own faults and to put to death the sins in his members, so that not only by his teaching but also by the example of his life he may make his sacrifice, which is the salvation of his disciples, acceptable to God. The Holy Spirit is the source of sanctification, and therefore the offering of the Gentiles which is made by Paul, in the role of priest, is said to be made acceptable to God by the Holy Spirit and not by the observance of the law. COMMENTARY ON THE EPISTLE TO THE ROMANS.[14]

PAUL'S FORM OF PRIESTLY SACRIFICE.
CHRY-SOSTOM: Now Paul raises his discourse to a loftier tone, speaking no longer of mere ministry only but of "priestly service" also. For Paul, his

---

[4]PCR 147. [5]CSEL 81.1:465. [6]See, e.g., 1 Cor 11:2; Gal 5:10. [7]NPNF 1 11:542. [8]ENPK 2:89. [9]PCR 147. [10]NTA 15:170. [11]ANF 1:257. [12]See, e.g., Ex 29:1; Lev 1:3, 10. [13]See 1 Tim 3:1-7. [14]CER 5:214-16.

preaching and evangelizing were a priestly service. It was his form of sacrifice. Nobody would reproach a priest for desiring to offer the most perfect sacrifice possible. Paul says this both to lift up their thoughts and show them that they are a sacrifice and to explain his own part in the matter, because he was appointed to this office. My sacrificial knife, he says, is the gospel, the word of my preaching. HOMILIES ON ROMANS 29.[15]

THAT THE OFFERING OF THE GENTILES MAY BE AN ACCEPTABLE SACRIFICE. AUGUSTINE: The Gentiles are offered to God as an acceptable sacrifice when they believe in Christ and are sanctified through the gospel. AUGUSTINE ON ROMANS 83.[16]

SANCTIFIED BY THE HOLY SPIRIT. PELAGIUS: By his example Paul was showing that what he performed with so much fear is holy. For some pass off as human what they proclaim as divine, with the result that what is holy seems to be unholy, since it is not done in a holy way. . . . Following Paul, however, the Gentiles become an acceptable sacrifice to God, sanctified and exalted not by fire but by the Holy Spirit. PELAGIUS'S COMMENTARY ON ROMANS.[17]

15:17 Paul's Work for God

PROUD IN CHRIST JESUS. ORIGEN: To be proud of one's work for God without Christ Jesus would be like saying one has glory in God's eyes without righteousness, wisdom or truth. COMMENTARY ON THE EPISTLE TO THE ROMANS.[18]

MY WORK FOR GOD. AMBROSIASTER: Believing and serving Christ Jesus with a pure conscience, Paul has made himself worthy in the sight of God the Father, to the point that he can say that there is nothing which Christ has not done through him for the encouragement of the Gentiles, by using him to perform signs and wonders that their power might support the preaching of the gospel. COMMENTARY ON PAUL'S EPISTLES.[19]

CHRYSOSTOM: After humbling himself, Paul here raises the tone, so as not to become an object of contempt in the eyes of his readers. HOMILIES ON ROMANS 29.[20]

GLORY IN GOD'S SIGHT. PELAGIUS: Paul has glory in the sight of God, even though he is defamed and attacked in the public eye. PELAGIUS'S COMMENTARY ON ROMANS.[21]

15:18 What Christ Accomplished Through Paul

THE PROOF OF HIS CALLING. CHRYSOSTOM: The miracles he performed and the obedience of the Gentiles were the proof that Paul had accomplished the purpose for which he was sent. . . . He does all he can to show that the whole thing was God's doing, not his own.[22] HOMILIES ON ROMANS 29.[23]

WHAT CHRIST WROUGHT THROUGH ME. PELAGIUS: Paul has not tried to claim that he has done anything in his own strength. God did all these things through him. PELAGIUS'S COMMENTARY ON ROMANS.[24]

15:19 Signs and Wonders by the Spirit's Power

THE POWER OF SIGNS AND WONDERS. ORIGEN: Signs differ from wonders in that signs are miracles which point to some future happening, whereas wonders are just miracles. COMMENTARY ON THE EPISTLE TO THE ROMANS.[25]

AS FAR ROUND AS ILLYRICUM. CHRYSOSTOM: Count up all the places Paul had been—not just in the Roman Empire but beyond its frontiers as well. Phoenicia, Syria, Cilicia and Cappadocia for a start, but also the back country—Arabia, Persia and Armenia. This is why he said "as far round as

---

[15]NPNF 1 11:543. [16]AOR 49. Cf. comments on 12:1. [17]PCR 147-48. [18]CER 5:216. [19]CSEL 81.1:467. [20]NPNF 1 11:543. [21]PCR 148. [22]See Acts 15:12. [23]NPNF 1 11:544. [24]PCR 148. [25]CER 5:218.

Illyricum," so that you would not only think of the direct route from Jerusalem to Illyricum but consider also all the surrounding countries as well. HOMILIES ON ROMANS 29.[26]

BY THE POWER OF THE HOLY SPIRIT. [PSEUDO-]CONSTANTIUS: Here Paul shows that the strength and power of Christ, of God [the Father] and of the Holy Spirit are one and the same. THE HOLY LETTER OF ST. PAUL TO THE ROMANS.[27]

PELAGIUS: Paul was talking not about words here but about miracles. The gospel is fully disseminated when the Gentiles also believe. PELAGIUS'S COMMENTARY ON ROMANS.[28]

THEODORET OF CYR: When Paul says "as far round as Illyricum," he means that he got to Illyricum in a roundabout way, via the eastern provinces, the Black Sea region, Asia Minor and Thrace. INTERPRETATION OF THE LETTER TO THE ROMANS.[29]

15:20 Preaching the Gospel

WHERE CHRIST HAD NOT BEEN NAMED. AMBROSIASTER: It was not without reason that Paul says that he tried to preach in places where Christ had not been named. For he knew that false apostles went about sharing Christ in ways which were wrong in order to ensnare the people by some other teaching under the name of Christ, which was then very difficult to put right afterward.[30] Therefore he wanted to get there first, in order to preach the right message. COMMENTARY ON PAUL'S EPISTLES.[31]

DIODORE: Paul was not trying to avoid the other apostles, but he thought it was wrong and unfair to steal the credit for what someone else had done. PAULINE COMMENTARY FROM THE GREEK CHURCH.[32]

LEST I BUILD UPON ANOTHER MAN'S FOUN-

DATION. CHRYSOSTOM: Paul was preeminent in this also, in that he did not go to places where the gospel had already been preached. So far was he from forcing himself upon other men's disciples that he even went to places where nobody had preached before.... He wrote all this to show that he was a stranger to vanity and to instruct them that it was not from any love of glory or of honor from them that he came to write but in order to fulfill his ministry, perfect his priestly service and love their salvation. HOMILIES ON ROMANS 29.[33]

PELAGIUS: A man who builds on someone else's foundation is not doing anything wrong, as long as he builds with gold and such.[34] Here Paul is referring to those false apostles who always went to converts and never to the Gentiles because they could not work miracles. Paul also shows that he had done a good job, for he both laid the foundation and also built on top of it. PELAGIUS'S COMMENTARY ON ROMANS.[35]

WHY HE HAD NOT VISITED ROME. GENNADIUS OF CONSTANTINOPLE: The explanation as to why Paul had not yet managed to visit the Romans seems to be that he believed that Peter had already come to them as their teacher, so he went to places where as yet no one had preached the gospel of Christ. PAULINE COMMENTARY FROM THE GREEK CHURCH.[36]

15:21 Those Who Have Never Been Told

THOSE WHO HAVE NEVER HEARD. AMBROSIASTER: Paul says that he was always quick to fill the Gentiles with the truth of the gospel, so that their understanding of the true Son of God might be correct and unshakable. COMMENTARY ON PAUL'S EPISTLES.[37]

---

[26]NPNF 1 11:54. [27]ENPK 2:90. [28]PCR 148. [29]IER, Migne PG 82 col. 213. [30]See 2 Cor 11:12-15. [31]CSEL 81.1:467-69. [32]NTA 15:111. [33]NPNF 1 11:544. [34]See 1 Cor 3:12. [35]PCR 148. [36]NTA 15:416. [37]CSEL 81.1:469.

NOTE WHERE PAUL GOES. CHRYSOSTOM: You see how Paul goes to where the labor is more and the toil greater. HOMILIES ON ROMANS 29.[38]

PELAGIUS: Paul shows that his work was foretold. Christ was made manifest in the apostles through the miracles which they performed in his name.[39] PELAGIUS'S COMMENTARY ON ROMANS.[40]

15:22 Hindered from Coming to Rome

WHY HINDERED. ORIGEN: Paul was not hindered by Satan, as some think, but by the fact that he was too busy planting churches in places where nobody had ever preached the gospel before. COMMENTARY ON THE EPISTLE TO THE ROMANS.[41]

WHY POSTPONED. AMBROSIASTER: Here Paul explains what he has already mentioned at the beginning of the epistle[42] and excuses himself by saying that although he wanted to come to them, he was obliged to shut out the wicked teachings of the false apostles.... These false apostles would have found the journey to Rome difficult, so Paul thought that it would do no harm if he postponed his visit for a while. COMMENTARY ON PAUL'S EPISTLES.[43]

RETURN TO HIS BEGINNING THEME. CHRYSOSTOM: At the end of his epistle he returns to what he said at the beginning.[44] HOMILIES ON ROMANS 29.[45]

---

[38]NPNF 1 11:544. [39]See Acts 4:7-10. [40]PCR 148. [41]CER 5:220-22. [42]Rom 1:13. [43]CSEL 81.1:469-71. [44]See Rom 1:13. [45]NPNF 1 11:544.

15:23-33 PAUL'S FUTURE PLANS

[23]*But now, since I no longer have any room for work in these regions, and since I have longed for many years to come to you,* [24]*I hope to see you in passing as I go to Spain, and to be sped on my journey there by you, once I have enjoyed your company for a little.* [25]*At present, however, I am going to Jerusalem with aid for the saints.* [26]*For Macedonia and Achaia have been pleased to make some contribution for the poor among the saints at Jerusalem;* [27]*they were pleased to do it, and indeed they are in debt to them, for if the Gentiles have come to share in their spiritual blessings, they ought also to be of service to them in material blessings.* [28]*When therefore I have completed this, and have delivered to them what has been raised,*ˣ *I shall go on by way of you to Spain;* [29]*and I know that when I come to you I shall come in the fulness of the blessing*ʸ *of Christ.*

[30]*I appeal to you, brethren, by our Lord Jesus Christ and by the love of the Spirit, to strive together with me in your prayers to God on my behalf,* [31]*that I may be delivered from the unbelievers in Judea, and that my service for Jerusalem may be acceptable to the saints,* [32]*so that by God's will I may come to you with joy and be refreshed in your company.* [33]*The God of peace be with you all. Amen.*

x Greek *sealed to them this fruit*   y Other ancient authorities insert *of the gospel*

Overview: Paul did not mean to suggest that he was only going to drop in on the Romans in passing, for he had longed to see them. Though delayed, he looked forward to being refreshed in their company. Paul first had to go to Jerusalem with aid for the saints, and he wanted the Romans to understand the importance of this. The Greeks had been generous in their almsgiving. The Fathers suggested that Paul was trying to spur the Romans to a similar effort. In any case, we know that when Paul got to Jerusalem he was arrested and was eventually sent to Rome to plead his case before Caesar. So he got his wish in the end, if not quite in the way he had originally intended.

15:23 Longing to Visit the Romans

No Room for Work in These Regions. Origen: "These regions" refer to Achaia, where Paul then was, and to the neighboring Macedonia, where he had been the first to preach the gospel.[1] Commentary on the Epistle to the Romans.[2]

I Have Longed for Many Years to Come. Chrysostom: He wrote to say he was coming to them but not because he wanted any glory from them. He was coming because he had . . . always wanted to visit them. Homilies on Romans 29.[3]

Pelagius: Where all the people have already heard the gospel, Paul has no reason for laying a foundation.[4] Observe from this that there are some desires which are good! Pelagius's Commentary on Romans.[5]

15:24 Go On by Way of You

I Hope to See You in Passing. Origen: This must not be understood to mean that Paul had so little love for the Romans that he was only going to drop in on them briefly while passing through on his way elsewhere. Look what he says [in the next few verses] and you will see that this cannot

be right. Commentary on the Epistle to the Romans.[6]

As I Go to Spain. Cyril of Jerusalem: Paul instructed imperial Rome and extended the zeal of his preaching even to Spain, sustaining countless conflicts and performing signs and wonders. Catechesis 17.26.[7]

Sped on My Journey. Chrysostom: Paul expresses himself in this way in order to keep the Romans from feeling proud. They were not used to being a mere stopover on a journey. Homilies on Romans 29.[8]

Once I Have Enjoyed Your Company for a Little. Pelagius: It is not certain whether Paul ever got to Spain. . . . The reason he says that he will enjoy their company "for a little" is that they did not need to come to faith but only to be strengthened in faith. Or it may mean that no amount of time can satisfy love. Pelagius's Commentary on Romans.[9]

15:25 Aiding the Saints in Jerusalem

With Aid for the Saints. Ambrosiaster: Paul wants the Romans to understand that they ought to be concerned with this sort of thing, for those who live because of mercy and who are justified before God ought to show their devotion to their brothers. Commentary on Paul's Epistles.[10]

Chrysostom: Paul explains his delay and in the process takes the opportunity to teach the Romans about the importance of almsgiving. Homilies on Romans 30.[11]

I Am Going to Jerusalem. Pelagius: In Jerusalem there were saints who had sold all their

---

[1]See Acts 16:9-10. [2]CER 5:222. [3]NPNF 1 11:545. [4]See 1 Cor 3:10. [5]PCR 148-49. [6]CER 5:222-24. [7]FC 64:112. [8]NPNF 1 11:545. [9]PCR 149. [10]CSEL 81.1:471. [11]NPNF 1 11:547.

possessions and laid them at the feet of the apostles,[12] devoting themselves to prayer, reading and teaching. It is clear from this text that their character was such that Paul is traveling in order to attend them in person, and he hopes that his offering will be received by them . . . thereby showing that it is more blessed to give than to receive.[13] PELAGIUS'S COMMENTARY ON ROMANS.[14]

15:26 Contributions for the Poor

CONTRIBUTIONS FOR THE POOR OF JERUSALEM. ORIGEN: Note how Paul subtly exhorts the Romans by praising the believers of Macedonia and Achaia. For if they could make some contribution, why could the Romans not do likewise? Most people think that Paul wanted the Romans to give to the same purpose as those of Macedonia and Achaia had done, but this interpretation seems to me to be too narrow. There were poor saints all over the place, and Paul wanted the Romans to develop a spirit of generosity toward them all. COMMENTARY ON THE EPISTLE TO THE ROMANS.[15]

PELAGIUS: They thought it would be good for them to make some collection for the expenses of the saints who had voluntarily become poor for their edification. PELAGIUS'S COMMENTARY ON ROMANS.[16]

REMEMBER THE POOR. THEODORET OF CYR: When St. Barnabas and St. Paul took on the task of preaching to the Gentiles, they made an agreement with Peter, James and John, promising them that they would encourage Gentile believers to come to the aid of believers in Judea. Paul mentions this in his epistle to the Galatians: "When they perceived the grace which was given to me, James and Cephas and John, who were reputed to be pillars, gave to me and Barnabas the right hand of fellowship, that we should go to the Gentiles and they to the circumcised; only they would have us remember the poor, which very thing I

was eager to do."[17] INTERPRETATION OF THE LETTER TO THE ROMANS.[18]

15:27 Sharing Spiritual and Material Blessings

SERVICE IN MATERIAL BLESSINGS. AMBROSIASTER: In this way the believers among the Jews would rejoice at God's providential saving of the Gentiles through their ministry. For these Gentiles, by giving themselves completely to the service of God and not caring at all about the things of this world, offered an example of good behavior to believers. Then too, the apostle wants us to be sympathetic and merciful so that we might feel obliged to give alms and to do good works with a willing heart, because whoever hopes for mercy from God must be merciful, in order to prove that he has some reason for his hope. For if a man is merciful, how much more is God! For this is the payment or reward, that those who receive mercy should be merciful. As the Lord said: "Blessed are the merciful, for God will be merciful to them."[19] COMMENTARY ON PAUL'S EPISTLES.[20]

THE GENTILES SHARE IN THEIR SPIRITUAL BLESSINGS. PELAGIUS: By example Paul incites the Romans to a similar effort, indicating that there was a good reason why it seemed good to them. The Gentiles had obtained teachers from the Jews and so . . . they ought to share their abundance with them.[21] PELAGIUS'S COMMENTARY ON ROMANS.[22]

15:28 Journeying to Spain

TO SPAIN. JEROME: Mark well the swiftness of the Word. It is not satisfied with the East but desires to speed to the West as well! HOMILIES ON THE PSALMS 57.[23]

---

[12]See Acts 4:34-35. [13]See Acts 20:35. [14]PCR 149. [15]CER 5:228-30. [16]PCR 149. [17]Gal 2:9-10. [18]IER, Migne PG 82 col. 216. [19]Mt 5:7. [20]CSEL 81.1:473. [21]See 2 Cor 8:14. [22]PCR 149-50. [23]FC 48:412.

15:29 Coming in the Fullness of Christ's Blessing

I Shall Come in the Fullness of the Blessing of Christ. Origen: What does Paul mean by this? I think he is talking here about the image of God, by which he means that there will be no admixture of any alien thought in the fulfilling of his task and no praise sought from men. He simply will offer all he has done to God in the simplicity of his heart. Commentary on the Epistle to the Romans.[24]

Ambrosiaster: "The fullness of the blessing" refers to the miracles through which the blessing is confirmed. Commentary on Paul's Epistles.[25]

Chrysostom: Paul is speaking here either about alms or about good deeds. For *blessing* is a name he very commonly gives to alms. Homilies on Romans 30.[26]

[Pseudo-]Constantius: The apostle would be taken to Rome in chains because of his preaching of Christ. He predicts that he will come in the fullness of blessing, as he was certainly aware that he did not have any less grace than the other apostles. The Holy Letter of St. Paul to the Romans.[27]

Pelagius: If the Romans behave well, Paul will be full of good teaching for them, for the teacher is incited to teach to the extent that the student shows progress. Pelagius's Commentary on Romans.[28]

15:30 Praying on Paul's Behalf

Strive Together with Me in Your Prayers. Ambrosiaster: Paul asks for their prayers . . . not because he deserves them but because he is following the principle that the church ought to pray for its pastor. For when many ordinary people come together and agree they become great, and the prayers of many can-

not be ignored.[29] Therefore, if the Romans want to see the apostle, let them pray earnestly that he may be set free so that they may receive him in the joy of brotherly love. Commentary on Paul's Epistles.[30]

The Love of the Spirit. Chrysostom: Here Paul mentions Christ and the Spirit but not the Father. I say this so that when you find him mentioning the Father and the Son or just the Father you will not devalue either the Son or the Spirit on that account. Note that he does not just say the Spirit but "the love of the Spirit," for the Spirit loves the world just as Christ and the Father do also. Homilies on Romans 30.[31]

When Many Pray. Pelagius: Paul asks the whole church to pray for him, because he knows that when many people pray together their prayers have great effect. When James was killed, Peter was set free from prison by the prayers of the brethren, who prayed not so much for his good as for their own, so that they could be strengthened by his teaching.[32] Spiritual love leads us to pray for one another. Pelagius's Commentary on Romans.[33]

15:31 Deliverance and Service

A Great Struggle Ahead. Chrysostom: Paul knew that a great struggle was about to befall him, and this was another reason why he asked for their prayers. Homilies on Romans 30.[34]

That I May Be Delivered from Unbelievers. Pelagius: Paul says this either so that they may all believe or else so that he may not fall into the hands of unbelievers while he is trying to serve believers, with the result that it would be

---

[24]CER 5:236. [25]CSEL 81.1:475. [26]NPNF 1 11:548. [27]ENPK 2:90. [28]PCR 150. [29]See 2 Chron 7:14; Mt 18:19. [30]CSEL 81.1:475. [31]NPNF 1 11:549. [32]See Acts 12:2-10. [33]PCR 150. [34]NPNF 1 11:549.

impossible for him to come to them. PELAGIUS'S COMMENTARY ON ROMANS.[35]

15:32 Joy and Refreshing

DELIVERING GOD'S GIFTS. AMBROSIASTER: Because Paul's mind is dedicated to delivering the gifts, he wants their mind to respond to him by the judgment of God so that, having understood his love for them, they might with one accord give thanks to God on his behalf. For he was a great blessing to them, in that by his ministry many were made happy and are now praising God. COMMENTARY ON PAUL'S EPISTLES.[36]

THAT I MAY BE REFRESHED IN YOUR COMPANY. CHRYSOSTOM: Note again Paul's humility. He does not say that he wants to come in order to teach them but in order that he may be refreshed by them! HOMILIES ON ROMANS 30.[37]

THAT I MAY COME TO YOU WITH JOY. PELAGIUS: Paul will come to Rome in joy if his offering is accepted at Jerusalem and will then speak the Word of God with peace of mind. . . . For heaviness of heart is a great hindrance to teaching. PELAGIUS'S COMMENTARY ON ROMANS.[38]

THEODORET OF CYR: Paul has no desire to do the right thing apart from God's will. INTERPRETATION OF THE LETTER TO THE ROMANS.[39]

15:33 The God of Peace

LIVING PEACEFULLY IN THE TRUTH. AMBROSIASTER: The God of peace is Christ, who said: "My peace I give to you, my peace I leave with you."[40] This is what he prays for them, knowing that the Lord said: "Behold I am with you always, even to the end of the world."[41] Paul therefore wants them to be the kind of people in whom the Lord Jesus Christ dwells, who has shown them that all the discord caused by human sin has been taken away and who has given them what is true, that they may live peacefully in that truth. COMMENTARY ON PAUL'S EPISTLES.[42]

CALLED TO PEACEFUL AGREEMENT. PELAGIUS: The God of peace dwells only in those who are peaceable. It is good that he has concluded with peace, because the two parties are here called back to peaceful agreement with each other. PELAGIUS'S COMMENTARY ON ROMANS.[43]

OVERCOMING SUSPICION. THEODORET OF CYR: Paul called God the "God of peace" here for a reason, because he was concerned about those at Rome who were battling one another or at least who were suspicious of one another. He wanted them to be at peace with each other because of the controversy which they were having over the observance of the law. INTERPRETATION OF THE LETTER TO THE ROMANS.[44]

---

[35]PCR 150. [36]CSEL 81.1:475. [37]NPNF 1 11:549. [38]PCR 150. [39]IER, Migne PG 82 col. 217. [40]Jn 14:27. [41]Mt 28:20. [42]CSEL 81.1:477. [43]PCR 150. [44]IER, Migne PG 82 col. 217.

16:1-16 PAUL'S PERSONAL GREETINGS

[1]I commend to you our sister Phoebe, a deaconess of the church at Cenchreae, [2]that you may receive her in the Lord as befits the saints, and help her in whatever she may require from you, for

she has been a helper of many and of myself as well.

³*Greet Prisca and Aquila, my fellow workers in Christ Jesus,* ⁴*who risked their necks for my life, to whom not only I but also all the churches of the Gentiles give thanks;* ⁵*greet also the church in their house. Greet my beloved Epaenetus, who was the first convert in Asia for Christ.* ⁶*Greet Mary, who has worked hard among you.* ⁷*Greet Andronicus and Junias, my kinsmen and my fellow prisoners; they are men of note among the apostles, and they were in Christ before me.* ⁸*Greet Ampliatus, my beloved in the Lord.* ⁹*Greet Urbanus, our fellow worker in Christ, and my beloved Stachys.* ¹⁰*Greet Apelles, who is approved in Christ. Greet those who belong to the family of Aristobulus.* ¹¹*Greet my kinsman Herodion. Greet those in the Lord who belong to the family of Narcissus.* ¹²*Greet those workers in the Lord, Tryphaena and Tryphosa. Greet the beloved Persis, who has worked hard in the Lord.* ¹³*Greet Rufus, eminent in the Lord, also his mother and mine.* ¹⁴*Greet Asyncritus, Phlegon, Hermes, Patrobas, Hermas, and the brethren who are with them.* ¹⁵*Greet Philologus, Julia, Nereus and his sister, and Olympas, and all the saints who are with them.* ¹⁶*Greet one another with a holy kiss. All the churches of Christ greet you.*

OVERVIEW: The Fathers made much of Phoebe and of the other women mentioned in Romans 16, because their names proved that there were women in the ministry in the first generation. By the fourth century that was becoming very rare, though it persisted in parts of the East longer than it did in the West. Priscilla and Aquila were well-known New Testament figures and old companions of Paul. There was and is disagreement over the name Junia(s). Most of the Fathers took it as masculine, but Chrysostom believed it referred to a woman who was so deeply respected that she was even counted among the apostles, thoughnot ofcourse as one of the Twelve. The precise identity of most of the names in this list was as uncertain to the Fathers as it is to us. It is obvious that they were guessing most of the time! Chrysostom's comment on the last chapter of Romans speaks volumes. The holy kiss was no longer a standard form of greeting by the fourth century, and it evidently caused the Fathers some embarrassment. Nevertheless, they were quite clear that its purpose was a spiritual one and warned Christians against taking liberties under the guise of obeying the apostle's instructions.

DO NOT RUSH THROUGH THIS GOLD MINE.

CHRYSOSTOM: I think there are many, even some apparently good commentators, who hurry over this part of the epistle because they think it is superfluous and of little importance. They probably think much the same about the genealogies in the Gospels. Because it is a catalog of names, they think they can get nothing good out of it. People who mine gold are careful even about the smallest fragments, but these commentators ignore even huge bars of gold! HOMILIES ON ROMANS 30.[1]

16:1 *Phoebe, a Deaconess*

WHETHER WOMEN WERE ORDAINED BY APOSTOLIC AUTHORITY. ORIGEN: This passage teaches that there were women ordained in the church's ministry by the apostle's authority. . . . Not only that—they ought to be ordained into the ministry, because they helped in many ways and by their good services deserved the praise even of the apostle. COMMENTARY ON THE EPISTLE TO THE ROMANS.[2]

PHOEBE'S RANK OF DEACONESS. CHRYSOSTOM: Note how many ways Paul dignifies

---

[1]NPNF 1 11:549-50. [2]CER 5:242-44.

Phoebe. He mentions her before all the rest and even calls her his sister. It is no small thing to be called the sister of Paul! Moreover, he has mentioned her rank of deaconess as well. HOMILIES ON ROMANS 30.[3]

NO DISCRIMINATION TOLERATED BETWEEN MALE AND FEMALE. [PSEUDO-]CONSTANTIUS: Here the apostle demonstrates that no discrimination or preference between male and female is to be tolerated, because he sends his letter to Rome by the hand of a woman and sends greetings to other women in the same epistle. Cenchreae is the port of Corinth. THE HOLY LETTER OF ST. PAUL TO THE ROMANS.[4]

WOMEN DEACONESSES IN THE EAST. PELAGIUS: Although the text of the letter is already finished, as it were, Paul has attached this material for the purpose of commendation and greeting, as was his custom.

Even today, women deaconesses in the East are known to minister to their own sex in baptism or even in the ministry of the Word, for we find that women taught privately, e.g., Priscilla, whose husband was called Aquila.[5] PELAGIUS'S COMMENTARY ON ROMANS.[6]

AT CENCHREAE. THEODORET OF CYR: Cenchreae is a village outside Corinth. It is interesting to note how quickly the gospel was spreading, in that it had already reached the villages. In fact the church at Cenchreae was so large that it even had a woman deaconess, and one who was famous and well known to boot. INTERPRETATION OF THE LETTER TO THE ROMANS.[7]

16:2 A Helper of Many

PHOEBE'S HELPFULNESS. ORIGEN: Paul commands that those who dedicate themselves to good works ought to be received by their brethren and be held in honor by being provided with whatever they might need. COMMENTARY ON THE EPISTLE TO THE ROMANS.[8]

THAT YOU MAY RECEIVE HER. AMBROSIASTER: Paul praises Phoebe as highly as he does because the more she appears to be an excellent person in the sight of others, the more she will receive the help owed to her in love. COMMENTARY ON PAUL'S EPISTLES.[9]

HER SAINTLINESS. CHRYSOSTOM: There are two reasons why Phoebe should be received by them. First, she has been received by the Lord, and second, she is herself a saint. HOMILIES ON ROMANS 30.[10]

HER SUPPORTIVENESS. PELAGIUS: Help her with expenses or support, says Paul, because she also helped many people as long as she had the means. PELAGIUS'S COMMENTARY ON ROMANS.[11]

HER HOSPITALITY. THEODORET OF CYR: It is probable that Phoebe helped Paul by offering him hospitality in her house at Corinth for the short time that he was there.[12] In return Paul opened the whole world to her, and throughout the Mediterranean she became a famous woman. INTERPRETATION OF THE LETTER TO THE ROMANS.[13]

16:3 Prisca and Aquila, Fellow Workers

PRISCA AND AQUILA. ORIGEN: It may be that these two, after having been expelled from Rome by the decree of Caesar and having come to Corinth, returned to Rome once the severity of the decree was relaxed. COMMENTARY ON THE EPISTLE TO THE ROMANS.[14]

COWORKERS WITH THE APOSTLE. AMBROSIASTER: These were Jews who, after they believed, became coworkers with the apostle because they had believed correctly and were thus able to persuade others to accept the right faith. Apollos, for

---

[3]NPNF 1 11:549-50. [4]ENPK 2:91. [5]See Acts 18:1-3, 24-26. [6]PCR 150-51. [7]IER, Migne PG 82 col. 218-20. [8]CER 5:244. [9]CSEL 81.1:477. [10]NPNF 1 11:550. [11]PCR 151. [12]Acts 18:18. [13]IER, Migne PG 82 col. 220. [14]CER 5:244-46.

example, although he was learned in the Scriptures, was nevertheless taught the way of the Lord more correctly by them. This is why Paul calls them his fellow workers "in Christ Jesus." COMMENTARY ON PAUL'S EPISTLES.[15]

LUKE'S TESTIMONY. CHRYSOSTOM: Luke also bears witness to them when he says that Paul dwelt with them[16] and that Priscilla [Prisca] had received Apollos and instructed him in the way of the Lord.[17] HOMILIES ON ROMANS 30.[18]

PELAGIUS: They are said to have established Apollos in the faith.[19] Paul calls them helpers because they helped him in his work of instruction.[20] PELAGIUS'S COMMENTARY ON ROMANS.[21]

FELLOW EVANGELISTS. THEODORET OF CYR: Paul adds "in Christ Jesus" to show that Prisca (or Priscilla; both forms are found in the manuscripts) and Aquila were not merely Paul's hosts but that they were fellow evangelists as well. INTERPRETATION OF THE LETTER TO THE ROMANS.[22]

16:4 Paul and the Churches Give Thanks for Them

THE MINISTRY OF HOSPITALITY. ORIGEN: This shows that Priscilla and Aquila were hospitable to Gentiles as well as to Jews. Hospitality is highly esteemed both by God and by man. COMMENTARY ON THE EPISTLE TO THE ROMANS.[23]

VIRTUOUS WOMEN NOT HINDERED BY THEIR SEX. CHRYSOSTOM: Here Paul hints at their hospitality and financial assistance, holding them in admiration because they had both poured forth their blood and had made their whole property available to everybody. Notice how noble were the women Paul named. They were in no way hindered by their sex from following the path of virtue, and this is only to be expected. "For in Christ Jesus there is neither male nor female."[24] HOMILIES ON ROMANS 30.[25]

THEY RISKED THEIR NECKS FOR MY LIFE. PELAGIUS: By supporting Paul's teaching, they exposed themselves to danger. Therefore all the churches thank them, for Paul was kept from harm by them. PELAGIUS'S COMMENTARY ON ROMANS.[26]

16:5 A House Church and a Notable Convert

THE FIRST CONVERT IN ASIA. AMBROSIASTER: Paul mentions Epaenetus's claim to fame, in order to show that important people believe and turn to the faith and in order to invite the leaders of the Romans to accept Christ, and if they have already done so, to become humble. COMMENTARY ON PAUL'S EPISTLES.[27]

THEIR HOUSE HAS BECOME A CHURCH. CHRYSOSTOM: Priscilla was noble enough to make their house a church, both by converting everyone in it and by opening it to strangers. Paul did not normally call houses churches, except when there was much godliness in them. . . . For even married people may become worthy of esteem and noble. These were married and became very honorable, even though their profession was that of tentmaker, which is far from honorable in itself.

Note how Paul calls Epaenetus "beloved," which is high praise indeed. For Paul did not use a word like this to show favoritism; rather, it was the result of calm, cool reflection. Moreover, he was the first convert in Achaea, either in time or in quality. . . . Given that it was likely that all these people were of humble birth, Paul shows what true nobility is and honors them accordingly. HOMILIES ON ROMANS 31.[28]

HOW THE ROMANS LEARNED FROM FOREIGNERS. PELAGIUS: Paul shows that a gathering of

---

[15]CSEL 81.1:479. [16]Acts 18:1-3. [17]Acts 18:26. [18]NPNF 1 11:550. [19]See Acts 18:24-26. [20]See Acts 18:19, 26. [21]PCR 151. [22]IER, Migne PG 82 col. 220. [23]CER 5:246. [24]Gal 3:28. [25]NPNF 1 11:550. [26]PCR 151. [27]CSEL 81.1:479-81. [28]NPNF 1 11:550-51.

believers is called a "church." Epaenetus was the firstborn of the church in Asia Minor. We learn from their names that all the people Paul greets were foreigners, and it is not unreasonable to suppose that the Romans came to faith through their example and teaching. PELAGIUS'S COMMENTARY ON ROMANS.[29]

THEODORET OF CYR: Evidently Prisca and Aquila had preached the gospel to their servants and converted them to the Lord. St. Luke mentions them [in Acts 18:24-28] and shows how they led Apollos to the truth. INTERPRETATION OF THE LETTER TO THE ROMANS.[30]

16:6 Mary, a Hard Worker

THE CONTRIBUTION OF WOMEN TO THE EMERGING CHURCH. ORIGEN: Paul is teaching here that women too ought to work for the churches of God. They work when they teach children how to behave, when they love their husbands, when they feed their children, when they are modest and chaste, when they keep a good household, when they are kind, when they are submissive to their husbands, when they exercise hospitality, when they wash the feet of the saints, and when they do all the other things which are allotted to women in the Bible. COMMENTARY ON THE EPISTLE TO THE ROMANS.[31]

MEN ARE PUT TO SHAME BY SUCH WOMEN AS THESE. CHRYSOSTOM: How can it be that yet another woman is honored and proclaimed victorious! We men are put to shame yet again. Or rather, we are not merely put to shame; we have a different honor conferred on us. For it is an honor to have such women as these among us, though we are put to shame in that we are left so far behind them. But if we come to know why they are so honored, we shall quickly overtake them.

What does Paul mean when he says that he does not permit a woman to teach?[32] He means to prevent a woman from coming forward publicly and preaching in the pulpit; he does not stop

them from teaching altogether. If this were the case . . . how would Priscilla have come to instruct Apollos? . . .

Mary worked hard among them, because along with teaching she performed other ministries besides. . . . The women of those days were more spirited than lions, sharing with the apostles their labors for the gospel's sake. HOMILIES ON ROMANS 31.[33]

YET ANOTHER WOMAN PRAISED. THEODORET OF CYR: Yet another woman who is praised because of her labors. INTERPRETATION OF THE LETTER TO THE ROMANS.[34]

16:7 Kinsmen and Fellow Prisoners

FELLOW PRISONERS. ORIGEN: It may be that these were Paul's kinsmen according to the flesh, but the expression "my fellow prisoners" is what fascinates me. When was Paul in captivity? It seems that this was the captivity of sin and that they were together with him in the blindness of unbelief. When Christ came they were set free, as was Paul. COMMENTARY ON THE EPISTLE TO THE ROMANS.[35]

PAUL'S KINSMEN. AMBROSIASTER: They were Paul's kinsmen in flesh and in Spirit, as the angel said to Mary: "Behold, your kinswoman Elizabeth."[36] COMMENTARY ON PAUL'S EPISTLES.[37]

A WOMAN WORTHY TO BE CALLED AN APOSTLE. CHRYSOSTOM: It was the greatest of honors to be counted a fellow prisoner of Paul's. . . . Think what great praise it was to be considered of note among the apostles. These two were of note because of their works and achievements. Think how great the devotion of this woman Junia must have been, that she should be worthy to be called an apostle! But even here Paul does

---

[29]PCR 151. [30]IER, Migne PG 82 col. 220. [31]CER 5:248. [32]1 Tim 2:12. [33]NPNF 1 11:554. [34]IER, Migne PG 82 col. 220. [35]CER 5:248-50. [36]Lk 1:36. [37]CSEL 81.1:481.

not stop his praise, for they were Christians before he was. Homilies on Romans 31.[38]

They Were in Christ Before Me. Theodoret of Cyr: Yet more praises. These people were companions of Paul in his sufferings and even shared imprisonment with him. Hence he says that they are men and women of note, not among the pupils but among the teachers, and not among the ordinary teachers but among the apostles. He even praises them for having been Christians before him. Interpretation of the Letter to the Romans.[39]

16:8 A Friend in the Lord

My Beloved in the Lord. Ambrosiaster: Paul greets him as a friend but as a friend in the Lord, because he had not shared Paul's work or his imprisonment. Commentary on Paul's Epistles.[40]

Greet Ampliatus. Chrysostom: Think what an honor it was to be loved by the apostle Paul. If Ampliatus had not been worthy of this, he would not have attracted Paul's love. Homilies on Romans 31.[41]

Theodoret of Cyr: This is no small praise, for Paul says that he is "beloved in the Lord," because he behaved uprightly and honestly. Interpretation of the Letter to the Romans.[42]

16:9 Beloved Fellow Workers

My Beloved Stachys. Chrysostom: Urbanus is praised more highly than Ampliatus, and Stachys receives a similar honor. Homilies on Romans 31.[43]

Greet Urbanus. Theodoret of Cyr: Paul praises Urbanus more highly than Stachys, because Urbanus had helped him in his preaching and in his struggles. Interpretation of the Letter to the Romans.[44]

16:10 A Friend Approved in Christ

The Family of Aristobulus. Origen: Paul does not say that those of the family of Aristobulus were beloved, or approved, or fellow workers in Christ. Perhaps they were not any of these things, and so he honors them only with a simple greeting. Commentary on the Epistle to the Romans.[45]

Greet Apelles. Ambrosiaster: Paul does not greet Apelles as a friend or fellow worker, but because he has been tried in temptations and found to be faithful to Christ. Aristobulus is to be understood as having assembled the brethren in Christ. Paul approves of this so much that he regards those whom he has gathered together to be worthy of greeting as well. Commentary on Paul's Epistles.[46]

Approved in Christ. Chrysostom: There is no praise like this, for the words "approved in Christ" include the whole list of virtues. . . . By setting out the praises particular to each, he sets before us their individual virtues. He does not excite envy by honoring one and not the other, but neither does he cater to cynicism by praising them all in exactly the same way. Homilies on Romans 31.[47]

Theodoret of Cyr: Paul bears witness to the great virtue of Apelles; there was nothing corrupt in him. Interpretation of the Letter to the Romans.[48]

16:11 Greeting Those in the Lord

The Family of Narcissus. Origen: Narcissus had a large family, but they were not all Christians, which is why Paul singles out "those

---

[38]NPNF 1 11:554-55. [39]IER, Migne PG 82 col. 220. [40]CSEL 81.1:481. [41]NPNF 1 11:555. [42]IER, Migne PG 82 col. 221. [43]NPNF 1 11:555. [44]IER, Migne PG 82 col. 221. [45]CER 5:252. [46]CSEL 81.1:483. [47]NPNF 1 11:555. [48]IER, Migne PG 82 col. 221.

in the Lord." COMMENTARY ON THE EPISTLE TO THE ROMANS.[49]

GREET THOSE IN THE LORD. AMBROSIASTER: When Paul calls Herodion his kinsman and nothing more, he shows that he was faithful in the love of the new birth, but he does not mention his perseverance. Narcissus is said to have been a presbyter of the time, and this is what we find in other manuscripts.... This presbyter Narcissus went about encouraging believers by his preaching. And since Paul did not know what the merits were of those who had been with him, he asks the Romans to greet those of his household who had put their trust in the Lord and who were therefore worthy of his greeting. COMMENTARY ON PAUL'S EPISTLES.[50]

THEODORET OF CYR: Paul seems to be implying that there were others in the family of Narcissus who did not yet believe. INTERPRETATION OF THE LETTER TO THE ROMANS.[51]

16:12 Workers in the Lord

GREET THE BELOVED PERSIS, WHO WORKED HARD IN THE LORD. AMBROSIASTER: Persis appears to be more honored than the other two, because she has worked hard in the Lord. This work is one of encouragement and of service to the saints for Christ's sake when they are under pressure and in need, because they had fled their homes and were being attacked by unbelievers. COMMENTARY ON PAUL'S EPISTLES.[52]

GREET THOSE WORKERS IN THE LORD. THEODORET OF CYR: Once more, praise for work which has been done. This presumably refers to hospitality, or fasting, or some other good work of that kind. INTERPRETATION OF THE LETTER TO THE ROMANS.[53]

16:13 Believers Eminent in the Lord

GREET RUFUS. AMBROSIASTER: For he [Rufus]

was chosen, that is, promoted by the Lord to do his work. Nevertheless he had such a holy mother that the apostle calls her his mother also. COMMENTARY ON PAUL'S EPISTLES.[54]

BELIEVERS BEFORE PAUL. PELAGIUS: These were Jews, and because they had suffered tribulation along with Paul but like him they had not been intimidated, they are deservedly held in esteem. Among others, they had been sent to further the progress of the Romans, and according to the testimony of Paul himself they are reported to have been believers before him. PELAGIUS'S COMMENTARY ON ROMANS.[55]

HIS MOTHER BY GRACE. THEODORET OF CYR: The mother of Rufus by nature had become Paul's mother by grace. INTERPRETATION OF THE LETTER TO THE ROMANS.[56]

16:14 Greetings for Other Believers

GREET HERMAS. ORIGEN: I think this Hermas was the author of the book called *The Shepherd of Hermas*, which seems to me to be a useful book and one which was inspired by God. I think the reason Paul does not praise him is that he himself tells us in his book that he was converted only after many sins. Scripture tells us not to rush to honor someone who has just repented from sin nor to give him praise as long as the angel of repentance is still over him. COMMENTARY ON THE EPISTLE TO THE ROMANS.[57]

THE BRETHREN WHO ARE WITH THEM. AMBROSIASTER: Paul greets these together because he knew that they agreed with one another in Christ and were loyal friends. He also greets the brethren who were with them but omits their names. COMMENTARY ON PAUL'S EPISTLES.[58]

---

[50]CSEL 81.1:483. [51]*IER*, Migne PG 82 col. 221. [52]CSEL 81.1:485. [53]*IER*, Migne PG 82 col. 221. [54]CSEL 81.1:485. [55]PCR 152. [56]*IER*, Migne PG 82 col. 221. [57]CER 5:256-58. [58]CSEL 81.1:485.

THEODORET OF CYR: This was another family of believers whom Paul thought worthy of praise. INTERPRETATION OF THE LETTER TO THE ROMANS.[59]

16:15 A Group of Saints

A HOUSEHOLD? ORIGEN: It is possible that Philologus and Julia were married and that the others named here were their domestic servants. COMMENTARY ON THE EPISTLE TO THE ROMANS.[60]

ALL THE SAINTS. AMBROSIASTER: These are understood to have been of one mind because it was for that reason that Paul greeted them together. COMMENTARY ON PAUL'S EPISTLES.[61]

FRIENDS RICH IN GRACE. PELAGIUS: By his example Paul teaches us what sort of friends we should greet in our letters, not those who are rich in worldly goods or honored with positions of rank but those who are well supplied in grace and faith. PELAGIUS'S COMMENTARY ON ROMANS.[62]

16:16 Greeting with a Holy Kiss

HOLY KISSING, NOT SHAMELESS. CLEMENT OF ALEXANDRIA: If we are called to the kingdom of God, let us walk worthy of the kingdom, loving God and our neighbor. Love is not proved by a kiss but by kindly feeling. But there are those who do nothing but make the church resound with a kiss, not having love itself inside them. For this very thing, the shameless use of a kiss, which ought to be mystic, occasions foul suspicions and evil reports. The apostle, however, calls the kiss holy. CHRIST THE EDUCATOR 3.11.[63]

TERTULLIAN: What prayer is complete if it is divorced from the holy kiss? ON PRAYER 18.[64]

SPEAKING ON BEHALF OF ALL THE CHURCHES. ORIGEN: From this and other statements like it, it appears that it was the custom to greet one another with a kiss after the prayers. The apostle calls this a holy kiss. How could Paul write that all the churches sent greetings, when he was only in one of them at the time? I think we have to understand this to mean that there was one spirit common to Paul and to all the churches, so that he could speak on behalf of them all. COMMENTARY ON THE EPISTLE TO THE ROMANS.[65]

ALL THE CHURCHES OF CHRIST GREET YOU. AMBROSIASTER: Paul asks that all those to whom he has written and whom he names be greeted with a holy kiss, that is, in the peace of Christ, not in the desire of the flesh, because these kisses are spiritual, not physical.

By saying "churches of Christ" Paul is saying that there is a church which is not Christ's. For David called the company of evildoers an assembly of the wicked.[66] COMMENTARY ON PAUL'S EPISTLES.[67]

KISS AS A SYMBOL OF EQUALITY BEFORE GOD. CHRYSOSTOM: By this salutation Paul intended to cast out of them any reason for pride. The great were not to despise the small, nor were the small to envy the great, but pride and envy were to be banished by the kiss, which made everyone equal. Therefore, he not only asks them to greet each other in this way, but he also sends them this greeting from the other churches. HOMILIES ON ROMANS 31.[68]

THE KISS OF JUDAS AND THE KISS OF PEACE. PELAGIUS: Not with a false and treacherous kiss, of the sort with which Judas betrayed the Savior.[69] For in the church the peace is proclaimed first, so that we may show that we are at peace with all who are about to partake of the body of Christ.[70] PELAGIUS'S COMMENTARY ON ROMANS.[71]

---

[59]IER, Migne PG 82 col. 221. [60]CER 5:258. [61]CSEL 81.1:487. [62]PCR 152. [63]ANF 2:291. [64]ANF 3:686. [65]CER 5:258. [66]See Ps 26:5. [67]CSEL 81.1:487. [68]NPNF 1 11:556. [69]See Mt 26:49; Mk 14:45. [70]1 Cor 10:16. [71]PCR 152.

16:17-27 PARTING ADVICE AND BLESSING

[17]*I appeal to you, brethren, to take note of those who create dissensions and difficulties, in opposition to the doctrine which you have been taught; avoid them.* [18]*For such persons do not serve our Lord Christ, but their own appetites,[z] and by fair and flattering words they deceive the hearts of the simple-minded.* [19]*For while your obedience is known to all, so that I rejoice over you, I would have you wise as to what is good and guileless as to what is evil;* [20]*then the God of peace will soon crush Satan under your feet. The grace of our Lord Jesus Christ be with you.[a]*

[21]*Timothy, my fellow worker, greets you; so do Lucius and Jason and Sosipater, my kinsmen.*

[22]*I Tertius, the writer of this letter, greet you in the Lord.*

[23]*Gaius, who is host to me and to the whole church, greets you. Erastus, the city treasurer, and our brother Quartus, greet you.[b]*

[25]*Now to him who is able to strengthen you according to my gospel and the preaching of Jesus Christ, according to the revelation of the mystery which was kept secret for long ages* [26]*but is now disclosed and through the prophetic writings is made known to all nations, according to the command of the eternal God, to bring about the obedience of faith—*[27]*to the only wise God be glory for evermore through Jesus Christ! Amen.*

z Greek *their own belly* (Phil 3.19)   a Other ancient authorities omit this sentence   b Other ancient authorities insert verse 24, *The grace of our Lord Jesus Christ be with you all. Amen.*

OVERVIEW: Troublemakers in the church were to be shunned. The Fathers described who they were and approved of the apostle's policies toward them. They coat poison with honey. The faithful are called to be wise as to what is good and guileless as to what is evil. The Fathers attempted as best they could to identify Paul's companions and kinsmen. They were praised for their obedience and encouraged in their adversities. The mention of Gaius and Erastus links this letter to Corinth, where Paul was probably residing when he wrote this letter. That at least is the conclusion that both the Fathers and the majority of modern commentators have come to. Romans 16:24 is found in some manuscripts as the conclusion. The last verses of Romans were displaced in some Greek manuscripts and are found at the end of Romans 14. John Chrysostom and Theodoret of Cyr reflect this in their commentaries. The letter concludes with a spiritual blessing in which the faithful are assured that Paul's gospel is based on the preaching of Jesus Christ.

16:17 *Avoid People Who Create Dissension*

AVOID JUDAIZING TEACHERS. AMBROSIASTER: Now Paul goes on to mention the false apostles, whom he warns against throughout the epistle just as he does here as well. But he attacks their teaching without saying what it is. They were forcing believers to become Jews and thereby making the benefits of God worthless.... They compiled long genealogies and used them to support their teaching, by which they were deceiving the hearts of the simple. COMMENTARY ON PAUL'S EPISTLES.[1]

---

[1]CSEL 81.1:489.

The Sources of Division. Chrysostom: Division is the subversion of the church. Turning things upside down like this is the devil's weapon. As long as the body is united he has no way of getting in, but harm comes from division. And where does division come from? From doctrines which are contrary to the teaching of the apostles. Homilies on Romans 32.[2]

Augustine: Paul is here discussing the same people he wrote about to Timothy[3] and to Titus.[4] See also Philippians [3:19]. Augustine on Romans 84.[5]

Theodoret of Cyr: The people Paul is referring to here were men who defended the law. Interpretation of the Letter to the Romans.[6]

16:18 Deceiving the Simpleminded

Coating Poison with Honey. Cyril of Jerusalem: The heretics do this by coating over their poison pills of godless doctrines with the honey of the name of Christ. The Catechetical Lectures 4.2.[7]

Flattering Words. Jerome: Flattery is always insidious, deceitful and bland. And a flatterer is well defined by philosophers as a bland enemy. Truth is harsh, bitter, stern, unpleasant and offensive to those who are reproved. Against the Pelagians 1.26.[8]

Chrysostom: It seems that Paul is talking here about the Jewish leaders. . . . Their words sound wonderful, but they are deceptive. However, they do not fool everyone but only the hearts of the simple-minded. Homilies on Romans 32.[9]

Pelagius: Paul is speaking of those who in his day came from among the circumcised and did away with fasts and abstinence. Disagreeing with apostolic teaching and setting obstacles before the brethren, they preached new moons and sabbaths and other feast days for the sake of their stomach. Pelagius's Commentary on Romans.[10]

16:19 Be Wise and Guileless

Be Guileless As to What Is Evil. Origen: This is similar to what Paul wrote to the Corinthians when he said: "Be babes in evil, but in your thinking be mature."[11] The Lord also said much the same thing: "The children of this world are wiser in their generation than the children of light."[12] Commentary on the Epistle to the Romans.[13]

The Hearts of the Innocent. Clement of Alexandria: The apostle admits that he rejoices because of the hearts of the innocent, and [in this verse] he gives a kind of definition of being as a child. Christ the Educator 1.5.[14]

Be Wise as to What Is Good. Ambrosiaster: Being "wise as to what is good" means doing good works, while being "guileless as to what is evil" means avoiding unrighteous deeds. Commentary on Paul's Epistles.[15]

Your Obedience Is Known to All. Pelagius: If you obeyed those you should not have obeyed, how much more should you obey us! For this is why these people came to you, because they knew that you could readily be led astray by unsuspecting obedience. I rejoice with you, because obedience is good only if it is reasonable. I want you to be wise in what is good, so that by being ignorant of evil you may bring the enemy down under the feet of innocence. Pelagius's Commentary on Romans.[16]

16:20 God Will Soon Crush Satan

---

[2]NPNF 1 11:559-60. [3]1 Tim 1:3-4. [4]Tit 1:10-12. [5]AOR 49. [6]IER, Migne PG 82 col. 224. [7]LCC 4:99. [8]FC 53:271. [9]NPNF 1 11:560. [10]PCR 152. [11]1 Cor 14:20. [12]Lk 16:8. [13]CER 5:264. [14]ANF 2:214. [15]CSEL 81.1:489-91. [16]PCR 152.

GOD WILL SOON CRUSH SATAN UNDER YOUR FEET. ORIGEN: It seems to me that "Satan" here refers to any spirit which is opposed to God. For in our language, *Satan* means "adversary."

But just as the apostle teaches that if they behave and demonstrate that they are the kind of people he says they are, then he promises that Satan will soon be crushed under their feet by the God of peace, so the same God of peace will stir up Satan in the hearts of those who do not keep his peace with a pure heart and a clean conscience. Thus whoever neglects the blessing of peace will suffer the bitter pangs of the adversaries until he remembers the sweetness of the peace which he has rejected. Therefore we are edified by both of these things, for God is said to stir up Satan against those who neglect him and to subdue him for the benefit of those who dedicate themselves to him, giving them the palm of victory over their vanquished foe and pouring out on them the rewards of victory. COMMENTARY ON THE EPISTLE TO THE ROMANS.[17]

AMBROSIASTER: Paul says this about his own coming to them, for then he will crush the devil so that they will be able to receive spiritual grace. Satan gets angry at that, because he wants people to remain in sin. The grace which he has promised he will give them when he comes he now prays that they will have. For if they deserve to receive that grace, then he is already with them in spirit. COMMENTARY ON PAUL'S EPISTLES.[18]

PELAGIUS: The Lord has given us power to tread upon scorpions and snakes and every power of the enemy[19] so that he may not prevail over us and so that we can walk over him with all our members free and unfettered. PELAGIUS'S COMMENTARY ON ROMANS.[20]

THE GRACE OF OUR LORD BE WITH YOU. THEODORET OF CYR: After revealing the enemy, Paul points to the Savior. Those who receive God's grace will never be defeated. INTERPRETATION OF THE LETTER TO THE ROMANS.[21]

16:21 Greetings from Timothy and Paul's Kinsmen in the Faith

TIMOTHY, MY FELLOW WORKER. ORIGEN: Timothy is well known from the Acts of the Apostles, where it is recorded that he was from Derbe, the son of a believing widow and of a Gentile father.[22] Paul asked him to remain at Ephesus in order to warn the people there not to teach anything different from what they had been taught nor to listen to myths and endless genealogies.[23]

Lucius may have been the same person as Luke the Evangelist, because names are sometimes given in the native form and sometimes in the Greek or Roman one.

Jason is the same person as the one who, when there were riots against Paul and Silas at Thessalonica, posted a bond for them so that they might have the freedom to preach.[24] Sosipater was the son of Pyrrhus, from Berrhoea.[25] . . . Paul calls them all his kinsmen because, although they were Gentiles, they were his brethren in the faith. COMMENTARY ON THE EPISTLE TO THE ROMANS.[26]

KINSMEN IN THE FAITH. AMBROSIASTER: Timothy was a fellow worker of Paul's as a cobishop, and he governed the church with great care. The Jews hated him to the point that he was circumcised because of it, in that his mother was Jewish and he could not be a teacher without being circumcised. Paul calls these people his kinsmen, partly by blood and partly by faith. COMMENTARY ON PAUL'S EPISTLES.[27]

THEODORET OF CYR: Timothy was circumcised at Lystra and Paul wrote him two letters. Jason is mentioned in Acts.[28] INTERPRETATION OF THE LETTER TO THE ROMANS.[29]

---

[17]CER 5:268-70. [18]CSEL 81.1:491. [19]Lk 10:19. [20]PCR 152-53. [21]*IER*, Migne PG 82 col. 224. [22]Acts 16:1. [23]1 Tim 1:3-4. [24]Acts 17:5-9. [25]Acts 20:4. [26]CER 5:272-74. [27]CSEL 81.1:491. [28]Acts 17:5-9. [29]*IER*, Migne PG 82 col. 224.

16:22 *Greetings from Tertius*

I, TERTIUS. AMBROSIASTER: Tertius was his name, not a number [third]. He was the scribe who wrote the epistle, and Paul allowed him to send his own greetings to the Romans. COMMENTARY ON PAUL'S EPISTLES.[30]

THEODORET OF CYR: Tertius was another of those who had accepted the apostle's teaching. Being rewarded for this with the gift of expression, he was told to send this letter to the Romans. INTERPRETATION OF THE LETTER TO THE ROMANS.[31]

16:23 *Greetings from the Church and Paul's Hosts*

PAYMASTER OF THE CITY OF GOD. ORIGEN: This is the same Gaius whom Paul mentioned as having baptized at Corinth.[32] Paul would not have mentioned that Erastus was the city treasurer if he did not intend a spiritual meaning as well, viz., that Erastus was the treasurer or paymaster of that city whose builder and maker is God. This is why he did not indicate in what city Erastus served as treasurer! COMMENTARY ON THE EPISTLE TO THE ROMANS.[33]

GAIUS THE HOST. AMBROSIASTER: I think that this is the same Gaius to whom John wrote rejoicing in the love which he showed to the brethren by being always ready to meet their needs.[34] COMMENTARY ON PAUL'S EPISTLES.[35]

MY HOST. CHRYSOSTOM: When you hear that Gaius was Paul's host, admire him not only for his generosity but also for his strictness of life. For if he were not worthy of Paul's standards, the apostle would never have lodged there.

Paul mentions Erastus's title with the purpose of showing that the gospel had taken hold among the great as well as among the rest of the population. . . . To a man who hears the Word, riches are not a hindrance, nor the cares of government, nor anything else of that kind. HOMILIES ON ROMANS 32.[36]

THEODORET OF CYR: The highest praise is reserved for hospitality on such a scale. . . . Gaius was a Corinthian, as appears from 1 Corinthians [1:14]: "I thank my God that I baptized none of you, except Crispus and Gaius." . . . Erastus is also mentioned elsewhere, in 2 Timothy [4:20]. INTERPRETATION OF THE LETTER TO THE ROMANS.[37]

16:24 *Grace to All*

GRACE AT THE END. AMBROSIASTER: Paul places Christ, through whom we were made and again remade by his grace, at the end of his epistle so that he might stick in our minds, for if we are mindful of his benefits he will always look after us, as he said: "Behold, I am with you always, even to the end of the world."[38] COMMENTARY ON PAUL'S EPISTLES.[39]

CHRYSOSTOM: This is where we ought to begin and end! The best proof of a generous teacher is that he benefits his learners not by word only but also by prayer. HOMILIES ON ROMANS 32.[40]

PELAGIUS: This is the closing formula, written in Paul's own hand, in all his letters. PELAGIUS'S COMMENTARY ON ROMANS.[41]

SURROUNDED BY THE FORTRESS OF GRACE. THEODORET OF CYR: Once again Paul offers them a spiritual blessing and surrounds them with the grace of God, which is like an impenetrable wall. This is how the epistle began and this is how it ends. We too may share in this grace, triumphing over temptations and, enlightened by it, following the right way free of all error. Walking in the apostle's footsteps we may be made worthy to

---

[30]CSEL 81.1:491. [31]*IER*, Migne PG 82 col. 224. [32]1 Cor 1:14. [33]*CER* 5:278. [34]3 Jn 1-3. [35]CSEL 81.1:491-93. [36]NPNF 1 11:561. [37]*IER*, Migne PG 82 col. 225. [38]Mt 28:20. [39]CSEL 81.1:493. [40]NPNF 1 11:561. [41]*PCR* 153.

behold the teacher and by his intercession receive the Lord's blessing and promises, by the grace and kindness of our Lord Jesus Christ, to whom with the Father and the Holy Spirit belong glory and honor, now and forever, world without end. Amen. INTERPRETATION OF THE LETTER TO THE ROMANS.[42]

WHETHER DELETED BY MARCION. ORIGEN: Marcion, who interpolated both the Gospels and the Epistles, deleted this passage [Romans 16:24] from the text, and not only this but everything [after 14:25] as well. In other manuscripts not edited by Marcion we find this passage in different places. Some have it immediately after [14:25], and others have it here, at the end of the epistle. COMMENTARY ON THE EPISTLE TO THE ROMANS.[43]

16:25 Revealing the Age-Old Mystery

THE REVELATION OF THE MYSTERY. ORIGEN: Paul wants to show that there are two ways in which those who believe in the gospel are strengthened. One is by his preaching, which is the preaching of Christ. The other is by the revelation of the mystery which was kept secret for long ages and which has now been revealed in Christ . . . not without suitable witnesses but with the backing of the prophetic Scriptures. COMMENTARY ON THE EPISTLE TO THE ROMANS.[44]

THE MYSTERY KEPT SECRET FOR LONG AGES. AMBROSIASTER: Paul gives glory to God the Father, from whom are all things, that he might be pleased to fill the congregation of the Romans with his grace, as he can do by confirming their minds in faith for the advancing of the gospel and the revelation of the mystery hidden for long ages, which has now been made manifest in Christ.[45] COMMENTARY ON PAUL'S EPISTLES.[46]

MY GOSPEL BASED ON THE PREACHING OF JESUS HIMSELF. CHRYSOSTOM: Here Paul prays

for them on the assumption that they are not yet firmly fixed but are still wavering. In order to back up what he says, he bases it all on "the preaching of Jesus Christ," by which he means the things that Jesus himself preached. For if Christ preached it, the teaching is not Paul's, but his. . . . Furthermore, to be let in on the secret, especially on one which had been kept for such a long time, is a sign of the greatest intimacy and friendliness. HOMILIES ON ROMANS 27.[47]

GOD WHO IS ABLE TO STRENGTHEN. PELAGIUS: God strengthens us with signs and teachings, so that you may live in the way that Paul has preached by the example and authority of Christ. PELAGIUS'S COMMENTARY ON ROMANS.[48]

THEODORET OF CYR: Paul says this in order to remind us of how old the gospel actually is. INTERPRETATION OF THE LETTER TO THE ROMANS.[49]

16:26 The Mystery Disclosed

MADE KNOWN TO ALL NATIONS. ORIGEN: Although the message is made known to all nations, it is not made known to all people, because only a few chosen ones are able to understand the wisdom and knowledge of God, of whom it is said: "Many are called, but few are chosen."[50] COMMENTARY ON THE EPISTLE TO THE ROMANS.[51]

NOW MADE KNOWN TO ALL. ORIGEN: Those who advance in the knowledge of Christianity do not treat the things written in the law with disrespect. On the contrary, they bestow even greater honor upon them, showing what a depth of wise and mysterious reasons is contained in these writings, which are not fully comprehended by

---

[42]IER, Migne PG 82 col. 225. [43]CER 5:280. [44]CER 5:280. [45]See 1 Cor 2:7-8; Col 1:26-27. [46]CSEL 81.1:495. [47]NPNF 1 11:534. [48]PCR 153. [49]IER, Migne PG 82 ad loc. [50]Mt 22:14. [51]CER 5:282.

the Jews, who treat them superficially and even as if they were to some extent mythical. AGAINST CELSUS 2.4.[52]

THROUGH THE PROPHETIC WRITINGS.
AMBROSIASTER: The mystery which is eternally hidden in God was revealed in the time of Christ, for God is not alone, but from all eternity he has his Word and the Paraclete with him. God decreed that every creature was to be saved by coming to a knowledge of this truth. For the truth of this mystery had been indicated by the prophets in symbols, and it was known only to God. . . . This wisdom is Jesus Christ, who is from God and was with God forever. COMMENTARY ON PAUL'S EPISTLES.[53]

NOW DISCLOSED. CHRYSOSTOM: By saying this Paul is releasing the weak person from fear. For this secret was contained in the law. Indeed, it is what the law was all about. We cannot ask why it should be disclosed now, for to do this would be to call God to account. We ought not to behave like busybodies but instead be content with what we have been given. HOMILIES ON ROMANS 27.[54]

LONG HIDDEN. PELAGIUS: The mystery of the calling of all the Gentiles, which through Paul's gospel, using the testimonies of the prophets, had now been plainly disclosed in Christ,[55] had long been hidden in the law. Although the prophets had said many things about the Gentiles, none had recognized as clearly as Paul how Gentiles and Jews would become one in Christ. For they had been able to determine that some should be admitted to the faith as proselytes. PELAGIUS'S COMMENTARY ON ROMANS.[56]

THE OBEDIENCE OF FAITH. THEODORET OF CYR: The obedience of faith is the result of the preaching of the gospel. INTERPRETATION OF THE LETTER TO THE ROMANS.[57]

16:27 Glory to the Only Wise God

THE LIMITS OF HUMAN WISDOM. ORIGEN: God cannot be called wise in the way that human beings are wise, because a wise man merely has a share in wisdom, whereas God is its author and source. COMMENTARY ON THE EPISTLE TO THE ROMANS.[58]

TO THE ONLY WISE GOD BE GLORY. JEROME: God alone is wise, although both Solomon and many other holy men were called wise.[59] AGAINST THE PELAGIANS 2.7.[60]

GLORY TO THE FATHER THROUGH THE SON IN THE SPIRIT. AMBROSIASTER: Without Christ nothing is complete, because all things are through him. It is acknowledged that praise is given to God the Father through him, because it is understood that "through Christ" means "through his wisdom," in whom he has saved believers. Therefore glory to the Father through the Son is glory to both in the Holy Spirit, because both are in the one glory. COMMENTARY ON PAUL'S EPISTLES.[61]

CHRYSOSTOM: Do not think that Paul said this in disparagement of the Son. For if all the things whereby his wisdom was made apparent were done by Christ and nothing was done without him, it is quite plain that the Son is equal to the Father in wisdom also. The word *only* is used in order to contrast God with every created being. HOMILIES ON ROMANS 27.[62]

GLORY FOREVER. PELAGIUS: God commanded that all the Gentiles obey and acknowledge God. He alone knew that this would one day happen, for he alone is naturally wise just as he is naturally good. Mankind is also called good, it is true, but we have the ability to be good or wise as a result of instruction, whereas God is good and wise by nature. To him be glory and honor

---

[52]ANF 4:431. [53]CSEL 81.1:495. [54]NPNF 1 11:534. [55]See Eph 3:1-13. [56]PCR 153. [57]IER, Migne PG 82 ad loc. [58]CER 5:284. [59]See 1 Kings 4:30-34; 7:14; 1 Chron 27:32; Dan 1:17; Mt 2:1. [60]FC 53:304. [61]CSEL 81.1:495. [62]NPNF 1 11:535.

through Jesus Christ forever. Amen. PELAGIUS'S COMMENTARY ON ROMANS.[63]

THE ONLY WISE GOD. THEODORET OF CYR: If the heretics try to use this [verse] to prove that Christ is not God, it should be remembered that Christ not only is called wise, he is even called *Wisdom.* INTERPRETATION OF THE LETTER TO THE ROMANS.[64]

---

[63]*PCR 153-54.* [64]*IER, Migne PG 82 ad loc.*

Appendix

Early Christian Writers and the Documents Cited

The following table lists all the early Christian documents cited in this volume by author, if known, or by the title of the work. The English title used in this commentary is followed in parentheses with the Latin designation and, where available, the Thesaurus Linguae Graecae (=TLG) digital reference or Cetedoc Clavis numbers. Printed sources of original language versions may be found in the bibliography of works in original languages.

Acacius of Caesarea

Pauline Commentary from the Greek Church (*Fragmenta in Epistulam Romanos*)	TLG 2064.002

Ambrose

Letters (*Epistulae*)	Cetedoc 0160
On the Death of His Brother Satyrus (*De Excessu Fratris Satyri*)	Cetedoc 0157
Paradise (*De Paradiso*)	Cetedoc 0124
Six Days of Creation (*Exameron*)	Cetedoc 0123

Apollinaris of Laodicea

Pauline Commentary from the Greek Church (*Fragments in Epistulam ad Romanos*)	TLG 2074.039

Athanasius

On the Incarnation of the Word (*De Incarnatione Verbi*)	TLG 2035.002

Augustine

Against Julian (*Contra Julianum*)	Cetedoc 0351
Against Lying (*Contra Mendacium*)	Cetedoc 0304
Augustine on Romans (*Exp. Quarumdam Propositionum ex Epistula ad Romanos*)	Cetedoc 0280
The City of God (*De Civitate Dei*)	Cetedoc 0313
Commentary on John (*In Iohannis Evangelium Tractatus*)	Cetedoc 0278
Continence (*De Gratia et Libero Arbitrio*)	Cetedoc 0352
Converts to the Creed (*Sermones*)	Cetedoc 0284
The Creed (*De Symbolo ad Catechumenos*)	Cetedoc 0309
Faith and Works (*De Fide et Operibus*)	Cetedoc 0294
Gift of Perseverance (*De Dono Perseverantiae*)	Cetedoc 0355
Grace and Free Will (*De Gratia et Libero Arbitrio*)	Cetedoc 0352
Faith and the Creed (*De Fide et Symbolo*)	Cetedoc 0293
Holy Virginity (*De Sancta Virginitate*)	Cetedoc 0300
Homilies on 1 John (*In Iohannis Epistulam ad Parthos Tractatus*)	Cetedoc 0279
Letters (*Epistulae*)	Cetedoc 0262
Lying (*De Mendacio*)	Cetedoc 0303

The Nature of the Good *(De Natura Boni)* — Cetedoc 0323

Of True Religion *(De Vera Religione)* — Cetedoc 0264

On Free Will *(De Libero Arbitrio)* — Cetedoc 0260

On Nature and Grace *(De Natura et Gratia)* — Cetedoc 0344

Predestination of the Saints *(De Praedestinatione Sanctorum)* — Cetedoc 0354

Question *(De Diversis Quaestionibus Octoginta Tribus)* — Cetedoc 0289

The Retractions *(Retractationum Libri Duo)* — Cetedoc 0250

Rudimentary Exposition of the Epistle to the Romans
(Epistulae ad Romanos Inchoata Expositio) — Cetedoc 0281

Sermon on Almsgiving *(Sermones)* — Cetedoc 0284

Sermon on the Mount *(De Sermone Domini in Monte)* — Cetedoc 0274

Sermons for Easter Season *(Sermones)* — Cetedoc 0284

Sermons for the Feast of the Nativity *(Sermones)* — Cetedoc 0284

The Spirit and the Letter *(De Spiritu et Littera)* — Cetedoc 0343

Tractates on the Gospel of John *(In Iohannis Evangelium Tractatus)* — Cetedoc 0278

The Trinity *(De Trinitate)* — Cetedoc 0329

The Way of Life of the Catholic Church *(De Moribus Ecclesiae
Catholicae et De Moribus)* — Cetedoc 0261

Basil of Caesarea

An Ascetical Discourse *(Prologus 5)* — TLG 2040.046

Concerning Baptism *(De Baptismo Libri Duo)* — TLG 2040.052

Exegetic Homilies *(Homiliae super Psalmos)* — TLG 2040.018

Hexameron *(Homiliae in Hexaemeron)* — TLG 2040.001

Homily Sixteen *(Homiliae super Psalmos)* — TLG 2040.018

Letters *(Epistulae)* — TLG 2040.004

The Long Rules *(Regulae Fusius Tractatae)* — TLG 2040.048

The Morals *(Regulae Morales)* — TLG 2040.051

Of Humility *(De Humilitate)* — TLG 2040.036

Bede the Venerable

Homilies on the Gospels *(Homeliarum Evangelii Libri II)* — Cetedoc 1367

Caesarius of Arles

Sermons *(Sermones Caesarii vel ex Aliis Fontibus Hausti)* — Cetedoc 1008

Chrysostom

Baptismal Instructions *(Catecheses ad Illuminandos)* — TLG 2062.382

Homiles on Genesis *(In Genesim Homilies 1-67)* — TLG 2062.112

Homilies on Romans *(In Epistulam ad Romanos)* — TLG 2062.155

Clement of Alexandria

Christ the Educator *(Paedagogus)* — TLG 0555.002

Stromata: Book Three *(Stromata)* — TLG 0555.004

Who Is the Rich Man That Shall Be Saved? *(Quis Dives Salvetur)* — TLG 0555.006

Clement of Rome

The First Epistle of Clement *(Epistula I ad Corinthios)*   TLG 1271.001

Cyprian

Exhortation to Martyrdom, to Fortunatus *(Ad Fortunatum)*   Cetedoc 0045

Jealousy and Envy *(De Zelo et Livore)*   Cetedoc 0049

On Morality *(De Mortalitate)*   Cetedoc 0044

On the Unity of the Church *(De Ecclesiae Catholicae Unitate)*   Cetedoc 0041

To Donatus *(Ad Donatum)*   Cetedoc 0038

Cyril of Alexandria

Explanation into the Letter to the Romans

    (Fragmenta in Sancti Pauli Epistulam ad Romanos)   TLG 4090.003

Letters *(Ad Monochos Aegypti)*   TLG 5000.001

Didymus the Blind of Alexandria

Pauline Commentary from the Greek Church

    (Fragmentum in Epistulam ad Hebraeos)   TLG 2102.046

Eusebius of Caesarea

Preparation for the Gospel *(Praeparatio Evangelica)*   TLG 2018.001

Eusebius of Emesa

Pauline Commentary from the Greek Church *(Fragmenta in Epistulam ad Romanos)*   TLG 4124.007

Gennadius of Constantinople

Pauline Commentary from the Greek Church *(Fragmenta in Epistulam ad Romanos)*   TLG 2762.004

Gregory of Nazianzus

Oration 28: On the Doctrine of God *(De Theologia)*   TLG 2022.008

Gregory of Nyssa

On Perfection *(De Perfectione Christiana ad Olympium Monachum)*   TLG 2017.026

On the Christian Mode of Life *(De Instituto Christiano)*   TLG 2017.024

On Virginity *(De Virginitate)*   TLG 2017.043

Gregory the Great

Dialogues *(Dialogorum Libri IV)*   Cetedoc 1713

Hilary of Poitiers

The Trinity *(De Trinitate)*   Cetedoc 0433

Ignatius

Epistle of Ignatius to the Ephesians *(Epistulae Interpolatae et Epistulae Suppositiciae)*   TLG 1443.002

To the Smyrneans *(Epistulae vii)*   TLG 1443.001

Irenaeus

Against Heresies (*Adversus Haereses*)   TLG 1447.007

Jerome

Against Rufinus (*Apologia Adversus Libros Rufini*)   Cetedoc 0613
Dialogue Against the Pelagians (*Dialogi Contra Pelagianos Libri III*)   Cetedoc 0615
Homilies on the Psalms (*Commentarioli in Psalmos*)   Cetedoc 0582
Homily 40 (*Tractatus LIX in Psalmos*)   Cetedoc 0592
Letters 14.10 (*Epistulae*)   Cetedoc 0620
Sermons (*Tractatus in Marci Evangelium*)   Cetedoc 0594

John of Damascus

Orthodox Faith (*Expositio Fidei*)   TLG 2934.004

Marius Victorinus

Against Arius (*Adversus Arium*)   Cetedoc 0095

Montanist Oracle

Testimonia (*Oracula*)   TLG 1771.001

Novatian

Jewish Foods (*De Cibis Iudaicis*)   Cetedoc 0068
Letter One (*Epistula xxx inter Opera Sancti Cypriani*)   Cetedoc 0072
The Trinity (*De Trinitate*)   Cetedoc 0071

Oecumenius

Pauline Commentary from the Greek Church (*Fragmenta in Epistulam ad Romanos*)   TLG 2866.002

Origen

Commentary on the Epistle to the Romans
   (*Commentarii in Epistulam ad Romanos*)   TLG 2042.037
Homilies on Leviticus (*Homiliae in Leviticum*)   TLG 2042.024
On First Principles (*De Principiis*)   TLG 2042.002
On Prayer (*De Oratione*)   TLG 2042.008
Origen Against Celsus (*Contra Celsum*)   TLG 2042.001

Polycarp of Smyrna

The Epistle of Polycarp to the Philippians (*Epistula ad Philippenses*) TLG 1622.001

Prudentius

The Origin of Sin (*Amartigenia*)   Cetedoc 1440

Severian of Gabala

Pauline Commentary from the Greek Church (*Fragmenta in Epistulam ad Romanos*)   TLG 1074.002

Tertullian

A Treatise on the Soul *(De Anima)*	Cetedoc 0017
Against Marcion *(Aduersus Marcionem)*	Cetedoc 0014
Against Praxeas *(Aduersus Praxean)*	Cetedoc 0026
An Answer to the Jews *(Adversus Iudaeos)*	Cetedoc 0033
The Chaplet *(De Corona)*	Cetedoc 0021
On Exhortation to Chastity *(De Exhortatione Castitatis)*	Cetedoc 0020
On Idolatry *(De Idololatria)*	Cetedoc 0023
On Modesty *(De Pudicitia)*	Cetedoc 0030
On Patience *(De Patientia)*	Cetedoc 0009
On Prayer *(De Oratione)*	Cetedoc 0007
On the Resurrection of the Flesh *(De Resurrectione Mortuorum)*	Cetedoc 0019

Theodore of Mopsuestia

Pauline Commentary from the Greek Church *(Fragments in Epistulam ad Romanos)*	TLG 4135.015

Theodoret of Cyr

Interpretation of the Letter to the Romans *(Interpretatio in xiv Epistulas Sancti Pauli)*	TLG 4089.030

Theophilus of Antioch

To Autolycus *(Ad Autolycum)*	TLG 1725.001

Timeline of Writers of the Patristic Period

Location / Period	British Isles	Gaul	Spain, Portugal	Rome* and Italy	Carthage and Northern Africa
2nd century				Clement of Rome, fl. c. 92-101 (Greek)	
				Shepherd of Hermas, c. 140 (Greek)	
				Justin Martyr (Ephesus, Rome), c. 100/110-165 (Greek)	
		Irenaeus of Lyons, c. 135-c. 202 (Greek)		Valentinus the Gnostic (Rome), fl. c. 140 (Greek)	
				Marcion (Rome), fl. 144 (Greek)	
3rd century				Callistus of Rome, regn. 217-222 (Latin)	Tertullian of Carthage, c. 155/160-c. 225 (Latin)
				Minucius Felix of Rome, fl. 218-235 (Latin)	
				Hippolytus (Rome, Palestine?), fl. 222-235/245 (Greek)	Cyprian of Carthage, fl. 248-258 (Latin)
				Novatian of Rome, fl. 235-258 (Latin)	
				Victorinus of Petovium, 230-304 (Latin)	

*One of the five ancient patriarchates

Alexandria* and Egypt	Constantinople* and Asia Minor, Greece	Antioch* and Syria	Mesopotamia, Persia	Jerusalem* and Palestine	Location Unknown
Philo of Alexandria, c. 20 B.C. – c. A.D. 50 (Greek)				Flavius Josephus (Rome), c. 37-c. 101 (Greek)	
Basilides (Alexandria), 2nd cent. (Greek)	Polycarp of Smyrna, c. 69-155 (Greek)	*Didache* (Egypt?), c. 100 (Greek)			
Letter of Barnabas (Syria?), c. 130 (Greek)		Ignatius of Antioch, c. 35–107/112 (Greek)			
Theodotus the Valentinian, 2nd cent. (Greek)	Athenagoras (Greece), fl. 176-180 (Greek)	Theophilus of Antioch, c. late 2nd cent. (Greek)			*Second Letter of Clement* (spurious; Corinth, Rome, Alexandria?) (Greek), c. 150
Clement of Alexandria, c. 150-215 (Greek)	*Montanist Oracles*, late 2nd cent. (Greek)				
Sabellius (Egypt), 2nd–3rd cent. (Greek)					Pseudo-Clementines 3rd cent. (Greek)
			Mani (Manichaeans), c. 216-276		
Letter to Diognetus, 3rd cent. (Greek)	Gregory Thaumaturgus (Neocaesarea), fl. c. 248-264 (Greek)				
Origen (Alexandria, Caesarea of Palestine), 185-254 (Greek)					
Dionysius of Alexandria, d. 264/5 (Greek)					
	Methodius of Olympus (Lycia), d. c. 311 (Greek)				

Timeline of Writers of the Patristic Period

Location	British Isles	Gaul	Spain, Portugal	Rome* and Italy	Carthage and Northern Africa
Period					
4th century				Firmicus Maternus (Sicily), fl. c. 335 (Latin)	
		Lactantius, c. 260- 330 (Latin)		Marius Victorinus (Rome), fl. 355-363 (Latin)	
				Eusebius of Vercelli, fl. c. 360 (Latin)	
			Hosius of Cordova, d. 357 (Latin)	Lucifer of Cagliari (Sardinia), d. 370/371 (Latin)	
		Hilary of Poitiers, c. 315-367 (Latin)	Potamius of Lisbon, fl. c. 350-360 (Latin)	Faustinus (Rome), fl. 380 (Latin)	
				Filastrius of Brescia, fl. 380 (Latin)	
			Gregory of Elvira, fl. 359-385 (Latin)	Ambrosiaster (Italy?), fl. c. 366-384 (Latin)	
			Prudentius, c. 348-c. 410 (Latin)	Faustus of Riez, fl. c. 380 (Latin)	
			Pacian of Barcelona, 4th cent. (Latin)	Gaudentius of Brescia, fl. 395 (Latin)	Paulus Orosius, b. c. 380 (Latin)
				Ambrose of Milan, c. 333-397; fl. 374-397 (Latin)	
				Paulinus of Milan, late 4th early 5th cent. (Latin)	
5th century				Rufinus (Aquileia, Rome), c. 345-411 (Latin)	
	Fastidius (Britain), c. 4th-5th cent. (Latin)	Sulpicius Severus (Bordeaux), c. 360-c. 420/425 (Latin)		Aponius, fl. 405-415 (Latin)	Quodvultdeus (Carthage), fl. 430 (Latin)
				Chromatius (Aquileia), fl. 400 (Latin)	
		John Cassian (Palestine, Egypt, Constantinople, Rome, Marseilles), 360-432 (Latin)		Pelagius (Britain, Rome), c. 354-c. 420 (Greek)	Augustine of Hippo, 354-430 (Latin)
				Maximus of Turin, d. 408/423 (Latin)	Luculentius, 5th cent. (Latin)
		Vincent of Lérins, d. 435 (Latin)		Paulinus of Nola, 355-431 (Latin)	
		Valerian of Cimiez, fl. c. 422-449 (Latin)		Peter Chrysologus (Ravenna), c. 380-450 (Latin)	
		Eucherius of Lyons, fl. 420-449 (Latin)		Julian of Eclanum, 386-454 (Latin)	

*One of the five ancient patriarchates

Alexandria* and Egypt	Constantinople* and Asia Minor, Greece	Antioch* and Syria	Mesopotamia, Persia	Jerusalem* and Palestine	Location Unknown
Antony, c. 251-355 (Coptic /Greek)	Theodore of Heraclea (Thrace), fl. c. 330-355 (Greek)	Eustathius of Antioch, fl. 325 (Greek)	Aphrahat (Persia) c. 270-350; fl. 337-345 (Syriac)	Eusebius of Caesarea (Palestine), c. 260/ 263-340 (Greek)	Commodius, c. 3rd or 5th cent. (Latin)
Peter of Alexandria, d. c. 311 (Greek)	Marcellus of Ancyra, d.c. 375 (Greek)	Eusebius of Emesa, c. 300-c. 359 (Greek)			
Arius (Alexandria), fl. c. 320 (Greek)	Epiphanius of Salamis (Cyprus), c. 315-403 (Greek)	Ephrem the Syrian, c. 306-373 (Syriac)	Jacob of Nisibis, fl. 308-325 (Syriac)		
Alexander of Alexandria, fl. 312-328 (Greek)	Basil (the Great) of Caesarea, b. c. 330; fl. 357-379 (Greek)				
Pachomius, c. 292-347 (Coptic/Greek?)	Macrina the Younger, c. 327-379 (Greek)				
Theodore of Tabennesi, d. 368 (Coptic/Greek)	Apollinaris of Laodicea, 310-c. 392 (Greek)				
Horsiesi, c. 305-390 (Coptic/Greek)	Gregory of Nazianzus, b. 329/330; fl. 372-389 (Greek)	Nemesius of Emesa (Syria), fl. late 4th cent. (Greek)		Acacius of Caesarea (Palestine), d. c. 365 (Greek)	
Athanasius of Alexandria, c. 295-373; fl. 325-373 (Greek)	Gregory of Nyssa, c. 335-394 (Greek)	Diodore of Tarsus, d. c. 394 (Greek)		Cyril of Jerusalem, c. 315-386 (Greek)	
Macarius of Egypt, c. 300-c. 390 (Greek)	Amphilochius of Iconium, c. 340/ 345- c. 398/404 (Greek)	John Chrysostom (Constantinople), 344/354-407 (Greek)			
Didymus (the Blind) of Alexandria, 313-398 (Greek)	Evagrius of Pontus, 345-399 (Greek)	Apostolic Constitutions, c. 375-400 (Greek) Didascalia, 4th cent. (Syriac)			
	Eunomius of Cyzicus, fl. 360-394 (Greek)	Theodore of Mopsuestia, c. 350-428 (Greek)		Diodore of Tarsus, d. c. 394 (Greek)	
	Pseudo-Macarius (Mesopotamia?), late 4th cent. (Greek)	Acacius of Beroea, c. 340-c. 436 (Greek)		Jerome (Rome, Antioch, Bethlehem), c. 347-419 (Latin)	
	Nicetas of Remesiana, d. c. 414 (Latin)				
Palladius of Helenopolis (Egypt), c. 365-425 (Greek)	Nestorius (Constantinople), c. 381-c. 451 (Greek)	Book of Steps, c. 400 (Syriac) Severian of Gabala, fl. c. 400 (Greek)	Eznik of Kolb, fl. 430-450 (Armenian)		
Cyril of Alexandria, 375-444 (Greek)	Basil of Seleucia, fl. 440-468 (Greek)	Nilus of Ancyra, d.c. 430 (Greek)		Hesychius of Jerusalem, fl. 412-450 (Greek)	
	Diadochus of Photice (Macedonia), 400-474 (Greek)			Euthymius (Palestine), 377-473 (Greek)	

Timeline of Writers of the Patristic Period

Location / Period	British Isles	Gaul	Spain, Portugal	Rome* and Italy	Carthage and Northern Africa
5th century (cont.)		Hilary of Arles, c. 401-449 (Latin) Eusebius of Gaul, 5th cent. (Latin) Prosper of Aquitaine, c. 390-c. 463 (Latin) Salvian the Presbyter of Marseilles, c. 400-c. 480 (Latin) Gennadius of Marseilles, d. after 496 (Latin)		Leo the Great (Rome), regn. 440-461 (Latin) Arnobius the Younger (Rome), fl. c. 450 (Latin) Ennodius (Arles, Milan, Pavia) c. 473-521 (Latin)	
6th century		Caesarius of Arles, c. 470-543 (Latin)	Paschasius of Dumium (Portugal), c. 515-c. 580 (Latin) Leander of Seville, c. 545-c. 600 (Latin) Martin of Braga, fl. 568-579 (Latin)	Epiphanius the Latin, late 5th–early 6th cent. (Latin) Eugippius, c. 460- c. 533 (Latin) Benedict of Nursia, c. 480-547 (Latin) Cassiodorus (Calabria), c. 485-c. 540 (Latin)	Fulgentius of Ruspe, c. 467-532 (Latin) Verecundus, d. 552 (Latin) Primasius, fl. 550-560 (Latin) Facundus of Hermiane, fl. 546-568 (Latin)
7th century				Gregory the Great (Rome), c. 540-604 (Latin) Gregory of Agrigentium, d. 592 (Greek)	
			Isidore of Seville, c. 560-636 (Latin) Braulio of Saragossa, c. 585-651 (Latin) Fructuosus of Braga, d.c. 665 (Latin)	Paterius, 6th/7th cent. (Latin)	
8th-12th century	Adamnan, c. 624-704 (Latin) Bede the Venerable, c. 672/673-735 (Latin)				

*One of the five ancient patriarchates

Alexandria* and Egypt	Constantinople* and Asia Minor, Greece	Antioch* and Syria	Mesopotamia, Persia	Jerusalem* and Palestine	Location Unknown
Ammonius of Alexandria, c. 460 (Greek) Poemen, 5th cent. (Greek) Besa the Copt, 5th cent. Shenoute, c. 350-466 (Coptic)	Gennadius of Constantinople, d. 471 (Greek)	John of Antioch, d. 441/2 (Greek) Theodoret of Cyr, c. 393-466 (Greek) Pseudo-Victor of Antioch, 5th cent. (Greek) John of Apamea, 5th cent. (Syriac)		Gerontius of Petra c. 395-c.480 (Syriac)	
Olympiodorus, early 6th cent.	Oecumenius (Isauria), 6th cent. (Greek)	Philoxenus of Mabbug (Syria), c. 440-523 (Syriac) Severus of Antioch, c. 465-538 (Greek) Mark the Hermit (Tarsus), c. 6th cent. (4th cent.?) (Greek)	Jacob of Sarug, c. 450-520 (Syriac) Babai the Great, c. 550-628 (Syriac) Babai, early 6th cent. (Syriac)	Procopius of Gaza (Palestine), c. 465-530 (Greek) Dorotheus of Gaza, fl. 525-540 (Greek) Cyril of Scythopolis, b. c. 525; d. after 557 (Greek)	Pseudo-Dionysius the Areopagite, fl. c. 500 (Greek)
	Maximus the Confessor (Constantinople), c. 580-662 (Greek)	Sahdona/Martyrius, fl. 635-640 (Syriac)	Isaac of Nineveh, d. c. 700 (Syriac)		(Pseudo-) Constantius, before 7th cent.? (Greek) Andreas, c. 7th cent. (Greek)
		John of Damascus (John the Monk), c. 650-750 (Greek)			
	Theophanes (Nicaea), 775-845 (Greek) Cassia (Constantinople), c. 805-c. 848/867 (Greek) Arethas of Caesarea (Constantinople/Caesarea), c. 860-940 (Greek) Photius (Constantinople), c. 820-891 (Greek) Symeon the New Theologian (Constantinople), 949-1022 (Greek) Theophylact of Ohrid (Bulgaria), 1050-1126 (Greek)		John the Elder of Qardu (north Iraq), 8th cent. (Syriac) Isho'dad of Merv, d. after 852 (Syriac)		

Biographical Sketches & Short Descriptions of Select Anonymous Works

This listing is cumulative, including all the authors and works cited in this series to date.

Acacius of Beroea (c. 340-c. 436). Syrian monk known for his ascetics. He became bishop of Beroea in 378, participated in the council of Constantinople in 381, and played an important role in mediating between Cyril of Alexandria and John of Antioch; however, he did not take part in the clash between Cyril and Nestorius.

Acacius of Caesarea (d. c. 365). Pro-Arian bishop of Caesarea in Palestine, disciple and biographer of Eusebius of Caesarea, the historian. He was a man of great learning and authored a treatise on Ecclesiastes.

Adamnan (c. 624-704). Abbot of Iona, Ireland, and author of the life of St. Columba. He was influential in the process of assimilating the Celtic church into Roman liturgy and church order. He also wrote *On the Holy Sites*, which influenced Bede.

Alexander of Alexandria (fl. 312-328). Bishop of Alexandria and predecessor of Athanasius, on whom he exerted considerable theological influence during the rise of Arianism. Alexander excommunicated Arius, whom he had appointed to the parish of Baucalis, in 319. His teaching regarding the eternal generation and divine substantial union of the Son with the Father was eventually confirmed at the Council of Nicaea (325).

Ambrose of Milan (c. 333-397; fl. 374-397). Bishop of Milan and teacher of Augustine who defended the divinity of the Holy Spirit and the perpetual virginity of Mary.

Ambrosiaster (fl. c. 366-384). Name given by Erasmus to the author of a work once thought to have been composed by Ambrose.

Ammonius (c. fifth century). An Aristotelian commentator and teacher in Alexandria, where he was born and of whose school he became head. Also an exegete of Plato, he enjoyed fame among his contemporaries and successors, although modern critics accuse him of pedantry and banality.

Amphilochius of Iconium (b. c. 340-345, d.c. 398-404). An orator at Constantinople before becoming bishop of Iconium in 373. He was a cousin of Gregory of Nazianzus and active in debates against the Macedonians and Messalians.

Andreas (c. seventh century). Monk who collected commentary from earlier writers to form a catena on various biblical books.

Antony (or Anthony) the Great (c. 251-c. 356). An anchorite of the Egyptian desert and founder of Egyptian monasticism. Athanasius regarded him as the ideal of monastic life, and he has become a model for Christian hagiography.

Aphrahat (c. 270-350 fl. 337-345). "The Persian

Sage" and first major Syriac writer whose work survives. He is also known by his Greek name Aphraates.

Apollinaris of Laodicea (310-c. 392). Bishop of Laodicea who was attacked by Gregory of Nazianzus, Gregory of Nyssa and Theodore for denying that Christ had a human mind.

Aponius/Apponius (fourth–fifth century). Author of a remarkable commentary on Song of Solomon (c. 405-415), an important work in the history of exegesis. The work, which was influenced by the commentaries of Origen and Pseudo-Hippolytus, is of theological significance, especially in the area of Christology.

Apostolic Constitutions (c. 381-394). Also known as *Constitutions of the Holy Apostles* and thought to be redacted by Julian of Neapolis. The work is divided into eight books, and is primarily a collection of and expansion on previous works such as the *Didache* (c. 140) and the *Apostolic Traditions*. Book 8 ends with eighty-five canons from various sources and is elsewhere known as the *Apostolic Canons*.

Arius (fl. c. 320). Heretic condemned at the Council of Nicaea (325) for refusing to accept that the Son was not a creature but was God by nature like the Father.

Arnobius the Younger (fifth century). A participant in christological controversies of the fifth century. He composed *Conflictus cum Serapione*, an account of a debate with a monophysite monk in which he attempts to demonstrate harmony between Roman and Alexandrian theology. Some scholars attribute to him a few more works, such as *Commentaries on Psalms*.

Athanasius of Alexandria (c. 295-373; fl. 325-373). Bishop of Alexandria from 328, though often in exile. He wrote his classic polemics against the Arians while most of the eastern bishops were against him.

Athenagoras (fl. 176-180). Early Christian philosopher and apologist from Athens, whose only authenticated writing, *A Plea Regarding Christians*, is addressed to the emperors Marcus Aurelius and Commodius, and defends Christians from the common accusations of atheism, incest and cannibalism.

Augustine of Hippo (354-430). Bishop of Hippo and a voluminous writer on philosophical, exegetical, theological and ecclesiological topics. He formulated the Western doctrines of predestination and original sin in his writings against the Pelagians.

Babai (c. early sixth century). Author of the Letter to Cyriacus. He should not be confused with either Babai of Nisibis (d. 484), or Babai the Great (d. 628).

Babai the Great (d. 628). Syriac monk who founded a monastery and school in his region of Beth Zabday and later served as third superior at the Great Convent of Mount Izla during a period of crisis in the Nestorian church.

Basil of Seleucia (fl. 444-468). Bishop of Seleucia in Isauria and ecclesiastical writer. He took part in the Synod of Constantinople in 448 for the condemnation of the Eutychian errors and the deposition of their great champion, Dioscurus of Alexandria.

Basil the Great (b. c. 330; fl. 357-379). One of the Cappadocian fathers, bishop of Caesarea and champion of the teaching on the Trinity propounded at Nicaea in 325. He was a great administrator and founded a monastic rule.

Basilides (fl. second century). Alexandrian heretic of the early second century who is said to have believed that souls migrate from body to body and that we do not sin if we lie to protect the body from martyrdom.

Bede the Venerable (c. 672/673-735). Born in Northumbria, at the age of seven he was put under the care of the Benedictine monks of Saints Peter and Paul at Jarrow and given a broad classical education in the monastic tradition. Considered one of the most learned men of his age, he is the author of *An Ecclesiastical History of the English People*.

Benedict of Nursia (c. 480-547). Considered the most important figure in the history of Western monasticism. Benedict founded many monasteries, the most notable found at Montecassino, but his lasting influence lay in his famous Rule. The Rule outlines the theological and inspirational foundation of the monastic ideal while also legislating the shape and organization of the cenobitic life.

Besa the Copt (5th century). Coptic monk, disciple of Shenoute, whom he succeeded as head of the monastery. He wrote numerous letters, monastic catecheses and a biography of Shenoute.

Book of Steps (c. 400). Written by an anonymous Syriac author, this work consists of thirty homilies or discourses which specifically deal with the more advanced stages of growth in the spiritual life.

Braulio of Saragossa (c. 585-651). Bishop of Saragossa (631-651) and noted writer of the Visigothic renaissance. His *Life* of St. Aemilianus is his crowning literary achievement.

Caesarius of Arles (c. 470-543). Bishop of Arles renowned for his attention to his pastoral duties. Among his surviving works the most important is a collection of some 238 sermons that display an ability to preach Christian doctrine to a variety of audiences.

Callistus of Rome (d. 222). Pope (217-222) who excommunicated Sabellius for heresy. It is very probable that he suffered martyrdom.

Cassia (b. c. 805, d. between 848 and 867). Nun, poet and hymnographer who founded a convent in Constantinople.

Cassian, John (360-432). Author of the *Institutes* and the *Conferences,* works purporting to relay the teachings of the Egyptian monastic fathers on the nature of the spiritual life which were highly influential in the development of Western monasticism.

Cassiodorus (c. 485-c. 580). Founder of the monastery of Vivarium, Calabria, where monks transcribed classic sacred and profane texts, Greek and Latin, preserving them for the Western tradition.

Chromatius (fl. 400). Bishop of Aquileia, friend of Rufinus and Jerome and author of tracts and sermons.

Clement of Alexandria (c. 150-215). A highly educated Christian convert from paganism, head of the catechetical school in Alexandria and pio-

neer of Christian scholarship. His major works, *Protrepticus, Paedagogus* and the *Stromata,* bring Christian doctrine face to face with the ideas and achievements of his time.

Clement of Rome (fl. c. 92-101). Pope whose *Epistle to the Corinthians* is one of the most important documents of subapostolic times.

Commodian (probably third or possibly fifth century). Latin poet of unknown origin (possibly Syrian?) whose two surviving works suggest chiliast and patripassionist tendencies.

Constitutions of the Holy Apostles. *See Apostolic Constitutions.*

Cyprian of Carthage (fl. 248-258). Martyred bishop of Carthage who maintained that those baptized by schismatics and heretics had no share in the blessings of the church.

Cyril of Alexandria (375-444; fl. 412-444). Patriarch of Alexandria whose extensive exegesis, characterized especially by a strong espousal of the unity of Christ, led to the condemnation of Nestorius in 431.

Cyril of Jerusalem (c. 315-386; fl. c. 348). Bishop of Jerusalem after 350 and author of *Catechetical Homilies.*

Cyril of Scythopolis (b. c. 525; d. after 557). Palestinian monk and author of biographies of famous Palestinian monks. Because of him we have precise knowledge of monastic life in the fifth and sixth centuries and a description of the Origenist crisis and its suppression in the mid-sixth century.

Diadochus of Photice (c. 400-474). Antimonophysite bishop of Epirus Vetus whose work *Discourse on the Ascension of Our Lord Jesus Christ* exerted influence in both the East and West through its Chalcedonian Christology. He is also the subject of the mystical *Vision of St. Diadochus Bishop of Photice in Epirus.*

Didache (c. 140). Of unknown authorship, this text intertwines Jewish ethics with Christian liturgical practice to form a whole discourse on the "way of life." It exerted an enormous amount of influence in the patristic period and was especially used in the training of catechumen.

Didymus the Blind (c. 313-398). Alexandrian

exegete who was much influenced by Origen and admired by Jerome.

Diodore of Tarsus (d. c. 394). Bishop of Tarsus and Antiochene theologian. He authored a great scope of exegetical, doctrinal and apologetic works, which come to us mostly in fragments because of his condemnation as the predecessor of Nestorianism. Diodore was a teacher of John Chrysostom and Theodore of Mopsuestia.

Dionysius of Alexandria (d. c. 264). Bishop of Alexandria and student of Origen. Dionysius actively engaged in the theological disputes of his day, opposed Sabellianism, defended himself against accusations of tritheism and wrote the earliest extant Christian refutation of Epicureanism. His writings have survived mainly in extracts preserved by other early Christian authors.

Dorotheus of Gaza (fl. c. 525-540). Member of Abbot Seridos's monastery and later leader of a monastery where he wrote *Spiritual Instructions*. He also wrote a work on traditions of Palestinian monasticism.

Ephrem the Syrian (b. c. 306; fl. 363-373). Syrian writer of commentaries and devotional hymns which are sometimes regarded as the greatest specimens of Christian poetry prior to Dante.

Epiphanius of Salamis (c. 315-403). Bishop of Salamis in Cyprus, author of a refutation of eighty heresies (the *Panarion*) and instrumental in the condemnation of Origen.

Epiphanius the Latin. Author of the late fifth-century or early sixth century Latin text *Interpretation of the Gospels,* with constant references to early patristic commentators. He was possibly a bishop of Benevento or Seville.

Epistle of Barnabas. See Letter of Barnabas.

Eucherius of Lyons (fl. 420-449). Bishop of Lyons c. 435-449. Born into an aristocratic family, he, along with his wife and sons, joined the monastery at Lérins soon after its founding. He explained difficult Scripture passages by means of a threefold reading of the text: literal, moral and spiritual.

Eugippius (b. 460). Disciple of Severinus and third abbot of the monastic community at Cas-

trum Lucullanum, which was made up of those fleeing from Noricum during the barbarian invasions.

Eunomius (d. 393). Bishop of Cyzicyus who was attacked by Basil and Gregory of Nyssa for maintaining that the Father and the Son were of different natures, one ingenerate, one generate.

Eusebius of Caesarea (c. 260/263-340). Bishop of Caesarea, partisan of the Emperor Constantine and first historian of the Christian church. He argued that the truth of the gospel had been foreshadowed in pagan writings but had to defend his own doctrine against suspicion of Arian sympathies.

Eusebius of Emesa (c. 300-c. 359). Bishop of Emesa from c. 339. A biblical exegete and writer on doctrinal subjects, he displays some semi-Arian tendencies of his mentor Eusebius of Caesarea.

Eusebius of Gaul, or Eusebius Gallicanus (c. fifth century). A conventional name for a collection of seventy-six sermons produced in Gaul and revised in the seventh century. It contains material from different patristic authors and focuses on ethical teaching in the context of the liturgical cycle (days of saints and other feasts).

Eusebius of Vercelli (fl. c. 360). Bishop of Vercelli who supported the trinitarian teaching of Nicaea (325) when it was being undermined by compromise in the West.

Eustathius of Antioch (fl. 325). First bishop of Beroea, then of Antioch, one of the leaders of the anti-Arians at the council of Nicaea. Later, he was banished from his seat and exiled to Thrace for his support of Nicene theology.

Euthymius (377-473). A native of Melitene and influential monk. He was educated by Bishop Otreius of Melitene, who ordained him priest and placed him in charge of all the monasteries in his diocese. When the Council of Chalcedon (451) condemned the errors of Eutyches, it was greatly due to the authority of Euthymius that most of the Eastern recluses accepted its decrees. The empress Eudoxia returned to Chalcedonian orthodoxy through his efforts.

Evagrius of Pontus (c. 345-399). Disciple and

teacher of ascetic life who astutely absorbed and creatively transmitted the spirituality of Egyptian and Palestinian monasticism of the late fourth century. Although Origenist elements of his writings were formally condemned by the Fifth Ecumenical Council (Constantinople II, A.D. 553), his literary corpus continued to influence the tradition of the church.

Eznik of Kolb (early fifth century). A disciple of Mesrob who translated Greek Scriptures into Armenian, so as to become the model of the classical Armenian language. As bishop, he participated in the synod of Astisat (449).

Facundus of Hermiane (fl. 546-568). African bishop who opposed Emperor Justinian's *post mortem* condemnation of Theodore of Mopsuestia, Theodoret of Cyr and Ibas of Edessa at the fifth ecumenical council. His written defense, known as "To Justinian" or "In Defense of the Three Chapters," avers that ancient theologians should not be blamed for errors tha became obvioust only upon later theological reflection. He continued in the tradition of Chalcedon, although his Christology was supplemented, according to Justinian's decisions, by the theopaschite formula *Unus ex Trinitate passus est* ("Only one of the three suffered").

Fastidius (c. fourth-fifth centuries). British author of *On the Christian Life*. He is believed to have written some works attributed to Pelagius.

Faustinus (fl. 380). A priest in Rome and supporter of Lucifer and author of a treatise on the Trinity.

Faustus of Riez (c. 400-490). A prestigious British monk at Lérins; abbot, then bishop of Riez from 457 to his death. His works include *On the Holy Spirit*, in which he argued against the Macedonians for the divinity of the Holy Spirit, and *On Grace*, in which he argued for a position on salvation that lay between more categorical views of free-will and predestination. Various letters and (pseudonymous) sermons are extant.

The Festal Menaion. Orthodox liturgical text containing the variable parts of the service, including hymns, for fixed days of celebration of the life of Jesus and Mary.

Filastrius (fl. 380). Bishop of Brescia and author of a compilation against all heresies.

Firmicus Maternus (fourth century). An anti-Pagan apologist. Before his conversion to Christianity he wrote a work on astrology (334-337). After his conversion, however, he criticized paganism in *On the Errors of the Profane Religion*.

Fructuosus of Braga (d. c. 665). Son of a Gothic general and member of a noble military family. He became a monk at an early age, then abbot-bishop of Dumium before 650 and metropolitan of Braga in 656. He was influential in setting up monastic communities in Lusitania, Asturia, Galicia and the island of Gades.

Fulgentius of Ruspe (c. 467-532). Bishop of Ruspe and author of many orthodox sermons and tracts under the influence of Augustine.

Gaudentius of Brescia (fl. 395). Successor of Filastrius as bishop of Brescia and author of twenty-one Eucharistic sermons.

Gennadius of Constantinople (d. 471). Patriarch of Constantinople, author of numerous commentaries and an opponent of the Christology of Cyril of Alexandria.

Gerontius (c. 395-c.480). Palestinian monk, later archimandrite of the cenobites of Palestine. He led the resistance to the council of Chalcedon.

Gnostics. Name now given generally to followers of Basilides, Marcion, Valentinus, Mani and others. The characteristic belief is that matter is a prison made for the spirit by an evil or ignorant creator, and that redemption depends on fate, not on free will.

Gregory of Elvira (fl. 359-385). Bishop of Elvira who wrote allegorical treatises in the style of Origen and defended the Nicene faith against the Arians.

Gregory of Nazianzus (b. 329/330; fl. 372-389). Cappadocian father, bishop of Constantinople, friend of Basil the Great and Gregory of Nyssa, and author of theological orations, sermons and poetry.

Gregory of Nyssa (c. 335-394). Bishop of Nyssa and brother of Basil the Great. A Cappadocian father and author of catechetical orations, he was a philosophical theologian of great originality.

Gregory Thaumaturgus (fl. c. 248-264). Bishop of Neocaesarea and a disciple of Origen. There are at least five legendary *Lives* that recount the events and miracles which led to his being called "the wonder worker." His most important work was the *Address of Thanks to Origen*, which is a rhetorically structured panegyric to Origen and an outline of his teaching.

Gregory the Great (c. 540-604). Pope from 590, the fourth and last of the Latin "Doctors of the Church." He was a prolific author and a powerful unifying force within the Latin Church, initiating the liturgical reform that brought about the Gregorian Sacramentary and Gregorian chant.

Hesychius of Jerusalem (fl. 412-450). Presbyter and exegete, thought to have commented on the whole of Scripture.

Hilary of Arles (c. 401-449). Archbishop of Arles and leader of the Semi-Pelagian party. Hilary incurred the wrath of Pope Leo I when he removed a bishop from his see and appointed a new bishop. Leo demoted Arles from a metropolitan see to a bishopric to assert papal power over the church in Gaul.

Hilary of Poitiers (c. 315-367). Bishop of Poitiers and called the "Athanasius of the West" because of his defense (against the Arians) of the common nature of Father and Son.

Hippolytus (fl. 222-245). Recent scholarship places Hippolytus in a Palestinian context, personally familiar with Origen. Though he is known chiefly for *The Refutation of All Heresies*, he was primarily a commentator on Scripture (especially the Old Testament) employing typological exegesis.

Horsiesi (c. 305-c. 390). Pachomius's second successor, after Petronius, as a leader of cenobitic monasticism in Southern Egypt.

Ignatius of Antioch (c. 35-107/112). Bishop of Antioch who wrote several letters to local churches while being taken from Antioch to Rome to be martyred. In the letters, which warn against heresy, he stresses orthodox Christology, the centrality of the Eucharist and unique role of the bishop in preserv-ing the unity of the church.

Irenaeus of Lyons (c. 135-c. 202). Bishop of Lyons who published the most famous and influential refutation of Gnostic thought.

Isaac of Nineveh (d. c. 700). Also known as Isaac the Syrian or Isaac Syrus, this monastic writer served for a short while as bishop of Nineveh before retiring to live a secluded monastic life. His writings on ascetic subjects survive in the form of numerous homilies.

Isho'dad of Merv (fl. c. 850). Nestorian bishop of Hedatta. He wrote commentaries on parts of the Old Testament and all of the New Testament, frequently quoting Syriac fathers.

Isidore of Seville (c. 560-636). Youngest of a family of monks and clerics, including sister Florentina and brothers Leander and Fulgentius. He was an erudite author of comprehensive scale in matters both religious and sacred, including his encyclopedic *Etymologies*.

Jacob of Nisibis (d. 338). Bishop of Nisibis. He was present at the council of Nicaea in 325 and took an active part in the opposition to Arius.

Jacob of Sarug (c. 450-c. 520). Syriac ecclesiastical writer. Jacob received his education at Edessa. At the end of his life he was ordained bishop of Sarug. His principal writing was a long series of metrical homilies, earning him the title "The Flute of the Holy Spirit."

Jerome (c. 347-420). Gifted exegete and exponent of a classical Latin style, now best known as the translator of the Latin Vulgate. He defended the perpetual virginity of Mary, attacked Origen and Pelagius and supported extreme ascetic practices.

John Chrysostom (344/354-407; fl. 386-407). Bishop of Constantinople who was noted for his orthodoxy, his eloquence and his attacks on Christian laxity in high places.

John of Antioch (d. 441/42). Bishop of Antioch, commencing in 428. He received his education together with Nestorius and Theodore of Mopsuestia in a monastery near Antioch. A supporter of Nestorius, he condemned Cyril of Alexandria, but later reached a compromise with him.

John of Apamea (fifth century). Syriac author of

the early church who wrote on various aspects of the spiritual life, also known as John the Solitary. Some of his writings are in the form of dialogues. Other writings include letters, a treatise on baptism, and shorter works on prayer and silence.

John of Damascus (c. 650-750). Arab monastic and theologian whose writings enjoyed great influence in both the Eastern and Western Churches. His most influential writing was the *Orthodox Faith.*

John the Elder (c. eighth century). A Syriac author who belonged to monastic circles of the Church of the East and lived in the region of Mount Qardu (northern Iraq). His most important writings are twenty-two homilies and a collection of fifty-one short letters in which he describes the mystical life as an anticipatory experience of the resurrection life, the fruit of the sacraments of baptism and the Eucharist.

John the Monk. Traditional name found in *The Festal Menaion,* believed to refer to John of Damascus. *See* John of Damascus.

Josephus, Flavius (c. 37-c. 101). Jewish historian from a distinguished priestly family. Acquainted with the Essenes and Sadducees, he himself became a Pharisee. He joined the great Jewish revolt that broke out in 66 and was chosen by the Sanhedrin at Jerusalem to be commander-in-chief in Galilee. Showing great shrewdness to ingratiate himself with Vespasian by foretelling his elevation and that of his son Titus to the imperial dignity, Josephus was restored his liberty after 69 when Vespasian became emperor.

Julian of Eclanum (c. 385-450). Bishop of Eclanum in 416/417 who was removed from office and exiled in 419 for not officially opposing Pelagianism. In exile, he was accepted by Theodore of Mopsuestia, whose Antiochene exegetical style he followed. Although he was never able to regain his ecclesiastical position, Julian taught in Sicily until his death. His works include commentaries on Job and parts of the Minor Prophets, a translation of Theodore of Mopsuestia's commentary on the Psalms, and various letters. Sympathetic to Pelagius, Julian applied his intel-

lectual acumen and rhetorical training to argue against Augustine on matters such as free will, desire and the locus of evil.

Justin Martyr (c. 100/110-165; fl. c. 148-161). Palestinian philosopher who was converted to Christianity, "the only sure and worthy philosophy." He traveled to Rome where he wrote several apologies against both pagans and Jews, combining Greek philosophy and Christian theology; he was eventually martyred.

Lactantius (c. 260-c. 330). Christian apologist removed from his post as teacher of rhetoric at Nicomedia upon his conversion to Christianity. He was tutor to the son of Constantine and author of *The Divine Institutes.*

Leander (c. 545-c. 600). Latin ecclesiastical writer, of whose works only two survive. He was instrumental in spreading Christianity among the Visigoths, gaining significant historical influence in Spain in his time.

Leo the Great (regn. 440-461). Bishop of Rome whose *Tome to Flavian* helped to strike a balance between Nestorian and Cyrilline positions at the Council of Chalcedon in 451.

Letter of Barnabas (c. 130). An allegorical and typological interpretation of the Old Testament with a decidedly anti-Jewish tone. It was included with other New Testament works as a "Catholic epistle" at least until Eusebius of Caesarea (c. 260/263-340) questioned its authenticity.

Letter to Diognetus (c. third century). A refutation of paganism and an exposition of the Christian life and faith. The author of this letter is unknown, and the exact identity of its recipient, Diognetus, continues to elude patristic scholars.

Lucifer (d. 370/371). Bishop of Cagliari and vigorous supporter of Athanasius and the Nicene Creed. In conflict with the emperor Constantius, he was banished to Palestine and later to Thebaid (Egypt).

Luculentius (fifth century). Unknown author of a group of short commentaries on the New Testament, especially Pauline passages. His exegesis is mainly literal and relies mostly on earlier authors such as Jerome and Augustine. The content of his writing may place it in the fifth century.

Macarius of Egypt (c. 300-c. 390). One of the Desert Fathers. Accused of supporting Athanasius, Macarius was exiled c. 374 to an island in the Nile by Lucius, the Arian successor of Athanasius. Macarius continued his teaching of monastic theology at Wadi Natrun.

Macrina the Younger (c. 327-379). The elder sister of Basil the Great and Gregory of Nyssa, she is known as "the Younger" to distinguish her from her paternal grandmother. She had a powerful influence on her younger brothers, especially on Gregory, who called her his teacher and relates her teaching in *On the Soul and the Resurrection*.

Manichaeans. A religious movement that originated circa 241 in Persia under the leadership of Mani but was apparently of complex Christian origin. It is said to have denied free will and the universal sovereignty of God, teaching that kingdoms of light and darkness are coeternal and that the redeemed are particles of a spiritual man of light held captive in the darkness of matter (*see* Gnostics).

Marcellus of Ancyra (d. c. 375). Wrote a rufutation of Arianism. Later, he was accused of Sabellianism, especially by Eusebius of Caesarea. While the Western church declared him orthodox, the Eastern church excommunicated him. Some scholars have attributed to him certain works of Athanasius.

Marcion (fl. 144). Heretic of the mid-second century who rejected the Old Testament and much of the New Testament, claiming that the Father of Jesus Christ was other than the Old Testament God (*see* Gnostics).

Marius Victorinus (b. c. 280/285; fl. c. 355-363). Grammarian of African origin who taught rhetoric at Rome and translated works of Platonists. After his conversion (c. 355), he wrote against the Arians and commentaries on Paul's letters.

Mark the Hermit (c. sixth century). Monk who lived near Tarsus and produced works on ascetic practices as well as christological issues.

Martin of Braga (fl. c. 568-579). Anti-Arian metropolitan of Braga on the Iberian peninsula.

He was highly educated and presided over the provincial council of Braga in 572.

Martyrius. *See* Sahdona.

Maximus of Turin (d. 408/423). Bishop of Turin. Over one hundred of his sermons survive on Christian festivals, saints and martyrs.

Maximus the Confessor (c. 580-662). Palestinian-born theologian and ascetic writer. Fleeing the Arab invasion of Jerusalem in 614, he took refuge in Constantinople and later Africa. He died near the Black Sea after imprisonment and severe suffering, having his tongue cut off and his right hand mutilated. He taught total preference for God and detachment from all things.

Methodius of Olympus (d. 311). Bishop of Olympus who celebrated virginity in a *Symposium* partly modeled on Plato's dialogue of that name.

Minucius Felix (second or third century). Christian apologist who was an advocate in Rome. His *Octavius* agrees at numerous points with the *Apologeticum* of Tertullian. His birthplace is believed to be in Africa.

Montanist Oracles. Montanism was an apocalyptic and strictly ascetic movement begun in the latter half of the second century by a certain Montanus in Phrygia, who, along with certain of his followers, uttered oracles they claimed were inspired by the Holy Spirit. Little of the authentic oracles remains and most of what is known of Montanism comes from the authors who wrote against the movement. Montanism was formally condemned as a heresy before by Asiatic synods.

Nemesius of Emesa (fl. late fourth century). Bishop of Emesa in Syria whose most important work, *Of the Nature of Man*, draws on several theological and philosophical sources and is the first exposition of a Christian anthropology.

Nestorius (c. 381-c. 451). Patriarch of Constantinople (428-431) who founded the heresy which says that there are two persons, divine and human, rather than one person truly united in the incarnate Christ. He resisted the teaching of *theotokos*, causing Nestorian churches to separate from Constantinople.

Nicetas of Remesiana (fl. second half of fourth

century). Bishop of Remesiana in Serbia, whose works affirm the consubstantiality of the Son and the deity of the Holy Spirit.

Nilus of Ancyra (d. c. 430). Prolific ascetic writer and disciple of John Chrysostom. Sometimes erroneously known as Nilus of Sinai, he was a native of Ancyra and studied at Constantinople.

Novatian of Rome (fl. 235-258). Roman theologian, otherwise orthodox, who formed a schismatic church after failing to become pope. His treatise on the Trinity states the classic western doctrine.

Oecumenius (sixth century). Called the Rhetor or the Philosopher, Oecumenius wrote the earliest extant Greek commentary on Revelation. Scholia by Oecumenius on some of John Chrysostom's commentaries on the Pauline Epistles are still extant.

Olympiodorus (early sixth century). Exegete and deacon of Alexandria, known for his commentaries that come to us mostly in catenae.

Origen of Alexandria (b. 185; fl. c. 200-254). Influential exegete and systematic theologian. He was condemned (perhaps unfairly) for maintaining the preexistence of souls while purportedly denying the resurrection of the body. His extensive works of exegesis focus on the spiritual meaning of the text.

Pachomius (c. 292-347). Founder of cenobitic monasticism. A gifted group leader and author of a set of rules, he was defended after his death by Athanasius of Alexandria.

Pacian of Barcelona (c. fourth century). Bishop of Barcelona whose writings polemicize against popular pagan festivals as well as Novatian schismatics.

Palladius of Helenopolis (c. 363/364-c. 431). Bishop of Helenopolis in Bithynia (400-417) and then Aspuna in Galatia. A disciple of Evagrius of Pontus and admirer of Origen, Palladius became a zealous adherent of John Chrysostom and shared his troubles in 403. His *Lausaic History* is the leading source for the history of early monasticism, stressing the spiritual value of the life of the desert.

Paschasius of Dumium (c. 515-c. 580). Translator of sentences of the Desert Fathers from Greek into Latin while a monk in Dumium.

Paterius (c. sixth-seventh century). Disciple of Gregory the Great who is primarily responsible for the transmission of Gregory's works to many later medieval authors.

Paulinus of Milan (late 4th-early 5th century). Personal secretary and biographer of Ambrose of Milan. He took part in the Pelagian controversy.

Paulinus of Nola (355-431). Roman senator and distinguished Latin poet whose frequent encounters with Ambrose of Milan (c. 333-397) led to his eventual conversion and baptism in 389. He eventually renounced his wealth and influential position and took up his pen to write poetry in service of Christ. He also wrote many letters to, among others, Augustine, Jerome and Rufinus.

Paulus Orosius (b. c. 380). An outspoken critic of Pelagius, mentored by Augustine. His *Seven Books of History Against the Pagans* was perhaps the first history of Christianity.

Pelagius (c. 354-c. 420). Contemporary of Augustine whose followers were condemned in 418 and 431 for maintaining that even before Christ these were people who lived wholly without sin and that salvation depended on free will.

Peter Chrysologus (c. 380-450). Latin archbishop of Ravenna whose teachings included arguments for adherence in matters of faith to the Roman see, and the relationship between grace and Christian living.

Peter of Alexandria (d. c. 311). Bishop of Alexandria. He marked (and very probably initiated) the reaction at Alexandria against extreme doctrines of Origen. During the persecution of Christians in Alexandria, Peter was arrested and beheaded by Roman officials. Eusebius of Caesarea described him as "a model bishop, remarkable for his virtuous life and his ardent study of the Scriptures."

Philo of Alexandria (c. 20 B.C.-c. A.D. 50). Jewish-born exegete who greatly influenced Christian patristic interpretation of the Old Testament. Born to a rich family in Alexandria,

Philo was a contemporary of Jesus and lived an ascetic and contemplative life that makes some believe he was a rabbi. His interpretation of Scripture based the spiritual sense on the literal. Although influenced by Hellenism, Philo's theology remains thoroughly Jewish.

Philoxenus of Mabbug (c. 440-523). Bishop of Mabbug (Hierapolis) and a leading thinker in the early Syrian Orthodox Church. His extensive writings in Syriac include a set of thirteen *Discourses on the Christian Life*, several works on the incarnation and a number of exegetical works.

Poemen (c. fifth century). One-seventh of the sayings in the *Sayings of the Desert Fathers* are attributed to Poemen, which is Greek for shepherd. Poemen was a common title among early Egyptian desert ascetics, and it is unknown whether all of the sayings come from one person.

Polycarp of Smyrna (c. 69-155). Bishop of Smyrna who vigorously fought heretics such as the Marcionites and Valentinians. He was the leading Christian figure in Roman Asia in the middle of the second century.

Potamius of Lisbon (fl. c. 350-360). Bishop of Lisbon who joined the Arian party in 357, but later returned to the Catholic faith (c. 359?). His works from both periods are concerned with the larger Trinitarian debates of his time.

Primasius (fl. 550-560). Bishop of Hadrumetum in North Africa (modern Tunisia) and one of the few Africans to support the condemnation of the Three Chapters. Drawing on Augustine and Tyconius, he wrote a commentary on the Apocalypse, which in allegorizing fashion views the work as referring to the history of the church.

Procopius of Gaza (c. 465-c. 530). A Christian exegete educated in Alexandria. He wrote numerous theological works and commentaries on Scripture (particularly the Hebrew Bible), the latter marked by the allegorical exegesis for which the Alexandrian school was known.

Prosper of Aquitaine (c. 390-c. 463). Probably a lay monk and supporter of the theology of Augustine on grace and predestination. He collaborated closely with Pope Leo I in his doctrinal statements.

Prudentius (c. 348-c. 410). Latin poet and hymn-writer who devoted his later life to Christian writing. He wrote didactic poems on the theology of the incarnation, against the heretic Marcion and against the resurgence of paganism.

Pseudo-Clementines (third-fourth century). A series of apocryphal writings pertaining to a conjured life of Clement of Rome. Written in a form of popular legend, the stories from Clement's life, including his opposition to Simon Magus, illustrate and promote articles of Christian teaching. It is likely that the corpus is a derivative of a number of Gnostic and Judeo-Christian writings. Dating the corpus is a complicated issue.

Pseudo-Dionysius the Areopagite (fl. c. 500). Author who assumed the name of Dionysius the Areopagite mentioned in Acts 17:34, and who composed the works known as the *Corpus Areopagiticum* (or *Dionysiacum*). These writings were the foundation of the apophatic school of mysticism in their denial that anything can be truly predicated of God.

Pseudo-Macarius (fl. c. 390). An anonymous writer and ascetic (from Mesopotamia?) active in Antioch whose badly edited works were attributed to Macarius of Egypt. He had keen insight into human nature, prayer and the inner life. His work includes some one hundred discourses and homilies.

Quodvultdeus (fl. 430). Carthaginian bishop and friend of Augustine who endeavored to show at length how the New Testament fulfilled the Old Testament.

Rufinus of Aquileia (c. 345-411). Orthodox Christian thinker and historian who nonetheless translated and preserved the works of Origen, and defended him against the strictures of Jerome and Epiphanius. He lived the ascetic life in Rome, Egypt and Jerusalem (the Mount of Olives).

Sabellius (fl. 200). Allegedly the author of the heresy which maintains that the Father and Son are a single person. The patripassian variant of this heresy states that the Father suffered on the cross.

Sahdona (fl. 635-640). Known in Greek as Martyrius, this Syriac author was bishop of Beth

Garmai. He studied in Nisibis and was exiled for his christological ideas. His most important work is the deeply scriptural *Book of Perfection* which ranks as one of the masterpieces of Syriac monastic literature.

Salvian the Presbyter of Marseilles (c. 400-c. 480). An important author for the history of his own time. He saw the fall of Roman civilization to the barbarians as a consequence of the reprehensible conduct of Roman Christians. In *The Governance of God* he developed the theme of divine providence.

Second Letter of Clement (c. 150). The so-called *Second Letter of Clement* is an early Christian sermon probably written by a Corinthian author, though some scholars have assigned it to a Roman or Alexandrian author.

Severian of Gabala (fl. c. 400). A contemporary of John Chrysostom, he was a highly regarded preacher in Constantinople, particularly at the imperial court, and ultimately sided with Chrysostom's accusers. He wrote homilies on Genesis.

Severus of Antioch (fl. 488-538). A monophysite theologian, consecrated bishop of Antioch in 522. Born in Pisidia, he studied in Alexandria and Beirut, taught in Constantinople and was exiled to Egypt.

Shenoute (c. 350-466). Abbot of Athribis in Egypt. His large monastic community was known for very strict rules. He accompanied Cyril of Alexandria to the Council of Ephesus in 431, where he played an important role in deposing Nestorius. He knew Greek but wrote in Coptic, and his literary activity includes homilies, catecheses on monastic subjects, letters, and a couple of theological treatises.

Shepherd of Hermas (second century). Divided into five *Visions,* twelve *Mandates* and ten *Similitudes,* this Christian apocalypse was written by a former slave and named for the form of the second angel said to have granted him his visions. This work was highly esteemed for its moral value and was used as a textbook for catechumens in the early church.

Sulpicius Severus (c. 360-c. 420). An ecclesiastical writer from Bordeaux born of noble parents. Devoting himself to monastic retirement, he became a personal friend and enthusiastic disciple of St. Martin of Tours.

Symeon the New Theologian (c. 949-1022). Compassionate spiritual leader known for his strict rule. He believed that the divine light could be perceived and received through the practice of mental prayer.

Tertullian of Carthage (c. 155/160-225/250; fl. c. 197-222). Brilliant Carthaginian apologist and polemicist who laid the foundations of Christology and trinitarian orthodoxy in the West, though he himself was later estranged from the catholic tradition due to its laxity.

Theodore of Heraclea (d. c. 355). An anti-Nicene bishop of Thrace. He was part of a team seeking reconciliation between Eastern and Western Christianity. In 343 he was excommunicated at the council of Sardica. His writings focus on a literal interpretation of Scripture.

Theodore of Mopsuestia (c. 350-428). Bishop of Mopsuestia, founder of the Antiochene, or literalistic, school of exegesis. A great man in his day, he was later condemned as a precursor of Nestorius.

Theodore of Tabennesi (d. 368) Vice general of the Pachomian monasteries (c. 350-368) under Horsiesi. Several of his letters are known.

Theodoret of Cyr (c. 393-466). Bishop of Cyr (Cyrrhus), he was an opponent of Cyril who commented extensively on Old Testament texts as a lucid exponent of Antiochene exegesis.

Theodotus the Valentinian (second century). Likely a Montanist who may have been related to the Alexandrian school. Extracts of his work are known through writings of Clement of Alexandria.

Theophanes (775-845). Hymnographer and bishop of Nicaea (842-845). He was persecuted during the second iconoclastic period for his support of the Seventh Council (Second Council of Nicaea, 787). He wrote many hymns in the tradition of the monastery of Mar Sabbas that were used in the *Paraklitiki.*

Theophilus of Antioch (late second century).

Bishop of Antioch. His only surviving work is *Ad Autholycum*, where we find the first Christian commentary on Genesis and the first use of the term *Trinity*. Theophilus's apologetic literary heritage had influence on Irenaeus and possibly Tertullian.

Theophylact of Ohrid (c. 1050-c. 1108). Byzantine archbishop of Ohrid (or Achrida) in what is now Bulgaria. Drawing on earlier works, he wrote commentaries on several Old Testament books and all of the New Testament except for Revelation.

Valentinus (fl. c. 140). Alexandrian heretic of the mid-second century who taught that the material world was created by the transgression of God's Wisdom, or Sophia (*see* Gnostics).

Valerian of Cimiez (fl. c. 422-439). Bishop of Cimiez. He participated in the councils of Riez (439) and Vaison (422) with a view to strengthening church discipline. He supported Hilary of Arles in quarrels with Pope Leo I.

Verecundus (d. 552). An African Christian writer, who took an active part in the christological controversies of the sixth century, especially in the debate on Three Chapters. He also wrote allegorical commentaries on the nine liturgical church canticles.

Victorinus of Petovium (d. c. 304). Latin biblical exegete. With multiple works attributed to him, his sole surviving work is the *Commentary on the Apocalypse* and perhaps some fragments from *Commentary on Matthew*. Victorinus expressed strong millenarianism in his writing, though his was less materialistic than the millenarianism of Papias or Irenaeus. In his allegorical approach he could be called a spiritual disciple of Origen. Victorinus died during the first year of Diocletian's persecution, probably in 304.

Vincent of Lérins (d. before 450). Monk who has exerted considerable influence through his writings on orthodox dogmatic theological method, as contrasted with the theological methodologies of the heresies.